İbrahim the Mad
and Other Plays

Middle East Literature in Translation

Michael Beard *and* Adnan Haydar, *Series Editors*

İBRAHİM THE MAD

AND OTHER PLAYS

✦   ✦   ✦

An Anthology of

MODERN
TURKISH
DRAMA

VOLUME ONE

◆   ◆   ◆

Edited by

Talat S. Halman and Jayne L. Warner

Syracuse University Press

First Edition 2008
08 09 10 11 12 13   6 5 4 3 2 1

Front cover: Müşfik Kenter in the title role of *İbrahim the Mad,* Kent Players Theater,
Istanbul, 1967. Courtesy of Müşfik Kenter.

The paper used in this publication meets the minimum requirements of American
National Standard for Information Sciences—Permanence of Paper for Printed Library
Materials, ANSI Z39.48-1984.∞™

For a listing of books published and distributed by Syracuse University Press,
visit our Web site at SyracuseUniversityPress.syr.edu.

ISBN-13: 978-0-8156-0897-4   ISBN-10: 0-8156-0897-7

Library of Congress Cataloging-in-Publication Data

Ibrahim the mad and other plays : an anthology of modern Turkish drama. Volume one /
edited by Talat S. Halman and Jayne L. Warner.
p. cm. — (Middle east literature in translation)
Includes bibliographical references.
ISBN 978-0-8156-0897-4 (pbk. : alk. paper)
I. Halman, Talât Sait. II. Warner, Jayne L.
PL237.I27 2008
894'.352408—dc22
2008008718

Manufactured in the United States of America

Contents

Preface   *vii*

Guide to Turkish Spelling,
Pronunciation, and Monetary Terms   *ix*

Introduction
An Overview of Turkish Drama (until 1970)   TALAT S. HALMAN   *xi*

The Neighborhood   AHMET KUTSİ TECER   *1*

A Ball for the Imaginative   TUNÇ YALMAN   *65*

Man of the Hour   HALDUN TANER   *87*

In Ambush   CAHİT ATAY   *143*

Sea Rose   NECATİ CUMALI   *159*

A Shanty in Istanbul   BAŞAR SABUNCU   *213*

The Mikado Game   MELİH CEVDET ANDAY   *271*

İbrahim the Mad   A. TURAN OFLAZOĞLU   *325*

Çiçu   AZİZ NESİN   *441*

Biographical Notes   *477*

Acknowledgments   *479*

Preface

I brahim the Mad and Other Plays, with its companion volume, *I, Anatolia and Other Plays*, represents the first major collection of Turkish plays to be published in English translation.[1] The nine plays in *İbrahim the Mad* span the decades from the 1940s through the 1960s, and those in *I, Anatolia* cover the 1970s through the end of the millennium.

For these volumes, the editors chose a representative selection from the vibrant and varied modern Turkish dramatic writing—a Western genre adopted and adapted by Turkish playwrights beginning in the latter part of the Ottoman Empire and the early period of the Turkish Republic. The selected plays include settings that are historical *(I, Anatolia; The White Gods)*, village/rural *(In Ambush)*, small town *(Bald Mehmet of Atça)*, urban *(The Mikado Game; Old Photographs)*, and international/universal *(Vladimir Komarov; A Ball for the Imaginative)*. The principal locale of two of the plays is the small-town or neighborhood coffeehouse found throughout Turkey *(The Neighborhood; Fehim Pasha's Mansion)*. The plays address a range of social, economic, and political issues and run the gamut from ribald comedy to dramedy to historical tragedy. Examples of musicals and vaudevilles have not been included because of the problems inherent in rendering these forms into another language. The plays range from one act *(In Ambush; My Lovely Scarf)* to four acts *(Man of the Hour)* and from a one-woman play *(I, Anatolia)* to two-character plays *(The Mikado Game; Old Photographs)* to those with more than thirty characters plus extras *(İbrahim the Mad; Bald Mehmet of Atça)*. Several of the plays are written primarily in free verse *(İbrahim the Mad; The White Gods; I, Anatolia)*.

The selections in these two volumes generally reflect the work of the leading Turkish playwrights from the period covered. The translators, many well known for their translations of Turkish literature, include some of the playwrights themselves.

The plays are arranged in chronological order by date of their original Turkish publication or production. The cast of each play is presented in the order of stage appearance. The editors have checked each translation against the Turkish original line by line and word by word—in some cases making substantial revisions (submitted when possible to the translators for approval) and frequently opting for more colloquial English.

---

1. A shorter collection is Talat S. Halman, ed., *Modern Turkish Drama: An Anthology of Plays in Translation*, which contains four plays. Published by Bibliotheca Islamica in 1976, it received wide critical acclaim.

By providing a representative sampling of the genre over six decades, the editors intend that these two volumes will help address the nearly complete omission of Turkish drama from general surveys of world literature and drama. It is also hoped that they will spark an interest in Turkish theatrical arts in the English-speaking world as well as provide enjoyable reading and scripts for possible staging.

Jayne L. Warner

◆ ◆ ◆

Guide to Turkish Spelling, Pronunciation, and Monetary Terms

Throughout this book, Turkish proper names and special terms conform to standard modern Turkish spelling. The pronunciation of the vowels and consonants is indicated in this guide:

a	(like *gun*); var. â (like *are*)	m	(as in English)
b	(as in English)	n	(as in English)
c	(like *jade*)	o	(like *eau* in French)
ç	(*ch* of *chin*)	ö	(like *bird* or French *deux*)
d	(as in English)	p	(as in English)
e	(like *pen*)	r	(*r* of *rust*)
f	(as in English)	s	(*s* of *sun*)
g	(*g* of *good*)	ş	(*sh* of *shine*)
ğ	(makes preceding vowel longer)	t	(as in English)
h	(*h* of *half*)	u	(like *pull*); var. û (like *pool*)
ı	(like second vowel of *portable*)	ü	(like *tu* in French)
i	(like *it*); var. î (like *eat*)	v	(as in English)
j	(like *measure*)	y	(*y* of *you*)
k	(*k* of *king*)	z	(as in English)
l	(as in English)		

Of the twenty-nine characters in the Turkish alphabet, six do not exist in English: ç, ğ, ı, ö, ş, ü. The letters *q, w,* and *x* are not in the Turkish alphabet, although they may occur in foreign names. The letter *ğ* has its own capital, *Ğ*, but it never starts a word. The undotted *ı* and the dotted *i* are separate vowels whose distinctions are strictly observed in pronunciation and spelling. These two letters have their individual capitals as well: *I* and *İ*, respectively.

The few exceptions to authentic Turkish spellings are words that have found their way into the English language and appear in standard English dictionaries often in anglicized forms—for example, *rakı, paşa,* and *efendi* are anglicized as *raki, pasha,* and *effendi*—as well as words that keep their Turkish spellings in English, such as *bey.* Exceptions include *molla, hacı,* and *ağa,* which have been kept in Turkish. *Ağa* has numerous meanings and connotations, and the specific use has been provided in plays where the term occurs.

Proper names have been kept in modern Turkish with two major exceptions: İstanbul and İzmir have been rendered with normal English spelling using *I* rather than *İ.* Names of Muslim Turks and members of ethnic minorities appear in the translations exactly as they are spelled in modern Turkish.

MONETARY TERMS

The plays in this collection and in its companion volume *I, Anatolia and Other Plays* cover a period of about sixty years during which currency values dramatically fluctuated. The changes owing to inflation, in particular the rampant increases in later decades, render the monetary references virtually meaningless. To give the reader an idea of the relative values, prices, and salaries, all the original numerical amounts have been kept, but lira and kuruş (one hundred kuruş equal one lira) have frequently been dropped (and *penny* is occasionally substituted for *kuruş*). References to gold and silver coins have been left as they appear in the original texts.

Introduction

An Overview of Turkish Drama (until 1970)

TALAT S. HALMAN

The date: 1 April 1873. The place: The Gedikpaşa Theater in Istanbul. The play: *Vatan yahut Silistre* (Fatherland or Silistria). The author: Namık Kemal, the patriotic poet, novelist, and journalist who was a severe critic of the Ottoman regime. The audience, responding to the play's rousing nationalistic spirit, broke into thunderous applause and clamored: "Author! Author!" The author appeared on stage, graciously acknowledging the ovation.[1] Leaving the theater, the audience continued the demonstration in the street: "Long live Kemal!" "Long live the nation!" The incident, although an explicit show of enthusiasm for the play and its author, was equally an implicit demonstration against the sultan and his entourage. The authorities were perturbed and uneasy about the public outcry. When the audiences at the second and third performances demonstrated with the same vigor, Sultan Abdülaziz struck back by closing the play and exiling Namık Kemal and some of his colleagues.

The vehement opposition seemed to have been crushed, but the *Vatan yahut Silistre* incident established once and for all the political significance of literature in Turkish life and for the first time the special impact of drama. From 1873 onward, the theater was to remain a vital core of the literary vanguard and an integral part of sociopolitical awareness and agitation.

Despite numerous periods of outright censorship imposed by the authorities or of acquiescence on the part of authors and directors, the modern history of Turkish drama has been notable for contributions to the awakening of nationalist sentiments, to cultural awareness, to progressive and innovative ideas, to public education, to the evolution of

---

For information on the evolution of Turkish drama after 1970, refer to the introduction "The Turkish Theater Since 1970" in *I, Anatolia and Other Plays: An Anthology of Modern Turkish Drama, Volume Two* (Syracuse, N.Y.: Syracuse University Press, 2008).

1. According to another version, Namık Kemal was not present at the premiere. The audience rushed out of the theater crying, "Long live Kemal," and marched to his newspaper office, where they left a letter of thanks for him.

the concepts of social justice, and to the absorption of the values of other cultures, mainly those of the West. To a far greater extent than in other Islamic countries and more so than in some European nations, the theater in Turkey has been a principal agent of sociopolitical change as well as a major vehicle of intellectual and literary transformation.

Long before the European-style legitimate theater came into being in the Ottoman Empire, the Turks had evolved various forms and traditions of drama. Traditional theatrical entertainment included a vast repertoire of dances, peasant plays, pageants, rites, processions, mock fights, festival acts, acrobatics, mimes, puppetry, marionette performances, clown acts, juggling, sleight-of-hand magic, and sectarian rituals, as well as the three major forms—the performances of a *Meddah* (panegyrist, storyteller, solo comedian), *Karagöz* (shadow play), and *Orta oyunu* (Turkish *commedia dell'arte*).

The Turkic dramatic tradition presumably goes back two thousand years. Scholars have made various classifications of the stages and different genres of the Turkish theater,[2] but the evolution followed the same general stages as the cultural history of the Turks:

Pre-Islamic (before the ninth century to the eleventh century A.D.)
Pre-Ottoman (eleventh century to the thirteenth century)
Ottoman (thirteenth century to mid–nineteenth century)
Westernized Ottoman (mid–nineteenth century to 1923)
Turkish Republic (after 1923)

Anatolia, the cradle of civilizations, offered the legacy of the Hittites, Phrygians, Lydians, Greeks, Romans, Arabs, Persians, and Byzantines to the Turks who came into it bringing their own language, literary traditions, sociopolitical norms, and performing arts. The Turks willingly availed themselves of the heritage they found in their new homeland and started to evolve a unique synthesis. Nüvit Özdoğru, a notable theater personality, observed: "Crude peasant plays, which have survived to this day through countless generations, have been traced to Central Asia as well as to festivals in honor of Dionysus and to Egyptian and Greek mysteries celebrated at Eleusis and elsewhere."[3] Metin And, a leading authority on the history of the Turkish theater, has published several studies tracing the Central Asian shamanistic, ancient Greek, Anatolian, and Turkish elements in the folk dances of modern Turkey.[4]

2. See Nicholas N. Martinovitch, *The Turkish Theatre* (New York: New York Theatre Arts, 1933), pp. 6–7; Metin And, *Geleneksel Türk Tiyatrosu* (Ankara: Bilgi, 1969), p. 11; *A History of Theatre and Popular Entertainment in Turkey* (Ankara: Forum, 1963–1964), pp. 9–13; Margot Berthold, *A History of World Theater*, edited by Edith Simmons (New York: Frederick Ungar, 1972; reprint, New York: Continuum, 1991), p. 30.

3. Nüvit Özdoğru, "Turkey: Traditional Theater," in *The Reader's Encyclopedia of World Drama*, edited by John Gassner and Edward G. Quinn (New York: Crowell, 1969), p. 865.

4. Metin And, *Dances of Anatolian Turkey* (Brooklyn, N.Y.: Dance Perspectives, 1959); *Dionisos ve Anadolu Köylüsü* (Istanbul: Elif, 1962); *Türk Köylü Dansları* (Istanbul: İzlem, 1965).

There is very little documentary evidence concerning Turkish dramatic arts prior to the emergence of the Ottoman state at the end of the thirteenth century. The resemblances and affinities between some ancient mysteries, rites, pantomimes, mythic enactments, processions, and dances, on the one hand, and current forms of entertainment among Turkish peasants, on the other, lead scholars to believe that there must have been direct continuity or substantial preservation of traditional forms and styles in many parts of Anatolia, particularly in those localities that have remained isolated. Irrespective of the patterns of continuity, the peasant plays and dances of contemporary Turkey reveal an impressive originality and the capability of making a synthesis of diverse borrowings. It is a near-impossible task to differentiate the ancient Turkic, Anatolian non-Turkic, and Ottoman or modern Turkish elements.[5]

The vast repertoire of peasant plays consists of indigenous and assimilated traditions. The Stag Play, based on themes of death and resurrection, is distinctly non-Islamic, even pagan, and may be traced back to an Anatolian Hittite origin[6] or to Central Asian Turkic lore. The *taklit*s (animal imitations) were probably taken over by Turks from the earlier inhabitants of Anatolia, in particular the Greeks. Regrettably, no systematic survey or recording of the peasant plays has been made. There must be scores of different village plays with their own original plots, characters, acting styles, props, costumes, and dramatic devices. The several dozen such plays that have been collected and studied clearly show the scope and significance of the peasant plays. The absence of scholarly interest is lamentable in two respects. First, as modern communications penetrate the villages, most of the peasant plays are rapidly disappearing, and unless they are filmed or carefully studied, they may be lost forever. Second, no use is being made of these plays for nurturing a national theater movement.

Traditional Turkish theater engendered three major types of entertainment that were substantially indigenous: the storyteller, the shadow play, and the theater-in-the-round. The storyteller originally started as a narrator of religious and heroic tales. He was therefore called a *Meddah,* which literally means "panegyrist, encomiast, extoller."[7] It is safe to assume that the early Turkish communities, before their conversion to Islam, had started enjoying story sessions in addition to the poetry and music programs of their resident bards and itinerant minstrels. The epic literature of pre-Islamic Turkish groups was probably disseminated not only by the troubadours, but also by the storytellers. After conversion to

---

5. Metin And estimates the number of Anatolian dances at about fifteen hundred. The variety of these dances defies the imagination, indicating that most of them must be original or at least autochthonous amalgams rather than borrowings ("Origins and Early Development of the Turkish Theater," *Review of National Literatures* [special issue: "Turkey from Empire to Nation"] 4, no. 1 [spring 1973], p. 55).

6. And, *A History of Theatre and Popular Entertainment,* p. 57.

7. The most informative and reliable source on the *Meddah* is Georg Jacob, *Vortrage türkischer Meddahs* (Leipzig: Mayer and Müller, 1923). Fuad Köprülü, "Meddahlar," in *Edebiyat Araştırmaları* (Ankara: Türk Tarih Kurumu, 1966, reprint, 1986; Istanbul: Ötüken, 1989), pp. 361–412, is an excellent survey.

Islam, the Turkish *Meddah*s told their traditional tales of heroism, religious narratives of the new faith, and myths and legends taken over from the Persians, Indians, and Arabs. The *Meddah*s not only provided live entertainment and a measure of intellectual stimulation, but also served the function of *propaganda fide,* proselytizing unbelievers and reinforcing the faith of the believers. But the evangelical function as well as the Islamic content of the *Meddah* stories were abandoned "when the Mohammedan clergy forbade any reference to the saints in the plays."[8]

Using secular topics and tales, the *Meddah*s became storytellers, with their repertoire concentrating on heroic deeds, daily life in their regions and communities, gnomic tales, and exhortations. Satire gradually started to form the core of their programs: humorous anecdotes about human foibles, impersonations of stock types and familiar individuals, mockery of social mores, and guarded or open stabs at people in high office, including sometimes the sultan. It was at this stage of its evolution that the *Meddah* program became a theatrical act.

The *Meddah* was the Turkish sit-down version of the American stand-up comic or the British music hall and burlesque comedian. Usually performing at coffeehouses, he would sit on a raised platform with no accoutrements except for several types of headgear and no props other than his handkerchief and cane, both of which he used for a variety of purposes. With a great deal of mimicry, a broad range of vocal modulation, and occasionally exaggerated gesticulation, he would present anecdotes and skits. To the aficionado, much of the *Meddah*'s material would be entirely familiar—but repetition was not necessarily a sign of the *Meddah*'s lack of imaginativeness. As in classical poetry, the art was in introducing subtle variations on the theme: a new turn, a slightly different accent, a fresh sight gag, or a satirical reference to a recent event.

In Ottoman life, the *Meddah*s were enjoyed by the sultan and the man in the street alike. They were particularly popular in the seventeenth and eighteenth centuries, and their popularity, despite rigorous censorship and the advent of the legitimate theater, lasted well into the twentieth century. The last masters were still practicing their art in the 1940s, after which no new *Meddah*s came along (except for moderately successful re-creations by some contemporary actors in the closing decades of the twentieth century and paltry revivals in the first decade of the twenty-first century).

The Ottoman Turks reveled in the illusionistic art of *Karagöz,* the shadow play. It was probably inspired originally by Chinese shadow puppets and acquired various elements from Indian versions, although numerous European scholars have advanced the theory that the shadow play originated in the eastern Mediterranean region, from where it moved to the Orient. Metin And says that *Karagöz* emerged in the Near East, where "shadow theatre existed in the eleventh, twelfth and thirteenth centuries, especially in Egypt," and it evolved in Turkey, where "references to shadow theatre made their appearances as early

---

8. Martinovitch, *The Turkish Theatre,* p. 22.

as the thirteenth and fourteenth century albeit merely as literary metaphors, rather than as definite references."[9]

The type of shadow play commonly known as *Karagöz,* whatever its origins and acquired elements, is authentically Turkish. Throughout Ottoman history, it captivated audiences in cities and towns and evolved into a philosophical, political, and satirical vehicle. Its influences may also be observed outside of Turkey—in most Near Eastern and North African countries, as well as in Greece, Romania, Bulgaria, and Yugoslavia.

The *Karagöz* "puppeteer" presents a one-man act in which he manually operates all the characters and impersonates all their voices. The figures are two dimensional; the best ones are made of leather, usually camel. Although painted in many bright colors, they appear on the linen screen mostly as shadows. Light from a candle, oil lamp, or electric bulb illuminates the screen, projecting the figures. The master operators sing various songs and recite poems in addition to voicing as many as six characters at a time, imitating different accents, using special styles, cadences, and modulations in order to make the silhouettes come alive.

The shadow play opens by proclaiming itself to be a faithful mirror of the world, implying also that life, being transitory and devoid of value, is a mere shadow, a fleeting image, yet, in a mystical context, a reflection of godliness. The protagonists are always Karagöz and Hacivat, who, like the "Odd Couple," are good friends frequently entangled in verbal and physical combat. Hacivat is an ill-educated man who uses big words to pass himself off as an intellectual, whereas Karagöz represents the common man. Theirs is a communication crisis depicted by the modern theater of the absurd.

Karagöz is peopled with dozens of characters, including Bey, the often inept gentleman; Çingene, the gypsy; Frenk, a Frenchman or a European in general; Zenne, a woman, sometimes presented with bare breasts; Türk, a bumbling Anatolian Turkish peasant; Tiryaki, the addict or chain smoker; Beberuhi, the dwarf; Yahudi, the wily Jew; Çelebi, the dandy; Acem, an Iranian; an Arab or a black man; Arnavut, an Albanian; and Mirasyedi, literally, an "inheritance-eater" or "playboy." Such figures and animals as dragons and snakes, forests, houses, boats, trees, donkeys, dogs, and buggies sometimes enhance the action and the visual impact.

The steady decline of the shadow play since the latter part of the nineteenth century was caused initially by censorship, but later by the growing appeal of the legitimate theater and

9. And, *A History of Theatre and Popular Entertainment,* p. 34. The best study of *Karagöz* is Georg Jacob, *Türkische Litteraturgeschichte in Einzeldarstellungen: Das türkisches Schattentheater* (Berlin: Mayer and Müller, 1900). Cevdet Kudret has published the definitive edition of all extant *Karagöz* plays in three volumes (Ankara: Bilgi, 1968, 1969, 1970). Hellmut Ritter's *Karagös: Türkische Schattenspiele,* 3 vols. (vol. 1, Hannover, Germany: Orient-Heinz Lafaire, 1924; vol. 2, Istanbul: Druckerei Universum, 1941; vol. 3, Wiesbaden, Germany: Deutsche Morgenländische Gesellschaft, 1953) is also a comprehensive compilation with an excellent introduction. Otto Spies's *Türkisches Puppentheater* (Emsdetten, Germany: Lechte, 1959) is recommended as a scholarly survey. Metin And's *Karagöz: Turkish Shadow Theatre* (Istanbul: Dost, 1975; rev. ed., 1979) is also highly recommended.

many other types of entertainment, in particular motion pictures, radio, and television, as well as by the wide distribution of books, newspapers, and magazines. But the primary reasons for the virtual disappearance of the shadow plays were their inherent limitations and their resistance to change. *Karagöz* failed to adjust to new theatrical tastes. It retained its stock characters, stereotyped plots, and recurring dialogue. In modern times, some unsuccessful attempts were made, occasionally by leading playwrights, to adapt *Karagöz* to the legitimate stage and to modern themes. The shadow plays do offer rich possibilities for animation and multimedia presentation, but unless an imaginative new approach is adopted, this art will remain moribund.

The most representational and realistic traditional theatrical art in Ottoman Turkey was the *Orta oyunu,* a type of comic theater-in-the-round. Originally called *Kol oyunu* (company play) or *Meydan oyunu* (play-in-the-round), the *Orta oyunu,* which literally means "play-in-the-middle," has often been described as the Turkish *commedia dell'arte.* The resemblances in basic features and the similarity of the words *arte* and *orta* have led many scholars to the assumption that *Orta oyunu* was a direct offshoot of the *commedia dell'arte,* perhaps imparted to the Ottomans by some Italian troupes performing in Istanbul. Even if one can prove that the disparities between the two forms outnumber the common features, the term "commedia dell'orta" would be justified.

The similarities are far more striking between *Orta oyunu* and *Karagöz.* Many of the same minor characters and the basic plots are common to both. The available texts prove how the two genres, one illusionistic and the other nonillusionistic, used the same story lines, scenes, gags, and characterizations. Because *Karagöz* is the older form, it has been speculated that *Orta oyunu* must have been its representational version.

As in *Karagöz,* most of the characters in *Orta oyunu* are stereotyped; the location is essentially abstract, although identified by some specific reference; the set is open or fluid; and slapstick is the salient comic element, with a heavy reliance on dialects, wordplay, spoonerisms, various speech defects, and similar devices.[10]

As a form of comedy, the *Orta oyunu* gradually fell into decay in the early decades of the twentieth century, and members of the Zuhuri Kolu (the elite corps of *Orta oyunu* players) passed from the scene. One of its aspects, *Tulûat,* improvisational theater based on extensive ad-lib, continued into the second half of the century, however.

Playwrights and other men of letters in modern Turkey have given a great deal of thought to reviving or modernizing the *Orta oyunu.* A leading intellectual, İsmayıl Hakkı Baltacıoğlu, was particularly energetic and resourceful in calling for a new lease on life for *Orta oyunu* with innovations. Numerous important modern plays, including *Keşanlı Ali Destanı (The Ballad of Ali of Keşan)* by Haldun Taner, have systematically utilized some

10. For a detailed description of the two main characters, Pişekâr and Kavuklu, see Martinovitch, *The Turkish Theatre,* pp. 17–18.

features of the *Orta oyunu*. Yet the traditional theater-in-the-round has failed to make a comeback either in its original form or as an old model for new creativity.

All traditional theater among Turks—peasant plays, court entertainment, *Karagöz, Meddah, Orta oyunu*—seems to have been in the comic vein. There is a conspicuous absence of serious drama, particularly tragedy. This phenomenon is all the more remarkable because the Turks were after all ensconced in part of the terra firma of Greek tragedy and came into frequent contact with the Persian *Ta'ziyeh* (passion play) and the Muharram festivals (held during the first month of the Islamic calendar), which were notable for their elements of tragedy.

A plausible explanation for the "tragic void" might be found in the seriousness with which the Ottoman Turks embraced the orthodox tenets of Islam or the doctrines of such sects as the Mevlevi, Bektaşi, and Yesevi, rather than a major denomination such as Shiism, which was dominant in Persia and engendered tragic depictions of martyrdom.

Islam, as its name signifies, is submissive to God's will. It accepts—it surrenders to—the fate, tragic as it may be, that God ordains. In this theological sense, tragedy does not actually exist because it is just another act or revelation of God. In the Sufi (mystic) tradition, the only suffering that has a human dimension is separation from God. Death, in mystical terms, is not tragic because, as an exercise of destiny, it represents man's return to and merging with God. Mystic poetry, a vast corpus composed by both elite poets and the minstrels, conveys the tragic feeling of the soul's search for God. Aside from this acute sense, however, Ottoman culture developed virtually no understanding of a dramatic situation in artistic terms, nor did it evolve any concept of a protagonist with heroic dimensions pitted against forces beyond his control, a protagonist with superhuman aspirations and a yearning to transcend himself, a defiant man.[11] This absence of formal tragedy or even of a structured tragic view or sense in traditional Turkish culture has probably been a factor in the slow evolution of modern tragedy in Turkey since the advent of the legitimate stage in the mid–nineteenth century.

The nineteenth-century phenomenon of systematic Westernization brought to the shrinking Ottoman Empire many innovations patterned after European models. The Ottomans, proud of their faith and conquests, had felt superior to the West until decline gradually set in. From the seventeenth century onward, there were defeats at the hands of European powers, deterioration of morale and of official institutions, and eventually the armed rebellions of some of the empire's non-Muslim minorities. The Ottoman ruling class became increasingly impressed with Europe's growing strength and technological achievements.

---

11. As the eminent Orientalist Louis Massignon has observed, "Art is allowed to be created only within the limits set by the faith. The Muslim is reluctant to fall into the trap of art. . . . Consequently, no dramatic art exists among the Muslims. Because of unquestioning acceptance of fate, the Muslim individual does not experience the clash of man *vs.* God. His submission negates tragedy" ("İslam Sanatlarının Felsefesi," in *Din ve Sanat,* translated by Burhan Toprak [Istanbul: Suhulet, 1937], pp. 17–18).

In 1839, the Tanzimat (Reforms) Period ushered in legal, administrative, educational, and cultural changes. Literature was both a concomitant and a major catalyst of change. New genres made their appearance—fiction, essay, journalistic article, and drama.

Prior to this period, the Ottoman Turks had acquired a limited knowledge of the European legitimate theater and its dramatic literature. Foreign embassies and consulates in Istanbul and Izmir were presenting plays (Corneille, Molière, Montfleury) in the late seventeenth and early eighteenth centuries. It was during the reign of the reformist sultan Selim III (ruled 1789–1807), who was himself a poet and composer, that the first theater was constructed in Istanbul around the turn of the nineteenth century. The sultan's active interest encouraged European troupes to perform frequently in the imperial capital. Many of them gave performances at Selim's court.

In 1828, the second major reformist sultan, Mahmud II, invited Giuseppe Donizetti, brother of the composer Gaetano Donizetti, to come to Istanbul to start a military band and an imperial orchestra. Donizetti's success accelerated theatrical activity. In Mahmud's reign, two amphitheaters were constructed in Istanbul, and numerous European troupes performed there regularly.

After Bartolomeo Giustiniani opened his French playhouse in the late 1820s, the Italian magician Bartholomew Bosco built a five-hundred-seat theater in Istanbul in 1839 to present French plays and operas in addition to his own acts.[12] The renowned French poet Gérard de Nerval, who visited Istanbul in 1843, wrote that the Ottoman capital had a rather active entertainment life: in addition to *Karagöz* performances, he watched *İki Dulun Kocası (Le mari des deux veuves)* in the theater district and a French production of Molière's *Monsieur de Pourceaugnac* presented at the court for the pleasure of Sultan Abdülmecid, who had specifically asked for a comedy by Molière.[13] This same sultan treated the British and Swedish ambassadors to play performances at the new Dolmabahçe Palace in 1859. It was also Abdülmecid who encouraged the earliest Turkish translations of Molière's comedies.

The year 1859 is a milestone in the history of Turkish drama and the beginning of the writing of dramatic literature in the Western vein: İbrahim Şinasi, poet, author, and translator, wrote the first Turkish play, *Şair Evlenmesi (The Wedding of a Poet)*;[14] published in 1860). A few earlier texts are probably not original plays, but translations or adaptations from the French. A play that looks plausible as an original, *Vakaayi-i Acibe ve Havadis-i Kefşger Ahmed* (The Strange Adventures of Ahmed the Cobbler), presumably written

12. Metin And, *Tanzimat ve İstibdat Döneminde Türk Tiyatrosu, 1839–1908* (Ankara: Türkiye İş Bankası, 1972), p. 25; *A History of Theatre and Popular Entertainment*, p. 66.

13. Gérard de Nerval, *Voyage en Orient* (Paris: Charpentier, 1862), vol. 2, p. 206.

14. The English translation by Edward A. Allworth, *The Wedding of a Poet: A One-Act Comedy,* was published in 1981 (White Stone, N.Y.: Griffon House) and reprinted in *An Anthology of Turkish Literature,* edited by Kemal Silay, Indiana University Turkish Studies and Turkish Ministry of Culture Joint Series no. 15 (Bloomington: Indiana University Turkish Studies, 1996), pp. 240–49.

in the first half of the nineteenth century by an unidentified author, lacks unassailable authenticity.[15] Şinasi's play, which was commissioned by the imperial court, is thoroughly Turkish in style, characterizations, dialogue, and dramatic devices. Nüvit Özdoğru summarized the basic features of *Şair Evlenmesi* in the following words:

> A one-act farce, it ridicules the custom of arranged marriages. This was a very advanced idea for the Turkey of that period. The play also reveals the corruption of some Muslim priests who did business by accepting bribes and suggests that people should not blindly follow the priests' teachings. The characters, more types than real persons, spoke in the vernacular of the day. With its broad humor and swift development of theme, the play is not altogether removed from Karagöz or Ortaoyunu. The form, diction, and the satirical content of the play set the pattern for other playwrights to follow.[16]

Many forces, urges, and elements converged to establish this European-style theater in nineteenth-century Turkey. The new cultural and technological orientation of the empire sought to Westernize life and letters. Also, the traditional theatrical arts had failed to regenerate or innovate themselves and were consequently suffering from a lack of creativity. The European companies brought to the Turks a whole new world of exciting drama with vivid characters. The non-Muslim communities of the empire added their own productions to the increasingly lively scene. The Armenians, for example, did not confine their activities to plays in the Armenian language, but started numerous professional companies specializing in productions in Turkish. Their contribution to the growth of the Ottoman theater was of immense value.

The earliest theaters in Istanbul (those owned by Michael Naum, an Armenian, and by the Italians Giustiniani and Bosco) catered to visiting European troupes, only occasionally presenting plays in Turkish. "By the third quarter of the nineteenth century, however," according to Metin And, "the Istanbul Armenians had established two companies that sought a wider Turkish audience. First a company called Şark (The Orient) and later another company called Vaspuragan came into existence, performing, translating, and adapting European plays bilingually."[17]

The Gedikpaşa Theater housed the repertoire company named the Ottoman Theater Company, under the direction of Güllü Agop, an Armenian who had converted to Islam. Agop's company "produce[d] a tragedy based on the Turkish romance *Leylâ vü Mecnun* by Mustafa Efendi,"[18] in which Turkish actors appeared on stage as salaried professionals.

In this period, classics and contemporary European plays found wide popularity among Istanbul audiences. Translations or adaptations (and occasionally the originals

---

15. This play was discovered by Fahir İz at the Österreichische Nationalbibliothek in Vienna in 1956. İz published the text under the title *Papuççu Ahmed'in Garip Maceraları* (Istanbul: Yenilik, 1961).

16. Özdoğru, "Turkey: Traditional Theater," p. 867.

17. And, "Origins and Early Development of the Turkish Theater," p. 60.

18. Ibid., p. 61.

performed by visiting European troupes) of the plays of Molière, Goldoni, Dumas, Schiller, Hugo, Racine, Corneille, Shakespeare, and many other leading or long since forgotten writers constituted a favorite repertoire for Turkish theatergoers and an education in playwriting for authors.

This growing theatrical activity stimulated indigenous playwriting. After the pioneering work of Şinasi, Ahmet Vefik Pasha and Âli Bey offered Molière adaptations; Namık Kemal wrote romantic, patriotic, and historical plays; Ali Haydar and Şemseddin Sami dramatized myths and legends; and Ahmet Midhat Efendi, following in the footsteps of Şinasi, turned out many plays exposing the folly of antiquated social mores.

The playwrights were acutely aware of their functions of educating the public, introducing progressive ideas, criticizing social and political institutions, and satirizing the types who were responsible for backwardness—for example, the religious fanatic, the bureaucrat, and the rabid conservative. The closing decades of the nineteenth century, however, were marked by censorship and suppression of works considered dangerous to the sultan and his regime. Plays dealing with revolutionary ideas such as strikes, overthrow of government, uprisings, and similar themes were banned. Mere references to such terms as *freedom, anarchy, dynamite, constitution,* and *equality* could lead to the prosecution of authors and directors. Because Sultan Abdülhamid had an enormous nose, *Cyrano de Bergerac* was banned. It was in this milieu that the patriotic uprising inspired by Namık Kemal's play *Vatan yahut Silistre* in April 1873 caused the Gedikpaşa Theater to suffer a temporary setback.

Under this censorship, innocuous light comedies flourished. Popular taste, too, was a major factor. Molière dominated the scene of comedy in nineteenth-century Turkey. Most of his plays were translated or adapted, and they served as models for scores of new plays by Turkish writers. Molière's principal characters found their counterparts in authentic Ottoman types. The misers, the misanthropes, and the hypochondriacs—Molière's antiheroes—became the butt of Turkish satire. The comedy of manners and satirical plays exposing foibles and frailties reached popularity that was to become pervasive and perennial. Light comedies were characterized by slapstick, clowning, *mal entendu,* horseplay, practical jokes, sight gags, fleecing, infidelity, and dialects and accents.[19]

The earliest specimens of European-style tragedy written by Turkish playwrights made their appearance in the 1860s. The evolution of the genre was to remain under the influence of Racine, Corneille, Shakespeare, and others. Greek tragedy seems to have wielded very little, if any, influence during the last decades of the Ottoman state. But Elizabethan and French tragedy offered nineteenth-century Ottoman playwrights effective models that they assiduously studied and, in some cases, partially plagiarized.[20]

19. Niyazi Akı, *XIX. Yüzyıl Türk Tiyatrosu Tarihi* (Ankara: Ankara Üniversitesi Basımevi, 1963), pp. 42–43.

20. Although such practices as adaptation without acknowledgment and outright plagiarism were more common in comedy, careful students of early Ottoman tragedies, principally Akı, have documented the specific debts to non-Turkish models (ibid., pp. 61–70).

Abdülhak Hâmit Tarhan, one of the dominant figures of Turkish poetry and literary Europeanization, owes much of his fame to the plays he wrote between 1872 and 1918. His early plays were melodramas steeped in sentimentality. Of his twelve tragedies, ten are in classical or syllabic verse, either in full or in part. Rhymes and the metric structure give the diction of these plays a forced and contrived quality. The plots are based on intrigue, impossible loves, heroism—all depicted in romantic terms and often set in places and periods unrelated to the Turkish experience.

The melodrama enjoyed popularity in Istanbul, becoming virtually a genre in itself. A major producer-director of Armenian origin, Mardiros Mınakyan, nurtured the public penchant for melodrama and catered to it. "A rough analysis of Mınakyan's Theatre, known as the Osmanlı Tiyatrosu (the Ottoman Theatre)," writes Metin And, "shows the bulk of the repertoire to be a considerable number of melodramas adapted or translated. . . . Most of his repertory consisted of dramas or dramatized versions of popular novels by such authors as Georges Ohnet, Xavier de Montépin, Octave Feuillet, Émile Richebourg. Also Victor Hugo, Alexandre Dumas fils, Émile Zola, and others were translated."[21] Mınakyan's theater and other companies produced many melodramas by native playwrights as well. The melodrama took root in the Turkish performing arts: it affected playwriting, acting, and the plots and the performances of Turkish films well into the second half of the twentieth century.

The era of constitutional government starting in 1908 gave new impetus to theatrical activity. Relatively wider freedoms and an atmosphere of hope and optimism spurred playwrights to dwell on social problems and to dramatize political themes. In his extensive study of the 1908–23 period, Metin And has listed the salient features of the new plays: explicit themes of liberty, reform, and innovation; a realistic conception of love rather than platonic and idealized love; a highly critical view of fatalism and of supernatural powers; emphasis on national development and on legal-political reforms; strong denunciation of oppression and injustice; advocacy of such ideologies as Turkism, Islamism, and socialism; pride in the glorious chapters and episodes of Turkish history; active interest in villages and in the peasant's plight; and the sanctity of the family.[22]

Turkish theater embarked on a new course of creativity with the establishment of the Municipal Theater in Istanbul in 1914. The prominent French director André Antoine "signed a contract with the Municipality of Istanbul to found a Conservatory of Music and Drama and run it as its General Director."[23] Although Antoine was forced to return to Paris after a six-week stay in Istanbul, the groundwork had already been laid, and the

---

21. And, *A History of Theatre and Popular Entertainment,* p. 78.

22. Metin And, *Meşrutiyet Döneminde Türk Tiyatrosu, 1908–1923* (Ankara: Türkiye İş Bankası, 1971), pp. 120–21, 180–82, 199–200, 285–87.

23. Tunç Yalman, "Turkey," in George Freedley and John A. Reeves, *A History of the Theatre,* 3rd rev. ed. (New York: Crown, 1968), p. 817.

theater raised its curtain in January 1916 with an adaptation of Émile Fabre's *La maison d'argile*. This city-subsidized repertory company, first called Darülbedayi (House of Fine Arts), then renamed Şehir Tiyatrosu (City Theater), formed the vital core of Turkish theatrical arts until midcentury.[24]

The City Theater of Istanbul came into its own in 1927, when Muhsin Ertuğrul, "the greatest name in contemporary Turkish theatre, returned from a prolonged stay in Russia and took the helm as its Artistic Director . . . and made it probably the best-run and most versatile theatre company in the Middle East."[25] Many actors at the City Theater described the era in which Muhsin Ertuğrul took the helm as "the Renaissance of Turkish theater." His nearly two decades as artistic director yielded dozens of productions of major classics and modern plays, stimulated native playwriting, and evolved a versatile professional repertory company. As director-actor-translator, Ertuğrul provided inspiration and impetus. In his sixty-five-year career, he also distinguished himself as Turkey's first major film director and as director general of the State Theater in Ankara. Among his memorable achievements are the creation of children's theater, systematic encouragement of Turkish playwrights, and the establishment of a network of regional theaters in the countryside.

Theater in Turkey has also been enhanced by many highly competent and dynamic private companies. After the establishment of Ertuğrul's Küçük Sahne (Little Stage) in 1952, several dozen independent theaters were founded. Some closed their doors because of intense competition, and some because of the impact of television, which began broadcasting in Turkey in the early 1970s. The best among the private theaters—especially the Kent Players Theater, established in 1958 by Yıldız Kenter, Turkey's greatest actress, and her brother, Müşfik Kenter—present productions and performances that often equal their counterparts in countries with a much longer tradition in the legitimate theater.

The establishment of the Turkish Republic in 1923 gave the theater fresh vigor. Mustafa Kemal Atatürk, the founder of the republic, placed strong emphasis on the dramatic arts as a vital ingredient of and a spur to the process of Westernization. Muslim women, who had first been allowed to appear on the stage in 1919, now found it easy to become actresses and began to enjoy publicity and prestige.

In the early years of the republic, an outpouring of patriotic plays sang the praises of the nation's glory in war and its emergence as a modern nation. Many were written in meter and rhyme. Some utilized the Turks' ancient heroics as their themes or plots. By and large, these plays were of a utilitarian and propagandistic type designed to strengthen national pride and solidarity.

Turkish dramatic literature since the establishment of the republic has been marked overall by continuing vitality, increasing diversity, and growing refinement of technique

24. For an excellent study of the history of the Municipal Theater, see Özdemir Nutku, *Darülbedayi'in Elli Yılı* (Ankara: Ankara Üniversitesi Basımevi, 1969).

25. Yalman, "Turkey," p. 817.

and aesthetics. The establishment of the State Conservatory, first in Ankara (1946) and later in Istanbul, and then the creation of drama departments and theater schools at numerous universities provided academic training for new generations of actors and directors. The "explosion" of theatrical activity, particularly since the early 1960s, has made Istanbul and Ankara very lively theatrical centers.

The Turkish passion for Shakespeare peaked in the early 1960s, when at Istanbul's venerable City Theater Engin Cezzar gave 170 consecutive performances as Hamlet, with a total of seventy thousand people watching. This number became a world record, which was broken six or seven years later by Richard Burton on Broadway.

During many seasons, Istanbul could boast as much theatrical activity as most European cultural capitals, and the range of interest ran from Greek tragedies to black comedy, from Argentinian melodrama to Brechtian epic theater, from Molière to Tennessee Williams. Virtually no major playwrights and very few great plays of world literature were neglected on the Turkish stage. The playwrights were on the whole well read in the classics and kept abreast of developments in world drama. State, municipal, and private theaters presented highly competent productions of classical and contemporary plays from many parts of the world. Scholars and critics of the theater, including reviewers, offered astute, sophisticated, erudite analyses and critical assessments. The wider freedoms provided by the Turkish Constitution of 1961 and the even greater freedoms that evolved from the mid-1980s onward enabled playwrights to deal with social and economic problems in less guarded or allegorical terms, bringing to the stage a whole spectrum of political themes and tensions. An ever-expanding cultural consciousness also spurred playwrights, especially after 1950, to dramatize previously neglected themes and historical periods: Ottoman history, Greek drama, ancient Near Eastern mythology, Turkish folklore and epic literature, and universal topics set in no identifiable country or locale.

The foremost pioneer of the study of the history of modern Turkish theater, Metin And, devised an encompassing typology in his books entitled *A History of Theater and Popular Entertainment in Turkey* and *50 Yılın Türk Tiyatrosu* (The Turkish Theater of the Past 50 Years): plays about idealistic heroes, social reformers, and political leaders battling against corruption, political tyranny, and social injustice; plays depending largely on character portrayal; plays on dreams, memory, and psychoanalytical themes; plays depicting women's and artists' problems; plays about the eternal triangle and marital problems in general; plays on social injustice, bureaucracy, urban-rural conflicts; detective plays, murder mysteries, suspense thrillers; family dramas, including those about the generation gap; verse melodramas; village dramas and plays about life in shantytowns; plays about the previous civilizations of Anatolia; plays about the maladjusted; dramas dealing with abstract concepts and hypothetical situations; light comedies and vaudevilles; satires of traditional values and current life; the play-within-a-play; modernizations of shadow plays and *comedia dell'arte*; plotless plays; dramas based on folk legends and Turkish history; expressionistic plays; sentimental dramas; epic theater; cabaret the-ater; plays based on Greek tragedy; theater of the absurd and musical drama.[26]

Another major scholar-critic, Sevda Şener, has observed the following about aspects of Turkish playwriting:

> The most conspicuous achievement of contemporary Turkish dramatic writing and pro-duction has been the conscious effort to create original native drama by making use of the formal and stylistic elements of traditional spectacular plays in a way to satisfy modern taste and contemporary intellectual needs. The main challenge to such an attempt is to preserve critical sensitivity and to discriminate between the easy attraction of the spec-tacular and the pleasure of witnessing the true combination of form and content.[27]

From the middle of the twentieth century onward, according to Dikmen Gürün, a notable theater critic, "the [Turkish] playwrights' quest was focused on the issues of rural migration, feudal social order and life in the slums. . . . [T]he system was questioned in all its aspects. In later years, influenced by the current political theater in Europe, the Turkish playwrights began to deal with the issue in a similar form and content. They employed the episodic form of epic and merged it with the traditional Turkish norms."[28]

Theater in Turkey, all its shortcomings and weaknesses aside, can still legitimately boast remarkable achievements, which have enabled it to move far ahead of theater not only in all developing countries, but also in many advanced countries that have a longer theatrical tradition and substantially greater resources. The record of Turkish dramatic arts is, by any objective criterion, impressive.

26. And, *A History of Theatre and Popular Entertainment,* pp. 102–10; *50 Yılın Türk Tiyatrosu* (Istanbul: Türkiye İş Bankası, 1973), pp. 490–637.

27. Sevda Şener, "Turkish Drama," http://sanat.bilkent.edu.tr/interactive.m2.org/Theater/SSener.html.

28. Dikmen Gürün, "An Excursion in the Turkish Theater," http://sanat.bilkent.edu.tr/interactive.m2.org/Theater/dikmen.html.

İbrahim the Mad
and other plays

◆   ◆   ◆

The Neighborhood

AHMET KUTSİ TECER

Translated by Nüvit Özdoğru

An Editor's Note

Turkey's State Theater raised its curtain in 1947 in Ankara and was to exert a profound influence on the country's theatrical life in the ensuing decades. Its first production featured *Köşebaşı (The Neighborhood)* by the distinguished lyric poet Ahmet Kutsi Tecer (1901–67). It was the first play to come from Tecer's pen. It blended the techniques of European-style playwriting with an authentic Turkish dramatic context and characters. The lavish production and a captivating set design, the likes of which had seldom been seen on the Turkish stage, proved an auspicious start for the involvement of the Turkish state in stimulating the dramatic arts. Scores of playwrights entered the theater world thanks to opportunities provided by the State Theater. By its sixtieth anniversary, this huge governmental undertaking could boast thirty-five stages in thirteen provinces.

Tecer earned a degree from the Department of Philosophy at the University of Istanbul after studying at the Sorbonne in Paris. He thereafter served as a teacher of literature and as a Ministry of Education official. From 1942 to 1946, he was a member of Parliament. He later taught at the State Conservatory in Ankara and spent about two years in Paris as his country's cultural attaché. On his return to Turkey, he was on the faculties of the Galatasaray Lycée, Istanbul Conservatory, Academy of Fine Arts, Journalism Institute, and Istanbul's Teachers College. Acclaimed as a highly accomplished poet, Tecer also attracted wide attention for his research and publications related to Turkish folklore. He made a contribution of abiding value to the development of scholarly studies and performances of Turkish folk music.

After *Köşebaşı,* Tecer wrote numerous plays, many of which had successful productions. Of them, the most outstanding was *Koçyiğit Köroğlu,* based on the traditional folk epic about the folk hero Köroğlu.

The term *köşebaşı* literally mans "street corner." Showing a slice of life in a small section of Istanbul, Tecer's play features familiar local characters who babble unaffected words, seem likable, and are refreshingly human. On the stage, it must have reminded its Turkish audiences of their traditional *Karagöz* (shadow play), which presents a host of one-dimensional characters who talk in colorful accents and parade over the screen without following a set story line. *The Neighborhood,* like *Karagöz,* has no dramatic action to speak of, no plot in the real sense, no theme development, and no denouement—just a variety of characters in swift traffic, a congeries of Istanbul types (grocer, junk dealer, matchmaker, city official, street cleaner, snob, *simit*[1] vendor, and a score of others) who amble or stumble in and out as elements of local color or as mere embellishments with little functional purpose.

The setting features a street corner with rundown houses and a café around which the neighborhood drama—what little there is of it—is acted out. Among the problems and conflicts are the tug-of-war between generations, the need to make ends meet, the gulf between citizen and city government, and vicious gossip—to all of which the play pays lip service without generating significant universal themes out of them.

The action, meager as it is, revolves around the so-called Stranger who mysteriously turns up in the neighborhood. He is in reality no stranger at all, but a man who had left the neighborhood in his youth some twenty years earlier when he fathered a girl out of wedlock. By an incredible coincidence, the Stranger has unwittingly arrived on the scene on the day when his father is buried in the morning and his daughter gets married at night. At the end, he leaves the neighborhood with his identity still unknown to all the characters but one.

The play's continuing relevance was proven once again when the State Theater of Ankara did a full-dress revival in 2007–8.

This neighborhood, like most of its counterparts all over the world, lives its life in small talk. In the play, no meaningful or interesting lines are spoken by any character. Ironically, one character sums up the neighborhood as well as the play itself in the following words: "It's better to let the neighborhood people talk. And they talk and talk and talk, but you still have to hunt for the truth."

The English translation by Nüvit Özdoğru (1920–2002) is remarkably successful. Özdoğru enjoyed fame in Turkey as a prominent actor, director, and translator. With his superb command of the English idiom, he has captured the play's mood and local color. Özdoğru was a graduate of Robert College, Turkey's premier American school and did graduate work at Washington State University and the University of Wisconsin. At the latter university, he staged his translation of the Tecer play in 1953; it was the first Turkish play ever to be produced in the United States. Reviewing it in a local newspaper, Jerry Schecter observed: "The intimate, mundane, humorous, and dramatic life in a small quarter of Istanbul was highly rewarding and slightly amazing in its success." Significantly, America's leading drama magazine of the time, *Theatre Arts*, ran a news item about the production along with a photograph and Özdoğru's comments concerning the play, its cultural context, and the set design. The item noted that "Dr. Joseph Shipley, president of the Drama Critics Circle, is reported to be interested in the play and is making plans for its production."[2] That prospect regrettably never materialized despite the enthusiasm of Dr. Shipley, who, according to a news report in the Turkish daily *Vatan*, observed that "*The Neighborhood* resembles the works of Chekhov and Gorky from the standpoint of universal problems and emotions."[3]—TSH

1. *Simit:* A bread roll in the shape of a large ring, covered with sesame seeds.
2. "First Modern Turkish Play in English," *Theatre Arts* (February 1953), p. 88.
3. *Vatan*, 24 January 1953.

Characters

NIGHT WATCHMAN

WOMAN

COFFEEMAN'S HELPER (NURİ), a young man about twenty-five

GROCER'S HELPER (MEHMET), a young man about eighteen or nineteen

BEGGAR

MILKMAN

WOMAN WHO BUYS MILK

SHOESHINE BOY

SİMİT VENDOR

MIDWIFE (KEVSER), an elderly woman

CARPENTER

GROCER, about fifty-five, plump and bald; talks with a slight provincial accent

STREET-CLEANING WOMAN

STRANGER

BREAD VENDOR

COFFEEMAN

JUNK DEALER

BEYAĞABEY[4] (NACİ), about forty, with heavy eyebrows and a short mustache

PAPERBOY

BEYBABA,[5] a sniffling, bearded man of about seventy, slightly stooped

BOY

OLD WOMAN

WOMAN WITH BASKET

WOMAN WITH BAG

CITY OFFICIAL

FIRST MAN, coffeehouse patron

SECOND MAN, coffeehouse patron

THIRD MAN, coffeehouse patron

FOURTH MAN, coffeehouse patron

GRANNIE, midwife's mother

MAN WITH DERBY, notary clerk

TINKER

WAITER

BEARDED MAN, committee member

4. *Beyağabey:* A respectful way of addressing an actual older brother or a mature man who is not necessarily a relative.

5. *Beybaba:* A respectful way of addressing or referring to one's father or a man of advanced age, not necessarily one's own father.

GRAY-HAIRED MAN, committee member

MAN WITH SIDEBURNS, committee member

SCHOOLBOY, Beyağabey's son, about nine or ten years old

FRIVOLOUS GIRL (ZEHRA), Beybaba's granddaughter

MAN

BACKGAMMON PLAYERS (FIRST PLAYER; SECOND PLAYER)

HEADMAN[6]

WOMAN AND HER BOY

MATCHMAKER

POLICEMAN

PASHA'S SON

FIRST WORKER

SECOND WORKER

FIRST MUSICIAN

SECOND MUSICIAN

THIRD MUSICIAN

FOURTH MUSICIAN

FIFTH MUSICIAN

YOUNG BOY, carpenter's son

YOUNG WOMAN

YOUNG MAN

The Neighborhood; sketch by Turgut Zaim from Ahmet Kutsi Tecer, *Köşebaşı* (Ankara: Kültür Basım ve Yayım Kooperatifi, 1947).

6. Headman (Turkish, *muhtar*): The elected head of a village or of a neighborhood within a town or city.

PROLOGUE

[*The setting represents one of Istanbul's old neighborhoods. It is a place where three streets meet. Left stage is a coffeehouse on a platform. It has a garden partly covered by a vine. An ancient tree casts its shadow over the entire garden. The coffeehouse is Turkish style with an enclosed interior where the kitchen is located. In the garden are several tables. This section can be used only when weather permits. Customers are usually old retired people, but many young men are among the frequenters. Alcoholic drinks are forbidden by the city laws.*

Right stage, opposite the coffeehouse, is a small grocery store that sells goods such as cheese, potatoes, dry beans, sausages, and canned vegetables, but no fresh vegetables. Next to the store is a house. Near the coffeehouse is a house with a bay window. Above its door is a sign on which is written "Midwife Kevser." From here to the grocery store, the street is closed for repairs. Rubbish is piled up on the street. A sign in the street reads "Street Closed."

There is a small water fountain up center. It is situated at the meeting place of two streets extending right and left. On two sides of the fountain is a wall in the old Ottoman style with iron-barred windows. Behind the wall is a small mosque surrounded by cypress trees.

The stage is dark. The only light comes from a streetlamp. The NIGHT WATCHMAN *comes strolling down the street. In his hand is a whistle tied to a chain.*]

NIGHT WATCHMAN: [*To himself.*] This is the one hundred and thirty-fourth night. Every day I have to send a slip to the station. Why, that would come to this much paper! [*Demonstrates with his hands.*] Take away one hundred from three hundred—that leaves you two hundred. Take away thirty-four from sixty-five—if it were thirty-five, that would leave thirty—so this leaves you thirty-one. There are two hundred and thirty-one more days to go to finish the year. What a world! What odd things are going on under the sun! I'd give my life to be a well-read man. What good does an ignorant goat like me do? All he can hope to be is a night watchman or a neighborhood watchman—it's all the same. [*Lights a cigarette.*] You have to watch something. Watch the night or watch the neighborhood: you have to watch for robbers, watch for fires, watch for people who may disturb the peace. Do we have to watch for unpleasant things all the time? Whoever you talk to, he'll tell you that a night watchman watches for harm that may come to the neighborhood. That's not true. A night watchman watches over sleep and sweet dreams. [*Stretches as he yawns.*]

What a strange thing, this sleep! When I see the first morning light, I feel drowsy—as if all the sleep of the neighborhood gathers on my eyelids. I never hear the racket of the day. But at night I almost hear the breathing of the people who sleep in their soft beds. [*Walks around.*]

One hundred and thirty-four nights! Oh my God! Look at the numbers! [*Blows his whistle. It is answered by a whistle in the distance.*] All is quiet. We're as many night watchmen as there are neighborhoods. If they really wanted to, they could let us live like well-to-do people. Why, just in this street here, there are eighteen houses. That one over there has eleven. If you counted all of them, why, they'd come to more than two hundred. Some pay ten a month, some pay twenty. They should at least figure it on a daily basis. What a dream!

Ours is a thankless job. There is no graft in our business. Once in a blue moon, someone may run to me for help. No, I don't mean to complain either. I get tips every so often, at holiday time. I send some of it home, keep the rest.

[*Blows his whistle.*] I'd better take it easy! No patrols around tonight! The chief of police, his aide—they all have their affairs tonight. As long as there's no labor forced on me, I'm all right. [*A dog howls.*] That's a sign of something; I hope it's good. [*Goes under the streetlamp.*] I really like it under these lights. [*Looks at his watch.*] It won't be long before morning. One more round and that'll do it. As soon as light appears in the sky, I turn around and come back to this corner here. The helper of Old Scarface there opens up the coffeehouse and makes me a cup of good hot coffee. I drink it and really get sleepy. The grocer's helper is there about to pull up the shutters. I get a handful of candy or some halvah or a slice of cheese. Whatever Allah gives! Well, that's the way the night becomes morning!

[*Walks around.*] Oh, the things that go one in these houses! Babies scream all night long, sick people squirm with pain, tired hearts beat quietly, sleepless old folks keep their lights burning and sit up all night, hardworking women climb out of their warm beds before sunrise to do their housework. Oh, so much going on! [*A train whistles and passes by in the distance.*]

Someone comes, someone goes. Someone dies, someone is born. That's the way it is with this neighborhood. Yesterday's children grow up, become men. The old ones go, the new ones come. You sweat and struggle, yet it is still the same old world. Nothing changes. I've been a watchman for twenty years, and it is still the same old neighborhood. Well, I'd better make another round. [*Blows his whistle, then takes a few steps. Just as he is about to make his exit, a* WOMAN's *voice is heard in the distance, "Watchman! Watchman!"*] For heaven's sake!

[*A young* WOMAN *comes running.*]

WOMAN: Please, dear Baba,[7] find us a doctor! He's taken a change for the worse. There was a doctor around here, but tonight he's on duty someplace else. I don't know any other doctor. Please, dear Baba!

---

7. *Baba*: Literally "father," but often used to address an older man respectfully.

NIGHT WATCHMAN: May Allah restore his health! It won't be long before morning. Is he very sick?

WOMAN: Friends and neighbors, they're all gathered at his bedside.

NIGHT WATCHMAN: Which house is it?

WOMAN: It is Macit Bey.

NIGHT WATCHMAN: Oh? Poor man. He's been sick for a long time now. So he's really bad, eh?

WOMAN: [*Crying.*] Please, old Baba, a doctor!

NIGHT WATCHMAN: You must never lose faith in Allah. Come with me! [*Both leave. The streetlamp goes off.*]

CURTAIN

ACT I

[*Morning. When the curtain opens,* NURİ, *the* COFFEEMAN'S HELPER, *is seen standing on a chair, checking the lightbulbs in the garden.* MEHMET, *the* GROCER'S HELPER, *is sweeping the street in front of the grocery store. A* BEGGAR *is sitting quietly by the wall of the mosque. The noise of a streetcar and ship and train whistles are heard. People are passing by. The* MILKMAN *enters from the street opposite the coffeehouse.*]

MILKMAN: Milk! Milk!

[*A* WOMAN'*s head appears at the window of the house next to the grocery store.*]

WOMAN WHO BUYS MILK: Milkman! Milkman! [*Comes to the door.*] Where have you been? It's almost noon. The poor child is crying for food, "Waa! Waa!"

MILKMAN: That's the way with the world. I stopped at their house yesterday morning. The poor man was alive. I stopped by this morning to deliver his milk, he was dead. It's so sad, lady.

WOMAN: Too bad! Who . . . who was it?

MILKMAN: Macit Bey.

WOMAN: Oh, no! What a good man he was! [*They go on with their conversation. A* SHOE-SHINE BOY *with his box slung from his shoulder enters from the side of the* MIDWIFE'*s house, walks around the coffeehouse, and heads in the direction of the mosque.*]

COFFEEMAN'S HELPER: [*To the* SHOESHINE BOY.] How's business?

SHOESHINE BOY: [*As he leaves.*] There's nothing around here. I'm going to the streetcar stop.

COFFEEMAN'S HELPER: Look at these streets! Of course you won't find any customers around here. [*Gets busy with the flowerpots.*]

SİMİT VENDOR: *Simit!* Fresh *simit!*

[*A* MAN *with a carpenter's box in his hand comes from the direction of the mosque and rings the doorbell of the* MIDWIFE's *house.*]

MIDWIFE: [*Sticks her head out the bay window.*] What is it, Son?

CARPENTER: It's any minute now, Auntie.

MIDWIFE: Don't be so nervous. This is not the first one, is it?

CARPENTER: No, the fifth.

MIDWIFE: May Allah protect them all.

CARPENTER: I'm late for work on account of this. If she gets more pains, they'll let you know. Please take good care of her!

MIDWIFE: Allah will protect them both! Don't worry. [*The* CARPENTER *waves good-bye and leaves. The* MIDWIFE *examines her flowerpots. As she goes in,* MEHMET, *the* GROCER'S HELPER, *appears singing.*]

GROCER'S HELPER: [*Calls to the* COFFEEMAN'S HELPER.] Nuri, my friend, you haven't asked me why I'm so late! We went to the movies last night.

COFFEEMAN'S HELPER: [*Comes to the edge of the platform.*] Was it any good?

GROCER'S HELPER: Laurel and Hardy. You must go and see it, too. It was really funny.

COFFEEMAN'S HELPER: It's a good thing your boss hasn't arrived yet. He's running after unpaid accounts again, I guess.

GROCER'S HELPER: If I make my boss angry, he won't give me any more privileges. I'd saved some halvah for the watchman. Poor guy, I guess he couldn't stop by.

COFFEEMAN'S HELPER: I made his coffee; he drank it and left.

GROCER'S HELPER: I came late.

COFFEEMAN'S HELPER: He came late, too.

GROCER'S HELPER: [*Anxiously.*] Did something happen?

COFFEEMAN'S HELPER: Yes, Macit Bey . . .

GROCER'S HELPER: Did he die?

COFFEEMAN'S HELPER: Last night. Just before sunrise.

GROCER'S HELPER: [*Walks toward the coffeehouse.*] He was a good man. Whenever I took things to his house, he always gave me something.

COFFEEMAN'S HELPER: He hadn't been around the coffeehouse for quite some time.

GROCER'S HELPER: He was very old.

COFFEEMAN'S HELPER: Retired twenty years ago.

GROCER'S HELPER: From what job?

COFFEEMAN'S HELPER: District accountant.

GROCER'S HELPER: He has a daughter and a wife and no one else.

COFFEEMAN'S HELPER: They have a little money, and the house is their own.

GROCER'S HELPER: How could they have money? The boss was grumbling the other day. He said their bill was getting bigger and bigger. They should at least pay it from month to month.

COFFEEMAN'S HELPER: They poured a lot of money into doctors and medicine.

GROCER'S HELPER: He should've married off his daughter at least.

COFFEEMAN'S HELPER: That's a difficult problem. If they could find a stranger, they might . . .

GROCER'S HELPER: Why do you say that, Nuri, my brother?

COFFEEMAN'S HELPER: She made a bad name for herself in the neighborhood.

GROCER'S HELPER: Do you believe all the things they say?

COFFEEMAN'S HELPER: No, but she became the talk of the neighborhood. Anyway, her mother, too, was . . .

[*The* GROCER *appears around the corner, huffing and puffing.*]

GROCER: [*Pushes his cap back. To his* HELPER.] You loafer, you! Leaving your work and chatting again, eh? [*His* HELPER *cringes and backs up.*] This is the millionth time I've caught you.

[*The* COFFEEMAN'S HELPER *is busy at the tables.*]

GROCER'S HELPER: I . . . Boss, I was telling him about the movie.

GROCER: There will be no more going to the movies at night! This is the last time. Do you understand?

GROCER'S HELPER: Boss . . .

GROCER: If you want to make a man of yourself, you'll have to forget about such nonsense. You lose both your money and your sleep, and you're late for work the next morning.

GROCER'S HELPER: Boss . . .

GROCER: In our day, there was no such thing as opening a store after the sun was up. The time to open the store was when you could begin to tell the white thread from the black thread. If you came late, people would say, "Did some relative get sick, or did someone die last night?"

GROCER'S HELPER: He's dead, he's dead!

GROCER: Who's dead?

GROCER'S HELPER: Macit Bey.

GROCER: I thought one of your relatives was dead. What am I talking about, and what are you talking about? What's it to you if Macit Bey is dead? Your job is to come to the store on time, open it up, set up the shop window, put out the sacks. Hey, tell me, has Macit Bey really died? It's a pity. He's gone too, eh? You could tell from the way he looked that he was going. He had a stroke, poor man. His face looked kind of crooked. Who told you?

GROCER'S HELPER: Nuri, my friend, told me. He got the news from the night watchman.

COFFEEMAN'S HELPER: [*Comes near them.*] He passed away last night before dawn. It seems they sent the night watchman for the doctor and to the drugstore, but it was no use.

GROCER: That's a lot of expense.

COFFEEMAN'S HELPER: They have a little money. And the house is theirs.

GROCER: Yes, it's theirs all right, but it's mortgaged. What money could they have? All they had was a government pension. Their account here grew and grew. They should've at least paid some of it when they got the pension every three months.

COFFEEMAN'S HELPER: They poured a lot of money into doctors and medicine.

GROCER: That's what riles me. You pay for the doctor, you pay for the medicine, and a man goes and dies just the same. And leaves a lot of debt behind in the bargain.

COFFEEMAN'S HELPER: Did you stop giving him credit?

GROCER: [*To his* HELPER.] You mind your own business, you loafer! What are you gawking at? No more movies or anything like that, either! This is the last time. Do you understand? [MEHMET *starts working, but keeps listening to the conversation.*] Nuri, my boy, I don't know when this fellow of mine will make a man of himself. What you were saying about Macit Bey's credit. Now, look, I wouldn't be so heartless. He was my customer for twenty years, ever since he retired and came here to live. I got a lot of his money. It wouldn't be fair to turn my back on him when he was hard up. "Put it on the books," he said, and I did. One page was filled and then another and pretty soon a whole book.

COFFEEMAN'S HELPER: You don't say!

GROCER: That's the way my trade goes. I have to give credit. There are people who pay cash, but a man who calls himself a grocer must be good at bookkeeping. It doesn't take much to put it in the book, but it takes a lot to get it out. It's still trouble whether you extend credit or not.

COFFEEMAN'S HELPER: We have to keep a book, too.

GROCER: Yours is no book account. It's a wall account. Draw a line, draw another one, and another one. Coffee is five, tea is five, everything is five. Count the lines, add them up, multiply them by five, and you have it.

COFFEEMAN'S HELPER: The hookah is twenty, soda is fifteen.

GROCER: What's the difference? Hookah? You put down four lines. Soda? Three lines. Ours is nothing like that. Bingo! In comes someone with a bottle in her hand. What is it you want? Vinegar for Macit Bey's house. Put it down! Bingo! In comes someone with a sack in his hand. What is it? Rice for Macit Bey. Write that down, too. In short, rice, beans, olive oil, butter, salt, kerosene—write it all down. Salt is twelve for a kilo, rice is forty-two, olive oil is sixty—everything is like that. It all depends on what it is.

COFFEEMAN'S HELPER: How much do you think you can collect?

GROCER: Collect? Yes, I'd like to collect, but how can I? You never know. Last month Mullah Mehmed's son-in-law died. His wife paid up every single penny from her inheritance. Thank Allah for his blessings! And last year—you knew the street letter writer,[8] didn't you? He died. His account had piled up, too. He didn't have any property, either.

---

8. Street letter writer (Turkish, *arzuhalci*): Person with a small table and typewriter set up on the street who types letters and petitions for the illiterate or those without typewriters. A common practice in the past, but occasionally still seen.

What does a street letter writer have anyway—just a typewriter. I had my eyes open and acted before his creditors could get there. I brought the machine down to the store, and that took care of the balance.

COFFEEMAN'S HELPER: Macit Bey has a daughter and a wife—no one else.

GROCER: Now wait, let me explain that to you. Macit Bey, may Allah rest his soul, came to this neighborhood twenty years ago. You should've seen it—one loaded cart after another. Piles and piles of luggage. Carpets, chests, trunks, everything you could ask for! [*Sees his* HELPER *leaving work to listen to them.*] You rascal, you! Leaving your work and listening to us, huh? If I twist your ear . . . So this is the type of man Macit Bey was. And his daughter, Dürdane, I don't remember whether or not she was born yet. She was probably a baby. Anyway, this is Macit Bey's second wife.

COFFEEMAN'S HELPER: Oh? I didn't know that.

GROCER: What do you know anyhow? Did you know the other things I told you?

COFFEEMAN'S HELPER: I'd heard a few things myself.

GROCER: A few things? Oh, you mean when he was district accountant? They made the poor man retire because of a "reorganization."

COFFEEMAN'S HELPER: He made his pile.

GROCER: No, that wasn't the reason. He was an İttihatçı. Remember the time when these were the two parties, İtilâfcı and İttihatçı?[9] You wouldn't know them. Well, he was an İttihatçı. What I mean is, he was one of the Young Turks.[10] Well, you wouldn't understand that either. But it's sometimes handy to know the background. You see, these Young Turks were the ones that forced Abdülhamid off the throne. This man, Macit Bey, had a lot of property to begin with—a lot. But it was in Bursa . . . left to him by his father and his father's father before him. If he hadn't had that, where would he be now? All he had was a skimpy pension. Could he have managed to get along with only that?

COFFEEMAN'S HELPER: They say he'd made his pile.

GROCER: That's what your boss said, but you listen to what I say. He started that rumor when they first came here, but later he changed his story—after Macit Bey started frequenting the coffeehouse.

COFFEEMAN'S HELPER: Yes, he used to come around a lot before he got sick.

GROCER: You see what I mean? When they first moved in, he'd never leave the house. That got your boss furious, see? When he bought a house and settled here, people started to talk. "Where can a retired man find all that money?" they wondered. And your boss built up the whole story. Your boss has an open ear, but a closed mind. Nuri, my boy, if you want to find out about this neighborhood, ask me. Your boss wouldn't know this either. But when I hear something, I dig to the bottom of it till I really find out the

---

9. İtilâfcı and İttihatçı: Turkish political parties formed after the oligarchic constitution of 1908.

10. Young Turks: Members of the Unionists (Ottoman Society of Union and Progress), the dominant political force in the Ottoman Empire from the revolution of 1908 until the end of World War I.

truth. What do you think? Is it easy to own a grocery store? Could I stay in business if I didn't know who I was putting on the books?

[*A* STREET-CLEANING WOMAN *appears near the fountain.*]

COFFEEMAN'S HELPER: I heard some other things, too.

GROCER: What other things? Oh yes, about his wife. They talked about her, too. Now, the truth is that this is Macit Bey's second wife. Twenty years ago when they came here, Macit Bey had a twenty-year-old son by his first wife.

COFFEEMAN'S HELPER: Hey, Boss, you talk just like a fortune-teller.

GROCER: That's no fortune-telling. I saw all this with my own two eyes. Macit Bey had a grown-up son.

COFFEEMAN'S HELPER: What happened to him? Did he die or something?

GROCER: No, nothing like that. His father disowned him. But why did he do it? Now, I wouldn't know that. Well, I heard things, but I wouldn't like to say unless I was sure. But the word was going around that the boy and the stepmother were . . . you know, she was young and pretty then.

COFFEEMAN'S HELPER: No wonder!

GROCER: Well, if it isn't true, I hope the man who lied about it pays for it. You wouldn't know. You're young yet, Nuri, my boy. When I hear something, I like to split hairs until I find the facts. I don't believe everything I hear, like your boss does. Oh, what things people say, what things! Of course, nobody means any harm, but this is a neighborhood. You can't keep a neighborhood from gossiping. If one wall is quiet, the other will talk. Plug one hole and another bursts. Sometimes the neighborhood people keep quiet. Days pass, and the people keep quiet—as if their mouths are sealed. One comes, one goes, one passes, one stops. This door . . . bang! It closes. That window . . . bang! It shuts. Something is going on, but the walls won't talk. In times like these I get scared. You know that something is going to blow up, but you wonder on whose head! You never can tell. I'd be scared of my own head, too. Suppose it blew up on my head! It's better to let the neighborhood people talk. And they talk and talk and talk, but you still have to hunt for the truth. That's the only thing to do. Now where were we? Oh yes, that's what people were saying. The truth of the matter is that the boy left town. That's all there was to it. And no one ever saw his face in the neighborhood again. And his name was forgotten. The whole thing just died down, but some people still wonder about the woman in the story. And that's the part you've heard. Do you get me? Would your boss know these things the way I do? Of course not.

[*A well-dressed man (*STRANGER*), about forty comes past the* MIDWIFE'*s house, looks around, and enters the coffeehouse. He sits at a table and scrutinizes the place.*]

COFFEEMAN'S HELPER: A customer has come, and I left the grill on. Boss, you're quite something. I'll see you later. [*Exits.*]

GROCER: [*Follows the* COFFEEMAN'S HELPER *with his eyes.*] That fellow is going to turn out to be somebody. You can tell it by the way he walks. And then look at this Mehmet here! If I go away, he takes off, too. Hey, Mehmet, look here, try to make a man of yourself. Movies and theaters—those things don't take a man anywhere. Look around you! There are movie theaters everywhere. Do you follow me, you miserable loafer? Now the customers are going to start coming in. What are you still loafing around for? Take the broom and come in here! [*Enters the store.*]

STRANGER: [*To the* COFFEEMAN'S HELPER, *who greets him with his hand.*] One cup of hot tea! Make it dark!

COFFEEMAN'S HELPER: [*Yells to the kitchen.*] Tea! Make it dark! [*Enters the kitchen.*]

GROCER'S HELPER: [*In front of the store with a broom in his hand.*] Every morning it's "open up the shutters, arrange the display window, set out the sacks, sweep the floor, dust off the counters, and then sweep the street, too." I can't figure it out. Am I a street cleaner or a grocer's helper? As for getting privileges, he even wants to know what I do at night. [*Gestures defiantly.*] This is the last time I'll sweep the street! [*Enters the store.*]

COFFEEMAN'S HELPER: [*Brings the tea.*] Here you are. [*Eager to converse.*] And a good morning to you!

STRANGER: Thank you.

COFFEEMAN'S HELPER: You're a stranger here, aren't you?

STRANGER: Yes.

COFFEEMAN'S HELPER: Are you looking for someone?

STRANGER: No, I was just passing through. What's the name of this place?

COFFEEMAN'S HELPER: Rüstempaşa.[11]

STRANGER: What's the name of that street? [*Points to the street between the coffeehouse and the mosque.*]

COFFEEMAN'S HELPER: Kuşkonmaz.

STRANGER: What about this one? [*Points to the street opposite the coffeehouse.*]

COFFEEMAN'S HELPER: Mihri Hatun. [*The* STRANGER *is silent.* NURİ *leaves. The* BREAD VENDOR *stops in front of the grocery store. He is pushing a covered handcart with two lids.*]

BREAD VENDOR: [*Loudly.*] Mehmet!

GROCER'S HELPER: [*Appears at the door.*] Hey, Boss! The bread has come. [*To the* BREAD VENDOR.] You're always late! [*As* MEHMET *approaches the cart, the* GROCER *comes to the door.*]

BREAD VENDOR: How are you, Boss? [*Lifts one of the lids.*]

GROCER: How do you expect? As if I haven't enough trouble already, I have to tussle with you. Every now and then they come and close your bakery. Why don't you pay your taxes and get it over with?

BREAD VENDOR: For the past ten years, the taxes have been piling up.

---

11. Rüstempaşa: A section of Istanbul on the European side, near the Mısır Çarşısı, the Spice Bazaar.

GROCER: You'll pay 'em in Hell.

BREAD VENDOR: [*Takes the loaves of bread, two by two, from the cart and throws them to* MEHMET.] One . . . two . . . three. [MEHMET *throws them to the* GROCER *in the same way.*] That's it.

GROCER: Half the time your bread is stale. Customers are complaining.

BREAD VENDOR: Stale? This bread?

GROCER: Tell your boss that! Let him send over some French bread for this evening. Don't you forget, now! [*Enters the store.*]

GROCER'S HELPER: [*As he enters the store.*] Don't forget the French bread.

BREAD VENDOR: All right, all right. [*Exits.*]

COFFEEMAN'S HELPER: [*Sees his boss coming, humming a folk tune.*] Good morning, Boss!

COFFEEMAN: [*Dressed in the old Külhanbeyi[12] fashion, he is tall and lean, and has a pock-marked face. His jacket is over his shoulders. Still sleepy, he comes tottering along from Mihri Hatun Street and enters the coffeehouse. He points to the mess in the street.*] Look at that! Is this a street or the morning after a fire? They piled up all this stuff and then left. Not a single cart has passed for a week. Even a pedestrian wouldn't pass through this mess if he didn't own a shop here or live here. He'd take some other street. [*Spits.*] Goddamn! Look at these shoes! If I didn't own this coffeehouse, I wouldn't set foot here myself. But what can a man do? I opened this shop and have been in business for twenty-five years. It wouldn't do to give it up now. And then I get to thinking and say to myself: "Curse the stinking shop and the whole rotten neighborhood. Why not take off to somewhere else?" [*Sits on a chair and twists his mustache.*] Stupid me! Why didn't I rent that place in Samatya[13] last year?

COFFEEMAN'S HELPER: Hey, Boss, tea or coffee?

COFFEEMAN: If I could have some raki with lemon, that would be better than anything. Last night I hit the bottle again. Damn it, today's rakis are nothing but alcohol. You could put 'em in the spirit lamp and burn 'em. It burns my guts out. I had some appetizers, too. Then I got up in the middle of the night, guzzled water from the jug—glug, glug, glug. The more I drank, the worse I felt. They don't make raki like they used to. Those were the good old days. You could gulp one liter, two liters, nothing would happen. Raki used to build you up and nourish you. If it weren't so, I would've been laid out in a wooden box by now. Good old raki! We had a Balta[14] Mehmet Bey, may Allah keep him in peace. He used to say, "Good raki doesn't burn you up. You can pour it on a fire and put it out." Mehmet Bey was the captain of our Fire Brigade—our Tulumba. He was a rich man. He didn't give a damn about the world. Whenever a fire started, he'd swing on his coat with the skill of an acrobat and be off. Well, Brother,

---

12. *Külhanbeyi:* Name given to hoodlums or roughnecks.

13. Samatya: A district on the European side of Istanbul, on the Sea of Marmara.

14. *Balta* (or *baltıcı*): Title for a halberdier in the old palace guard of the sultans.

I've been raised in the Tulumba myself. I'd slip on my shoes and run wherever the fire had started. [*Gets carried away.*] Haaaaayt! Here we come, the brigade of Rüstempaşa! Mehmet Bey with the lantern in front and blowing the horn. The fire wagon would be like a boat taken off its rollers—swish, out to sea, to where the fire was. But forget that now! Make me a strong one! I always like my coffee strong.

COFFEEMAN'S HELPER: [*Loudly.*] Make a strong one! [*Goes to the kitchen.*]

COFFEEMAN: What kind of "make a strong one" is that? Like a mosquito! A coffeeman's voice must boom and rumble! [*Twists his mustache. Takes out his cigarette case and lights a cigarette.*]

JUNK DEALER: [*His voice is heard from afar, and then he enters.*] Rags! Old clothes! Old hats! Old shoes!

COFFEEMAN: Count them up, you old rat, count them up! Streets, houses, people . . . we've all turned to old rags. [*Comes face to face with the* STRANGER *and greets him in the traditional manner.*][15] Good morning! Good to see you!

STRANGER: Good morning.

[*People are busy in front of the fountain. A customer (*BEYAĞABEY*) comes past the* MID-WIFE*'s house and approaches the* COFFEEMAN*'s table.*]

COFFEEMAN: Have a seat! [*Moves and shows him a seat.*]

BEYAĞABEY: What's wrong? Had a good time last night, I take it. Aren't you over your hangover yet?

COFFEEMAN: Beyağabey, may Allah convince you, the raki we get these days isn't fit to drink. [*Yells to* NURİ.] Bring a good strong one for Beyağabey—on me! [*To* BEYAĞABEY.] So we can enjoy it together.

STRANGER: [*Examines the newcomer. Says to himself.*] Naci, that's him all right. [*Stands up.*] It's senseless that you came here. Are you going to let them know who you are? [*Sits down again, but in such a way as to conceal his face.*]

BEYAĞABEY: They turned the neighborhood upside down again. What kind of city is this? As long as I can remember, repairs, repairs, repairs!

COFFEEMAN: I'm fed up, Beyağabey, fed up. [*The* PAPERBOY *appears in front of the mosque.*]

PAPERBOY: [*Chanting.*] Murder! Murder! Read all about it! Woman murders husband!

BEYAĞABEY: Paperboy!

PAPERBOY: [*As he approaches.*] Papers! All papers! *Tanin, Tasvir, Vakit, Cumhuriyet.*

BEYAĞABEY: [*Hands him some money.*] Give me a *Cumhuriyet.* [*The* PAPERBOY *leaves;* BEYAĞABEY *examines the paper.*]

---

15. Traditional manner: Reference to an old-fashioned greeting by putting the right hand down with the palm turned upward, bringing it up to the mouth, and pretending to kiss the foot or the hem of the person who is being greeted or welcomed. In this form of greeting, no kissing is involved, but a sort of imitation of it in the manner described.

COFFEEMAN: What's going on in the world? [*Blows cigarette smoke.*]

BEYAĞABEY: A treaty has been signed with Britain. Negotiations are going on with France. Hardly anything else on the subject, though.

COFFEEMAN'S HELPER: [*Brings the coffee.*] Welcome, Beyağabey, welcome.

BEYAĞABEY: Thank you, Nuri. [*Points to the newspaper.*] Murder in big print on the front page again. Papers are no fun anymore, either.

COFFEEMAN'S HELPER: There's news in our neighborhood, too. Macit Bey . . .

BEYAĞABEY: [*Lays aside his paper.*] What about him?

COFFEEMAN'S HELPER: He's gone, but may you have a long life!

[*The* STRANGER *looks up startled.*]

BEYAĞABEY: Oh, no!

COFFEEMAN: He was a fine man, may Allah rest his soul.

BEYAĞABEY: He'd been seriously ill.

COFFEEMAN: He'd had a stroke, poor man.

COFFEEMAN'S HELPER: He suddenly took a turn for the worse.

[*The* STRANGER *follows the conversation intently.*]

BEYAĞABEY: The woman wore him out. Yakety, yakety-yak.

COFFEEMAN: It isn't that, Beyağabey. When you reach seventy, that's about it. They were husband and wife for so many years. Besides, he wasn't the kind of fellow to be taken in by a woman's pestering. He just died of old age.

BEYAĞABEY: Drop by drop, water will crack a rock. Never mind about his last sickness. She drove him to it. Too bad. May he rest in peace. He was a good man. [*The* STRANGER's *head droops.*]

COFFEEMAN: "Captain!" He used to call me "captain." And I'd call him "patron," in our way. Macit Bey's gone, so I'm no longer captain. The neighborhood has lost its flavor. Well, this is all he had for his lot, poor man.

COFFEEMAN'S HELPER: He left the grocer holding the bag for a good sum.

BEYAĞABEY: That's not a disgrace in times like these.

COFFEEMAN: [*Looks up.*] The grocer brought it on himself, the fool!

BEYAĞABEY: What have you against the grocer, anyway?

COFFEEMAN: Beyağabey, you don't know him as I do. Since I opened this coffeehouse, we've been neighbors. You live around here, too. You know what I mean. I don't really drink. I just toss a few quick ones down every night. I do so right in front of our kitchen. [*With the back of his hand, he smoothes his mustache.*] And with a few tidbits, too. And nobody even senses it. I don't harm anybody, do I, my brother? Hey, Nuri, you tell me, does anyone have any complaints?

COFFEEMAN'S HELPER: Of course not, Boss, why should they?

COFFEEMAN: If I didn't have any worries, would I be drinking this damn poison? They out-
lawed the Fire Brigade, so I gave in to drinking. And this grocer is supposed to be my
neighbor. Businesspeople shouldn't stab one another in the back. The neighborhood
filed a complaint with the city: "In Istanbul, at Rüstempaşa, at the Mescitönü place, at
the crossroads, the old number 25, the new number 56 coffeehouse is face to face with
the Rüstempaşa mosque. Inasmuch as alcoholic drinks are certainly being consumed
at the above mentioned premises. . ." The bastard made it out just like a lawyer.

BEYAĞABEY: Why do you say "the neighborhood"? You're making me angry. You do everything yourselves and then blame the neighborhood for it.

COFFEEMAN: No, Beyağabey, no! The neighborhood doesn't even know about it. The grocer
wrote a petition and had the old women and children put down their seals or thumbs.
Most of them don't even know how to read or write. They all thought they were signing the account book. He filled the whole paper with signatures. That's the kind of
bastard he is.

BEYAĞABEY: I know the grocer, and I know you, too. You talk as a best friend when you're
with him, and then you charge him with all sorts of crimes.

COFFEEMAN: No, Beyağabey, I don't talk behind anybody's back. In the name of the Fire Brigade, if it's a lie, may Allah strike me dead. I'd say it to his face, too. Wouldn't I, Nuri?

COFFEEMAN'S HELPER: Sure, Boss. What about the petition they signed against him about
the way he wets the soap and salt, adds water to the soda and kerosene, and mixes
stones with the rice? There are seventeen more complaints like that on the list. Did
you forget, Boss?

BEYAĞABEY: If I asked him about it now, he'd say it was you who incited the whole neighborhood. Leave such empty talk aside. Live in peace like good neighbors.

COFFEEMAN: No, Beyağabey, there's nothing between us. We're getting along fine. We've
never quarreled either. Beyağabey, you're a member of the council; you know I didn't
make any petition or anything. Do I look like the kind of man who would do a thing
like that? The neighborhood made an agreement and wrote a petition to complain
about the grocer. They came to me and insisted that I sign it, too. They really insisted,
Beyağabey! And I, just for their sake . . . if you were in my place, Beyağabey, would
you disappoint customers?

BEYAĞABEY: Forget it, man, forget it! [*Folds his newspaper. As* NURİ *goes to the kitchen,*
BEYAĞABEY *and the* COFFEEMAN *stand up.*] Poor Macit Bey! It's a pity. [*Takes a step
and stops.*] What happened to his son, I wonder? [*The* STRANGER *gets excited, takes his
sunglasses from his breast pocket, and puts them on.*] You know, he had a son just about
my age. [*The* COFFEEMAN *shakes his head.*] I'd better go home and ask the womenfolk
to go see his family, and then I must go and prepare the funeral. [*Leaves. In front of
the mosque, he meets a man (*BEYBABA*) walking with the support of a cane. They greet
each other and talk.*]

COFFEEMAN: [*As he is about to go to the kitchen, approaches the* STRANGER. *The* STRANGER *looks at him. The* COFFEEMAN *greets him informally with his hand.*] What would you like to have—coffee or tea?

STRANGER: I've just had my glass of tea.

COFFEEMAN: This one is on me.

STRANGER: Thank you, I just had one.

COFFEEMAN: No, mister, it's the honor of the coffeehouse! [*Yells to* NURİ.] Make two glasses of tea on me! [*To the* STRANGER.] It's clear you're not from this neighborhood. You're a stranger. I imagine this is your first trip to this neighborhood. I know well how to pay my respects to gentleman like you. I am the servant of my guests.

STRANGER: Not at all, not at all.

COFFEEMAN: [*Sits beside the* STRANGER.] You're an engineer working on this road? No engineer would come here at this hour. You're a doctor? No doctor would sit here at this hour. You're a city tax collector? A tax collector comes here only at a time when this place is teeming with taxpayers. I wonder what I should call you. Pardon my asking, mister, but what is your business?

STRANGER: Well . . . I . . . I'm just a traveler. Came to Istanbul from a great distance.

COFFEEMAN: That's nothing for you to keep secret. Anyone who looks at your clothes and manners can tell you're a gentleman.

STRANGER: Thank you. I had some business to take care of down here. Not even that . . . I came just to look around, see the place.

COFFEEMAN: Good old Istanbul! Travel in it forever, you still can't see it all.

[BEYAĞABEY *leaves* BEYBABA, *goes to Mihri Hatun Street, and gives alms to an old* BEGGAR *near the fountain.* BEYBABA *enters the grocery store.*]

STRANGER: The street is in quite a mess. When I saw your coffeehouse, I stopped to rest for a while.

COFFEEMAN: Mister, these roads really make me bitter about the whole neighborhood. I can't help getting mad at the municipality. If they can't afford to build new roads, why in Allah's name do they come around and mess up the whole street? They piled all this rubbish here and then left. It's been like this for a week. But when it comes to collecting taxes, they really get them out of us. Every day officials and more officials! As soon as one goes, another one comes. Tax collectors, building inspectors, policemen, controllers, comptrollers, sanitary inspectors! Coffee or tea for every Allah-forsaken one of them! Figure for yourself how much that would run me! Everything I have is sunk into this place. How am I supposed to break even? You saw for yourself, mister—not a soul has shown up all morning. [*With his head he signals as though saying, "Look, there's no one."*]

STRANGER: If you order things for everybody, as you did for me, only Allah can help you. You are too generous, my friend.

COFFEEMAN: A gentleman like you is priceless! You're a man of breeding; I can tell it by the way you hold yourself. A gentleman can always tell another when he sees one. You knew right away that I'm generous. I can't help it, sir; it's in my nature. My mother, may Allah keep her spirit bright, before I was born promised a sacrifice to a saint so that she might have a son. Allah is great; he accepts the vow, and I am born. After I am born, she wraps me up, gets two candles, and takes me to the mausoleum of a saint to pray that I be blessed with riches as long as I live. But while praying, she gets tangled up. Instead of saying, "May his riches be great," she says, "May his generosity be great." That's the story my dear late mother used to tell.

STRANGER: [*Smiles. Takes off his sunglasses and puts them in his breast pocket.*] If I were from this neighborhood—that is, if I lived in this neighborhood—I'd come down to your coffeehouse every day.

COFFEEMAN: Your word is enough, sir. By Allah, let me be the dust under your feet. My coffeehouse is your coffeehouse. You can honor us whenever you wish. If you see any neglect in our service, I hope you'll forgive us. [NURİ *brings the tea.*] Give it to the beyefendi,[16] my boy. The beyefendi is my permanent guest today. Whatever he drinks, it's on me.

[BEYBABA *comes out of the grocery store with a package of cigarettes in his hand and goes to the coffeehouse. The* GROCER *says good-bye at the door.*]

STRANGER: Many thanks. But this won't do. Let me . . .

COFFEEMAN: Allow me, sir. Let me kiss your foot, Beyefendi! If I said anything I didn't mean, I hope you'll forgive me. [*As* BEYBABA *comes in.*] Come right in, Beybaba. [*To the* STRANGER.] He is the grandfather of our neighborhood. [BEYBABA *sits at a table near them.* COFFEEMAN *to* NURİ.] Make Beybaba's coffee. [NURİ *leaves.*] Who says that Beybaba is a retired man? If all the government employees went to their offices on time the way Beybaba comes down to our coffeehouse, by Allah people's problems would be straightened out overnight. He is like clockwork, our Beybaba.

BEYBABA: No joy is left in the neighborhood.

COFFEEMAN: No more joy is left in the whole world.

BEYBABA: The world? What world are you talking about? This one or the next?

COFFEEMAN: This one, of course, Beybaba.

BEYBABA: What do you talk about this world for? What did you see, what did you get out of it? Everybody's world is for himself. And your world is this coffeehouse, this neighborhood.

[*A* BOY *enters the grocery store.*]

COFFEEMAN: We came to this world, all right, but what did we find, Beybaba?

---

16. *Beyefendi:* A polite honorific for a man, "sir."

BEYBABA: How long ago did you come to this neighborhood?

COFFEEMAN: A few years before Macit Bey moved here.

BEYBABA: May Allah keep him in peace. [*Coughs.*]

COFFEEMAN: May your life be long, Beybaba. [*The* STRANGER *looks depressed.* NURI *brings* BEYBABA's *coffee.*]

COFFEEMAN'S HELPER: Here you are, sir.

BEYBABA: [*Philosophically.*] There will always be new ones to drink after we are gone. Give it here, Son!

STRANGER: [*Gets up. To the* COFFEEMAN.] Let me stroll around for a while.

COFFEEMAN: [*Gets up.*] Just give the order, sir, and I'll come along with you. I know this neighborhood like the back of my hand. Let's go together. I won't let you feel like a stranger in this town.

STRANGER: Thank you, but it's better if I wander by myself. I don't want to bother you. Thank you very much. You've a lot of things to do. Thank you again. [*Exits.*]

COFFEEMAN: Come again, sir. I'll be waiting. My coffeehouse is a good stopping place. Come again. [*Sees the customer to the door, then sits beside* BEYBABA.]

BEYBABA: Who was that man?

COFFEEMAN: A stranger, Beybaba.

BEYBABA: Has he inherited something, is he looking for some land to buy, or is he after somebody? What's his business in this neighborhood, I wonder?

COFFEEMAN: He's wandering around, Beybaba. He says he came to Istanbul on a trip.

BEYBABA: I'm surprised at you, my good man. Is this the place to see for a man who's come to Istanbul on a trip? What have we to offer here? Do we have mosques of sultans, palaces, gardens, or parks? In my whole life I've never seen anyone come to this section without some definite business in mind. Even a native doesn't call here, to say nothing of a stranger. What do you think Istanbul is? People from all over the world, from the far corners of the world, are assembled in this city. Even a native of Istanbul doesn't know Istanbul. Where is Fatih, where is Cihangir, and where's Üsküdar? One who lives in Vefa may never know what Topkapı is like. One who lives in Fatih may never know Ayvansaray. One neighborhood doesn't know the other neighborhood. One section doesn't know the other section. People coming to Istanbul scatter in all directions from the Galata Bridge. Who'd ever want to come here? What I mean to say is, this man must have some definite business in mind.

COFFEEMAN: You got me worried now, Beybaba!

BEYBABA: Well, it makes no difference to us one way or another.

COFFEEMAN: You can't tell, Beybaba! Suppose this fellow is an inspector or something.

BEYBABA: Does it matter to you?

COFFEEMAN: Too bad this is the way I am, Beybaba, I never keep my foolish mouth shut! Do you think I made a blunder somewhere . . . huh? May Allah punish him! No, he doesn't look like one of those fellows, does he, huh? [*Shouts.*] Hey, Nuri, come over here!

BEYBABA: Take it easy, my man! What is it you think you said? What's all this excitement about?

COFFEEMAN: It's no easy matter, Beybaba. Along comes the meeting of the Tradesman's Guild. If I attend, it's no good. If I don't attend, it's no damn good, either. If you go, they say you messed it up; if you don't go, they say you messed it up all the same. It doesn't matter what the cockeyed thing is about—whether it's the city elections or the headman elections or whatever the hell elections it is. [NURI *enters.*] Hey, Nuri! He's an inspector; this stranger is an inspector! Do you think we messed it up somewhere—one of us?

BEYBABA: No, my friend, no! That's not the way an inspector would look. Go on, boy, go on with your work. Your boss is a little turned around today. Besides, what does it matter? What's it to you? You're pretty well off after all.

COFFEEMAN: Good for you, Beybaba! After all, I'm pretty well off. I'm jogging along somehow, and I don't poke my nose in anybody's business either—like some people I know.

COFFEEMAN'S HELPER: [*Angrily.*] Come what may, you always take it out on me, Boss. I didn't even open my mouth. You were the one who was talking to him man to man.

COFFEEMAN: Oh, cut it out! What I want to know is, did this stranger ask you any questions?

COFFEEMAN'S HELPER: He asked me the name of the neighborhood. He asked me the names of the streets, that's all.

COFFEEMAN: Well, it sounds all right. He's come here just to look around. There's a lot to what you say, Beybaba, but this fellow is, maybe, a little different. Curiosity! That's what it is. No one can say that our Rüstempaşa's not a lovely little place. Its air is fine, it has tap water, and for drinking it has spring water. Bring me a glass of water, Nuri. My guts are on fire again.

COFFEEMAN'S HELPER: You pick on me all the time. I heard Macit Bey had made quite a pile, huh?

COFFEEMAN: Goddamn grocer! [*Points in the direction of the grocery store.*] No doubt he's filled your ears with gossip again.

BEYBABA: Such talk makes me angry. If you're retired, you're supposed to eat what everyone else eats, wear what everyone else wears. If you're a little well off in the neighborhood, you must be prepared to wear the label of graft as long as you live—as if retirement means becoming a hermit for the rest of your life. Now, talking about Macit Bey . . . [*They get into deep conversation.*]

[*The* BOY *dashes out of the grocery store and disappears. The* GROCER *rushes out after him.*]

GROCER: You wicked bastard, you! While I'm busy weighing the olives, you go and pinch the candy, eh? If I ever get a hold of you . . . [*Shows his fist. As he is glaring in the* COFFEEMAN's *direction, an* OLD WOMAN *comes to the store.*]

OLD WOMAN: What are you glaring at like that? Don't you go into a trance again!

GROCER: Wherever I look, I see a dirty crook. [*Turns to the* OLD WOMAN.] What would you like to have?

[NURİ *goes to the kitchen.*]

OLD WOMAN: Give me a kilo of that rice I bought the other day.

GROCER: Where's your bag?

OLD WOMAN: I didn't bring it along today. Put it in a paper sack.

GROCER: You buy the stuff cheaper than water from me. If it is bulk goods, I weigh it on the tray of the scales. I sell you goods on credit, and now you make me waste the paper sacks on you in the bargain. Don't you have any fear of Allah in you?

OLD WOMAN: Are you speaking all those words to me? By Allah, you have no feeling of shame at all. I buy on credit, yes, but have I once failed to pay the bill every month, regularly?

GROCER: You're not the only customer.

OLD WOMAN: What is it to me what the other customers are doing? Why are you scolding me?

GROCER: It isn't that, my good woman. I'm stuck in a swamp today, and I can't get out of it.

OLD WOMAN: Who told you to wander in swamps?

GROCER: No, my good woman, no, you don't understand. It's this Allah-forsaken city! Where shall I begin? Sinking, climbing—pretty soon we'll sink our whole lives in these roads. But that's not what I'm talking about. Today one of my customers died.

OLD WOMAN: May Allah give him peace and give you mercy! [*In response to a gesture of disgust by the* GROCER.] And I took pity on you for a moment! Haven't you any conscience or a feeling of kindness? The poor man is dead. All you do is worry about your money.

GROCER: You can't die with the dead. Besides, do you know who it was?

OLD WOMAN: It makes no difference who it was! He's still Allah's creature. He must've been a poor soul if he's been buying on credit and unable to pay the bill. May Allah never leave anyone so low.

GROCER: Did I hear you say "poor," "low"? Would you call a man poor when he owns a house, all that property, furniture? His rugs alone would be valued at a fortune. What do you say to that? And the government pension. Yes, I forgot the pension.

OLD WOMAN: Who was this man?

GROCER: Macit Bey.

OLD WOMAN: Oh no! Oh, what a good man he was! He'd never let anyone down. He'd run to the rescue of the whole neighborhood. Oh, what a pity! Give me that rice and let me go. It's really a pity, really a pity!

GROCER: [*As he enters the store.*] Two hundred and twenty-nine lira!

OLD WOMAN: [*As she enters the store after the grocer.*] Poor man, what a pity!

[*Two* WOMEN *appear in the distance, with basket and bag respectively. They come slowly.* NURİ *brings the* COFFEEMAN'S *water.*]

COFFEEMAN: [*Indicates* BEYBABA *to* NURİ.] He says they finally found a man for the girl. [*Drinks his water.*]

BEYBABA: And a good one, too. He's quite a gentleman. You know Ali Rıza from Daghistan in the Bazaar? This is his son. They are pretty well-to-do, but the girl didn't want him, it seems.

COFFEEMAN: Her nose is up in the air, huh, Beybaba?

BEYBABA: All the girls nowadays are like that. I have a granddaughter—Zehra.

COFFEEMAN: Yes, I know . . . the druggist's daughter.

BEYBABA: She's my elder daughter's daughter.

COFFEEMAN'S HELPER: Who doesn't know Zehra, Beybaba?

BEYBABA: And my son-in-law, may Allah give him brains, boasts that he has trained and educated his daughter. I asked Zehra the other day, "My girl! What type of husband would you like to have?"

COFFEEMAN: With money, no doubt.

COFFEEMAN'S HELPER: Of course.

BEYBABA: Nothing like that. I wish it were so. Most girls wish to have wealthy husbands so they may realize all their dreams—clothes, shoes, rings, earrings, this and the other. Well, there is something to that perhaps. But this one of ours! Can you guess what type of husband she would like to have? [*Coughs.*] "He must," she said, "dance well!" Dance! Can you believe it?

COFFEEMAN: [*With surprise.*] We came to this earth too early, I guess, Beybaba.

[NURİ *bites his knuckles with surprise.*]

BEYBABA: This Dürdane is like Zehra, too. Why shouldn't she want him? You can't make sense out of this modern generation.

COFFEEMAN'S HELPER: Yes, Beybaba, but they're in debt up to their necks.

BEYBABA: Did you say debt? Is there anyone in this day and age who is not in debt?

[*A* CITY OFFICIAL *comes to the coffeehouse. He wears a uniform and has a pile of papers in his hand.*]

COFFEEMAN: Uh oh, here he comes again! [*Springs from his seat, goes to the* OFFICIAL. *They enter the coffeehouse together.* NURİ *and* BEYBABA *continue talking.*]

OLD WOMAN: [*Meets the two approaching* WOMEN *as she leaves the store.*] Good morning to you, Sisters.

WOMAN WITH BASKET: Good morning to you. What have you bought? Sugar?

OLD WOMAN: My old man likes rice pilaf very much.

WOMAN WITH BASKET: We came to buy some bread.

OLD WOMAN: Go get your bread. I'll wait for you here.

[*The two* WOMEN *enter the store.*]

COFFEEMAN'S HELPER: Where is Macit Bey's son now, Beybaba?

BEYBABA: We once heard that he was working for the government in the east, but no one really knows if he's dead or alive.

[*People come to the coffeehouse in twos and threes. Most of them are older men, and it is apparent that they are from the neighborhood.* NURI *leaves* BEYBABA *and receives the newcomers. He greets them, shows them to tables, and provides them with chairs. The patrons act informally and order tea or coffee.*]

COFFEEMAN'S HELPER: [*Waiting on the customers.*] Coffee with sugar on the side! Two strong coffees, five glasses of tea!

[*The* COFFEEMAN'S HELPER *goes to the kitchen. Some of the men greet* BEYBABA *with their hands as they go past him. One or two younger ones kiss his hand.*]

BEYBABA: [*Greets each person differently depending on who it is.*] Salaam, salaam! May Allah bless you my son. [*Everyone sits down. To the relatively older men near him.*] Merhaba! Good day!

OLD WOMAN: [*To the two* WOMEN *who have come out of the store.*] Did you get what you wanted?

WOMAN WITH BASKET: May Allah never show worse days. But look, dear, how stale it is!

OLD WOMAN: May Allah blind that grocer. Because he's given Macit Bey two hundred and nine liras' worth of goods on credit, he's not leaving anything unsaid behind the poor man's back.

WOMAN WITH BAG: It's a pity this happened to the poor man.

WOMAN WITH BASKET: And his wife, wretched one, is left a widow like me.

WOMAN WITH BAG: She'll hardly wait for the forty days of mourning. If someone proposed to her, she'd marry him right now. She isn't like us, dear. All she wants is to live and enjoy life. I heard it several times with my own two ears. She used to say, "How difficult it is to live with an old husband. We both can't be blessed together; it is either him or me." That's the way she sent the poor man off to the grave!

BEYBABA: [*As he leaves, to the person near him.*] I'm an old man, Son; let me go early and wash for prayers. [*They exchange good-byes. More people come to the coffeehouse.*]

OLD WOMAN: I take pity on the girl, though.

WOMAN WITH BASKET: Not that fickle good-for-nothing.

[*The* WOMEN *leave, talking to each other.* NURI *brings coffee and tea to the tables.* MEHMET *appears at the door of the grocery store.* NURI *walks to the edge of the platform and signals* MEHMET, *who comes to the platform.*]

COFFEEMAN'S HELPER: [*Whispers to* MEHMET.] Tell your boss the official is here.

GROCER'S HELPER: Is it a petition or something again?

COFFEEMAN'S HELPER: No, no, it's the road.

GROCER'S HELPER: What road? Our road?

COFFEEMAN'S HELPER: It seems they are going to tear down both our coffeehouse and your store in order to widen this road.

GROCER'S HELPER: Widen the road? [*Enters the store with excitement.*] Boss! Boss! [*As* NURİ *turns toward the kitchen, the* STRANGER *slowly and meditatively comes to the coffeehouse.*]

COFFEEMAN'S HELPER: [*Receives the* STRANGER.] Welcome, Mr. Inspector! Come on in! [*The* STRANGER *does not pay any attention. He sits where he sat before.*] Coffee? Tea?

STRANGER: No, thank you. [NURİ *returns to the kitchen. The* GROCER *and* MEHMET *appear at the door. They anxiously look toward the coffeehouse and then enter the store with sorrowful faces.*]

FIRST MAN: [*Looks at his watch.*] It's almost time for prayers.

SECOND MAN: He has a grown-up daughter. No other relatives.

THIRD MAN: He was at an age to have grandchildren.

[*The* STRANGER *pays more attention.*]

FOURTH MAN: He had a son. They used to say he'd become an actor or something.

THIRD MAN: I'd rather be buried alive than have a son like that.

SECOND MAN: He was quite a rascal.

THIRD MAN: Never once did he remember his old father.

SECOND MAN: I wouldn't be at all surprised if he turned up all of a sudden to get his share of the inheritance.

FIRST MAN: They don't have much of anything except a house.

FOURTH MAN: And they've mortgaged that.

CITY OFFICIAL: [*Appears with the* COFFEEMAN *at the threshold.*] Just about everybody is here for the funeral! [*Salutes and goes toward the grocery store.*]

COFFEEMAN: [*Rolls up his sleeves with the air of a man just starting work.*] Damn this municipality! [*Goes to the kitchen.*]

GROCER'S HELPER: [*Calls out from the door of the store.*] Boss!

[*The* GROCER *comes out panting, greets the* CITY OFFICIAL *and takes him into the store. The* BEGGAR *who has been sitting by the wall of the mosque gets up and enters Mihri Hatun Street.*]

FIRST MAN: He suffered a long time. It's hard on anyone not to be able to move.

SECOND MAN: He's been suffering for twenty years.

THIRD MAN: Both his wife and his daughter are left without support.

SECOND MAN: She might get a husband someday.

FIRST MAN: She's pretty modern, too!

FOURTH MAN: Look at the mother and marry the daughter.

FIRST MAN: [*Stands up.*] Come, let's wash for prayers.

[*At the courtyard of the mosque, movement indicates that the coffin is being brought. Those assembled at the coffeehouse turn their eyes in the direction of the mosque. Then they all get up, some putting out their cigarettes, some leaving their cups half full. Some pay* NURİ. *In small groups, they leave the platform and slowly walk in the direction of the mosque.*]

COFFEEMAN'S HELPER: Boss, the funeral party is leaving.

[NURİ *leaves after the crowd. The* COFFEEMAN *puts his jacket on his shoulders and joins the crowd with quick steps. The* STRANGER *gets up with the hesitancy of a man without a will. He follows the crowd with faltering steps. As the funeral party moves, he falls behind. He can no longer walk; he stops and covers his face with his hands.*]

CURTAIN

ACT II

[*As the curtain opens, the* GROCER *is measuring the area in front of the grocery store with a meter stick. He is followed by* MEHMET, *who is imitating his boss's actions. The* GROCER *walks toward Kuşkonmaz Street and the coffeehouse. He pantomimes drawing lines with his arms. Both of them look depressed. It is around noon; the neighborhood appears deserted. There is no one in the coffeehouse except* NURİ, *who walks onto the platform once in a while. Ship and train whistles and streetcar bells are heard.*]

GROCER: I can't understand it. Why should they tear down my store to widen the road? I can't figure it out. The surveyor isn't going to measure it any other way, either. I use the same measurements that he will. A meter stick is a meter stick. Mehmet, go to Kuşkonmaz Street and walk toward me! Look me straight in the eye. Don't be a slowpoke! If the store goes, it'll be good-bye for both of us. I can't open a new store, and you won't find a boss like me. [MEHMET *walks toward Kuşkonmaz.* GRANNIE, *with glasses and a cane, comes out of the* MIDWIFE's *house and walks in the direction of the mosque.*]

MIDWIFE: [*From the window.*] Don't be late, Grannie.

GRANNIE: No, my dear. I'm soft-hearted. I can't stand sobbing and tears. I'll just offer my condolences, tell them we must go on living, and then come back. That's the pious thing to do, my girl. [*As she goes past the grocery store, the* GROCER *is taking off his cap and scratching his head.*] What's the matter, Boss Grocer? You're scratching your bald head again.

GROCER: [*Puts on his cap.*] Everything's rotten, Grannie. Enough already. Why should they tear down this store? What will they gain by that? Why should anyone put in a road from Kuşkonmaz Street to here? There is nothing there; it's all been burned down.

GRANNIE: Don't just stand there like a scarecrow. Go tell the city fathers that it all burned down.

GROCER: There's someone putting pressure on the municipal people, that's certain. Who'd ever listen to me? Everyone in the neighborhood uses this street—the grocer, the butcher, the baker, the shoemaker, every one of us. [*Points in the direction of the* MID-WIFE's *house.*]

GRANNIE: How would the municipal people know, Son? In the last big fire over there, our house burned to the ground along with the mansion of Zekâi Pasha. Who in the world hasn't heard about that? A million thanks to Allah, my late husband—may Allah keep him in peace—had built this house here out of mud and twigs when he was still alive. He said we might need it someday. Need it we did! After the fire, we took shelter here and weren't left in the street. My poor daughter Kevser's dowry also burned. Poor girl's luck burned down with it.

GROCER: You don't say, Grannie!

GRANNIE: Oh, yes. That no-good son-in-law-to-be! He had his eyes on the house and not on the girl.

GROCER: [*Mockingly.*] That's the way to marry!

GRANNIE: This should be a warning to people who have daughters old enough to marry. After that, my poor Kevser grew bitter against the whole world; she became a midwife. The other day I was sitting with her. Knock! Knock! Knock! There stood before me a big, stupid monster. I said to him, "What is it, Son? Do you have a pregnant one or a backache, or have you got worms in your belly? What is it you want?" And what do you think he said? He said, "You haven't paid your tax bill. If you don't pay it right away, we'll take your property." I got so angry blood rushed to my head. My Kevser found and brought the tax receipts. The no-good looked them over, and it turns out he had a tax bill on the house that burned down!

GROCER: Oh, Grannie, what a pity!

GRANNIE: I'll go to the higher-ups, by God, I'll go to the higher-ups! [*Walks away.*]

GROCER: High officials, low officials, councilmen, surveyors, may Allah take you all!

GRANNIE: What's this coffeehouse doing here, right in the middle of the street? It sticks out like a sore thumb, without any shape at all.

GROCER: [*Mumbling to himself.*] That pig of a coffeeman! I think he's found a way to pull a dirty deal on me again. The official seemed like a nice man to me, but one never knows what people are really like. What did he and the coffeeman speak about at length? [*During this conversation, he has not noticed that* MEHMET *has walked back as he was told.*] You slowpoke, are you still here? Didn't I tell you to walk to Kuşkonmaz Street and back?

GROCER'S HELPER: I just came back, Boss.

GROCER: [*Takes a step toward him.*] When did you come back? You haven't left yet! Come on, get going!

GROCER'S HELPER: [*Runs, repeats the movements.*] Boss, can I come back now?

GROCER: "Boss! Boss!" May Allah take you and your boss! Come on, step on it! [*Points his finger to his forehead.*] Walk without taking your eyes off my forehead! May the devil take you! I told you not to fool around there. Step on it!

GROCER'S HELPER: I'm coming, Boss, I'm coming! [*Stumbles and falls in the mud.*] Oh! Mama! [*The* COFFEEMAN'S HELPER, *who has been watching him, laughs loudly.*]

GROCER: Oh damn! As if I'm not having enough trouble—now he has to go and break his skull. Nuri, my son, this dolt will always fall into the mud like that. [*To* MEHMET.] Now you don't look any different than a gutter rat! How did I ever hire you as a helper?

COFFEEMAN'S HELPER: [*Comes near the edge of the platform. Mockingly.*] What did you discover down there, Mehmet?

GROCER'S HELPER: Shame on you, Brother Nuri! I'll get even with you!

GROCER: Go to the fountain and wash yourself. Don't come near me with all that mud on you. [MEHMET *goes toward the fountain.*] Nuri, my son, this street business will sink us all into a hole. [*Calls* NURI *with his hand.*] Come here, I want to talk to you.

COFFEEMAN'S HELPER: [*Approaches him.*] What's up, Boss?

GROCER: [*Slyly.*] Where's your slave driver?

JUNK DEALER: [*The* JUNK DEALER *appears near the mosque. Chants.*] Old shoes, old hats, any old bottles or papers or clothes! The old-clothes man is here today.

GROCER: [*Turns his head in the direction of the* JUNK DEALER'S *voice.*] Macit Bey's clothes, shoes, and hat. The junkman made a profit there! [*To* NURI.] Where is your boss?

COFFEEMAN'S HELPER: He's napping on the bench.

GROCER: Of course, he's taking it easy with an assistant like you. I suppose he's finished his business with the official. [NURI *shrugs.*] The pig knows what he's doing. Nuri, my son, you saw what a wreck this Mehmet is. He'll never make a man of himself. Where can a man find an assistant like you? You're a worker—that's what you are. Now ask me to open a store for you, and I'd open it just out of spite for that stingy boss of yours. If you wanted to, we could be partners and work together. What do you say?

COFFEEMAN'S HELPER: Honest?

GROCER: I'm fed up with bill collecting anyway. And this neighborhood . . . why, I wouldn't mind if I never saw it again for the rest of my life. The rich and the poor, they're all the same—debts, debts, debts. Spreading 'em around like seeds on the ground. I have to wait all winter before they shoot up so I can harvest my share. If the customer dies, I'm in for it. I'm sick and tired of running from one neighborhood to another to collect bad debts. We can close this store and open a coffeehouse in Sirkeci.[17]

COFFEEMAN'S HELPER: Suppose this plan turns out to be like the last one?

GROCER: No, no, no!

COFFEEMAN'S HELPER: We'll be partners, huh?

GROCER: I'll put up the capital.

---

17. Sirkeci: A business district on the European side of Istanbul.

COFFEEMAN'S HELPER: We'll run it together?

GROCER: You'll do the work. I'm getting pretty old now.

COFFEEMAN'S HELPER: You're not teasing, are you, Boss?

GROCER: Your boss is the one to make jokes about a thing like this. I'm not teasing you. [*Schemingly, mincing his words.*] And what's more, by the order of Allah and the word of the Prophet, you and my daughter . . . [*Pats* NURI, *who is all smiles, on the shoulder. The* GROCER *laughs slyly. They laugh together.*]

COFFEEMAN'S HELPER: [*Abruptly.*] Now I know what I'll do to him!

GROCER: That's my boy!

COFFEEMAN'S HELPER: The soles of my feet are calloused from working for him for ten years.

GROCER: He doesn't even appreciate it.

COFFEEMAN'S HELPER: This way I could never have a shop of my own before my next trip to this earth.

GROCER: Don't change your mind, though, after talking to him.

COFFEEMAN'S HELPER: [*Takes off his apron.*] From this day forth, I have nothing to do with the coffeehouse or with this neighborhood.

GROCER: How's Sirkeci for a location, huh?

COFFEEMAN'S HELPER: To hell with this apron of his!

GROCER: Or better still, let him put it around his waist and do a belly dance before the official. [*Laughs.*]

COFFEEMAN'S HELPER: No, before the whole committee!

GROCER: [*Suddenly collects himself.*] What committee?

COFFEEMAN'S HELPER: The surveying committee. They'll be coming today.

GROCER: My God! Did you say today?

COFFEEMAN'S HELPER: I heard it when my boss and the official were whispering to each other.

GROCER: [*Getting carried away.*] The bastard! He's trying to catch me in a web. It'd be the end of me if they came when I wasn't around. I was going to take off after those unpaid bills again. The official told me the committee was going to come here, but he didn't say today. No doubt they've made a secret arrangement. [*Shakes his fist in the direction of the coffeehouse.*] I'll fix you so that you won't forget it for the rest of your life!

COFFEEMAN'S HELPER: [*Same gesture.*] I'll show you what's what!

GROCER: [*Craftily.*] But don't tell him anything until it's all over.

COFFEEMAN'S HELPER: I'll make him good and sorry.

[NURI *angrily goes to the coffeehouse. Just then, a middle-aged* MAN WITH DERBY *comes to the coffeehouse. He has a briefcase under his arm.*]

GROCER: [*Behind* NURI.] Well, I got all the information out of him all right, but it doesn't sound so good. So the committee will come today, huh? Devil take you with your traps! [MEHMET *comes, wringing his apron.*] Mehmet, my boy, when are you going to make a man of yourself? Let that Nuri be an example to you. He has sharp ears and a smooth tongue. Even if people whisper, he hears them. He wouldn't fall into a ditch like you, either. And whatever he hears, he sings like a nightingale.

GROCER'S HELPER: Boss, may I go home and come back?

GROCER: He hasn't even been listening to me! He doesn't even know what I've been talking about! That kind of fellow would drive a man into a ditch.

GROCER'S HELPER: [*Insists.*] To change my clothes.

GROCER: [*Walks toward the store.*] Allah give me patience!

GROCER'S HELPER: Just an hour's break.

GROCER: Come in here. [*Enters the store.*]

GROCER'S HELPER: [*In front of the store, behind his boss.*] I won't come in; I won't listen to you! Give me my back pay now! [*Enters the store.*]

[NURİ *nervously pushes a chair here and a table there. The* MAN WITH DERBY *gapes at him.*]

MAN WITH DERBY: Psst! Come here!

COFFEEMAN'S HELPER: [*Nervously.*] What do you want?

MAN WITH DERBY: Cup of coffee!

COFFEEMAN'S HELPER: What's it to me? Ask the coffeeman!

MAN WITH DERBY: [*Stutters nervously.*] I'm a n-nervous man.

COFFEEMAN'S HELPER: Then go to the doctor!

MAN WITH DERBY: Allah help me! Don't you work here?

COFFEEMAN'S HELPER: [*Making a ball out of the apron he has been holding in his hand.*] Can't you see?

MAN WITH DERBY: So you've been fired! It doesn't surprise me in the least.

[NURİ *bangs his fist on the table and stalks to the kitchen. The* COFFEEMAN, *awakened by the noise, drowsily looks out the window.*]

COFFEEMAN: [*Shouts to the* MAN WITH DERBY.] Look here, friend, what's all this noise out there? Are you firing cannons in Ramadan,[18] or do you think you're in the heavy artillery? Hey, Nuri, take care of that fool out there! [*In answer,* NURİ *throws his apron on one of the tables.*] Take it easy, now! The customer is always right. [*Straightens up.*] Satan's curses! Suppose this one's an inspector, too. [*Rushes out, rubbing his eyes. To the* MAN WITH DERBY.] What'll you have, mister, coffee or tea?

MAN WITH DERBY: [*Angrily.*] What kind of coffeehouse are you running here? Is this any way to treat a customer? The helper and the boss are two of a kind.

---

18. During the month of Ramadan (Turkish, Ramazan), when Muslims fast from sunrise to sunset, residents were traditionally awakened each morning before sunrise by the firing of cannons so they could prepare the morning meal.

COFFEEMAN: Forgive us, mister.

MAN WITH DERBY: How can I? Your coffeehouse and your coffeeman, your whole neighborhood and street and road . . .

COFFEEMAN: What about them?

MAN WITH DERBY: Are dumps, dumps, dumps!

COFFEEMAN: [*Sits beside the* MAN WITH DERBY. *Amiably.*] Don't say any more, friend! You look like a talkative man. I like customers like you. Let's have a cup of coffee together. [*Pushes his cigarette case toward the man, then helps himself.*] Nuri, draw two! [*They light their cigarettes. The* COFFEEMAN *sees that* NURI *is not paying any attention.*] Nuri!

COFFEEMAN'S HELPER: Make it yourself!

MAN WITH DERBY: See what I mean?

COFFEEMAN: Never mind, we all are human, after all. You can't tell from one minute to another—fair wind in the morning, foul wind in the evening.

COFFEEMAN'S HELPER: Cut it short! Hand me my pay!

MAN WITH DERBY: Send him away! Send him away!

COFFEEMAN: [*To* NURI.] Is it money you want? [*Takes some money from his pocket.*] Here are five lira. [*Puts it on the table.*]

COFFEEMAN'S HELPER: I'm quitting. Hand over my back pay!

MAN WITH DERBY: Throw him out!

COFFEEMAN: Business is slow today. Take the day off. Go any place you want. It's all right with me. But come back early tomorrow.

COFFEEMAN'S HELPER: I'm not going to work here anymore.

MAN WITH DERBY: Get rid of him!

COFFEEMAN: You can have time off until Sunday. That'll make three days, counting today. Isn't that enough?

COFFEEMAN'S HELPER: I'm going to have another job.

MAN WITH DERBY: Too much patience is too much!

COFFEEMAN: Never mind. [*Points to the* GROCER, *who has just appeared at the door of the grocery store.*] What's he giving you this time? Money or the girl?

COFFEEMAN'S HELPER: Both!

MAN WITH DERBY: That doesn't sound bad at all.

COFFEEMAN: May Allah give you brains!

COFFEEMAN'S HELPER: We'll be partners.

COFFEEMAN: [*Signals the* GROCER *to come.*] Partner! Come, come! Coffee is on me.

GROCER: [*To* MEHMET.] If anyone comes from the committee or something, tell him I'm at the coffeehouse. Keep your eyes open! [*Goes to the coffeehouse.*]

MAN WITH DERBY: Is this the generous father-in-law? Giving away both the money and the girl, eh?

COFFEEMAN: [*Shows the* GROCER *the chair near him.*] Sit down.

GROCER: [*As he starts to settle his fat body down.*] What business are you talking about?

COFFEEMAN: [*Abruptly.*] Sit down.

GROCER: [*Sits.*] I thought you were talking about business.

COFFEEMAN: You've led the poor lad on again. You've done it often before, but it'll be hard to go back on what you've said this time.

GROCER: I don't know what you're talking about.

COFFEEMAN: Don't give me that. You could never find a son-in-law like Nuri.

GROCER: After all, my daughter isn't an old maid. I'll give her to anyone I choose. Nuri or Mehmet—that's my business.

[BEYAĞABEY *enters.*]

COFFEEMAN: Welcome, Beyağabey! [*Gets up. The* GROCER *is edgy.* BEYAĞABEY *sits down.*] Nuri, bring the coffee! [NURI *doesn't move.*] Enough of this! Let's drink to the engagement, shall we, partner? [NURI *goes to the kitchen without saying a word.*]

BEYAĞABEY: May he rest in peace! He was Allah's faithful. The whole neighborhood was there.

GROCER: May Allah reward them! Some of us couldn't make it.

BEYAĞABEY: Frankly, you ought to have come.

COFFEEMAN: Beyağabey, may Allah convince you, he's the black sheep of the guild. [*To the* GROCER.] He was your customer for twenty years. Have you no fear of Allah? It was your duty to go. Am I not right, Beyağabey?

GROCER: [*To* BEYAĞABEY.] Don't listen to him! [*To the* COFFEEMAN.] Was it me or you who was lying down on the bench just now? [*The* COFFEEMAN *is taken aback.*]

BEYAĞABEY: That's a shame, too.

COFFEEMAN: May Allah convince you, I had to leave right away after the mosque ceremony. I've a bad liver, Beyağabey.

GROCER: My foot! He just wanted to take it easy. [*Attempts to leave.*]

COFFEEMAN: [*Holds the* GROCER *by the arm.*] Don't leave us! We're just having a pleasant conversation here, that's all. Am I not right, Beyağabey? [*To the* GROCER.] If no one else had gone to the funeral, I still would've gone. Why? Because we've been neighbors for twenty years. I owe him my friendship.

GROCER: Big mouth! I wish that damn mouth of yours was a potato sack so I could tie it shut.

COFFEEMAN: May Allah convince you, I didn't say anything to hurt you. [*To* NURI, *who has just brought the coffee.*] Did I . . . huh, Nuri? I wouldn't. Why not? Because, one, we're good neighbors; and two, you're going to have Nuri as your son-in-law.

GROCER: [*To the* MAN WITH DERBY.] Don't mind him, mister. That's the way a drunkard's mind works. [*Gets up angrily.*] I have a lot of work to do.

COFFEEMAN: [*Pulls him down by the arm.*] Sit down, for Allah's sake. We're enjoying a pleasant conversation here.

BEYAĞABEY: Sit down, man! Are you leaving because I came?

TINKER: [*Chants as he passes by.*] Shine your pots and pans . . .

GROCER: [*Makes a gesture showing impatience. To* BEYAĞABEY.] I'm sorry. [*Points to the* COFFEEMAN.] But he's going to make me use some dirty language. [*Sits down.*]

COFFEEMAN: That doesn't matter. You can give it to the tinker and have it shined.

MAN WITH DERBY: [*Stands up.*] Gentlemen, with your permission . . .

COFFEEMAN: Sit down, for God's sake.

MAN WITH DERBY: I'm not from this neighborhood. I've just stopped here for a while on some business.

COFFEEMAN: So much the better. The business of the whole neighborhood is settled here. The district headman and the council members all end up here. [*Points to* BEYAĞABEY.] He's one of the six members. Tell him what your troubles are.

MAN WITH DERBY: [*Looks at their faces with a strange expression. To the* COFFEEMAN.] Are you serious?

COFFEEMAN: Why shouldn't I be?

MAN WITH DERBY: You said he was one of the six members.

BEYAĞABEY: I see why you're surprised. You probably thought of that old gang of six rough-necks. It's nothing like that, though. This is the name that the neighborhood gave us. That's what they call our neighborhood council.

COFFEEMAN: It's not for nothing that the neighborhood talks about such things. [*Looks at the face of the* MAN WITH DERBY.] What are you anyway . . . a director or an inspector or what?

MAN WITH DERBY: Never mind.

COFFEEMAN: These gentlemen, they are most important. They carry all the burden of the neighborhood. They do all the work. They are the council. They are the Chamber of Commerce. They are the Red Crescent.[19] They are the Protection of Children, etc., etc.

BEYAĞABEY: [*To the* MAN WITH DERBY.] Let's hear what your troubles are. [*The* MAN WITH DERBY *puts his bag on the table and takes out a piece of paper.*]

MAN WITH DERBY: [*Reading.*] Mihri Hatun Street . . . yes, that's it . . . Mihri Hatun Street . . . where is that street?

BEYAĞABEY: Right here. This is it.

MAN WITH DERBY: I'm looking for number forty-two.

BEYAĞABEY: That's Macit Bey's house. [*The* GROCER *and* COFFEEMAN *listen carefully.*]

MAN WITH DERBY: [*Looks at the paper.*] Yes, Macit Bey's. That's what it says here.

BEYAĞABEY: He passed away.

GROCER: What relation are you to Macit Bey?

---

19. Red Crescent: Humanitarian organization in Turkey; official name, Türkiye Kızılay Derneği. Part of the international Red Crescent group. Counterpart of the Red Cross and International Red Cross.

MAN WITH DERBY: I'm no relation of his. I'm a notary clerk.

COFFEEMAN: [*Opens his arms to the side.*] Why didn't you spit it out before that you were a clerk, Brother?

MAN WITH DERBY: The creditors have submitted a lien. I'm to report it to him.

GROCER: You're a little late, my friend.

BEYAĞABEY: May he rest in peace.

MAN WITH DERBY: When did he die?

BEYAĞABEY: We buried him today.

MAN WITH DERBY: Curse my luck! I won't be able to report it to him, then?

COFFEEMAN: Go to his new address if you want to—under the cypress, no number, newly arrived, Topkapı Cemetery. May Allah forgive me!

BEYAĞABEY: [*Seriously.*] Don't commit a sin like that.

GROCER: Who served the lien?

MAN WITH DERBY: The bank.

GROCER: [*To the* COFFEEMAN.] In plain language, the house is mortgaged to the rafters.

COFFEEMAN: [*Teasing.*] In plain language, the bank doesn't allow a man to own a house for nothing. [*Taps the* MAN WITH DERBY.] How much did the fellow owe you?

GROCER: That's none of your business. [BEYBABA *comes in. The* COFFEEMAN *shows him a place.*]

BEYBABA: [*Remains standing.*] What's the topic of your conversation?

BEYAĞABEY: [*Fidgeting.*] An unpleasant business. Macit Bey has mortgaged the house at the bank, and now the bank has served him a lien.

BEYBABA: What a day for that! [*Sits down.*]

MAN WITH DERBY: [*Makes an attempt to leave.*] With your permission, sir.

BEYBABA: Who's this gentleman?

COFFEEMAN: He's a notary clerk.

BEYBABA: [*To the* MAN WITH DERBY.] Look here, Son!

MAN WITH DERBY: Yes?

BEYBABA: You'll say he's dead in your report, won't you?

MAN WITH DERBY: I'm just doing my duty. [*Remembers something.*] Oh, yes. [*Takes out a piece of paper.*] Will you sign here, please?

BEYBABA: What for?

MAN WITH DERBY: Let's write in the report that he's dead. [*Sits down, mumbling to himself as he writes on the paper.*] The person whose name appears on this notice . . . yes, name and address . . . died today. It is certified by us on this day, the fourteenth of May 1939. That's it. [*Gives the pen to* BEYAĞABEY.] Here.

BEYAĞABEY: [*As he signs.*] May light always shine on his soul.

MAN WITH DERBY: [*Gives the pen to the* COFFEEMAN.] You sign it, too, please!

COFFEEMAN: [*Signs with apparent difficulty.*] That's good. [*Gives the pen to the* GROCER.] You do the same!

GROCER: If you're a creditor, this is what you end up with. [*The* MAN WITH DERBY *takes the pen from the* GROCER *and passes it to* BEYBABA.]

BEYBABA: [*Searches his pockets.*] I don't have my glasses with me, but that's all right. Give it here.

COFFEEMAN: Allah will reward you, Beybaba.

MAN WITH DERBY: [*Takes the pen from* BEYBABA *and puts it in his pocket.*] Now the matter is in the hands of the court. The heirs may or may not accept the debts. What do I know! [*Puts his papers into the bag. The* GROCER *sighs.*]

BEYBABA: You wouldn't know, of course, but he left behind a wife and a daughter. How will they manage, poor things?

GROCER: He had a son, too.

BEYBABA: I hope they won't be left without shelter.

MAN WITH DERBY: I wouldn't know one way or the other. [*About to go.*] With your permission?

COFFEEMAN: [*From where he is sitting.*] Good-bye. Come again.

MAN WITH DERBY: [*As he passes by* NURI.] Be more civil next time!

GROCER'S HELPER: [*Shouts from the grocery store.*] Boss! Boss!

GROCER: You and your boss! [*Gets up anxiously and goes to the store.*]

[*A* WAITER *comes to the coffeehouse.*]

COFFEEMAN: Who are you looking for?

WAITER: You!

COFFEEMAN: I don't even know you. How do you know me?

WAITER: [*Impertinently.*] Ah, that's our vocation. What good is a waiter if he doesn't know people? One look at a man's face and I ought to be able to tell whether he's a businessman, a playboy, a government official, a contractor, a crook, a tramp, a cop, or a . . .

COFFEEMAN: Cut it out! What do you want?

WAITER: Saffet Hanım[20] has sent her regards.

COFFEEMAN: And who are you?

WAITER: I wait on tables, and they hired my boss to take care of the wedding.

COFFEEMAN: Say so then!

WAITER: We're short of chairs. There'll be a big crowd tonight. We need fifteen or twenty more chairs.

COFFEEMAN: We have none to spare.

WAITER: We'll pay rent.

COFFEEMAN: [*Makes believe he is leaving.*] Get them somewhere else.

WAITER: [*Hands him an envelope.*] This is for you.

COFFEEMAN: What is it?

---

20. *Hanım:* A title meaning "Miss" or "Mrs." (used after a first name).

WAITER: An invitation.

COFFEEMAN: For tonight?

WAITER: To the dinner, too.

COFFEEMAN: Why didn't you tell me that before? The chairs will be ready tonight. [*Pats the* WAITER *on the shoulder.*] Understand?

WAITER: That's the spirit, Boss!

COFFEEMAN: All right, all right. Come and get them tonight. [*The* WAITER *leaves.*] Where the hell did my helper disappear to?

[*The* GROCER, *while talking with his own* HELPER, *looks in the direction of Kuşkonmaz, then hastily walks there.* BEYAĞABEY *and* BEYBABA *talk between themselves, occasionally eavesdropping on the* WAITER.]

BEYAĞABEY: The grocer's going to Kuşkonmaz.

[*Three men,* COMMITTEE MEMBERS, *appear from Kuşkonmaz, engrossed in a discussion.*]

COFFEEMAN: [*Astonished.*] It's the committee.

BEYBABA: What committee is it this time?

COFFEEMAN: The Technical Committee. Damn it! So he's put the fix on the officials. He's pulled a fast one on me, eh? Suppose I'd gone to the Fish Bazaar to get drunk and forget my worries or something? He really would have done me in then. I'll show him what's what! [*Rushes up to the men. The* COMMITTEE MEMBERS *carefully examine the whole area. One of them is bearded, another is gray haired, and the third one is a young man with sideburns and a pipe. The* GROCER *and the* COFFEEMAN *follow them with anxious looks.*]

BEYAĞABEY: These committees come and go, but the road is still unfinished. It is still in a mess!

BEYBABA: Once a thing is wrecked, it isn't repaired easily. A pipe around here burst the other day. The whole water system got wrecked. They still need to repair it. People are lining up in front of the fountain, day and night, night and day. They shut off the gas for repairs, and it still hasn't come back on. And coal is being sold for a pretty penny. It's just like old age—rheumatism, gall stones, hardening of the arteries, dizzy spells. And you can never get repaired again.

BEYAĞABEY: The neighborhood has grown old, Beybaba.

BEYBABA: If it goes on like this, it's going to die one of these days. The whole neighborhood has changed. It's almost deserted now. Anyone who can afford to is selling everything and moving someplace else.

BEYAĞABEY: Do you have a mind to do likewise, Beybaba?

BEYBABA: Are you out of your mind, Son? Nobody is tying my hands. If I'd wanted to, I could've moved long ago. I'm going to die here, Son. That's what I'm going to do. [*A moment's silence. A* SCHOOLBOY *wearing a uniform comes to talk to* BEYAĞABEY. BEYBABA *looks at the* SCHOOLBOY.] Praise Allah! He's grown big and tall.

SCHOOLBOY: Father, I'm going to buy a notebook. Teacher said so.

BEYAĞABEY: Kiss Beybaba's hand, like a good boy! [*The* BOY *kisses* BEYBABA's *hand.*]

BEYBABA: May you have a long, long life, my child!

BEYAĞABEY: It's getting so we buy a notebook every day. What do you do with all these notebooks—eat them?

SCHOOLBOY: This one is for drawing, Father.

BEYAĞABEY: Haven't you one already?

SCHOOLBOY: I had one, Father, but my brother tore it.

BEYAĞABEY: [*Hands him money.*] It's your fault. You shouldn't leave it lying around. If you don't take good care of this one, I'll never buy you another notebook. Is that clear?

SCHOOLBOY: Yes, but, Father, why don't you tell my brother not to take my notebooks? [*Leaves running; enters the grocery store.*]

BEYBABA: [*Follows the* BOY *with his eyes.*] I wonder if we were like this, too, when we were young? Of course not! In our day, could a child this age enter a coffeehouse and talk to his father this way?

[*The* COMMITTEE MEMBERS *together with the* COFFEEMAN *and the* GROCER *approach the grocery store, talking all the while.*]

BEYAĞABEY: The committee's coming here, I think.

COFFEEMAN: [*To the* BEARDED MAN.] Gentlemen, won't you honor us by having a cup of coffee?

GROCER: [*Pointing to the front of his store.*] Come on over, gentlemen! I'll set up the chairs right away.

BEARDED MAN: [*Pays no attention; goes on talking.*] Now look at these marks on the basement wall. They start right over here. These definitely indicate that the real catacomb—yes, the catacomb—is situated at this spot. [*Points toward the store.*] Exploration is necessary in this direction.

GROCER: [*Pleads.*] Have pity, sir, have pity!

COFFEEMAN: Cata . . . catastrophe, huh?

GRAY-HAIRED MAN: The angle ties, characteristic of Byzantine architecture, are present here, too. [*Points toward the coffeehouse.*] If you ask my opinion, there must be a line coming right through here.

COFFEEMAN: [*Bewildered.*] No, no, no, no, sir, you're wrong!

GROCER: [*As if answering him.*] You see what you've done? [*The* COFFEEMAN *frowns.*]

GRAY-HAIRED MAN: [*Turning to the* COFFEEMAN.] Are you the owner of the coffeehouse?

COFFEEMAN: My coffeehouse is famous, sir.

GROCER: This corner is known for its grocery store, sir.

BEARDED MAN: [*To his colleagues.*] Let's rest a while at this coffeehouse. We can discuss it there. [*The* COMMITTEE MEMBERS *move toward the coffeehouse, saying, "OK." The* COFFEEMAN *is happy.*]

COFFEEMAN: Nuri! Come right in, gentlemen. Nuri! Gentlemen, come in, come in.

GROCER: [*Groaning.*] That's the end of me! [NURİ *comes running, greets the* MEMBERS, *shows them seats. They sit down. The* GROCER *follows them and stands in a corner in an attitude of respect, with his hands clasped in front.*]

COFFEEMAN: What's your order, sir?

BEARDED MAN: [*Casually dressed, wearing a bow tie.*] What do you serve?

COFFEEMAN: Coffee, tea, soda, Turkish delight, the hookah, juices, buttermilk, lemonade, ice cream.

MAN WITH SIDEBURNS: Ice cream!

COFFEEMAN: Please forgive me. We're out of ice cream right now. [*To the* BEARDED MAN.] How about a good glass of hot tea—tradesman style?

BEARDED MAN: [*Smiles.*] Excellent. [*The others also order tea.*]

COFFEEMAN: [*Shouts.*] Pour three! Steep it.

[NURİ *leaves running.* COMMITTEE MEMBERS *discuss among themselves. The* GROCER *approaches the* COFFEEMAN.]

GROCER: Can you figure it out?

COFFEEMAN: If you heed what this tall one says, my coffeehouse is gone.

GROCER: That's nothing. If you listen to what this one with the glasses says, my store will be torn down.

COFFEEMAN: Things look bad!

[*A* GIRL, *seventeen or eighteen, comes hopping and skipping near* BEYBABA. *She has the manners of a frivolous girl and wears loud clothes.*]

BEYBABA: What brings you here, Zehra?

FRIVOLOUS GIRL: [*Embraces her* GRANDFATHER.] Bonjour, Grandpa! [*To* BEYAĞABEY.] Bonjour, sir.

BEYAĞABEY: Welcome, my girl.

BEYBABA: Did you stop at the house?

FRIVOLOUS GIRL: I don't have to stop at the house to see you, dear Grandpa. [*To* BEYAĞABEY, *informally.*] I'm really surprised at the kind of life you lead. All your life passes between this coffeehouse and home. What is there at this filthy coffeehouse to make you want to spend all your time here? Is it all for the shade of this vine? If you wish to see each other, you should have at-home days and see each other that way. What do you have here? Black cypress trees, a stumpy old minaret, a mausoleum, and a graveyard. I'd be bored stiff if I had to spend my time here.

BEYAĞABEY: That's not a fair statement at all.

BEYBABA: [*To* BEYAĞABEY.] Don't listen to her outbursts.

FRIVOLOUS GIRL: And on that corner is a filthy, filthy, filthy grocery store! I wouldn't buy a thing from that place. And look at the condition of this street! My shoes are a shambles. [*Sits down, adjusts her shoes. Bursts out.*] Grandpa, I've a surprise for you! Can you guess what it is? Impossible! You won't ever guess! I'm so excited! Why don't you make a guess, Grandpa dear?

BEYBABA: How can I ever guess your nonsense?

FRIVOLOUS GIRL: Nonsense! That's what you always say. [*Suddenly.*] I'm going to Paris!

BEYAĞABEY: [*Curiously.*] To Paris?

BEYBABA: [*To* BEYAĞABEY.] Didn't I tell you?

FRIVOLOUS GIRL: [*To her* GRANDFATHER.] Don't you believe it?

BEYBABA: Was Paris mentioned in a novel that you've read?

FRIVOLOUS GIRL: Grandpa dear! What's the Paris of the novel or even the Paris of the cinema compared to the Paris inside me? The Eiffel Tower, the River Seine, Cathédrale de Notre Dame, Montparnasse, Grand Palais, Champs Élysées, Versailles, Printemps, music, dance, opera, theater—it's all so *chic, chic, chic!*

BEYAĞABEY: To live in Rüstempaşa and make all this trip in your imagination! It's a pretty inexpensive trip.

FRIVOLOUS GIRL: You don't believe me, either?

BEYBABA: Tell me, did you pass your examinations?

FRIVOLOUS GIRL: Oh, Grandpa, I'm going to Paris to finish my education. Father is going to do everything he can for me. He wants me to have a fine education. What can I learn here? The Academy of Fine Arts is so provincial, provincial, provincial! Wouldn't it be a pity to let my talents go to waste?

BEYBABA: [*Straightening up.*] So?

FRIVOLOUS GIRL: Father is going to take me there himself. I'll get myself a room in a boardinghouse, and then he'll return here.

BEYBABA: So, your father humors you in this. No wonder your foolish ideas have gotten so big. Who will manage the drugstore while he's gone?

FRIVOLOUS GIRL: His assistant, of course, Grandpa.

BEYBABA: [*Angrily.*] If you have a business, you should run it yourself. As soon as he leaves this place, that will be the end of his shop. [*To* BEYAĞABEY.] I would be dead right if I said that man doesn't even have the brains of a child! That's my son-in-law! The girl is exactly like her father.

FRIVOLOUS GIRL: Grandpa dear, you never liked my father. And he says, "People your grandpa's age never appreciate the spirit of youth." But I think you're right, too, Grandpa. Father is *demi-éclairé.*

BEYBABA: What did you say?

FRIVOLOUS GIRL: I mean, he is only half educated.

BEYBABA: Did you say "half"? He's not even quarter educated. He's plain ignorant.

BEYAĞABEY: Can't be that bad.

BEYBABA: But it is.

FRIVOLOUS GIRL: Grandpa dear, Father is very strong in science. What he lacks is . . .

BEYBABA: Yes?

FRIVOLOUS GIRL: *Musique, peinture, architecture, littérature.*

BEYBABA: What he lacks is brains.

FRIVOLOUS GIRL: In other words, *beaux arts.*

BEYBABA: Bizarre? Yes, he is bizarre.

FRIVOLOUS GIRL: Grandpa, I mean he lacks general *culture.* I'll make up for what he lacks.

BEYAĞABEY: What'll you be studying in Paris?

FRIVOLOUS GIRL: *Peinture.*

BEYAĞABEY: I beg your pardon?

FRIVOLOUS GIRL: That's painting.

BEYAĞABEY: Wouldn't it be better if your father bought you a good camera?

FRIVOLOUS GIRL: *Pardon,* sir, but . . . [*Bites her lip.*] Oh, I couldn't explain it to you. It would take so long!

BEYBABA: May Allah give you brains.

FRIVOLOUS GIRL: [*To* BEYAĞABEY.] Raphael, Michelangelo, Picasso. Shall I go on?

BEYAĞABEY: Excuse me, but who are all those people?

FRIVOLOUS GIRL: Don't you know them? They are great painters.

BEYAĞABEY: No, I never mix with foreigners.

FRIVOLOUS GIRL: We will never understand each other, sir.

BEYBABA: Who can understand you, anyway?

FRIVOLOUS GIRL: [*Embraces her* GRANDFATHER.] You, Grandpa dear, you!

BEYBABA: Don't be insolent! Now explain to me how this thing happened.

FRIVOLOUS GIRL: [*Sits down.*] What thing, Grandpa dear?

BEYBABA: This Paris thing. Where did your father get this idea of Paris?

FRIVOLOUS GIRL: Oh, Grandpa dear, can't you understand at all? Who's going to Paris?

BEYAĞABEY: Weren't you talking of going to Paris all this time?

FRIVOLOUS GIRL: I wish I could! I was just telling you what was going on in my mind.

BEYBABA: So you're not going to Paris, then?

FRIVOLOUS GIRL: [*Sighing.*] I'm afraid not, Grandpa.

BEYBABA: I'm very glad to hear that.

[*A moment's pause. Ship and train whistles are heard.*]

FRIVOLOUS GIRL: [*Dries her eyes inconspicuously.*] These train and ship whistles are getting on my nerves, my dear Grandpa.

[*The* COMMITTEE MEMBERS *by this time have finished drinking the tea* NURİ *brought them. They are now busy with a sketch they have laid on the table.*]

GROCER: [*To the* COFFEEMAN.] Let's sail over and see what all this talk is about.

COFFEEMAN: Go ahead. I'll come in from the starboard. [*The* COFFEEMAN *stands in front of the* GROCER, *and the* GROCER *comes near the* COMMITTEE MEMBERS *sideways.*]

GROCER: [*Coughs.*] Excuse me, sir. [*The* COMMITTEE MEMBERS *turn toward him.*] We've been around this neighborhood for some time, so if there's any information you may care to have, we would . . . [*To the* COFFEEMAN.] Wouldn't we?

COFFEEMAN: [*Approaches.*] We're not what you call natives of this city, sir, but we're fairly close to it. There's no such thing as a native of Istanbul, anyway, sir. There are only natives of neighborhoods.

BEARDED MAN: [*To the* GROCER.] Are you the headman of this neighborhood?

GROCER: [*Straightens up.*] The neighborhood wanted it a lot, sir, but I didn't accept the honor.

BEARDED MAN: Is that store yours?

GROCER: [*Getting excited.*] Yes, yes, sir! I'm a very poor man, believe me. I have three little girls and a son, eight years old. It's a big family! This store is all I have to feed all those mouths. I am at your mercy.

COFFEEMAN: May the Great Allah convince you, sir, that there is no profit in this coffeehouse business at all, but the whole future of my family rests on what I get out of it. If you're a coffeeman in times like these, you're sunk. [*Slaps his neck.*] But if you sell groceries, you're sitting pretty. You buy stuff for nothing and sell it for four times what it's worth. In the coffee business, may Allah convince you, you can't make more than two hundred cups from a kilo of coffee. I buy the coffee for a price. Add to that the cost of the sugar, coal, rent, gas, cups, plates, broken dishes, torn napkins. You figure the rest for yourself, sir.

GROCER: Sir, there are grocers, and then there are grocers. But an honest man who tries to do an honest business is Allah's beloved if Allah loves the poor. You have to have capital to run a grocery store. Now, if I had a grocery store in Yağkapanı or Unkapanı,[21] or even in the Fish Bazaar, then I'd call five hundred or a thousand just small change. Mine is only a small business. If I had the brains I should've had, I'd have opened a coffeehouse and made a pile. You buy the coffee wholesale; you buy the sugar wholesale. You buy everything wholesale and cheap. After making the coffee, you save the grounds, mix it with some new coffee, and serve it all over again. You steam the tea leaves in hot water, and Allah gives you the water. People come to play backgammon, you serve 'em a couple of pieces of candy. People come to play cards, you serve 'em the same, and it costs you almost nothing.

BEARDED MAN: [*To the* GROCER *and the* COFFEEMAN.] You've given us extensive information about the problems of the grocery and the coffeehouse business. We are very obliged to you. [*The* COMMITTEE MEMBERS *go back to the sketches.*]

COFFEEMAN: [*To the* GROCER.] Do you like what you've done?

GROCER: You could've shut your big mouth, too.

COFFEEMAN: You made 'em angry. Did you have to shoot your mouth off like that?

21. Yağkapanı and Unkapanı: Business districts in Istanbul.

GROCER: I used to think you had a head on your shoulders. Now clean up the mess you've made.

[*Gestures and mimicry between the* GROCER *and the* COFFEEMAN.]

FRIVOLOUS GIRL: Where's my soda, Grandpa dear? I won't leave until I have it.

BEYBABA: All right, all right!

FRIVOLOUS GIRL: Coffeeman! Coffeeman!

COFFEEMAN: [*Without turning his head.*] What do you want? [*To the* GROCER.] Those snobs came here to investigate, and you tried to teach them about the grocery business, you stupid ass.

GROCER: You're the stupid ass. Were you going to hire 'em as handymen, you fool?

COFFEEMAN: [*Makes a fist.*] You moose!

GROCER: [*Does the same.*] Pig!

FRIVOLOUS GIRL: [*Impatiently.*] My soda! [*Pounds the table.*]

COFFEEMAN: [*Shouts.*] It's coming! [*Goes over to* BEYBABA.] What'll you have, Beybaba?

FRIVOLOUS GIRL: [*Frowns and says to the* COFFEEMAN.] Rude man!

COFFEEMAN: [*Looks the* GIRL *up and down, then turns to* BEYBABA.] May I help you, Beybaba?

FRIVOLOUS GIRL: One asks the ladies first. You ought to learn this.

COFFEEMAN: [*Unable to take it any longer.*] Don't talk as if you're not from this neighborhood, Sister!

FRIVOLOUS GIRL: Stop it! I'm not going to talk to you. Bring me the soda!

COFFEEMAN: Take it easy, Sister. It's a difficult time. We couldn't get any soda today.

FRIVOLOUS GIRL: Grandpa dear, I can't bear the sight of this impolite man. What rudeness! He doesn't even know how to talk to ladies. I'll never set foot in this place again. Perihan invited me to her wedding; that's why I came here. I wouldn't even go to the wedding if there weren't going to be dancing. This coffeehouse makes me feel bitter against the whole neighborhood. Whenever I ask Grandma where you are, she always answers, "Your grandpa is at the coffeehouse, like he owns the place." And then I come down here, and it's always like this. I wish they'd move this coffeehouse. It ought to be torn down!

COFFEEMAN: Go easy on us, Sister!

FRIVOLOUS GIRL: [*Turns her back to the* COFFEEMAN. *To her* GRANDFATHER.] I stopped at Dürdane's before I came here. Her eyes were all swollen from crying. I got bored there. Came down here only to get more bored. Now I don't even feel like going to Perihan's wedding. But they say the band is going to be marvelous tonight. [*Embraces her* GRANDFATHER.] Good-bye, Grandpa! [*To* BEYAĞABEY.] Good-bye, sir. [*To the* COFFEEMAN.] Rude man!

MAN WITH SIDEBURNS: [*Suddenly gets up, looks at* ZEHRA.] Zizi!

FRIVOLOUS GIRL: [*Turns toward the sound and speaks in the same manner.*] Kiki!

[*The other* COMMITTEE MEMBERS *give them strange looks.*]

MAN WITH SIDEBURNS: [*Extends both hands.*] I can't believe my eyes! What a wonderful coincidence! And in this *décor,* you're just like a madonna! Showering us poor peasants with the gifts of your beauty. Extraordinary.

GRAY-HAIRED MAN: [*Looks at the* BEARDED MAN, *who looks back. They shake their heads meaningfully and go back to the sketches.*] You see?

BEYBABA: [*Gets up as* ZEHRA *holds the young man's extended hands. In a rage.*] Good for you, my boy! Showering the poor peasants with gifts is a good deed. What do you do for a living?

FRIVOLOUS GIRL: *Pardon,* Grandpa dear! Let me introduce my friend to you. He got the Premier Prix in architecture this year.

BEYBABA: What?

FRIVOLOUS GIRL: Premier Prix—that is, he got the first prize at the Academy of Fine Arts. He'll go to Paris!

COFFEEMAN: Well, I'll be damned!

FRIVOLOUS GIRL: [*Continues.*] Kiki—*pardon,* Kemal and I are friends from both the lycée and the academy. He calls me Zizi. I call him Kiki.

MAN WITH SIDEBURNS: [*Bows before* BEYBABA *very politely.*] I'm fortunate to know your granddaughter, sir.

BEYBABA: [*Shaking his head.*] I can see that.

MAN WITH SIDEBURNS: [*To* ZEHRA.] I'd like you to meet my colleagues. [ZEHRA *and the* YOUNG MAN *go to the table where the* COMMITTEE MEMBERS *sit. The* GIRL *offers her hand to the* MEN *as she is introduced. The* GRAY-HAIRED MAN *is cold. The* BEARDED MAN *is more courteous. They shake hands and offer each other seats.*]

COFFEEMAN: What's going on here, Beybaba?

BEYBABA: [*Sadly.*] Well, you couldn't understand it unless you were a grandfather yourself. One of my sons was killed in the war. Another one has no children. One daughter is in Erzurum. And this is what's left to me.

[GRANNIE, *the* MIDWIFE*'s mother, appears at Mihri Hatun Street. A* MAN *enters the grocery store.*]

BEYAĞABEY: This new generation! [*Shakes his head.*]

COFFEEMAN: [*Points out the* MAN WITH SIDEBURNS *to* BEYBABA.] I suppose he knows how to dance well!

GROCER: [*To himself.*] There's a woman's hand in this.

GROCER'S HELPER: [*Calls from the store.*] Boss! Come collect the money!

GROCER: Collect the money! [*Hurries out, goes toward the store, stops, and starts back.*] The committee . . . [*Turns again and goes toward the store.*] Yes, I must get the money.

STREET-CLEANING WOMAN: [*Rests on her broom and talks to* GRANNIE.] I work, too. It's not a shame to work with your hands.

GRANNIE: Yours is work, Daughter. [*Points to the* FRIVOLOUS GIRL.] But what about this one? By God, she's frivolous, that's what she is. It's the end of the world! Thank Allah if the earth doesn't split open and we don't all sink. [*Walks away.*]

STREET-CLEANING WOMAN: [*As she sweeps.*] She's been to school. Of course she won't sweep the streets like me.

MAN WITH SIDEBURNS: [*To* ZEHRA.] What we've observed here is very interesting, you know!

BEARDED MAN: When they dug these roads around here for repairs, they came across some signs of ancient buildings. The municipality, presuming that these buildings might be works of antiquity, has found it necessary to have them examined by experts before starting the repairs.

GRAY-HAIRED MAN: [*To the* BEARDED MAN.] We have completed the details necessary for the main points in our report. We two are agreed. As far as our friend is concerned . . .

MAN WITH SIDEBURNS: *Pardon!* I'm *d'accord* with the conclusions you've reached. Where I differ is, *théoriquement parlant,* on an artistic issue. [*To* ZEHRA.] *N'est-ce pas?* [*To the others.*] An artistic point!

GRAY-HAIRED MAN: [*Angrily.*] All right, all right. You can write a report of your own. [*To the* BEARDED MAN.] There is nothing more to be discussed. We may as well leave now.

BEARDED MAN: Coffeeman!

COFFEEMAN: [*Anxiously hurrying over toward him.*] Yes, sir?

BEARDED MAN: [*Attempting to hand him some money.*] The check, please!

COFFEEMAN: Oh, no, sir! You're my guests.

BEARDED MAN: [*Lays the money on the table.*] Keep the change! [*They all get up.*]

COFFEEMAN: Let me be your slave, sir! Take your money, sir! You can pay next time you come. You brought honor to my coffeehouse. Please come again! I'll be waiting. [*Puts the money back in the hand of the* BEARDED MAN.]

BEARDED MAN: How can this be?

COFFEEMAN: It's our pleasure, sir, believe me. [*Pleadingly.*] If you don't mind, I'd like to ask you a question. There isn't any danger to my coffeehouse, is there?

BEARDED MAN: I don't know what you're talking about.

COFFEEMAN: You won't tear down the coffeehouse or anything because of the road, will you?

BEARDED MAN: Oh, did you think we came to survey the road? [*The* COFFEEMAN *nods in assent.*] We have nothing to do with it. The City Engineering Committee looks after the road situation. We came to look for antiquities. Is that clear to you now?

COFFEEMAN: [*With joy and surprise.*] Did you say antiquities?

BEARDED MAN: Of course!

COFFEEMAN: By God, we have an antiquity right here!

BEARDED MAN: Something different from what we've seen already?

COFFEEMAN: It's this fellow here, sir, this grocery man. [*The* COMMITTEE MEMBERS *laugh.*]

GRAY-HAIRED MAN: Shall we go? [*The others nod.*] Come along, then! [*Returns the money to the* COFFEEMAN'*s palm. The* COFFEEMAN *stares.*]

MAN WITH SIDEBURNS: [*To the* FRIVOLOUS GIRL.] Be careful of your shoes . . .

FRIVOLOUS GIRL: They can't get any worse. I'll buy some new ones.

[*The group leaves the platform and goes toward the grocery store.* MEHMET *appears and disappears at the door. The* GROCER *dashes out, panting. He is holding two separate bundles of money in his hands. He approaches the* BEARDED MAN.]

GROCER: Sir, how about my store?

BEARDED MAN: What do you want? You're doing all right, aren't you?

GROCER: [*Puts his hands behind his back.*] I'm a poor man, sir. Please don't do anything to my store—for the sake of my children.

GRAY-HAIRED MAN: The coffeeman is an oddity, and the grocer is another. [*To the* GROCER.] We are specialists on works of antiquity. We've nothing to do with the road situation.

BEARDED MAN: [*To the* GROCER.] To put it so you will understand—antiques.

GROCER: [*Astonished.*] Oh, you mean you're antique dealers? [*Straightens up.*] I carry some myself. Very cheap, too, sir. Bring it, Mehmet, bring the sack! I didn't get them whole-sale. I got them straight from the factory. They're real cheap, sir. [MEHMET *hurries.*]

BEARDED MAN: [*Turns to the others.*] The coffeeman's right. He's really an antique.

GROCER: [*Excited.*] He's a liar, sir, believe me, he's a liar! I had no thought of offering . . . [*Hides the money behind his back.*] Devil take that coffeeman! [*The* COMMITTEE MEM-BERS *don't pay any attention and leave. Both the* GROCER *and the* COFFEEMAN *stand staring at them until they disappear. Their eyes meet. The* COFFEEMAN *sees the money that the* GROCER *is holding in his hands, then looks at the money in his own hand.*]

COFFEEMAN: [*Blurts out in a loud voice in the* GROCER'*s direction.*] Baldy! [*Makes a face.*]

GROCER: [*In a loud voice in the* COFFEEMAN'*s direction, blasting the* COFFEEMAN.] Crack-brained brute! [*Makes faces.*]

CURTAIN

ACT III

[*Evening. Two* MEN *are playing backgammon at the coffeehouse. The* COFFEEMAN *is watching them. The* HEADMAN *is busy with some papers at a table. Opposite him sit a poor* WOMAN AND HER BOY, *three or four years old. The* WAITER *is carrying the chairs. The* STREET-CLEANING WOMAN *is working. Ship and train whistles are heard. Streetcar bells clang.*]

GROCER: [*Sees a customer to the door.*] Good-bye. [*Looks in the direction of the coffeehouse.*] Mehmet!

GROCER'S HELPER: [*Enters.*] Yes, Boss?

GROCER: Go find out where the chairs are going.

GROCER'S HELPER: Yes, Boss. [*Goes to the coffeehouse.*]

GROCER: [*Still at the door. To the* MATCHMAKER *who is passing by.*] What's the good word? Where are you going?

MATCHMAKER: Are you sleeping? Yakety-yak-yak, the whole neighborhood's talking about it. There's a wedding at Saffet Hanım's.

GROCER: Is it tonight? How can I keep a straight head with all these worries about the bills? Just think, Auntie, it's quite a bit of money.

MATCHMAKER: Who hasn't paid up his bill?

GROCER: If they pay, it's the will of Allah; if they don't, that's the will of Allah, too.

MATCHMAKER: What does that mean?

GROCER: What can it mean? [*The* STRANGER *comes slowly to the store.*] It means there is no contract or anything. It's all on the books. It is Macit Bey's bill. [*To the* STRANGER.] What would you like to have?

STRANGER: [*Hands him money.*] Give me a pack of cigarettes.

GROCER: [*Talks to the* MATCHMAKER *as he enters the store.*] Please stay! I want to tell you something.

GROCER'S HELPER: [*To the* COFFEEMAN'S HELPER.] Brother Nuri, where are those chairs going? Is there a meeting at the party headquarters?

COFFEEMAN'S HELPER: No, they're going to the wedding at Saffet Hanım's.

GROCER'S HELPER: Oh really! Is it tonight? I should've known that.

COFFEEMAN'S HELPER: She doesn't trade with you, that's why.

GROCER'S HELPER: Yes, ours is a poor man's grocery store. [*Leaves.*]

COFFEEMAN'S HELPER: [*Behind the* GROCER'S HELPER.] Mehmet!

GROCER'S HELPER: [*Stops.*] What is it, my brother?

COFFEEMAN'S HELPER: My wedding is coming pretty soon, too.

GROCER'S HELPER: Really! Has your boss agreed to it?

COFFEEMAN'S HELPER: What did you think? [*The* GROCER *taps* MEHMET *on the back.* MEHMET, *hopping and skipping, enters the store. The* GROCER *goes back to the front of the store, hands the* STRANGER *the pack of cigarettes, and then puts many coins in his hand.*]

GROCER'S HELPER: Boss! The chairs are going to the wedding of Saffet Hanım's daughter.

GROCER: [*Pays no attention. The* STRANGER *is startled. The* GROCER *drops a coin and picks it up.*] The coffeeman's going to make a pretty penny on those chairs, lucky guy. [*Blows the dust off the coin and puts it in the* STRANGER'*s palm. To the* MATCHMAKER.] If I had any luck . . .

MATCHMAKER: What are you waiting for? Many of the girls in the neighborhood have been given away. I don't know what you're waiting for.

GROCER: I'm waiting for the number of girls to dwindle a little more.

MATCHMAKER: So that you can sell yours at a higher price? Nothing doing. This is not the same as the grocery business. A girl blossoms one morning just like a flower. Even if there's no wind or rain or frost to touch her, some morning you'll find that she has withered away. Besides, listen to me, I have a lucky touch.

GROCER: All right, find a husband for my older daughter!

GROCER'S HELPER: [*Interrupts.*] Brother Nuri, Boss?

GROCER: You rascal, you! You're leaving your work and listening to us, huh? It's almost dark now. When are you going to deliver all these groceries? Come on, get to work! I've had enough of this cockroach. Auntie, who did you get for Saffet Hanım's girl? Is he a wealthy man with a lot of property and so on?

MATCHMAKER: Yes, he has everything. Even if his income doesn't overflow, it's small and steady. He didn't make Saffet Hanım spend a single lira for the wedding.

GROCER: In our day, people wouldn't just go and take a girl for a wife. The family elders would go and find out about the girl and her family.

MATCHMAKER: It isn't any different now. She's a girl from a fine family. She's the navy man's daughter.

GROCER: [*Chuckles knowingly.*] You know the facts as well as anyone else, but they wouldn't suit your purpose.

MATCHMAKER: The matchmaker has made the match, and the man's willing to marry her! That's all there is to it. It's a sin to talk like this.

GROCER: Don't be angry with me, Auntie. I didn't go out in the street and shout the name of the girl's real father.

MATCHMAKER: [*Angrily.*] Don't make me angry so early in the evening! Look at me and listen. If I want to, I can say Saffet Hanım's girl is the navy man's daughter, and your daughter is the coffeeman's. Do you understand? They call me the Matchmaker! [*Walks away.*]

GROCER: [*Snaps back.*] Allah help me with these matchmaking women! [*To the* STRANGER.] I guess you can get just about anything if you pay for it. [*Suddenly.*] Is there anything else you would like?

STRANGER: I just want to buy some matches. [*Hands him money.*]

GROCER: Forgive me. The damn woman distracted me. [*Enters the store.*]

STRANGER: [*To himself.*] How can I ask him?

GROCER: [*Comes back, gives him the box of matches. The* STRANGER *walks to the coffeehouse without saying anything. The* GROCER *puts his hand against his temple.*] Something doesn't seem right here! The coffeeman must be up to something!

HEADMAN: [*Hands the* WOMAN WITH HER BOY *a piece of paper.*] Here you are, my good woman.

WOMAN: [*After taking the paper.*] Where do I go now?

HEADMAN: Take that paper to a lawyer and file a suit for child support.

WOMAN: That hardhearted scoundrel says this is not his child. My little bundle of joy, my darling! This is my destiny, I guess. Some men take another man's bastard daughter and cherish her as if she were their own flesh and blood, and this man of mine kicks his own child out into the cold. [*Tears come to her eyes.*] Come along, Son, let's go. May Allah keep you. [*Leaves.*]

HEADMAN: [*As she leaves.*] Stop by the Children's Aid Society tomorrow and get a pair of shoes for the child.

WOMAN: [*As she disappears.*] God bless you!

HEADMAN: [*Bangs on the table.*] Nuri!

COFFEEMAN'S HELPER: [*Comes running.*] Yes, my headman?

HEADMAN: Take away these papers, will you? It's almost dark now. No one from the council showed up today. Make me a good cup of strong coffee—traditional style.

COFFEEMAN'S HELPER: Make one, traditional style! [*Goes to the kitchen.*]

COFFEEMAN: [*Leaves the* BACKGAMMON PLAYERS *and sits beside the* HEADMAN.] Are you through working, Brother Headman?

HEADMAN: When some unpleasant matter comes up, there's no fun in being a headman.

COFFEEMAN: [*Sees the* STRANGER.] Come on in! Come on in! [*The* STRANGER *comes over to them, takes his hat off, and greets them. The* COFFEEMAN *returns the greeting with his hand.*]

HEADMAN: Good day to you!

STRANGER: [*As he sits down.*] My legs are tired from walking. [*Rubs his knees.*]

COFFEEMAN: [*Introducing the* STRANGER.] This is our headman. [*Points to the* STRANGER.] And this is a guest here.

HEADMAN: Welcome. How are things in Ankara?

STRANGER: I come from Izmir.

HEADMAN: Fine! Whose guest are you?

STRANGER: Whose guest? I, well . . . [*Points to the* COFFEEMAN.] I'm the boss's guest. [*They chuckle.*]

COFFEEMAN: Thanks. I'm honored! He's our guest, Brother Headman. He came to see Istanbul.

HEADMAN: I'm not asking that. What I mean is, where is the gentleman staying?

STRANGER: Well, I don't stay in this neighborhood. I stay at a hotel. I'm a stranger here. While wandering around the city, I came across this place.

HEADMAN: [*Grimly.*] This is all there is to this neighborhood, Brother. There is nothing to see. I asked that question just out of habit. As you know, I'm a headman. [*To the* COFFEEMAN.] There is no joy in being a headman, though.

COFFEEMAN: Take it easy, my headman!

HEADMAN: I take it to heart when I have to deal with such matters. How can I take it easy? You saw the condition of that woman who just left. She's both hungry and wretched. I asked her to come tomorrow and get a pair of shoes for her child from the Children's

Aid Society. Her husband deserted her and says the child isn't his. Everybody knows that it is his child. She's not that type of woman. But that's bad fortune. As she was saying herself, some other fellow—this is just between you and me—claims someone else's bastard as his own daughter, and this good-for-nothing is disowning his very own son. That's the way of the world. What do you say to that?

STRANGER: It takes all kinds.

HEADMAN: But, sir, you can't easily find the kind of woman I've been talking about. You wouldn't know, of course. In this neighborhood, we have a famous one—the notorious Saffet Hanım! In her younger days she was quite a flirt. She came here as the young bride of a navy man. He was a nice, fatherly fellow. But he was at home for a week and away for a month. There wasn't an older, level-headed person in the house, either. So, to cut a long story short, the woman started to cast her eyes around. And on that street over there—the woman used to live on this street here—well, on that street over there, we had our Macit Bey. He passed away today, may he rest in peace. He'd just arrived in this neighborhood at that time. He had a son about her age. Quite a Casanova and good looking, too. Well, this Saffet Hanım led the boy astray. People started to talk, but the matter was soon hushed up because, whatever happened, Macit Bey would never talk about it, so we didn't insist. But Macit Bey disowned his son. And that's not the end of the story. One day Saffet Hanım had a daughter. Every soul in the neighborhood knew who the father was, but . . . [BEYBABA *enters.*] Come on in, Beybaba! [*They all straighten up.*]

BEYBABA: [*As he settles down.*] You seem to be having quite a conversation!

COFFEEMAN: We're talking about the Saffet Hanım affair, Beybaba.

BEYBABA: Quite a coincidence, isn't it? The girl's wedding falling on the same day as her grandfather's funeral.

HEADMAN: Yes, you're right.

COFFEEMAN: You've said it, Beybaba!

BEYBABA: The navy man left a great deal of property. He was a pasha's son.

HEADMAN: Just the house they live in is worth a fortune. [*To the* COFFEEMAN.] Wouldn't you say so?

COFFEEMAN: Sure thing, my headman.

BEYBABA: They say she's getting her daughter a good home. It's a good thing the new in-laws didn't investigate in the neighborhood.

COFFEEMAN: That's right, Beybaba, they didn't.

HEADMAN: Of course they did! They asked me. I wouldn't get in the way of a girl's happiness, though. It's a sin to wreck a home—a nest. [*Teases the* COFFEEMAN.] Of course, you don't pay much attention to such things.

COFFEEMAN: In the name of the Fire Brigade, my headman, this is a matter of honor. By God, I never even opened my mouth. [*To* NURİ, *who has brought the coffee.*] Did I, Nuri? Did I say anything about Saffet Hanım's daughter? Never, my headman, never!

May the Koran strike me dead. [*Takes the invitation out of his pocket.*] Look, she even invited me to the wedding!

[*The* STRANGER *leans over to see the invitation, but the* COFFEEMAN, *not noticing him, puts it back in his pocket. One of the* BACKGAMMON PLAYERS *bangs the set and gets up.*]

FIRST PLAYER: [*Loudly.*] Double six.

SECOND PLAYER: It isn't fair. I didn't see the dice.

FIRST PLAYER: None of your fast tricks with me!

COFFEEMAN: [*To the* SECOND PLAYER.] You've lost your touch!

SECOND PLAYER: Why, he's lucky like Saffet Hanım. He threw double six and won the game. [*The two* PLAYERS *argue and then leave.*]

HEADMAN: Anyway, we never again saw or heard Saffet Hanım do anything she shouldn't do. And when the navy man died . . .

BEYBABA: That was in the old days when she was young and pretty. She used to wear high-heeled shoes then.

COFFEEMAN: Good for you, Beybaba, you really have a fine memory!

BEYBABA: I can't remember recent things very well, though, Son. [*Looks at the* STRANGER.] For example, I have a feeling I've seen this gentleman before, but I can't remember where.

COFFEEMAN: You saw him today, Beybaba, before noon.

BEYBABA: Yes, that's right. You see, I couldn't remember. To me, it seems as though it was a long, long time ago.

STRANGER: People look alike.

BEYBABA: That's right, too. Well, when the navy man heard about the matter, he said she was his daughter and settled the whole thing. If he had divorced the woman, both she and the child and he himself would have been miserable. He said, "Let her sin be hers," and performed a good deed. The poor man didn't live long after that. But he did accomplish that good deed and deserved to go to Paradise.

HEADMAN: The boy must now be just about the age of Naci. I was a bit older than them, a few years their senior.

COFFEEMAN: You still are their senior, their headman.

HEADMAN: He did what he did out of ignorance. He was a Casanova, that's all. Otherwise, he was a fine lad. Ask Naci, he'll tell you. He was intelligent, diligent, and a good friend. The woman led him astray.

BEYBABA: [*Thoughtfully.*] Nonsense. That was his destiny.

[*The* BOY *who was seen running away from the grocery store in Act I runs past the* MIDWIFE'*s house. A* POLICEMAN *comes panting after him.*]

COFFEEMAN: Are you after him again, Officer?

POLICEMAN: [*Stops, takes off his cap, and dries his perspiration as if he has given up the chase.*] If I ever catch him, I'll make him good and sorry.

COFFEEMAN: What did he pinch this time?

POLICEMAN: The grocer complained to me today. He snitched some candy and things from the store.

COFFEEMAN: Don't pay any attention to what he says. He's a weirdo. [*The POLICEMAN puts on his cap, salutes with his hand, and goes to the grocery store.*]

BEYBABA: [*Gazes at the sky.*] Well, it looks like the shades of night have fallen again. [*Gets up.*] Let's be on our way! [*Everybody gets up.*]

HEADMAN: [*To the STRANGER.*] Are you going to stay here?

STRANGER: I think I'll rest here a while. Good-bye! [*Tips his hat to them. The HEADMAN responds by putting his hand on his chest.*]

BEYBABA: [*Standing, turns back and speaks to the COFFEEMAN.*] The irony of it! From that street over there, we took a man to his grave today. Tonight we'll recite prayers for him. And on that street over here there will be a wedding.

COFFEEMAN: What can you do? Everything was set for tonight.

BEYBABA: They used to set dates for weddings in our day, too. But if someone died in the neighborhood—to say nothing of the next street—all the music and dancing would stop. The guests would have their dinner, the older folk would go to their homes, and the younger ones would talk quietly among themselves.

HEADMAN: Times were different then.

BEYBABA: I'm telling you so you'll know it—I already have one foot in the grave. After I join my maker one of these days, this neighborhood will go to the dogs. That's what I'm afraid of. [*Leaves with the HEADMAN. One goes right, the other left. The COFFEE-MAN sits down.*]

STRANGER: What a pleasant man, this Beybaba!

COFFEEMAN: He is very pleasant, my brother. You sit down, sir, I'll be right back.

STRANGER: Get on with your work. [*The COFFEEMAN goes to the kitchen. The STRANGER speaks to himself.*] All the things I hear at this coffeehouse! [*Plunges into thought.*]

POLICEMAN: [*Comes out of the store, followed by the GROCER. As he leaves.*] You're really making me work!

GROCER: Don't worry, I'll make it worth your while. Just keep an eye on the store.

POLICEMAN: Lock it up good and tight and leave the rest to me.

GROCER: If you want to catch that little brat, go to Saffet Hanım's tonight. You'll be sure to find him at the wedding!

POLICEMAN: I'm glad you reminded me. I'll see you later. [*Leaves.*]

GROCER: Mehmet!

GROCER'S HELPER: [*Comes closer.*] Yes, Boss?

GROCER: Mehmet, my boy, when are you going to make a man of yourself? Didn't I tell you not to eavesdrop when I'm talking to somebody?

GROCER'S HELPER: Well, Boss, Nuri, my brother . . .

GROCER: Nuri, my brother, Nuri, my brother . . . I'm sick and tired of you and your Nuri!

GROCER'S HELPER: He said his wedding wasn't far off.

GROCER: He talks, but it doesn't mean a thing. You open your eyes and be a man, and I'll give my daughter to you.

GROCER'S HELPER: [*Stupefied.*] Serious, Boss?

GROCER: [*Sarcastically.*] No, just joking! Why should I joke with you?

GROCER'S HELPER: [*As he goes away, skipping and hopping.*] It won't take me long to be a man now! [*Turns toward the coffeehouse.*] So much for you, Nuri, my brother!

GROCER: [*To himself.*] Come to think of it, that wouldn't be so bad. [*As he enters the store, a man about thirty, the* PASHA'S SON, *comes down the street smoking a cigarette. He is very particular about the way he walks and is meticulously dressed.*]

PASHA'S SON: [*From the entrance of the store.*] Will you give me a box of matches, please?

GROCER: [*Comes out with the matches.*] Here you are. You're the pasha's son, right?

PASHA'S SON: How's everything?

GROCER: If you have a daughter, you're in for it! How are you?

PASHA'S SON: Is it possible to be well?

GROCER: What's the trouble?

PASHA'S SON: Gossip, *mon cher.*

GROCER: You haven't been around here for a long time.

PASHA'S SON: This neighborhood holds no thrills for me. I'm staying in Şişli[22] at a high-class rooming house. I told my landlady the other day that I was going to the Princes' Islands[23] for the summer, but came here instead.

GROCER: That's fine. When are you moving to the Princes' Islands?

PASHA'S SON: [*Bitterly.*] To the Princes' Islands? If I can pay the back rent on the room, then I can move to the Princes' Islands.

GROCER: What about the estate—your grandfather's lands and so on?

PASHA'S SON: My grandfather, Zekâi Pasha, has really left a lot of property. If I win the case, I'll be stupendously rich.

GROCER: You don't say! What'll you get from the inheritance?

PASHA'S SON: Well, my share will be a fortune.

GROCER: [*Opens his eyes wider.*] Heavens!

PASHA'S SON: Mehmet, give me a bottle of raki, a can of sardines, a lemon, a loaf of French bread, one package of cigarettes, and some cheese.

GROCER: [*To* MEHMET.] Give it to him, Son, give it to him. [*To the customer.*] So you'll be rich, eh?

PASHA'S SON: I'll win the case.

---

22. Şişli: A fashionable district in Istanbul.

23. Princes' Islands: An archipelago of nine islands in the Sea of Marmara, near Istanbul.

GROCER: I pity the girl.

PASHA'S SON: You mean Lili?

GROCER: Who's Lili?

PASHA'S SON: The landlady's daughter.

GROCER: I'm not talking about her. I'm talking about Saffet Hanım's daughter, Perihan. They should've married her to you.

PASHA'S SON: Lili is cuter, though. Perihan has more sex appeal.

GROCER: Sixty bucks! Where would you get it?

PASHA'S SON: I mean "sex appeal."

GROCER: Good for you. You're a real pasha's son, and you made all this come out into the open. No wonder they say, "Like mother, like daughter." [MEHMET *hands the* PASHA'S SON *a bag. The latter grabs it.*]

PASHA'S SON: That's it, right?

GROCER'S HELPER: Two lira.

PASHA'S SON: [*As he walks away.*] I'll pay you later. Good-bye.

GROCER: [*Stupefied.*] That rascal got the better of me. The inheritance and the court decision took my mind off business. What's happened to my brains? Mehmet, my son, don't forget to remind me. Let's at least put it down in the book. He may or may not pay it. There's another thing. Mehmet!

GROCER'S HELPER: Yes, Boss?

GROCER: Pull down the shutters!

GROCER'S HELPER: It's early yet, Boss.

GROCER: Pull down the shutters!

GROCER'S HELPER: Yes, Boss. [*Carries the goods inside and starts pulling down the shutters.*]

GROCER: I don't know which of my troubles I ought to worry about most! The customers are driving me bankrupt! I can't give my daughter away; she'll remain with us. They're going to pull the store down! [*Pessimistically.*] I hope they do it someday so I can get away from the whole rotten business. [*Enters the store.*]

[*The* STREET-CLEANING WOMAN *comes with tired steps and lights the red signal lantern. The old* BEGGAR *seen in Act I enters and rings the doorbell of the house next to the grocery store. The door opens, and the profile of a* WOMAN *appears. She is the one who bought milk previously. The* BEGGAR *gets alms, puts his hand on his heart, and quietly leaves. The* STREET-CLEANING WOMAN *enters the grocery store. The voice of the* SİMİT VENDOR *is heard in the distance.*]

SİMİT VENDOR: Evening *simit* . . . good and hot! [*This voice reminds the* STRANGER *of a previous experience; he sniffs the scent of the hot* simits. *The* STREET-CLEANING WOMAN *comes out of the grocery carrying two loaves of bread. The* CARPENTER *hurriedly passes by.*]

STREET-CLEANING WOMAN: Where are you going so fast?

CARPENTER: Oh, is that you? I'm in such a hurry I didn't see you.

STREET-CLEANING WOMAN: What's your hurry? Let's walk together.

CARPENTER: It's any minute now.

STREET-CLEANING WOMAN: Her belly was almost reaching her nose.

CARPENTER: I'll see you later!

STREET-CLEANING WOMAN: Best of luck! I hope she has an easy time of it.

CARPENTER: Thank you. [*Starts walking.*]

STREET-CLEANING WOMAN: [*Shouts after him.*] What are you hoping for? A girl or a boy?

CARPENTER: A boy, I hope. [*Leaves.*]

STREET-CLEANING WOMAN: I wish I was born a boy, too. [*Puts her broom on her shoulder.* NURI, *who has been collecting cups from the tables, comes to the edge of the platform.*]

COFFEEMAN'S HELPER: [*To the* STREET-CLEANING WOMAN.] Sister! Why don't you go and serve at the wedding? You may get a little money.

STREET-CLEANING WOMAN: Did you say money? I'd rather go to Macit Bey's house and serve Allah.

[NURI *goes back to his work. The* COFFEEMAN *comes out twisting his mustache, starts toward the* STRANGER, *then stops.*]

COFFEEMAN: Nuri! Turn on the middle one! [NURI *twists the bulb in the socket, and a pleasant light filters through the leaves of the vine. To the* STRANGER.] Forgive me, I left you alone, sir. [*Sits by him, continues twisting his mustache, then lights a cigarette and speaks off and on.*]

STREET-CLEANING WOMAN: [*To a* WORKER *passing by.*] Good evening to you!

FIRST WORKER: Thank you, Sister.

STREET-CLEANING WOMAN: Do you like your new work?

FIRST WORKER: I'm getting along, Sister.

STREET-CLEANING WOMAN: How is the pay?

FIRST WORKER: We'll know tomorrow if we get a raise.

STREET-CLEANING WOMAN: Well, Allah be with you! [*To the* SECOND WORKER.] Aren't you going to say "good evening"?

SECOND WORKER: Of course I will. Good evening! We never see you in our neighborhood anymore.

STREET-CLEANING WOMAN: How would you know? You're never home.

SECOND WORKER: You should've listened to me and got that job in the factory.

STREET-CLEANING WOMAN: That's easy to say! Who can I leave the babies with? I'm not working as a street-cleaning woman in this neighborhood just for the pleasure of it. Every so often I go and look at my babies.

SECOND WORKER: Have you heard from your husband?

STREET-CLEANING WOMAN: Maybe there's a letter on the way, but it never gets here. Poor man has to be so far away.

SECOND WORKER: Mardin[24] is a long way from here. I hope he'll soon get rid of that uniform. [*Walks away.*]

STREET-CLEANING WOMAN: I don't know. [*Walks away.*]

[BEYAĞABEY *comes from Mihri Hatun Street and turns into the street where the* MIDWIFE *lives. As he passes by the platform, the* COFFEEMAN *calls to him.*]

COFFEEMAN: Where are you going at this hour, Beyağabey?

BEYAĞABEY: I'm going to buy some incense, candles, and aloe wood for Macit Bey's tonight.

COFFEEMAN: [*Noticing that* BEYAĞABEY *is looking at the* STRANGER.] The gentleman is a stranger. You wouldn't know him.

BEYAĞABEY: Oh? I felt for a moment that I knew the gentleman. See you later. [*Leaves.*]

COFFEEMAN: If you say so, Beyağabey. [*Automobile horns are heard. To the* STRANGER.] Come to think of it, I feel like I've seen you before, too.

STRANGER: We're beginning to know each other, that's why.

COFFEEMAN: God knows, I wouldn't leave you alone tonight, but if I don't go to the wedding, people will take offense. Like always, they'll make me talk—just for laughs.

STRANGER: [*Attempting to ask something.*] This wedding . . .

[*Five* MUSICIANS *enter in single file, slopping through the mud in the street. The* COFFEEMAN *turns in the direction of the noise.*]

FIRST MUSICIAN: I hope we can go through here without sinking deeper into the mud.

SECOND MUSICIAN: There's a coffeehouse! Let's duck in there!

FIRST MUSICIAN: That's good! To the coffeehouse!

COFFEEMAN: [*Jumps up.*] Come on in! Come on in! This way, please! [*Receives the* MUSICIANS *and shows them seats.*] Nuri! Hey, Nuri!

THIRD MUSICIAN: [*Shakes the dirt off his trousers.*] Who'd believe we took a taxi?

COFFEEMAN: Forgive us, our road is in a mess. [*The* SHOESHINE BOY *enters from the direction of the mosque.*]

THIRD MUSICIAN: Shoeshine boy! [*The* SHOESHINE BOY *comes toward the coffeehouse.*] This is lucky, at least.

FIRST MUSICIAN: Where's the wedding? Is it far?

COFFEEMAN: No, in that street there. A stone's throw!

FIRST MUSICIAN: Let's not waste time, then. Let's go straight to the house.

FOURTH MUSICIAN: It's better if we tidy ourselves a little.

COFFEEMAN: Do come in, gentlemen, do come in! Coffee, tea? Saffet Hanım will hear that you've arrived. That's the way it is with a neighborhood.

24. Mardin: A city in southeastern Turkey.

SECOND MUSICIAN: Some hot tea wouldn't be bad at all.

ALL BUT THE FIFTH MUSICIAN: Tea! Glass of tea . . .

COFFEEMAN: [*To the* FIFTH MUSICIAN.] How about you, Brother?

FIFTH MUSICIAN: I don't care for anything! [*To the* COFFEEMAN'S HELPER.] Take this, Son! Go get me a pack of cigarettes. [*Hands money to* NURI, *who leaves.*]

THIRD MUSICIAN: [*To the* SHOESHINE BOY.] Just the polish.

COFFEEMAN: [*Loudly.*] Tea coming up! [*Goes to the kitchen. The* MUSICIANS *straighten their clothes.*]

COFFEEMAN'S HELPER: [*In front of the grocery store.*] Hey, Mehmet, what are you sulking about?

GROCER'S HELPER: What's it to you? [NURI *enters the store.*]

FIRST MUSICIAN: [*To the* SHOESHINE BOY.] Clean these up, too. [*The* SHOESHINE BOY *does what he is told and leaves.*]

COFFEEMAN'S HELPER: [*Comes out of the store. To* MEHMET.] What is it this time? Did you fall in the ditch again?

GROCER'S HELPER: [*Snaps back.*] Are you talking to me?

COFFEEMAN'S HELPER: [*As he goes back to the coffeehouse.*] Stupid!

GROCER'S HELPER: [*Angrily.*] Stupid fool!

GROCER: [*From the store.*] Mehmet! Who are you bickering with? I told you to pull down the shutters!

GROCER'S HELPER: [*Behind* NURI'*s back.*] I'll show you what's what! [*Enters the store.*]

COFFEEMAN: [*From the kitchen.*] Nuri!

COFFEEMAN'S HELPER: I'm coming. [*Gives the package to the* MUSICIAN, *goes to the kitchen, comes out with the tray, and starts serving the tea.*]

[*A* YOUNG BOY, *the* CARPENTER'*s son, comes running from Mihri Hatun Street and excitedly rings the doorbell of the* MIDWIFE'*s house. The* GROCER *and* MEHMET *have closed the store and are about to leave.*]

YOUNG BOY: Auntie, Auntie! [*Rings again.*]

GROCER: [*Looks in the direction of the* MIDWIFE'*s house.*] Mehmet, my boy, my heart stopped. For a moment I thought the midwife was coming to my house. I certainly have a soft heart! [*Pantomimes swinging a baby in his arms.*] When you take the little newborn on your lap, its head smells of musk, like the earth of Heaven! [*Pantomimes smelling.*] Ah! [*Stands in a state of ecstasy. Then to* MEHMET.] Come along! [*Starts walking toward Mihri Hatun Street.* MEHMET *follows him.*]

MIDWIFE: [*Opens her door.*] Her pains are coming faster, I guess.

YOUNG BOY: Please be quick, Auntie!

MIDWIFE: I'm ready to go, Son. I'll just get my bag and my lantern. [*Goes in and then reappears with a bag in one hand and a lantern in the other. As she leaves.*] Heaven knows, I may be late arriving at Saffet Hanım's, but if I don't show up, she'll be offended. We'll see what happens. [*The streetlamp goes on.*]

COFFEEMAN: [*Comes twirling his mustache.*] Nuri, turn on the light. [*Another light goes on over the platform. To the* MUSICIANS.] How did you like my tea? [*The* MUSICIANS *answer, "Fine, just fine . . . "*]

FIFTH MUSICIAN: [*Takes a bottle out of his pocket.*] Let's have a little snort!

COFFEEMAN: [*As the* MUSICIAN *brings the bottle to his mouth.*] No, no, no! You're my guest. [*Takes a bottle out of his own pocket and offers it.*] Let me be your servant. Alcohol kills the germs.

FIFTH MUSICIAN: [*Guzzling the drink.*] Drink up, sinners! [*Hands the bottle back to the* COFFEEMAN.]

COFFEEMAN: Drink up, sinners! [*They drink to each other.*] Nuri, turn out the lights inside! [*The lights go off.*]

FIRST MUSICIAN: [*Takes his zither from its case and examines it.*] I almost fell on my face. This thing hit against the wall. I hope it isn't broken. [*Plays it a little.*]

FOURTH MUSICIAN: [*Takes his clarinet from its case and blows it. A foul sound comes out. To* NURI.] Son, will you bring me a glass of water? [*The others also tune their instruments;* NURI *brings the water. The* FOURTH MUSICIAN *wets the reed of his clarinet.*]

COFFEEMAN: Nothing like good Turkish music! [*Passes the bottle to the* FIFTH MUSICIAN.]

FIFTH MUSICIAN: Thank you! [*Guzzles the drink. Hands it back to the* COFFEEMAN.] Do you like jazz, too?

COFFEEMAN: [*Guzzles his drink.*] What if I do like it? [*Mimics Turkish dancing.*] If you don't know this dance, what's the use? We were born thirty years too soon, my friends—thirty years too soon. [*Stops dancing.*] Good old Turkish music!

FIFTH MUSICIAN: [*Gulps from his own bottle.*] Tonight we'll have everything. Both Turkish music and American music!

COFFEEMAN: [*With his bottle in his hand.*] My, my, my! Is another band coming, too?

FIFTH MUSICIAN: No, friend, we're it! On even hours we play Turkish music, and on odd hours we play American music. That's the way things are! I'm a violinist, but I can play the mandolin and the clarinet and other instruments, too. And in a tight spot, I can play the accordion and saxophone as well. The trumpet is no stranger to me, either. Well, I have to make a living somehow, you know. One has to keep up with the times.

COFFEEMAN: It's the end of the world! [*They guzzle their drinks.*]

FIFTH MUSICIAN: [*Sings.*] "The neighborhood tavern . . . its door is of vine." [*Sings each line twice.*]

COFFEEMAN: [*Excitedly.*] The walls have ears, old friend! Don't say "the neighborhood tavern"! Say "the neighborhood coffeehouse"!

FIFTH MUSICIAN: [*Sings.*] "The neighborhood coffeehouse . . . " [*Just then the* WAITER *enters.*]

WAITER: [*To the* MUSICIANS.] Boss, instead of settling down here, why don't you all come over to Saffet Hanım's? She's been waiting for you.

FIRST MUSICIAN: Yes, we took it easy here. It's dark already. [*The* MUSICIANS *get up.*]

COFFEEMAN: Friends! I'm not a stranger myself. I'll go with you. [*The* COFFEEMAN *forgets about the* STRANGER. *He leaves the coffeehouse with the* WAITER *and the* MUSICIANS. NURİ, *in a hurry, picks up some table covers and cups, puts out the lights in the vine, and then locks the door to the kitchen.*]

COFFEEMAN'S HELPER: [*To the* STRANGER.] Forgive us, Mr. Inspector! [*Leaves in a hurry.*]

[*The* STRANGER *gets up like a ghost and descends to the street. He slows down, then stops; he turns back and comes to the spot where the three streets meet.* BEYAĞABEY *returns from shopping. They come face to face.*]

STRANGER: [*As if he cannot help himself.*] Naci!

BEYAĞABEY: [*In great surprise.*] Is it you? [*They embrace.*] How come I didn't recognize you? You were sitting at the coffeehouse, weren't you? I never thought you'd come. In fact, we didn't even know you were alive. Shame on you! We never heard from you. [*Forces a smile.*] But that's all right. You are here now. [*Notices the* STRANGER*'s silence.*] Did you stop at the house? [*The* STRANGER *shakes his head no.*] Good! Come over to my place! [*Takes him by the arm.*]

STRANGER: [*Doesn't move. Haltingly.*] Naci . . . I know . . .

BEYAĞABEY: [*Tries to drag him by the arm.*] My God, we can't talk like this in the middle of the street. Come, let's go to my place! You've been gone twenty years. We're going to have a good long talk. Come along!

STRANGER: [*Doesn't budge.*] No, no. Let's not do that. Stay with me a while. It was stupid of me to come here in the first place, but as a man gets older, he gets soft, I think, and starts to feel nostalgic about the old days. But the world goes on. Or do I feel some sort of repentance? I don't know what it is exactly, but last night I couldn't get a wink of sleep. I twisted and turned all night. I remembered the old days.

BEYAĞABEY: So you came here yesterday?

STRANGER: For twenty years I didn't set foot in this neighborhood. Yesterday when we docked, I didn't have it in my mind—or did I really? Well, when I was still on board the ship, I didn't even look in this direction. Last night I went to a restaurant in Beyoğlu with a few friends. Then we went to the theater. I returned to the hotel and went to bed, but as soon as I put my head on the pillow, there was a new theater for me—old memories.

BEYAĞABEY: You never even remembered us.

STRANGER: What good is there in remembering the old days? Even if I did return to Istanbul once in a while . . . bitter memories! My father, may he rest in peace, was a peevish, quarrelsome man. If he hadn't been that way, the whole matter would've been forgotten. He could've allowed for my age, but he didn't. When the word got around, my stepmother didn't miss the opportunity. What stepmother can stand the children of her husband's previous wife? You know how fanatical my father was in matters of family honor. One day—I'll never forget the scene—I overheard her say, "How can I be mother to a scoundrel almost my age? When you married me, you should've thought of that. Both of us can't live under the same roof. Either he goes or I go." And then she started to cry. "We've become the talk of the whole neighborhood," she said. The door of the room was closed, so I came closer. My father was asking her, "Why should we be the talk of the town?" She said, "I wasn't going to tell you, but you're forcing me to say it. That lover son of yours and that navy man's wife, Saffet . . . " There was a moment of silence. And then she said, "When the neighborhood pulls a raid one of these days, you'll believe it." Think of it! You know what a severe and conservative man my father was. "I'll disown him!" I heard him cry as if he were choking. In one moment I was crushed—ashamed to death. Then suddenly I was filled with rebellion. I rushed down the stairs and slammed the door of the house. As I turned the corner of the street, I saw my stepmother's shadow going back and forth at the window. That's the last I saw of the whole family.

BEYAĞABEY: What did you do then?

STRANGER: Well, I didn't have money enough to buy a crust of bread. All the relatives were scattered after the Great War. I went to Bursa. My uncle was dead, and both his sons were in the army. There was not a soul in the house. My other uncle was in Egypt—prisoner of the British. Only Allah knows how I spent that year. I worked as a waiter, a public letter writer, an actor, a deckhand, and finally a stoker on a ship. That way I ended up in Marseilles. It's a long story after that. I went to school there, got a diploma, came back to Istanbul. Then I went to Ankara. For a time I worked for the government, traveling around the country. Then I started to work freelance—a commission agent, a contractor, the representative of a firm, now this, now that— and finally today I'm doing all right. I got married. Have three children, all of them boys. I wanted to have a girl, too, but . . . [BEYAĞABEY *does not say anything.*] How mysterious, how complex is the life of a neighborhood! The things I've heard at the coffeehouse! [*Sighs.*]

BEYAĞABEY: What will you do now?

STRANGER: What will I do? [*A pause.*] Nothing. Everything will be kept under the cover of this night. I've seen a lot of things in life, but never before have I had to struggle so much to come to a decision. I couldn't leave the neighborhood after this morning. I walked from street to street. For a moment after the funeral, I hid behind the cypresses in the old cemetery and gazed at our house. It looked so desolate! Women were going in and out the door. I saw you a couple of times, too. You can't imagine the things I felt as I watched you. For a minute I saw a young girl by the window. She was crying. She must have been my . . . she was fair skinned and blonde.

BEYAĞABEY: That's she.

STRANGER: I was about to turn back and go. Then I stopped at this corner. My goodness! That grocer and this coffeeman! They are the living histories of the neighborhood.

BEYAĞABEY: Then you must have heard?

STRANGER: Yes, I heard everything. And that dear old man, Beybaba . . . I felt as though he were my father. I didn't know what to do, whether to kiss his hand or embrace him or what. Then the headman . . . there was no place to hide; we sat face to face. Luckily, he didn't recognize me. Well, I couldn't leave, you see.

BEYAĞABEY: I don't know what to say. You've heard everything! Come, let's go to my house. You must stay with us tonight. Bitter or sweet, we should eat and speak whatever God has given us.

STRANGER: No, thank you. Now listen. Would you do me a favor? I'll start for Izmir tomorrow. Before I leave, though, I'll send you a check. Pay the mortgage on our house and the grocery bill and whatever else there is to pay. And what remains can go to Dürdane's trousseau. Will you do this for me?

BEYAĞABEY: Certainly.

STRANGER: I'll send you another check. That'll be in Saffet's name. Give it to her in secret. It'll be for our daughter. Will you do that, too?

BEYAĞABEY: Of course!

STRANGER: Well, it's time to leave now. Please don't let anyone know about me. [BEYAĞABEY *does not answer.*] Promise?

BEYAĞABEY: Yes.

STRANGER: It's good that I'm forgotten here. It's better that way. Better, that is, for a family man. I was almost going to make another mistake after all these twenty years. The past is past, though. One mustn't stir it. The neighborhood may get in one's way, sometimes. OK, good-bye. [BEYAĞABEY *does not move. The* STRANGER *pats him on the back.*] Well, good-bye!

BEYAĞABEY: Let me come to the hotel with you.

STRANGER: No, thank you.

BEYAĞABEY: Let me take you to the streetcar stop, then.

STRANGER: Wouldn't be worth the trouble. [BEYAĞABEY *takes a step to go with him, then changes his mind.*]

BEYAĞABEY: Good-bye, then. [*They shake hands.*]

STRANGER: Good-bye. [*Follows* BEYAĞABEY *with his eyes as* BEYAĞABEY *leaves.*]

[*A* YOUNG COUPLE, *going to the wedding party, appears from the side of the* MIDWIFE'S *house. The* YOUNG WOMAN *walks in front, not paying attention to where she is stepping.*]

YOUNG WOMAN: [*Stops.*] Help me! Oh, help me! Give me a hand! My shoes! My shoes! Oh no!

YOUNG MAN: [*Holds his wife by the hand.*] Step right here, dear. [*The* YOUNG WOMAN *moves.*] That's it!

YOUNG WOMAN: [*Nervously.*] What shall I do? We can't go to the wedding like this. We tried to save the shoes, and now look at my skirt! Let's go back.

YOUNG MAN: Never mind, dear, they know us in this neighborhood. Is it our fault? [*Puts his arm in hers. Dance music is heard in the distance. They continue walking.*]

YOUNG WOMAN: [*About the* STRANGER.] He must be drunk. Why does he turn and look at us so?

YOUNG MAN: [*Walking. Looks at the* STRANGER. *To his wife.*] He's a stranger.

STRANGER: [*As the couple disappears, to himself.*] A stranger . . .

CURTAIN

EPILOGUE

[*The setting is the same as that of the Prologue. A few stars in the sky. The* NIGHT WATCHMAN *appears.*]

NIGHT WATCHMAN: I hope it's a lucky night tonight! I'd like to see the carpenter now that he has a son. He has five of 'em now. But he doesn't even think about it. The oldest one is only fourteen. Well, as long as Allah gives him strength, the rest is easy, I guess. [*Laughter and Turkish music are heard from a distance.*] They really have stretched that wedding! This time of night, and they still haven't broken it up yet. I just don't understand these modern weddings. In place of sweet pilaf they have raki and wine. They offered me the wine and the appetizers. Heaven forbid! I wouldn't touch either of them. She's quite a woman, though. Just like a man. She's the Saffet Hanım of the neighborhood. Managing the whole crowd single-handedly! [*A whistle is heard. He whistles back.*] The patrols are here tonight to keep an eye on the place. Their chief is probably invited to the wedding, too. And then to think of Macit Bey! That's life!

[*The* STRANGER *appears; he looks haggard. His coat lapels are drawn up. The* NIGHT WATCHMAN *stops under the streetlamp and stares at him.*]

STRANGER: Hello!

NIGHT WATCHMAN: Hello. Have you been to the wedding?

STRANGER: I've been to quite a place all right!

NIGHT WATCHMAN: You're right. That doorway is really something to see. [*The* STRANGER *half turns back in the direction from which he has come.*] All the scum of the neighborhood is there. Not only at the doorway, either. Go around the garden, and every crack in the wall has someone peeping through it. I don't know what they're looking for. That's curiosity.

STRANGER: Did you see the bride?

NIGHT WATCHMAN: I did.

STRANGER: She's lovely, isn't she?

NIGHT WATCHMAN: Well, yes . . .

STRANGER: Yes, what?

NIGHT WATCHMAN: I mean . . . well, may Allah give them both health and strength.

STRANGER: She looks beautiful in the bridal gown, doesn't she?

NIGHT WATCHMAN: Yes, beautiful, beautiful. Well . . .

STRANGER: Well, what?

NIGHT WATCHMAN: In times like this, all that expense? Well, that's the way with the world, I guess. Some are in misery and debt, and some are living it up. [*Shakes his head.*]

STRANGER: How long have you been in this neighborhood?

NIGHT WATCHMAN: More than twenty years.

STRANGER: [*Turns his face toward the* NIGHT WATCHMAN.] Who knows how many things you have seen here! [*The* NIGHT WATCHMAN *makes a gesture meaning "plenty."*]

NIGHT WATCHMAN: [*Looks attentively at the* STRANGER.] You're not from this neighborhood, are you?

STRANGER: It shows, doesn't it?

NIGHT WATCHMAN: The roads are in a mess. Let me take you to the main street.

STRANGER: No, thank you. I'll get there somehow. [*Gives money to the* NIGHT WATCHMAN.] It's not much, but . . . [*Starts walking away.*]

NIGHT WATCHMAN: Thank you. [*Sees that it is a large bill.*] Sir, by mistake . . . [*Attempts to return the money.*]

STRANGER: It isn't a mistake, it isn't. [*Leaves.*]

NIGHT WATCHMAN: By God! He came like a savior, this man. My poor wife was whining in her last letter again. [*Walks around. Gazes at the stars.*] Twenty years. It's easy to say! But nothing like this ever happened to me before. Who knows what more things are hidden in this world! Who knows who that man was! [*Gazes at the stars.*] That star up there is shining bright tonight. This one up here is shining, too. And that one over there just fell. They're all gates of destiny. Some open before you, and some close. [*A whistle is heard.*] All's quiet in the neighborhood! [*Blows his whistle.*] The hundred and thirty-fifth night. [*Walks away. Dance music is heard from a distance.*]

CURTAIN

◆   ◆   ◆

A Ball for the Imaginative

TUNÇ YALMAN

An Editor's Note

Tunç Yalman (1925–2005) was an all-around personality of the theater par excellence—artistic director, playwright, actor, stage director, translator, and teacher. He came from a prominent Istanbul family. His father, Ahmet Emin Yalman, was a highly influential newspaper publisher and journalistic pioneer well known for his books in Turkish and in English (published in the United States). His mother, Rezzan A. E. Yalman, achieved recognition as a prolific translator. Tunç Yalman graduated from the prestigious Robert College in Istanbul, the oldest American college outside the United States. His class of 1944 is notable for having produced a prime minister, an Istanbul mayor, a World Bank vice president, a director-general of Turkey's Press and Information Agency, and the sheikh of a Sufi sect. Yalman became the theatrical star of that class.

In the 1940s, he reveled in the life of drama at Robert College, appearing in major roles in that school's almost professional productions in English and Turkish. He later attended the Yale Drama School, where he excelled in playwriting. His play entitled *The Myrmidons* was selected for a full-dress production of the Yale Drama School graduating class. After graduation, another play he had written in English, *A Ball for the Imaginative*, came close to getting an Off-Broadway production. The present anthology is giving this intriguing play its first exposure. Yalman's original script is published intact here except for minor bits of editing.

In the 1950s, Yalman joined the editorial staff of his father's daily, *Vatan*, first as its arts reporter, then as a columnist, and finally as the editor of the arts supplement. But because his heart was in the theater, he abandoned journalism and became involved with the Istanbul City Theater under the aegis of the eminent actor-director-administrator Muhsin Ertuğrul in the 1960s. Yalman's many years as a moving force at that galvanizing theater secured his fame as a great director of both the classics and modern plays, although many critics refused to give him credit for his acting.

The 1970s saw the emergence of Yalman as artistic director of the Milwaukee Repertory Theater, where he received kudos for his riveting productions. During his two forays into directing in New York City, Tunç Yalman attracted attention for his staging of Amran Ducovny and Leon Friedman's *The Trial of Lee Harvey Oswald* on Broadway and of Joe Orton's *Entertaining Mr. Sloan* Off Broadway. In the 1980s, he was a professor of drama at the prestigious North Carolina School of the Arts, where he also directed numerous plays. He spent fifteen of his last years in New York City, where with a voracious appetite he saw many hundreds of plays, adding this number to his presumably unparalleled record of several thousand he had seen in Turkey, Europe, England, and the United States before he fell victim to a relentless disease that kept him incapacitated in Turkey.

A Ball for the Imaginative is Yalman's only play to see publication. It stands as a testament to the talents of one of Turkey's greatest theatrical figures. It is a youthful yet mature work, filled with quaint characters, sparkling dialogue, and scintillating action.—TSH

Characters

TOTO, asylum inmate

SIMON, asylum inmate

IN CARNATION, asylum inmate

NAPOLEON, asylum inmate

NURSE MESOPOTAMIA

COUNTESS PALACHINKA

DR. ROSE, inspector

INSPECTOR SAGE

TWO MALE NURSES

[*The action takes place in* COUNTESS PALACHINKA's *former residence on the outskirts of a small city. The countess has turned her house into a privately run asylum for those who cannot adjust.*

A pentagonal setting representing part of a large room in COUNTESS PALACHINKA's *privately run experimental asylum. A heavy red curtain masks the entrance to the room.*

Before the play begins the audience hears the strains of a quaint, cheerful, and unusual melody.

At the rise of the curtain, TOTO, SIMON, IN CARNATION, *and* NAPOLEON *are seen executing a merry barn dance to the accompaniment of this same tune. The music presently comes to an end. They stop dancing.* SIMON *goes over to the gramophone and removes the record.* NAPOLEON, *who is wearing a Napoleonic hat, sits on the sofa.* TOTO *places a stool under his feet.*]

NAPOLEON: This is a charming ball. A very charming ball indeed! We are very pleased with it.

TOTO: Thank you, sire. I am glad Your Imperial Highness is having a good time.

SIMON: [*Casually, while looking at the records.*] Napoleon.

NAPOLEON: Yes, Simon?

SIMON: Did you ever think about the problem of lighting those large ballrooms in palaces? They used candles, of course, but candles give such little light.

IN CARNATION: They must have used hundreds of them.

NAPOLEON: Nay, thousands!

TOTO: Maybe that's why there were so many revolutions. Because all the money went to the lighting of ballrooms.

SIMON: What are candles made of?

IN CARNATION: Of wax.

SIMON: I know. What's wax?

NAPOLEON: It is white, and it bends.

IN CARNATION: Yes, but what is it made of?

NAPOLEON: Of stuff that is white and that bends!

TOTO: Candles are made of wax.

IN CARNATION: All women must have been beautiful in those days. All women are beautiful by candlelight. I know.

SIMON: Next time we have a ball, let's have it at night, and let's ask Nurse Mesopotamia to give us candles.

IN CARNATION: She won't.

SIMON: Why not?

IN CARNATION: Fire regulations.

TOTO: Maybe she will if we invite her to the ball.

IN CARNATION: She won't accept. She has no imagination!

SIMON: Yes, poor girl, and, what's more, she doesn't show the slightest desire or tendency to develop one. She isn't like Countess Palachinka. Palachinka has imagination.

NAPOLEON: Of course. Palachinka has everything! But this girl—it's sad when you think of the unlimited opportunity she has working in a place like this. What's the use of being a nurse in Countess Palachinka's asylum for the imaginative if one is not going to benefit by it?

TOTO: She will never find a husband. That's what will happen to her. I, for one, would never marry a woman who carries a watch.

NAPOLEON: Nay, she carries two of them. One on her wrist and one in the pocket of her uniform. It's disgusting.

SIMON: God has no concept of time. It is immoral and impious for man to invent such a concept and then to go and become a slave to it. Besides, it is so inconvenient to measure an unseen, nonexistent thing like time.

NAPOLEON: In the old days, they at least made amends for it by having beautiful clocks and watches. Every watch was a work of art. But now they are not even made—they are manufactured! Having beautiful watches is acceptable to a point, but turning out millions of hideous little timekeepers is simply unpardonable.

TOTO: Napoleon, how old would you have been now if you had been the real Napoleon?

NAPOLEON: When was he born, In Carnation? I always forget.

IN CARNATION: He was born in 1769.

NAPOLEON: I would have been more than two hundred years old, my dear Toto, and, what's more, I am a real Napoleon.

TOTO: When were you born?

NAPOLEON: How should I know?

TOTO: When were you born, In Carnation?

IN CARNATION: On the eighth of May, in the year 1921.

TOTO: And you, Simon?

SIMON: I don't know.

TOTO: I wonder when I was born. I used to know, but I forgot.

NAPOLEON: The devil is getting into us. Mesopotamia's watches are bewitching us. We must stop talking about time. There is no time! Let us talk of things that exist. Let us talk of love.

SIMON: Tell us a tale of mythology, In Carnation.

IN CARNATION: All right. Do you want a tale of real mythology or one of my own?

SIMON: Eat the grape and don't ask which vineyard it comes from.

IN CARNATION: What?

SIMON: An old proverb.

[IN CARNATION *takes a wooden chair, places it in the center of the stage, climbs up on it, and prepares to tell his tale.* NAPOLEON *and* SIMON *sit and prepare to listen,* TOTO *is lying on the floor.*]

IN CARNATION: There once was a hippopotamus with a pocket on his belly.

NAPOLEON: That's a kangaroo.

IN CARNATION: No, it was a hippopotamus. The Queen of the Bees fell madly in love with this hippopotamus, whose name was Rhododendron. But she did not know about the curse on the belly.

TOTO: Why did he have a pocket on his belly?

IN CARNATION: The Goddess of Love had put it there because she had not been invited to his christening. She had prophesied that Rhododendron would fall in love with a woman smaller in size than himself and that this pocket would separate him from his love, at the same time causing him great bodily pain.

SIMON: And he fell in love with a queen?

IN CARNATION: Yes, he fell in love with the Queen of the Bees.

TOTO: Was it a great love?

IN CARNATION: It was the greatest love of their generation. After a suitable period of courtship, they decided to get married. It was agreed upon that the queen was to move into Rhododendron's pocket and that she was to bring with her thirty-three servants to look after the habitat and to make honey.

SIMON: How big is a hippopotamus?

IN CARNATION: Much bigger than thirty-four bees! How can I go on telling you stories when you doubt the credibility of what I say? Why, this pocket was large enough to hold one hundred bees, but the queen just happened to bring a mere thirty-three. And you think even that is too many!

SIMON: I humbly apologize, In Carnation. I have never seen a hippopotamus. I did not know.

NAPOLEON: It is a rare animal, In Carnation. I beg you to accept Simon's apologies and to go on with your story.

IN CARNATION: [*Comes down off the chair.*] I have stepped into another mood now, Napoleon. I'll finish it tomorrow.

TOTO: Just tell us what happened. Tell us very quickly. You must tell us.

IN CARNATION: Well, very quickly then. On the night of the wedding, the Queen of the Bees entered the pocket with her servants. But the Goddess of Love had put stingers on the bodies of the bees, and then she sealed the opening of the pocket with honey so that they were imprisoned inside. The bees stung the hippopotamus until he died of the pain, and they died of suffocation. Ever since that fateful day, bees have had stingers, and hippopotamuses have not had pockets on their bellies. That was the way in which the Goddess of Love got her revenge, and thus the prophecy was fulfilled. [*Pause.*]

NAPOLEON: What injustice! Why should poor Rhododendron be punished because his parents had failed to send an invitation?

IN CARNATION: That, my dear Napoleon, is the moral of the story. Children often suffer for the faults of their parents.

TOTO: But, In Carnation, sometimes the exact opposite occurs. If my parents had not been what they were, I would have been withering in an office or behind a counter instead of living in this heavenly asylum.

IN CARNATION: True, Toto, quite true. We may assume, then, that the issue depends on the particular fault of the particular parents.

SIMON: As I always say, everything is relative anyway.

IN CARNATION: Simon, it is my turn to apologize now. I humbly apologize for having been slightly impatient with you just now.

SIMON: Thank you, In Carnation, you are very considerate.

IN CARNATION: [*Goes over to* SIMON.] Let's shake hands. [IN CARNATION *and* SIMON *shake hands.*]

NAPOLEON: Let's all shake hands. We haven't done so since Toto's egg fell on the floor at breakfast.

TOTO: But nothing has happened since my egg fell on the floor.

NAPOLEON: For shame, Toto. Must something happen for us to shake hands? Must we wait for a fitting occasion in order to show our love for one another? Love should never be taken for granted, lest it wither and die! Let's shake hands, my friends, let's shake hands!

SIMON: I shake your hand, Toto, and am thy brother.

TOTO: I shake your hand, Simon. May thy present bliss be perpetual.

SIMON: I shake your hand, In Carnation, and am fond of thee.

IN CARNATION: I shake your hand, Simon. Thou canst always depend on my love. [*To* TOTO, *who has come up behind* SIMON.] And thee, Toto.

SIMON: I shake your hand, Napoleon.

NAPOLEON: And I thine, Simon. God be blessed for having made thee. [TOTO *is following* SIMON *around the room.*] I shake your hand, Toto. It is a rare pleasure to know thee.

IN CARNATION: [*To* NAPOLEON.] I shake your hand, my friend.

NAPOLEON: I shake your hand, In Carnation. May your carnations never wither.

TOTO: And now let us pray, please. I feel like praying.

NAPOLEON: Yes, of course, Toto. Whose turn is it?

IN CARNATION: I spoke this morning. I think it's Simon's turn.

SIMON: But is it proper to pray at a ball? Don't forget—this is a ball!

NAPOLEON: Don't be silly, Simon! What difference does it make where you pray? Besides what place could be more fitting than a ball? That is where people are most likely to forget.

SIMON: Yes, Napoleon, you are right. Let's shake hands!

[SIMON *and* NAPOLEON *shake hands once again.* IN CARNATION *and* TOTO *kneel.* NAPOLEON *joins them.* SIMON *stands in front of the kneeling men, directly facing the audience, and begins to pray. They all are looking up to Heaven.*]

O God in Heaven, and if there is no God and if there is no Heaven, then O Power that we love, O Power that created us and the universe, we thank thee for our existence. We thank thee for having sent our parents to bed on that particular night when we were in them; we thank thee for having discarded all the other seeds that surrounded us and for having chosen us from among the thousands of others. We thank thee for our having been born. We are sorry for all our brothers and sisters who died unborn, but we know that one had to be chosen, and we thank thee for our luck in having been chosen. Twins are rare and quintuplets the limit, that we know. Most of the seeds have to perish—we understand and are not sorry for them. And then, we thank you for our lives after our birth, we thank you for having made us so happy. [*Looks down and almost automatically adds.*] And for making Palachinka like us and take care of us. [*Looks up again.*] We are happy, O God, and if there is no God, then O Imaginary Power that we love, it is to thee we speak, to thee we give our thanks!

[*The four* INMATES *are still looking up at the ceiling when the red curtain on the wall is suddenly pushed open and* NURSE MESOPOTAMIA *is seen closing the door behind her.*

MESOPOTAMIA, *in her immaculate uniform, and the white door, now revealed in all its nakedness, are in complete contrast with the rest of the room. We are reminded, and some of us are perhaps reassured, that this definitely is a hospital of some sort. Somehow there can be no mistake about it anymore.* MESOPOTAMIA *is young, pretty, and probably very competent in her profession. Before the* INMATES *have had time to return to a less pious mood, she speaks in a pleasant voice.*]

NURSE MESOPOTAMIA: Why are you all kneeling on the floor?

TOTO: We were praying, Mesopotamia. [*Gets up.*] We are finished now.

NURSE MESOPOTAMIA: I thought you were having a little party this afternoon.

NAPOLEON: We are having a great ball, Mesopotamia. But we just felt like praying between dances.

NURSE MESOPOTAMIA: You pray very often, don't you? Tell me, do you always say the same prayers?

IN CARNATION: No, it's something different every time. But we don't say prayers, woman, we . . . we just pray.

NURSE MESOPOTAMIA: To whom do you pray?

IN CARNATION: To the Imaginary Power whom we love.

NURSE MESOPOTAMIA: To God, you mean?

IN CARNATION: We aren't sure if there is a God or not; nobody can be sure. But that doesn't matter, you see, because we love God and what he stands for regardless of whether he actually exists or not.

NURSE MESOPOTAMIA: [*After having thought this over.*] I . . . I don't think I understand.

NAPOLEON: Sometimes, Mesopotamia, you seem to forget that it is very difficult for you to understand these things—or else you wouldn't carry a watch!

IN CARNATION: She has two watches.

NURSE MESOPOTAMIA: Only one today, In Carnation. I broke my wristwatch.

IN CARNATION: Congratulations.

NURSE MESOPOTAMIA: That's a nice thing to say! It'll cost me a small fortune to have it repaired!

NAPOLEON: You're hopeless, Meso, but I think I'll shake your hand nevertheless. [*Goes to her and shakes her hand.*] Basically, we like you very much.

NURSE MESOPOTAMIA: Thank you, Napoleon.

IN CARNATION: We welcome you to the ball, Mesopotamia. Put a record on, Simon, and let's dance to the master's voice!

NURSE MESOPOTAMIA: I am sorry, In Carnation, but I can't. I am very busy this afternoon. With all your talk, you almost made me forget I came to tell you that the countess is on her way to your room.

SIMON: Palachinka!

TOTO: She will dance with us!

NAPOLEON: How nice of her to have accepted our invitation!

IN CARNATION: But we didn't send her one, did we?

NAPOLEON: No, that's why it's so nice!

NURSE MESOPOTAMIA: Now listen. This isn't one of her regular visits. There are two inspectors with her; one of them is a doctor, and I think the other one comes from the Statistics Bureau.

NAPOLEON: What are they inspecting?

NURSE MESOPOTAMIA: The Municipal Health Department has sent them for a general inspection. Now, we must make a very good impression on those two men. You know how particular municipalities are about private institutions and hospitals like this. Countess Palachinka had great difficulty in obtaining permission to open a home of this kind for men like you. So be careful while you talk to those two men. They already know that you are wise, so you don't have to prove it to them. And I warn you, they don't look very understanding. Please don't try to convert them to anything. I am sure they wouldn't appreciate it. They have already visited most of the other rooms, and they do seem to be a little shocked by the decorations, but I don't think that matters, really. [*Looks around the room.*] They're supposed to know all about our experimental policy. Now, you will be nice to them, won't you?

TOTO: [*Has picked up a thick, leather-bound volume from one of the beds.*] We are always nice!

IN CARNATION: To everybody!

NURSE MESOPOTAMIA: I know you are, but I thought I would warn you anyway.

TOTO: [*Holding the book.*] You left this book here this morning, Mesopotamia. I read a few pages. It is very interesting, but there are so many characters in it that I got confused after a while. [*Looks at the title, then gives it to her.*] It is called *The Telephone Directory.* [*Turns to the others.*] That's my favorite joke.

NURSE MESOPOTAMIA: Thank you, Toto. I've been looking for it everywhere! The inspectors will be here any moment now. I'll tell them you are having a party, and then maybe they won't stay very long.

NAPOLEON: [*Produces a pack of playing cards from his pocket, gives* MESOPOTAMIA *two cards.*] On the contrary, we shall be delighted to have them. You can give them these invitations.

NURSE MESOPOTAMIA: [*Takes the cards.*] All right.

[NURSE MESOPOTAMIA *leaves the room.* SIMON *puts on a record—a waltz. The four IN-MATES hold each other by the hand and begin one of their merry and fantastic dances. After a short while,* MESOPOTAMIA *excitedly reenters and tries to stop the dance.*]

Shh! They're coming.

[*The* INMATES *stop dancing and look at the door.* COUNTESS PALACHINKA *enters with the two* INSPECTORS. *She is a stout, impressive-looking woman in her fifties. It is obvious, even at first sight, that she must be fond of experimenting with the color of her hair.*]

She does not seem to have yet found the right tone. She is rather pleasantly overdressed. Her tailored suit looks quite severe. The temptation to alleviate its seriousness with two silver foxes dangling from her shoulders and with brooches and pins and whatnot must have been irresistible to her. Her hat is not extravagant.

She is a very sensible woman in spite of the fact that people judging her by conventional standards of behavior are apt to disagree. She has money, thinks that it ought to be spent, and spends it—usually for some worthwhile purpose or for some purpose that she believes to be worthwhile. Bureaucrats and philistines hate her for it.

One of the inspectors, DR. ROSE, *is a short, ordinary man. The other,* MR. SAGE, *has a lean and hungry look. He keeps caressing his brow with nervous fingers. The* INMATES *look at the newcomers.]*

COUNTESS PALACHINKA: [*To the* INSPECTORS, *as she enters the room.*] And this is my favorite room. It used to be my bedroom in the old days when I lived here. [NURSE MESOPOTAMIA *leaves.*]

NAPOLEON: [*Goes over to the* COUNTESS *and gallantly kisses her hand.*] In the name of our little assembly, I feel honored in welcoming you and your illustrious entourage to our ball, Your Highness.

COUNTESS PALACHINKA: [*Makes a little curtsy.*] The honor is all mine, sire. [*And then cheerfully to the others.*] Hello, Toto! Hello, Simon! Hello, In Carnation!

TOTO, SIMON, and IN CARNATION: [*In unison.*] Hello, Palachinka!

COUNTESS PALACHINKA: These two gentlemen have come to ask you if you are happy. [*Points to the* INSPECTORS, *who remain silent.*]

SIMON: How very nice of them!

TOTO: Thank you.

NAPOLEON: How thoughtful of the municipality to employ men who go around asking people if they are happy! How very thoughtful!

IN CARNATION: But, gentlemen, what about yourselves? Is there anybody to see to it that the inspectors are happy? [*To the* COUNTESS.] They don't look very happy, do they, Palachinka?

COUNTESS PALACHINKA: Now, now, boys, you're supposed to answer questions today. That's what these gentlemen are here for.

DR. ROSE: [*Looks at* TOTO, *who happens to be looking at him.*] Are you men satisfied with the food?

TOTO: What food?

DR. ROSE: The food you eat.

TOTO: Why do you ask?

DR. ROSE: [*Decides to try a more direct approach.*] Did you have an egg for breakfast this morning?

TOTO: No.

DR. ROSE: [*Turns to the* COUNTESS.] I thought you said that you gave them eggs every morning.

COUNTESS PALACHINKA: I do nothing of the sort.

DR. ROSE: But you said just now, in the other room, that they had eggs for breakfast!

COUNTESS PALACHINKA: They do, but I don't give them to them!

DR. ROSE: Why didn't this man have an egg for breakfast?

COUNTESS PALACHINKA: How should I know! I live thirty miles away! Why didn't you have an egg for breakfast, Toto?

TOTO: Because it fell on the floor.

DR. ROSE: Where is it?

TOTO: What?

DR. ROSE: The egg.

TOTO: Mesopotamia took it away.

DR. ROSE: Who?

TOTO: Mesopotamia. [DR. ROSE *looks despairingly at the* COUNTESS.]

COUNTESS PALACHINKA: Who's that, Toto? Anybody I know?

TOTO: We call Riabuchinska Mesopotamia this week!

DR. ROSE: And who's Riabuchinska?

COUNTESS PALACHINKA: That's what they called her last week.

DR. ROSE: Called who?

TOTO: [*Shouts impatiently.*] Mesopotamia!

DR. ROSE: This is a madhouse!

COUNTESS PALACHINKA: This is the second time you have used that expression, Doctor! I must ask you to choose your idioms more carefully! [NURSE MESOPOTAMIA *enters while* COUNTESS PALACHINKA *is making her indignant remark.*]

NURSE MESOPOTAMIA: Did you call me?

COUNTESS PALACHINKA: Why, no, my dear.

NURSE MESOPOTAMIA: I thought I heard somebody calling my name. [*Prepares to leave the room.*]

DR. ROSE: Wait a minute! Is your name Mesopotamia?

NURSE MESOPOTAMIA: Yes. I mean . . . no . . . it's Washington.

TOTO: But we call her Mesopotamia.

SIMON: This week!

NAPOLEON: There was a time when we called her Plo . . . P-L-O . . . Plo!

DR. ROSE: Miss Washington, was this man given an egg for breakfast today? [*Points to* TOTO.]

NURSE MESOPOTAMIA: Yes.

DR. ROSE: Did it fall on the floor?

NURSE MESOPOTAMIA: Yes.

DR. ROSE: Did you clean up the floor?

NURSE MESOPOTAMIA: Why, yes.

DR. ROSE: Hmm. I have so little faith in the management of this place, I am ready to expect anything! [*Takes a few steps around the room.*] Just look at this room! Look at it!

COUNTESS PALACHINKA: Don't forget this is an experimental institution, Doctor!

NURSE MESOPOTAMIA: The men are rather fond of disorder, Doctor, but you can be sure that the rooms are scrubbed and dusted regularly.

COUNTESS PALACHINKA: Thank you, my dear. [NURSE MESOPOTAMIA *exits.*]

IN CARNATION: Fat women come and sweep the floor, sir, every time we go out to the garden. The countess takes good care of us. We are very happy here.

COUNTESS PALACHINKA: Thank you, In Carnation.

INSPECTOR SAGE: What is your name?

IN CARNATION: In Carnation.

DR. ROSE: [*Interrupts.*] Why?

IN CARNATION: What's your name?

DR. ROSE: [*Answers automatically.*] Theodore Rose.

IN CARNATION: [*He and* DR. ROSE *are now directly facing each other.*] Why?

DR. ROSE: What do you mean, why?

IN CARNATION: I mean exactly what you meant when you asked me why!

DR. ROSE: But I am not called "Incarnation."

IN CARNATION: Of course not. I am called "In Carnation."

DR. ROSE: That's a funny name.

IN CARNATION: It may be funny, but it's my name. "In" for Ignatius.

DR. ROSE: And your surname is Carnation?

IN CARNATION: Yes, Dr. Rose!

NAPOLEON: My favorite flower is the tulip.

DR. ROSE: [*Turns to him suspiciously.*] What's your name?

NAPOLEON: My name?

DR. ROSE: Yes.

NAPOLEON: Napoleon.

DR. ROSE: Don't you know there is a Napoleon in practically every lunatic asylum in the world?

COUNTESS PALACHINKA: Dr. Rose!

NAPOLEON: Is there?

DR. ROSE: Yes, there is. But you, I imagine, pride yourself in really and truly being Napoleon.

NAPOLEON: Yes.

DR. ROSE: Don't you know that Napoleon has been dead for a long time now?

NAPOLEON: You mean the emperor?

DR. ROSE: Yes, I mean the emperor!

NAPOLEON: Of course he's dead. What was the date of his death, In Carnation?

IN CARNATION: 1821, Napoleon.

DR. ROSE: Well then?

NAPOLEON: "Well then" what?

DR. ROSE: If you admit that he is dead, who are you?

NAPOLEON: I am Napoleon.

DR. ROSE: [*Impatiently turns to* INSPECTOR SAGE.] I'm to blame for this. I should never have started arguing with them.

NAPOLEON: [*To the* COUNTESS.] He doesn't believe me. You tell him, Palachinka!

COUNTESS PALACHINKA: Dr. Rose, this man is called Napoleon! He can't help it if some French emperor happened to have the same name, can he?

DR. ROSE: Why didn't he say so in the first place?

COUNTESS PALACHINKA: He did.

DR. ROSE: [*Angrily to* NAPOLEON.] Why do you wear that silly hat then?

NAPOLEON: Why not?

DR. ROSE: This is a madhouse!

COUNTESS PALACHINKA: You are a very tactless psychoanalyst, Dr. Rose!

DR. ROSE: Who told you I was a psychoanalyst?

INSPECTOR SAGE: [*Has hardly moved since he entered the room.*] He is a general practitioner.

COUNTESS PALACHINKA: Who obviously belongs to the old school!

DR. ROSE: I do, Countess, and I am proud of it. I want a spade to be called a spade!

NAPOLEON: Why not?

DR. ROSE: How many more rooms do we have to visit?

COUNTESS PALACHINKA: Just two more. You don't have to visit them, though.

DR. ROSE: Oh, I do, I do. I must see everything before I turn in my report.

COUNTESS PALACHINKA: You are a very conscientious man, aren't you, Doctor?

DR. ROSE: Yes, yes. Come along, Sage, let's go and get it over with.

INSPECTOR SAGE: Wait a minute, Dr. Rose, I haven't asked them anything yet.

DR. ROSE: Oh my God, at the rate we're going we'll never get out of here. Countess, why don't you and I go into the next room and start questioning the others? Sage can join us when he's through with these men. If he ever is through!

COUNTESS PALACHINKA: As you wish, Doctor. The next two rooms are at the end of the corridor, Mr. Sage. I think first we shall go into the one on the right.

INSPECTOR SAGE: Thank you, Countess.

COUNTESS PALACHINKA: [*Heard speaking to* DR. ROSE *on her way out.*] I really don't see why you are being so impatient, Doctor. After all, we have only twenty-four guests. [*The* COUNTESS *and* DR. ROSE *exit.*]

INSPECTOR SAGE: [*This is just a boring routine for him, and yet from the way he looks at the men, it is obvious that he is curiously fascinated by them. He is very tired.*] The countess told us that we could talk with the men on this floor on any subject. That means that you are on your way to recovery. Now, tell me what you would like to do when you are discharged?

NAPOLEON: Mr. Sage, I, for one, will never leave this place while I am alive. I don't intend to do so; I don't want to do so; and, unless Palachinka runs out of money, I don't think I will do so. And I think that my friends think this way, too.

INSPECTOR SAGE: May I ask why you . . . why you were sent to live here?

NAPOLEON: I wasn't sent, I was chosen—by Palachinka. She picked us all up from the street or from other places at different times.

INSPECTOR SAGE: But why?

NAPOLEON: I was what they call a drug addict, that's why!

INSPECTOR SAGE: I see.

NAPOLEON: I used to take drugs because I was unhappy. When I took them, I was happy. But here I am happy without having to take anything. I'm just happy. So why should I want to leave?

TOTO: Why should he want to leave, Mr. Inspector? He is happy. We all are happy. We have the large garden. We have large beds to sleep in and food to eat. We talk and sleep and talk and sleep again, and sometimes we just sit still and do nothing. And sometimes we think about things. We have solved all the mysteries; we have found answers to everything. They may not be the right ones, but they satisfy us. I was in another place once. It was all white and bad. But here we decorate our rooms and even our corridors. We can do anything we like. And the nurses are different here. We are so happy, Mr. Inspector, that we pray several times a day. And each time it is a different prayer.

INSPECTOR SAGE: I don't want to appear indiscreet, but what was your main problem?

TOTO: I was what they call an epileptic. I still am, I think, but seizures come very, very seldom now.

NAPOLEON: You are a very polite man, sir.

INSPECTOR SAGE: Thank you, Napoleon.

IN CARNATION: But you are also a man who is full of sorrow, are you not?

INSPECTOR SAGE: What makes you say that?

IN CARNATION: Your silence while that man was asking us silly questions. Your sad eyes. Your habit of clearing your brow with your hand. [INSPECTOR SAGE's *fingers automatically repeat the gesture.*] You see!

INSPECTOR SAGE: What else do you see in me?

IN CARNATION: Blackness. There is something . . . something restless within you. I can see you walking down crowded streets. Great crowds all around you, and you are alone. Alone with yourself, and you don't like yourself.

INSPECTOR SAGE: No.

SIMON: Be yourself, man, and get it off your chest. Tell us what it is. We might be able to help.

INSPECTOR SAGE: It's nothing, really. It's nothing. I suppose I do look tired . . . I have been a little nervous lately . . . I don't sleep very well . . . that's why. I . . . I think I'll go now.

IN CARNATION: [*As* INSPECTOR SAGE *is awkwardly retreating toward the door.*] Wait! You are married, aren't you?

INSPECTOR SAGE: [*Stops.*] Yes.

IN CARNATION: And you have a child . . . perhaps two?

INSPECTOR SAGE: Yes, I have a son and a daughter. But . . . how do you know?

IN CARNATION: I am what they call a mind reader. That's how I used to earn my living. You don't like your family, do you?

INSPECTOR SAGE: [*Looks at* IN CARNATION *for a moment, then slowly speaks.*] No, I don't like my family. [*Then quickly adds.*] I didn't mean to say that.

IN CARNATION: Say it, my friend. Once you accept it as a fact, you will feel much better. I hated my wife, too. I know exactly what you are going through. I suffered and suffered until I reached a decision. And then, afterward, everything seemed so clear all of a sudden.

INSPECTOR SAGE: What did you do?

IN CARNATION: I killed her.

INSPECTOR SAGE: [*Smiles ironically.*] I couldn't do that. [*Slowly begins to let himself go.*] Besides, you see, it isn't only that woman and her children that I don't like. The trouble is, there is nothing I do like. I hate my work. I hate the streets I walk in. I hate the rooms I am in. I hate the look of the buildings and walls that surround me. Everything is so monotonous, so deadly monotonous! People say the same silly things, eat the same tasteless meals, drink the same bitter stuff, over and over again. I want some change. I need some change. And yet I know it will never come. Nothing ever happens to me. I don't even have anyone I can talk to.

TOTO: You can talk to us.

INSPECTOR SAGE: Thank you. What is your name?

TOTO: Toto.

INSPECTOR SAGE: Thank you, Toto.

IN CARNATION: What are you going to do?

INSPECTOR SAGE: I don't know.

NAPOLEON: For us, the world is very beautiful and meaningful, but it's no use trying to convince you, is it?

INSPECTOR SAGE: No. I know all that you or anybody else can possibly tell me about the beauty of the world. Sometimes I see it myself, but not often enough.

NAPOLEON: I am sorry.

INSPECTOR SAGE: You said you might be able to help me. Nobody can help me. I just happen to have that kind of mind.

SIMON: [*In a very calm voice.*] Kill it.

INSPECTOR SAGE: How?

SIMON: By killing yourself.

INSPECTOR SAGE: I can't.

SIMON: Why not?

INSPECTOR SAGE: I can't. I tried, and I couldn't. [*Takes a little bottle from his pocket.*] Do you see this?

IN CARNATION: Poison?

INSPECTOR SAGE: Yes. If I were to drink this, I would be dead in a minute. And the doctor said it causes hardly any pain.

IN CARNATION: Dr. Rose?

INSPECTOR SAGE: Yes, I got it from Dr. Rose. I told him I wanted to kill an unhappy old dog I had.

TOTO: It has a very nice color.

INSPECTOR SAGE: Just think of it. If I drank this now, I would die almost instantly. No more wife, no more children, no more inspections and keeping of silly statistics, no more anything. It would be good-bye to stuffy rooms; good-bye to the knife and to the fork and to the spoon; good-bye to food, to small talk, to small worries; it would be good-bye to my overcoat and to my ugly shoes and socks.

NAPOLEON: Remember, it would also be good-bye to the sea and the sky and the trees, to the sun and the rain and the thunder.

INSPECTOR SAGE: Where are they? Were is the sky? Where is the sea? The sea! I haven't seen the sea for the past ten years! I haven't touched a tree, a real tree, since I was a boy. I already said good-bye to them long ago, Napoleon. They are not part of my world. My life is all petty and small.

IN CARNATION: Change it. Go away. Change everything.

INSPECTOR SAGE: I can't. Maybe I could have once, but now I can't. I am too tired to do anything about it.

SIMON: There is no hope then?

INSPECTOR SAGE: No hope. [*Holds up the tiny bottle.*] Only this.

IN CARNATION: Drink it.

INSPECTOR SAGE: Do you really think I should?

SIMON: Yes, you should. You have nothing to lose. Drink it and be done with it. What are you waiting for, if you're so miserable? [INSPECTOR SAGE *suddenly uncorks the bottle and swallows the poison.*] I humbly apologize, Inspector, for having been slightly impatient with you just now.

INSPECTOR SAGE: [*In a very quiet voice.*] Thank you, my friends.

[*There is silence as the four* INMATES *gaze at* INSPECTOR SAGE. *His head suddenly falls on his shoulders. He is dead. They go to him and cover part of his body with a bedcover.* SIMON *goes to the gramophone and puts on a record—"Jumbo's Lullaby."*]

SIMON: Let's dance for his soul.

[*The four* INMATES *assemble in the middle of the room and begin to dance. In a moment,* COUNTESS PALACHINKA *enters in a flurry.*]

COUNTESS PALACHINKA: The doctor is getting very impatient. Where is the other inspector? [*Does not see the body because the* INMATES *are standing in front of it.*]

TOTO: He died.

COUNTESS PALACHINKA: [*Stops the record, which is still playing.*] He what?

NAPOLEON: He took poison and died.

COUNTESS PALACHINKA: [TOTO *and* NAPOLEON *have moved away from the body while talking to her. Now she sees it and crosses to it.*] But why?

IN CARNATION: He was a very unhappy man, Palachinka.

COUNTESS PALACHINKA: Are you sure you had nothing to do with it?

NAPOLEON: Of course not, Palachinka. He wanted to die because he hated everything. He had all the reason in the world to live; he was free, and yet he thought everything was closing in on him. He just couldn't see any meaning to life and decided to put an end to it.

SIMON: He hadn't touched a tree since he was a boy.

COUNTESS PALACHINKA: What are we going to do? Oh my God, what shall I say to the doctor?

IN CARNATION: We shall tell him the truth.

COUNTESS PALACHINKA: Oh, my darlings, I'm so worried.

NAPOLEON: About us?

TOTO: Oh, Palachinka, Countess Palachinka, don't let them do anything to us. Give money to the doctor, give him lots of money! Tell him that this is what his friend wanted. Tell him we didn't kill him!

IN CARNATION: But we didn't kill him, Toto. We have nothing to fear.

TOTO: I'm afraid. Please, Palachinka, please don't let them take us away!

COUNTESS PALACHINKA: [TOTO *is kneeling in front of her; she caresses his hair.*] Nobody will take you away, Toto. I won't let them. [*Music is suddenly heard.* SIMON, *who had been standing near the gramophone, has put on a record.*]

SIMON: Let's dance for his soul.

[*The four* INMATES *assemble at the center of the room. Presently their limbs begin to react to the strange tempo of the music—a rather lively rhythm with occasional strains of melancholy. The* COUNTESS *watches them for a moment, then takes hold of the bedcover that partly covers* INSPECTOR SAGE's *body and looks at him.*]

COUNTESS PALACHINKA: Yes, he does seem to be happier now.

[*Just as* COUNTESS PALACHINKA *is about to pull the bedcover over the body,* DR. ROSE *enters, followed by* NURSE MESOPOTAMIA: DR. ROSE *sees* INSPECTOR SAGE *lying on the sofa and goes over to him. The four* INMATES *stop dancing.* SIMON *goes to the gramophone and stops the music.* NURSE MESOPOTAMIA *stands near the door.*]

DR. ROSE: [*Examines the body, finds the bottle, and sniffs it.*] This is what happens, Countess, when deranged persons are let loose in private, experimental institutions. Do you have a telephone on this floor?

COUNTESS PALACHINKA: Now, listen to me, Doctor. These boys had nothing to do with your friend's suicide.

DR. ROSE: How do you know?

COUNTESS PALACHINKA: They told me so, and I believe them. I know they never lie. Tell him how it happened, In Carnation!

IN CARNATION: He was very unhappy, Doctor. He took that poison out of his pocket and drank it. He was very, very unhappy.

DR. ROSE: [*To* COUNTESS PALACHINKA.] I gave him this bottle myself the other day. He said he wanted to kill a useless old dog he had. [*Turns to* NURSE MESOPOTAMIA.] Call for an ambulance, Nurse. And you can have the body taken downstairs. [NURSE MESOPOTAMIA *goes out.* DR. ROSE *pulls the cover over* INSPECTOR SAGE'*s body.*] But suicide or no suicide, I shall see to it that these men are transferred to a state asylum and get the kind of treatment they deserve. I don't think the mayor will like this, Countess! We all disapprove of this place, anyway. And I think this will be the end of your little establishment! A man attached to the municipality dying in such a strange way in an experimental mental asylum! Public opinion and the local press will simply demand that the place be closed down! It was a mistake to give you permission to start it in the first place. I have said so all along! If you want to waste your money, waste it on something else! And now this—this is the last straw! People will get even more suspicious after this! It will have to be closed down!

COUNTESS PALACHINKA: Not if you submit the right kind of report!

DR. ROSE: What do you mean?

COUNTESS PALACHINKA: Not if you say that this man killed himself while you were in the room! Your conscience need not trouble you; he did what he wanted to do. This place won't be closed down if you can just be sensible enough to think of the good of these men! Why should you punish them because of some prejudice you happen to have against the way I spend my money?

DR. ROSE: I don't have any prejudices, Countess. I have principles, and I live by them. I disapprove of this place. I do not believe this is the way to run a mental hospital. Just look at this room! Look at this room!

[*Two* MALE NURSES *in white uniforms enter the room. They are carrying a stretcher. They place the body on the stretcher and exit carrying it.*]

COUNTESS PALACHINKA: [*Has decided to play her trump card.*] So you have principles?

DR. ROSE: Yes.

COUNTESS PALACHINKA: [*Quite bluntly.*] Would you let me dictate your report if I gave you five thousand?

DR. ROSE: I don't take bribes.

COUNTESS PALACHINKA: Ten thousand.

DR. ROSE: No.

COUNTESS PALACHINKA: Very well. You have principles. Tell me, Doctor, do you ever bet on horses?

DR. ROSE: Yes, sometimes.

COUNTESS PALACHINKA: So you have nothing against betting?

DR. ROSE: No.

COUNTESS PALACHINKA: [*To the* INMATES.] You wanted to dance, my friends, didn't you?

SIMON: [*Mumbles.*] Yes, for his soul.

COUNTESS PALACHINKA: You were having a ball, weren't you? And you invited two gentlemen to your ball? You sent them playing cards for invitations—that was very charming of you. Unfortunately, one of them had to leave early—he wanted to leave, and he left! But the other gentleman is still here. The other gentleman still has to be entertained. Go on, dance, my friends. Go on and dance!

[SIMON, *who is standing near the gramophone, puts on a record, a little-known waltz; then he goes to the center of the stage and joins the others. The music is not very loud. They very slowly begin to dance.*]

[COUNTESS PALACHINKA *stops* DR. ROSE, *who has taken a step toward the door.*] Wait a minute! Dr. Rose, let us make a bet, shall we? Let us bet that if I can persuade you to join my friends' dance during the next three minutes, you will let me dictate your report.

DR. ROSE: This is preposterous, Countess! I must go and telephone the authorities immediately.

COUNTESS PALACHINKA: Will you hand in a favorable report if I persuade you to dance with these men during the next three minutes? [*Looks at her watch. The* INMATES *have stopped dancing. They are looking at her, trying to grasp the situation. The music is still heard.*]

DR. ROSE: Nothing could make me dance with four madmen!

COUNTESS PALACHINKA: Do you accept my challenge, then?

DR. ROSE: This is unheard of, Countess!

COUNTESS PALACHINKA: Do you?

DR. ROSE: [*Shouts almost impatiently.*] Yes, I do!

COUNTESS PALACHINKA: The recompense for turning in the middle of the room with these four gentlemen is twenty thousand! Each one of them will offer you five thousand for the honor you will bestow upon him by your condescension! [*To the* INMATES.] Go on! Dance, my friends! Think of it, Dr. Rose, a fortune! Just by moving your feet two or three times!

[*Looks at her watch.*] You have exactly one minute and forty seconds to win your bet! This is a double bet really, isn't it? By winning one thing, you lose another! But, after all, isn't money everything? Isn't it, Dr. Rose? Just think of what you can do with twenty thousand! You have twenty seconds left, Dr. Rose! You must decide!

[*The four* INMATES *are rhythmically turning in the center, holding hands.* DR. ROSE *slowly approaches them, two of the* INMATES *extend their hands and gently pull him into the circle. The* DOCTOR *moves about grotesquely. After a moment, the record comes to an end.* SIMON *goes over to the gramophone.*]

You go on dancing, my friends! Dr. Rose and I have to go down and settle a few things. You go on with your party. [*She is near the door now.*]

TOTO: Will everything be all right, Palachinka?

COUNTESS PALACHINKA: Yes, Toto, everything will be all right. Are you coming, Doctor?

[DR. ROSE *slowly advances toward the door and goes out with the* COUNTESS. *She waves her hand to the* INMATES *before she closes the door. The four* INMATES *stand motionless for a moment. Then* SIMON *stands in front of the others, takes the same position he had during the previous prayer scene, and speaks in a soft voice.*]

SIMON: You are not angry with us, are you? We could have prevented him from drinking his stuff, but what need was there to prevent him?

TOTO: It had such a beautiful color!

SIMON: If he hadn't done it here, he would have done it somewhere else. There was no hope for him. He was all empty inside. Perhaps you would have liked us to invite him to come and live with us. I think we all thought of it for a moment. Palachinka would have accepted. She would even have been glad. [*Smiles impishly.*] And the doctor . . . he would have been angry. Oh, he would have been so angry! But it was too late. The world had been too much with him, as they say. It made the soul you gave him dry up and shrink and wrinkle. Why do you allow some men to become like that, O God! Why do you keep your elements, your stars, your trees, your sky, your seas, your cleansing winds away from them?

IN CARNATION: He knows what he is doing, Simon.

NAPOLEON: I hope so.

IN CARNATION: If he exists, he knows what he is doing, and if he doesn't, it makes no difference one way or the other! Let's go on with our ball! Let's dance!

[SIMON *slowly goes over to the gramophone and puts on a record—the same one that had been playing at the opening of the play.* IN CARNATION *goes to the door and pulls the curtain. The white hospital door connecting the room with the outside world is once more hidden behind the heavy red curtain. The four* INMATES *meet at the center of the stage and begin to dance.*]

CURTAIN

◆   ◆   ◆

Man of the Hour

HALDUN TANER

Translated by Clifford Endres and Selhan Savcıgil-Endres

An Editor's Note

In 1953, *Man of the Hour,* the first play from the pen of the outstanding short-story writer Haldun Taner (1915–86), was taken into the repertory of the Istanbul City Theater. He had written it four years earlier, but had kept it in the drawer of his desk, waiting for a more opportune time for this patently political play to see the light of day. Having accepted the play, the City Theater distributed the roles and proceeded with rehearsals. But, coming alive on the stage, *Man of the Hour* did cause concern among the authorities that cabinet ministers, politicians, and parliamentarians might take offense. The playwright had taken care to avoid giving the impression that any person in particular or any individual country was being made the butt of criticism: he had introduced his play as taking place "anywhere in the world at an indeterminate time" and had listed his *dramatis personae* not by personal names, but by such characterizations as "professor, wife, secretary-general, man," and so on. Yet the play ran afoul of possible official recrimination. City Theater administrators took up the matter with the governor of Istanbul, who referred it to the minister of the interior, who in turn sought the advice of the prime minister and the president of the Turkish Republic. This tragicomical rigmarole ended with the banning of the production.

The ban made the play into a cause célèbre—and, as a prominent critic Fikret Adil wrote in a major daily, "Taner himself became 'a man of the hour.'"[1]

Taner, a graduate of the French-language lycée Galatasaray, had been sent to Heidelberg University on a government scholarship in 1935 to study economics and political science, but cut his studies short when he contracted tuberculosis and returned home in 1938. During his treatment, he wrote numerous radio plays for Radio Ankara. In 1950, he graduated from the Department of German Philology at Istanbul University, where he also obtained certificates in Turkology and the history of art. Upon graduation, he became an instructor in the history of art at that university and later taught theater classes as well. In 1955, he went to Vienna to study drama and directing, where he gained experience as assistant stage director at various Viennese theaters for nearly two years. Returning to Turkey in 1956, he wrote a column in the daily *Tercüman.* He later had a twelve-year stint as a columnist for the leading Istanbul daily *Milliyet.*

---

1. Fikret Adil, *Yeni İstanbul,* 14 September 1953.

The 1960s and 1970s were banner decades for Taner's theatrical creativity. His Brechtian epic play *Keşanlı Ali Destanı* (translated into English as *The Ballad of Ali of Keshan* by Nüvit Özdoğru and published in *Modern Turkish Drama,* edited by Talat S. Halman) became a sensational success, with an estimated 2,000 performances in Turkey and no less than 240 performances abroad. It is a musical (with a captivating score by the prominent Turkish composer Yalçın Tura) depicting life and colorful characters in a big-city shantytown terrorized by bosses and bullies.

The Ballad proved epoch making, and the play elicited hosannas from Turkish and foreign critics. Prominent scholar and critic Özdemir Nutku declared in a newspaper statement: "With this play, Haldun Taner points the direction in which the Turkish theater should move." William Saroyan, who watched the Istanbul production, reportedly stated: "This play is good enough to be produced anywhere in the world." According to various reports that came out in the Turkish press, the *Frankfurter Zeitung* wrote that the Turkish theater could now compete with the European theater, and the *Nürnberger Zeitung* stated that German critics regarded *The Ballad of Ali of Keshan* as the *Threepenny Opera* of Turkey.

Encouraged by the overflow of rave reviews, Taner went on to write many more major plays of social satire and opened Turkey's first-ever cabaret theater in Istanbul in 1967. His Ostrich Cabaret Theater and the new genre achieved instant success, remaining prominent for more than ten years until the Ostrich's demise in the early 1980s.

Taner's plays, film scripts, newspaper columns, and collections of short stories won a multitude of awards in Turkey and abroad from the late 1940s to the mid-1980s. It would be safe to assert that few playwrights if any have exerted a greater creative influence on the Turkish theater than did Haldun Taner.

Man of the Hour, Taner's most explicitly political play, appears in this anthology in a smooth translation by a husband-and-wife team, Clifford Endres and Selhan Savcıgil-Endres, both of whom teach American literature at Kadir Has University, one of Istanbul's private institutions of higher learning, where in 2000 they started the Department of American Literature and Culture. Clifford Endres, a Fulbright lecturer in 1985, has also taught at Boğaziçi, Ege, and Başkent Universities. He is the author of several books, and his articles have appeared in numerous U.S. periodicals. Selhan Savcıgil-Endres has taught at Hacettepe and Başkent Universities and has written articles on various Turkish and American authors. Their translations, which include a collection of the selected poems of Enis Batur, have appeared in a variety of anthologies and journals.[2]—TSH

2. The Endreses gratefully acknowledge the support provided for the translation of *Man of the Hour* by the Cunda Workshop for Translators of Turkish Literature.

Characters

WIFE of the professor

FATHER-IN-LAW, wife's father

REPORTER

ASSOCIATE (PROFESSOR)

PROFESSOR, later minister of industry

CROWD

MAN IN CROWD

SERVANT in the professor's home; later CLERK in the minister's office

FIRST PARTY OFFICIAL

SECOND PARTY OFFICIAL

SECRETARY-GENERAL of the Yellow Party

BROTHER-IN-LAW of the professor; later PRIVATE SECRETARY to the minister

PHOTOGRAPHER

SON of the professor

ANNOUNCER

NEW ANNOUNCER

SECRETARY to the minister

SECOND REPORTER

ASSISTANT DIRECTORS

MAN

ACT I

[*The* PROFESSOR's *study. A desk stands in front of a window at stage right. On the wall behind the desk is a large portrait of a man in half-profile, with a small white beard and soft, gentle eyes. At stage center is a door leading to the entrance hall of the house. The door is flanked by two large old bookcases; the shelves are filled with rows of books. The curtain rises on the* WIFE *talking on the phone. The* FATHER-IN-LAW *is holding a newspaper but attentively listening to his* DAUGHTER.]

WIFE: No, he's not back yet. . . . Well, why on earth should I lie to you? . . . The professor is my what? . . . He happens to be my husband. . . . I could have told you that if you'd asked before. . . . No, not at all. . . . Yes, he was summoned to the capital yesterday. An important meeting. . . . Yes, I know what time it is; we have a clock here too, thank God. . . . No, he hasn't come back yet. . . . Yes, thank you, too. Good-bye. [*Hangs up the phone.*] This is the fourth reporter to call since morning. And the least polite.

FATHER-IN-LAW: So it's true then. I didn't believe it when I read it in the *Daily Truth*. Thought it must be a lie . . .

WIFE: All the same, you came.

FATHER-IN-LAW: Of course. It's natural, isn't it? I was just about to fly off to close that iron ore deal, but as soon as I read the news, I dropped everything and flew here. It's hard to imagine.

WIFE: It's true, all right. But he can't make up his mind.

FATHER-IN-LAW: Is he crazy, this guy? With an opportunity like this at hand . . .

WIFE: He's become an insomniac. He won't talk even to me. He keeps to himself all the time. When the telegram came, he got up in the middle of the night and went to talk to his old professor.

FATHER-IN-LAW: His professor! But he's been dead for years!

WIFE: Yes, of course. I'm not talking about a live person. [*Points to the portrait.*] He talks to the dead man.

FATHER-IN-LAW: That's just why I came. I know how deluded he can be. Somebody has to push him or provoke him or fire up his courage as necessary.

WIFE: If it were up to him, he'd say yes, but it's his associate professor. That guy is something else again!

FATHER-IN-LAW: What would he know about politics?

WIFE: Nothing, that's what scares him. "Oh my goodness, dear Professor, don't be foolish. By all means, dear Professor, be careful. Whatever you do, dear Professor, don't get swept away. Academia is safe ground, but politics may not suit your calculations."

FATHER-IN-LAW: What nonsense! "Not suit your calculations!" Why, I can calculate in five minutes how much he'll make if he says yes.

WIFE: His associate says they'll exploit his dear professor's name.

FATHER-IN-LAW: [*Sneering.*] As if he had a name to exploit! I hope they'll talk him into it in the capital.

WIFE: Yes, I hope so, I really do . . .

FATHER-IN-LAW: How much time is left until the deadline for submitting names for the ballot anyway? It's only a matter of hours. Where's the meeting being held?

WIFE: At the opposition party's headquarters, with the members of the committee. The secretary-general happens to be his old classmate. Do you know what he said? He said that the moment the professor is kind enough to accept the nomination, he can just name what ministry he'd like to have in the new cabinet.

FATHER-IN-LAW: Really! You mean he's going to be a minister? Frankly, I never expected this. But of course they'd make him a minister. Can they find anybody better? To be fair, there's nobody in his field who can top him.

WIFE: A minute ago you weren't talking this way.

FATHER-IN-LAW: I've always praised my son-in-law's knowledge. In fact, I admit I'm proud of what he's done. What he lacks is the will to fight. In politics and business alike, you can't get ahead without the ability to fight.

WIFE: He's so timid, there's no end to it. At the beach, he can't even go into the water without being pushed.

FATHER-IN-LAW: Don't I know? That's how he was on his wedding night. But don't worry, he'll get used to it. And we'll support him as much as we can. A businessman is a politician of sorts.

[*Footsteps. A* REPORTER *enters, covered with dust.*]

REPORTER: [*Shakes off the dust.*] I'm sorry. Good morning.

WIFE: Who are you?

REPORTER: I'm a reporter.

WIFE: How did you get in?

REPORTER: The back door. The gardener wasn't letting anyone in the front. I'd like to interview you, sir.

FATHER-IN-LAW: You're mistaken, young man. I'm not the professor.

REPORTER: Please. It's obvious that you know nothing about me or my newspaper. Do you think a reporter such as I could make a gross mistake like that?

FATHER-IN-LAW: Who the hell you are I don't know, but I'm the father-in-law. Of that I'm sure.

REPORTER: [*Surprised. Looks at the* WIFE.] Then where's the professor?

WIFE: Not back.

REPORTER: [*To the* FATHER-IN-LAW.] But your driver told us you just came from the airport.

FATHER-IN-LAW: I was on the plane from the south.

WIFE: Don't you know who my husband is, for God's sake?

REPORTER: Did anybody know him until that newspaper story and cartoon?

WIFE: Oh, is there a cartoon of him? Let me see. [*Takes the newspaper from the* REPORTER.] This doesn't look like him.

FATHER-IN-LAW: What do those scales mean?

REPORTER: One pan represents the opposition party, the other the ruling party.

FATHER-IN-LAW: When my son-in-law steps on the opposition's pan, that side grows heavier. How intelligent! Let's subscribe to this newspaper immediately.

REPORTER: OK, I'll sign you up as soon as I get back. At least then my trip will count for something.

FATHER-IN-LAW: Well, you seem to be a good reporter—you managed to sell a subscription. Come back a little later. If you want my advice, bring a photographer along. My son-in-law will be along soon, or he would have wired.

REPORTER: Sir, you're just as sharp as we are. I'm going now, but I'll be back in half an hour.

WIFE: By the back door again?

REPORTER: No, the front door next time.

WIFE: Oh Dad, this is all like a dream to me! In fact, I can't believe it.

FATHER-IN-LAW: You'll believe it when you're a minister's wife.

WIFE: Which ministry will it be, do you think? I'll tell him to ask for Foreign Affairs. Yes, foreign minister ... as you know, I've wanted to be a diplomat's wife ever since my teens—official receptions, banquets, big game hunts. Think about it—our pictures in the papers, cocktail glasses in hand, joking with the British ambassador. Just think, Dad, "Her Excellency"! That's what they'll call me if he becomes a minister, won't they?

FATHER-IN-LAW: Maybe.

WIFE: "His Excellency's lady"! Oh Dad, do you think they'll make him a minister?

FATHER-IN-LAW: I don't see why not. He knows a little French, doesn't he?

WIFE: Well, yes.

FATHER-IN-LAW: Can he figure out how to eat with his left hand?

WIFE: Of course he can.

FATHER-IN-LAW: Then no problem. The rest is just "Bonjour, Monsieur," "Bonsoir, Madame." It's the United Nations that sets foreign policy anyway.

WIFE: [*To herself.*] No, they wouldn't give him Foreign Affairs. They'd pick a professional, probably. [*To her* FATHER.] You'll see. Since his field is economics, they'll assign him to something like Finance or Economy.

FATHER-IN-LAW: Never mind the field. In ministries, credentials come after the fact. Look, what was the former profession of the current minister of commerce?

WIFE: I don't know. What was he?

FATHER-IN-LAW: A urologist.

WIFE: No!

FATHER-IN-LAW: I swear. And the minister of health?

WIFE: If the minister of commerce is a doctor, the minister of health must be a businessman.

FATHER-IN-LAW: Bravo! You're learning. A textile manufacturer. As fate would have it ...

WIFE: But those were the old days. When the opposition takes office, surely they'll appoint qualified people.

FATHER-IN-LAW: I doubt it. People who know what they're doing would be afraid to take the job.

WIFE: Oh, how I want Foreign Affairs ...

FATHER-IN-LAW: Well, the Ministry of the Interior isn't bad, either. Then there's Commerce. And Customs. I don't think Industry would be so terrible. Do you know which one I'd like?

WIFE: [*Surprised.*] You?

FATHER-IN-LAW: I mean for your husband, of course. If only I could be someone who thinks only of himself! No, I personally would prefer him to be in charge of Industry. That would be the most beneficial for the family.

WIFE: Oh, don't say that, Dad. These are just illusions anyway. Let him accept the nomination first. Once he's in the cabinet, the rest will be easy, won't it?

FATHER-IN-LAW: Right. [*The doorbell rings.*] This must be him.

WIFE: No, he doesn't ring like that.

[*Enter the* ASSOCIATE, *a shrewd and arrogant-looking man in his midthirties.*]

ASSOCIATE (PROFESSOR): [*Greets them.*] The professor's not here yet, apparently.

WIFE: Not yet. Dad, have you met this gentleman? He's my husband's associate.

ASSOCIATE: I believe we met at your birthday party.

FATHER-IN-LAW: Oh yes, I remember. You made a great impression on me that day.

ASSOCIATE: [*To the* WIFE.] Is it true that he went to the capital? The faculty and students, all of us, are dying to find out.

WIFE: Of course you are!

ASSOCIATE: What I most feared has happened then. How awful!

WIFE: What is it that's so awful?

ASSOCIATE: The fact that he's floundering this way.

FATHER-IN-LAW: Floundering, you say, or flourishing?

ASSOCIATE: Floundering, sir, of course. I don't think it's good that a scholar of his standing should appear so frivolous.

FATHER-IN-LAW: What's so frivolous about becoming a minister?

ASSOCIATE: Why, certainly it's frivolous to be driven along by the flow of events like a cork on the current!

FATHER-IN-LAW: What would you do if you received the same offer?

ASSOCIATE: I would reject it. If you love him, you'll put a stop to all this. His real place is at his professorial post.

WIFE: How many years has it been since he was given that post? And what's he gotten out of it? Nothing but unadulterated honor.

ASSOCIATE: You don't like honor?

FATHER-IN-LAW: It's all well and good, but the thing we call honor won't buy your bread and butter.

WIFE: For goodness' sake! Isn't a minister's honor as great as a professor's?

FATHER-IN-LAW: Of course, and more.

WIFE: Whenever these polls come out in the papers, they always run a professor's picture. Surely a minister's . . .

ASSOCIATE: An apt criterion. Ah, but madam, is it so important to get one's picture in the newspapers? These days what we generally see in the papers are pictures of football players and pop singers.

FATHER-IN-LAW: [*Looks at his* DAUGHTER.] Weren't we talking about pictures with the British ambassador?

ASSOCIATE: [*Astonished.*] The British ambassador!

FATHER-IN-LAW: Or the American one. Maybe both. For example . . .

ASSOCIATE: So you're hoping for Foreign Affairs?

WIFE: It's possible, isn't it?

ASSOCIATE: I doubt it. A lot of people have an appetite for that one. [*Sardonically.*] Oh, come on, is it really necessary to have pictures taken with ambassadors? Suppose he gets Commerce.

FATHER-IN-LAW: Would that be so bad? Let's hope he does.

ASSOCIATE: [*To the* WIFE.] In that case, he'll have his picture taken with wholesale dealers. Bales of cotton everywhere. Or else at the Livestock Association, surrounded by sheep of every kind: stump-tailed sheep, fat-tailed sheep, curly-tailed . . .

WIFE: Stop joking, please.

FATHER-IN-LAW: I don't care what office they hand out, as long as it's something.

ASSOCIATE: Poor professor! Is he going to discard those noble robes for this?

FATHER-IN-LAW: A man with a wife and children should show common sense when a golden opportunity comes along. I know what I'm talking about.

ASSOCIATE: I've never heard him complain about his situation, though.

FATHER-IN-LAW: But we complain.

ASSOCIATE: You?

FATHER-IN-LAW: Yes, me. My daughter. The whole family—all of us. And not just us—the whole nation, all the taxpayers. Look at what the newspaper says. [*Takes a newspaper from his pocket, puts on his reading glasses, finds a spot in the lead article, and then begins to read.*] "The moral integrity and ethical concern with which he opposed, on grounds that it violated human rights and the Constitution, the tax bill introduced to cover the budget deficit . . ."

ASSOCIATE: [*Interrupting.*] Pay no attention to those papers. They write whatever they want. They're actually the ones who brought everything to this point, and now things have gotten out of hand.

FATHER-IN-LAW: Which hand?

ASSOCIATE: I mean they've made a mountain out of a molehill. It's these reporters who have turned the poor professor into the man of the hour. Just like that!

WIFE: They just put his comments in the newspapers, that's all.

ASSOCIATE: Do you really think he made those remarks all by himself?

WIFE: Then who did?

ASSOCIATE: [*Smiles.*] The professor and a political comment? You know how far away he stays from such things. He's never uttered a word in his life to a newspaper about the government.

FATHER-IN-LAW: Then who did he say those things to?

ASSOCIATE: Probably a friend, maybe two. In private, just talking idly.

WIFE: Just talking idly!

ASSOCIATE: Yes, just to make conversation. And then some busybody politician who happens to overhear it passes it on to his reporter pal, who doesn't lose a second in dressing it up as a political statement, then tacking on a big photo, and putting it in the paper. Next day there's a great brouhaha in the government. I was with him when the news broke—he could have cried.

FATHER-IN-LAW: Then why didn't he refute it? He could have denied that he ever made a statement to the press.

ASSOCIATE: He intended to, but the ideas were his own, and he couldn't bring himself to repudiate them once he had somehow expressed them. As you can see, this is a case of "Out of the frying pan, into the fire."

WIFE: Is that so?

ASSOCIATE: You know the rest. The opposition party used the professor's thesis in Parliament to back the prime minister into a corner. If they'd had four more votes, the whole cabinet would have been toppled. And, of course, what made things worse was the official reprimand of the professor by the university, which was put up to it by the government. That really stirred things up. So the professor has been turned into a victim and become the people's number one darling. Well, that's the "story of a hero," as summarized from backstage.

WIFE: You seem a little jealous of my husband.

ASSOCIATE: How can you think a thing like that, madam?

WIFE: Yes, you are, you're jealous of my husband! You're trying to belittle what he's done.

ASSOCIATE: Please. Nobody can appreciate the professor like I do, not even you. But let's be frank: it's purely a chain of coincidences that's brought the professor to this point, despite himself.

WIFE: Not true. He disapproves of the ruling party, and he stepped into the limelight to help the opposition.

ASSOCIATE: Those are the very words of the agitprop newspapers, madam. I hope you don't believe what you're saying! Both the government and the opposition know what's really happening. The opposition's real aim is to use the professor as a puppet. To put a respectable and beloved name like his at the top of their list would surely elevate the prospects of the candidates below.

FATHER-IN-LAW: OK, let's say that's what it's about. What's wrong with that? [*At this point, a roar from the street is heard: "Hurrah! Hurrah! Pro-fes-sor! Pro-fes-sor!" The* WIFE *and the* FATHER-IN-LAW *rush anxiously to the window. The* ASSOCIATE *goes over and stands behind them. Standing on his tiptoes, he looks out over their heads.*] Look, they're carrying him on their shoulders. That means he said yes.

WIFE: They stopped his car as it turned into the street.

FATHER-IN-LAW: What a wonderful and heartfelt expression of love!

ASSOCIATE: Organized by the opposition party, probably.

WIFE: Look how big the crowd is! [*The* CROWD—*all men—continues to roar: "Pro-fes-sor! Pro-fes-sor!" The* WIFE *dabs at her tears. The* FATHER-IN-LAW *embraces her.*] Come on, let's go and welcome him ourselves. Hurry!

[*The* ASSOCIATE *backs away with a bemused look. Just as the others are about to exit at stage center, they are pushed back into the room by the* CROWD *that pours in, carrying the* PROFESSOR *on their shoulders. He is expostulating, pleading for moderation. Slight of stature, he seems less an academic than a file clerk, with crew-cut graying hair and a mild-mannered appearance. The people cheering him wear expressions of respect and admiration, even awe. They lower him to the floor.*]

PROFESSOR: [*Puts his hands over his eyes and remains motionless for a moment.*] I don't know why, but I get dizzy when my feet are in the air. [*Opens his arms wide to the* CROWD.] Thank you, my friends. This is most kind. I am grateful to you indeed.

MAN IN CROWD: It is we who are grateful to you. We'll do anything for you. [*With gestures of obeisance, the* CROWD *withdraws.*]

PROFESSOR: Did you see that? Did you see how they carried me in?

WIFE: Of course we did. You were on their shoulders.

FATHER-IN-LAW: Thank God you said yes. And rightly, my dear son. I was right to be proud of you.

PROFESSOR: No.

ASSOCIATE: [*Heatedly.*] Of course you rejected it, sir.

PROFESSOR: No. I left it up in the air. [*Silence.*] Hey look, everybody, it's not an easy thing to decide.

WIFE: Still?

PROFESSOR: [*Approaches the cactus plants in pots on a shelf and makes gestures of petting them.*] I hope you haven't forgotten to feed my rabbits while I was gone.

WIFE: They're being fed, all right? What about us, and what about you?

ASSOCIATE: Is it so hard for you to throw a resounding "no" at their heads? The professor I know . . .

PROFESSOR: The professor I knew would have done that, but . . .

ASSOCIATE: Maybe I didn't know you all that well.

PROFESSOR: It's nothing. What's more important is that I never knew myself that well. The secretary-general of the party described me in such terms that it is a great surprise not to see a statue of myself already erected.

FATHER-IN-LAW: It will happen; it will surely happen one day. All you have to do is say yes.

PROFESSOR: [*To the* ASSOCIATE.] Do you know when it is that we truly arrive at the realization that we don't know ourselves? It's when we have to make an important decision. Deciding things looks like an easy job—a hardly noticeable act of the jaws and tongue muscles and a one-syllable sound: *yes* or *no*. But do you know how much effort it takes to produce those one-syllable words?

FATHER-IN-LAW: Now you're exaggerating.

PROFESSOR: Well, why shouldn't I? It's not just my past but my whole future that's tied to this one syllable. And not a question merely of my future, but that of my wife, my children, my grandchildren, and all the generations to come.

FATHER-IN-LAW: And of their prosperity.

PROFESSOR: [*Not listening.*] It's a tremendous position. Yes, why hide it? I'm wavering. It's true I've been brought to this crossroads by external currents, but why not make the most of the situation?

FATHER-IN-LAW: Now you're talking! Why not, indeed?

WIFE: Sometimes, darling, you make good sense.

PROFESSOR: [*Continues.*] And let's not forget that, after all, I'll never find what I'm looking for in my scholarship.

FATHER-IN-LAW: Like what?

PROFESSOR: Let's be honest. Never mind the university, in my whole life, I've never managed to be first in anything. I'm inclined by nature to stay in the background. I'm hardworking and a good teacher they say, but that's all. Maybe that's why it took me until two years ago to get the promotion and the chair that I deserved for so long. The fiasco of that humiliating vote in the election for dean is still a stain on my honor.

ASSOCIATE: Let's not talk about that now, sir.

PROFESSOR: Why not? It's the truth. What am I to all these people? [*Looks at his* WIFE.] After all, am I not a timid and annoyingly passive professor with no particular virtues beyond a handful of books and his principles?

ASSOCIATE: Not at all, sir.

WIFE: Don't be silly, dear.

PROFESSOR: No, don't make excuses for me. They call me "a good man, a valued scholar," but what do they say behind my back? "A mild-mannered sort, a naive man. Knock him down and take away his marbles." Am I right? Tell me the truth.

ASSOCIATE: Not at all, sir.

PROFESSOR: Yes, that's how it is, just like that. [*Pause.*] You have no idea what a nuisance it is to be like this and to be treated accordingly. [*Looks at his* WIFE.] Sometimes I want to show people that I'm not really like that. I'm sick and tired of getting pitied. May I be frank?

FATHER-IN-LAW: Absolutely, Son! Speak up! Assert yourself!

PROFESSOR: [*To his* WIFE.] Do you remember last year when the minister of education came to the university?

WIFE: No, I don't.

PROFESSOR: [*To the* ASSOCIATE.] Remember how on top of everything else, in front of three other professors, he scolded me as if I were a student of his? Why? Just because I'd failed the daughter of a minister!

ASSOCIATE: I do remember.

PROFESSOR: How low I felt that day—so desperate. Miserable. Though I was justified. [*Pause.*] It was on that day, my friends, that my longing for power began.

FATHER-IN-LAW: That's my boy! When you get to be minister, that's the day you start paying them back.

PROFESSOR: Power is a good thing, friends . . . but there's a terrible feeling of responsibility that goes along with it.

SERVANT: [*Enters.*] Sir, two officials from the party's district executive committee are here to see you.

PROFESSOR: Oh darn, I was about to visit my rabbits in the garden. Well, let's see what they want. Show them in.

WIFE: We're just leaving. [*Goes to the side door. The* FATHER-IN-LAW *hesitates, undecided whether to go or stay. Finally he follows her. The* ASSOCIATE *does not move. The* OFFICIALS *who enter are dressed formally in black dinner jackets, bow ties, and pinstriped pants. One is older, the other middle-aged. They are nearly expressionless and clearly steeped in politics. They have apparently been sent; it is obvious that their show of admiration is rehearsed. Their manners are artificial, their movements almost mechanical.*]

FIRST PARTY OFFICIAL: Sir, we have come in the name of our party's district executive committee to convey our kind regards.

PROFESSOR: Thank you. Come in.

FIRST PARTY OFFICIAL: We won't disturb you for long. It is our distinct honor to convey to you the formal request of the executive committee.

SECOND PARTY OFFICIAL: The executive committee of the Yellow Party for our district would consider your permission to place your name at the top of its list of candidates as an honor without measure.

PROFESSOR: I'm honored. I'll consider it.

FIRST PARTY OFFICIAL: [*Mechanically.*] There are scarcely three hours before the deadline for submission of the list of parliamentary candidates. In these waning moments, as we await your decision—which we are confident will come down in favor of our party—we have approached you in order to seek the favor of your presence and to communicate the committee's warmest affection and deepest respect, in hopes of facilitating the "yes" pan of the scales to weigh a bit more heavily in the balance.

SECOND PARTY OFFICIAL: Perfect.

PROFESSOR: My thanks. I'll consider it.

FIRST PARTY OFFICIAL: The nation will be grateful to you.

SECOND PARTY OFFICIAL: Our party will not forget the largesse you have bestowed upon it.

FIRST PARTY OFFICIAL: The candidates of our district will be deeply honored to appear on the same ballot.

ASSOCIATE: I can believe that. Thanks to the professor, their chances of getting elected will increase.

SECOND PARTY OFFICIAL: Our party will record your name in golden letters in its book of honor.

FIRST PARTY OFFICIAL: We shall await your historic decision with keen anticipation.

PROFESSOR: OK, I'll think about it.

SECOND PARTY OFFICIAL: Very well. We respectfully ask your permission to depart. Farewell, sir.

PROFESSOR: Go with my blessing.

[*The* OFFICIALS *leave. The* SERVANT *enters.*]

SERVANT: Sir, the secretary-general have arrived.

PROFESSOR: How many?

SERVANT: Only one.

PROFESSOR: Then why the plural?

SERVANT: Even if there's only one, such respected and important people should be addressed as if they are many. My lady has taught me the use of the royal *they*.

ASSOCIATE: Well, I see you would quite easily qualify as a clerk at the ministry.

[*The* SERVANT *shrugs and exits. The* FATHER-IN-LAW *enters, holding a tea glass and chewing.*]

FATHER-IN-LAW: The secretary-general is here.

[*The* SECRETARY-GENERAL *enters. He is a typically expressionless, cold-blooded professional politician, about the* PROFESSOR'*s age but fitter.*]

SECRETARY-GENERAL: Greetings, Professor!

PROFESSOR: Greetings.

SECRETARY-GENERAL: [*Although he acknowledges the others, he speaks only to the* PROFESSOR.] Well? Your decision?

PROFESSOR: I haven't made it yet.

SECRETARY-GENERAL: Oh come on, enough already of this melancholy pensiveness. Thinking is for old folks and women. A man's job is to make decisions.

PROFESSOR: Without thinking?

SECRETARY-GENERAL: A statesman is a man who thinks and acts instantly.

ASSOCIATE: In a jiffy.

SECRETARY-GENERAL: [*As if noticing the* ASSOCIATE *for the first time.*] Oh, you have guests.

PROFESSOR: My associate. My father-in-law. Have you met before?

[*The* FATHER-IN-LAW *has been behaving like a sycophant, nodding and beaming, his expressions and gestures confirming the* SECRETARY-GENERAL'*s words.*]

FATHER-IN-LAW: I had the honor to meet the secretary-general on a previous occasion.

SECRETARY-GENERAL: Really?

FATHER-IN-LAW: It was during the past session of Parliament. I appeared before the Finance Committee to ask for the tax on iron products to be lowered. You were on the committee.

SECRETARY-GENERAL: Oh yes. [*Proudly.*] As an MP.

FATHER-IN-LAW: We couldn't explain ourselves properly to the others, but you followed our petition with interest.

SECRETARY-GENERAL: I don't remember the details.

FATHER-IN-LAW: You said you would work on it and pass it on to Parliament.

SECRETARY-GENERAL: And then?

FATHER-IN-LAW: Due no doubt to more important concerns of yours, our petition did not meet with success.

SECRETARY-GENERAL: Yes. Very important concerns. Elections in particular. But once we're in power again, we'll have the final say, and then we'll overcome all these bothersome impediments.

FATHER-IN-LAW: Of course, sir. We hope so, sir. Thank you, sir.

SECRETARY-GENERAL: [*To the* PROFESSOR.] Well, my friend, I'm going to turn in the list now. I took the trouble to drop everything and come here, but still you're dragging your feet like a coy bride. Is it really so hard for you to part with your cactus plants and rabbits?

PROFESSOR: You can imagine the mental state I'm in.

SECRETARY-GENERAL: [*As if reciting a maxim.*] In politics, there are no mental states.

FATHER-IN-LAW: I myself don't see any sense in wallowing in a mental limbo.

SECRETARY-GENERAL: Your attitude is annoying our people at the central office. What is it you find so attractive at the university? You've been a professor for ever so many years, and you haven't even become university president.

PROFESSOR: The presidency belongs mostly to the political side of academic life, Honorable Secretary-General. It is characterized by promises, compromises, vote hunting, and threats of all kinds. In my opinion, what makes a real scholar does not include those things. A scholar has his own work to do. And when he gets it done, it should be published in the international arena.

SECRETARY-GENERAL: Never mind that. Who would read it? Who would pay any attention? Do you know what I compare a scholar to?

PROFESSOR: No, what?

SECRETARY-GENERAL: An ostrich with its head buried in the sand.

PROFESSOR: [*Finds this extremely amusing and laughs loudly.*] Exactly! How true.

ASSOCIATE: OK then, why don't we get rid of them once and for all since they're all utterly useless?

SECRETARY-GENERAL: Oh, not totally. They can be good for something.

ASSOCIATE: Like what, for example?

SECRETARY-GENERAL: Like inventing rationales for our activities, for example. [*To the* PROFESSOR.] Actually, sir, we need you. Leave scholarship to the intellectuals, who are incapable of doing anything else. If you're able to act, why stick to theory? If your mind's alive, grab the power; bring to life the things you imagined. If you yourself don't bring the seriousness and high moral quality of the scholarly world to politics, who will?

FATHER-IN-LAW: Definitely. One should definitely think about himself and consider his family.

PROFESSOR: [*On the verge of tears.*] May I have an hour, please?

SECRETARY-GENERAL: He still wants more time, does he? You're as stubborn as a mule, for God's sake! Don't you understand this is a life-and-death struggle, and those who aren't with us are against us? It's either "yes" or "no." Get over this fence-sitting attitude—"maybe" is no answer. [*Sounds of applause from outside.*] If you're on your feet, you have to walk. And what does walking mean? Giving direction to your footsteps. If you open your mouth, you have to speak. And what does speaking mean? Saying one thing and meaning another. Whether you want to or not, you're going to use your brilliance for the country's welfare, Mr. Professor.

ASSOCIATE: You mean "for your party's welfare."

SECRETARY-GENERAL: [*As if reciting a maxim.*] What's good for the party is good for the country. What's more, hesitation by those of whom much is expected is nearly the same as their throwing down their guns and deserting the battlefield.

FATHER-IN-LAW: Absolutely. Ungrateful not just to the country, but to the family and to themselves.

SECRETARY-GENERAL: We need bold, dedicated people to run the country. Are you one of those people or not? Your decision will tell us. Real service is possible only when the desire for self-sacrifice is there.

ASSOCIATE: [*Sarcastically.*] Self-sacrifice? I see. All this hullabaloo over ballot boxes is about dedication and self-sacrifice.

SECRETARY-GENERAL: Can it be anything else?

ASSOCIATE: Winning the election, possibly?

SECRETARY-GENERAL: If you said something like that anywhere else, they'd laugh you out of the room. You can't truly believe that all our hard work is only for that!

ASSOCIATE: What else then?

SECRETARY-GENERAL: [*As if reciting a maxim.*] For the sake of protecting the seat of power from those unfit for it. [*Takes a box of cigarettes from his pocket.*] Look, Professor. Draw a line down the middle of this. On the left, list the pluses; on the right, the minuses.

FATHER-IN-LAW: Active and passive.

SECRETARY-GENERAL: Then make your calculations and get back to me in half an hour.

ASSOCIATE: Sounds easy.

SECRETARY-GENERAL: Erase the right side completely because this job has no minuses.

FATHER-IN-LAW: Absolutely.

SECRETARY-GENERAL: I hope everything is understood, Professor. Take until seven. The party chairman is expecting your answer. Consider well, and let us know.

[*The* SECRETARY-GENERAL *makes a grand exit, pleased with his performance. When the door opens, applause pours in from outside. The* PROFESSOR's *attitude during the scene has been one of contemplation. He occasionally mutters a word or two, then goes back to his thoughts.*]

ASSOCIATE: [*Sardonically, to the* FATHER-IN-LAW.] You'll get along very well with the secretary-general.

FATHER-IN-LAW: He's a very understanding man.

ASSOCIATE: He'd make a good salesman.

WIFE: [*Enters.*] What happened? You said yes, didn't you? I heard the noise outside.

PROFESSOR: No, dear. He's expecting my answer at seven.

WIFE: Still undecided?

PROFESSOR: Please, everybody, can you leave me alone for fifteen minutes?

ASSOCIATE: Of course, sir. [*To the others.*] Let's go. [*To the* PROFESSOR.] Don't forget, there are six people in this room.

PROFESSOR: Six? [*Points to people in the room one by one, counting.*]

ASSOCIATE: [*Points to the portrait on the wall.*] He's waiting for your decision with as much interest as the rest of us. [*The* PROFESSOR *looks at the portrait. As he does, the* ASSOCIATE *continues in a clear voice.*] In your moments of indecision, you've always sought inspiration from him. "What would he do if he were in my shoes?" you used to ask and then make your decision accordingly. Do it like that. If he were you, he'd throw this pack of dogs out on their ears!

PROFESSOR: Enough. Please don't try to influence me. I want to make my choice in tune with my own heart, without outside pressure. [*Noise from outside:* "Hurrah! Hurrah!]

FATHER-IN-LAW: Never mind the portraits and listen to the voice of reason, Son. A windfall like this doesn't come along twice! The future belongs to those who know how to make a decision.

ASSOCIATE: You've taken up aphoristic language, too, apparently. [*Exits.*]

[*All except the* PROFESSOR *exit. Lights dim. Emphasizing the silence, the ticktock of the clock on the table, unnoticed until now, becomes audible. The applause of the* CROWD *outside continues. The* PROFESSOR *cradles his head in his hands in a contemplative position. Now and then he glances at the box of cigarettes left by the* SECRETARY-GENERAL *and scribbles a note on it. At this point, the people who have exited appear together under different lighting. The remainder of the stage goes dark. It remains in total darkness for a short period. When the lights go up, the set is illuminated in a completely different hue.*]

WIFE: [*Happily.*] At last! For the first time in your life, you've made a wise decision.

FATHER-IN-LAW: [*Overwhelmed with emotion, takes the* PROFESSOR'*s hand to his lips.*] My beloved son, my tiger!

[*The* SERVANT, *who witnesses this scene from the doorway, throws up his hands.*]

ASSOCIATE: I don't know what to say. A world has been shattered before my very eyes. [*Covers his face with his hands.*] I'm sorry. Excuse me.

BROTHER-IN-LAW: [*Enters.*] My dear brother-in-law! Can it be true? I heard it from the servant. [*The* PROFESSOR *looks on, astonished.*] You'd never believe how hard I prayed. But we're in luck. Here's your new personal secretary!

PROFESSOR: Where?

BROTHER-IN-LAW: Here. Me, of course. Can you find anyone better? I don't think so.

SERVANT: [*Enters.*] The reporters are here.

PROFESSOR: So soon!

SERVANT: They were already at the door. I just gave them the good news.

PROFESSOR: You gave them the good news?

SERVANT: [*Shyly and proudly.*] Yes, actually.

FATHER-IN-LAW: Let them in. We can't keep them waiting at the door.

WIFE: Maybe you'd like to speak to them privately?

PROFESSOR: To reporters? God forbid!

[*Enter the* REPORTER *and the* PHOTOGRAPHER.]

REPORTER: [*As he enters.*] First of all, congratulations! Forgive the rush, but we want to get this in the evening edition. What's your special field?

PROFESSOR: After long consideration, it seemed to me that the right course was to accede to the desires of the people. [*Chants of "Hurrah!" are heard from outside.*] I do not consider serving my fellow citizens, who have exhibited so much affection toward me, to be a vocation any less valuable than serving in my scholarly field. [*The* ASSO-CIATE *shakes his head.*]

REPORTER: [*Taking notes.*] I see.

PROFESSOR: We ought to serve our country whenever and wherever it calls on us, whether it be at a university or in Parliament . . . or on the battlefield.

[*The* PHOTOGRAPHER *is meanwhile shooting pictures from odd angles with the flash— kneeling, lying on his back, and so on.*]

REPORTER: [*Notices the portrait.*] Your professor, I presume?

PROFESSOR: Yes. I owe everything to him. First I was his student, then his associate for years. When he died, I replaced him.

REPORTER: [*Not listening.*] What are your prospects of becoming a minister?

PROFESSOR: It's too early to answer that question.

REPORTER: [*Writing.*] I see, I see. [*Scratches his head.*] Your biography has already been typeset.

ASSOCIATE: And his bibliography?

REPORTER: [*Shrugs.*] Not necessary.

PROFESSOR: So your newspaper will be the first to announce my candidacy?

REPORTER: Oh, that story's out already.

PROFESSOR: But I just this moment accepted.

REPORTER: The secretary-general told us to run it. He was sure of your answer.

PROFESSOR: Amazing! Before I'd made up my own mind.

ASSOCIATE: [*Mimicking the* SECRETARY-GENERAL.] In politics, it's parties, not people, who make decisions. Even decisions about people's private lives. You're merely at the threshold. Just wait and see.

PHOTOGRAPHER: We need a picture of you all as a family.

[*Family members arrange themselves in front of the portrait. The* PROFESSOR *sits, his* WIFE *behind him with her hand on his shoulder. All pose with cheerful smiles.*]

SON: [*Bursts in explosively and grasps the situation at a glance.*] Don't tell me, Dad, you said yes! [*Rushes to his* MOTHER *and starts dancing a tango with her.*]

WIFE: Oh, don't be silly.

[*The phone rings.*]

PROFESSOR: Hello. [*His expression changes.*] Thank you very much indeed, sir. [*To his* WIFE.] The party chairman congratulates me. [*The members of the family—*WIFE, SON, FATHER-IN-LAW, *and* BROTHER-IN-LAW—*are now lined up in a row next to the* PROFESSOR. *They whisper the news from one to the other. The* PROFESSOR *continues.*] Don't mention it, please. We're grateful to you, sir, everybody here. [*To his* WIFE.] He's inviting us to dinner. [*Into the phone.*] Good-bye, sir.

SON: Were you taking a picture without me? [*They all line up again.*] Will this be in tomorrow's papers?

REPORTER: This evening's. Why?

SON: I want to send one to the principal of my school. Tomorrow's the day for teachers to issue final reports.

PHOTOGRAPHER: Squeeze a little closer to each other. Smile, please. [*To the* FATHER-IN-LAW.] Not you, your smile is big enough already. [*The* WIFE *smiles and tries to straighten her hair. As she does, the flash goes off.*]

WIFE: Oh! You took it already?

PHOTOGRAPHER: It's OK, no problem. One more now.

[*The* SON *is in the rear, standing on tiptoe to be seen. He jumps up. At this, there is a loud crash, and the portrait falls from the wall. All heads turn in that direction.*]

CURTAIN

INTERLUDE

[*During the interlude we hear the soothing voice of an* ANNOUNCER *emanating from the radio in the parlor.*]

ANNOUNCER: We now bring you election results from the southeast. Yellow Party: 586,685. Orange Party: 211,112. Blue Party: 111,222. Although counting remains incomplete for Districts Two and Three, the Yellow Party has taken the overall lead in the eastern region. The Orange Party continues to hang onto a small lead in District Four of the eastern region and District Five of the western region. We will continue to broadcast the results as we receive them. [*Marching songs and anthems.*]

[*Some time later.*] Your attention, please. It is now possible to announce the final results in the national elections for parliamentary office. In the final count, the Yellow Party has won 281 seats and therefore a majority in Parliament. The Orange Party has won 200 seats, and the Blue Party 80 seats. That is to say, the two opposition parties combined will have one MP less than the new ruling party. According to the chairman of the Orange Party, the situation is favorable for the implementation of democratic rule. [*A loud crash.*] We apologize for this untimely interruption, which has been regrettably caused by technical difficulties. I now yield my chair to the new announcer from the newly victorious party. Good evening to you all.

NEW ANNOUNCER: Good evening, ladies and gentlemen. Please allow me to introduce myself as the new radio announcer from the newly victorious party. My dear fellow citizens, countrymen, party members, and all of those who share the same vision: henceforth, it will be my honor to relay to you over your unbiased radios the news of the new achievements of the new order. Let us celebrate this new day for the nation. Your mission is ours; our mission is yours. Let us all cherish our one and only mission. The Yellow Party takes pride in having won its leadership position by means of the people's vote. From Yellow Party organizations around the country a flood of telegrams is pouring in; heartfelt joy is spreading throughout the nation as people take to the streets to celebrate this momentous success with parades, festivities, and fireworks, even though it is still daylight. [*Applause and sounds of celebration.*]

CURTAIN

ACT II

[*Office of the minister of industry. The set is almost the same as that of Act I: the desk is to the right of the window, which is in the same place. The bookcases are replaced by file cabinets. There is again a large framed portrait on the wall, but this time it is that of the party chairman, who is characterized by stern looks and large jowls. At stage left, a second door has been added. As the curtain rises, the* BROTHER-IN-LAW, *who has become the* PRIVATE SECRETARY, *is walking toward the ringing phone.*]

PRIVATE SECRETARY: Hello, this is the Ministry of Industry. . . . No, the minister hasn't arrived yet, sir. I am the private secretary, sir. . . . Certainly, sir, with pleasure. I'll tell him as soon as he arrives. [*Hangs up. A knock is heard.*] Come in.

SON: [*Pokes his head in.*] Hello, Uncle. The old man's not here, I see.

PRIVATE SECRETARY: Not yet.

SON: [*Enters carrying a bouquet of red roses.*] And his secretary?

PRIVATE SECRETARY: Just left for the file clerk's office. You're here to try to get a date, eh?

SON: What's wrong with that? You don't like it? Come over here and look out the window, then talk. Let's see if she'll be so cool to me now.

PRIVATE SECRETARY: [*Is dragged to the window by the* SON *and looks out.*] Wow! Whose car is that?

SON: Whose do you think? Another school year is over, you know.

PRIVATE SECRETARY: Your father bought this for you?

SON: Are you kidding? It's a present from me to myself.

PRIVATE SECRETARY: How can you afford it?

SON: Dealer loan. Plus a whopping discount. The guy greatly respects the old man.

PRIVATE SECRETARY: What brand?

SON: Hampton, '65 model. Eight cylinders. Automatic. They don't put clutches in these cars, you know. A smooth drive, this car. [*Points to the* SECRETARY'*s desk.*] I'd like to take her for a spin in it.

CLERK: [*Enters. He is the* SERVANT *of Act I.*] Telegram.

PRIVATE SECRETARY: Didn't I tell you to put them all on my desk?

CLERK: Yes, but since you're here . . .

PRIVATE SECRETARY: It doesn't matter if I'm here.

SON: On your desk, Uncle? How come?

PRIVATE SECRETARY: I keep them arranged in order of importance, that's why. [*Puts the telegram into his pocket.*]

SECRETARY: [*Enters carrying file folders. She is a commonplace, talkative, coquettish girl wearing a short-sleeved blouse and skirt.*] Those old congress reports aren't back there. Can they be here, I wonder? [*Climbs onto a chair and rummages in a file cabinet.*]

SON: Can I help?

SECRETARY: [*Finds what she's looking for and jumps down.*] No, it's not necessary. Thanks.

SON: [*Approaches her and hands her the flowers.*] These are for you.

SECRETARY: Thanks. Put them over there. [*To the* PRIVATE SECRETARY.] I left some maps from the Planning Office on my desk. Have you seen them?

PRIVATE SECRETARY: [*Slightly upset.*] They must have gotten mixed up with the other files by mistake. Oh! Here they are.

SECRETARY: [*Takes them and puts them on the* PROFESSOR's *desk.*] He wants to see them when he comes in.

PRIVATE SECRETARY: The secretary-general called. He wants us to move up the fact-finding trip.

SECRETARY: Is that so? I wonder why.

SON: Umm, I have a new car. If you'd like to . . .

SECRETARY: I saw it outside. Drive safely.

SON: Well, what I actually meant was . . . if I might ask . . .

SECRETARY: Don't ask. Next week is the Industrial Congress. We don't even have time to scratch our heads.

CLERK: [*Enters.*] Two reporters are here.

PRIVATE SECRETARY: Get rid of them.

SECRETARY: No, call them in. Remember what the minister said. [*The* CLERK *exits.*]

SON: Hey, what about me? You didn't give me an answer.

SECRETARY: How many times have I told you to find somebody your own age? Go tour the countryside with your cute little car.

SON: But I . . . [*Leaves his sentence unfinished as the* REPORTERS *enter, but whispers to the* SECRETARY *on leaving.*] I'll wait in front of the building until you come out. [*Exits. The* SECRETARY *shakes her head as if hoping he will come to his senses.*]

REPORTER: [*Greets the* SECRETARY *and continues the sentence he has begun outside.*] If the Budget Committee continues to resist . . .

SECOND REPORTER: It won't matter if he's the last man on his feet. The professor will defend his proposals to the end. He's a man of principle . . .

REPORTER: You never know.

SECOND REPORTER: This ministry has never seen a man with so much integrity or such a high degree of honor. Even the smear campaigns by the opposition bounce right off him. Why? Because he's the only politician who values common sense over party interest.

REPORTER: Mighty big words.

SECOND REPORTER: It's his sixth month in office. If there was anything suspicious, it would be stinking to high heaven by now.

REPORTER: What do you say to the rumors about his father-in-law?

[*The* PRIVATE SECRETARY, *who is discussing a document with the* SECRETARY, *is startled upon overhearing these words.*]

SECOND REPORTER: Well, I'm not so sure about him. But you'd better keep an eye on the secretary-general.

REPORTER: Oh, they say he gave that famous singer her walking papers.

SECOND REPORTER: Actually, his real favorite is the stables. They say he's teaching VIP wives how to ride.

REPORTER: He wasn't always like this, was he?

SECOND REPORTER: Welcome to power, pal. What's in it that makes whoever has it suddenly potent, in every sense of the word?

PROFESSOR: [*Enters, wearing the same clothes as before, but looking much younger.*] Hello, gentlemen. Go ahead, shoot. What are you burning to ask?

REPORTER: [*Approaches with a notebook in hand.*] Certain opposition circles accuse you of obstinacy in defending your funding scheme for the new industrial project. They claim it will torpedo the budget.

PROFESSOR: It's true I defend my funding scheme, but it's incorrect that it might torpedo the budget.

REPORTER: Then why all the fuss?

PROFESSOR: Lack of vision. Or else it's ill-will. [*Smiles.*] Let them believe whichever they like.

REPORTER: What's your opinion on the ruling party's wanting to raise MP salaries after only six months in power?

PROFESSOR: It's well known how I have opposed that from day one. But it's interesting to note that it's the only topic on which the ruling and opposition parties can agree.

REPORTER: Let's get to the major issue—the new tax bill.

PROFESSOR: We handled it. The bill will be withdrawn.

SECOND REPORTER: But isn't it true that the Yellow Party leaders don't see eye-to-eye with you?

PROFESSOR: Well, at the beginning, yes, but . . .

SECOND REPORTER: But you vigorously opposed them.

PROFESSOR: The bill will be withdrawn, I tell you.

REPORTER: Yes, perhaps for a while. But with their mentality, how can you guarantee they won't submit it again later?

PROFESSOR: If they do, you can be sure I won't be one of its supporters. I vetoed it as a cabinet member; I'll do the same as an MP in Parliament.

SECOND REPORTER: I admire how you hang in until the bitter end. [*To the* REPORTER.] See, didn't I tell you?

REPORTER: If I may ask a personal question?

PROFESSOR: Sure.

REPORTER: They say there's a light burning in your window all night. Is that true?

PROFESSOR: [*Modestly.*] Well, maybe I do work a little harder than I should.

SECOND REPORTER: Don't you get tired? Shouldn't you take a rest once in a while?

PROFESSOR: I've put off resting until the big sleep. I'll take perpetual leave then.

SECRETARY: Please don't talk like that.

REPORTER: How about your staff? Can they keep up with you?

PROFESSOR: They do their best. [*The* SECRETARY *squeezes in a document for his signature.*] For example, this poor girl, bless her heart, even outside office hours she tries to help me, over my objections.

SECOND REPORTER: I don't think we should keep you any longer. Thank you very much.

REPORTER: Yes, thank you, Professor.

SECOND REPORTER: Good day.

PROFESSOR: Farewell. [REPORTERS *exit*.]

SECRETARY: The secretary-general called, sir. It's about the fact-finding tour.

PROFESSOR: The fact-finding tour? I was going to take that trip next week. Has there been a change? [*On the phone.*] Get me the secretary-general. [*To the* SECRETARY.] Have the newspapers come?

SECRETARY: Here they are. [*Hands the* PROFESSOR *newspapers on wooden dowels.*]

PROFESSOR: [*Glances at them while speaking into the phone.*] Hello. Not there? . . . On the way here? . . . Even better. Thanks. [*Hangs up, continues to scan the newspapers.*] Those unprincipled bums! I think this paper is obsessed with me. Look at the stuff they're making up now.

SECRETARY: Don't mind them.

PROFESSOR: But I'm a sensitive person.

SECRETARY: I know. But is it worthwhile to get your feelings hurt with everyday political dogfights?

PROFESSOR: Maybe you're right, my child, but one mustn't let these people cast aspersions on one's honor.

SECRETARY: [*Reaches automatically for her notebook.*] I understand, sir. We're going to write another refutation.

PROFESSOR: [*Dictates.*] On the twenty-fifth of the month, in the lead editorial of your newspaper on the topic of the recent appointee to the Purchasing Committee of our ministry, the allegations of his close ties with my father-in-law . . .

SECRETARY: Are totally contrary to the truth. [*The* PROFESSOR *looks at her in surprise. She gestures as if to show that she is experienced in these matters.*] Leave the rest to me.

PROFESSOR: Rest of what?

SECRETARY: The items of the press law—article, paragraph, number . . . I've seen quite a few ministers come and go here.

PROFESSOR: How many?

SECRETARY: Counting you, five.

PROFESSOR: Well, well. Ministers come and go, and you stay, is that it?

SECRETARY: I'm above political parties. [*Smiling at her own joke, she goes on writing.*] In conformity with Article Five of the law, corrections to the above-mentioned page and column . . .

PROFESSOR: [*Stands behind her to see what she is writing.*] What now? Why did you stop?

SECRETARY: I don't know. I thought you were going to take my hand in yours.

PROFESSOR: What a strange idea! What made you think that?

SECRETARY: I don't know. Instinct, I guess.

PROFESSOR: How odd! What sort of nonsense is that?

SECRETARY: How should I know? It just came out. Actually, the previous minister used to like to do that sometimes. Do you think pleasing the people you work with now and then is so strange?

PROFESSOR: I didn't mean that. I just meant you're like a daughter to me. What if I did take your hand, anyway? But not here and now. Why on earth . . .

SECRETARY: Oh, don't mind me. I'm just the moody, crazy-girl type. I'm sorry. It was just wishful thinking. Anything to add to this? *Un point c'est tout.*

PROFESSOR: Where did you come up with that?

SECRETARY: The former minister used to say that when he wanted to close a subject.

PROFESSOR: [*Smiles.*] What a clever little fool you are.

SECRETARY: Just a minute. [*Takes a small notebook from her purse and cheerfully jots down a few words in it.*]

PROFESSOR: What's that?

SECRETARY: My diary. I write down memorable phrases that I run across in novels or movies. Or life. Like this.

PROFESSOR: I didn't say anything memorable.

SECRETARY: [*Puts her notebook away.*] Think whatever you want. For me, it was priceless.

SECRETARY-GENERAL: [*Enters.*] Oh, you're busy, pardon me.

PROFESSOR: No, not at all, come right in. What's this about the fact-finding trip?

SECRETARY-GENERAL: I came to talk to you about that. You weren't planning to leave until next week, were you?

PROFESSOR: That's right.

SECRETARY-GENERAL: Well, we've decided to push the trip up slightly. There's been a bit of unpleasantness down south, and the party chairman thinks that as the most popular and most respected cabinet member in the country, you might have a calming effect. It would be good if you can go today instead of next week. Of course, it's up to you.

PROFESSOR: That's not a bad idea at all. It might even be better this way. I can be back in the capital for the Industrial Congress next week.

SECRETARY-GENERAL: It's settled then.

PROFESSOR: [*To his* SECRETARY.] Please tell the driver to get my station wagon ready. I'm leaving on my fact-finding tour tonight.

SECRETARY: If the repairs are finished.

SECRETARY-GENERAL: Now look. This ministry has two Cadillacs. It looks funny for the minister to use an old station wagon while his deputies are riding in Cadillacs.

PROFESSOR: Oh, she's my old faithful. I used that car for the entire election campaign. What was our slogan? Wasn't it that we were going to put an end to the Cadillac regime?

SECRETARY-GENERAL: That was before the elections. [*The* SECRETARY *exits. The* SECRETARY-GENERAL *follows her with his eyes.*] What a cute little piece you've got there!

PROFESSOR: Hey, you know I don't approve of such language.

SECRETARY-GENERAL: Maybe we should exchange secretaries. Mine is an old bird in her sixties, but she types three hundred words a minute.

PRIVATE SECRETARY: [*Enters.*] Hey, is it correct, what I'm hearing? Are you heading out on that trip today?

PROFESSOR: Yes, why?

PRIVATE SECRETARY: You wanted me to prepare for the Industrial Congress, remember?

PROFESSOR: That's right. Then you'd better stay and finish the job. I'll go alone.

PRIVATE SECRETARY: Yes, Minister. [*Exits.*]

SECRETARY-GENERAL: So what else is new around here?

PROFESSOR: Some reporters were here again this morning. That tax bill . . .

SECRETARY-GENERAL: [*Anxiously.*] You didn't make any new statements, I hope.

PROFESSOR: Why not?

SECRETARY-GENERAL: The party chairman wasn't so happy with what you told the reporters the last time. When will you learn to get used to party discipline? Just between you and me, this 281 to 280 majority of ours is awfully thin. It has to be propped up. We have to be very careful.

PROFESSOR: But didn't we come into power by opposing a tax bill that was against the Constitution and human rights?

SECRETARY-GENERAL: Yes.

PROFESSOR: Then how come we're now supporting an identical bill that's against the Constitution and human rights?

SECRETARY-GENERAL: My dear professor, will you get over this way of thinking? [*Clasps the* PROFESSOR's *shoulders in a brotherly embrace and offers sincere advice.*] In politics, you always keep your eye on the opposition. If they're against a bill, you're for it. If they're for it, you're against it. That's how it works. So what if we said something earlier? Or if we didn't say something earlier? It's in the past either way, so forget it. It's history.

PROFESSOR: I never eat my own words.

SECRETARY-GENERAL: Big deal. Noble language. OK, so you caused the bill to be withdrawn, but you damaged the party's reputation.

PROFESSOR: That's a matter of perspective. [*Points to a newspaper.*] I sent this paper a correction a minute ago. Rumor has it that my father-in-law is abusing his privileged situation.

SECRETARY-GENERAL: [*Suddenly interested.*] Let me see. [*Reads.*] This is bad. But the real mistake is yours.

PROFESSOR: Mine? Why?

SECRETARY-GENERAL: Certainly yours. If I'm not wrong, this reporter's brother wanted you to give him a position as a committee member.

PROFESSOR: Yes, he did.

SECRETARY-GENERAL: Well, if you'd agreed to it, you wouldn't be in this jam now. You've got to throw a bone to the wolves now and then.

PROFESSOR: OK, but there's never an end to it then, is there? They eat one up and howl for more.

SECRETARY-GENERAL: Then throw them another one. We're the butchers, aren't we?

PROFESSOR: I won't throw bones or anything else.

SECRETARY-GENERAL: Then they'll bite. They'll growl. Why make a big deal of it? All it would have taken was a committee membership.

PROFESSOR: What if he's not qualified?

SECRETARY-GENERAL: Qualification is in the hands of the appointing minister.

PROFESSOR: Every day holds a new revelation for me.

SECRETARY-GENERAL: Keep your mind open, Professor. If politics were as simple as science, everybody would be a politician. Relax. Throw a bone to the wolf. If you don't, I will.

PROFESSOR: You will?

SECRETARY-GENERAL: Of course. For your sake.

WIFE: [*Enters clad in a riding outfit, including high leather boots, and carrying a whip.*] Oh! I see you're not alone.

SECRETARY-GENERAL: I'm giving a lesson in politics to this big baby. [*Kisses her hand.*]

WIFE: [*To the* PROFESSOR.] I hear you won't be able to join us for that meeting. A pity.

PROFESSOR: [*Surprised.*] Where did you hear that?

WIFE: [*Taken aback.*] Oh, umm . . . I don't remember. From, from . . .

SECRETARY-GENERAL: [*To the* PROFESSOR.] Didn't you ask for the driver a little while ago?

WIFE: [*Relieved.*] Oh yes, I was wondering how I knew.

PROFESSOR: It wasn't clear that I was going to come to that meeting even if I didn't go on the fact-finding mission.

WIFE: Well, I'd have dragged you along with us. [*The* SECRETARY *enters and busies herself with documents.*]

SECRETARY-GENERAL: It used to be home, university, library. He didn't know anything else. Like a performing horse. All year long. Now it's ministry, Parliament, prime minister's office. Then prime minister's office, Parliament, ministry. [*To the* PROFESSOR.] You never could bring yourself to join the social life. Last week you dodged the minister of finance's reception.

PROFESSOR: They make you drink a lot there. It's not good for me. I don't know what I'm doing afterward. [*The* SECRETARY *perks up at this.*]

SECRETARY-GENERAL: Nonsense, that's just talk. You're a grown man, aren't you? [*To the* WIFE.] I ought to leave now. [*To the* PROFESSOR.] Let me just go downstairs to see the undersecretary for five minutes. [*Exits.*]

WIFE: When are you setting out?

PROFESSOR: I think in the evening, when it's cool.

WIFE: We won't be back from our meeting by then. So good-bye, if we don't see each other. I'll tell them to pack your suitcase. Which suits do you want?

PROFESSOR: How many do I have besides the one I'm wearing? The light-colored one.

WIFE: This is nothing but posturing! People dress up to show off. And you're boasting about having that sorry old car and your old clothes. I wish God would put some sense into your head! [*Exits.*]

SECRETARY: [*To the* PROFESSOR, *who has turned pensive.*] What are you thinking?

PROFESSOR: [*Collects himself.*] Nothing. Nothing at all.

SECRETARY: Brooding doesn't become you. When you smile, you look fifteen years younger. Oh yes, speaking of age, now I remember! [*Goes to the desk, picks up her flowers, and gives them to the* PROFESSOR.] Happy birthday!

PROFESSOR: What birthday?

SECRETARY: Isn't today the tenth of May?

PROFESSOR: Why, yes it is. Even I forgot about it. How did you know?

SECRETARY: I wrote it down when the papers ran your biography.

PROFESSOR: I'm touched.

SECRETARY: Don't mention it.

PROFESSOR: When I remember your birthday, we'll be even.

SECRETARY: Oh, I don't think so.

PROFESSOR: I'd like to do something for you in return. [*Strokes the flowers.*] You've been looking very tired these last few days. How about a week's vacation? Go to the beach. Swim. Have fun till I come back.

SECRETARY: Oh no, sir, I don't want that. But would you really like to do something for me?

PROFESSOR: Yes, of course.

SECRETARY: Oh, no, no . . . I changed my mind. Don't listen to what I say. I'm just a crazy, moody girl.

PROFESSOR: No, tell me, let's hear what it is.

SECRETARY: Promise me you'll do it?

PROFESSOR: Of course I will if I can.

SECRETARY: Take me with you on your fact-finding tour. It will be a change for me, and you won't be left without a secretary.

PROFESSOR: Fine, but . . .

SECRETARY: But?

PROFESSOR: How would it look? How could we . . .

SECRETARY: We what?

PROFESSOR: I mean . . .

SECRETARY: [*Giggles loudly.*] Are you afraid?

PROFESSOR: Oh come now, what do you mean? You're like a daughter to me.

SECRETARY: Well, in that case you must be like a father to me.

PROFESSOR: That's something to think about! [*They laugh, and the* PROFESSOR *pats her affectionately.*]

SECRETARY: But promise me . . .

ASSOCIATE: [*Entering.*] Oh! Pardon me.

PROFESSOR: [*Somewhat disconcerted.*] Oh! Why, where did you come from? Come in.

SECRETARY: [*Quietly.*] I'm going home to pack my suitcase.

PROFESSOR: Wait . . .

ASSOCIATE: I'm afraid I've disturbed you. [*The* SECRETARY *exits.*]

PROFESSOR: No, certainly not. Sit down. What brings you to town?

ASSOCIATE: I came to the capital on university business. It's good to see you looking so well. You've grown younger.

PROFESSOR: The fruit of hard work. And a feeling of accomplishment.

ASSOCIATE: Aha. So you're happy with life?

PROFESSOR: Full to the brim. It's as though I hadn't lived until now. I feel like a newborn baby. [*Takes one of the flowers and sniffs it.*] Like a plane tree when the sap rises in the spring. Like there's a second childhood in me.

ASSOCIATE: I understand completely.

PROFESSOR: I threw that old worthless diffidence into the wastebasket. At last I've become somebody. I command much more respect now . . . definitely.

ASSOCIATE: You were well respected in the past, too.

PROFESSOR: Oh? Who was it who used to come to meet me at the train station when I came back from those academic conferences? Only you and a few shiftless students I'd failed who were trying to impress me. But now when I go to a party congress, the stations can't hold the crowds who come to see me.

ASSOCIATE: The voice of the people is the voice of truth.

PROFESSOR: Like a patient who understands the meaning of health, I've realized the meaning of power. [*Strokes the arms of his chair.*] They call this the chair of power. From where you are, it looks like an ordinary chair. You have to come to this side to really see. [*Stands and extends his hand toward the audience.*] From where I stand, people look like ants. [*Goes to the dictaphone.*] See this dictaphone? If I speak an order into it, hundreds of thousands of arms and legs will carry it out in ten minutes. [*Picks up the phone.*] This phone connects me to every division and unit of my ministry. [*Indicates the intercom bells.*] Look at these bells. There are eight of them. [*Plays them like piano keys with his fingers. Three* ASSISTANT DIRECTORS *immediately enter through the center door, the* PRIVATE SECRETARY *and the* CLERK *from the side door on the right, and the* SECRETARY *from the adjacent door. The* ASSOCIATE *is amazed. The* PROFESSOR *to the subordinates.*] I'm sorry, I hit the call bells by mistake with my elbow. [*All leave, bowing and scraping. To the* ASSOCIATE.] Did you see that? [*Points.*] The one who came from over there is my undersecretary. [*Points.*] The one who came from there is my private secretary. The one from the right . . .

ASSOCIATE: Yes, this is your second childhood, all right. One day I hope you'll be prime minister. People can change so much . . .

PROFESSOR: [*Smiles.*] I am what I've always been.

ASSOCIATE: So you think. But you're not yourself anymore.

PROFESSOR: Then who am I?

ASSOCIATE: In politics, there's no "me" or "you." There's only "us" and "them." You've become the party's man, its property, its puppet.

PROFESSOR: What about my character?

ASSOCIATE: Sooner or later one's character melts in the frying pan of the party's character.

PROFESSOR: [*Smiles.*] That means you don't know me at all! [*Pause.*] Despite everything, though, I'm very fond of you. I've been thinking of something for you for a while.

ASSOCIATE: [*Surprised.*] For me?

PROFESSOR: I want you to be my undersecretary. I'm going to meet with the prime minister soon. I'll get the OK in three days. Let's serve the nation together and be proud.

ASSOCIATE: [*Laughs loudly.*] You've got be joking! While I'm trying to pull you out of the pit, you're trying to pull me in. Are you aware, dear professor, that you're becoming more and more ridiculous? If you'll permit me, I have some advice for you.

PROFESSOR: Go ahead.

ASSOCIATE: Before the ship you're on goes aground, try to disembark at the first port. [*Gets ready to leave; picks up his briefcase.*]

PROFESSOR: Wait. Stay a little longer.

ASSOCIATE: I've got other things I must do.

PROFESSOR: Well then, let's leave together. I'm going to stop by the prime minister's office. [*They exit.*]

PRIVATE SECRETARY: [*Enters as they leave, takes a file folder from the* PROFESSOR's *desk drawer, and removes a map showing land registration. Picks up the phone.*] Hello, long distance? Get me 12 34 56. Urgent. [*Hangs up and lounges in the armchair as he lights a cigar and studies the map. The phone rings.*] Hello, Dad. . . . Sure, they're all fine. My sister's gone to a meeting, and my brother-in-law's out fact finding. Now listen. The industrial site is going to be a little south of where we thought. Look at the map in front of you. Follow the river and come south. Imagine a circle fourteen centimeters in diameter with that olive grove in the center. That's the land for the site. You'll need to move quickly. . . . What do you mean, four million? I tell you, we'll make at least six and half million. Now how about the ship-catering deal? Bids are due on the twenty-second. They'll drop their price. . . . No, listen. To meet it we just cut the quality again. Now what about that pipe deal, any news? . . . Ah, good. [*Noise outside.*] Uh oh! Somebody's coming. I'm hanging up. [*Hangs up.*]

SON: [*Enters, with dust and blood on his clothes.*] Where's my dad, where's my dad?

PRIVATE SECRETARY: What the devil happened to you? [*Sound of an ambulance passing with its siren on.*]

SON: Uncle, I just ran over a man!

PRIVATE SECRETARY: You ran over a man? Where? When?

SON: Just now, down the street. [*Slumps down.*] I was waiting downstairs in my car for Dad's secretary. She ran out in a hurry. I wanted to take her for a ride. But she jumped into a taxi. So I chased after them. There was a traffic jam at the intersection. I lost the taxi. When the road cleared, I stepped on the gas. I was going to cut them off and pull her into my car. Like they do in the movies.

PRIVATE SECRETARY: How fast were you going?

SON: A hundred, hundred and ten maybe.

PRIVATE SECRETARY: Idiot!

SON: I caught up with the taxi. I veered right. He veered right. I went left. He went left. Then a bicycle came out of nowhere, I don't know how, and I hit it. The guy took two somersaults and landed on the road. To top it off, the taxi was the wrong one. The guys in it jumped out and started beating me up. So I stepped on the gas and shot back here.

SECRETARY-GENERAL: [*Enters.*] OK, so we've had coffee with the undersecretary too. I'm going now, Professor. [*Not seeing the* PROFESSOR, *to the* PRIVATE SECRETARY.] He's not here?

PRIVATE SECRETARY: He was planning to drop by the prime minister's office.

SECRETARY-GENERAL: [*Notices the* SON.] What's wrong with you?

PRIVATE SECRETARY: He ran over a man.

SECRETARY-GENERAL: [*Goes to the* SON.] Ran over a man! Now hold on, don't panic. We'll find a way out. What's your license number?

SON: I still have temporary license plates.

SECRETARY-GENERAL: So much the better. Now go wash up. Tidy up a bit. Then go straight home. Don't leave the house. If the man's still alive, we'll find a way out.

SON: What if he's dead? [*Cries loudly.*] If he's dead, what will become of me?

CURTAIN

ACT III

[*A room at a rustic mountain hotel. A bed and a toilet on the side. Balcony in the background. Night. Outside, the noise of crickets. As the curtain rises, the* PROFESSOR, *wearing his glasses and a bathrobe, is writing by the light of a lamp. He looks tired. He occasionally rubs his eyes. It is obvious that he is suffering from a headache. The balcony door opens halfway, and the* SECRETARY *pokes her head in.*]

PROFESSOR: [*Startled.*] Who's there?

SECRETARY: [*Opens the door farther.*] It's me. I was worried about you.

PROFESSOR: Thanks. Haven't you gone to bed yet?

SECRETARY: I tried to, but I couldn't sleep.

PROFESSOR: Maybe it's the aftershock of the problem with the car.

SECRETARY: What if the car had broken down in a really remote place?

PROFESSOR: Umm hmm. We were so lucky to find this mountain hotel. [*Points to the phone.*] I asked them to call home for me a little while ago. I thought my wife might get worried and call the hotel in the city.

SECRETARY: How's your headache?

PROFESSOR: Aspirin hasn't done any good.

SECRETARY: Wait a minute. I know a better medicine. [*Exits by the balcony door. The phone rings.*]

PROFESSOR: Hello . . . Ah, is that you, Son? Why are you so scared? . . . You thought it was the police? What police? . . . You must have been dreaming. Did I wake you? . . . Why don't you put your mother on for a minute? [*The* SECRETARY *enters with a bottle of whisky, fills a glass.*] She's not home yet? [*Looks at his watch.*] How can that be? It's midnight. . . . No, don't say anything to her when she comes in. [*Hangs up.*]

SECRETARY: [*Sarcastically.*] She obviously hasn't been worrying about you.

PROFESSOR: That's odd. I hope nothing's happened to her.

SECRETARY: After the meeting, there was to be a dinner. After the dinner, a ball . . .

PROFESSOR: Odd.

SECRETARY: I brought something for your headache. This is the best medicine for headaches.

PROFESSOR: [*Drinks absentmindedly, then bursts into a coughing fit.*] Why, this is whisky!

SECRETARY: Yes, it is. Opens the veins. Lowers the tension. Chases away the headache.

PROFESSOR: No, not for me. I don't touch alcohol.

SECRETARY: Oh, a little bit never hurt anyone. [*Behaving like a nurse.*] Come on, let's see you take your medicine. [*He drinks.*] That's right. Now put your work aside. Your eyes are bloodshot.

PROFESSOR: I was taking notes on today's investigations.

SECRETARY: Funny, isn't it? You're a typical Taurus, exploited because of your good heart.

PROFESSOR: Taurus?

SECRETARY: I mean people born under that sign. May tenth is Taurus . . . the Bull.

PROFESSOR: So I'm a Bull, eh?

SECRETARY: Oh, you don't know what a Bull you are! How about another whisky?

PROFESSOR: No, no.

SECRETARY: That's not good enough. Here. [*Hands him the glass.*] Think of it as medicine. Hold your nose and drink it.

PROFESSOR: What next?

SECRETARY: What's your wife's sign?

PROFESSOR: I have no idea. [*Takes a small notebook from his pocket.*] Her birthday is July twentieth.

SECRETARY: Cancer. I guessed that already. [*Takes a magazine from the table and reads.*] Listen: "Taurus and Cancer cannot get along with each other."

PROFESSOR: Is that so?

SECRETARY: Do you know what's the ideal spouse for a Bull?

PROFESSOR: A cow?

SECRETARY: [*Laughs.*] Oh, that's good. You're cute. No, a Capricorn.

PROFESSOR: What's your sign?

SECRETARY: I don't know. I was born on December twenty-third.

PROFESSOR: What sign would that be?

SECRETARY: [*Hands him the magazine.*] See for yourself.

PROFESSOR: [*Reads.*] Capricorn.

SECRETARY: Is that so? What a strange coincidence. [*Sighs.*]

PROFESSOR: Eh? What are you thinking?

SECRETARY: Nothing. Nothing at all. A cloud came and went, that's all. Don't take everything I say seriously. I'm a moody . . .

PROFESSOR: . . . crazy girl. Clearly.

SECRETARY: You're always making fun of me.

PROFESSOR: No, I'm not. I'm only joking.

SECRETARY: Is your headache a little better now?

PROFESSOR: This whisky's really made a difference. Amazing.

SECRETARY: [*Fills their glasses again.*] Then here's to your health!

PROFESSOR: And to yours!

SECRETARY: I'm actually surprised at you. You don't seem to know that you're alive.

PROFESSOR: Why, who said that? I'm . . .

SECRETARY: [*Has been looking out the window. Suddenly puts her hand over the* PROFESSOR*'s mouth.*] Ssshhh!

PROFESSOR: [*Frightened.*] What is it?

SECRETARY: A shooting star. If you make a wish on a shooting star, it's bound to come true.

PROFESSOR: What did you wish?

SECRETARY: [*Flirtatiously.*] I'll never tell! It's my secret. [*Drinks.*] Do you know what my dream is? To have a big farm somewhere far away from people, like this hotel. Chickens, roosters, cows . . .

PROFESSOR: Rabbits.

SECRETARY: Rabbits of course. Especially rabbits. How did you know I love rabbits?

PROFESSOR: I love them, too. That's why I mentioned them. I have rabbits at home. [*Suddenly melancholy.*] I mean, I used to.

SECRETARY: Why did you go into politics, anyway? Politics is not for delicate souls such as yourself. Do you know what I compare politics to? A capsizing boat. First it's right side up, then it's upside down. [*Laughs.*] Here's to your health!

PROFESSOR: What are we drinking to now?

SECRETARY: To everything except politics. To life! To spring! [*Goes to the balcony and opens the doors wide.*] The full moon! [*A bit sadly.*] And to lovers.

PROFESSOR: The last part sounded a bit weak. Why haven't you ever gotten married?

SECRETARY: I don't know.

PROFESSOR: Have you ever been engaged?

SECRETARY: Once.

PROFESSOR: And?

SECRETARY: It was a mistake. Puppy love. [*Sighs and drinks.*]

PROFESSOR: What put you off?

SECRETARY: Everything. Especially his unreliability. Most men are like candidates running for election. When they get what they want, they forget all their promises. [*Sighs.*]

PROFESSOR: [*Touched.*] My, my, my, what a pity. Poor child.

SECRETARY: [*Shakes off the mood.*] No, it was a lucky thing.

PROFESSOR: Eh?

SECRETARY: Because later on I meet my soul mate.

PROFESSOR: Well, OK then. No problem.

SECRETARY: The new one is the exact opposite—instead of being self-centered, he's self-sacrificing.

PROFESSOR: I'm very glad to hear it.

SECRETARY: That one was a troublesome boy; this one is mature. My diary is full of him. I want to be his, but at the same time I hate him.

PROFESSOR: Hate him?

SECRETARY: Because he's married.

PROFESSOR: That's bad news.

SECRETARY: The fact that he has a world and a life other than me drives me mad. I don't let on, but I torture myself. Sometimes I just want to hurt him. I want him to be as unhappy as I am. I feel like scratching his face. Scratching him like a cat. Then I feel guilty and want to hug him and make him feel better. Maybe it's true love.

PROFESSOR: Is this from a novel or from your diary?

SECRETARY: The last sentence is from a novel. The first part is my true feelings. Believe me, I love him with all my heart, with butterflies on the inside. I like everything about him.

PROFESSOR: Like what, for instance?

SECRETARY: Everything. His eyes, his absentmindedness, the way he looks at people over his glasses. [*The* PROFESSOR *chokes, coughs, and drops a vase on the table.*] The clumsy way he's always dropping things. [*Pauses.*] Even how slow he is to catch on to some things. [*Raises her glass.*] Never mind. To your health.

PROFESSOR: To yours.

SECRETARY: And once again to lovers. God's blessed children.

PROFESSOR: Hear! Hear!

SECRETARY: I'm sure you were in love once yourself. Can there be a human being who's never been intoxicated by love?

PROFESSOR: How did we get on this subject?

SECRETARY: Oh, please tell me. I'm dying of curiosity.

PROFESSOR: God forbid.

SECRETARY: Never at all intoxicated?

PROFESSOR: Maybe a little. This whisky's going to my head.

SECRETARY: I didn't ask if you were drunk. Don't play word games, please.

PROFESSOR: Maybe I was, then.

SECRETARY: With your wife?

PROFESSOR: I loved her once.

SECRETARY: [*Curious.*] And then?

PROFESSOR: Oh, let's forget all this.

SECRETARY: And before your wife?

PROFESSOR: [*Nods.*] I was seventeen. There was a large fig tree in front of my window.

SECRETARY: Were you in love with the fig tree?

PROFESSOR: No, with the neighbors' daughter. The fig tree was between her window and mine.

SECRETARY: Very interesting.

PROFESSOR: One Sunday my parents went to visit my aunt. I stayed home studying for an exam.

SECRETARY: [*Goes closer to his chair and sits on the floor with her legs crossed, listening interestedly.*] Sooo?

PROFESSOR: Alas, she happened to be home alone that day, too.

SECRETARY: What was she doing alone?

PROFESSOR: It was too long ago to remember exactly. Making quince jelly, I think.

SECRETARY: I'm really curious about this girl. What was she like? What kind of girl?

PROFESSOR: She had a turned-up nose, and her eyes were blue. A cute little thing. A lot like you.

SECRETARY: Oh, this is lovely! I'm dying to hear the rest. Then what happened?

PROFESSOR: [*Pulls himself together.*] Oh, why am I blathering on like this?

SECRETARY: Don't be a party pooper. You started—you have to finish.

PROFESSOR: Oh, don't.

SECRETARY: I'm waiting.

PROFESSOR: Dear girl, I think I'm getting drunk.

SECRETARY: Says who?

PROFESSOR: Are you sure?

SECRETARY: Sure.

PROFESSOR: Then you must be drunk.

SECRETARY: Oh no, never.

PROFESSOR: OK, I'll tell you.

SECRETARY: God bless you!

PROFESSOR: You too.

SECRETARY: OK, out with it.

PROFESSOR: It's funny, isn't it? I'm a bit embarrassed.

SECRETARY: Don't be silly! Here, this will encourage you. [*Fills his glass again.*] I can turn the lights down if you want. [*Turns off the ceiling light so that only the table lamp is on.*] The night likes to cover up our foolishness.

PROFESSOR: She called to me from her window.

SECRETARY: What did she say?

PROFESSOR: "How wonderfully ripe the figs are," she said.

SECRETARY: Good tactic.

PROFESSOR: I wasn't all that fit when I was young, either. But somehow I found myself in the top of the tree.

SECRETARY: Bravo!

PROFESSOR: I was holding out to her the ones I'd picked. The tree is here, the window there. Can you imagine all this? Then suddenly she says, "Wouldn't you like to come in so that we can eat them together?"

SECRETARY: Oh bravo, I like this!

PROFESSOR: If I can just stretch my leg a bit farther, I'm in, it's done.

SECRETARY: OK, do it.

PROFESSOR: She was leaning halfway out the window, reaching for my hand.

SECRETARY: Bravo! And so you plopped right in.

PROFESSOR: Of course not. I fumbled and tumbled and fell.

SECRETARY: Out of the tree?

PROFESSOR: Of course, out of the tree. I fainted from the excitement. I split my head. It took them half an hour to bring me around again.

SECRETARY: What a pity! And then?

PROFESSOR: That was it. Not much before or since.

SECRETARY: Did you see the girl again?

PROFESSOR: Whenever she saw me after that, she would giggle and run away. [*Sighs.*] That was the first and last love adventure of my life.

SECRETARY: What a pity!

PROFESSOR: Yes, that's how it was. [*Holds out his glass to her.*] Drink. Drink up. This is the best medicine for pity. [*The* SECRETARY *drinks and laughs at this last sentence. The* PROFESSOR *laughs, too. They laugh a while together and then slowly turn serious. They stare at each other in wonder, as if seeing one another for the first time.*]

SECRETARY: It's funny, isn't it?

PROFESSOR: On the contrary, it's serious.

SECRETARY: Definitely.

PROFESSOR: Incredible.

SECRETARY: You're surprised?

PROFESSOR: Are you sure we're talking about the same thing?

SECRETARY: Without a doubt.

PROFESSOR: How can this be?

SECRETARY: Fate. The working of destiny.

PROFESSOR: OK, but . . .

SECRETARY: There are no ifs or buts in this business.

PROFESSOR: This is impossible. I'm drunk.

SECRETARY: If you only knew how much I'd like to scratch you. [*Drinks.*] This is also the best medicine for bringing out your true feelings.

PROFESSOR: How can this be? How can this be?

SECRETARY: [*Walks to the window and points to the silhouette of a fig tree.*] How wonderfully ripe the figs are.

PROFESSOR: [*Stands and walks to her, then stops and holds his head.*] I'm dizzy . . .

SECRETARY: Hey, come on, don't faint again, please. Not this time.

CURTAIN

ACT IV

[*The set is as it was in Act II, the office of the minister of industry. As the curtain rises, the* PRIVATE SECRETARY *and the* FATHER-IN-LAW *are engaged in conversation.*]

FATHER-IN-LAW: I'm glad to see the end of that business of the run-over bicyclist. The secretary-general covered it up quite handily. Good for him!

PRIVATE SECRETARY: If my brother-in-law had heard about it, he'd have handed his son over to the authorities himself.

FATHER-IN-LAW: It's incredible, his foolish obsession with honor. How's the boy now? Has he wised up any since his accident?

PRIVATE SECRETARY: He's become a little strange, actually. He's calmed down, but he's taken up drinking nonstop. He's like those drugged hyenas in the circuses. My sister's probably told you all this already.

FATHER-IN-LAW: Oh, is it so easy to see your sister these days? She was out at a ball again last night.

PRIVATE SECRETARY: Still, the most ticklish thing may be this cabinet crisis.

FATHER-IN-LAW: So the rumors are true.

PRIVATE SECRETARY: It's the party chairman's obstinacy. All these months my brother-in-law's been resisting it with his every nerve and fiber. I myself heard him say that if the government brings up this tax bill in Parliament, it will be signing its own death warrant.

FATHER-IN-LAW: What impudence!

PRIVATE SECRETARY: Thank God the Blue Party voted for it. That bailed us out. If the opposition parties ever managed to act in unison, they could have a majority with my brother-in-law's vote.

FATHER-IN-LAW: Let's talk about our own affairs. What about that industrial site?

PRIVATE SECRETARY: It caused a big stink at the commission. They found ten lira per square meter awfully high.

FATHER-IN-LAW: Those fools! We bought that land for two. Did they expect us to give it away for two and a half? Anyhow, after all that whining and hand wringing, they agreed on six.

PRIVATE SECRETARY: Even so, our profit will be about five and a half million.

FATHER-IN-LAW: That's two and a half less than I first estimated.

PRIVATE SECRETARY: Never mind, let it be your donation to the government. And if we get the construction contract, that'll be another eight million.

FATHER-IN-LAW: You mentioned another cement company.

PRIVATE SECRETARY: Yes, I did. [*Opens a drawer in the* PROFESSOR's *desk.*] Should be here somewhere. [*Finds it.*] Here. Twenty-two and a half dollars a ton, FOB. Letter of credit in tax-free dollars to a Swiss bank.

FATHER-IN-LAW: A good price. We can't beat it.

PRIVATE SECRETARY: Don't worry. If we can't beat the price, we can lower the quality again. Like with the catering.

FATHER-IN-LAW: You're a genius!

PRIVATE SECRETARY: You're too kind.

FATHER-IN-LAW: [*Points to the* PROFESSOR's *chair.*] That chair should be yours.

PRIVATE SECRETARY: [*Points to his own office.*] People like me work better behind the scenes.

FATHER-IN-LAW: How much longer will he be with the prime minister?

PRIVATE SECRETARY: As long as necessary.

FATHER-IN-LAW: Then I may as well stop in and see our people downstairs. Back in fifteen minutes. [*Exits.*]

PRIVATE SECRETARY: [*Rummages for another file, finds it, and rings a bell. The* CLERK *enters.*] The secretary in yet?

CLERK: She went to the doctor this morning.

PRIVATE SECRETARY: Here, take this to Accounting. [*The* CLERK *exits.*]

MAN: [*Barges in explosively.*] Where's that scumbag of a minister?

PRIVATE SECRETARY: [*Heading to his own office.*] First of all, sir, this is not how a minister's office should be entered.

MAN: Who are you, and who do you think you're teaching etiquette to?

PRIVATE SECRETARY: I'm the minister's private secretary.

MAN: I'm looking for the minister himself.

PRIVATE SECRETARY: The minister's not in yet.

MAN: Why not?

PRIVATE SECRETARY: Because he's not. I don't need to give you a reason.

MAN: [*Holds his wristwatch up to the* PRIVATE SECRETARY*'s nose.*] Look at the time! Ten past ten. Doesn't the workday start at nine? You can go. I'll wait here.

PRIVATE SECRETARY: This is not the place to wait. Go to the next room and take a number.

MAN: [*With an angry gesture.*] Ha! You think you can brush me off just like that?

PRIVATE SECRETARY: [*Rings a bell; the* CLERK *enters.*] Take this gentleman to the waiting room.

CLERK: [*To the* MAN.] The minister's not here yet, sir. Please, let's go to the waiting room.

MAN: Take your hands off me! [*Noise from outside; the* MAN *goes to look.*] Ha! Here he is.

PRIVATE SECRETARY: [*Goes to the window and looks down. Sound of a car door closing.*] Yes, here he is. But you go on out now.

MAN: [*Goes to the corner and sits down.*] I'm not going anywhere.

PRIVATE SECRETARY: God, what a nuisance!

PROFESSOR: [*Enters.*] What's all this? [*To the* MAN.] Who are you?

MAN: I'll tell you who I am, all right? But first tell these people to leave.

PROFESSOR: [*To the* PRIVATE SECRETARY *and the* CLERK.] Go on out. I'll deal with it. [*To the* MAN.] Go ahead, please, I'm listening.

MAN: Tell me, what good are you in that chair?

PROFESSOR: [*Flabbergasted.*] I beg your pardon! Pull yourself together. It is a minister to whom you are speaking.

MAN: Minister, schminister, what difference does it make? I'm still a ruined man.

PROFESSOR: Now tell me, who are you?

MAN: Do you mean to say you really don't know who I am?

PROFESSOR: Unfortunately, no, I don't.

MAN: I'm the man who sent you at least five nine-hundred-word telegrams, one after another, over the past several months.

PROFESSOR: We get hundreds of telegrams here every day. But an eight-hundred-word one . . .

MAN: [*Corrects him.*] Nine hundred.

PROFESSOR: I never got one with nine hundred words. About what?

MAN: [*Turns to the audience.*] "What was it about?" he asks. Look at him. Can you believe this? I'm at my wit's end. Are you making fun of me, Mr. Minister? [*Changing tone.*] All right, then, do it, do it. Everybody's doing it anyhow. I'm worse than crazy already. [*Showing his teeth, smiles bitterly.*] Crazy, ya haaa! [*With a horrible and bitter laugh, he reaches toward the* PROFESSOR *as if to take him by the neck.*] No, don't be afraid, I won't strangle you. [*Suddenly turns serious.*] But am I the kind of man to act this way? How shameful. How embarrassing. [*His face has become beet red. Tries to loosen his collar with his fingers.*]

PROFESSOR: You're going to choke. Get yourself under control.

MAN: I wish I would choke and get it over with. Every evening the mockery of my wife and kids, the expressions of pity and ridicule on the faces of my friends. [*Excitedly.*] I'm ruined, Mr. Minister. Three months ago I was a happy family man, my work was going well, I was a proper citizen like anyone else. But now? I'm a jobless man, a miserable person. I've taken to drink. [*Offhandedly, with a leering wink.*] Yeah, yeah, what else to do, so much on my mind . . . [*Takes out a handkerchief almost the size of a tablecloth and wipes his face, then bursts into a heartrending song of sorrow.*] Alas, alas, woe is me!

PROFESSOR: [*Watches the* MAN, *partly horrified and partly fascinated. Appalled, he seems to grow smaller in his chair. At one point, he rings the bell. The* CLERK *enters.*] Please bring a soda water with ice for this gentleman.

MAN: [*Wipes his face and loosens his collar further.*] Please excuse my irritability, Mr. Minister. Sometimes I lose my control. [*The* CLERK *brings soda, pours it into a glass, and hands it to the* MAN. *He drinks it with pinky finger extended, then wipes his mouth.*] Oh, thank you.

PROFESSOR: Do you feel better now? I'm listening.

MAN: I'll tell you everything, but I really don't know where to start.

PROFESSOR: Begin at the beginning.

MAN: Right. That's the best way. One must begin at the beginning. [*Looks up at the ceiling and thinks hard. Suddenly.*] Sir, all of a sudden the water was cut off.

PROFESSOR: [*Astonished.*] What did you say?

MAN: I said "water." All of a sudden the water was cut. I was shampooing my hair. There was soap all over my face and in my eyes. I rang the bell, of course.

PROFESSOR: What is the relevance of this to your complaint?

MAN: Hang on a second and listen, my friend. This is happening at the hotel, at night. I'm covered with soap, right? When I push the button, in comes the bellboy, naturally. "What kind of scandal is this?" I ask. "What can I do, sir, the water's cut off," he says. "But don't worry, I'll bring a bucket of water from downstairs." And so he did. Who would have thought? So I wash off the soap. I look around. No robe . . . no bathrobe. Well, I think to myself, it belongs to the hotel, after all. But still, I'm as naked as the day I was born.

PROFESSOR: Not good.

MAN: Thank God my room is just across the hall from the shower. Now, if you were me, what would you do?

PROFESSOR: Sneak quickly into my room.

MAN: Bravo! So I peek carefully out the door. Nobody in the hall. And I race to my room.

PROFESSOR: Good.

MAN: Only to find out I'd locked the door.

PROFESSOR: The key?

MAN: Fell into the water. Where was the water? The cow drank it. Now where could the key have been, my friend? The key was in the pocket of the bathrobe.

PROFESSOR: I see the problem.

MAN: Now the door of the room on the right—no, on the left; no, let me see, on the right; no, no, the one on the left . . .

PROFESSOR: Never mind which one.

MAN: The one on the left, yes, it was definitely the door of the room on the left that opened. It's a woman in a negligee. Seeing me in that condition, she claps her hands to her face and starts screaming: "Help! Help! there's a maniac on the loose, help!"

PROFESSOR: Run back into the bathroom.

MAN: Right! I race back to the bathroom. Unfortunately, this time I mistakenly break into the room of a woman with a child at her breast. She faints, the baby starts crying . . . all the other guests pour into the corridor shouting, "Catch him! Maniac! Assassin! Pervert!" All the bells are ringing like crazy in a huge commotion. I was so scared that I ran upstairs looking for an empty room to hide in. But they caught me. They beat the hell out of me and threw a blanket over me. And they took me in that condition to the police station. "Caught red-handed," as they say.

PROFESSOR: But how!

MAN: Listen, Minister. They kept me that night, the next day, and the next night. They wouldn't even let me call home. I was cut off completely from the outside world. Finally, after three days, I managed with the greatest difficulty to explain myself and was set free. But of course by that time I'd missed the deadline for the bid.

PROFESSOR: What bid?

MAN: The one your ministry opened. For textile machinery. Don't you understand? It was all a con game. The bellboy, the screaming woman. It was like a murder they'd planned down to the last detail just to trap me.

PROFESSOR: Very strange indeed.

MAN: If it hadn't been this game, it would have been another one. They've done it to so many.

PROFESSOR: What sort of game?

MAN: One friend of mine was arrested as a draft dodger. Again on the night before a bid. These are ruthless men. They work just like a gang. It's really my fault, though. I didn't pay enough attention to those threatening letters.

PROFESSOR: Did they send threatening letters, too?

MAN: Of course they did. "Stay out of this business, or it won't be good for your health." That kind of letter. But I laughed it off. I thought I was hardened in such matters. They also sent people to spy on my business when I wasn't in my office, to find out what bids we planned to submit. And when they saw that they couldn't beat our bids . . .

PROFESSOR: I'm simply amazed.

MAN: Not surprisingly, the company fired me the next day. Well, why not? They're foreigners—quite proper. After all, I was naked and locked out without a key. Would they listen to me? They'd say keep your eyes open and don't take the bait. They were right, of course. Did they pay our salaries for nothing? On top of everything else, my wife suspected me of having something to do with that woman at the hotel and sued me for divorce.

PROFESSOR: What a pity. But who is it doing all these things to you?

MAN: EKB, Inc.

PROFESSOR: I beg your pardon?

MAN: EKB, Inc. Every Kind of Business, Incorporated.

PROFESSOR: Who are they?

MAN: Why, they're your people. It's your father-in-law's company. Come now, sir, don't pretend you don't know who I mean.

PROFESSOR: But isn't my father-in-law's company in the iron business?

MAN: What, is there any kind of business they're not into? They've got their fingers in every pie there is. From the catering business to shipyards to selling overpriced land for industrial sites. Too bad for you I have to pipe up about it. Oh! Speaking of plumbing, they're in that business, too. They dig up perfectly good pipes and replace them with their own. Well, I wish you many more prosperous days. You're on the inside; they're on the outside. A fine piece of work, actually.

PROFESSOR: [*Angrily.*] Watch your language, sir.

MAN: [*Without changing his tone.*] Hard to blame you. It's just the facts of life. Everywhere in the world it's like this. The ones who build the railroads are the minister of transportation's relatives. The ones who hit the jackpot in the markets are the minister of trade's pals. It's OK. We don't mind it all that much. But there ought to be limits, don't you agree? Have some mercy. We have families to feed, too.

PROFESSOR: Pull yourself together, sir. I can't let you go on like this. I'll look into what you said. If it's true, the guilty parties will be brought to justice. But I'm going to take you to task for putting those people and me in the same . . .

MAN: If you're not in cahoots with them, why didn't you answer my telegrams?

PROFESSOR: I swear on my honor that I never saw them.

MAN: [*Thinking.*] Why, those unprincipled rascals! They've got the post office in it, too. I never thought of that.

PROFESSOR: I don't think the post office has anything to do with it. [*Rings a bell. The* CLERK *enters.*] Call my private secretary. Now things will become clear.

PRIVATE SECRETARY: [*Enters.*] You called for me?

PROFESSOR: Those eight-hundred-word telegrams that came for me . . .

MAN: [*Corrects him.*] Nine hundred . . .

PROFESSOR: Those nine-hundred-word telegrams. Why didn't I get them?

PRIVATE SECRETARY: I don't know what you're talking about, my dear brother-in-law.

PROFESSOR: How so? He says he sent five of them.

MAN: [*Leaps up from his chair.*] I've got it!

PROFESSOR: Got what?

MAN: I see it all now.

PROFESSOR: How?

MAN: [*Points to the* PRIVATE SECRETARY.] Didn't this man call you "brother-in-law" just now?

PROFESSOR: Yes.

MAN: Then that explains it. The gang that made my life hell belongs to your father-in-law. Haven't you figured it out yet, Mr. Minister? Father and son belong to the same gang. While the father is pulling the wool over my eyes to get the bids, the son is busy losing my telegrams.

PRIVATE SECRETARY: [*As if insulted.*] I beg your pardon! You can't talk to me like that. I'll show you what happens to those who blacken our honor with no evidence.

PROFESSOR: You keep quiet.

PRIVATE SECRETARY: How can I? He's insulting me.

[*At this moment the* FATHER-IN-LAW *enters, in a cheerful mood.*]

MAN: [*Sees him.*] Well, look at this! Here's the man! And he came in with no help from me! [*Puts his hand in his back pocket and moves toward the* FATHER-IN-LAW, *who, with unexpected speed for his age, ducks into the* PRIVATE SECRETARY's *office. He locks the door behind him. Meanwhile the* CLERK *and the* PRIVATE SECRETARY *try to restrain the* MAN.]

PROFESSOR: Hey, what's all this? Calm down, everybody.

MAN: [*Breathing hard.*] Please excuse my outburst, Mr. Minister. [*Sits down again.*] I don't know what I'm doing. I'm like a madman.

PRIVATE SECRETARY: There, he confesses it himself. If you're mad, go see a shrink. Don't toy with people's honor with no proof.

MAN: He keeps harping on evidence and proof. It's true I don't have hard evidence. But there's such a thing as conscience. Conscience isn't completely dead yet. [*To the* PROFESSOR.] Excuse my words earlier, Mr. Minister. You're a man of conscience. An honest man. After all, you're a professor. Professors don't make good thieves. So I put my fate in your hands. [*Takes two slips of paper from his pocket.*] This one is my company's claim for reimbursement. And this one is my own.

PROFESSOR: Let's see. [*Examines the claims.*] What's this hotel bill for 850 lira?

MAN: My wife won't let me in, ever since that day. Am I to sleep on the street?

PROFESSOR: [*Examines the claims again.*] Five hundred and seventy lira? Oh, this is for those eight-hundred-word telegrams.

MAN: [*Corrects him.*] Nine hundred.

PROFESSOR: A thousand lira for false teeth? What's this about, for goodness' sake?

MAN: I told you about the rough handling. They broke two of my teeth in that hotel fracas. I had to get new ones. Am I to go around toothless?

PROFESSOR: Let me have these. Your rights will be protected. [*To the* PRIVATE SECRETARY.] I'm placing you in the custody of the ministry. You'll have to account for all those games you've been playing. You and your father.

PRIVATE SECRETARY: But my dear brother-in-law . . .

MAN: [*Tries to kiss the* PROFESSOR's *hand.*] I kiss your blessed hand, Mr. Minister. You're a true man of honor. You're the pride of our country.

PROFESSOR: [*Pulls his hand away.*] No, please don't mention it.

MAN: I'm leaving now, Mr. Minister. I'll wire my company immediately. Nine hundred words. [*Exits.*]

PROFESSOR: [*To the* PRIVATE SECRETARY.] Are you still here? Go on, get out of my sight! Take your briefcase and leave the ministry.

PRIVATE SECRETARY: For the sake of a crazy man?

PROFESSOR: It's not him. It's me who's crazy for never suspecting a thing until now.

[*The* PRIVATE SECRETARY *goes to his office. The door is locked. He knocks. From inside comes the* FATHER-IN-LAW's *voice.*]

FATHER-IN-LAW: Has that man left yet?

PRIVATE SECRETARY: Yes. [*The door opens. The* FATHER-IN-LAW *comes out and goes toward the* PROFESSOR.]

PROFESSOR: Don't say anything because nothing will work.

FATHER-IN-LAW: You're exaggerating. It's not such a big deal. A little excess of enthusiasm on the part of my men, that's all. It's not so hard to fix. Why, I'll pay for the man's losses right now.

PROFESSOR: How easy for you. And what about my honor?

FATHER-IN-LAW: What does any of this have to do with your honor?

PROFESSOR: For people who have no honor themselves, nothing, of course. Now will you please leave? I may not be able to hold my tongue. Go, and stay out of my sight.

[*The* FATHER-IN-LAW *wants to say something to the* PROFESSOR *but realizes that it would be unconvincing. He leaves the office. The* PRIVATE SECRETARY, *without looking at the* PROFESSOR, *follows his* FATHER. *As they are about to exit, the* SECRETARY *enters and looks closely at the* FATHER-IN-LAW, PRIVATE SECRETARY, *and the* PROFESSOR. *She becomes aware that something is up.*]

SECRETARY: What's going on in here?

PROFESSOR: Nothing. Nothing at all. [*The phone rings.*] Hello. . . . Yes, sir. Yes, I read the report by the American expert. Production is up 70 percent. . . . Am I a fortune-teller? Ha ha, a fortune-teller! Well, I'll take it as a compliment. [*Hangs up.*]

SECRETARY: You didn't even look at me today.

PROFESSOR: I'm sorry, I'm a little upset.

SECRETARY: Such things aren't worth getting upset about. [*Moves closer.*] You didn't even ask where I was today.

PROFESSOR: You told me you were going to the doctor. Are you sick?

SECRETARY: A little.

PROFESSOR: What did the doctor say?

SECRETARY: [*Moves closer and toys with his shirt buttons.*] Correct.

PROFESSOR: What was correct?

SECRETARY: My guess.

PROFESSOR: What guess?

SECRETARY: Three and a half months. The result of that trip.

PROFESSOR: [*Horrified, leaps out of his chair.*] What?

SECRETARY: Don't shout. You'll bring everyone in here.

PROFESSOR: [*Grips the desk.*] You're joking, aren't you? This is a joke, isn't it? Tell me you're joking. I don't feel so well.

SECRETARY: I'm sorry to hear this from you. I thought you'd be very happy.

PROFESSOR: [*His voice cracking.*] That means . . . oh my God!

SECRETARY: Three and a half months.

PROFESSOR: Why? But why?

SECRETARY: [*Now very close to the* PROFESSOR, *she straightens his tie and looks up at him with a kind of unfocused but seductive gaze.*] Please forgive me, my darling. It was out of my hands. Do you remember that night? How I made a wish on a shooting star?

PROFESSOR: What did you wish for?

SECRETARY: You asked me on that night, too, but I didn't tell. I wanted to have your child. I knew all the trouble it would bring, but since when does love listen to reason? I wanted to feed a child of your blood with my own blood. Oh, don't look at me with that hard look. I'll kill myself.

PROFESSOR: Is it possible to get rid of it?

SECRETARY: You're crazy! I just told you it's three and a half months. Anyway, even if it were possible, I wouldn't do it. Listen. If flowers bloom and trees bear fruit according to the eternal laws of nature, it was inevitable that our divine love would grow, too. This is the flower of that love.

PROFESSOR: What a thoughtless thing to do!

SECRETARY: Just be patient for another five months. When you see its face, you'll be sorry for these words of yours. [*Strokes his face.*] Don't frown at me so. If you do, I tell you, I'll commit suicide.

PROFESSOR: You can't have a baby here. Do you understand? Not here! My honor would be worthless. I'll send you to Europe. You can have the baby there and come back.

SECRETARY-GENERAL: [*Enters.*] Oh! You're busy, I see.

PROFESSOR: No, not really. [*To the* SECRETARY.] We'll talk later.

SECRETARY-GENERAL: No, talk now. I'm no stranger. [*The* SECRETARY *exits. To the* PROFESSOR.] What's wrong? You look a little pale.

PROFESSOR: Just tired, nothing unusual.

SECRETARY-GENERAL: Come on, my friend, don't wear yourself out like this. Do you get good rest at night?

PROFESSOR: So-so.

SECRETARY-GENERAL: Blood pressure?

PROFESSOR: No idea. Haven't checked it lately.

SECRETARY-GENERAL: You have to check it regularly. How about sugar in the urine? Albumen? Blood cholesterol?

PROFESSOR: No. No. None of that, I hope.

SECRETARY-GENERAL: You're tiring yourself out, Brother. Nobody in the cabinet works as hard as you do. Even the party chairman says so.

PROFESSOR: What did he say exactly?

SECRETARY-GENERAL: He said, "The professor should take a little rest." He said, "He'll be of great service to us in the future." "I don't want him to burn out so soon," he said.

PROFESSOR: That sounds a bit tongue-in-cheek.

SECRETARY-GENERAL: Yeah, you got it. I'll get right to the point. He wants you to get sick for a while.

PROFESSOR: Meaning I've been chosen to be the scapegoat.

SECRETARY-GENERAL: [*Respectfully corrects him.*] Not a scapegoat, a hero. The party needs a friend to rescue it and the cabinet from the crisis they've got themselves into.

PROFESSOR: Uh-huh. Let's look at this a minute. Who's the one who's been trying to rescue the cabinet and the party from this crisis by trying to withdraw the tax bill that got them into it in the first place?

SECRETARY-GENERAL: You.

PROFESSOR: And who's the one who, despite all my warnings over the past few months, seemed convinced, yet caused this crisis by treating it as a fait accompli?

SECRETARY-GENERAL: The party chairman.

PROFESSOR: Then why doesn't he resign?

SECRETARY-GENERAL: [*In a pitying tone.*] You talk like a child. Do you know what it means to have a cabinet crisis just now? Don't forget, a party in power with a majority of 281 to 280 has to act carefully. If the opposition parties can manage to form a coalition, we can say good-bye to power.

PROFESSOR: And what about me and my personal honor?

SECRETARY-GENERAL: In politics there's no personal honor. God save the party!

PROFESSOR: However . . .

SECRETARY-GENERAL: Be reasonable. You'll make a little sacrifice, that's all.

PROFESSOR: Forget it. I'm not such an idealist.

SECRETARY-GENERAL: Try.

PROFESSOR: And if I can't?

SECRETARY-GENERAL: We'll convince you.

PROFESSOR: Aha! This is a threat.

SECRETARY-GENERAL: Don't exaggerate. Look. The first thing you do—you resign. Of course, we'll find a good reason for that. The best is illness. Or overwork is good, for example. Then you send a farewell message. In it, of course, you express your pleasure at having marched in tune with the party chairman, and you close with words like these: "Like a soldier on a tour of duty, I pass the torch to my successor." [*Hands him a slip of paper.*] Here's a sample from a former minister. I remind you that our party chairman will never forget this sacrifice of yours. The next time it won't be a problem for you to become a minister again or ambassador to a European capital. Only at the beginning might there be a little trouble. Some unkind headlines in the newspapers for a day or two, maybe. But don't mind them. Some talking behind your back at the commission—but it's meaningless anyway. And, of course, for the party newsletter I'll produce an article scolding you. But pay no attention to that. You may even find that some of your friends stop greeting you. Pay no attention to that either. University clubs, young people, the man in the street . . .

PROFESSOR: [*Suddenly loses patience.*] Enough! None of this is going to happen. I'm not going to resign. Do you understand? I'm not a pawn in your game. You and your party chairman pushed me forward when you were in trouble and scared off the king. Declared "checkmate" to the Orange Party. And now, because I won't go along with you in this, you want to sacrifice me in another gambit. That's it, isn't it? Why beat around the bush?

SECRETARY-GENERAL: All right! Even if it's like you say, what's wrong with that?

PROFESSOR: I'm not resigning. I won't resign. We'll all sink or swim together. Go and tell that to your bosses!

SECRETARY-GENERAL: Whoa! If you start raising your voice like that, I'll have to change my language, too. If it comes to pigheadedness . . .

PROFESSOR: It's already come to that. So what?

SECRETARY-GENERAL: I'll be forced to use other means.

PROFESSOR: Like what?

SECRETARY-GENERAL: Some information we obtained about your private life.

PROFESSOR: I don't understand.

SECRETARY-GENERAL: You understand just fine. For example, that secretary of yours, whom you couldn't bear to be away from on your fact-finding trips, is suddenly now at the gynecologist's door.

PROFESSOR: [*Stumbles and grabs his desk.*] My secretary . . . my secretary . . .

SECRETARY-GENERAL: [*Takes a small notebook from his pocket.*] Yes, your secretary. Can you read this handwriting? Diary notes. This is a diary. A diary I've had in hand for the past ten minutes. The newspapers would swarm around a scandal like this just like flies on a garbage heap. Come on, let's see what's left of the legend of the professor and his famous honor in twenty-four hours.

PROFESSOR: Would you really stoop as low as that?

SECRETARY-GENERAL: It's all in your hands.

PROFESSOR: I hope you kept records of my father-in-law's swindles, too. They'll be no less valuable to the newspapers.

SECRETARY-GENERAL: Oh, they're not that important. Ordinary stuff, really.

PROFESSOR: Is that so? Ordinary stuff! Ordinary! [*Looks fiercely into the* SECRETARY-GENERAL's *eyes.*] How long have you been in bed with them?

SECRETARY-GENERAL: What? You've got to be kidding. God forbid, in bed with them!

PROFESSOR: Ordinary stuff! Those bums! And you're part of their gang. Sure. Maybe the head of it. Yes, it's clear now. Everything. Just like the naked man at the hotel said.

SECRETARY-GENERAL: What naked man?

PROFESSOR: Exactly like he said. First, the water was cut off.

SECRETARY-GENERAL: [*Frightened now.*] Are you in shock?

PROFESSOR: Yes. He said, "Suddenly the water was cut. There was foam all over my face. I couldn't see anything." Who would have thought? And in the confusion, you stole the key.

SECRETARY-GENERAL: What the hell are you talking about, my friend?

PROFESSOR: Everything was organized beforehand. Everything. Your negotiations with my father-in-law and then forcing me to appoint that dolt of a brother-in-law as my private secretary. It was all planned. You stole that man's key, and you stole my reputation. Now you want to leave me in the corridor stark naked. And as if that's not enough, you want to throw a blanket over me and drag me into court red-handed, don't you?

SECRETARY-GENERAL: I'll call a doctor for you.

PROFESSOR: No, I'm not crazy. [*Shows his teeth in a bitter smile.*] I'm not crazy yet. [*Laughs bitterly and loudly.*] Don't be afraid, I won't strangle you. [*Turns serious.*] Doesn't my situation resemble his precisely? The one on the right—no, on the left; no, on the right—wait, let me see, the one on the left. [*Looks toward the* SECRETARY's *office.*] Yes, yes, you have a woman ready behind the door on the left. A woman in a negligee. That one was going to cause a ruckus at the hotel. This one was going to fill up her belly and do the same here. You organized the whole thing like the plot of a detective novel. That fact-finding tour. That mountain hotel.

SECRETARY: [*Enters in tears.*] Lies! Lies! Believe me, it's all a lie. How could I possibly be such a nasty human being? [*To the* SECRETARY-GENERAL.] You ought to be ashamed of yourself!

PROFESSOR: Then how did this diary get into their hands?

SECRETARY: They must have stolen it. Or had it stolen. Believe me. [*Noise from outside.*]

CLERK: [*Enters.*] It's your son. He says he has to see you.

SON: [*Rushes in.*] Oh Dad, please forgive me.

SECRETARY-GENERAL: You're here?

SON: [*Kneels and clasps his* FATHER's *legs.*] Forgive me, Dad. When he saved me after the accident . . .

PROFESSOR: What accident?

SON: I ran over a man four months ago. The secretary-general covered it up. After that, I turned into a puppet in his hands. He forced me to spy on you. [*Looks at the* SECRE-

TARY.] And when jealousy is also involved . . . I'm disgusted with myself. [*Sobs loudly.*] I hate myself.

SECRETARY: And well you should. [*Goes to the* PROFESSOR *and caresses him.*] Please don't be so worried. [*To the* SECRETARY-GENERAL.] So what if you got hold of my diary? I admit I'm guilty. If I have to feel guilty for falling in love with an angelic, pure-hearted, honest person, then I take the blame on myself. Yes, lay everything out to the public if you want. Let the people judge. Go ahead, play your game.

SECRETARY-GENERAL: This is just idle talk.

SON: [*Suddenly starting to dash out.*] I can't look you in the eye anymore. You won't see me again for years.

PROFESSOR: [*With paternal feeling, tries to stop him.*] No, wait. Listen.

SECRETARY-GENERAL: We're sending him to Brazil to study jazz on a state scholarship. Don't worry.

SECRETARY: [*To the* SECRETARY-GENERAL.] I'm just curious about one thing. How did you steal this?

SECRETARY-GENERAL: He must have reached in through the kitchen window.

SECRETARY: [*Opens her purse, takes out a notebook, and shows it to the* PROFESSOR.] Here it is.

PROFESSOR: What is it?

SECRETARY: My diary.

SECRETARY-GENERAL: What's this then? This is your handwriting, isn't it?

SECRETARY: Yes.

SECRETARY-GENERAL: Then?

SECRETARY: He stole the wrong one. That was the first one I had. I wrote some entries on the first few pages. And farther on, notes on a page or two.

PROFESSOR: And then?

SECRETARY: Then a friend gave me this one. I turned the other one into a shopping list.

SECRETARY-GENERAL: [*Riffling through the pages.*] Shopping list?

SECRETARY: [*Goes to his side and reads.*] Look. Olive oil, one kilo; tomatoes, two kilos; parsley. [*As the* SECRETARY-GENERAL *turns the pages.*] Sardines, apples. Again two kilos of tomatoes. Shall I read on?

SECRETARY-GENERAL: That's enough. [*Gives the notebook to the* SECRETARY.]

PROFESSOR: I'm sorry. [*Goes to her side.*] For a moment, it looked like the whole world was against me.

SECRETARY: You're right, you're not used to these tactics. [*Goes to the fireplace, strikes a match and starts to burn the notebook the* SECRETARY-GENERAL *has just handed to her.*] You never know. One day they might steal it again. I'll burn it now.

PROFESSOR: That's a pity.

SECRETARY: Don't worry, I memorized the whole thing.

SECRETARY-GENERAL: [*Smiles calmly.*] OK, so you got rid of it. But I'm curious. How are you going to hide the other one?

SECRETARY: None of your business. [*Exits.*]

SECRETARY-GENERAL: So much unpleasantness is not really necessary, Professor. If you agree nicely . . .

PROFESSOR: [*To the* SECRETARY-GENERAL.] Is there anything nice left in this business? Not when you're capable of stealing keys in the shower to win bids, there's not. Your dirty trick didn't work, pal. And it's never going to work. I'm firing you all. I'm taking my in-laws to court. I'm going to appoint a whole new staff. As for you, no more easy money from this ministry. Go and find another friend to play your games with.

SECRETARY-GENERAL: This is just hot air, Professor. If you take your father-in-law to court, you'll disgrace yourself. As for appointing a new staff, leave that to the new minister.

PROFESSOR: I told you, I'm not resigning.

SECRETARY-GENERAL: If not today, you'll have no choice but to do it tomorrow. Tomorrow is the party's executive committee meeting. Decisions are made unanimously there, you know.

PROFESSOR: If we're acting out of pigheadedness, I'll leave on a fact-finding trip and won't come back for three months.

SECRETARY-GENERAL: With a new secretary this time? I wouldn't recommend it. Besides, those mountain roads are extremely dangerous.

PROFESSOR: What does that mean?

SECRETARY-GENERAL: I'm saying an accident can easily happen.

PROFESSOR: Nothing you say surprises me anymore.

SECRETARY-GENERAL: Not to worry. We'd arrange a state funeral for you. [*Smiles.*] And the party chairman would see that your widow enjoyed a hefty pension.

PROFESSOR: Fine, but what did I do wrong . . . believing all of you and accepting the candidacy?

SECRETARY-GENERAL: No, of course not. Disrespecting party rules and discipline. Not listening to anyone.

PROFESSOR: Didn't my power come from that very quality?

SECRETARY-GENERAL: Your power has become the party's liability.

PROFESSOR: No pressure and no power can stop me from defending my principles. Now I know what I'll do. Straighten up and face me, sir. I'm throwing down the gauntlet. I've seen your true face at last. I resolve to bring ethics back to politics.

SECRETARY-GENERAL: I can see you're taking this far too seriously. That's just stuff from archaic schoolbooks. Drop these high-and-mighty airs and live a real life! You're nothing but fine words . . . all idle talk. This impertinence of yours is the way three or four retired teachers talk at the coffeehouse, but that's all. You're preaching to the deaf.

PROFESSOR: "The most powerful man in the world is a man on his own," a philosopher once said.

SECRETARY-GENERAL: What stupidity! Who cares about "a man on his own," even if he could dream the impossible dream? If you want to be heard, you've got to talk through a party microphone. These days a man on his own counts for nothing.

PROFESSOR: That's why you don't want me on my own. You said it quite well yourself, actually. And you're right from top to toe. Yes. Maybe. But think a second. [*Quietly.*] A man on his own is still the most powerful man in the world—especially in our Parliament.

SECRETARY-GENERAL: I don't get it.

PROFESSOR: Open your mind and take it in.

SECRETARY-GENERAL: [*Slowly seems to understand.*] What? That is, you mean . . .

PROFESSOR: You guessed it. With one word, I can turn a 281 to 280 majority into a 280 to 281 minority.

SECRETARY-GENERAL: You mean you're going to join the Orange Party?

PROFESSOR: Just to spite you. Temporarily. Until I can bring you down and turn over a new, clean page.

SECRETARY-GENERAL: Well, this is more than I expected out of you. I was quite wrong, to be sure.

PROFESSOR: I'll use your own weapons against you. Come on, stand up. I challenge you.

SECRETARY-GENERAL: You've learned well what I taught you, I see.

PROFESSOR: How else?

SECRETARY-GENERAL: I understand. You're surprised and shaken. You were used to rising. Coming down so suddenly is now making you dizzy. Listen to me, Professor. [*Takes a box of cigarettes from his pocket.*] Just draw a line down the middle of this. On the left, list the disadvantages of this business; on the right, the advantages. On the left, scandal, humiliation. On the right, temporarily a low-profile MP and then a European ambassador at least. Guaranteed. Lisbon or the Vatican. [*Winks.*] You'll take your secretary with you, sir? Yes? I'm crossing out the left-hand side.

PROFESSOR: Just like seven months ago.

SECRETARY-GENERAL: [*Looks at his watch.*] We've talked too long. I have work stacked up to here. You've got until seven. The party chairman is expecting an answer. Think. Think hard. We'll be waiting for your answer. [*Exits.*]

PROFESSOR: [*To his back.*] Then you'll be waiting for nothing. I told you what I'm going to do. You'll be 280 to 281.

CLERK: [*Enters.*] Sir, officials from the party district executive committee.

PROFESSOR: They can go to hell.

[*The two PARTY OFFICIALS of Act I enter in the same attire.*]

FIRST PARTY OFFICIAL: It is a great pleasure for us to convey to you the kind regards of the district executive committee of our party.

PROFESSOR: Will you please leave?

SECOND PARTY OFFICIAL: We deeply sympathize with your anger, but we have no doubt that you will regain your senses, overcome your anger, and once more consider the good of the party as superior to your own concerns.

FIRST PARTY OFFICIAL: Very good.

PROFESSOR: I said, go to hell.

SECOND PARTY OFFICIAL: The enormity of the troubles you have undergone will be engraved in the history of our party in golden letters.

FIRST PARTY OFFICIAL: Our party . . .

PROFESSOR: [*Grabs a seal from his desk.*] Will you get out? Or else there's going to be an accident.

SECOND PARTY OFFICIAL: [*Shields his head with his hands.*] Our party . . .

PROFESSOR: Your party has hit the wall, gentlemen. You're talking rubbish.

FIRST PARTY OFFICIAL: But our party . . .

SECOND PARTY OFFICIAL: We have to tell you . . .

PROFESSOR: [*Threatens them; they run out.*] Shut up! [*Throws the seal in his hand at the picture on the wall. It shatters.*] Cowards! Traitors! I'm not going to resign. I won't! I won't!

SECRETARY: [*Enters with a suitcase in hand.*] Come on, let's go.

PROFESSOR: What for? I'm not going anywhere. I'm here. I'm staying here. Nobody else is going to sit at this desk. [*Turns on the dictaphone.*] Please take down this statement. . . . Hello! [*Plays nervously with the bells.*] What's this, is no one working? [*Rings another bell.*] Where's my clerk? Or don't these bells work, either? [*Madly presses all the bells for his assistants, but nobody comes.*] Good lord, nobody's here!

SECRETARY: They're capable of anything. Let's get out of here before they come and take you away. [*Takes a bankbook from her purse.*] I had a few thousand lira in my bank account. I took them out. We can go to the village where my aunt lives and hide out. And then you can divorce your wife and marry me. I even found the farm that we imagined. Cows, chickens, rabbits . . .

PROFESSOR: Don't talk nonsense.

SECRETARY: From now on you're mine. Everybody else has abandoned you. I'm the only one left. I'll be with you to the very end—the light of your dark days. Yes, your dark days. Someday we'll write all this down and be rich.

PROFESSOR: I'm not going. [*Runs to his chair and grabs its arms.*] I won't leave! I won't leave even if the world stops turning. They can't tear me away. Death before dishonor. [*The phone rings.*] Hello . . . Party chairman? Is the secretary-general with you? . . . Yes, that's my decision. . . . I see nothing to laugh at. . . . [*Opens his eyes in amazement.*] How? What? . . . Two Orange Party MPs just died? Today? . . . So now, if I switch parties, it will be 280 to 279. [*To the* SECRETARY.] What an unhappy coincidence! [*Laughter is heard from the phone.*] Damn! What? . . . My wife's there, too, by coincidence?

How come? . . . Is she offering me advice? . . . I don't want it. Damnation! [*Hangs up.*] I understand everything now . . .

SECRETARY: What did I tell you? Let's run away without losing more time. [*The* PROFESSOR *opens his desk drawer and rummages frantically for his revolver. Finds it.*] No, don't do this. Not like this. First me. Then you. We have to stick together no matter what. [*Jumps in front of him.*] No, me first. Me first. Hand in hand.

PROFESSOR: [*Pulls the trigger, then looks in the cylinder.*] Those unprincipled thugs! They took out the bullets. Now what am I to do? [*Cradles his head in his hands and begins contemplating, in the same position as in Act I. Lights go out. The* SECRETARY *disappears in the dark. Ticktock of the clock. Marches and anthems (same as in Act I). Again the applause from outside ("Hurrah! Hurrah!"). On the wall, we again see the framed picture of the old professor with a beard. The file cabinets turn into bookcases. The same set as in Act I. The clock ominously strikes seven. The* PROFESSOR *takes the box of cigarettes left by the* SECRETARY-GENERAL. *Throws it away. As the music rises to a climax, he reaches for the phone. In contrast to his previous frantic behavior, he speaks in a calm and pitiable manner.*] Hello? Secretary-General? . . . No, unfortunately I won't be able to accept your offer of candidacy. I thank you for the honor, but please accept my apologies. . . . What have I been thinking? I've been thinking a lot of things. I can't explain it on the phone. As you know, I have a bit of an unhealthy imagination. . . . Groundless worries? Perhaps . . . Prone to exaggeration? Possibly. Forgive me. It's impossible. [*Family and household members, who have been waiting outside with great curiosity, rush in, dressed as they were in Act I.*]

ASSOCIATE: This is exactly what we expected from you, Professor. My congratulations.

FATHER-IN-LAW: You ruined the whole damn thing, Son.

WIFE: [*To her* FATHER.] Didn't I tell you that he was losing his mind?

PROFESSOR: [*Puts his hands over his eyes.*] I had a terrible nightmare.

ASSOCIATE: [*Knowingly.*] I can imagine.

SON: [*Barging in explosively.*] Did you say yes, Dad?

WIFE: Unfortunately no, dear. He's ruined the first and last chance of his life.

SON: You were my last hope. Tomorrow is the faculty meeting at school. That means I've flunked again.

PROFESSOR: May that be all we lose.

SON: But you promised me a motorcycle if I passed.

PROFESSOR: I wouldn't have bought it for you even if you'd passed.

SON: Why not?

PROFESSOR: You'd probably run over somebody again and get us into trouble. [*The* SON *looks at his* MOTHER, *and she signals that the* PROFESSOR *is unbalanced. The* PROFESSOR *opens his drawer and takes out a revolver-shaped lighter to light his cigarette.*] Oh, this is a real relief. What a nightmare, what a nightmare. I'm as overjoyed as if I were born into a new world.

BROTHER-IN-LAW: [*Enters.*] Your decision, dear brother-in-law? The nation is waiting for it. And I nominate myself as your personal secretary from now on. Don't promise anyone else.

FATHER-IN-LAW: [*Shakes his head.*] Useless.

SERVANT: [*From the door.*] The reporters are still waiting.

PROFESSOR: No need for them. Why would they want to see me? I'm no longer the man of the hour.

ASSOCIATE: [*Looks at the portrait on the wall in a kind of ecstasy.*] Even he's smiling on your momentous decision.

PROFESSOR: I'm going out to the garden to see my rabbits. [*Exits.*]

FATHER-IN-LAW: All this wasn't worth going without food since morning. [*To his* DAUGH-TER.] Don't people eat dinner here? My stomach is growling.

WIFE: Sure, let's go downstairs. [*All except the* WIFE *and the* ASSOCIATE *begin to exit.*] Won't you come, too?

ASSOCIATE: [*Starts to go with the others, but suddenly stops.*] You go on down, I'll be along in a minute. [*Stands in the doorway until he is sure they are downstairs, then picks up the phone. Speaks quietly, covering his mouth with his hand.*] Hello. Ruling party? It's me. I convinced the professor to turn down the opposition party's offer. It wasn't easy, but it's done. I'm a man of my word. Don't worry about this district. I'll be at the club soon. I'd like my commission this evening. . . . Yes, the figure we agreed on. No checks. Cash . . . Not at all. . . . Absolutely! Good-bye and good luck. [*The portrait on the wall suddenly falls and shatters. The* ASSOCIATE *draws back in fear and amazement. Turns to look at the portrait.*]

CURTAIN

◆　　◆　　◆

In Ambush

CAHİT ATAY

Translated by Talat S. Halman

An Editor's Note

Pusuda *(In Ambush)* is a small-scale tour de force that enjoyed impressive success in Turkey's major cities and in some rural towns. Although hardly a masterpiece, it ranks among the better achievements of modern Turkish theater. In a brief introduction Cahit Atay (b. 1925) wrote when the play was published in book form in 1961, he mentions that he felt akin to Yeats, although he seems to have a closer resemblance to O'Casey. Atay is vitally attuned to his soil and his people, both dramatically and politically.

Cahit Atay is at his best when dealing with short dramatic treatments, compact plots, and few characters. *In Ambush* displays the playwright's strengths (as well as some of his forgivable weaknesses). The action is built around three characters: Yılanoğlu the Ağa, a small-time feudal lord; Dursun, a numbskull peasant, a sort of village idiot; and Yaşar, the university-educated son of a local family. The Ağa has his eye on a girl betrothed to Yaşar, who, having just received his law degree, is imminently expected to return to the village. Anxious to remove Yaşar from his path, the Ağa, after much ballyhoo and bullying, persuades Dursun to shoot Yaşar. The incident, the Ağa claims, will catapult Dursun to the exalted status of a hero. Yaşar makes his appearance, taking Dursun by surprise. They happen to be old friends, and Yaşar deftly talks Dursun out of the bloody deed. The Ağa, infuriated because his prey has evaded the ambush, lashes out at Dursun, who, quite by accident, shoots the Ağa himself, thereby attaining the promised heroic stature.

Out of the tiny plot, Atay derives several morals that hold social significance for Turkey as well as philosophical connotations in a more universal context. Feudal domination, he implies, is doomed to crumble before the alliance of the underprivileged and the intellectual, even though the alliance may seem fortuitous. Heroism tends to assert itself less by what man creates than by what he destroys. Usurpation ultimately brings its own downfall.

Naive as these morals sound, they had an acute relevance in the Turkey of the 1960s, where the problem of landowners versus peasants (or the exploiter versus the exploited) erupted as a burning social issue. The timeliness of its morals accounted in part for *Pusuda*'s popularity with diverse Turkish audiences, urban and rural alike. The play, however, derives much of its impressive appeal from its dramatic merits—the hilariously comic

145

element in Dursun's character, Atay's crisp and lilting usage of colloquial Turkish, and the earthy impact of the three sharply delineated *personae*.

The action, though brief, has swift, inept, and inexplicable turns. Because the plot does not follow a well-structured cause-and-effect pattern, it seems clipped or disrupted at times. The trio of characters does not form a triangular dramatic relationship. *Pusuda* might have been more forceful in conveying its valid message had the playwright brought the Ağa and Yaşar together on the stage. One conjectures that the play would have benefited substantially from a wider scope of character treatment in terms of motives and conflicts.

Atay had a very limited formal education. Quitting high school, he had brief stints as a village teacher, staff member of the Meteorological Institute, clerk at an attorney's office, designer, and the like. He also wrote radio plays for Radio Ankara.

In 1950, he founded the Yurt Theater. His first major success came in 1959 when the Turkish State Theater staged his first full-fledged play entitled *Pervaneler* (The Moths). In this play and several subsequent ones, as in *In Ambush*, which was first produced in 1961, Atay concentrated on the problems of rural Turkey—blood feud, the ruthlessness of feudal lords, the peasants' inability to adjust to living and working in the urban areas, and so on. He also tried his hand at a few vaudevilles, but his principal contributions to Turkish dramatic literature have been bittersweet rural tragicomedies.

Some of Atay's plays, which left their imprint on dramatic realism, were made into films. Among the numerous awards he won is the Ministry of Culture Prize in 1993.

The translation is by Talat S. Halman, whose biography appears on pp. 477–78.—TSH

Characters

AĞA, a big landowner and minor feudal lord, whose actual name is YILANOĞLU (literally, "Son of a Snake")

DURSUN, a farmhand

YAŞAR, a young attorney fresh out of law school

[*The action takes place in rural Turkey around the middle of the twentieth century.*

A desolate spot by a bumpy country road. Across from it, a small mound covered with bushes and brambles. Fields stretch to the mountains in the background.

A sunny morning. YILANOĞLU *enters left. His thick eyebrows, big mustache, and enormous watch chain immediately catch the eye. He is the typical* ağa *with his shiny boots, velvet riding trousers, navy-blue vest, and double-breasted jacket. He wears his faded felt hat slightly slanted to the left.*

He appears annoyed and anxious as he looks down the road. He dips his hand into his vest pocket and takes out his watch. He gets so impatient and jittery that he becomes

almost mechanical as he glances in quick succession at the watch, the left side of the road, and then the right side. It is apparent that he is in a great hurry and waiting for someone. Another glance to his left, and his strange mechanical motions stop. Greatly relieved, he sticks his watch back into the vest pocket. With his hands clasped behind his back, he stands and waits, as if that nervous man is gone and has been replaced by someone who is hard as rock and cold as ice.

In a moment, DURSUN *enters, panting and sweating. Everything he is wearing is tattered. Except for the occasional glimmer of the double-barreled hunting shotgun hanging from his shoulder, he looks shabby and dismal from top to toe. He is a young man with a stupid look in his eyes. There are big patches on the haunches and knees of his trousers, and the cuffs have been tucked into his embroidered wool socks. He has on old, large army boots. His shirt is filthy. On his head, he wears an old straw hat with the brim practically gone. Over his left shoulder hangs a makeshift hunting bag made of cloth.*]

AĞA: Damn it, where have you been?

DURSUN: [*Frightened.*] I'm real sorry, Boss . . . I was doing . . . I mean . . . in the field . . .

AĞA: Never mind the field!

DURSUN: [*Guilelessly.*] Don't say that, Boss. The field is all I got.

AĞA: Damn you, what did I tell you?

DURSUN: [*Cheers up.*] You sure told me. When you asked me to get my double-barrel and come here, I figured it all out anyway. I said to myself, "We're going partridge hunting." [*Suddenly.*] Let's go up to Forkhill! How about it, Boss? Right now, all those bushes must be teeming with partridges. [*Eyes the* AĞA.] Now, you ain't gonna hunt with these clothes on, are you? Besides, where's your gun?

AĞA: Well, you got yours, right?

DURSUN: Sure thing. Gee, I'm stupid. The boss ain't gonna run up and down hills and valleys, is he now? Boss, just don't give it another thought. Come, sit under the tree. Make yourself at home. Meanwhile, I'll take a look around. Believe me, if I want to, I can wipe out all the partridges around here. Look, you want me to come back with enough of them for you and your drinking buddies to eat for a whole week? Man, I tell you, I can fill this bag with partridges in no time. Just wait and see, Ağa. You're gonna be so proud of your farmhand Dursun.

AĞA: [*Imperiously.*] Go behind that mound over there. [DURSUN *does as he is told. The* AĞA *walks over to the right side of the road, turns around, and takes slow steps toward the mound.*] Aim! Take aim at me!

DURSUN: [*Stunned.*] At you, Boss? God forbid!

AĞA: Look, I didn't say shoot, did I? Save your appetite for later.

DURSUN: What is this? You testing me?

AĞA: Idiot. We're just rehearsing a plan.

DURSUN: Come off it. Nothing is easier than shooting a man from here. God knows, every day I shoot five, ten crows in the field.

AĞA: [*Looks to the right of the road; then walks over to* DURSUN.] Come out. [*Kneels by the mound. Takes out his cigarette case, taps it on the side, and opens it. To* DURSUN.] Go on, kneel. [DURSUN *crouches reluctantly, rests the shotgun on his lap. Frightened, eyeing the* AĞA, *he waits for him to speak. Rolling a cigarette, the* AĞA *talks sternly.*] You're gonna lie there—behind the mound. [*Brusquely.*] Get it?

DURSUN: [*Without having understood anything.*] Yeah. I get it, all right.

AĞA: Atta boy! [*Holds out the cigarette case as if doing a great act of kindness.*] Take it. Roll one.

DURSUN: [*Doesn't dare.*] No. You mind if I don't?

AĞA: I'm telling you to roll one. [DURSUN *takes the case as if he is holding fire. Looking incredulous, he starts to roll a cigarette with shaky hands. The* AĞA *sticks his cigarette into his amber cigarette holder and lights it.*] You're gonna hold the gun—and fire. That's all. [DURSUN *looks absentminded as he struggles with the cigarette, as though rolling a cigarette with tobacco from the* AĞA's *case has made him deaf. The* AĞA *blares.*] Tell me, is there anyone bigger than me in this town?

DURSUN: [*Stops rolling the cigarette.*] No such thing.

AĞA: [*Challenging.*] Can anyone dare take a stand against me? Is anyone brave enough? [DURSUN *gets frightened. Gives up his struggle to roll a cigarette, which he is unable to do anyway. Hands the cigarette case back to the* AĞA.] And how about you, man? What's with you? [*Angrily puts the case in his pocket.*]

DURSUN: [*Cringes, still thinking of the cigarette case.*] I . . . I just couldn't roll it.

AĞA: Man, try to make something of yourself. What can you expect from being a farmworker? [*Like an orator.*] Listen here, you scum! Have you no sense of honor? Have you no integrity? Have you no dignity? You and the rest of you poor bastards—you people are like sheep, you know!

DURSUN: [*Inches away from where he was crouching.*] God knows, Boss . . .

AĞA: You ever go to the coffeehouse?

DURSUN: Uhh . . . after a day's work in the field . . .

AĞA: Well, let's say you went to the coffeehouse. Who gives a damn? You're nobody. Working in that field, you've turned into a scarecrow. No one in the coffeehouse will even look at you, you know that. Man, you're no better than the butcher's dog. [*Pause.*] But me?

DURSUN: They're scared of you, Boss. Most of those people haven't got the guts to come near you.

AĞA: You bet your life that's the way it is. But why?

DURSUN: Your name is Yılanoğlu. You've got a name! You're the lord here.

AĞA: That mantle didn't fall on my shoulders from Heaven, did it, now? I earned it all with hard work, with the sweat of my brow. You better get that straight! I toppled a couple of fellows, that's how. Just mowed them down in the street, at the marketplace. I've committed enough crimes to last my family for seven generations. My sons and their sons can just lie on their backs and enjoy themselves. No one will dare come near them, let alone touch them. [*Pause.*] How about you?

DURSUN: [*Dejected.*] You're absolutely right. Nobody gives a damn about me. Like you said, just a scarecrow. Crows mock me—they're not afraid or anything—they come and sit on the scarecrow, on me, all the time.

AĞA: [*Points to the shotgun.*] But once you fire that! See, that's why I want to do you a big favor.

DURSUN: [*Full of hope.*] I knew it, I knew it. The Great Yılanoğlu . . . I said to myself, "If Yılanoğlu, whose fame has spread all over these parts, calls me in, there's got to be something to it."

AĞA: [*Gives him advice.*] This is the opportunity of a lifetime. Use your head, man. Get it into your head that someone is fond of you. There's a whole bunch of guys in this town who'd love to volunteer for this job. If I'd had an announcement made on the PA system at the public square, you wouldn't even have gotten into the waiting line. That's why I didn't let anyone know. I swear to God I just want to give a poor fellow a little boost.

DURSUN: [*As if the AĞA has made him a gift of a whole farm.*] How can I thank you enough?

AĞA: Well, you can get a good rest in the pen. Five years, maybe ten. It's like a school. You'll learn how to write petitions. And you'll get a chance to talk to people.

DURSUN: What do you mean—"the pen"?

AĞA: No, no, no. You're not going to have any thoughts of escaping. A real man never escapes. If you do something, make sure it's perfect, my son. Escape? That's what a woman does. Now, what's that you were saying?

DURSUN: You know best.

AĞA: Besides, your old lady—instead of staying home and going to waste, she can work in the field and open up a little bit. Once you come out of the pen . . . oh boy, when you are released, the minute you walk into that coffeehouse, just imagine all the wonderful things that'll happen to you. God knows, they'll lead you to the best table. You can just name all the things you want. Tea and coffee will flow like anything. All those girls walking by this road here—they'll fall all over Dursun. I bet you might even marry into one of the town's wealthy families. You want me to keep telling you about all the benefits? You're gonna own orchards and gardens, fields and lots. Man, maybe you'll get a horse, too.

DURSUN: [*Dreamily.*] You don't say, Boss?

AĞA: You bet your life. [*Looks at the road.*]

DURSUN: [*With great excitement, grabs the AĞA's hand and kisses it.*] You're a great boss . . . the best . . . I knew it, I knew there was something in all this. Great Yılanoğlu. You want me to be your slave? I'll be your slave for life. You know, there are guys who say, "Yılanoğlu is cruel." Goddamn liars!

AĞA: [*Doesn't hear; keeps watching the road.*] Tell me, lad, you know how harmful those crows are for your field. [*Points to the road.*] That son of a bitch is bad for the whole town. Upstart, that's what he is. You follow me? Look here, anyone can shoot partridges and crows. [*Pause.*] He'll come this way in just a short while. You know him. Yaşar . . .

DURSUN: The son of the Kulaksız family?

AĞA: That's him.

DURSUN: Sure, I know him. He grew up in our neighborhood. [*Tries to find a grudge against* YAŞAR.] We used to play knucklebones, and he used to beat me.

AĞA: There you are. You ought to hold that against him.

DURSUN: Didn't he go to school, Boss?

AĞA: He did, damn it. I wish he hadn't. His uncle took care of his education.

DURSUN: I know him, too—Blind İbrahim.

AĞA: We told him: "Man, don't send this youngster to school. Have him work for you." But how can you talk to the blind about colors? He sold his land and orchards and put the lad through school. A big school, one of the top schools, too. Now they say Yaşar is going to open a law office in town. There you are. [*Angrily.*] And they say he's going to marry Zehra. You know, the widow's daughter. He's going to squander everything she owns. Well, we did our best to warn them, but what do they know? They're waiting for that son of a bitch. Zehra's mother—they say—bought God knows how many pounds of meat from the butcher. A huge amount. Hey, wake up!

DURSUN: Oh my God!

AĞA: All for him—get it? You know, you're gonna do a great service. Once he feels he's on top of the world, no one can hold him back, I tell you. [*Points to the shotgun.*] That's different, though. [*Points at the mound.*] Lie back there, like before. Remember the way I was walking toward the mound? Yeah, like that . . . [*Taps* DURSUN *on the shoulder, then looks at his watch.*] He must be on his way. My horse is back there by the big plane tree. I'd better go there and take a nap. When I hear the shots, I'll come running. You have nothing to worry about. I'll take care of the rest.

DURSUN: [*Proudly.*] With God's permission, I'm gonna do it, Boss.

AĞA: Well, so long for a while. [*Comes back before exiting.*] In military service, they make you repeat your orders. I was a sergeant. [*Sternly.*] What'll you do?

DURSUN: [*Instinctively stands at attention.*] I mean . . . like . . . well . . .

AĞA: That won't do. You're supposed to say: "I lie in ambush behind the mound and fire at the Kulaksız boy, sir!"

DURSUN: Just don't worry about it.

AĞA: All right, then.

DURSUN: [*Imagines himself as important as the* AĞA.] Good-bye, Yılanoğlu.

AĞA: [*Returns.*] Did you just call me "Yılanoğlu"? Only two people call me "Yılanoğlu": Rifat, my friend who owns the club, and my wife. Damn it, right away you grow too big for your britches. You're gonna do a measly little thing, that's all. In the middle of nowhere, you're gonna take a couple of shots from an ambush.

DURSUN: [*Cowers.*] Forgive me . . . I mean . . . I was gonna say "Boss."

AĞA: Everyone should know who he is and what his place is in life. [*Rubs it in.*] You're quite a fella, you know. [*Forces a smile.*] Hold the shotgun over to the other side, will you, sonny? [*Points to the road.*]

DURSUN: [*Stares behind him after he is sure that the* AĞA *is gone.*] God must be on my side. What a windfall . . . I used to wrack my brains about this son of a gun. Now look what happens. Who would have thought—Yılanoğlu spilling his secrets to Dursun the farm boy? [*Strokes the shotgun and grins stupidly.*] So, this is the way it is, eh? Well, this is the only life I'm gonna live. [*Faces the side where the* AĞA *made his exit.*] It's a godsend for sure. . . . Son of a gun really sang this time. [*Suddenly grimaces; holding his groin, he writhes in pain.*] Oh my God . . . [*As if weeping.*] You reap what you sow. When you work like a dog and get no rest, you sure get a lot of bellyache. I better lie down for a moment. [*Remembers* YILANOĞLU.] I know, Boss, I know. [*Pulls himself together, but when the pain starts again, he sits down by the mound, holding onto the shotgun. Yawns.*] It's killing me—all this hoeing, all this farmwork. I tell you, I'm finished. [*His eyes droop. He falls asleep. The gun slides out of his hands.*]

[*In a moment,* YAŞAR *enters right, off the road. He has spectacles. He is a young man with a bright, breezy face and a kindly expression. He is wearing a sports shirt and casual trousers. There is a handkerchief around his neck—presumably to keep perspiration away. He carries a small suitcase. Notices* DURSUN.]

YAŞAR: [*Walks over to* DURSUN *and takes a close look.*] Ah, this is my friend Dursun.

[*Without making any noise,* YAŞAR *takes the gun away. Moving impishly and tiptoeing, he goes over to the bushes and hides the gun. Then he crouches beside* DURSUN *and whistles in his ear the tune of their school song.* DURSUN, *in his sleep, begins to mumble the tune.* YAŞAR *whistles the tune louder.* DURSUN *sings it louder.*]

DURSUN: [*As if dreaming.*] Oh boy, we really sang that song. All of us together. The big house next to the school used to echo when we sang. Women and girls would rush to the windows. [*Opens his eyes; looks in the direction of* YAŞAR, *who is still whistling.*] My God. [*His eyes bulge.*] Yaşar? [*Still reminiscing.*] They used to kick me out of school, saying I was too dumb. And boys always made fun of me. [*To* YAŞAR.] When you wanted to play hooky, you always made me take your place during roll call. Remember, pal? [YAŞAR *nods and goes on whistling.* DURSUN, *nostalgically.*] Yeah, man. In those days, you used to whistle just like now. Your nickname was "Whistling Boy." Remember how that religious guy once chased you with a big stick?

YAŞAR: [*Laughs.*] I sure do. He kept saying, "Whistling Boy attracts all the demons to the neighborhood!" [*Gets up and spreads open his arms.*] Come, my friend. You are my childhood—my carefree, colorful childhood.

DURSUN: [*With great excitement, rises to his feet and embraces* YAŞAR.] Hey, friend! My one and only black-eyed Yaşar. [*Is suddenly embarrassed about his tattered clothes; lets his arms drop to his sides.* YAŞAR *insists on hugging him, though.*]

YAŞAR: [*Not letting go, he keeps hugging.*] My friend Dursun!

DURSUN: [*Breaks away, hesitant, his eyes filled with tears.*] So that's the way it goes, huh? You've become a gentleman. But me . . . [*Angrily.*] I'm a measly little farmhand. [*Suddenly starts looking around.*] Where the hell is my gun?

YAŞAR: What gun? Are you out hunting, Dursun?

DURSUN: [*Keeps looking about.*] That gun is all I got. Without it . . . my hands will be tied. Crows will ravage the field. [*Turns around and glares at* YAŞAR.] Never mind the field . . .

YAŞAR: Don't worry, Dursun. [*Walks over and takes the gun from where he had hidden it.*] I put it away. Just a joke. [*Returns the shotgun to* DURSUN.]

DURSUN: [*Grabs the gun and immediately takes his position behind the mound, aiming at* YAŞAR.] Hope you don't mind, pal, but I gotta shoot you!

YAŞAR: [*Laughs incredulously.*] Shoot me? Why?

DURSUN: What do I know? I take a shot at a flock of crows, and one crow falls dead.

YAŞAR: Well, maybe there is good reason to shoot crows.

DURSUN: Say what you want. I gotta kill you.

YAŞAR: Dursun . . .

DURSUN: Go on, tell me.

YAŞAR: Are you serious? [*Gently.*] Oh, Dursun . . . you're being a kid all over again. At this age, you're playing cops and robbers, huh?

DURSUN: [*Harshly.*] It sure breaks my heart, but it's gotta be this way.

YAŞAR: Which means . . . you . . . well, then, what's the reason?

DURSUN: [*On the verge of tears.*] Goddamn. Am I supposed to stay this way forever? Tell me, should I creep and crawl all the time? Like the butcher's dog. Am I not even supposed to go to the coffeehouse, huh? I shouldn't have my own field and tools, my own horse, is that it? And am I not supposed to get married? [*Timidly.*] Now, if I . . . I mean, if I do this to you . . . if I shoot you—excuse me, pal—people will think highly of me, you see.

YAŞAR: I get it, Dursun, now I know. It's always this way. In order for one person to amount to something, another person has to be done away with. What a shame.

DURSUN: Why must you hammer it in? I told you, one crow will fall dead.

YAŞAR: One crow falls. All right, dear friend, shoot. But something must have gone wrong between the two of us. [*Tries persuasion.*] I feel sorry for you. Dursun, the killer feels more pain than the victim does. When you go into the coffeehouse, a voice will rise above that din and ask you: "What had he done to you?" Won't it? Let's say you're all settled; you have your land and house and your wife, and you're about to dip your spoon into your soup, when you suddenly hear that voice asking you: "Crows had to be killed because they were digging up all the seeds. But Yaşar? How about Yaşar?" Tell me, when you hear that question, aren't you going to drop your spoon? Will you be able to walk by these thickets of red berries and remain calm? Will you be able to rip open the cool, bloodred watermelon? Tell me.

DURSUN: You used to beat me at knucklebones.

YAŞAR: But who saved you from drowning in the lake?

DURSUN: Yeah, man, you're right. I'd forgotten that. [*Walks up to* YAŞAR.] You're a good kid, Yaşar. [*Implores him.*] Let's find some reason, huh? We got ages till nighttime. [*Keeps pleading.*] Please, Yaşar, please.

YAŞAR: Let's find something.

DURSUN: You know how dumb I am. You went to school and all. Come on, prove yourself.

YAŞAR: I'll do my best, Dursun. [*Pondering.*] Is there a blood feud between us?

DURSUN: [*Hopefully.*] Is there?

YAŞAR: I can't think of anything like that.

DURSUN: You're right, damn it. [*Pauses. Keeps pulling up his pants and ponders anxiously.*]

YAŞAR: [*Stretches, looking at the sun.*] Oh, such a marvelous day.

DURSUN: [*Annoyed.*] This is no time to talk about the weather, is it, pal? [*He, too, cannot help yawning and stretching.*] Wouldn't it be just great to take a nap under the plane trees? [*As he is about to lie down, he remembers* YILANOĞLU, *straightens up, and mutters to himself.*] He wouldn't come to us. Who are we, after all? He is the big man around here.

YAŞAR: Well, OK, but there has to be a reason for what you're talking about. If it was wartime, that would be different: You'd drop your hoe, I'd throw away my pen—we'd both go. When the sky is as ruthlessly blue as it is now . . . instead of dying like this, we would try to kill or even to die, for that matter. But in wartime there would be plenty of reasons: that's when we would pull the trigger to get rid of the infidel and the enemy. [*Emphatically.*] Are there any such orders, Dursun?

DURSUN: [*Evasively.*] No.

YAŞAR: Then what are we supposed to do? We have no old grudge. [*Suddenly.*] How about it? Let me insult you . . . spit in your face . . .

DURSUN: What's the matter with you, man?

YAŞAR: Just trying to find a good cause. I feel I'm letting you down, and it breaks my heart to do that. You see, I am a humanist.

DURSUN: [*Aims at* YAŞAR *immediately.*] Now say that again.

YAŞAR: Say what?

DURSUN: You said something, remember?

YAŞAR: Humanist.

DURSUN: Man, I used to think of a communist like an eagle or an owl. So you are one of those types, huh? Well, buddy, you gave yourself away. You're a communist, and you expect me not to shoot you?

YAŞAR: Don't mix them up. Some of our educated people mistake one for the other. But must you? "Humanist," not "communist." Also, I admire the Greeks.

DURSUN: My, my! He fell into his own trap again. He is a friend of the Greeks!

YAŞAR: Of the ancient Greeks.

DURSUN: If you think you can put me on . . . there's no such thing as an old infidel and a new infidel. You're not playing this game right, you know. I got things to do.

YAŞAR: And how about me? [*Dreamily.*] I'm going to open a law office and start serving the townsfolk.

DURSUN: I swear to God, they'll make life miserable for you. They're such a bunch of swindlers. Remember the mayor? No matter how hard he tried, he couldn't make a go of it. In the end, he hanged himself. You better listen to what I say, brother. You'll get sick and tired; you'll go searching for some other place where you can die in peace. Forget it, huh? You were doing all right with that Greek stuff. What do you say?

YAŞAR: That's fine. Let's leave everything until the day I go searching for a place where I can die in peace.

DURSUN: [*Offended, he lowers his gun.*] Oh, it's just dandy, ain't it? I'll remain the scum of the earth, working as a farmhand. Day in and day out I'll look into your eyes, asking you, "You wanna die?" so that I'll lead a better life at long last. No, buster, I won't go in for that stuff. [*All of a sudden screams with joy.*] Yippee! I got an idea! Some years back, your father had my father beaten. My mother used to tell the story. I understand they went to court. Now, what have you got to say to that? [*Aims the shotgun.*]

YAŞAR: [*Shakes his head.*] No. I heard it from my uncle. The way it happened, Yılanoğlu arranged the whole thing and then tried to blame it on my father.

DURSUN: Yılanoğlu doesn't go in for beatings. He wipes the guys out.

YAŞAR: Well, buddy, you can take a look at the court records.

DURSUN: Let's go, then.

YAŞAR: Actually, my father was acquitted.

DURSUN: [*Just as they are about to exit.*] Shucks! You know what? The government building burned down the other day—and all the court records with it.

YAŞAR: That's true. I read about it in the papers. They claim one of the big shots had it burned down.

DURSUN: Honest?

YAŞAR: What else do you expect? Undoubtedly someone from Yılanoğlu's party.

DURSUN: Man, I wish that son of a bitch were here instead of you.

YAŞAR: You mean Yılanoğlu?

DURSUN: [*Fearfully.*] Are you kidding? Who is brave enough to pull a gun on Yılanoğlu? You don't think bullets could go through that son of a bitch, do you? [*Obsessed with the idea.*] The man who shoots Yılanoğlu is bound to become famous all over the world. You know, they'd write ballads about him.

YAŞAR: [*Emotionally.*] I don't care for those songs. They are as sharp as knives, as bitter as poison. They oppress the heart. How will you listen to them, Dursun, when they are saying, "They shot Yaşar on the way from the railroad station"? Do you think you would be able to listen to a song like that?

DURSUN: [*Saddened.*] I just couldn't. Man, it would tear my heart out. Remember the ballad about that poor young man—"They shot Recep by the bridge." His fiancée wrote that song.

YAŞAR: You know, Dursun, I have a fiancée, too—Zehra.

DURSUN: [*Pulls himself together.*] You don't think the widow's daughter is gonna sing a song of lament for you, do you? No, brother, don't eat your heart out. You needn't worry about her.

YAŞAR: Why's that?

DURSUN: Never mind. Just listen to what I'm saying.

YAŞAR: Oh. Zehra is free and open. She's on her own. She sings. She's not like some of the girls who used to be kept behind lattices and veils. But the townspeople . . .

DURSUN: Well, each person's sins . . .

YAŞAR: [*Sensitive about all matters relating to Zehra.*] I don't follow.

DURSUN: I hear she's flirting with Rıza, the hosiery guy.

YAŞAR: As I said, it's all gossip. When Zehra goes into Rıza's shop to buy socks, people think something goes on in there. Those are narrow-minded people.

DURSUN: What have you got to say about Yılanoğlu?

YAŞAR: [*Emphatically.*] Did Yılanoğlu stick his nose into this, too?

DURSUN: The man is the lord of this region. He does whatever he damn pleases. What can you do about it?

YAŞAR: Zehra and Yılanoğlu. [*Laughs as if he is anxious to chase bad thoughts away.*] My Zehra is like a sunflower, Dursun. The sunflower always follows the sun or the moon or whatever sheds light. [*Contemptuously.*] What would she do with that man who is like the darkest night?

DURSUN: Whatever Yılanoğlu wants, Yılanoğlu gets. I hear even his wife says she likes the girl.

YAŞAR: Did you say his wife? Yılanoğlu's wife?

DURSUN: I said his wife, all right. I am told that the wife says she is going to get Zehra to be Yılanoğlu's second wife. That woman is such a pig. She knows what she's doing. She claims she's gonna arrange the second marriage herself. You get it, don't you? She's doing it because when Yılanoğlu takes Zehra, he'll come home instead of spending his nights away. The woman knows she is washed up.

YAŞAR: [*Almost mumbling to himself.*] It's frightful. Even talking about it is horrendous. A wife who arranges for a second wife for her own husband. My God, it's so disgusting. It's impossible to live a life like this.

DURSUN: [*Aims the gun.*] You said it. Buddy, you've come around to my view, haven't you?

YAŞAR: [*Pensively.*] That couldn't be. There are such things as conscience and justice.

DURSUN: [*Misunderstands him.*] You said it's impossible to live, right?

YAŞAR: [*Doesn't hear, absorbed in thought.*] Give me that thing.

DURSUN: [*Gleefully hands him the gun.*] That's what I call a hero. You're gonna do it your-self, huh?

YAŞAR: [*Looks at the gun with contempt.*] This double-barrel . . . cold steel . . . gunpowder . . . buckshot . . .

DURSUN: Yeah, all that.

YAŞAR: [*Takes aim at DURSUN and keeps talking.*] The gun that was aimed at me . . .

DURSUN: [*Frightened.*] Heaven help me, am I the target now?

YAŞAR: Remember the enmity between us?

DURSUN: [*Trembling.*] For heaven's sake, Yaşar, my best friend Yaşar, we couldn't find any reason for a grudge . . .

YAŞAR: [*Continues.*] Treachery . . . animosity, blood, death.

DURSUN: [*Imploring.*] You're already the man you always wanted to be, Yaşar, and now you're gonna kill me, and you're gonna add honor to all the honor you already got, is that it?

YAŞAR: [*Goes on.*] The hand that tries to grab your field, someone else's orchard, another man's house . . . that hand now tries to grab Zehra, huh?

DURSUN: I swear to God, it ain't me. It's Yılanoğlu.

YAŞAR: He is all the evil things I've been talking about. He is the pistol on the hip . . . the knife . . . the hatred. Yes, this gun, too. [*Flings the gun away.*] Don't take it in your hands, Dursun. You ought to hold on to friendship and love and affection. [*Hugs DURSUN and kisses him on the cheeks.*] There's nothing like the smell of the soil, of human warmth, of friendship.

DURSUN: [*Cheerfully, with one eye on the gun.*] Never mind what the townsfolk say. They'll say anything. Oh, you know what? I hear the widow and her daughter are expecting you. They've bought a lot of meat, too. They're sure waiting for you.

YAŞAR: I know. [*Looks with emotion in the direction of the town.*] I hope the town is waiting for me, too. There are so many things I want to do there. [*Enthusiastically picks up his suitcase.*] I'd better get going. Dursun, you have to come to my wedding. [*Spiritedly walks left.*]

DURSUN: [*Quickly picks up the gun.*] What will Yılanoğlu say to me? [*Gets hold of himself, aims at YAŞAR's back.*]

YAŞAR: So long. [*Looks back as he is about to exit.*] Dursun, what's going on? Is it Yılanoğlu again?

DURSUN: [*Embarrassed; aims in the air.*] I was going after the crows. I mean, like, I wanted to fire in the air.

YAŞAR: Go ahead. Pull the trigger in our honor, to announce our friendship. [*YAŞAR waits. DURSUN pulls the trigger, and suddenly there is a downpour of confetti all over the stage.*

Astounded, they first look up, then gaze at each other. YAŞAR *gets hold of himself. Extending his free hand, he cheerfully walks over to* DURSUN.] Confetti . . .

DURSUN: What's comfy? God in heaven! These are flowers, man, apricot flowers. [*Holds his hand under the confetti.*] Damn it, what is this?

YAŞAR: You said it, Dursun, flowers. [*Points to the sky.*] Heaven's answer . . . flowers of happiness from the huge blue tree. [*Deliriously.*] You weren't going to be able to shoot me, Dursun. You couldn't have done it.

DURSUN: [*Bewildered.*] I stuffed the buckshot into this damn thing myself—and the gunpowder.

YAŞAR: [*Triumphantly.*] It turned into paper. Tiny round pretty pieces of paper. When you come to my wedding, bring your gun along. You can fire as much as you like. The whole place will light up, will be filled with the loveliest colors. [*Runs out happily.*]

DURSUN: [*Breaks and locks the shotgun.*] Satan has gotten into this. God Almighty! He has strange ways. [*Not having noticed* YAŞAR's *exit.*] Buster, you say I wasn't gonna be able to shoot you, huh? God doesn't want it.

AĞA: [*Enters at lightning speed.*] Damn you, butcher's dog! Damn coward! You let the bastard go! [DURSUN, *frightened, jumps behind the mound.*] Stupid bastard! Now you hide, huh? What were you doing a couple of minutes ago? Couldn't hit the target, is that it?

DURSUN: [*Feels guilty.*] I couldn't have, Boss.

AĞA: [*Stands with all of his awesome bulk in the middle of the road, facing* DURSUN.] Why didn't you tell me before? See how you messed everything up? You're such a coward.

DURSUN: This thing doesn't shoot, Boss.

AĞA: What thing?

DURSUN: The shots turn comfy or something . . . like paper, you know. I've never seen anything like it.

AĞA: You're raving mad. What does that mean?

DURSUN: I still can't get it.

AĞA: How can something like that happen?

DURSUN: It can. I'll swear on anything. Tiny pieces of paper . . . like snowflakes. May God strike me dead if I'm lying.

AĞA: Shut up, you dog.

DURSUN: I swear to God, I'm telling the truth. [*In a daze, points the barrel at the* AĞA.] If you don't believe me, let's try it. I'll fire the left cartridge, and you'll see for yourself.

AĞA: You bastard, you're gonna shoot me, huh?

DURSUN: Have no fear. Nothing will go wrong. Those aren't buckshot in there—just paper. [*Fires.*]

AĞA: [*Takes one step.*] You dog! [*Tumbles over at the bottom of the mound.*]

DURSUN: [*Stunned, he can't believe what has happened. After a brief pause.*] You're putting me on, Boss. This thing doesn't kill a man. [*Listens, then straightens up fearfully, and walks over to the* AĞA's *corpse.*] God Almighty! Yılanoğlu is full of holes. [*Scared.*] I swear, I . . . I'm not guilty. I just wanted to give it one more try. [*Talking to the corpse.*] Boss . . . Boss . . . My one and only boss. Get up, for heaven's sake. You sure scared me. [*Panic-stricken, he looks around.*] He's dead . . . Great Yılanoğlu . . . [*Wants to run away.*] Yılanoğlu is dead! [*Dips into his hunting bag and looks into it.*] We came to hunt partridges and just look at all the things that happened to us, man. Dursun the farmhand finished off Yılanoğlu, huh? [*Suddenly looks proud of himself.*] Why the hell shouldn't I finish him off? Isn't Dursun a real man? Don't I have my own reputation? Can't I go into the coffeehouse? [*Posing like a hero.*] "Dursun, my boy, you felled Yılanoğlu like a pine tree, didn't you?" [*Standing tall.*] "That's the way I am, pal. I shoot them down. And that's no joke, I mean business. Anyone can kill Yaşar, that's easy." [*Leans over the* AĞA's *corpse, removes the* AĞA's *watch with its chain, his cigarette case and holder, and stuffs them into his hunting bag. Throws his hat away and puts the* AĞA's *enormous hat on his own head, pulling it all the way down until it covers his ears.*] "I swear I'm not lying, pal." [*As if showing the bag to someone.*] "The watch and the cigarette case . . . all of them belonged to the Ağa. You want witnesses, you want evidence—here they are." [*The hat practically covers his eyes. With the double-barreled gun hanging down his shoulder,* DURSUN *walks left, standing erect.*] "If you don't believe me, go to the road that leads to the railway station. There, by the mound, you'll find his carcass." [*Walks out like a hero.*]

CURTAIN

◆　　◆　　◆

Sea Rose

NECATİ CUMALI

Translated by Nilbahar Ekinci

An Editor's Note

Necati Cumalı (1921–2001) was one of Turkey's most prodigious writers—a prominent poet, major novelist, excellent translator, stimulating essayist, and writer of consummate short stories. He wrote approximately thirty plays, some of which had superb productions in Turkey and abroad. No Turkish anthology featuring any twentieth-century literary genre would be complete without selections from Cumalı's work.

A lawyer by profession, Cumalı held a variety of jobs—with the Publications Office and the Directorate of Fine Arts of the Turkish Ministry of Education, Turkey's Press Office in Paris, and Radio Istanbul. He also spent some years in Tel Aviv, where his wife was stationed. In Turkey, Cumalı is remembered and admired for his engaging poems, powerful fiction, and riveting plays, which are notable especially for their depiction of female disenchantment.

Cumalı's *Boş Beşik* (Empty Cradle) was awarded the first prize at Germany's Erlangen International Theater Festival in 1955. One of his novellas, *Susuz Yaz*, which he later adapted to the stage, was made into a film that won the top award at the prestigious Berlin International Film Festival in 1963. (The play version of this novel, translated into English by Nüvit Özdoğru as *Dry Summer*, appeared in the 1976 anthology *Modern Turkish Drama*, edited by Talat S. Halman.) This prolific writer was also the recipient of numerous major Turkish awards, including the 1978 Muhsin Ertuğrul Best Play Prize and the 1981 Ministry of Culture Theater Award.

Here, Cumalı is represented by the play *Derya Gülü (Sea Rose)*, featuring the name of Captain Haşim's fishing boat, also a figurative allusion to his wife, Meryem. Cumalı himself observed in the play's revised second edition that

> *Sea Rose* takes place around the classical triangle of the theater; that of the relationship between the woman, the husband, and the lover. However, what makes the play different is that it takes place in surroundings and a setting which in turn give it a reality that reflects the daily lives of the people of the sea. While looking for happiness, the characters come across unexpected circumstances. In vain they try to set up a link between their present and their future, as all their attempts to do so are obstructed and restructured by factors beyond their control.[1]

---

1. Necati Cumalı, *Derya Gülü Aşk Duvarı, Zorla İspanyol*, 2nd rev. ed. (Istanbul: İmbat, 1969); quote translated in Talat S. Halman's review of Necati Cumalı, *Sea Rose*, translated by Nilbahar Ekinci, *World Literature Today* 66 (1992), pp. 575–76.

The three-character play, which premiered at Istanbul's Kent Players Theater during the 1963–64 season, has a great deal of concentrated power. The agon looms large from virtually the first words spoken as the curtain rises and continues unabated to the end. The tragedy of the triangle seems to have no hubris or nemesis; nothing is preordained except the inner passions. The motivating force is not concupiscence. The playwright presents his story and his protagonists within the metaphor of the sea: human tragedy, like the sea, is timeless, limitless, all-powerful, self-creating.

The language is variously terse, lyrical, intense. It is predictably the language of an accomplished poet, sometimes to such an extent that the reader or viewer may wonder if it is realistic in the case of the characters portrayed.

Sea Rose has both the raw power and the tenderness of the sea. It is one of the most moving plays to come out of Turkey, which cherishes its vibrant theatrical life.

It has regrettably proved impossible to obtain any biographical data on the translator, Nilbahar Ekinci. All we know is that she was equal to the task of doing this English translation.—TSH

Characters

MERYEM, Haşim's common-law wife in her midtwenties
CAPTAIN HAŞIM, a fisherman in his fifties
SİNAN, Haşim's hired hand, a twenty-seven-year-old fisherman

ACT I

Scene 1

[*The south coast of the Bay of Izmir; a beach near Kilizman.*

On the left: A fisherman's boat, pulled ashore. The boat has been set on a wooden wedge and is buttressed on both sides by supports. It has been covered with canvas set up in the shape of a tent, painted in lively colors (such as orange and green). On the prow, one can read the name Sea Rose *written clumsily. Beneath the writing is a crudely drawn picture of a rose.*

On the right: A one-room fisherman's hut, seen through a vertical cross section and built on a stone base half a meter high, reminding one of a shanty. On the side of the hut closer to the audience, there are two rough stone steps leading to the door. Inside, on the left and running wall to wall, is a bunk on which HAŞIM *and his common-law wife,* MERYEM, *sleep. At the head of the bunk, there is a rolled mattress. A kerosene lamp is on the wall. All around the hut there are fishing equipment, fish boxes, nets, and the broken-down furniture of a poor fisherman. Although the hut looks poor, run down, and cheap, cleanliness and tidiness strike the eye. The furniture has been kept clean and is arranged as well as possible.*

In the forefront between the boat and the hut: A tripod of stakes with a pot hanging from it. Around the fire, there are fish boxes used as chairs and a big stone.

On the outer walls of the hut hang fishing nets, left to dry.

In the background: The sea.

The season is the beginning of fall, and the time is late afternoon.

When the curtain rises, MERYEM *is squatting rear stage, near the sea, with her back to the audience. She is washing pots and pans. She goes on doing this for a while after the curtain rises. For a moment, she smoothes her skirt with a quick movement of the hand and with her shoulder straightens the hair falling over her face. She finishes what she's been doing with quick movements. She gets up and pours into the sea the water from the pot she was washing. With her elbows and the back of her right hand, she straightens her underwear and dress, which have ridden up while she was squatting. She shakes herself and, after picking up the other pots and pans and the wooden spoons, rushes to the hut. She puts down the things she is carrying right inside the door and covers them up with a cloth. She dries her hands on her skirt. She unties the small kerchief on her head, straightens her hair, and then ties the kerchief again. She takes a dress from the top of the bunk and holds it in front of herself. She holds the dress between her chin and chest, presses it down on her body and walks around, trying to see how it suits her.*

HAŞİM *enters from the right with a small wicker basket held between his right hand and his hip. He looks in the direction of the boat and turns toward the hut.*]

HAŞİM: Meryem!
MERYEM: [*From inside the hut.*] What's the matter?
HAŞİM: Are you in there?
MERYEM: Didn't you hear me?

[HAŞİM *puts the wicker basket down on the ground near the fire.*]

HAŞİM: Has anybody been here asking for me?
MERYEM: [*Still interested in the dress and without paying attention.*] No.
HAŞİM: [*Indecisive; after a short pause.*] Meryem!
MERYEM: [*To herself.*] Go to hell! [*Raises her voice.*] I said, "What's the matter?"
HAŞİM: Where the hell have you been?
MERYEM: I'm here!
HAŞİM: Answer me properly.

MERYEM: I'm here, go on!

HAŞİM: What're you doing in there?

MERYEM: [*Mumbling.*] I've had enough. [*Aloud.*] I'm coming.

HAŞİM: [*Goes near the door.*] Where did you find that dress?

MERYEM: [*Shrugs.*] Isn't it beautiful?

HAŞİM: So nobody came around looking for me? When did you come back?

MERYEM: A little while ago.

HAŞİM: Where did you find that dress?

MERYEM: The lady gave it to me.

HAŞİM: Money?

MERYEM: She gave me my money, too. [*Hands* HAŞİM *a five-lira bill that she takes out of her dress pocket.*] Here.

HAŞİM: Only five lira?

MERYEM: [*Indifferent.*] How much more should she give me? She gave me the dress, too. Whenever I go to work for her, she always gives me something I can use plus the day's wages. Last time she gave me a pair of shoes, and this time she gave me this dress.

HAŞİM: Good. Just be happy that your lady collects her old things for you.

MERYEM: Of course I'm happy. Can't you see that I'm nearly naked? What have I got to put on? [*Starts trying the dress on again.*] Isn't it beautiful?

HAŞİM: It's not for you.

MERYEM: [*Pretends not to understand.*] It's just right for me.

HAŞİM: If she was going to give you a dress, she should have given you a suitable one.

MERYEM: What's wrong with this one?

HAŞİM: It's not right for you.

MERYEM: You may not like it, but I do.

HAŞİM: You can't wear that dress, and that's that!

MERYEM: Why can't I wear it?

HAŞİM: You can't.

MERYEM: The hem is deep. It just needs to be let down a little.

HAŞİM: [*Pulls the dress out of her hands.*] Are you blind? It's got no sleeves.

MERYEM: Of course not, it's for the summer. [*Reaches out suddenly to grab the dress.* HAŞİM *throws it onto the bunk.* MERYEM *grabs it.*] All the lady's dresses are like this. Don't you see them when you walk past beautiful houses? All the women's dresses are sleeveless.

HAŞİM: [*Pulls the dress out of her hands again, crumples it up, and hurls it onto the bunk.*] You are no lady. You're Captain Haşim's wife.

MERYEM: Even Captain Haşim's wife has to live.

HAŞİM: Take a look at fishermen's wives like yourself. I won't let you go around with bare arms in front of the man who lives in this boat. So you'd better get that into your head!

MERYEM: Instead, you let me go around in rags like these.

HAŞİM: With you, one would let go of his good intentions even if he were the Prophet himself. I fired Dursun only this morning and just because of you.

MERYEM: What am I supposed to have done to Dursun?

HAŞİM: What else could you do? You took his wits away.

MERYEM: [*Lightly.*] He had no wits anyway.

HAŞİM: [*Looks for something under the bunk.*] You think you're the only clever one, but I'm cleverer than you. [*Takes out an empty wine bottle from under the bunk and gets up.*] Who drank it?

MERYEM: Well, I'll be darned. Again?

HAŞİM: Go on. Who drank it?

MERYEM: Who could drink it? You did. [*Smooths the dress and folds it.*]

HAŞİM: [*Confused.*] Me?

MERYEM: No, me, not you!

HAŞİM: [*Undecided.*] When did I drink it?

MERYEM: When? Last night, of course.

HAŞİM: Don't lie. I drank before I came home last night.

MERYEM: Just as well. When you came, the bottle was half full, and you knocked it all off.

HAŞİM: It was half full. [*Tries to remember.*] That's what I'm trying to say.

MERYEM: Well, I'm telling you. You drank it.

HAŞİM: Good heavens!

MERYEM: Leave Heaven out of it. You did drink it!

HAŞİM: It's strange. I wasn't even drunk last night.

MERYEM: [*Mocking.*] Oh no, you weren't. You were real drunk last night! Let the ones who saw you speak.

HAŞİM: I wasn't. [*Remembers.*] I gave Dursun his money and came home. I wasn't drunk last night. Don't act as if I'm getting senile. Tell me, who drank it?

MERYEM: If you're not getting senile, then keep track yourself of what you drink. Don't get me mixed up in this. Who would drink your wine? I didn't give it to my lover, did I?

HAŞİM: Mind what you're saying and don't talk dirty.

MERYEM: You mind what you're saying. You're always like this. You knock off the glass in front of you, and then you wonder who drank it. Why don't you think about this while you're drinking?

HAŞİM: Very strange. All right, isn't there any more wine in the house?

MERYEM: No.

HAŞİM: I thought we had about half a bottle.

MERYEM: Then go and find it. [*A short pause.*]

HAŞİM: So nobody came looking for me? Wherever is this lout?

MERYEM: [*Pauses while she is tidying up the room.*] Which lout?

HAŞİM: Someone was going to come to replace Dursun. I hired him and sent him here.

MERYEM: [*Continuing her work.*] He didn't come.

HAŞIM: [*Takes out the five-lira bill and then puts it in his pocket again.*] I'll go and see where he is.

MERYEM: [*Icily.*] Go and look.

HAŞIM: You can't trust this sort. Maybe he's got himself another job. I'll go and find someone else.

MERYEM: [*Mumbles half intelligibly.*] Do whatever you want to do.

HAŞIM: What are you mumbling about?

MERYEM: What should I mumble about? May God take my life and rid me of you!

HAŞIM: I'm going fishing in the morning. I need a hand.

MERYEM: Go on, go wherever you want to go. Don't fuss.

HAŞIM: I'll be back soon. The bait's outside.

MERYEM: [*Leaves the room before* HAŞIM *does.*] OK.

[HAŞIM *puts the empty wine bottle into the back pocket of his trousers and covers the bottle with his shirt.*]

[MERYEM *takes the bait basket and walks toward the seaside.*] The dirty drunkard. [*Dips the bait basket into the sea a few times and comes back.*] All he ever thinks about is the tavern.

HAŞIM: [*Comes out and starts walking in the direction that he came from.*] I'll be back soon.

MERYEM: [*Puts the bait basket on the ground near the fire.*] What shall I tell him if he comes while you're away?

HAŞIM: Tell him to sit down and wait for me. I'll be back in a quarter of an hour.

MERYEM: Leave all the cash you have on you with me.

HAŞIM: I said I'll be back.

MERYEM: You won't be back until you spend all the cash at the tavern.

HAŞIM: I have no such intention. Go on. You sit down and start preparing the bait. [*Starts to go away.*]

MERYEM: Don't be late. I wouldn't know what to do with a stranger.

HAŞIM: If he shows up, tell him to sit down and prepare the bait. [*Goes out.*]

MERYEM: [*Grumbles.*] I hope you never come back. You old drunkard. Now that you have the five lira, go drown yourself.

[MERYEM *goes into the hut. She looks out for a minute and then closes the door. She quickly takes off the dress she's wearing and puts on the dress given to her by the lady. Her new dress reaches about two inches below her knees and is long enough for a woman living in the city, but, compared to her old dress, is oddly short for a fisherman's wife.*

SİNAN *enters left. He's got his clothes in a bundle over his back. He's a hefty, handsome young man. He appears shy. He looks around irritatedly. He moves closer to the boat;*

murmuring to himself, he reads the name of the boat and moves his fingers over the picture of the rose.

MERYEM *opens the door of the hut, and with her back against the edge of the door she follows* SİNAN's *movements.*

SİNAN *turns toward the hut and sees* MERYEM.

MERYEM *at first heads back into the hut, but then pulls herself together quickly. Without changing her stance, she looks at* SİNAN *for a while.*]

Who are you looking for?

SİNAN: Is this Captain Haşim's boat?

MERYEM: Yes.

SİNAN: I'm looking for Captain Haşim. Is he here?

MERYEM: No.

SİNAN: Hasn't he come yet?

MERYEM: He's been and gone.

SİNAN: To the coffeehouse? Then I'll come back later. [*Starts to go away.*]

MERYEM: [*Goes down the stone steps.*] Are you the hand he hired?

SİNAN: [*Hesitates.*] That's me.

[MERYEM *walks past* SİNAN *and goes near the boat.*]

MERYEM: That's all right then. Get settled down in the boat and wait. [*Takes a look inside the boat.*] I'll just look to see if Dursun left anything behind.

SİNAN: Who?

MERYEM: The hired hand before you. He went away this morning. [*As she moves away from the boat.*] Nothing's left. You get settled.

[MERYEM *goes back to the hut, closes the door, and puts on her old dress.*

SİNAN *puts his bundle down on the ground in front of the boat, sits on it, leans against the boat, and lights a cigarette. Even at the first whiff, his eyes wander to the door of the hut and search for* MERYEM.

He gets up a little later, looks the boat over, and feels the stern and the canvas with his hands. He looks at the door again and picks up his bundle. MERYEM *comes out of the hut.*]

Where are you going?

SİNAN: Nowhere. I'm here.

MERYEM: Don't you like it?

SİNAN: [*Puzzled.*] Like what?

MERYEM: Not me, for sure. The boat of course.

SİNAN: It's a strong boat.

MERYEM: Why don't you put your bundle in the boat?

> [SİNAN *puts his bundle down in the steerage.* MERYEM *picks up the bait basket and points to the empty box on the other side of the basket.*]

> Sit down over there. [SİNAN *sits. They begin to prepare the bait.*] Are you a stranger?

SİNAN: Yes.

MERYEM: Where are you from?

SİNAN: Marmaris.

MERYEM: I'm from Bodrum.

SİNAN: So you're from Bodrum!

MERYEM: Why are you so surprised?

SİNAN: Well, Captain Haşim's from the Black Sea coast.

MERYEM: He's from the Black Sea coast, and I'm from Bodrum. [*Sighs.*] Surprising, but that's the way it is.

SİNAN: Bodrum's very nice. I used to go to Bodrum a lot in the old days. [*A short pause.*]

MERYEM: [*Livelier.*] It's been seven or eight years since I left Bodrum. Who knows when I'll go there again. Maybe I'll never go.

SİNAN: [*Livelier.*] I've been everywhere from İskenderun to Istanbul. The Black Sea is the only place I haven't been. But there's no castle like the one at Bodrum.

MERYEM: You're a man. A man goes wherever he wants. Of course you know all those places. I've been only in Bodrum and here.

SİNAN: I'm the one who went away from home to make a living. You always go where the bread is. But a man should have a home to live in.

MERYEM: What's wrong with it? If I were a man, I'd do the same. I'd go around. I'd see the world. Do you often go to Marmaris?

SİNAN: I haven't been there since I came back from my military service.

MERYEM: How long has it been since you came back?

SİNAN: A little more than six years.

MERYEM: That's a long time. Don't you have any relatives back there?

SİNAN: Sure I do.

MERYEM: If you have relatives, why don't you look them up?

SİNAN: I haven't had the chance. I just didn't happen to go that way.

MERYEM: Nonsense. Who do you have over there?

SİNAN: There was my mother. Who knows, maybe she's still alive. We were a big family. I had brothers and sisters. We got separated. Each one is somewhere else now, just like me.

MERYEM: Don't you ever hear from them?

SİNAN: I get news whenever somebody comes from there. It's been more than a year since I heard from my mother. She was alive then.

MERYEM: What about your brothers and sisters?

SİNAN: That's why I came here. There was one older than me. They said that he works on the boats here. Maybe I'll find him.

MERYEM: [*Thoughtful.*] What would be the use even if you found him?

SİNAN: That, you can never tell. All the same, I'm looking for him because he's my brother.

MERYEM: I don't even hear a word from my folks.

SİNAN: Where are they?

MERYEM: How would I know? I guess they're in Bodrum. [*A short pause.*] Don't you have anyone else?

SİNAN: Who do you mean?

MERYEM: Your fiancée? [*A short pause.*]

SİNAN: No.

MERYEM: Didn't you ever want to get married?

SİNAN: To want to is not enough.

MERYEM: Who knows? If you had wanted to badly enough, maybe you would have gotten married.

SİNAN: I've been working on the sea for years. How could I have got married?

MERYEM: You could have if you were a villager. All villagers are married.

SİNAN: It's because they have land. Where I come from, it's just like your Bodrum. If you have land, you plow it, get married, and have children. The one who doesn't have land is left with a piece of wood. And once you sail out to the sea in it, you can't easily settle down.

MERYEM: I'm glad you're like this. I don't like villagers.

SİNAN: Me neither.

MERYEM: It's better this way. Villagers are always stingy.

SİNAN: [*Becoming more at ease.*] I used to be a sponge diver.

MERYEM: [*Admiringly.*] Really?

SİNAN: Yes, I was a sponge diver. If I had kept on doing it, maybe I'd have had a house by now, but I quit.

MERYEM: You would, indeed. They make good money.

SİNAN: They do, but pay no heed to it. That money goes as quickly as it comes.

MERYEM: Why should it? Does anybody take it out of your pocket?

SİNAN: It just does in the sponge business. Once you know you're alive above the sea, you never think twice about the money you spend. All you have flies away in two or three days. Then you find yourself ready to go down into the depths of the sea again. You don't care whether you spend a lot of money or not. The bottom of the sea is not like the top. Say that you're in a boat on the sea, and there's a storm. The boat is wrecked and sinks. Either you drown or you survive. But once you get the bends, you've had it.

Maybe you won't die, but you'll be a cripple for life. After that, you can't do anything properly. Even if you want to beg, you won't be able to open your palm.

MERYEM: You can have an accident in every business. It isn't always that you get the bends.

SİNAN: If you're in the sponge business, you do. At sometime or another, you do. The sponge fools you. You go down twenty fathoms. Your shoulders begin to ache. But you see a sponge cluster a fathom deeper. If you're fooled and you go down and try to pull it out, you've had it.

MERYEM: Don't go down then.

SİNAN: You can't resist. The sponge fools you and pulls you down. We also used to get a share of the profit. We got shares of whatever we brought up. When you see a sponge, you say that one share of it is yours, one is the captain's, and one the boat's. Then you can't let it go. I worked for three years in the sponge business and couldn't save a penny. When Kerim got the bends, I quit.

MERYEM: Who's Kerim?

SİNAN: He was my friend. We had dived together. He got struck right next to me. They pulled him up. I didn't work in the sea after that.

MERYEM: Then what happened?

SİNAN: Nothing. Would've been better if he'd died. He didn't die, but became bedridden.

MERYEM: And you?

SİNAN: I lost my enthusiasm. [*A short pause.*]

MERYEM: So you were afraid?

SİNAN: Anybody can be afraid, depending on the situation. But fear is one thing, and what I feel is something else.

MERYEM: Yours is fear, too.

SİNAN: No, it isn't!

MERYEM: What is it, then, if it's not fear?

SİNAN: I've never known myself to be afraid of a person I see with my two eyes. You feel a pain, a weight on your shoulders, under the sea. It's as if you've got a whole camel load on your shoulders. You feel as if two hands have grabbed you and pushed you to the bottom of the sea. You take a look right and left under the water, but you can't see those two hands. You never have a tangible enemy in front of you.

MERYEM: [*Distracted.*] So you're not a coward?

SİNAN: As far as I know, I'm not, but who knows? Maybe someday I'll get scared; maybe someday there'll be someone to fear, too.

MERYEM: I'm not afraid, either. I'm not afraid of anyone. I feel afraid only when I'm sleeping. You can't protect yourself while you're asleep, that's why.

SİNAN: Right. The bottom of the sea is just like that, too. It's exactly like it is when you're asleep.

MERYEM: What is it like?

SİNAN: Just like in sleep—under the sea, you can't call anyone, you can't move about easily, and you can't hear if anyone calls you. [MERYEM *laughs*.] Why are you laughing?

MERYEM: You make me laugh.

SİNAN: Why?

MERYEM: You tell things in a different way. Kind of strange. But nice. Go on, tell me more. [SİNAN *is silent*.] Go on.

SİNAN: Is Captain Haşim usually late?

MERYEM: You never know.

SİNAN: [*Prepares the bait faster*.] Don't you know when he comes back?

MERYEM: [*Shrugs*.] It's none of my business. He can come whenever he wants to. [*Sees that* SİNAN *can't make sense of what she's said, but goes on*.] You can never tell with him. He says he'll just go for a short stroll and be back soon, but only God knows when he'll be back again.

SİNAN: Are you his wife?

MERYEM: [*Shrugs*.] Well, yes. But he's much older than me.

SİNAN: He must be in his fifties.

MERYEM: Maybe more. Who knows, maybe he's older than my father. [*Gets up*.] Are you hungry?

SİNAN: I'm not.

MERYEM: Come on, don't hesitate. I'll give you something to eat if you're hungry.

SİNAN: When I'm hungry, I'll say so.

MERYEM: You must be hungry. When are you going to eat? See, it's nearly evening.

SİNAN: I can eat any old time. Wait till the captain comes.

MERYEM: Don't wait for him to come back. [*As she goes into the hut*.] Who knows when he'll be back. [*Returns with a plate and spoon in her hand. Gives* SİNAN *the spoon and pours some soup into the plate from the pot hanging over the fire*.] Anyway, God knows when he'll be back. Sometimes he can't see what's under his nose. [*Gives the plate to* SİNAN.] Here's some fish soup.

SİNAN: Does he drink very much?

MERYEM: He's never sober. He drinks all day long. Whenever he gets hold of some money, he drinks.

SİNAN: [*Pensive*.] So he drinks a lot?

MERYEM: You know what they say—if you struck a match, he'd catch fire. He stinks of wine like an uncovered wine barrel.

SİNAN: Is he very quarrelsome?

MERYEM: Why do you ask?

SİNAN: If he starts swearing, we won't get along very well.

MERYEM: He's not that kind. You wouldn't know whether he drank or not unless you smelled his breath. Oh, and another thing is that he forgets things. He forgets very quickly what he's said or what he's done.

sİNAN: That's OK then. Let him drink.

MERYEM: Don't you drink?

sİNAN: Sometimes. I used to drink a lot when I was a sponge diver. I was also quarrelsome.

MERYEM: How do you mean?

sİNAN: Just quarrelsome. I used to pick fights with those around me for no reason at all. I was really strange in those days. But the habit passed gradually.

MERYEM: [*Smiles.*] How did you pick a fight? Tell me.

sİNAN: [*Gives the plate back and wipes his mouth with the back of his hand.*] I just did. How can I remember how now?

MERYEM: I'll give you another helping.

sİNAN: Don't bother.

MERYEM: Let me. Finish off your bread. [*Fills the plate and gives it to him.*] I wasn't hungry, but seeing you eat has made me want some. Come on, tell me. Why did you pick fights?

sİNAN: You don't need to have a reason to pick a fight. Is everything going so smoothly that you don't have to pick one?

MERYEM: Who did you fight with?

sİNAN: I don't know. I just did. Anyone would do. Owners of boats. [*Starts to get angry.*] The bastards! You put your life into it, and they bargain with you for every penny. You ask for an advance, and they tell you they don't have any money. They try to take away what is rightfully yours. This is life! It's damn well not measured with their money! Of course I didn't shut up. That's why they didn't like me. I had lots of enemies.

MERYEM: You did well. Let them not like you. What's the use if everybody loves you in this world? You'll be a nothing.

sİNAN: Sure enough. [MERYEM *laughs.*] Why are you laughing now?

MERYEM: You say "sure" to everything I say.

sİNAN: [*Gives the plate back and shrugs.*] Well, isn't that so? It was delicious. [MERYEM *walks toward the seaside with the plates in her hand.*]

MERYEM: Did you find this place easily?

sİNAN: First I walked right past here and then found it on the way back.

MERYEM: Did you ask anyone?

sİNAN: No, I didn't. I knew the place when I saw the boat. Then I asked you. I had the name of the boat in mind. I knew this was the place when I read it.

[*Holding in her hands the plates she has rinsed at the shore,* MERYEM *straightens up.*]

MERYEM: So nobody saw you come here?

sİNAN: [*Not making any sense out of it.*] No. Why should they? [MERYEM *comes near* sİNAN.]

MERYEM: Do you know how to read?

sİNAN: I try to as well as I can. Anyway, there is the picture of a rose under the name of the boat. You'd know even if you don't know how to read.

MERYEM: I don't know how to read. Neither does Captain Haşim.

SİNAN: It's very easy. You could learn quickly if you wanted to.

MERYEM: I wanted to very much, but I never had the chance. I could have learned if somebody had taught me. Why don't you teach me?

SİNAN: All right.

MERYEM: You know the beautiful houses a little way off? I work in those houses. [*Gesturing with her hands.*] In those houses, even the little children know how to read. The children, the ladies, they all read books. Newspapers. Whenever I can lay my hands on them, I look at the pictures in those books and newspapers. When did you learn?

SİNAN: When I was doing my military service.

MERYEM: Do you think I could learn, too?

SİNAN: Well, if you want to. They used to teach everybody in the army. But some learned and some didn't. The ones who didn't learn didn't want to, that's why.

MERYEM: Write "Meryem" for me.

SİNAN: "Meryem"?

MERYEM: "Meryem." Meryem's my name. [SİNAN *writes "Meryem" on the sand with his finger.*]

SİNAN: Mer . . . yem.

MERYEM: Is that "Meryem"?

SİNAN: This is M, this E, this R, this Y, this E, this M; that's "Meryem."

MERYEM: This is M, this E, this R, this . . .

SİNAN: Y . . .

MERYEM: [*Continuing.*] This is Y, and this E . . . [*Compares it with the other letter.*] They're the same.

SİNAN: Sure.

MERYEM: [*Happily.*] And this is M. The same as the first one.

SİNAN: Why shouldn't it be the same?

MERYEM: How should I know? By God, it's easy.

SİNAN: Not as easy as you think, but you'll learn quickly.

MERYEM: What's your name?

SİNAN: Sinan.

MERYEM: Write "Sinan" too.

SİNAN: [*Says the syllables as he writes.*] Si . . . nan.

MERYEM: [*Thoughtful.*] So this is "Sinan"? [*Moves her fingers over the letters and says the syllables.*] Mer . . . yem . . . Si . . . nan. How nice. Can you write anything you want?

SİNAN: I can.

MERYEM: Write *Sea Rose.*

SİNAN: [*Spells.*] S . . . E . . . A . . .

MERYEM: [*Interrupts him.*] This is E.

SİNAN: Yes, E. [*Goes on.*] R . . . O . . . S . . . E . . .

MERYEM: [*Compares the writing on the boat and the writing on the sand.*] They're both the same.

SİNAN: No, they're not.

MERYEM: Yes, they are.

SİNAN: The writing on the boat is wrong. The R is the wrong way round. The correct one is like the one I wrote.

MERYEM: Look what I did. I got them mixed up.

SİNAN: Wait a minute, don't hurry.

MERYEM: [*Sighs quietly and changes the subject.*] Do you like the name of the boat?

SİNAN: Well, you can see that name everywhere.

MERYEM: Sure, because it's a beautiful name.

SİNAN: I didn't say it isn't.

MERYEM: When the captain married me, he used to call me "Sea Rose." But I was beautiful then.

SİNAN: You're still beautiful.

MERYEM: Liar.

SİNAN: Why?

MERYEM: Just because you're a liar. Do you lie to all women like this? [*Gets up before waiting for his reply.*]

SİNAN: I did not lie to you.

MERYEM: That's all right then. [SİNAN *doesn't know what to say.* MERYEM, *before entering the hut, stops and turns around.*] Er . . .

SİNAN: What's the matter?

MERYEM: Never mind. [*Just as she is about to enter the hut, she changes her mind.*] Because the captain is very jealous. [*Goes into the hut and closes the door.*]

SİNAN: [*Draws some shapes in the sand with a stick. Without being aware of what he's doing, he says the syllables.*] Mer . . . yem. [*As he gets up, he throws the little stick on the ground with force.*]

Scene 2

[*Same day. Early hours of the night. The hut is illuminated by the light from the kerosene lamp.*

In the fireplace outside, there is a fire that is about to die out.

The sound of the sea is heard.

SİNAN *is sitting near the fire in the same place as in Scene 1. He's waiting for* CAPTAIN HAŞİM's *return. Once in a while he stirs the fire and throws on some more wood. He takes a burning stick from the fire and lights his cigarette. He is more interested in what's going on in the hut than in* CAPTAIN HAŞİM's *return. The door of the hut is open a crack.*

MERYEM *is sitting on a fish box in the hut. She is sitting with her head in her hands. Then she removes her hands from her head and straightens up.*

SİNAN, *too, sits up just at that moment and listens to the sounds coming from the hut.*

MERYEM *gets up and starts to walk toward the door. She is hesitant.*

SİNAN *gets up.*

MERYEM *comes to the door. She holds the door handle and waits hesitantly for a while behind the door. Her excited state is very obvious.* SİNAN *waits, facing the door.*

MERYEM *turns back slowly. She makes the bed, climbs up onto the bunk without getting undressed, and turns down the kerosene lamp before lying down on her back.*

SİNAN *sits down slowly.*]

Scene 3

[*An hour later.*

HAŞİM *enters the hut and closes the door. He is holding an empty birdcage in his hand. He puts it down on the floor. He is too drunk to notice the low-burning lamp. With his other hand, he is holding a goldfinch hidden underneath his shirt. He gropes around for some matches. After finding them, he strikes one and goes toward the lamp as if to light it.*

MERYEM, *still lying down, turns toward him quickly.*]

MERYEM: What are you doing?

HAŞİM: I'm going to light the lamp.

MERYEM: [*Sits up and pulls* HAŞİM *back.*] It's already lighted. Get away from it. [HAŞİM, *seeing that the match has gone out, strikes another one.*]

HAŞİM: I saw Captain Hüseyin. We chatted.

MERYEM: [*With her back to* HAŞİM, *adjusts the wick of the lamp.*] I can see.

HAŞİM: It's been a long time since we last met.

MERYEM: Oh, I'm sure you made up for all that lost time.

HAŞİM: [*Tries to pull himself together.*] Didn't you sleep? [*After adjusting the wick of the lamp,* MERYEM *turns toward* HAŞİM. *While she is blowing out the match in his hand, she sees the empty cage on the floor, near the door.*]

MERYEM: What's that?

[MERYEM *tries to catch hold of* HAŞİM's *hand beneath his shirt.* HAŞİM *pulls his hand back quickly and walks toward the cage. From under his shirt, he takes out the goldfinch wrapped up in a yellow handkerchief.*]

HAŞİM: A guest. My guest.

MERYEM: Did you bring that thing here again?

HAŞİM: [*Puts the bird in the cage and shuts the door.*] I've brought Fakir back.

MERYEM: As if all we needed in this house was Fakir.

HAŞİM: You're right. Of course all we needed was him.

MERYEM: No wonder things didn't go right these past few days. [HAŞİM *picks up the cage from the floor. He makes an attempt to hang it on the nail in the ceiling plank, but fails. He succeeds on his second try.*] There's not enough space even for you and me in this hut. Who's going to look after him?

HAŞİM: [*Looks at the bird.*] I will. I'll look after him. [*Sits on the fish box.*] Only God knows who makes it too crowded. Maybe me, maybe you. Maybe God gave us a roof over our heads just for Fakir's sake. You never know. Nobody but God knows who makes a crowd in this world. [*Takes a bottle of wine from his back pocket and drinks from it.*] Nobody knows that for sure except God. Don't you forget it!

MERYEM: [*Puts out her hand to take away the bottle.*] Haven't you had enough of that?

HAŞİM: Mind your own business. Let go.

MERYEM: Go on. Take off your clothes and go to bed.

HAŞİM: Only God can account for those who are alive in this world. Nobody in the world has the right to think of anyone else as one too many. God gives a life to each who is alive . . . and only He takes it away. Don't you forget it!

MERYEM: Do whatever you want.

HAŞİM: Didn't you get undressed?

MERYEM: I will.

HAŞİM: [*Gets up.*] I kept looking at that nail for days and days. Each time I saw it, I felt pangs of regret. See, his place is up there. [*Goes near* MERYEM.] And your place is . . . [*Tries to fondle her.*]

MERYEM: [*Pushes* HAŞİM's *hand away.*] Don't touch me.

HAŞİM: [*Repeats the same move.*] You are my rose. My Sea Rose.

MERYEM: I said don't get fresh. Leave me alone.

HAŞİM: Your hair . . .

MERYEM: I don't want it . . .

HAŞİM: Your hair . . . just a little . . .

MERYEM: Let go of me. You're drunk. You shouldn't have drunk so much. I'm not in the mood to amuse a drunkard.

HAŞİM: You should be ashamed. Look, Fakir is looking at you.

MERYEM: [*Pushes him back again.*] All we needed was a goldfinch in this ruined place, and now we have that, too. God give me patience! [HAŞİM *goes back to where he left the wine bottle and sits down.*]

HAŞİM: I was always planning to bring Fakir back. I didn't take him away forever. I just took him to the coffeehouse for safekeeping.

MERYEM: Ha! Look, he left the bird for safekeeping.

HAŞİM: [*Drinks from the bottle.*] That's exactly what I did.

MERYEM: Don't forget what you're drinking, and tomorrow don't ask me for your bottle of wine. [*Tries to take away the bottle.*]

HAŞİM: Let go of it. Who's asking you to take the bottle? I left him for safekeeping. I could see him all the time in the coffeehouse. Then I saw that he couldn't get used to the coffeehouse. He got depressed. Goldfinches aren't like you or me; they get depressed. The smoke in the coffeehouse wasn't good for the boy. I could see that if I left him there any longer, he was going to die. So I brought him back.

MERYEM: Why don't you come clean and tell me that you sold him? For safekeeping! Why don't you say that you couldn't find any money to buy wine and that you sold him to the owner of the coffeehouse? Obviously, he gave him back to you because he's had enough of looking after him.

HAŞİM: I did not sell him. I left him for safekeeping. I owed the owner of the shop some money, but that's got nothing to do with it. And I paid him back.

MERYEM: With what? You had only five lira.

HAŞİM: I told you I paid him back; therefore, I must have done so. I would spare Fakir even if I knew that I'd die of thirst. You'd better remember this. What's money, anyway? It's the dirt of your hand. I have a good name even if I don't have any money. But few have a good name.

MERYEM: Did Captain Hüseyin pay you back?

HAŞİM: Captain Hüseyin, Captain Hasan, or whoever it is. If you have a good name, everybody pays you back. Didn't you get undressed?

MERYEM: Are you blind?

HAŞİM: [*Bottle in hand, walks toward the cage. Mockingly.*] Fakir! You rascal, did you recognize your aunt? See, your auntie hasn't got undressed. She's waited for us. [*Drinks from the bottle and knocks over the fish box.* MERYEM *puts the box back in its place and helps him sit down.*]

MERYEM: Don't knock the place down. If you have to drink, do so while you're sitting down.

HAŞİM: Why didn't you get undressed?

MERYEM: Oh, not that again.

HAŞİM: [*Catches* MERYEM's *wrist.*] Ha? Why didn't you get undressed?

MERYEM: [*Shakes herself free.*] A stranger outside and me alone inside, and I was supposed to get undressed. Oh, God.

HAŞİM: When did he come?

MERYEM: Who?

HAŞİM: The one outside.

MERYEM: He came whenever he was supposed to come.

HAŞİM: Why didn't you send him over to the coffeehouse?

MERYEM: Here we go again. Didn't you tell me to tell the man to sit down and wait for you?

HAŞİM: So you sat up together till this hour.

MERYEM: We did. [*Snapped back.*] We chatted.

HAŞİM: So you sat up. What did you tell him?

MERYEM: What could I tell him? That I married you and now I'm as happy as can be.

HAŞİM: All right. Why didn't you get undressed then?

MERYEM: Oh, shut up. I've had enough. Leave me alone, will you? Didn't you see that we prepared the bait?

HAŞİM: Don't let it be with this one like it was with Dursun. Do you get me? Don't let it be like it was with Dursun. Don't you forget this. What did he tell you?

MERYEM: Go ask him.

HAŞİM: [*Finishes off the wine in the bottle and gets up.*] I will. I'll ask him now. [*Loses his balance and holds onto* MERYEM; *she helps him lie down on the bunk.* HAŞİM *catches* MERYEM *by her wrist.*] Come here, near me.

MERYEM: I'm here. Come on, lie down.

HAŞİM: Why didn't you get undressed? Come here. Your hair, just a little . . . just a little . . . your hair . . .

[HAŞİM *goes to sleep, sprawled all over the bunk.* MERYEM *struggles for a while to lay him straight and to make space for herself, but she can't move him. She is about to cry in anger. She turns down the lamp and goes out of the room. She sits on the doorstep and cries. Sounds of music float from one of the summer residences nearby.* SİNAN, *who is sitting near the fire, gets up and approaches her.*]

SİNAN: Are you crying? [MERYEM *doesn't answer. She wipes her eyes.*] Why are you crying? [MERYEM *keeps quiet and goes on sighing quietly.*] What happened? Why are you crying? Did he beat you? [SİNAN *is very close now.* MERYEM *gets up and holds his hand. Then she drops his hand and takes a few steps toward the fire. She looks extremely depressed. They sit on the fish boxes.*] Don't cry.

MERYEM: I'm not crying anymore.

SİNAN: Why did you cry?

MERYEM: It's better if you don't ask why.

SİNAN: Tell me. Why did you cry?

MERYEM: Ugh . . . let it go. Don't ask.

SİNAN: Go on, tell me.

MERYEM: [*Wipes her eyes with the hem of her skirt.*] It's nothing. It's over.

SİNAN: What did he do? Tell me.

MERYEM: I'm out of luck . . . terribly out of luck.

SİNAN: Why?

MERYEM: You've seen what kind of a man he is. I've been putting up with his drinking for years and years. I've had enough. Enough. [*Sighs.*]

SİNAN: [*Excited.*] Don't worry. Have patience.

MERYEM: [*Sobs.*] How can I be more patient? It's been the same every night for years. Every single night. My youth has passed away this way. I have a right to live, too! My God, if only I could be rid of him!

SİNAN: [*Wants to reach out and hold* MERYEM's *hand, but doesn't have the courage. With his hand reaching out, he points to the hut.*] What happened?

MERYEM: What could have happened? He dozed off. Oh, I hope he dies. I hope he never wakes up. He ruined my youth.

SİNAN: [*Hesitant.*] Did something happen between you two?

MERYEM: What could have happened? Nothing happens between him and me. Because I don't want it to happen . . .

SİNAN: Isn't he your husband?

MERYEM: So what? He disgusts me. My hair stands on end when he touches me. Oh God. Let me be rid of him. [*Toward the hut.*] Dirty old drunkard! Swine!

SİNAN: Still, he's your husband.

MERYEM: [*Sighs.*] So what? I didn't want to marry him.

SİNAN: Then why don't you get rid of him?

MERYEM: Where can I go?

SİNAN: [*Grabs* MERYEM's *arm and gets up.*] Come here.

MERYEM: [*With slight resistance.*] Where to?

SİNAN: Come a little.

MERYEM: Don't, please.

SİNAN: Come on.

MERYEM: [*While* SİNAN *embraces her.*] Don't—I don't have any strength.

Scene 4

[*Fifteen minutes later. Near the fire.* MERYEM *and* SİNAN *are sitting as they were in Scene 1.*]

MERYEM: I'm not in my right mind.

SİNAN: Are you sorry?

MERYEM: Not yet, but . . .

SİNAN: But what?

MERYEM: God knows what you'll think about me later on.

SİNAN: What should I think about you? Nothing?

MERYEM: We'll see.

SİNAN: Like what?

MERYEM: Who knows, maybe you'll think that I do the same thing with everybody.

SİNAN: Don't you?

MERYEM: See, you've started thinking that way.

SİNAN: I didn't ask because of that.

MERYEM: Then why did you ask?

SİNAN: Just so that I know.

MERYEM: Nonsense!

SİNAN: Didn't you?

MERYEM: [*A little cross.*] Of course I didn't.

SİNAN: [*A little surprised.*] So you didn't.

MERYEM: Of course I didn't. What did you think? That I'm common property? Don't worry, I won't pester you because of what happened.

SİNAN: I'm not worried about that.

MERYEM: You men. All of you are the same. I was very weak this time. I didn't have the chance to pull myself together. Forget it. Let's both of us forget it. And don't you ever try to do it again.

SİNAN: [*Tentatively.*] If you want . . .

MERYEM: Go on. Why did you stop?

SİNAN: If you want, I'll marry you.

MERYEM: Did you think before saying that?

SİNAN: I'm very sincere about it.

MERYEM: How quick. You saw me yesterday for the first time. Anyway, there's him. What'll happen to him?

SİNAN: Doesn't matter. We'll run away together.

MERYEM: Run away? Where?

SİNAN: Doesn't matter where. We'll run away and find a place. If you want, we'll go back to Bodrum or to Marmaris.

MERYEM: You think it's that easy. Just wait till you see him awake tomorrow morning. He's as cunning as a fox. Anyway, you never know—maybe he'll come to in a little while. You just wait and see him like that. He takes you into the palm of his hand. He'll make you do whatever he wants. He doesn't show it, but he's ever so jealous, too. If he realizes that there's something between you and me, God knows he'll kill us both for sure.

SİNAN: It's not that easy.

MERYEM: Difficult for him? It's not important to him. He has just one or two more years to live anyway. He'll kill you and me and spend the last two years of his life in prison. There's nothing for him to be afraid of.

SİNAN: Do I have something to be afraid of?

MERYEM: You're young. Your life is more precious.

SİNAN: Just let him try.

MERYEM: What would you do? Would you kill him?

SİNAN: Maybe I would, if he tried to kill me.

MERYEM: [*Hopefully.*] Would you? Would you really kill him?

SİNAN: Since I don't want to die . . .

MERYEM: Then kill him.

SİNAN: Why should I kill him for nothing? [MERYEM *gets up.*] Stop. Where are you going?

MERYEM: To take a look at him.

SİNAN: What are you going to do? [MERYEM *wants to go, but* SİNAN *keeps her back by holding her arm.*]

MERYEM: Just a minute.

SİNAN: Not now.

MERYEM: Not to kill him.

SİNAN: Then why?

MERYEM: Just to see if he's waking up.

SİNAN: Go look then. [*Lets go of* MERYEM*'s arm. She goes into the hut, takes a look at* HAŞİM, *and comes back to her former place.*] How is he?

MERYEM: Like a log.

SİNAN: Won't he wake up?

MERYEM: You never know when or how he wakes up. Sometimes he wakes up suddenly.

SİNAN: Maybe we should go to bed, too.

MERYEM: Doesn't matter, let's sit up.

SİNAN: What if he wakes up?

MERYEM: So what if he wakes up? Is it a sin to sit and talk? You said you weren't afraid. What about it?

SİNAN: All right. We'll do what you want.

MERYEM: Good. Listen. The best thing is to kill him. There's no other way to get rid of him. To run away won't do. Wherever we go, he'll come and find us.

SİNAN: It seems as if he's frightened you a lot. How can he find us?

MERYEM: He will. I know him. He's like a cat. You know how you throw cats away and they find their way back home just by looking at the stars? He's just like that. There's nowhere he doesn't know. So don't have any hopes about running away. The best thing is to kill him.

SİNAN: Don't soil your hands with blood.

MERYEM: The best way is to kill him. [*Carried away by the thought of killing him, she's very passionate and excited.*] I've thought about how he can be killed. I've thought about it for a long time.

SİNAN: Since when?

MERYEM: Since the first day we were together. I've been thinking about how he can be killed since the day he married me. It'll be very easy for you.

SİNAN: Why haven't you killed him?

MERYEM: I didn't have anyone to help me. Once or twice I tried to do it by myself, but I couldn't.

SİNAN: Why?

MERYEM: Because it didn't work out.

SİNAN: Why?

MERYEM: Once I made him eat from a copper plate not coated with tin.

SİNAN: But he didn't die.

MERYEM: He turned purple, he had pain. [*Imitating him.*] He said, "I have a stomachache."

SİNAN: Yes?

MERYEM: Then he went to the seashore, and he was sick. Everything that was inside him came out. And then he was as good as new in half an hour. The swine has seven lives.

SİNAN: Then how can he be killed now, if he has seven lives?

MERYEM: Now it'll be easy because you're here. It'll be very easy for you. I've thought about everything.

SİNAN: How can it be easy? With no reason . . .

MERYEM: [*Begging.*] Get rid of him for me. Please. Get rid of him. I'll be your wife, your servant, your slave. Beat me, kill me if you want, or drag me on the ground. It won't hurt. Just rid me of him. I've never had a happy day near him. I always feel very out of place near him. I feel that he'll die and I'll be left all alone. Besides, I'll become much uglier by the time he dies. My skin will sag. Nobody's going to look at my face then. Please kill him. If you love me just a little, please kill him.

SİNAN: [*Doubtful.*] Couldn't you find someone to help you before now?

MERYEM: I didn't look for anyone.

SİNAN: Surely I'm not the first one you've found . . . since you decided to kill him such a long time ago.

MERYEM: [*A little hurt.*] If I'd looked for someone, maybe I could have found someone. I thought you were different. It doesn't matter now.

SİNAN: What about Dursun, then?

MERYEM: What about him?

SİNAN: Didn't Dursun agree to help you?

MERYEM: Why should he? There wasn't anything between him and me.

SİNAN: That's not what I heard in the coffeehouse before I came here.

MERYEM: What did you hear?

SİNAN: I just heard something.

MERYEM: They said, "His wife is beautiful and you're lucky," didn't they?

SİNAN: How do you know?

MERYEM: Is that so difficult to figure out? Everyone says what crosses his mind. After tonight you have the right to believe what you've heard.

SİNAN: What I heard wasn't exactly what you said. They said that Dursun didn't encourage you, so you laid a trap for him and caused him and the captain to fight.

MERYEM: Nonsense. Dursun would do anything I'd say. He'd do whatever I wanted, but I didn't ask him.

SİNAN: Why didn't you?

MERYEM: Because I didn't love him. What would I do with him? I didn't love him. The captain and him, they're both the same to me. Better to live with Captain Haşim. At least he knows how to please me every once in a while.

SİNAN: They said at the coffeehouse that Dursun was a very honest man, that he wouldn't double-cross the man who gave him his bread.

MERYEM: Does such a man exist in this world?

SİNAN: I . . . [Doesn't know what to say.]

MERYEM: Why didn't you go to bed?

SİNAN: I wasn't able to sleep.

MERYEM: Because of me?

SİNAN: I don't know. I just couldn't sleep.

MERYEM: [Gets up.] You see. I couldn't sleep just as you couldn't. I'm alive, too! I'm not an angel. [Begins to walk toward the hut.] Anyway, I've learned my lesson.

SİNAN: [Catches MERYEM by her arm.] Stop, don't go!

MERYEM: So, what if I don't go?

SİNAN: Stay here and let's talk.

MERYEM: What more do we have to talk about?

SİNAN: Sit down.

MERYEM: You've let the cat out of the bag. Now I know the way you're thinking. Anyway, he'll wake up anytime now; he'll look for me.

SİNAN: Let him. Sit down.

MERYEM: You've changed. Better if I go. You'll be sorry later if I sit down now.

SİNAN: I won't.

MERYEM: You will. If I sit down, we'll have to finish it off.

SİNAN: Sit down. We'll do it if necessary. [MERYEM decides not to go, picks up a thick log from the ground, and gives it to SİNAN.]

MERYEM: Take this. [SİNAN takes the log.] Hit him with this.

SİNAN: With this?

MERYEM: [Sits down. Excited and furious, she describes the plan.] Right on the top of his head. Just swing it this way and hit him, that's enough. You see, it's very easy.

SİNAN: Then?

MERYEM: Then the rest is easy. They say that you won't be punished if you've killed someone in self-defense. Haven't you ever heard that?

SİNAN: Yes, but . . .

MERYEM: [Interrupts him.] When they catch you, you are going to say that he attacked you with a knife and that you grabbed this log to save your own life and swung it and that it hit him by accident.

SİNAN: I'll say so, but do you think the prosecutor will believe me?

MERYEM: Let him not believe you. What choice does he have other than believing you? You just explain everything like I say and leave the rest to me. The prosecutor and the gendarmerie have to believe what I say. They don't have any other witnesses. I'm the only witness. I know just what to say to the prosecutor.

SİNAN: Tell me what you're going to say to him.

MERYEM: Everybody knows about his drinking. Everybody will have seen the state he was in when he left the tavern tonight. I'll say that I was sitting near the fire and that you were waiting for his return to talk to him about this job. When the captain saw us sitting together, he thought there was something between us. I'll say that first he swore at you and then pulled out his knife and attacked you. That you were taken unaware, that you moved back a little and were between the sea and the captain when he attacked you again. You were desperate and grabbed a log from the ground and started to defend yourself. That is when the captain attacked again. He slipped, and the log hit his head. I'll say that you aimed the log at the hand that held the knife. How about that?

SİNAN: What if the prosecutor says that we planned this together?

MERYEM: He can't say that. He can never say that. You came just this evening. What's more, nobody saw when you came. He could say it if it were two or three months later, but not now. Some time must have passed since the time we met in order for us to have planned this together. [*Gives the log, which* SİNAN *had set on the ground, back to him again.*] Hold it. We've got only this evening to do this. Otherwise, we can't do it.

SİNAN: [*Puts the log back down on the ground.*] It's better if we run away.

MERYEM: I've told you, I can't run away. So long as he's alive, I'll have no peace of mind. If he discovers this, he'll kill us both. [*Picks up the log.*] Just hit him once. Do you understand? He should die with the first blow. [*Shows him how.*] Hit him real hard like this in the middle of his forehead. [*Holds out the log.*] Go on, take it.

SİNAN: [*Doesn't take the log.*] I can't do it.

MERYEM: [*Leans on the log as if it were a walking stick.*] Why?

SİNAN: I can't.

MERYEM: Is it that difficult?

SİNAN: I don't like death.

MERYEM: Or are you afraid?

SİNAN: It's not because of fear.

MERYEM: Of course it's because of fear. Why don't you be honest and say that you're afraid? You quit diving and say that it's not because of fear. You can't hit a drunk man with a log, and you say it's not because of fear. What is fear, then?

SİNAN: I can't spend a miserable life in prison. Even if he were to draw out his knife to stab me, I'd twist his wrist and take the knife away.

MERYEM: [*Pulls herself up.*] Look here, do you want me to be your wife or not?

SİNAN: I do.

MERYEM: [*Gets up.*] Then he's got to die.

SİNAN: But why?

MERYEM: Simply because there's no other solution for both of us.

sİNAN: I asked you to run away with me.

MERYEM: I can't run away.

sİNAN: Let's run away. That way we'll live, and he'll live, too.

MERYEM: He's lived long enough. He should let me live a little, too.

sİNAN: Let's run away. Nobody'll ask us anything. Neither the prosecutor nor the gendarmerie.

MERYEM: I can't run away. Get that into your head. He won't let us, do you get it? I've been his wife for so many years . . . isn't that enough? He's worn me out all these years! I've suffered enough. If he's going to die, let him die now. Why should he live any longer? Let him drink fewer barrels of wine.

sİNAN: Do others do anything differently? Isn't that how it goes with everybody else? [MERYEM *moves nearer to* sİNAN *and puts her arm around his neck.* HAŞİM *stirs inside the hut.*]

MERYEM: You won't be sorry if you listen to me. You'll see how good it'll be when he's no longer between us. I'll love you like nobody ever did. Anyway, just think, where would we run away to? You don't have anyplace to hide.

HAŞİM: [*From inside.*] Meryem . . .

MERYEM: [*Gives the log to* sİNAN *again.*] Go on—hold it and get it over with. That's it. He's even coming out here of his own will.

sİNAN: [*Wants to go back to the boat.*] I'll go now.

MERYEM: [*Holds* sİNAN'*s hands so that he can't let go of the log.*] Hold it, don't drop it. Let's move a little closer . . . like this. So that when he comes, he'll see us knee to knee and mouth to mouth. [*Moves the box she's sitting on nearer to* sİNAN.]

HAŞİM: [*From inside.*] Meryem! Where are you, girl?

MERYEM: Go to hell! Come and see. [*Raises her voice.*] I'm sitting here. [sİNAN *holds the log more tightly.* HAŞİM *gets down from the bunk and moves toward the door. The log falls out of* sİNAN'*s hand.* MERYEM *wants to move her box nearer to* sİNAN, *but* sİNAN *stops her. He moves back slightly.*] Don't move. Let him see us like this.

HAŞİM: [*From the threshold.*] Meryem, what happened to you, girl? Didn't you hear me call? [*Stretches.*]

MERYEM: Well, I didn't run away, did I? Here I am. [*To* sİNAN *in a low voice.*] Like I told you, in one blow.

sİNAN: [*Pushes away the log with his foot.*] Don't be crazy.

HAŞİM: [*Comes closer.*] Were you here?

MERYEM: [*Pushes the log over to* sİNAN *with her foot.*] I can't sleep in the chicken coop, can I?

HAŞİM: Near the fire! Well, well, that's good! [*Sits down on the third box near the fire.*] I think the wine's gone to my head. I fell asleep. [*Turns to* sİNAN.] How long did I sleep? [*Behind* HAŞİM, MERYEM *makes signs to* sİNAN, *trying to tell him to pick up the log and hit him.*]

sİNAN: [*Confused by* HAŞİM'*s question and* MERYEM'*s gestures.*] Well, a little . . .

HAŞİM: How long?

SİNAN: About half an hour.

HAŞİM: [*Turns his back to* SİNAN.] Let me see . . . [*Looks at the stars.*] The Pleiades are still over Foça. They're not even over Karşıyaka. Like you said, it must've been half an hour or three-quarters of an hour at the most. [*While* MERYEM *is repeating her gestures, he turns around. To* MERYEM.] Give me a little water. [MERYEM *gets up. To* SİNAN.] You don't sleep much like me, do you? [*Shouts to* MERYEM, *who's entering the hut.*] See if we have any coffee in the jar. If we have some, bring it over here. [*To* SİNAN.] What was your name, friend?

SİNAN: Sinan.

HAŞİM: I must have forgotten. [*Shouts to* MERYEM.] Sinan is our guest tonight. Bring over the coffeepot and the sugar. Let's make some coffee. [*To* SİNAN.] Wine doesn't go to my head usually, but, then, I forget easily. I remember everything later on, though. You don't sleep much, either, do you?

SİNAN: I don't.

HAŞİM: But you're young. How old are you? About twenty-five?

SİNAN: A little older.

HAŞİM: At your age, you sleep the moment you put your head on the pillow. You should've seen me when I was your age.

[MERYEM *comes back with water, coffee, and a coffeepot. While approaching them, she repeats her gestures from behind* HAŞİM's *back.*]

[HAŞİM *turns to* MERYEM.] Why did you take so long? [*Turns back to* SİNAN.] Are you worrying about something?

SİNAN: Worrying about something?

HAŞİM: If you don't sleep at your age, you must be worrying about something. Either you have something on your mind and you're thinking about that, or you're in love! Well? Are you in love?

SİNAN: [*Puzzled.*] I'm not.

HAŞİM: Don't be shy, tell me. I'm like your father. If you're in love, tell me the girl's name; I'll get you married. I'll go and ask for the girl's hand for you. It's pretty difficult to say no to me. If they say no, we'll do something about it. If you're going to get married, do it now. You are a man; you can get married anytime you like, but it's better if you get married now. [MERYEM *makes signs to* SİNAN, *telling him not to believe* HAŞİM.] You see, I was a little late in getting married. I don't feel too good about it. I always have this worry that should I die, Meryem will be all alone. Isn't that so, Meryem? Would you cry if I died? Would you shed tears for me? [MERYEM *rapidly stirs the coffee in the coffeepot.* HAŞİM *tries to stroke* MERYEM's *hair.* MERYEM *moves her head back.* HAŞİM *laughs heartily. He continues.*] I tease her once in a while. Why should anyone shed tears over me? But I won't die yet. You've let the fire burn down.

SİNAN: I was going to go to bed in a little while.

HAŞİM: How do you like the boat? Is it warm inside? But you haven't gone to bed yet. The weather's fine anyway. But I like to have a fire going during the nights. It takes away the dampness of the night and cheers you up. [*Picks up the log lying near* SİNAN'*s feet.*] We have to feed the fire. [*Hands the log over to* SİNAN.] Take this and break it. [SİNAN *moves back involuntarily.* MERYEM *excitedly makes signs to him to take the log.*] Come on, break it up. You're younger than me. Why did you stop? [*Turns back to* MERYEM.] Don't meddle, it's still early. [*Takes the log from* SİNAN.] Don't you have any strength? Give it to me. I'll show you how to break it. [*Breaks it in two on his knee while throwing the pieces one by one into the fire.*] When there's a fire going at night, it seems to me as if it's burning right inside me. Fire is good. It takes away your sorrow. See how it crackles. You'll see how good it makes you feel in a little while. If you have something on your mind at night and you can't sleep, just sit by the fire for five or ten minutes, watch the fire, and light a cigarette. Whatever is on your mind will go away. [*Gives* SİNAN *a cigarette and lights one for himself.*] See if there are any other logs around. [*They look around.*] Yes, there's one over there; grab it, will you? [SİNAN *takes it.*] Now you break that one. Let's celebrate the night. [MERYEM *gives* HAŞİM *his coffee.* SİNAN *breaks the log on his knee. While* SİNAN *is throwing the pieces one by one into the fire,* MERYEM *gives him his coffee. The flames light up their faces.* HAŞİM, *after sipping his coffee.*] This is good. [MERYEM *and* SİNAN *turn toward* HAŞİM.]

CURTAIN

ACT II

Scene 1

[*Early afternoon a fortnight later. The setting is the same as in Act I. The weather is bad; the roar of the sea can be heard all through Act II.* MERYEM *is sitting on the stone steps in front of the hut and sewing.* SİNAN *approaches, looks around him carefully, and grabs* MERYEM'*s arm.*]

SİNAN: Come on.

MERYEM: [*Frees her arm.*] Are you crazy?

SİNAN: There's no one around. The shutters of all the houses are closed.

MERYEM: [*Tries to calm him down.*] Please don't.

SİNAN: You go into the hut; I'll come in after you.

MERYEM: It's daytime! Are you out of your mind?

SİNAN: You've been saying no for the past fifteen days. When?

MERYEM: When we get married.

SİNAN: You said, "Let's get married," and I said, "All right." Well, isn't it enough?

MERYEM: Please don't insist. He might come any minute.

SİNAN: He usually doesn't come at this time of the day.

MERYEM: Please understand me. Not before I'm your wife. First, let's get married. [*Gets up, changes her place, and sits on one of the boxes near the fire.* SİNAN *starts to mend the fishing nets.*]

SİNAN: You didn't act like this the first night I came here.

MERYEM: I wasn't in my right mind that night.

SİNAN: What's this story you're making up? Do you think I'm that naive? Who knows how many others took your mind away before me.

MERYEM: Let me die this minute if I ever thought about someone else in that way before you came. You came and seduced me.

SİNAN: Ahh, come on! [*Puts the mended nets into the basket. As he bends down and gets up again, it's apparent that his shirt has become unstitched.*]

MERYEM: The sleeve of your shirt has come apart. Take it off, and I'll mend it for you.

SİNAN: No, thank you. I'd rather ask a favor from the Devil himself than you.

MERYEM: Come on, take it off. Don't be so stubborn. [*Thoughtful.*] If you only knew how I married Captain Haşim.

SİNAN: [*Takes off his shirt and gives it to* MERYEM.] Take it.

MERYEM: I was just fifteen. My father had recently died. I had six brothers and sisters, all of them younger than me. After my father died, Captain Haşim started to come to our house. He used to bring flour, oil, and fish. I used to think that he was after my mother. I was in love with a young boatman like you. I wanted to marry him. He used to work for the captain.

SİNAN: Was he Dursun?

MERYEM: All you ever think about is Dursun. It wasn't Dursun. I saw Dursun here for the first time. He came to work for the captain about seven or eight months ago. I used to think about that boatman. Then one day the captain talked to my mother, she agreed, and he married me.

SİNAN: What happened to that boatman?

MERYEM: He was a shy boy. Whenever you looked him in the eye, he used to bow his head.

SİNAN: You said you never thought about anyone else in that way.

MERYEM: You two are different. He wasn't like you at all. When I looked at his face, I didn't know a thing about the facts of life. [*Shrugs.*] I was a child then, and he was naive.

SİNAN: So nothing happened between you two, eh?

MERYEM: When I married the captain, he went away. I've never forgotten to this day how angry he was when he looked at me. His name was Mehmet. I never saw him again. The captain took me away from Bodrum and brought me here. He built this hut.

SİNAN: So it looks as if whoever starts to work for the captain goes away because of you.

MERYEM: Why don't you go away?

SİNAN: Who knows? Maybe I will, too.

MERYEM: [*Startled.*] If you go away, I'll shoot myself, do you understand me? May God curse me if I don't!

SİNAN: You won't, don't worry. That boat won't be empty for too long!

MERYEM: Cross my heart and hope to die!

SİNAN: Tell me truthfully, did anything happen with someone else before me?

MERYEM: No.

SİNAN: Swear that nothing happened!

MERYEM: I swear that nothing happened.

SİNAN: With neither Dursun nor the boatman, is that so?

MERYEM: Dursun was a coward. [*A short pause.*] And Mehmet was a child.

SİNAN: And me?

MERYEM: You're a man. Your heart is warm. No woman could resist you.

SİNAN: I'm not a man! I'm not trustworthy!

MERYEM: You are. You did everything that an honest man would do. My heart was covered with ice before you came along. You warmed it. [*They look in each other's eyes for a while without talking. Then* MERYEM *lowers her eyes to her sewing.*] This is why I'm sorry I surrendered to you. I knew that night that you'd think in this way later on, but we couldn't help what happened. Anyway, did you see how he wouldn't give us the opportunity again?

SİNAN: He's drunk day and night. He can't see the end of his nose. He wouldn't realize it if you were to sleep with another on your left while he's sleeping on your right!

MERYEM: If I were to do that, I'd have you. I never did. [*Worried.*] Tell me truly, are you going to go away?

SİNAN: [*Distant.*] We'll see.

MERYEM: You won't . . . you won't leave me, will you? Tell me. But get this into your head: if I ever go out that door and not see you, I'll die. That first night you came, I'd had just about all I could take. Do you understand? I couldn't resist you.

SİNAN: And I've had enough of your whims! This place has turned into Hell with all three of us here together. I can't bear this kind of hypocritical and deceitful affair. I can't look the man straight in the eye. Don't you see that no evil crosses his mind?

MERYEM: Why can't you look him in the eye? Didn't I tell you that he's as cunning as a fox? See how he's softened you? He knows what to do better than you and me. It's not for nothing that he's gentle with you.

SİNAN: He's the same with everyone. He's good to everyone.

MERYEM: So you say. You ask me about his good nature. He never thinks about anyone but himself. If he'd been that good, he wouldn't have ruined my youth. What's that if it's not badness? You don't expect him to strangle a man every day, do you? You have no need to be ashamed. He married me by winning my mother's heart. And he did it with a kilo of oil and a sack of flour. I gave myself to you of my own will. I couldn't resist you that night, but I'm not sorry. He should be ashamed when you look at my face. [*Gives him back his shirt.*] Go on, take this and put it on. If you have anything else to be mended, bring it along, and I'll do it. And don't forget that I haven't jilted the captain yet, and I haven't jilted myself. Don't worry; I have more honor than the ones who say they have honor. Any other woman in my place would have jilted him with the first man who came along and in the first week, too. [sinan *puts on his shirt.*]

sinan: He's coming.

meryem: Let him.

sinan: Do whatever you'll do, but talk to him.

meryem: Well, things won't go on like this for long.

haşim: [*Enters from the right. To* sinan.] How's everything? [*To* meryem.] Did you mend Sinan's shirt?

meryem: It had come apart.

haşim: Good! It caught my eye, too, at noon. [*To* sinan.] Everything is ready?

sinan: [*Distant.*] Yes.

haşim: What's the use? The weather's terrible. Nobody's happy about it at the coffeehouse. Do you have a cigarette?

sinan: I threw away the empty packet a little while ago.

haşim: [*Takes a box of cheap cigarettes out of his pocket.*] Take this. [*Turns toward the sea.*] The son of a bitch. It's like a monster. Looks like there's a slight fog over the bay, doesn't it?

sinan: Yes.

haşim: If it goes on like this, it'll calm down before morning. Everyone's unhappy at the coffeehouse. [*Goes into the hut.*]

sinan: [*To* meryem.] Go on, you go in, too.

meryem: Not now.

haşim: [*Looks around for something in the hut. Feels the empty bottles and calls.*] Meryem!

meryem: [*Enters the hut.*] What? What are you looking for?

haşim: [*Stops searching.*] Do you have any money?

meryem: How can I have any money?

haşim: You're the type who saves for a rainy day. You must have put aside a few kuruş.

meryem: I haven't.

haşim: Come on, don't be mean. Give me some if you have any. I'll give you more after I come back from the sea tomorrow. You can put that aside.

meryem: I told you I haven't got any. Didn't you hear me?

haşim: I think it'll be better if I give everything I earn to you from now on, eh?

meryem: I said I don't have any. I gave all that I had to you.

haşim: [*Examines the side wall of the hut.*] There's a big crack in this wall. It needs to be repaired.

meryem: At last you've seen it.

HAŞİM: I saw it, but the weather was still warm even three days ago. [*Looks into the cage.*] Fakir is going to freeze to death here.

MERYEM: Think about yourself before Fakir.

HAŞİM: What can happen to you and me? Look, he's all shriveled up.

MERYEM: I get it. Take him and give him to whomever you promised to give him to.

HAŞİM: I talked to the man at the coffeehouse. It's full of smoke there, but still it's warmer than here. [*Takes down the cage.*] Come on, you go on with whatever you're doing. [*Puts his finger into the cage and plays with the bird. Then he takes out his handkerchief, opens the door of the cage, takes Fakir out of the cage, and wraps him up in the handkerchief.*]

SİNAN: [*To* MERYEM, *who has stepped outside.*] What did he say?

MERYEM: I'll tell you later.

SİNAN: Did you talk to him?

MERYEM: He's going in a minute. I'll tell you then.

SİNAN: Well, tell him first and then . . . [HAŞİM *stops and listens to the conversation taking place outside the hut.*]

MERYEM: Ssh! Quiet! I haven't talked to him yet. [HAŞİM *comes out of the hut with the cage in one hand and Fakir wrapped in the handkerchief in the other.*]

HAŞİM: Sinan.

SİNAN: Yes?

HAŞİM: [*Holds out the cage.*] Take this. [*Also holds out the handkerchief.*] And this. Don't hold too tight. Hold him well, don't let him escape, but don't squeeze him. Right. That's the way. I wrapped him up in a handkerchief so that he won't be cold. After all, he isn't used to this kind of weather. Take them to Recep at the coffeehouse. I talked to him about it. [SİNAN *exits. To* MERYEM.] Come in for a minute, will you?

MERYEM: [*Busy by the fire.*] Don't you see that I've got things to do?

HAŞİM: Come in, let's talk a little. [*Enters the hut.*]

MERYEM: [*Enters the hut after him.*] What's the matter?

HAŞİM: Sit here in front of me.

MERYEM: [*Sits on the fish box.*] Tell me . . .

HAŞİM: [*Lights a cigarette.*] Sinan's a good boy, eh? What do you say?

MERYEM: Now, what's this got to do with us?

HAŞİM: Just tell me . . .

MERYEM: I don't know. He's your man.

HAŞİM: A good boy. I like him. And he's good on the sea, too.

MERYEM: It's all the same to me. What would it matter if he's good or bad?

HAŞİM: [*Softly.*] What did Sinan tell you?

MERYEM: When?

HAŞİM: A little while ago, outside.

MERYEM: What do you mean, "what did he say"?

HAŞİM: A little while ago, when you went outside.

MERYEM: I don't know. Let me think for a minute. He said something, but what? I forgot.

HAŞİM: Go on, remember.

MERYEM: What for?

HAŞİM: I, too, want to know what he said.

MERYEM: Oh yes. He wanted to know if you had anything for him to do.

HAŞİM: [*Doesn't insist.*] All right. [*Changes the subject.*] Sinan's a good boy, but there's something bad about him.

MERYEM: What?

HAŞİM: He's single.

MERYEM: [*Shrugs.*] What if he's single?

HAŞİM: I must marry him off. Being single is not good for ones like him.

MERYEM: [*Gets up.*] That's not anything for you or me to worry about, is it?

HAŞİM: Sit down. It'll be good for us as well as him if he gets married. Well?

MERYEM: I hadn't thought about it.

HAŞİM: Being single is not good for some people. Frankly speaking, loneliness is not good for them. They're like stray dogs, walking on the street with no collars. If you stroke them a little, they come closer and start to rub themselves against you.

MERYEM: I don't understand why you say these things.

HAŞİM: I found a girl for him.

MERYEM: [*Interested.*] Who's the girl?

HAŞİM: A poor and honest girl just like us.

MERYEM: Tell me who she is.

HAŞİM: You know her.

MERYEM: Is it Aliye?

HAŞİM: How'd you know?

MERYEM: You'd found her for Dursun, too.

HAŞİM: She wasn't suitable for Dursun, but she is for Sinan.

MERYEM: [*Nervous.*] Aliye isn't good for Sinan.

HAŞİM: Why? What's wrong with her?

MERYEM: How would you know her real character? I said she isn't good for Sinan, and she isn't. Don't make me say unpleasant things.

HAŞİM: You said the same things in connection with Dursun.

MERYEM: Is there a single man on this shore that Aliye hasn't run after? Honest, my foot! Nobody's more fickle than her. And I told you the same things about her that I'm saying now. Why do you want to get Dursun or Sinan into this?

HAŞİM: Sinan will be good for her.

MERYEM: What's more, Sinan hasn't even got a roof over his head.

HAŞİM: He'll build four walls for himself, just like us.

MERYEM: You finish building your own four walls before you think about somebody else's walls and marriage.

HAŞİM: Sinan must get married. That's all I know.

MERYEM: What's it got to do with you, anyway? Did he come to you and ask you for a wife?

HAŞİM: Look here, it's no use getting furious. I know you just as well as I know the speed of the boat when I hold the tiller. Don't make me say it!

MERYEM: Go on, tell me what you know so well?

HAŞİM: Don't play around with Sinan!

MERYEM: Who? Me?

HAŞİM: Yes, you! I'm not blind.

MERYEM: Are you saying all this because I mended a few things for him?

HAŞİM: Not only because of that. But you made him get used to you in a bad way!

MERYEM: So what if I mended his things? I'll do whatever I like for whomever I like! You don't think I have to mend only your things every day, do you?

HAŞİM: I'm telling you to watch your step and not to play around with him. That's all.

MERYEM: It's all right when I scrub somebody's hall and clean his windows, isn't it? If I took money from Sinan and gave it to you for wine, you wouldn't say a word, would you?

HAŞİM: Shut up! Hold your tongue!

MERYEM: What if I don't shut up? I've had enough!

HAŞİM: I'll do something I never did till this day! Don't make me any madder than I already am. What did you tell him out there?

MERYEM: I told him whatever I wanted to tell him. It's none of your business. Go on, now—do whatever it is that you're going to do. You haven't got a kuruş in your pocket, and you intend to marry someone else off!

HAŞİM: I told you to shut up!

MERYEM: I've had enough! I'm sick and tired of you. I just can't sit down and listen to you swear because you don't have any wine to drink and because I couldn't find you money for any, do you get it? You dirty drunkard!

HAŞİM: I said shut up!

MERYEM: You're drunk, that's what you are! You old coot! [HAŞİM *slaps* MERYEM *twice.*] You dirty drunkard! You scoundrel! You son of a bitch! [*She attacks* HAŞİM.] I'll show you . . .

HAŞİM: Go on, show me. [*They fight, but* HAŞİM *gets the upper hand.*] Come on, show me.

MERYEM: You've hit me! I'll show you!

HAŞİM: [*Straightens up.*] You asked for it.

MERYEM: [*Attacks him again.*] I asked for it, did I?

HAŞİM: [*Holds* MERYEM *by her wrists and pushes her back.*] Yes, you.

MERYEM: [*Breathless, she straightens her dress.*] You hit me! I'll show you! See if I'll stay with you another minute.

HAŞİM: The door is open. Just you try going away.

MERYEM: The door is open, eh? You'll be the one who'll go, do you understand? I'll show you. If I don't make you pay for this . . .

HAŞİM: See if you can make me pay.

MERYEM: So you can be forceful with me! You become a lion when you're with a woman who's young enough to be your daughter, but there's sure to be someone who'll get even with you someday!

HAŞİM: Get this into your head! Nobody can talk to me the way you do. Doesn't matter if he gets even with me or if I get even with him. I'll make him eat his words before he opens his mouth! I've kept quiet till now only because you're a woman.

MERYEM: So nobody speaks to you like this? You sent him to the coffeehouse just so you could slap me, didn't you? Oh, I understand now. You were afraid, weren't you?

HAŞİM: Afraid of who?

MERYEM: You know who very well. Why don't you slap me near him?

HAŞİM: Well, I might try that, too.

MERYEM: Slap him if you're that strong!

HAŞİM: I'll do that if it's necessary.

MERYEM: [*Slows down and starts to cry.*] What am I to you? Just think. What right do you have to hit me? What have you given me? What have I had from you except your breath stinking of wine? Anyone would give me a bite to eat if I gave him what I've given you. I would get as much consideration as I get from you if I gave him what I've given you. How dare you hit me? How? So what if I mended his shirt? He's your man. What's so bad about my helping him?

[*While* MERYEM *is crying,* HAŞİM *goes off stage at the right.* MERYEM *sits there and thinks for a while.* SİNAN *comes back. He goes straight to the boat and picks up his clothes. When* MERYEM *hears footsteps outside, she gets up and goes out of the hut. She goes toward* SİNAN.]

What happened? [SİNAN *doesn't reply. He puts his clothes in a bundle.*] Where are you going? [SİNAN's *back is turned to* MERYEM. *She tries to take the bundle.* SİNAN *doesn't answer her and bruskly frees himself from her.*] Are you going away? Tell me, are you going? What happened? Did he sack you? Are you cross with me? Tell me, are you cross with me? [SİNAN *ties up his bundle and turns away.*] Are you? Tell me you're not.

SİNAN: [*About to move away. With a slight gesture of his hand.*] Go away!

MERYEM: [*Insists.*] Oh, it's all my fault. Stop. If you go, I'll come with you, too.

SİNAN: There's no need for that.

MERYEM: Or are you running away from me? Tell me, what have I done to you? Please don't think badly of me.

SİNAN: I said go away.

MERYEM: Or did they tell you something about me?

SİNAN: Go away. I know what kind of a girl you are now.

MERYEM: [*Interrupts him.*] It's a lie. I swear whatever they told you is a lie.

SİNAN: All right. So be it.

MERYEM: Don't go yet. Don't go. Maybe I am bad, but I've done you no harm. I love you. Please stay. Don't even look at my face if you don't want to.

SİNAN: I can't stay here any longer.

MERYEM: Please say something. Tell me to my face what I've done wrong. Beat me if you want, kill me. Is it because I didn't talk to him?

SİNAN: That's enough!

MERYEM: Stay for tonight. I'll talk to him as soon as he comes.

SİNAN: No need. [*Moves as if he wants to walk away.*]

MERYEM: Good God. Or . . . or are you angry because I said no to you? [*Stops him.*] Please forget it. Forget what happened just for this once. Oh, you don't know me well. Who knows what lies you've heard about me. I'm not like I was that first night you came.

SİNAN: [*With contempt.*] And what are you like?

MERYEM: I was like a leaf in the wind that night. I wasn't in my right mind. I would have gone to anyone who held my hand. I wish you hadn't seen me like that. Now I've changed; I've changed a lot. I'm in love with you. I can't bear to have you think badly of me.

SİNAN: [*With anger and hatred.*] I see. [*Walks away.*]

MERYEM: [*Tries to stop him again.*] I have no other hope, no one else to trust. Please believe me. All right, then. [*Suddenly grabs hold of* SİNAN's *wrist.*] Come.

SİNAN: [*Slaps* MERYEM *on both cheeks.*] This is for you!

MERYEM: Don't!

SİNAN: Can you think properly now?

MERYEM: [*Feels her face where he slapped her and moves back a step or two.*] You, too. You hit me, too. Go away. Go away and don't let me see you ever again. Go to hell.

SİNAN: [*Stops just as he is about to leave.*] Coward!

MERYEM: [*After him.*] Don't take too long! Go away! You're like all of them. Go away! [SİNAN *exits.*]

Scene 2

[*Nighttime: three hours later.* HAŞİM *has drunk himself to sleep on the bunk.* MERYEM *sits on the doorstep. She is absorbed in thought. Music is heard.* SİNAN *comes back from the direction he left earlier. He leaves his bundle in the boat.* MERYEM *straightens up.* SİNAN *turns toward the hut. He's a little drunk.* MERYEM *throws herself at him.*]

MERYEM: You've stayed, haven't you? You're staying, aren't you? [*Puts her head on* SİNAN's *chest.*] I was terrified you'd go. Please listen to me. Only I know what I've gone through since the evening. You're not going, are you?

SİNAN: [*Strokes* MERYEM's *hair lightly.*] I'm not going.

MERYEM: You won't go. You'll never go. Oh, my darling. My life. My man.

SİNAN: It's cold now. Go inside.

MERYEM: I won't.

SİNAN: Go on, go in; don't start again.

MERYEM: [*Embraces* SİNAN *again.*] Tell me, do you love me, too?

SİNAN: I don't know.

MERYEM: You're drunk. Did you get drunk because of me? [SİNAN *doesn't answer.*] You're not cross with me—you're not angry with me, are you? Oh, what a fool I was, my precious. Why couldn't I understand it? I didn't realize till this evening that I love you so. Where have you been? I've missed you so much. If you go away, I won't stay here another moment. I'll come after you. Come on, kiss me, take me in your arms. [*Turns* SİNAN's *head, which was facing the hut, toward her.*] He fell asleep. [SİNAN *takes* MERYEM *in his arms.*] Hold me tight, tight. [*They kiss.*] Kiss me again. Oh, I'll never let you go. [*A long kiss.*]

Scene 3

[*A little later. As* MERYEM *and* SİNAN *are settling down by the fire.*]

MERYEM: Are you hungry?

SİNAN: Not really.

MERYEM: I've kept you something to eat. [*Fills the plate from the pot.*] Come on, eat this.

SİNAN: [*Takes the plate.*] So you didn't believe that I'd go?

MERYEM: Of course I didn't.

SİNAN: I was going to go, but . . .

MERYEM: Maybe you'll go one day, but not now.

SİNAN: How do you know?

MERYEM: How should I know? Maybe because I don't want to let you go. Such things are mutual.

SİNAN: I was going to go away tonight, but . . . it doesn't matter now.

MERYEM: Why didn't you, then?

SİNAN: I went up to the coffeehouse, and I couldn't go any farther. It was as if somebody threw a rope at me, and my feet got tied together.

MERYEM: [*Happily.*] It's a lie.

SİNAN: Cross my heart . . .

MERYEM: . . . and hope to die.

SİNAN: [*Kisses the bread and touches it to his forehead.*] Let this piece of bread curse me if I'm lying.

MERYEM: See? Don't ever try to escape again . . . or I'll tie your feet together like that.

SİNAN: [*Changes the subject.*] When did he come?

MERYEM: About an hour ago. He was drunk. He talked nonsense for a while and then went to bed. It wouldn't be like this if I were your wife. This is my ordeal.

SİNAN: Come on, don't complain about nothing.

MERYEM: Of course it's an ordeal! Am I wrong? I want to be his wife—I can't. I wish to be your lover—I can't again. I don't know what to do. Seems as if I am far too soft and good-hearted. I made this mistake once. I take no comfort so long as he lives.

SİNAN: I said let's run away.

MERYEM: The weather's getting worse.

SİNAN: Don't change the subject.

MERYEM: And I told you that I can't run away. He's more in love with me than you are. Would he let us run away? [Pensively.] All right. Why did you call me a coward today?

SİNAN: You are a coward. Isn't that true?

MERYEM: Why?

SİNAN: Would you be with him now if you weren't a coward? Is he suitable for you? You look like some sort of stolen goods when you're with him. If you weren't a coward, you'd run away with me.

MERYEM: What if you leave me later on?

SİNAN: Why should I leave you if you behave like a proper woman?

MERYEM: Who knows, maybe you'll get tired of me.

SİNAN: First of all, you should have confidence in yourself. Then start thinking. Now go inside.

MERYEM: I don't want to.

SİNAN: Why not?

MERYEM: I'm all right here, near you.

SİNAN: You weren't like this in the afternoon. You were scared to death in case he'd see us or hear something.

MERYEM: Let him see or hear from now on! I don't give a damn!

SİNAN: Excellent. I can see real progress in you this evening!

MERYEM: Please don't talk to me about this evening anymore. Don't remind me of this evening.

SİNAN: We'll see how you feel tomorrow, too.

MERYEM: We will. And you'll regret these words sometime.

SİNAN: Look here. Does he still make advances to you?

MERYEM: Heaven forbid! May God save me!

SİNAN: What do you mean?

MERYEM: Well, he makes advances, but unless I want it to happen . . .

SİNAN: So there isn't anything between you anymore, is there?

MERYEM: I haven't touched him since the day you came.

SİNAN: How do you handle him?

MERYEM: I make up a lie and distract him. Then I turn my back on him and go to sleep.

SİNAN: Look here. If I ever hear something else, I'll . . .

MERYEM: That's what I'm afraid of.

SİNAN: What?

MERYEM: It can't go on like this forever. For two weeks now I've kept him at bay saying, "I'm tired," "I'm sick," or "You're drunk." But what about later on?

SİNAN: [*With growing jealousy.*] What about later on?

MERYEM: He's sure to insist someday. He's my husband after all.

SİNAN: Who says he's your husband? You've had only a religious service. You haven't had a legally valid marriage.

MERYEM: Instead of saying this, why didn't you just hit him with the log that first night you came here?

SİNAN: I couldn't have done it.

MERYEM: [*Excited.*] Listen, I've got an idea.

SİNAN: What?

MERYEM: He's drunk now. You hold him by the arms, and I'll hold him by the legs. Let's put him on the road over there. We'll both be rid of him when a truck runs over him.

SİNAN: No!

MERYEM: Yes! Don't think he'll wake up. Everybody will say that he fell asleep there on the road on his way back from the tavern.

SİNAN: Are the truck drivers blind? They'll see him. [*A short pause.*]

MERYEM: [*Gets excited again.*] All right. I have another idea!

SİNAN: Tell me.

MERYEM: Push him over the side of the boat into the sea when you're fishing.

SİNAN: And then?

MERYEM: You'll say that he fell overboard.

SİNAN: What if they ask me why I didn't save him?

MERYEM: You dive into the sea, too, get wet, and then say that you couldn't save him.

SİNAN: What if he saves himself?

MERYEM: Don't let him.

SİNAN: This is not such a good idea, either.

MERYEM: [*Absorbed in thought.*] Or should I poison him?

SİNAN: You said yourself that didn't work.

MERYEM: The best was to hit him on the head with the log. [*Thinks for a moment.*] I got it.

SİNAN: What is it now?

MERYEM: Let's all three of us go out to fish tonight.

SİNAN: What do you mean all three of us?

MERYEM: Let's take him by the arms and legs, put him in the boat. Then let's go out on the sea.

SİNAN: In this weather?

MERYEM: What better than this weather? The boat will capsize before we go very far.

SİNAN: Then?

MERYEM: Then somehow I'll save myself. And you yourself. Let him save himself if he can in this condition. How about it?

SİNAN: This is more plausible, but . . .

HAŞİM: [*From inside.*] Meryem!

SİNAN: He's calling you.

MERYEM: [*Gets up. To* HAŞİM.] Drop dead, will you! Go to hell!

HAŞİM: [*Comes to the door and then closer.*] Are you here?

MERYEM: Sinan came a little while ago; I gave him his dinner.

HAŞİM: I'm hungry, too.

MERYEM: Sit down and eat. [*Goes inside to fetch the plates and everything.*]

HAŞİM: [*Stands up, his face turned toward the sea, breathes deeply, and stretches.*] Ohh. Good weather. Just the weather I like. [*To* MERYEM, *who has come back.*] Fill my plate up. [*To* SİNAN.] Once upon a time, I would go out on the sea in such weather no matter what happened. Folks wouldn't want to go out of their houses, but me, I would sail on the sea as easily as if I were playing tipcat. The sea won't eat you up . . . so long as you know her ways. [MERYEM *and* SİNAN *look at each other.* HAŞİM *takes his plate and starts to eat hungrily.*] It's been three days since I touched seawater. I'm rotting away here. [*Takes a deep breath.*] I've come alive. The deepwater fish must have come near the shore by now. We'll catch lots of fish. [*To* SİNAN.] How about going fishing tonight? [MERYEM *motions to* SİNAN *to accept.*]

SİNAN: [*Puzzled.*] You're the boss. You give the orders.

HAŞİM: [*Goes toward the shore with the plate in his hand.*] Let me take a closer look.

MERYEM: [*Softly, to* SİNAN.] Let me come, too. We'll turn the boat over and get rid of him.

SİNAN: [*With a hopeless expression on his face.*] It'll be difficult.

HAŞİM: The weather is going to go on like this. Look. Get up and take a look. [SİNAN *gets up.*] Come here, near me. Look ahead, over at Foça. It's getting foggy, you see? The weather will continue like this. You don't know the sea here as well as I do. You're a stranger. Anyway, it wouldn't matter even if you weren't a stranger. Nobody around this bay knows the sea better than me. [*Makes a sudden decision.*] Go on, get the boat ready.

SİNAN: With oars?

HAŞİM: Oars? No, with sails. [SİNAN *starts to pull off the tarp that covers the boat.*]

MERYEM: I'll come, too.

HAŞİM: You take this plate out of my hands. [*Indicates the hut with his head.*] That is where you belong.

SİNAN: Is the *Sea Rose* going to survive this weather?

HAŞİM: She's seen worse. You wait till I hold the rudder. [MERYEM, *who had taken the plate into the hut, comes back.*] See, there are no boats on the sea. [*To* MERYEM.] Go and make yourself useful. Light the lantern in the hut. [*To* SİNAN.] All the empty boxes will be full by tomorrow morning. [*Puts the nets and other equipment into the boat.*] You'll see how plentiful the fish will be tonight. Come on, go over to the prow, and let's push the boat. Fix the oars. [*Calls.*] Meryem . . . bring the lantern! [*To* SİNAN.] Let Meryem come, too. The boat will be heavier. We'll sail better that way. [MERYEM *comes back with the lit lantern.* HAŞİM *takes it from her and hands it over to* SİNAN, *who is in the boat. He then holds* MERYEM *by the arm.*] Go on . . . you, too . . . jump in. [*He helps her step into the boat as he is pushing it into the sea.*]

CURTAIN

ACT III

Scene 1

[*The next night. The stage is lit up by a sailor's lantern and the flames from the fire. The* Sea Rose *is where it was previously. And Fakir's cage has come back.* MERYEM *and* SİNAN *are by the fire.*]

MERYEM: Why are you sulking?

SİNAN: I don't feel well.

MERYEM: Do you think I do?

SİNAN: Then don't talk so much!

MERYEM: Oh, all right, do whatever you want!

[MERYEM *half turns where she is sitting so that he faces her side. She puts her elbows on her knees and props her chin on her fists.* SİNAN *fills his glass from the wine bottle at his feet and puts the bottle back on the ground. He drinks.* MERYEM *reaches out to take the bottle.*]

Give me that bottle.

SİNAN: [*Prevents her.*] Leave it.

MERYEM: Give it to me. Don't drink any more.

SİNAN: Don't interfere!

MERYEM: Don't drink. You become quarrelsome.

SİNAN: I know myself.

MERYEM: I can see that. [*Sits back in her former position; a short pause.*]

SİNAN: [*Sips from his glass. Deep in thought.*] I can't understand what kind of a woman you are.

MERYEM: [*Hurt.*] As if you understand other women. [*Shrugs.*] I'm just like other women.

SİNAN: You're not.

MERYEM: So what kind of a woman am I? [SİNAN *takes another small sip.*] Go on, tell me.

SİNAN: [*Changes the position of his feet while still sitting down.*] I don't know. You're different. I haven't figured you out yet.

MERYEM: Do you mean to say I'm bad? [*Turns to* SİNAN.] Don't start blaming me. I'm just like any other woman. [*Regretfully.*] Bad luck.

SİNAN: What bad luck?

MERYEM: My whole life has been full of bad luck. Who knows, if I had married you a long time ago, maybe I wouldn't have been like this. [*Sighs.*] Fate. This is my fate. Whew! My mind gets confused when I think about it all.

SİNAN: [*Mocking.*] You think too much.

MERYEM: Don't make fun of me! You didn't come into my life for all these years. You had to come into it when everything had turned into a mess!

SİNAN: I've heard all this too many times! Forget these old stories.

MERYEM: [*Thoughtfully.*] If only you'd showed up in those days. I would have run away with you at the slightest sign from you. I wasn't like this in those days.

SİNAN: What's wrong with you now?

MERYEM: [*Stoically.*] I don't know. Gone are those days. I'm tired. I have no more wishes. I feel bored, and our affair is in vain. The best thing to do is to cut it short . . .

SİNAN: Is this one of your whims? What did you think? That you could play around with me just as you liked?

MERYEM: I'm not playing around with you, and I have no such intentions. Whatever I told you, it was all true. And this is true, too. The thing we have is in vain. [*Looks behind her as if she's expecting someone, obviously bored by being left alone with* SİNAN.]

SİNAN: You were quick to change your mind.

MERYEM: Am I wrong? You were there, too, last night. As he was going from the prow to the stern, he slipped and was going to fall, but you grabbed him by the waist and saved him.

SİNAN: That was all I could do! I can't attack a man who doesn't attack me!

MERYEM: I got that.

SİNAN: So what?

MERYEM: If you really were in love with me, if you wanted me to stay with you, you wouldn't have saved him.

SİNAN: That's not the same thing.

MERYEM: Maybe you're right from your own point of view, but I'm right, too.

SİNAN: What do you mean?

MERYEM: One of you two is an extra for me! I can't be a wife to both of you! And there is no solution to our problem. So, you find yourself someone suitable, and I'll go back to my husband. [*Looks behind her.*]

HAŞİM: [*As he is entering.*] Sinan, fill up the glasses. [*Enters and takes the glass* SİNAN *gives him as he is sitting down.*] The sea has calmed down. The son of a bitch! It was like a monster last night. And it's like a lamb tonight. There won't be any fish in this weather. [*Turns to* SİNAN.] Did you ever think that we might sink last night?

SİNAN: [*After glancing at* MERYEM.] If we hand sunk, I would have saved myself anyway.

MERYEM: [*After glancing at* SİNAN.] I used to beat the men in swimming when I was at Bodrum.

HAŞİM: [*Drinks.*] And I would have saved myself. [MERYEM *and* SİNAN *look at each other.*] Accidents happen to whoever tries to avoid them. I've never thought about death or an accident until today. It's God's will. Death never happens to you without you thinking about it beforehand. It's been fifteen or twenty years. I used to work on a motorboat. A storm broke out between Sinop and Zonguldak. We fought against it for an hour or two, and in the end the boat sank like a piece of paper. There were seven of us. They couldn't even find the corpses of the other six. I got saved. [MERYEM *and* SİNAN *look at each other involuntarily.* HAŞİM *can't make sense of their furtive glances.*] What happened?

MERYEM: [*Shrugs.*] Nothing? What should have happened?

HAŞİM: [*Drinks.*] Or don't you believe me? That's the way it is, though. You never die before you say that you're dying. [*To* MERYEM.] If Azrael[2] were to take my life away every time he appeared, I'd have died a hundred times before today. If you only knew what I've gone through.

SİNAN: [*After glancing at* MERYEM.] Maybe she knows about some of it.

HAŞİM: She knows some, but she doesn't know this. [*After taking a small sip.*] Look here, Sinan. Listen. [*Lights a cigarette.*] When I was a year old, I got sick. My mother used to tell me all about it. May she rest in peace. People didn't know about doctors in those days. The doctors in those days were *hocas*[3] and old wives. Old wives' tales and old wives' medicines. When my fever didn't go down after about two days, my mother went to the *hoca*. And the *hoca* told her to wrap me up and leave me at the cemetery for a night. What stupidity! Is a cold cemetery the right place for a twelve-month-old baby? So my helpless mother took me to the cemetery and left me there. When she came the next morning, she found me crying with my eyes wide open. My poor mother was surprised when she saw me howling after a week of unconsciousness. She took me back and fed me. My mother was ignorant, and I am, too. But I wouldn't leave a child in a cemetery no matter which *hoca* or imam told me to. What I want to say is that if you're destined to live, you live.

MERYEM: [*After looking at* SİNAN.] Must be so.

HAŞİM: [*Continues.*] Sure, you're surprised. Anyone would be surprised. Meryem, did I ever tell you about when I was about seven years old? Do children ever sit together peacefully? We used to wrestle with each other. I was the champion. The adults would

---

2. Azrael: Name traditionally attributed to the angel of death in Islam.

3. *Hoca*: A religious teacher.

surround us. [*Accompanies his speech with head and hand gestures.*] They used to tease us and watch us. They used to have a good time like that. Once they had me wrestling with a boy three years older than me. We started wrestling. The boy saw that I was strong. He tried to catch my foot, but no go! He caught my arm—again no go! The adults started to tease him. I don't know how it happened, but he was half a foot taller than me, and I was caught unaware; he caught me by the waist and turned me upside down. My head hit a stone, and I fell down unconscious. I don't remember the rest. Everyone expected me to die at any moment, but I opened my eyes three days later. I still carry the scar on my head. [*Takes off his woolen cap, bends his head, and points to the scar with his finger.*] Right there. [MERYEM *and* SİNAN *bend down to see. They look at each other.* HAŞİM *straightens up.*] Couldn't you see it? Well, it's pretty dark out now. You can't see it easily. I'll show it to you both tomorrow. [*Puts on his cap.*] If it's not destined, you don't die. That's what I want to say.

SİNAN: That's right.

HAŞİM: [*Remembers another incident.*] What a thing to happen. [*Slaps* SİNAN's *knee.*] I was enlisted, and I went to battle. So many men died around me for three years in the war, but I didn't have as much as a nose bleed; I didn't even think about death. [*Fills his glass and passes the bottle to* SİNAN. MERYEM *and* SİNAN *look at each other.*] Maybe you'll believe it, maybe not, but let me tell you a story anyway. Listen! What madness it was! [*Slaps* SİNAN's *knee again.*] I had separated two people who were fighting. Even till today I can feel Azrael's hand on my back. It was madness. We were at the coffee-house. After fishing, a fight started about shares. There was a rowdy fisherman. He attacked the captain. After some kicking, slapping, and hitting with chairs, the captain grabbed his knife. I don't know where the fisherman got it, but I saw a curved knife in his hand. Those who had wanted to stop them dispersed immediately. I was the only one left between them. I was young in those days. I was rowdy, too. A knife in the air on one side and a curved one on the other. I didn't think at all. I pushed the captain's chest; he went back three steps and fell down in a chair. I turned around, held the fisherman by his waist, threw him over my shoulder, and took him out of the coffeehouse. I swear that one knife went over my arm, and the other one missed the vein in my neck. They just missed me. They were going to stab me instead of each other. Even if it hadn't hit the vein in my neck, a wound made by a curved knife never heals. [*Drinks.*] What I want to say is that God doesn't take back the life he's given until the appointed hour. Death comes on the destined day. [*Sits up a little and is suddenly hit by a strong heart attack. While he's pressing on his heart with one hand, he squeezes the wine glass in his other hand. He writhes with pain.*]

MERYEM: [*Jumps up.*] What's happening?

SİNAN: [*Jumps up at the same time.*] What's wrong?

HAŞİM: [*Gives the glass in his hand to* MERYEM *and tries to calm them down by motioning to them. With difficulty.*] Stop!

MERYEM: What's wrong? Tell me.

HAŞIM: [*With difficulty.*] A pain . . . what a pain. [*Doubles up in pain. Grabs the collar of his flannel undershirt.*]

SINAN: [*Trying to make him sit up.*] Sit up; don't bend; it's better if you sit up.

HAŞIM: It's like a press. [*Breathes with difficulty.*] It's squeezing my heart. It's going to smother me.

MERYEM: [*Worried.*] I'll get some water. [HAŞIM *says no with his hand and writhes in pain.*]

SINAN: Make an effort. [*Puts* HAŞIM'*s arm around his neck and tries to make him get up.*] Walk a little. You'll get better.

HAŞIM: [*Motions for* SINAN *to leave him alone.*] Stop. Never did something like this happen to me before. My God. It's going to break my bones. I can't breathe. [MERYEM, *not knowing what to do, fans* HAŞIM'*s face with two hands. Then she stops. She tries to unbutton his shirt.*]

MERYEM: If you'd lie down a little.

HAŞIM: [*Breathes deeply.*] It's getting better now.

MERYEM: Come on. Go in and lie down a little.

HAŞIM: I couldn't move. [*Holds his chest.*] It crushed my ribs.

SINAN: Don't move again.

HAŞIM: It's gone. It went away quickly. Really, if anything were to kill me, this would have been it. [*To* MERYEM.] Sit down.

MERYEM: Perhaps you caught cold.

HAŞIM: I've never had a cold in my life.

SINAN: Maybe a vascular strain?

HAŞIM: Not like that, either. This is different. I didn't understand what it was. Suddenly I couldn't move. But it doesn't matter now. Let's not stop chatting because of this. It's over. [*Drinks, fills his glass again, and passes the bottle to* SINAN.] Look at the sea. [*After looking at the sea, to* SINAN.] It's getting calmer and calmer. Won't be two hours before it gets rough again. The sea's sly tonight. You never know what'll happen. Before you go to bed tonight, pull up the boat a little. [*Drinks. After he has retrieved the bottle and filled his glass again, he gives the bottle back to* SINAN.] You can take a lot of drink, too.

SINAN: [*Fills his glass. Puts the bottle down on the ground.*] I drink now and then. I drink when I'm with a friend and chatting.

HAŞIM: Alcohol is my friend. I was never harmed by it. You know, the kind of friend who does whatever you want, who goes wherever you go. Alcohol and me are like that. When I catch lots of fish, I feel happy; I drink and become happier still. If I've got nothing to do, it keeps me busy and makes me forget my boredom. I have lived all these years and never had a better friend.

MERYEM: One can see the pleasure you're getting out of it tonight.

HAŞİM: It's both a pleasure and not a pleasure. It doesn't taste good tonight, anyhow.

SİNAN: I never want to drink when I'm alone.

HAŞİM: Well, you're young yet. Your head is still full of some raw dreams. But it's those dreams that fool you. I drink whenever I have money. What good is a man who doesn't drink?

MERYEM: What good is a man who drinks? When you drink, you start stammering. It's better if you don't drink and don't stammer.

HAŞİM: What do you know? If you're going to choose yourself a friend, do it at the tavern. A man who doesn't drink is like a closed box. You never know what's inside, diamonds or dung. When he drinks his quota, he tells you everything that's in his mind. He might look like a coward, but turn out to be brave.

MERYEM: [After glancing at SİNAN.] And some look brave and turn out to be cowards.

HAŞİM: [Continues.] That's right. He looks brave, but he turns out to be dishonest. Alcohol scrapes away a man's paint. You can see that those walking around like lions are in fact pussycats. By now I've seen all kinds. [Drinks. To SİNAN.] Come on. [SİNAN doesn't drink. He puts his glass down on the ground.] I've seen gentlemen you wouldn't hire as servants when they get drunk. I've seen generous ones who turned out to be misers. They try to make the waiter or the bartender pay for their drinks. To me, alcohol is the only measure that doesn't go wrong. [To SİNAN.] Go on, drink.

SİNAN: [Icily.] Could it be that you've been testing me?

HAŞİM: [Smiles.] What's up with you?

SİNAN: I don't like to be tested!

HAŞİM: And I don't like to fight when I'm drinking.

SİNAN: Then don't try testing me!

MERYEM: [Agitated.] What if he does test you?

SİNAN: [Harshly.] I don't get it!

MERYEM: If he wants, he'll test you. Aren't you his man?

SİNAN: He's the captain only on the sea. This is a friend's table.

HAŞİM: [To SİNAN.] That's enough! Watch your tongue! We have a woman with us.

SİNAN: First teach your wife to shut up!

HAŞİM: [Shaken.] What did you say?

SİNAN: [Still icily.] You heard what I said.

HAŞİM: [Recovers himself.] What is it you want? To start a fight?

SİNAN: I said I won't have you testing me. That's all.

MERYEM: What nonsense!

HAŞİM: [To MERYEM.] You shut up!

MERYEM: [Agitated.] Are you the captain, or is he? Are you going to explain yourself to him?

HAŞİM: I said shut up, or go away.

SİNAN: Go away and let him try.

HAŞİM: [*To* SİNAN.] Don't be so naive. I've tested you when I wanted to.

MERYEM: [*To* SİNAN *at the same moment.*] I'll go away if I want to. I wouldn't move an inch just because you told me to.

HAŞİM: Meryem. [*To* SİNAN.] I've tried you when I wanted to. If I hadn't, I wouldn't have sat and drunk with you at a table. I never lay a trap for someone while drinking. Come on. [*Picks up his glass.*] Let's drink if you're going to. If not, it's your business. [*To* MERYEM.] And you sit down. I'm not explaining myself to anyone. [*Drinks and wipes his mouth with the back of his hand. To* SİNAN.] Are you pleased now?

SİNAN: Whether I'm pleased or not, I'm leaving tomorrow.

HAŞİM: We'll talk about that tomorrow.

SİNAN: We can talk about it now. I decided to this morning.

MERYEM: [*Regretting her outburst, turns to* HAŞİM.] Ask him why he's leaving!

HAŞİM: That's for him to know.

SİNAN: I'll look up my brother.

HAŞİM: As you wish. I'll say good-bye whenever you say good-bye. Now forget about being angry and let's drink. [*Picks up the bottle to fill his glass. It's empty.*] Do we have any more?

MERYEM: How can we have any more?

HAŞİM: [*Looks for the bottles.*] There were three bottles. This is the first one . . .

MERYEM: You've drunk all three bottles.

HAŞİM: [*Looks around.*] This is one, this is two—three?

SİNAN: [*Picks up the third empty bottle on his right and turns it upside down.*] It's here.

MERYEM: And that's the third one.

HAŞİM: By God. All three of them are empty. And I haven't had enough yet.

MERYEM: [*Gets up.*] That's enough for tonight. And it's not as pleasant anymore, either.

HAŞİM: Oh, if you're good friends, you always have small arguments.

MERYEM: [*Looks around.*] In the other hunts, everybody has gone to bed. It's getting late.

HAŞİM: [*Gets up.*] I'm not sleepy, but still . . . let's go to bed if you want. [*To* SİNAN.] Go on, you go to bed, too. But, first, let's pull up the boat a little. You go around to the stern. [HAŞİM *and* MERYEM *move over to each side of the boat and hold the supports.*] Push hard. [*The boat moves forward on the props.*] That's enough. [*To* SİNAN.] Go over to the prow. Heave. [SİNAN *heaves the boat by the prow.* HAŞİM *and* MERYEM *move the props forward.*] The boat's OK now. Have a good night. [MERYEM *picks up the lantern by the fire. She stops for a moment as if she's going to tell* SİNAN *something, but then walks toward the hut and goes in.* HAŞİM *stops before going into the hut and turns to* SİNAN.] This business of your going away—think it over in the morning, will you?

SİNAN: We'll see. Let's wait till the morning. [HAŞİM *goes into the hut and shuts the door.* SİNAN *stays by the boat for a short while, lights a cigarette, and then takes his place by the fire again.* MERYEM *puts the lantern on a kerosene can turned upside down.* HAŞİM takes off his jacket and cap and hangs them on a nail near the door. He turns around and stops by Fakir's cage and plays with the bird.]

HAŞİM: How are you, sonny? Are you sleepy?

MERYEM: [*Takes off her dress. She now has on only her slip. She puts a fish box near the lantern, sits on it, and starts to unfasten her hair.*] Stop playing with him and go to bed.

HAŞİM: [*Sits on the edge of the bunk and starts to take off his boots.*] All right. I've stopped. You have your way, too. [*Pushes his boots under the bunk, takes off his pants and climbs into bed. After pulling the blanket up to his knees, he hangs his pants on a nail at the foot of the bunk.* MERYEM *combs her hair with a tortoiseshell comb.* HAŞİM, *with his face turned toward* MERYEM, *stretches out and props himself up with his elbow on the cushion.*] What's the matter with Sinan?

MERYEM: What do you mean?

HAŞİM: He was so peevish tonight. What do you think is the matter with him?

MERYEM: I wouldn't know about that.

HAŞİM: [*Very calm.*] What happened between you two?

MERYEM: [*Acts surprised.*] What could have happened between him and me?

HAŞİM: You had a tiff. He was arguing with you, not me.

MERYEM: I was angry because he acted like a bully. I don't have to act humbly toward everyone like you do, do I?

HAŞİM: [*After watching* MERYEM *comb her hair for a short while.*] All right. Come on, get into bed.

MERYEM: Can't you see? I'm combing my hair.

HAŞİM: I'm not drunk at all tonight, so don't start making excuses.

MERYEM: It's no use, so don't insist.

HAŞİM: Why?

MERYEM: I just don't want to.

HAŞİM: Come over here.

MERYEM: My hair is all matted. It's tangled. Let me comb it.

HAŞİM: Your hair is always beautiful. Even the wives of those rich guys in those beautiful houses don't have hair like yours.

MERYEM: Oh, I'm not beautiful anymore.

HAŞİM: What a beautiful girl you were! You were beautiful even when you were a kid! And you got even more beautiful as you grew up. I couldn't take my mind off you in those days when I used to come to your house.

MERYEM: Well, so you got your wish and turned me into this.

HAŞİM: What's wrong with you? You're still beautiful. You're at the height of your beauty now. You're not worn out at all.

MERYEM: [*Feeling better.*] You talk like that when it suits you.

HAŞİM: I always talk like this. But what's the use? I met you too late. I'm going to die disappointed because I didn't have as much time with you as I would have liked.

MERYEM: I've never seen a man like you. Even at this age, you lie like a little kid.

HAŞİM: I'm not lying. I said I met you too late.

MERYEM: You're right about that.

HAŞİM: I met you too late, but even in my youth my heart never beat the way it did when I first saw you. I was a rake in my youth. I never fell in love with anyone.

MERYEM: And by God, you appreciated my worth only too well, didn't you?

HAŞİM: Sure I did. I first felt sorry that I was getting old when I met you. And even today, I feel sorry now and then. If only I were ten or fifteen years younger . . .

MERYEM: So what would have happened then?

HAŞİM: Only God knows about that. Maybe you'd have been closer to me, eh? Would you?

MERYEM: I can never tell with you.

HAŞİM: Well, would you?

MERYEM: Don't keep asking me stupid questions.

HAŞİM: Listen, you know Sinan . . . well, I was stronger and more cheerful than him in my youth. Everywhere I went would become a carnival. I never knew unhappiness or distress. Everyone would seek my company. Friends never started drinking without me. Women didn't like to let me go. They used to cry with their arms around my neck. I wouldn't care a bit. Maybe I was made of stone or something. I obviously had no feelings and no conscience. Listen . . . when I think about the way I was then, I don't want to go back to Sinan's age. If I were to meet that twenty-five-year-old Haşim now, by God I would spit in his face. I hurt lots of people. I was just like an obstinate goat. I never appreciated the value of something beautiful or any sort of goodness. The only thing I believed in was my brute strength. Then, later, I calmed down.

MERYEM: Probably because you lost your strength.

HAŞİM: [*Proudly.*] Me, lose my strength? May God never let me see the day! It's not because of that. I came to my senses and calmed down, that's why. I would like to be younger now, but not Sinan's age; I'd like to be at the age I calmed down. It would be enough for me if I were forty or forty-five.

MERYEM: Why do you keep mentioning Sinan? What do you want from him?

HAŞİM: What else but his youth? He's the only one around who's the same age as you are. I don't have his youth. He's young and fresh. I'm old in both ways in your eyes. Every woman has an ideal in her head, and she flirts with everyone she meets till she gets to know him. You probably feel affectionate and motherly toward him.

MERYEM: To whom? Sinan?

HAŞİM: To Sinan or to anyone else.

MERYEM: It's never occurred to me to think that way.

HAŞİM: Oh yes it has.

MERYEM: Oh, go on, don't talk nonsense. As if I don't have other things to worry about. [*Belittling.*] Ha! Me, feeling affectionate toward Sinan. What rot.

HAŞİM: What I'm trying to say is that there must've been times when you were sorry that you spent your youth with me. But don't be sorry. The young ones don't have my experience. A young one would have hurt you or offended you from the first day. In all these years I only hurt you yesterday. And that was because . . . well, forget about that, too.

MERYEM: I never said that the young ones were better than you.

HAŞİM: [*Pushes aside the blanket.*] Come, let me touch your hair a little.

MERYEM: Wait, I haven't finished combing it yet.

HAŞİM: Come. Look what a beauty you are. There's the picture of a mermaid in the coffee-house; you look like her.

MERYEM: How you make up all these lies.

HAŞİM: I'll be damned if I'm lying. There's no woman better than you all the way from here to Bodrum.

MERYEM: [*Smiles.*] By God, nobody's better at lying than you.

HAŞİM: Come on, don't be coy. Bring your hair closer to me.

MERYEM: [*Gets up.*] Only my hair?

HAŞİM: [*Makes room for her.*] Only your hair. [MERYEM *gets into bed. Before lying down, she bends over the side of the bunk and turns the lantern down.* HAŞİM *slowly starts to fondle her hair.*]

MERYEM: You've tricked me again.

[*Outside the hut,* SİNAN *throws his cigarette to the ground and steps on it with his foot.*]

Scene 2

[*Next morning. It's about dawn. In the semidarkness, the horizon over the sea is a deep pink.* SİNAN, *just as in Act I, is sitting near the boat and waiting.* HAŞİM *has just died. He's lying lifeless on the bunk. Bewildered,* MERYEM *puts on her dress in a hurry. In sorrow, she weeps and mumbles to herself.*]

MERYEM: Oh, God. [*Runs to the door in fear.*] Sinan, Sinan, come here, quick. [*Goes near the bunk and then runs to the door again.*] Sinan, quick.

SİNAN: [*As he is going into the hut.*] What's the matter?

MERYEM: Come quick. [*Makes way for* SİNAN *by stepping aside.*] He's dead! I think he's died!

SİNAN: [*Puzzled.*] Dead? [*Goes closer and feels* HAŞİM's *chest and pulse.*]

MERYEM: [*In fear.*] He collapsed suddenly. Is he dead?

SİNAN: [*Thoughtful.*] Yes.

MERYEM: [*Exhausted, she goes near the door. Looks at* SİNAN's *bundle near the boat. With her back to him.*] Are you still going to go?

SİNAN: [*Doubtful.*] Or? [*Moves closer, grabs* MERYEM's *wrist, and turns her to face him.*] Tell me, what have you done to him? How did you kill him?

MERYEM: [*Without resistance, she looks into his eyes for a while. Calmly.*] He died naturally.

SİNAN: That's a lie! [*Shakes off* MERYEM's *wrist and turns his back to her.*]

MERYEM: [*Calmly.*] I felt him squeeze my wrist, and I jumped up. He had the same pains he had last night. He was suffocating. I wanted to give him some water, but he didn't want any. I unbuttoned his collar and tried to make him feel cooler. He said it was like being in a press. He said it was going to break his bones and make him die. He told me to take off everything he was wearing. Then he fell on his back and didn't move again.

SİNAN: Why didn't you call me?

MERYEM: It all happened so suddenly. He died like a boat with a hole in it. As if he sank into the sea. I saw him stop breathing, and I ran to call you.

SİNAN: [*Thoughtful, looking at* HAŞİM's *dead body.*] You had your mind set on killing him.

MERYEM: That was when he was alive.

SİNAN: And now?

MERYEM: I don't know. I'm terribly confused. All my hatred has gone away. Oh, what did I do wrong? I was young. I'm still young. I'm not done with life yet. For years he drank and dropped off to sleep, and for years I lay down next to him without any sleep. We were like a pair of oars, one shorter than the other one. Can such a boat make speed? And yet he was the only one I could hold onto. And now he's gone. [*Goes over to Fakir's cage and pours some bird food into it from a paper bag.*]

SİNAN: If he had answered me back last night, I could have killed him.

MERYEM: Last night was unusual. It was stormy. Neither of you was in your right mind. Now the storm is over. [*Puts the paper bag down.*]

SİNAN: It did stop, but only after washing ashore everything you've been keeping inside.

MERYEM: I see, so you're going.

SİNAN: I'm not going to stay just because he died.

MERYEM: How about me? Have you ever thought of what will happen to me?

SİNAN: I don't know.

MERYEM: You must know! Who am I going to stay with?

SİNAN: You were the one who wanted me to go last night.

MERYEM: Last night I was desperate.

SİNAN: And you're desperate now, too.

MERYEM: You can't have started to hate me so much in one day. You were the one who wanted it. You dragged me into it. You seduced me. You can't leave me now. [*Throws herself into his arms.*] You can't leave me all alone.

SİNAN: That was before yesterday.

MERYEM: [*Squeezes* SİNAN *in her arms.*] It's a lie. It's still the same. You loved me, and I loved you. We loved each other.

SİNAN: [*Pushes her away.*] Pull yourself together!

MERYEM: Tell me, didn't you love me?

SİNAN: What was between us wasn't love.

MERYEM: [*Her pride hurt.*] What was it, then?

SİNAN: It was anger, it was hatred, pity! It was a quarrel and a war! It was something like that!

MERYEM: And what's love? This is love.

SİNAN: It must be a different sort of feeling.

MERYEM: It's not! This is love! It's anger and calming down. It's hatred and happiness. It's a quarrel and making up. It's a headache, it's dizziness. You can never tell the difference between them when you're in love.

SİNAN: Even so, it's not for me.

MERYEM: Do you think so?

SİNAN: Yes. You're not for me, and I'm not for you.

MERYEM: [*Angry.*] I see. I understand what you want. Go find someone sluggish like yourself. I'm not going to beg you for favors. I'm not that old yet; neither am I so ugly. I'm not going to stay alone either.

SİNAN: [*Raises his hand in anger.*] Shut up. Don't make me sin on my way out . . . and with this corpse lying here.

MERYEM: Don't you dare hit me!

SİNAN: [*As he leaves the hut.*] Go back in! Don't let me see you again!

MERYEM: [*After him.*] What did you think? That I would die with him? That I would mourn for the rest of my life? This roof and this boat are mine now! I'm nobody's slave! I also have a right to live just the way I like!

SİNAN: [*Picks up his bundle. As he goes out from the right.*] You're the Devil! You're the Devil himself!

MERYEM: [*Goes out of the hut, down the steps. Shouts after* SİNAN *with increasing confidence.*] You're still jealous of me! Still worried to death in case I might be someone else's! You still want to hold me in your arms! All right, go away! Let's see you go. See how far you get this time around!

CURTAIN

A Shanty in Istanbul

BAŞAR SABUNCU

Translated by Nermin Menemencioğlu

An Editor's Note

Başar Sabuncu (b. 1943) is without a doubt one of Turkey's most versatile directors. He is known for his daring and innovative staging of both the classics and modern plays.

After graduating from Istanbul's French-language Saint Joseph Lycée, he worked as an actor with private theaters in Ankara and Istanbul and later as director and actor for Radio Ankara's play productions. Following training he received in stage directing in France, he joined the Istanbul City Theater. When he was dismissed from there for political reasons in 1981, he became a film director. In the 1980s and early 1990s, some of Turkey's best films were the directorial work of Başar Sabuncu. He later returned to his position with the City Theater.

Şerefiye (A Shanty in Istanbul) was Sabuncu's first full-length play. It had its premier in 1966 at the Ankara State Theater. An early short version was published, but the original of our English version remains unpublished. In 1968, the Ankara Art Lovers Association awarded *Şerefiye* the prize for the best Turkish play. Sabuncu shared this prize with Yaşar Kemal—a great honor for a twenty-five-year-old newcomer. Sabuncu also won awards for other plays and for his film and stage direction, including an honorable mention from the Euro Théatre.

This play's Turkish title, *Şerefiye,* is a term that refers to a tax levied on firms, individuals, and real estate in connection with improvements made in a section of a city. The play takes place inside a shanty (*gecekondu* in Turkish, literally meaning a squatter's house illegally put up in one night). In the lean years following the end of World War II, hundreds of thousands of rural people migrated into Turkey's urban areas in search of jobs. Those who found employment and even large numbers of families that remained unemployed built overnight ramshackle dwellings on vacant government land. So long as the roofs were thatched by daybreak, these shanties had immunity, under the law, from being torn down. Huge numbers of such shanties survived throughout decades in and around cities where a new class of rural-urban workers evolved. This class eventually made forays into the mainstream and joined the country's political blocs. This Sabuncu play dramatizes the tensions between the decadent urban bourgeoisie and the struggling shanty-dwellers. It is a compelling depiction of moral values challenged by urban economic and cultural reorientation.

Nermin Menemencioğlu (Streater) (1910–94), the translator of *A Shanty in Istanbul*, was well known for her translations of Turkish poetry, plays, and short stories into English. She rendered into English many of Anday's poems, including the book-length poem *Kolları Bağlı Odysseus* (Odysseus Bound). Menemencioğlu held a B.A. from Brown University and an M.A. from Columbia University. She edited the *Penguin Book of Turkish Verse* (1978).—TSH

Characters

SABRİ ŞENGİL, a night watchman at a factory

SAADET, Sabri's daughter, age six

SABİHA, Sabri's wife

GRANDFATHER, Sabri's father

YILMAZ, Sabri's son, age nineteen or twenty

TAHSİN MAHİROĞLU, Sabri's boss

NEZAHAT, Tahsin's wife

ACT I

[*Main room of* SABRİ ŞENGİL's *newly built shanty. It has a small window bought from a junk dealer and two doors that do not match—one is the front door, the other leads to* SABRİ *and* SABİHA's *bedroom. One corner of the room, provided with a small sink, a wire-mesh cupboard, and a few plate shelves, serves as a kitchen. Another corner, separated from the rest of the room by a curtain of cheap, flowered cotton, serves as* GRANDFATHER's *bedroom. The rest of the room, whose walls are not properly plastered yet, has shoddy furniture—a table and chairs, a divan that at night becomes a bed for* YILMAZ. *Obvious efforts have been made to clean the room and prepare it for a special occasion. Bits of embroidery, remnants of* SABİHA's *dowry, have been tossed on the table, the radio, the metal trunk, and every other conceivable object. On the wall behind the divan hangs a framed picture of Queen Soraya[1] wearing her crown; it has been cut out of an old magazine. There are vivid artificial flowers in a vase.*

SABRİ, *in his vest, is shaving at the sink, above which hangs a broken mirror. A copper pot is boiling on the gas burner.* SAADET *is sitting on the patched rug, humming a lullaby to her rag doll.*]

SAADET: [*To the doll.*] Shhhh, shhhh . . . rock-a-bye baby . . .

---

1. Soraya Esfandiary Bakhtiari (1932–2001), the second wife of Mohammad Reza Pahlavi, the last shah of Iran.

[*The hush is broken by a scream as* SABİHA *comes in through the front door, loaded with plates and cutlery.*]

SABİHA: They're burning . . . for goodness' sake, the beans are burning! [*Dumps the plates on the table.*]

SABRİ: [*Has cut himself.*] Ow!

SABİHA: [*Runs to the pot.*] Scorched! Oh, what a pity! Ruined!

SABRİ: [*In pain.*] Goddamn razor blade!

SABİHA: [*Turns off the gas burner.*] They're scorched, stuck to the bottom! We're disgraced!

SABRİ: [*Heedlessly.*] What?

SABİHA: The beans!

SABRİ: Whaaat!

SABİHA: Couldn't you have stirred them? Would they have stuck to your hand?

SABRİ: Take a look at my face.

SABİHA: I could smell them burning from around the corner. Give me a cloth.

SABRİ: Stuck, eh? [*Pulls the cloth from under the dishes, one plate falls with a clatter.*] Hell!

SABİHA: Oh, go away, go away! It would be better if you don't touch anything!

SABRİ: If we must, we can always replace . . .

SABİHA: They're not our property! I was embarrassed to have to borrow them.

SABRİ: [*Lifts the lid of the pot.*] Inedible, are they?

SABİHA: First, think of a way of explaining why one plate is missing.

SABRİ: [*Tastes the beans.*] How much smoked beef did you put in these?

SABİHA: A quarter pound.

SABRİ: Not enough!

SABİHA: If you'd bought more, I'd have used more!

SABRİ: Don't start again!

SAADET: [*To her doll.*] Quiet, baby, quiet! Or I'll give you to the bogeyman!

SABİHA: It never seemed right to me—beans for guests!

SABRİ: They themselves asked for beans.

SABİHA: With smoked beef?

SABRİ: With smoked beef!

SABİHA: Well, at least I didn't just do beans. I added something on the side!

SABRİ: So what's it to me? I just told you what they said—no more, no less! "It's been a long time since we have had some really delicious beans with smoked beef! Tell your lady to go to no other trouble." That's exactly what Tahsin Bey[2] said.

SABİHA: [*Sweeps up the fragments of the plate.*] Well, then, why did you badger me so?

---

2. *Bey:* "Gentleman" or simply "Mr." (used after the first name).

SABRİ: Go on, I bet you bragged plenty when you were borrowing those plates. Don't I know you!

SABİHA: [*Patronizingly.*] Go on yourself!

SABRİ: [*Tenses up.*] Who in this neighborhood has had such distinguished guests, I ask you? With a raise for me in sight, too! And all sorts of things, girl.

SABİHA: Hmm! I wonder!

SABRİ: Didn't I get a raise year before last, ungrateful creature?

SABİHA: [*Patronizingly.*] You did, and we acquired this palace!

SABRİ: Ah, but this time it's going to be a good raise. Yesterday Tahsin Bey had them tell him about the incident all over again. And he asked them once more who the brave fellow was who caught the thief. That's probably how he found out about our shanty.

SABİHA: You stop talking and get on with your shaving.

SABRİ: This is no razor blade—it's a blunt saw!

SABİHA: The boy uses it three times a day.

SABRİ: You leave him alone!

SABİHA: I'm only telling you.

SABRİ: Where is he, anyway?

SABİHA: Didn't you send him to get the guests? Who knows where he got stuck.

SABRİ: How would they get here if I hadn't sent him? Is this a house? It hasn't even got an address! [*Resumes his shaving.*] Where are the stuffed grape leaves? I don't see them anywhere.

SABİHA: In Selime Hanım's[3] fridge. We've been here only three days, and already it's ice cubes, food in her fridge, plates and cutlery on loan. I hardly dare to look her in the face.

SABRİ: Stop rubbing it in. Let me get my raise of a few pennies, then I'll set the table for forty-eight people. [*Pauses.*] Say, where's my father?

SABİHA: Searching for things in some garbage dump, I suppose. [*Tidies up the room.*] Time for you to get dressed. You're not going to face your guests in those rags, are you?

SABRİ: [*Washing his face.*] My clothes ready?

SABİHA: Fifteen suits ready, twenty at the cleaner's!

SABRİ: All right, all right, what I mean is, have you pressed my suit?

SABİHA: You've not worn it since the last holiday. Everything's laid out on the bed.

SABRİ: [*On his way to the bedroom.*] See if the meatballs are keeping hot.

SABİHA: And you get a move on. There's the table to be set. [*Starts tidying up the place again.*]

SABRİ: [*From the bedroom.*] I see you're taking an interest at last.

SABİHA: Who wants to be embarrassed?

SABRİ: Where's my green tie?

3. *Hanım:* A title meaning "Miss" or "Mrs." (used after the first name).

SABİHA: The boy must have put it on.

SABRİ: Stop blaming him for everything!

SABİHA: Well, doesn't he wear your ties?

SABRİ: What if he does? He's young, isn't he?

SABİHA: So he's young!

SABRİ: Oh, shut up now and think of the presents our guests will bring us!

SABİHA: [*As she dusts.*] Who'll bring what presents?

SABRİ: "We're not coming empty-handed, of course. Our gift for the new house shall be tucked under our arm." That's what Tahsin Bey said as he slapped me on the back.

SABİHA: You should have helped yourself to your own gift. With all that money right there in front of you.

SABRİ: What do you mean, girl?

SABİHA: They'd have thought the thief had taken it. "Dropped it as he was running," they'd have said.

SABRİ: [*Appears half-dressed in the bedroom door.*] How can a man bite the hand that feeds him and do a dirty thing like that, eh?

SABİHA: If you'd taken one small handful, who'd have thought of asking you?

SABRİ: A man trusts you with his goods, his belongings, his factory, he makes you night watchman, and you . . . you've got no mercy, girl!

SABİHA: Didn't the thought ever cross your mind?

SABRİ: So help me God, it didn't. [*Crosses to the mirror.*]

SABİHA: With that head on your shoulders, we'll never make ends meet. Maybe they'll erect a statue of you and make speeches in front of it!

SABRİ: Look here, are you trying to get a rise out of me, or . . . [*Suddenly remembers.*] The beans! They're going to get cold!

SABİHA: I'll warm them up when it's nearly time for the guests. What time is it now?

SABRİ: Twenty minutes to seven . . . they'll be here any minute now!

SABİHA: [*Runs around.*] And we're still in a mess. We'll be so embarrassed!

SABRİ: Has the dessert cooled off?

SABİHA: It's in the mesh cupboard.

SABRİ: You made the syrup good and thick?

SABİHA: I didn't wait for your instructions. [*Hands him a broom.*] Take this.

SABRİ: What for?

SABİHA: Go on, sweep.

SABRİ: Now you're going too far! [*Throws the broom on the floor.*]

SABİHA: I've got to get the child ready.

SABRİ: You'd better do something about your own hair first!

SABİHA: There's never any time for me. [*On her way out.*] You won't raise dust, will you? Wet the broom before you sweep.

SAADET: [*To her doll.*] Good little girls do not get their faces and hands dirty.

SABRİ: [*Nervously.*] Cut it out!

SABİHA: [*Takes* SAADET *by the hand.*] Come on, girl. [*To* SABRİ.] Don't forget to clean under the pictures.

[SABİHA *and* SAADET *go into the bedroom.*]

SABRİ: May God give me patience! [*Takes a few steps, wets the broom under the faucet, then begins to sweep while grumbling.* GRANDFATHER *comes in, dressed in a nightshirt and with a cap on his head.*]

GRANDFATHER: [*Grumbling to himself.*] Damn the whole neighborhood and damn all the people who live here. [*Sees* SABRİ *and continues in a mocking tone.*] Good luck with your task.

SABRİ: Thanks, Father. What are you up to? Cursing at the world again?

GRANDFATHER: What's more to the point is, what are you up to? First tell me that.

SABRİ: [*Embarrassed.*] Well . . .

GRANDFATHER: A man should not be seen doing this! It's always Sabiha, that bitch!

SABRİ: Once in a blue moon . . .

GRANDFATHER: Even so!

SABRİ: There are guests coming.

GRANDFATHER: Aha! [*Mockingly.*] That explains why the place looks so tidy. Good, good, very good!

SABRİ: [*Swallows some dust and coughs.*] I've had it!

GRANDFATHER: [*Softly.*] Shhh . . . Sabri . . .

SABRİ: Hmm?

GRANDFATHER: Come here, come, come . . .

SABRİ: What's up?

GRANDFATHER: But you're not to tell Sabiha.

SABRİ: [*Walks up to* GRANDFATHER.] I won't tell her.

GRANDFATHER: You're scared of her, so you'll tell her, but never mind. [*Opens his clenched hand.*] What's this?

SABRİ: [*Innocently.*] A stamp.

GRANDFATHER: [*Mockingly.*] Well done, such brains and at your age, too! Look carefully— it's a German stamp!

SABRİ: All this fuss for a stamp?

GRANDFATHER: You think it's easy to find such a stamp in a neighborhood of this sort?

SABRİ: How the hell should I know?

GRANDFATHER: What kind of a home is this? Years go by, and no one writes a letter, no one ever receives one! [SABRİ *laughs good-humoredly.* GRANDFATHER *sees the dishes.*] Where in the world did these come from?

SABRİ: They're the neighbors!

[*As* GRANDFATHER *picks up one of the dishes,* SABİHA *comes out of the bedroom, holding* SAADET *by the hand.* SAADET *is wearing her holiday best.*]

SABİHA: [*Hastily.*] Put down that plate, put it down. Your hands are not all that steady.

GRANDFATHER: Shame on you!

SABİHA: Sabri, you're still chattering, and the guests are almost here!

SABRİ: [*Nervously.*] I'm through sweeping.

GRANDFATHER: What's happening? Are the Russians coming?

SABİHA: Guests.

GRANDFATHER: Fine, I got that.

SABİHA: [*Sees the stamp in his hand.*] What's that? Not another of your stamps?

GRANDFATHER: None of your business!

SABİHA: Give it to me!

GRANDFATHER: Oh, for heaven's sake! Attend to your own affairs!

SABİHA: All the glasses are sticky with glue from your stamps.

GRANDFATHER: So what am I to do?

SAADET: [*Innocently.*] Do as you are told, Granddad. If people don't do as they are told, the bogeyman gets them.

GRANDFATHER: [*Pushes her away.*] Shut up, you little bastard! Just look at that child! [SAADET *screams her head off.*]

SABİHA: Don't you call my child a bastard!

GRANDFATHER: And don't you interfere with me.

SABİHA: You're always going for my child, never his . . .

SABRİ: [*Tries to smooth matters over.*] Sabiha . . .

GRANDFATHER: I loved my previous daughter-in-law more than I love you. Have you anything to say about that? Her tongue didn't hang out a mile.

SABİHA: [*Stubbornly.*] But God took her away . . . serves you right!

GRANDFATHER: The good do not live long.

SABİHA: I'm going to explode any moment now.

GRANDFATHER: Go ahead!

SABRİ: [*Comes between them.*] Time for you to get dressed, Father.

GRANDFATHER: I'm satisfied with these clothes.

SABRİ: But I've told you, we've got guests.

GRANDFATHER: For any guests in this house, a nightshirt is quite good enough! [*To* SABİHA.] The occasion seems to call for the treasures of your trousseau, though they were too good to use on your wedding night!

SABİHA: Sabri, get this man to stop, or I'll . . .

GRANDFATHER: Why don't you hang up your wedding nightgown in the bedroom, for good measure?

SABRİ: Listen, Father, in a little while Tahsin Bey and his wife are coming.

GRANDFATHER: Who, who?

SABRİ: The owner of our factory.

SABİHA: [*Proudly.*] That's who.

GRANDFATHER: No one asked you! [*To* SABRİ.] You don't mean it.

SABRİ: That's how it is, so you see . . .

GRANDFATHER: [*In a sudden flap; to* SABİHA.] Is my blue suit pressed?

SABİHA: I sold it to the junk dealer last year!

GRANDFATHER: Yes, to spite me. Very well, I'll put on the brown suit. Get the ironing board ready.

SABİHA: No ironing in here. I've just tidied up.

GRANDFATHER: Is brushing up forbidden, too? [*To* SAADET.] Bring me the brush.

SABİHA: Saadet is not your servant.

GRANDFATHER: Am I not her grandfather?

SABİHA: You don't sound like it.

GRANDFATHER: What do you mean? [*Mockingly.*] You mean Sabri is not her father?

SABİHA: [*Loses her temper.*] I mean maybe you're not Sabri's father—could be, couldn't it?

SABRİ: Stop it, both of you! Shame on you!

GRANDFATHER: Just look at that bitch!

SABRİ: [*Soothingly.*] The brush is in our room, Father. Go along now.

GRANDFATHER: OK, OK, I'm going! [*To* SABRİ, *mockingly.*] And good luck to you! [*Takes a few steps toward the bedroom.*]

SABİHA: Hey, are your shoes clean? Goddamn . . . God give me patience!

GRANDFATHER: Coming home I stepped into water-buffalo shit, but my shoes are clean compared to this place. [*Goes out.*]

SABRİ: [*Looks at* SAADET.] The girl looks all right.

SABİHA: There's not much left to dress her with. [*To* SAADET.] Saadet, child, run to your aunt Selime's and say, "My mother gave you a dish to put in your fridge." You bring it back. That's a good girl.

SAADET: All right.

SABRİ: I've just thought—we should've got some beer. These people always drink beer with a meal.

SABİHA: Wait a moment, child. [*To* SABRİ.] How many bottles?

SABRİ: We don't have to drink beer ourselves. Two bottles will do.

SABİHA: [*To* SAADET.] Get two bottles of beer from the grocer and be careful not to break them. [*To* SABRİ.] Why don't you give her the money?

SABRİ: Haven't you got some?

SABİHA: You're out of your mind! What day of the month is this? And guests on top of everything else.

SABRİ: Let him write it down in his book. Tell him your father sends greetings.

SABİHA: [*Runs after* SAADET.] Take the string bag with you, the bag! [*Hands* SAADET *the bag.* SAADET *goes out.*]

SABRİ: Sabiha, you really mean you have no money left?

SABİHA: You think I'm lying? How far do you think I can stretch the pittance you give me?

SABRİ: Well, I can't steal, girl; you have to have some self-respect.

SABİHA: Thank heaven our self-respect reaches up to the sky! [*Points at the table.*] Get hold of this. [*They move the table.*] A little more—that's it.

SABRİ: Shall I set the table?

SABİHA: No, no, never mind, you might drop another plate.

GRANDFATHER: [*From the other room.*] Hey, where are my trousers?

SABİHA: Damn you! Where they always are!

[GRANDFATHER, *in his long underwear, takes a pair of trousers from under his bed. On his way back, he sees the table.*]

GRANDFATHER: Knives on the right, forks on the left, spoons on top, with their handles to the right. [*Goes out.*]

SABİHA: God grant him mercy!

SABRİ: [*Setting the table.*] What was that about spoons? [SABİHA *withers him with a glance.*] What about the beans—should we put them back on the gas burner?

SABİHA: I've got the meatballs on now.

SABRİ: Well, they'll be here any minute. [*Grabs the pot.*] It's ice cold!

SABİHA: Get the little alcohol burner pumped up!

SABRİ: [*Walks toward the burner.*] And you change into something decent.

SABİHA: What have I got to change into?

SABRİ: That print dress you bought for the last holiday. Go put that on.

SABİHA: It's cotton!

SABRİ: Whatever it is, it's pretty!

SABİHA: All right, I'll wear that. [*Opens the bedroom door.*] Oooh!

GRANDFATHER: [*From the bedroom.*] Can't you knock before you come in? What's the great hurry?

SABİHA: There you have it. Your father gets all the attention, and nobody else counts in this house.

SABRİ: [*Struggles with the burner.*] Got a pin?

SABİHA: There, on the shelf with the pans.

SABRİ: Where's the alcohol?

SABİHA: Haven't you got eyes? There! [*Hands him the alcohol.*]

GRANDFATHER: [*Comes out fully dressed in a black-tie outfit, one hand behind his back.*] How do I look?

SABİHA: [*Heads toward her bedroom.*] At last!

GRANDFATHER: [*To* SABİHA *in a conciliatory tone.*] Look, Sabiha . . .

SABİHA: What is it now?

GRANDFATHER: Let's make up!

SABİHA: Well, well!

GRANDFATHER: I can't stand being cross with anyone for long.

SABİHA: You don't just stand it, you love it.

GRANDFATHER: I swear I don't.

SABİHA: [*Notices that he has one hand behind his back.*] What are you hiding in that hand?

GRANDFATHER: Nothing, nothing.

SABİHA: Come on, come on!

GRANDFATHER: [*Produces an old photograph in a frame.*] Here.

SABİHA: Weeell?

GRANDFATHER: A photograph of me with the late minister of health. He was one of our customers. I thought, maybe . . .

SABİHA: Out with it, what did you think?

GRANDFATHER: How about tacking it up, maybe on this wall?

SABİHA: Oh, tack it up, tack it up . . .

GRANDFATHER: [*Hurries to the wall.*] Bless you, my girl, bless you. [*Hangs up the photograph.*] You know it's old age that makes me grumble, don't you? God knows I think of you as a daughter. [*Looks at the photograph.*] How's that?

SABRİ: [*Looks up from his struggle with the burner.*] It's crooked. [GRANDFATHER *straightens the photograph.*]

SABİHA: Old fool! [SAADET *comes in, balancing a dish of food in one hand and holding the string bag with the bottles of beer in the other.*] Is that you, girl? Put that dish on the table. Sabri, you take the beer from her. I'm going to get dressed. [*Goes into the bedroom.*]

SABRİ: I've had it up to here! [*While he is taking the beer bottles from* SAADET, GRANDFATHER *studies his son's appearance.*]

GRANDFATHER: That won't do!

SABRİ: What?

GRANDFATHER: You can't wear blue socks with that suit, my boy!

SABRİ: [*Back at the burner.*] For heaven's sake, Father, leave me alone!

GRANDFATHER: Go change them at once.

SABRİ: My other socks are dirty.

GRANDFATHER: Dirty they can be, blue they cannot.

SABRİ: Go away, Father, stop pestering me!

GRANDFATHER: You want to show off, but where's your savoir faire? Let's have a look at the table. [*Goes over to the table.*] Oh my God, oilcloth! How can one eat off oilcloth?

SABRİ: [*Irritably.*] We do it every day, don't we?

GRANDFATHER: You do it, but that's different. At least you've had sense enough to get those plates. That's fine.

SABRİ: [*Mutters between his teeth.*] Hmmm!

GRANDFATHER: [*Changes the glasses around.*] What sort of a man is this Tahsin Bey?

SABRİ: A fatherly sort of man.

GRANDFATHER: What do you mean?

SABRİ: [*Pumps the burner.*] Just that.

GRANDFATHER: [*Folds the napkins in restaurant style.*] I can't place him—I wonder if he ever came to us for meals?

SABRİ: In the days when you were a waiter at that restaurant you keep telling us about nonstop, he was playing marbles with other kids!

GRANDFATHER: Where are your manners? Headwaiter. I was headwaiter. Your Sabiha's father was only a waiter.

SABİHA: [*Has heard the last words as she comes out of the bedroom. Angrily.*] You say that in front of the guests, and . . .

GRANDFATHER: It's true, isn't it?

SABİHA: And what were you?

GRANDFATHER: Headwaiter.

SABİHA: Humph!

GRANDFATHER: Humph to you! Don't you forget how you were always underfoot in the kitchen, a drooling child, an ugly little thing, and I felt sorry for you. Your father couldn't afford to get food for you all by himself.

SABİHA: Look at yourself! Did you or did you not drag Sabri out of school when he was barely in the second year instead of educating him properly?

GRANDFATHER: [*As though he hadn't heard.*] Your father couldn't even tie his bow tie himself! I had to do it for him—the sniveler!

SABİHA: God have mercy! Here, Sabri, pull up the zipper on this dress, for heaven's sake!

SABRİ: [*Does so.*] I've got the beans warming on the burner.

SABİHA: Keep the flame down, then. [*Walks toward the bedroom.*] And don't make a mess.

SABRİ: [*Turns the flame so low that it goes out.*] Hell, it's out! That godforsaken burner!

GRANDFATHER: That's no sort of job for you, my son.

SABRİ: [*Impatiently.*] For God's sake, Father!

GRANDFATHER: [*Lifts the lid off the pot.*] Here, let's have a taste. [*Tastes.*] What a bland stew!

SABRİ: [*Peeved.*] It's fine; I'm sure we can eat it! [*Tops up the alcohol in the burner.*]

GRANDFATHER: It's not me I'm thinking about, Son. Your guests are important people, isn't that right?

SABRİ: That's right!

GRANDFATHER: Well, you see?

SABİHA: [*Returns, holding onto her zipper.*] It's so embarrassing!

SABRİ: Wait a minute, wait!

SABİHA: It won't stay closed, see?

SABRİ: Oh, God! [*Leaves the burner and struggles with the zipper.*]

SABİHA: [*To* SAADET, *who is playing on the floor with her doll.*] Don't sit on the floor, girl! And pick up all those rags!

SAADET: I won't, I won't, I won't give my dolly to the bogeyman!

GRANDFATHER: [*Studies himself in the mirror.*] If only there were time to press my suit!

SABRİ: There, now, the zipper's fine.

SABİHA: Never a minute to myself. No wonder I look like a witch.

GRANDFATHER: All you need is a broom! [*Laughs at his own joke.*]

SAADET: [*Laughs. To* GRANDFATHER.] Witches fly on broomsticks, don't they, Granddad?

SABİHA: [*To* SAADET, *angrily.*] What are you laughing at, you little bastard?

GRANDFATHER: [*Laughs more loudly.*] She said "bastard"! She said "bastard"!

SABRİ: Father, pull yourself together, for heaven's sake!

[SAADET, *who has no idea what is being said, joins her* GRANDFATHER *in laughter until* SABİHA *gives her a slap. Her loud cries drown out* GRANDFATHER's *laughter. At that moment, a car stops outside the shanty and blows its horn. Except for* SAADET, *the characters stand petrified and listen intently. Then the hustle begins.*]

They're here, they're here!

SABİHA: What a scandal!

GRANDFATHER: [*Pushes* SABİHA.] Get away from that mirror!

SABİHA: Oh, it's broken again! Sabri, my zipper's broken!

SABRİ: [*Grabs a sweater from the top of the divan.*] Here, put this on!

SABİHA: Are you mad? In this heat?

GRANDFATHER: [*Someone has stepped on his foot.*] Look where you're going!

SABİHA: [*Tries to calm* SAADET.] Quiet, girl, shut up now, or I'll . . .

SABRİ: The beans, the beans!

SABİHA: Didn't you light the burner?

SABRİ: It went out, the son of a gun!

SABİHA: How humiliating!

[SAADET *cries at the top of her lungs. As the family rushes to the door, it is flung open by* YILMAZ. TAHSİN *and* NEZAHAT MAHİROĞLU *come in. They are fairly simple people, unostentatiously dressed. There is a fixed smile on their faces.*]

SABRİ: Come in, please come in!

SABİHA: [*To* SAADET.] Stop it, girl, I'm warning you!

TAHSİN: [*With exaggerated friendliness.*] Well, Sabri, my boy, how are you?

NEZAHAT: [*Also exaggerating.*] Oh, what a darling place!

SABİHA: It's wonderful having you here.

SABRİ: May I introduce my wife, sir? Sabiha.

NEZAHAT: How are you, Sabiha Hanım?

SABİHA: Thank you. I am well.

TAHSİN: I say, you've got a nice place here. Well done, well done!

SABRİ: Thanks to you, sir.

TAHSİN: No "sir" here, that's for the office. Here you call me Tahsin.

NEZAHAT: [*Sees* SAADET, *who is still crying.*] Oh, what a sweet child! [*Goes toward her.*] Darling!

SAADET: [*Frightened.*] Mother!

NEZAHAT: Now, now, you mustn't be frightened!

SABİHA: She's not used to strangers, madam.

NEZAHAT: Who's the brute who made you cry? [*Takes* SAADET *in her lap.*] Come on, whoops!

TAHSİN: Well, Sabri, what a good idea it was to come and visit you!

SABRİ: It's an honor, sir.

TAHSİN: Come on, come on, call me Tahsin.

SABRİ: I just can't!

GRANDFATHER: [*To show that he is there.*] Ahem!

SABRİ: My father, sir.

TAHSİN: Pleased to meet you, pleased to meet you.

GRANDFATHER: I'm honored, Tahsin Bey!

TAHSİN: Sir, you can pride yourself on having brought up a hero!

GRANDFATHER: Thank you!

NEZAHAT: Oh, she stuck out her tongue at her auntie! She stuck out her tongue!

SABİHA: [*Unable to understand why* NEZAHAT *is so cheerful about it.*] You little brat!

TAHSİN: Nezahat, come here, come here!

NEZAHAT: And who is this?

TAHSİN: Sabri's father.

NEZAHAT: What a nice little old man! Your father-in-law is a dear, Sabiha Hanım. [*Tries to grab* GRANDFATHER's *hand.*] Let me kiss your hand, Father.

GRANDFATHER: [*Pulls his hand away.*] No, no, young lady.

TAHSİN: [*In a loud voice.*] Come now, Sabri, take us around your house.

SABRİ: [*Embarrassed.*] Err, this is all there is, sir.

TAHSİN: [*Unflappable.*] That's fine, take us around this room, then.

SABİHA: It's in a bit of a mess, I'm afraid . . .

NEZAHAT: I know how it is, my dear; we all know what housework means.

SABRİ: Sir, my father and Yılmaz sleep in this room.

TAHSİN: Really, where?

NEZAHAT: [*Whispers to her husband.*] Careful, Tahsin!

TAHSİN: Hmm, yes, naturally. Let's see now, would it be behind this curtain?

GRANDFATHER: [*Sourly.*] I sleep there.

NEZAHAT: Are you comfortable there, sir?

GRANDFATHER: [*Trying to get them to pity him.*] I had no choice in the matter; that was the corner for me.

TAHSİN: Why do you say that? [*Sits down on* GRANDFATHER'*s bed.*] See how nice and soft your bed is.

GRANDFATHER: [*Blandly.*] A mattress filled with hay.

TAHSİN: [*Pretends he is amazed.*] You don't say . . . extraordinary! The springs must be very good, then.

GRANDFATHER: My bed's made of orange crates.

TAHSİN: [*Unflappable.*] Really? See, Nezahat, my dear? Do I not always say our people are so intelligent . . . that they can create miracles with their ingenuity?

SABİHA: We use Yılmaz's bed as a couch in the daytime.

TAHSİN: Look, Nezahat, it's made of orange crates!

GRANDFATHER: [*Cutting in.*] Four.

TAHSİN: Four orange crates underneath and one bale of hay can produce this!

NEZAHAT: [*Straining to say something.*] It's wonderful! [*Suddenly.*] And look at the design of this curtain!

SABİHA: [*Bashfully.*] I bought it on sale[4] three or four years ago. So, of course, it has been washed many times.

NEZAHAT: We need some curtains for the kitchen, Tahsin. Do remind me in the morning, and I'll drop in at the same store.

TAHSİN: So we are to have the same curtains! What do you say we get suits made of the same material, Sabri, my boy? [*Laughs heartily.*] Well done, well done! You have fitted everything snugly into a place no bigger than the palm of one's hand, yet we suffocate in our eight rooms!

NEZAHAT: [*Nudges her husband.*] Not at all like the palm of one's hand, darling, it's quite spacious!

TAHSİN: [*Correcting his gaffe.*] Well, yes, of course, spacious . . . it's spacious! No doubt you know more about it, Nezahat, but it seems to me we haven't got a room this big?

NEZAHAT: [*Sighs.*] I should say not.

GRANDFATHER: [*Sincerely sorry.*] Ah, a pity. But then, there are so many rooms.

TAHSİN: [*Excitedly.*] Nezahat! Come and look at the kitchen!

NEZAHAT: Wonderful! Look, Tahsin, spotless embroideries even on top of the cooking stove!

SABİHA: [*Timidly.*] I embroidered those as a girl.

TAHSİN: Where can one find such exquisite work nowadays? Everything's machine made now.

SABİHA: [*Timidly.*] They're not bad, either, those machine-made articles.

NEZAHAT: That's lazy work. [*To the* GRANDFATHER.] Your daughter-in-law is very clever with her hands.

---

4. The original Turkish text refers to the Sümer Bank, which manufactured and retailed dry goods at low prices.

GRANDFATHER: [*Reluctantly.*] Hmm, yes . . . that is so, young lady.

NEZAHAT: I simply cannot do anything with my hands. It's always a sore subject with me.

TAHSIN: [*Sees the bedroom door.*] I thought you said there was no other room? There must be another one beyond this door.

SABRI: That's where we sleep, sir. And the girl.

NEZAHAT: Let's see the bedroom, do let's.

SABRI: [*Uneasily.*] Well, the roof isn't on yet, you see . . .

TAHSIN: What of it, what of it? You get the summer breezes that way, what's wrong with that?

SABIHA: As soon as we can afford it . . .

NEZAHAT: Never mind, my dear, never mind. [*Goes into the bedroom.*]

SABRI: [*Embarrassed, to* TAHSIN.] You see, the timber ran out, so one side of the roof . . .

NEZAHAT: [*Excitedly from the bedroom.*] Tahsin! Do come and see! It's simply marvelous! The sky's so blue!

SABRI: [*Apologetically, to* TAHSIN.] While this good weather lasts . . .

TAHSIN: [*At the bedroom door.*] Fantastic, it's simply fantastic!

NEZAHAT: Isn't it?

TAHSIN: [*Exaggerating even more.*] Look here, Sabri, you're not really thinking of extending the roof over this room, are you?

SABIHA: [*Apologetically.*] We moved in at once so as not to have to pay rent, otherwise . . .

GRANDFATHER: I told them to wait, but who listens to me?

NEZAHAT: Please forgive me, but you must be out of your mind . . . mad. Isn't it charming, Tahsin darling? Think of it—you lie in bed looking at the stars, and in the morning the dew falls on you!

SABRI: No, there's a roof over the bed, it's the other side . . .

TAHSIN: [*Jovially.*] What are we waiting for, then? Let's push the bed over to the other side. [*Goes into the bedroom.*] Give me a hand, Sabri. [SABRI *goes into the bedroom.*]

SABIHA: What if it should rain all of a sudden?

NEZAHAT: [*Leaves the bedroom.*] You'll think of something then. But if you ask me, it's a crime to have a roof over this room. How long does summer rain last anyway? A minute or so.

TAHSIN: [*From the bedroom.*] Here, Sabri, my boy, get hold of this end.

SABRI: [*From the bedroom.*] Very well, sir.

NEZAHAT: [*Pretending to scold, calls out to the bedroom and then goes back in.*] Tahsin! Set the foot of the bed toward the North Star, darling! The North Star!

TAHSIN: Come along and help, all of you.

SABIHA: [*As she goes toward the bedroom.*] Our bed is a great big clumsy thing.

[*They all are in the bedroom. Their voices can be heard.*]

NEZAHAT: Darling, I think the trunk must be moved, too.

TAHSİN: That's it. Push the bed toward me a bit. Push, push, push!

NEZAHAT: A little more, a little more—place it directly under the hole.

TAHSİN: That's it, now push it against the wall.

SABRİ: Very good, sir.

TAHSİN: Tahsin.

NEZAHAT: [*Joyfully.*] That's lovely!

TAHSİN: Now let's tackle the trunk.

> [*Sound of a large object being moved. While this is going on,* YILMAZ *comes in through the street door. He stands still for a while, then goes up to* SAADET, *who is playing with her rag doll, and strokes her hair. He pulls a sweet out of his pocket and hands it to her. He is hastily making for the street door when the others emerge from the bedroom.*]

[*Jovially.*] Why are you running off, young man?

YILMAZ: [*Stops briefly.*] I'm not running off.

TAHSİN: [*Points to the divan.*] Come and sit here, beside me. [YILMAZ *does not move. To* SABRİ.] Your son is not very talkative, Sabri. All I could get out of him on the way here was "turn right, turn left."

SABİHA: True, he isn't talkative.

TAHSİN: [*Sits on his feet.*] Nothing like a divan for comfort! [*To* YILMAZ.] Come along now, why do you stand so aloof? [YILMAZ *approaches indifferently. He sits stiffly at one end of the divan.*] Come on now, pull up your legs in the old Turkish style, make yourself comfortable!

YILMAZ: [*Blandly.*] I'm more comfortable this way.

TAHSİN: [*Laughing, to the others.*] He's shy. [*They all laugh.*] Well . . . [*Slaps* YILMAZ *on his back.*] How did you like my car, eh? [*To* SABRİ.] Your young man went wild over my car. [*To* YILMAZ] Automatic gears . . . just sucks up the gas, though.

SABRİ: [*Hastily.*] Coming up the track, it must have got covered with dust. I had better wash it at once.

TAHSİN: Certainly not, don't move. Your road is fine!

NEZAHAT: So it is . . . just fine!

TAHSİN: Did you see me bounce over the ditches? That's good tires for you.

NEZAHAT: Instead of bragging about your car, why don't you let the boy drive it someday? Then he can judge for himself.

TAHSİN: [*Enthusiastically.*] Let him—of course I'll let him. [*To* YILMAZ.] You have a license?

YILMAZ: [*Matter-of-factly.*] No.

SABRİ: [*Timidly.*] You got it last year, driving Recep's truck, remember?

YILMAZ: I've lost it.

TAHSİN: You should get another, my boy. It might come in handy at some unexpected time.

NEZAHAT: Yes. You might come across a car for sale, at a bargain price.

SABİHA: As though that were all that's needed!

TAHSİN: Why not, Sabiha Hanım, one can never tell, you know. If I had dreamed—say, fifteen years ago—that I would someday own my own car, I'd have thought it pure fantasy, and yet . . .

SABİHA: You worked for it, sir. Not like this loafer . . .

TAHSİN: God is my witness, I did work. Killed myself at it. [*To* YILMAZ.] Shall I hire you as my chauffeur, eh?

NEZAHAT: That's it, our chauffeur has gone to his village on leave. We can always tell him we've found someone better when he returns.

TAHSİN: What do you say, eh?

SABRİ: [*Excitedly.*] He's had six months' driving experience as assistant on a truck.

GRANDFATHER: [*To* YILMAZ.] Say thank you, my son.

TAHSİN: I'll pay for your food and lodging, and your monthly pay will be . . .

YILMAZ: [*Curtly.*] I wouldn't like being a chauffeur.

NEZAHAT: [*Startled.*] But why not?

TAHSİN: [*Is put out, but tries not to show it.*] Well, then, you must get yourself a job that you do like. There are plenty of jobs . . . plenty of jobs, but no bread for him who does not work.

YILMAZ: [*Smiles. Responds gently.*] And for him who does?

SABRİ: What kind of a question is that, Son?

TAHSİN: [*Changing the subject.*] We're not forgetting the beans, are we?

SABRİ: The beans?

TAHSİN: Well, why are we here?

SABİHA: [*Hastily.*] Sabri, did you light the burner?

NEZAHAT: We'll light it if he hasn't, my dear.

GRANDFATHER: Please come to the table and let's begin. The beans can come later.

NEZAHAT: [*As if surprised.*] You mean there is something else as well?

SABİHA: [*Timidly.*] How can one serve only beans? That's no way to take care of guests.

NEZAHAT: [*With an exaggeratedly friendly tone.*] But we are not guests, my dear, for heaven's sake!

TAHSİN: [*Jokingly scolding* SABRİ.] Sabri, did I not say we wanted nothing else? That you were not to make Sabiha Hanım work too hard?

NEZAHAT: [*Laughs. To* SABİHA.] Did Sabri Bey not give you the message, perhaps?

SABİHA: He did, all right, but if I were to listen to him . . .

[*As they all settle down,* SABİHA *takes a dish from the top of the gas burner.* TAHSİN *remains sitting cross-legged on the divan. No one seems to notice that* YILMAZ *remains standing.*]

SABRİ: [*Aside, to* SABİHA.] I'm putting the beans on the burner.

NEZAHAT: Tahsin, come along, darling. Your meatballs are going to get cold.

TAHSİN: Oh, meatballs! Wonderful!

NEZAHAT: [*With a great deal of joy.*] I adore them!

GRANDFATHER: [*Shows a place to* TAHSİN.] You sit here, sir.

TAHSİN: [*Cheerfully.*] No, don't spoil my fun! I'm quite happy where I am!

> [*Having placed the beans on the burner,* SABRİ *goes to the mesh cupboard and returns with a dish of stuffed grape leaves.*]

NEZAHAT: [*With excessive show of pleasure.*] Look, Tahsin, stuffed grape leaves!

TAHSİN: This is the good life!

GRANDFATHER: I'll do the serving.

TAHSİN: Just put everything on the same plate, sir.

GRANDFATHER: As you wish.

SABİHA: [*Nudging* GRANDFATHER.] That isn't done! We have enough plates!

NEZAHAT: Tahsin likes to eat everything together, my dear.

TAHSİN: It's all going to the same place, isn't it?

SABRİ: [*To* SAADET.] You go play outside for a while, girl.

NEZAHAT: But isn't the child going to have some food? Eh, Sabiha Hanım?

SABİHA: I'll feed her later. [SAADET *goes out with her rag doll.*]

NEZAHAT: [*Behind* SAADET.] Oh, what a cute thing!

GRANDFATHER: [*Serving the guests.*] The potatoes are a bit soft, but . . . [SABİHA *gives him a harsh look.*]

TAHSİN: Please be generous to me, sir. I intend to eat until I burst!

NEZAHAT: [*Half-jokingly.*] Oh, come on now, Tahsin!

TAHSİN: If one is in the mood, what's wrong with that? Aren't we among friends?

SABİHA: Father, that's a very small helping for the lady.

NEZAHAT: I must leave room for the beans—you know how it is! [*Makes a gesture of being fat.*]

TAHSİN: I'm not going to wait for anyone.

GRANDFATHER: Bon appétit!

NEZAHAT: With all this good food in front of him, I'm afraid my husband has forgotten his manners, Sabiha Hanım!

SABİHA: I can't imagine him forgetting his manners!

SABRİ: Yılmaz, Son, bring the beer bottles from the cupboard.

TAHSİN: You shouldn't have bothered. What's better than pure water?

NEZAHAT: [*Feigning.*] I agree. [*To* SABİHA.] Sabiha Hanım, what a lot of spice you've put in these stuffed grape leaves!

SABİHA: [*Timidly.*] Should I not have used spices?

GRANDFATHER: [*To* NEZAHAT.] It's a tiny bit too much, isn't it? [SABİHA *gives him a dirty look.*]

NEZAHAT: No, no, I like them this way!

[YILMAZ *brings the beer.*]

TAHSİN: You're not eating, young man?

SABRİ: Go ahead, sit down, Son.

YILMAZ: I'm not hungry.

TAHSİN: [*Cheerfully.*] You don't have to be hungry to enjoy this delicious food. My compliments to you, Sabiha Hanım!

SABİHA: Enjoy it!

NEZAHAT: [*Excitedly.*] Tahsin, do you smell that?

TAHSİN: [*Again with unnecessary exuberance.*] Hey, smoked beef! Well done, Sabri, well done, bravo! I now realize I'm living. We simply vegetate in our apartment!

NEZAHAT: [*Butts in.*] Besides, we pay rent, too!

TAHSİN: That's right. You, at least, have a roof of your own over your heads!

NEZAHAT: And such a darling place it is!

TAHSİN: I could almost say I'm jealous. [*Suddenly.*] What if I pick up these meatballs with my fingers?

NEZAHAT: [*With a forced smile.*] Why not, darling?

[*Throughout the meal, the shanty family members are as anxious to display their knowledge of etiquette as* TAHSİN *and* NEZAHAT *are to put them at ease with their bad manners.* TAHSİN *obviously assumes that eating with the fingers is the norm in this household.* SABRİ *tries to use his knife and fork gracefully, and* TAHSİN *thinks he is making his hosts happy by putting the stuffed grape leaves into his mouth with his hand. A laughable situation, but also a bit pathetic.*]

TAHSİN: Tastes much better this way, eh, Sabri?

NEZAHAT: [*Objecting falsely.*] But, Tahsin, darling, you were going to ask Sabri Bey to tell us the story of the burglar, weren't you? I'm dying to hear it!

TAHSİN: [*Speaks with a full mouth.*] That's right, Sabri. On the way here, I told Nezahat briefly about the incident. She insisted she wanted the whole story from the hero's own mouth!

NEZAHAT: [*To* GRANDFATHER.] Do you know the full details, sir?

GRANDFATHER: [*Unimpressed.*] I've heard something about it.

TAHSİN: Well, then, we shall hear the full story now.

NEZAHAT: We're all ears, Sabri Bey.

SABRİ: [*Embarrassed.*] I'm not sure what to say.

NEZAHAT: Your husband is very modest, Sabiha Hanım.

TAHSİN: Come on, now, don't keep us in suspense, Sabri!

SABRİ: [*Swallows a mouthful of food, then begins haltingly.*] Well, I was on my second round . . . [TAHSİN *and* NEZAHAT *whisper to each other.*] I was on my second round . . .

TAHSİN: What?

SABRİ: I was on my second round . . .

TAHSİN: [*Pretends to be interested.*] Yes, Sabri, you were on your second round.

SABRİ: Eleven P.M., it was. I clocked in near the toilets.

GRANDFATHER: [*Softly.*] Never mind the toilets!

SABRİ: Then I came to the accounting office . . . I thought I saw a light at the door. I stopped in my tracks. Then . . . a sort of creaking noise . . .

NEZAHAT: [*Pretends to be afraid.*] Oooh!

SABRİ: Yes, of course I had the key. But first I tried the handle of the door . . . quietlike.

NEZAHAT: So you have the keys to every room, do you?

TAHSİN: We trust Sabri completely.

SABRİ: Thank you, sir.

NEZAHAT: Go on! What happened then?

SABRİ: I pulled out my gun, just in case.

NEZAHAT: Was it loaded?

TAHSİN: Shhh, Nezahat!

SABRİ: [*Embarrassed, cuts his story short.*] I went in . . . and caught the fellow red-handed.

NEZAHAT: [*Disappointed.*] Ooooh!

TAHSİN: Don't give us the bare outline; we want the details!

SABRİ: [*Half-heartedly.*] I opened the door quietly. With one hand firmly on the trigger, I turned on the light and saw . . .

NEZAHAT: [*Pretends to be afraid.*] A gangster!

TAHSİN: For heaven's sake, Nezahat!

SABRİ: A fellow standing by the open safe . . . ready to empty it and run!

TAHSİN: [*Exaggerating.*] Sabri then placed his gun against the fellow's forehead.

SABRİ: No, no, I didn't get all that near to him, sir. You cannot tell what a fellow like that might do. I picked up the telephone without taking my eyes off him.

TAHSİN: [*To* NEZAHAT.] You remember that was the night I went dashing back to the factory at midnight.

NEZAHAT: What a husband, Sabiha Hanım! You've every reason to be proud of him!

SABİHA: Bless you.

TAHSİN: That's no joke, I assure you. In Sabri's place, my knees would have buckled under me!

SABRİ: I was frightened quite a bit myself, sir.

TAHSİN: Oh, come on, the police told me the story at the precinct later. You weren't ruffled at all. But we must be grateful to this thief, Sabri, my boy. You've worked for me all these years, and we have not exchanged even a good morning up to now.

NEZAHAT: Ah, had you never seen Sabri Bey before?

TAHSİN: When would I have seen him, darling? As I leave the office, he checks in. The manager told me yesterday when we were going over the records, or I would not have known about Sabri's nice family or his new home. Our friendship is a recent one, but firm nevertheless, eh, Sabri?

NEZAHAT: So we owe this delicious food to that terrible thief.

SABRI: [*Embarrassed.*] Well, he wasn't so terrible, really. Not to make any comparisons, but he couldn't have been any older than Yılmaz here. To look at him, you'd think he was a law-abiding youngster.

TAHSIN: One must not be deceived by appearances, Sabri, my boy.

SABRI: He was so angry . . . he used bad language.

NEZAHAT: [*Inquisitively.*] What did he say, what did he say?

SABRI: [*Embarrassed.*] Begging your pardon, he called me a silly cow!

NEZAHAT: What a vulgar guy.

TAHSIN: Guilty and self-righteous at the same time! Because Sabri does not steal other people's money, because he is content to live on what he earns, he is a silly cow!

NEZAHAT: God forbid!

TAHSIN: Think of it, Nezahat, when Sabri went into the office, the safe was wide open. All that money within his reach, that is. And how much money? Let's see . . . more money than you can put in a suitcase.

GRANDFATHER: Oh my God!

TAHSIN: Salaries, wages, overtime . . . the fellow had chosen his day, I tell you. Well, if it had been some other watchman instead of Sabri, and he'd let the thief go and then slipped half of it into his own pocket and said the rest was all he had found, what could we have done?

NEZAHAT: Not a thing.

SABIHA: [*As if in a dream.*] Yes, it would have vanished.

TAHSIN: A man's mind can go blank, a thousand evil thoughts can flash through it. But what does Sabri do? He does not even glance at the money, just as he ignores personal danger.

NEZAHAT: [*With exaggerated enthusiasm.*] You are a hero, Sabri Bey!

TAHSIN: [*Follows up with a rambling speech.*] Listen to what I say, Nezahat. Listen to me. If today you and I are able to live a life of prosperity and happiness, we owe it not to the increasing abundance of worldly goods, not to greater knowledge or scientific progress, but only to the presence of honest men on earth, men whose numbers, alas, are decreasing daily!

[TAHSIN *is about to continue, but* YILMAZ, *who has been nervously twirling a plate in his hands suddenly drops it on the floor. It breaks with a crash.*]

NEZAHAT: Aah!

TAHSIN: What happened, my son?

YILMAZ: [*Blandly.*] It slipped out of my hands.

SABRI: Why did you have to spin it?

NEZAHAT: Never mind, Sabri Bey, after all, it's only . . .

YILMAZ: [*To* SABRİ.] Sorry, I didn't know you owned such a beautiful plate. [*Mockingly to* SABİHA, *who is looking as though she is going to devour him.*] Let's enjoy using these.

TAHSİN: [*With forced joviality.*] So, my dear Nezahat, that is the sort of man Sabri is. No matter how hard you search, you can never find another like him.

SABRİ: [*Very embarrassed.*] You are too kind, sir.

NEZAHAT: You are a very lucky boss, darling.

TAHSİN: [*His mouth full.*] Hey, stop me if I've said this, but these meatballs are fantastic!

SABİHA: I'm glad you like them.

GRANDFATHER: Sabri, serve the gentleman another meatball.

TAHSİN: No, no, bless you, my dear Sabri. If I were to eat like this every day, I'd need a wheelbarrow for my bulging belly!

NEZAHAT: [*Sighs.*] Where would you find food like this every day?

TAHSİN: Where indeed?

SABRİ: Are the beans warm, Sabiha? Have a look.

TAHSİN: Why, of course, the beans are yet to come!

NEZAHAT: Oh, the smell of the smoked beef makes one feel faint!

TAHSİN: If I didn't have to watch my figure, I'd gobble up the whole potful myself. Sabri, a brother's advice to you, don't put on too much weight!

SABRİ: I won't, sir.

TAHSİN: Once it's there, its difficult to melt away.

NEZAHAT: [*To* GRANDFATHER.] Unfortunately, Tahsin has got an appetite—what an appetite . . .

TAHSİN: But what do I eat, my darling? A grilled steak and salad . . .

NEZAHAT: Too much is too much, even if grilled. [*To* GRANDFATHER.] And, of course, when I see him devouring his meals with such enthusiasm, I get carried away, and I overeat, too. Look at your daughter-in-law; she is as slender as a reed!

GRANDFATHER: So she is, young lady.

TAHSİN: The truth is, Sabri, your wife is beautiful.

NEZAHAT: See how her hair shines! What do you wash you hair with, Sabiha Hanım?

SABİHA: [*Bringing the beans, embarrassed.*] Plain white soap.

TAHSİN: It's years since I've had a cake of that soap in my hands.

GRANDFATHER: I know. They do say they use sheep tails in making soap nowadays.

TAHSİN: All that fancy soap with perfume, cream, and whatnot, it's a swindle . . . that's what it is, a swindle! Everything is best in its pure state, its natural state. That's why I like your house so much. What's more beautiful than an unpainted wall?

SABİHA: [*Hurt.*] The moment we can afford it . . .

TAHSİN: [*Ignoring her.*] One must learn to see the charm in traces of soot above the stove.

SABRİ: [*Embarrassed, changes the subject.*] Won't you help yourself to the beans?

TAHSİN: [*Exuberantly.*] Beans! The king of dishes!

[GRANDFATHER *passes the beans around.*]

NEZAHAT: Tahsin, this gentleman serves a meal beautifully, doesn't he?

TAHSİN: Yes, I noticed that.

GRANDFATHER: [*Boastfully.*] I was once headwaiter at the Gusto Restaurant, sir.

TAHSİN: Ah? Ah yes. Unfortunately I've never been there. What great food I must have missed, eh, sir?

GRANDFATHER: They say it has gone down now. In my day, all the gentlemen of distinction were our clients. One moment, sir. [*Walks to the photograph on the wall.*]

YILMAZ: [*Softly.*] Granddad, stop it, now.

GRANDFATHER: Don't you interfere! [*Takes down the photograph and hands it to* TAHSİN.] A photograph of me with the late minister of health. He always sat at my table.

NEZAHAT: [*Looks at the photograph, then mincingly.*] I swear you haven't changed at all.

GRANDFATHER: [*Pleased.*] How can that be, young lady? It must have been at least twenty years ago.

TAHSİN: Nezahat is absolutely right. What do you think, Sabri?

SABRİ: [*Embarrassed.*] I don't know what to say, sir.

TAHSİN: You have not aged one bit, sir, not one bit. And why? Because you have always lived close to nature. You complain because the road to the house is unpaved, but, believe me, nothing is more harmful than concrete buildings and asphalt roads.

GRANDFATHER: I don't understand.

NEZAHAT: Harmful and appalling!

SABİHA: [*At a loss.*] Are they? What a pity!

TAHSİN: [*Suddenly.*] Do you know what I have just decided, Nezahat? I am going to have a divan built right around our living room, and all that furniture goes out!

NEZAHAT: Er . . . that would be lovely!

TAHSİN: And I'm going to sleep out on the terrace. That's it!

NEZAHAT: But look what you've done, Sabiha Hanım! You've sent the little girl outside; she must be starving!

SABİHA: I'd forgotten all about her! I'll give her something to eat right away.

SABRİ: Yılmaz, my son, go and bring Saadet in. [YILMAZ *goes out without saying a word.*]

TAHSİN: Oh! [*Pats himself on the stomach, then picks up his plate, and noisily gulps the remainder of the sauce.*]

NEZAHAT: [*Softly.*] Tahsin!

TAHSİN: The best part of a meal is the sauce, Nezahat. Come on, you do the same!

NEZAHAT: Never! [*Sees that the hosts are watching her; hastily.*] Yes, the sauce is very tasty! [*Sips from her plate.*]

TAHSİN: [*To the others.*] What are you waiting for? Pick up your plates. Let's see what name is written on the bottom! Pick them up, pick them up!

GRANDFATHER: [*Startled.*] But . . . is it done?

NEZAHAT: We did it, didn't we?

TAHSİN: [*As if giving an order.*] On your mark . . . one, two . . . three! [SABİHA, SABRİ, *and* GRANDFATHER *helplessly pick up their plates and sip the sauce. But this is not enough for* TAHSİN.] And now let's pick our teeth.

SABİHA: Sabri, get the toothpicks.

TAHSİN: What for? Our fingers are good enough! [*Places a finger in his mouth.*] We were a little quick in gobbling up everything, eh, Nezahat?

NEZAHAT: I'm absolutely stuffed.

TAHSİN: A feast for the soul. Look here, Sabri, my boy, I like your house, I like everything. I must do something for you in return for all this. Tell me, what would you like? You have but to make a wish.

SABRİ: All I want is your good health, sir.

TAHSİN: Never mind that sort of thing; ask for a gift.

[YILMAZ *and* SAADET *come in.*]

NEZAHAT: Psst, Tahsin.

TAHSİN: What? [*They whisper to each other.*]

SABRİ: [*To* SAADET.] Is that you, my little girl?

SABİHA: [*To* SABRİ *in an undertone.*] Now is your chance, you fool.

SABRİ: How can I?

SABİHA: Of course you can!

SABRİ: [*Embarrassed.*] You feed the child now.

SABİHA: Don't be a fool! Ask! [*Fills a copper bowl with beans for* SAADET.]

TAHSİN: [*Loudly.*] Listen, Sabri—what's the name of your little girl?

SABRİ: Saadet.

NEZAHAT: [*Goes up to* SAADET, *who is eating her beans, and pinches her cheek.*] What a sweet name—just right for her! You sweet thing!

SABİHA: [*To* TAHSİN.] Shall I bring the dessert now, or . . . ?

TAHSİN: Hear that, Nezahat? There's dessert as well.

NEZAHAT: [*With feigned happiness.*] These people are going to kill us with kindness, darling!

GRANDFATHER: Sabiha, serve the dessert.

NEZAHAT: Tahsin and I will share one portion.

SABİHA: Surely that's not enough? [*Brings the dessert.*]

TAHSİN: [*Loudly.*] What was I about to say? You've made me forget. [NEZAHAT *signals to him discreetly.*] Ah, yes. Look here, Sabri, we have taken quite a fancy to your daughter. Isn't that so, Nezahat?

NEZAHAT: [*Turning toward* SAADET.] We simply adore her. Look at the darling way she is sitting in the corner eating her beans.

TAHSİN: [*To* SABRİ.] So we thought we'd do you a favor—a real favor.

SABİHA: [*Passes the dish of sweet cakes.*] Help yourself, please.

TAHSİN: You listen, too, Sabiha Hanım. What I say is . . . [*Stops, then suddenly.*] Let us have Saadet!

SABİHA: [*Startled.*] Sir?

NEZAHAT: Have her for our child, that is.

TAHSİN: We have no children of our own. As one grows older, one needs children, they say. How true that is! A little soul mate. You can come and see her from time to time, and when she grows up, she can come and see you.

NEZAHAT: [*Strokes* SAADET's *head.*] Little darling!

TAHSİN: [*As if settling the bargain.*] That's it, then.

[SABİHA *and* SABRİ *stare at each other.* YILMAZ *stirs nervously. Only* GRANDFATHER *seems pleased with this proposition.*]

GRANDFATHER: [*To* SABRİ.] Answer the gentleman, my son, do not keep him waiting.

TAHSİN: [*Gently.*] Yes?

SABRİ: [*Wrings his hands.*] What should we say? [*As if asking for help.*] What do you think, Sabiha?

SABİHA: [*Trembling.*] How can it be?

NEZAHAT: She'll receive royal treatment, dear Sabiha, don't worry at all.

SABİHA: That's not what I meant.

NEZAHAT: Well, then?

GRANDFATHER: It will be one mouth less for Sabri to feed.

YILMAZ: [*On edge.*] What's come over you, Granddad?

GRANDFATHER: You stay out of this.

TAHSİN: [*Tries to lessen the tension.*] Why don't we eat our dessert, meanwhile. Eat our dessert and talk sweetly. [*Laughs loudly, but no one seems to share his pleasure.*] I think this dessert is just marvelous. [*They all pick up their forks, but without any enthusiasm.*]

NEZAHAT: [*Forcing it.*] Did you make it with milk, Sabiha Hanım, or with honey?

SABİHA: [*Quietly.*] With milk.

NEZAHAT: It's delicious. [*Eats a forkful of the dessert.*]

GRANDFATHER: [*When nobody says anything.*] Enjoy it!

NEZAHAT: [*Her mouth full.*] But it's made with honey, not with milk.

SABİHA: [*Surprised.*] That . . . that's what I meant to say. I'm confused! [*Another embarrassed silence.*]

TAHSİN: Of course, we were thinking of your own good. It's for you to decide.

NEZAHAT: She shall be the daughter of the house and learn how to do a few odd jobs in her spare time.

TAHSİN: Nothing much, we have plenty of servants.

NEZAHAT: Plenty of time to think about it, but when the occasion presents itself, we shall marry her to someone suitable.

TAHSİN: I'll supply the trousseau!

SABRİ: [*Gulps.*] Of course, you know best. Sabiha?

NEZAHAT: We don't mean to take her at once. She can stay with you for another few days. You bring her to see us, and when she is used to the idea . . .

GRANDFATHER: You can say what you will, but I think there is something in the idea.

TAHSİN: Isn't that so, sir?

GRANDFATHER: What kind of a life will she have here? Whom would she marry? [*With a belittling tone.*] The butcher, the baker!

TAHSİN: It is the duty of us all to think of our children's future.

NEZAHAT: Come, now, dear Sabri, you're not going to disappoint me, surely. We have really fallen in love with her.

TAHSİN: [*Half-threateningly.*] I'll begin to think you do not trust me, Sabri, my boy.

SABRİ: God forbid, sir. It's not that, but . . . [*Chokes on the words.*]

TAHSİN: [*With a fatherly tone.*] I understand, Sabri. A child is dearer than one's soul. But you must put up with the separation for the sake of your daughter.

NEZAHAT: Think of the cooking lessons she will receive from the cook—as good as a golden bracelet around her wrist!

GRANDFATHER: Now that is something.

TAHSİN: She's such a tiny little thing. If she only does the dusting, helps Nezahat around the house a bit . . .

NEZAHAT: Hardly anything at all. If you stand in her way now, your conscience will trouble you later. I'm sure of it.

TAHSİN: Well, we've said what we had to say, Nezahat; we have done our duty. The rest is now . . .

NEZAHAT: [*Earnestly to* SABİHA.] You agree, Sabiha Hanım?

SABİHA: [*Reluctantly.*] If it's for her good . . .

NEZAHAT: She's going to have a great time, my dear. [*Winks at* SABİHA.] And, after all, you are young; you can have another child.

SABİHA: [*Looks at* SABRİ, *as though asking for help.* SABRİ *bows his head. Then suddenly as if feeling tired.*] All right, then, so be it.

NEZAHAT: [*Turns to* SAADET.] Where's my little darling?

TAHSİN: [*His hand on* SABRİ's *shoulder.*] Believe me, you'll be naming us in your prayers someday.

[SABRİ *does not lift his head. Even* GRANDFATHER's *eyes have suddenly grown dim. He dares not look anyone in the face.* YILMAZ *takes out a cigarette and lights it.*]

SABRİ: [*Angrily.*] I didn't know you smoked!

YILMAZ: [*Indifferently.*] For the past four years.

SABRİ: What!

YILMAZ: Always this brand.

SABRİ: [*Mutters through his teeth.*] Bastard!

TAHSİN: [*Loudly to break the tension.*] Hey, Nezahat, we haven't given them our gift yet. What's the matter with us?

NEZAHAT: [*In a forced tone.*] Aah, that's right, we forgot, my darling.

TAHSİN: Out with it, out with it.

NEZAHAT: [*Takes a small, elegant parcel out of her handbag and hands it to* SABİHA.] Use this in good health.

SABİHA: You shouldn't have bothered. [*Places the package on the table.*]

TAHSİN: Aren't you going to open it?

GRANDFATHER: Open it, my son. [SABRİ *silently opens the package. A small silver dish is revealed.*]

SABRİ: [*Without enthusiasm.*] Thank you.

GRANDFATHER: [*Admiringly.*] It's real silver!

NEZAHAT: Read the inscription, Sabri Bey.

SABRİ: [*Reads with an expressionless voice.*] "To our hero, Sabri Şengil . . . "

TAHSİN: It's only a small token, of course.

NEZAHAT: How does the saying go? One gives what one can.

GRANDFATHER: Sabiha, why don't you place it on the radio?

NEZAHAT: Place it so that the inscription can be read, my dear.

GRANDFATHER: Yes, stand it upright. [SABİHA *places the dish on the radio.*]

TAHSİN: [*Enthusiastically.*] It looks very good there, very good. Sabri, whoever comes to your house now will want to know what heroic deed you performed. And you must tell them, but not as you told us, not so offhandedly. Linger over the details, puff up your chest.

NEZAHAT: [*To* GRANDFATHER.] You must feel great pride in knowing that you have brought up a brave son, sir.

GRANDFATHER: Bless you.

NEZAHAT: [*Giggling, to* SABİHA.] And you are a very lucky woman, my dear Sabiha.

TAHSİN: [*Punches his stomach.*] We're all sluggish, my friends. We have eaten too well. I feel the smoked beef coming to life in my stomach. We must melt some of the fat away!

SABRİ: Sabiha, a coffee for the gentleman.

TAHSİN: No, there's an easier way. Do you know the pumpkin game?

NEZAHAT: What on earth is that?

TAHSİN: A marvelous game. Look . . . [*Continues with great bursts of laughter, while* SABİHA *and* SABRİ *look on in amazement.*] Someone stands in the middle—anyone. "I can't be a pumpkin!" he says. He holds his hands thus. [*Points upward with the index finger of each hand.*] And at the same time he goes hop, hop, hop on one foot. Then the others ask, "Who'll be a pumpkin?" And he says, for instance, "Tahsin!"

GRANDFATHER: He couldn't be a pumpkin!

TAHSİN: It's just a game! What was I saying? Ah . . . then the person named stands in the middle, and he too hops on one foot. It will be easier to understand once we start playing.

NEZAHAT: Let me be first. Please let me be first!

TAHSİN: As I explained!

NEZAHAT: [*Lifts her fingers and hops on one foot in the manner described by* TAHSİN.] I can't be a pumpkin! I can't be a pumpkin!

TAHSİN: Then who'll be a pumpkin?

NEZAHAT: [*Laughing her head off.*] Tahsin will be a pumpkin.

TAHSİN: [*Stops the game.*] Remember we're supposed to ask together?

NEZAHAT: [*Starts the game again.*] I can't be a pumpkin! I can't be a pumpkin!

THE OTHERS: Who'll be a pumpkin, who'll be a pumpkin?

NEZAHAT: Yılmaz will be a pumpkin.

YILMAZ: [*Curtly.*] I'm not playing.

TAHSİN: [*Hops on one foot.*] I can't be a pumpkin! I can't be a pumpkin!

THE OTHERS: Then who'll be a pumpkin?

TAHSİN: Sabiha Hanım will!

SABİHA: [*Feeling obliged to take part in the game.*] I can't be a pumpkin! I can't be a pumpkin!

THE OTHERS: Then who'll be a pumpkin?

SABİHA: Father will.

GRANDFATHER: [*Joins the game enthusiastically.*] I can't be a pumpkin . . . I can't be a pumpkin!

THE OTHERS: Then who'll be a pumpkin?

GRANDFATHER: Sabri will!

SABRİ: [*Has been watching the game from a distance. Stands up.*] I can't be a pumpkin! I can't be a pumpkin!

THE OTHERS: Then who'll be a pumpkin?

[SAADET *now leaves her place and joins in the game. She is enjoying it more than anyone else.* TAHSİN *and* NEZAHAT *pretend to enjoy themselves.* GRANDFATHER *is as happy as a child.* SABRİ *and* SABİHA *have expressions that are not in keeping with the game.* YILMAZ *watches these ridiculous proceedings angrily.*]

TAHSİN: [*Breathlessly.*] Oh! [*They all stop.*] Too much for us, eh, Sabri? Too much!

NEZAHAT: I've never laughed so much! [*Plops into a chair.*] But it is getting late. Don't you think . . .

TAHSİN: We're having fun, Nezahat. Don't be a spoilsport.

NEZAHAT: [*In an undertone.*] We're dining out this evening, you haven't forgotten?

TAHSİN: So we are.

NEZAHAT: And I've had beans up to here!

TAHSİN: My new evening jacket?

NEZAHAT: It's been delivered. And I trust you won't think that sitting cross-legged is indicated. [YILMAZ *has heard this exchange. He turns his back.*]

TAHSİN: [*Loudly.*] You're right, it is getting late!

NEZAHAT: The time has simply flown!

GRANDFATHER: Can you not stay a little longer?

TAHSİN: The travelers must take to the road, alas.

SABRİ: Sabiha, the gentleman's jacket.

TAHSİN: No, no, I'll get it!

NEZAHAT: We did have such a good time, didn't we, Sabiha dear?

SABİHA: You must come again.

TAHSİN: It was a good idea, eh?

GRANDFATHER: It was an honor for us.

TAHSİN: [*Exaggerating.*] God bless you, Sabiha Hanım. I have never eaten such delicious food in my life!

SABİHA: I'm glad you enjoyed it.

TAHSİN: Your wife is a gem, Sabri. You're a gem, too, of course. A perfect match.

GRANDFATHER: Since you're not taking the child right away . . .

TAHSİN: The child? Oh, yes . . . Nezahat?

NEZAHAT: As we agreed, darling. You can send the chauffeur for her at the end of the week.

TAHSİN: All right, Sabri?

SABRİ: You know best, sir.

NEZAHAT: [*Pulls* TAHSİN *by the arm.*] Pssst, Tahsin . . .

TAHSİN: Yes, what is it? [*They whisper.*] Very well. [*Aloud.*] If the child has no decent clothes . . . [*Makes the gesture of pulling out his wallet.*]

SABRİ: Please, sir!

SABİHA: As long as we're able . . .

NEZAHAT: Why not, my dear, remember she is going to be our daughter, too, from now on!

TAHSİN: [*Slips a few bills into* SABRİ's *hand.*] This will cover any little thing she might need.

SABRİ: [*Embarrassed.*] Thank you.

TAHSİN: What was I saying? Yes . . . your little home is as snug as a bird's nest. May you live in it in good health.

NEZAHAT: [*To* SAADET.] Won't you say "come again" to Auntie, dear?

SAADET: Come again.

NEZAHAT: [*Hugs* SAADET *and keeps kissing her.*] Darling! [*Hugs* SABİHA.] If you'll come with her the first time, Sabiha Hanım, it will give me great pleasure to see you again.

SABİHA: [In a subdued manner.] God willing.

[*They walk toward the street door.*]

NEZAHAT: [*To* GRANDFATHER.] Good-bye, sir.

GRANDFATHER: Come again, young lady, come again.

TAHSİN: I had a great time! Bravo, Sabri, good for you!

GRANDFATHER: Come back again.

TAHSİN: Of course we'll come. We are relatives now! [*Laughs.*]

SABRİ: Shall I ask the boy to show you the way, sir?

TAHSİN: No need, we'll manage. [*To* YILMAZ.] Thank you, my boy.

YILMAZ: [*In a matter-of-fact tone.*] Good-bye.

TAHSİN: I have not forgotten my promise! Get your license, and you can drive my car. All right?

NEZAHAT: [*Impatiently.*] Come along, Tahsin!

TAHSİN: We're late, aren't we? And it's time for you to go to work, Sabri.

SABRİ: At once, sir. I'll just change my clothes and go.

TAHSİN: That is what I like about Sabri—work is one thing, friendship another! [*Pats* SABRİ *on the back.*] I would have dropped you off at the factory, but we must run a few errands. You don't mind, do you?

SABRİ: Of course not, sir.

[*Everyone has gone out except* YILMAZ *and* SAADET. *The* OTHERS *can be heard talking outside the shanty.*]

TAHSİN: [*Loudly.*] I envy you! You have it made.

THE OTHERS: Good-bye, good-bye . . . come again . . . an honor . . . good-bye . . .

[*A car can be heard starting; the horn is blown repeatedly. The sounds grow weaker as the family returns to the living room.*]

SABİHA: [*After a tense silence.*] Well, where's the raise?

SABRİ: For God's sake. [*Undoing his buttons, walks toward the bedroom.*] Isn't it enough that they came to see us?

SABİHA: So they've come and gone—how much?

SABRİ: [*Points to the silver dish.*] What's this worth?

SABİHA: A piece of tin!

SABRİ: That's what you think. Instead of griping, bring me my work clothes, and quickly.

SABİHA: Guilty and self-righteous at the same time! [*Goes muttering into the bedroom.*]

SABRİ: [*To* SAADET.] Have you had enough to eat, child?

GRANDFATHER: She had an enormous helping of beans.

SABRİ: [*Tersely.*] I wasn't asking you, Father.

GRANDFATHER: All right, all right. [*To* SABİHA, *who has returned with* SABRİ's *uniform.*] I'm taking one of these dirty glasses.

SABİHA: [*Angrily.*] Don't you start bothering me as well, Father!

GRANDFATHER: For God's sake! What is the matter with you all?

SABRİ: [*Changing his clothes; to* SABİHA.] Put some of the leftovers in my box. I get famished in the middle of the night.

SABİHA: With that head on your shoulders, be thankful for dry bread.

SABRİ: [*Shouts.*] I said I get famished, woman! Must you always think of an answer? [*Sees* YILMAZ *stepping toward the street door.*] Where are you going?

YILMAZ: [*Indifferently.*] For a walk.

SABRİ: [*Exploding.*] Well, that is one of a thousand blunders you've made today!

SABİHA: [*Adding fuel to the fire.*] The way he lit that cigarette!

SABRİ: Whatever made you smoke in front of your elders?

YILMAZ: I felt like it.

SABRİ: Would you like to know what I feel like, right now?

YILMAZ: Go ahead, do what you feel like doing.

SABRİ: Since you intended to sulk like an ox, why didn't you make yourself scarce?

YILMAZ: [*Smiling.*] I stayed for the show.

SABRİ: [*Completely angry.*] What is this, a tent at a fair? Let me tell you, I have no intention of feeding a loafing bum forever.

YILMAZ: Don't feed me! [*Takes another step.*]

SABRİ: [*Enraged.*] Don't you like your father, you dog? [YILMAZ *stops and looks him straight in the eye.*] You don't like your father, do you?

GRANDFATHER: [*Comes between them.*] Sabri, my son, don't get carried away by Sabiha; she's trying to . . .

SABİHA: Look at him now!

SABRİ: Did he light a cigarette?

GRANDFATHER: That he did, but . . .

SABRİ: [*To* YILMAZ.] Out with it! You have no respect for your father, isn't that right?

YILMAZ: [*Matter-of-factly.*] That's right, no respect.

SABRİ: [*Lunges toward his son.*] I'm going to break your . . .

GRANDFATHER: Sabri, my son! [*Stands between them.*]

YILMAZ: [*Belittlingly.*] All of a sudden you're roaring like a lion.

SABRİ: Watch your manners, you bastard! So I'm an unimportant man. What can I do?

YILMAZ: You're right, you can do nothing. [*Stays calm.*]

SABRİ: [*Furiously.*] Look at the fellow! Look at him! [*As* YILMAZ *prepares to go out.*] Whose tie is that around your neck, eh, whose?

YILMAZ: Yours.

SABRİ: Take it off!

YILMAZ: [*Removes the tie and tosses it on the floor.*] There!

SABRİ: Go to hell!

SABİHA: [*To* SAADET, *who has begun to cry out of fear.*] Stop it, girl, stop it!

SABRİ: And never step inside this house again!

GRANDFATHER: Children, children!

YILMAZ: I won't.

SABRİ: Bastard!

[YILMAZ, *without replying, goes to* SAADET. *He hunts in his pockets for something to give her, finds nothing, picks up the rag doll from the floor and places it in the child's lap.* SAADET *stops crying and looks at him in amazement. A brief, tense silence.*]

YILMAZ: Good-bye! [*Goes out.* SAADET *resumes her crying.*]

SABİHA: You stop it this minute, or I'll fill your mouth with pepper.

GRANDFATHER: This is not a home; it's a ward for crazies!

SABRİ: [*Now more tired than angry.*] He said he would never come back, didn't he?

GRANDFATHER: That's what you told him to do, my foolish son!

SABRİ: [*Defeated. To himself.*] You wild man! You wild man! Was that the way a decent youngster would address his father?

SABİHA: What can he do but come back? Of course he'll come back and eat out of your hand!

SABRİ: [*To himself, with a pained expression.*] Why, why? What time is it?

SABİHA: You've got your watch on.

SABRİ: [*Looks at his watch.*] Good, I've still got time. Sabiha, the grocer may still be open. Go get me a small bottle.

GRANDFATHER: Son, not before going to work . . .

SABİHA: The grocer will stop letting us have things on credit, and we'll be in a real fix. Is that what you want?

SABRİ: [*Produces the money* TAHSİN *gave him.*] Pay as you buy.

SABİHA: Well, honestly, Sabri. What about the girl's clothes, then?

SABRİ: [*Suddenly angry again.*] So I must account to you for my actions as well, must I?

SABİHA: [*Alarmed.*] You know best.

SABRİ: [*Shouting at the top of his lungs.*] Yes, I know best!

[SABİHA *takes her sweater and rapidly goes offstage.* SABRİ *sinks down onto the divan.*]

GRANDFATHER: [*To himself.*] You'd think I was going to eat her glass, the stingy woman!

[SABRİ *gives his father a tired, defeated look, then hands him one of the glasses on the table.* GRANDFATHER *takes the glass happily, pats his son on the back, and goes to the corner where he hid his stamps.* SABRİ *looks first around the shanty as if he is seeing it for the first time. Then his eyes become fixed on* SAADET, *who is playing on the floor. He goes over to her and gently strokes her hair.*]

SABRİ: [*Almost choking.*] I don't know shit!

CURTAIN

ACT II

[*The same room, four or five days later. In contrast to Act I, the room is now in great disarray. It has been raining, the roof has been leaking, and the furniture has been piled up in the only dry corner of the room. Wet clothes, underwear, and sheets are hanging bedraggled from a rope stretched across the room.*

SABIHA *is lying on the divan with a patched quilt over her. She coughs from time to time.* GRANDFATHER *is huffing and puffing as he irons a sheet at the table.* SABRI, *barefoot and with the sleeves of his uniform rolled up, is mopping the floor with a large rag.*]

SABRI: [*Angrily tosses the rag into a pail.*] I'm going to wreck this shack! I'm going to pour gas on the foundations and set it on fire!

SABIHA: [*Exhaustedly.*] For heaven's sake, Sabri!

SABRI: It's easy for you to lie there and crow, of course!

GRANDFATHER: And how!

SABIHA: Do you think I'm enjoying myself, you merciless creatures? I'm simply too weak to stand on my feet.

GRANDFATHER: [*Mutters to himself.*] Here I am ironing sheets, at my age!

SABRI: [*Hands him the rag.*] I'll be happy to swap jobs with you, if you prefer mine.

GRANDFATHER: I don't need another job.

SABRI: That's fine, then. Without dealing with all this shit and muck, you can still feel useful for once in a blue moon!

GRANDFATHER: I suppose you are making me pay for my two mouthfuls of food.

SABRI: Let's not have you spin that tale again.

GRANDFATHER: Have I no rights in this house, I ask you? Have I not given you everything I had?

SABRI: Many thanks, as usual. [*Straightens up.*] Oh my back!

SABIHA: Don't talk to me about pains!

SABRI: [*Points at the clothes on the rope.*] Could you not have saved some of these at least?

SABIHA: We're lucky to have saved our lives. The rain came so suddenly! The bed was drenched in no time, and I was wet to the bone before I even woke up!

GRANDFATHER: A summer drizzle!

SABIHA: Look, while you're so busy tossing words about, don't let me see you burn a hole in that sheet!

SABRI: Stop it, you two! I'm sick to death . . . I simply haven't got the strength to listen to your jabber.

GRANDFATHER: That's what happens when you're unable to make your wife do what you tell her. So keep diving into that pail!

SABRI: If you two hadn't just turned over and slept, this would have been finished long ago.

GRANDFATHER: [*Tosses one end of a sheet to* SABRİ.] Get hold of this!

SABRİ: Hell! [*Drops his rag and helps* GRANDFATHER *fold the sheet.*]

SABİHA: I mopped the floors until the skin came off my hands, and you talk of me lying in bed.

SABRİ: I was talking to my father.

GRANDFATHER: Is it my fault if I didn't get wet?

SABİHA: I prodded you I don't know how many times. Why didn't you show any sign of life?

GRANDFATHER: I was half asleep; I didn't understand what it was all about, and by the time I was wide awake it was too late. And if even I'd gotten up earlier, I wasn't going to hold an umbrella under the holes in the roof!

SABRİ: If you'd lent a hand, you could have helped save the trunk.

GRANDFATHER: If the trunk was so precious, then why didn't Sabiha do something about it?

SABİHA: God grant you the gift of mercy! I was in no state to think of trunks.

GRANDFATHER: Fine, so why do you both lash out at me? [*Returns to the table with the folded sheet.*]

SABRİ: [*Points at the clothes on the rope.*] Those are never going to dry in this kind of a place.

SABİHA: When the clothes outside are dry, you can hang this lot there.

SABRİ: So . . . every job is for me! "Sabri, here, there, everywhere!"

SABİHA: I told you I'm shivering, my teeth are chattering. Sabri, why can't you understand?

SABRİ: [*Wringing out his rag.*] What kind of a shower was this . . . not a dry spot left anywhere?

GRANDFATHER: What do you mean, a shower? It was a flood! I don't sleep properly in any case and to go mopping floors at my age!

SABRİ: You'd think I got out of a soft bed to do the mopping! I spent the whole night wriggling like a dog who has singed his bottom . . . dreaming of bed, longing for the moment when I could collapse into it—then what do I have to do? Come home to this mess!

SABİHA: Why scold me? What do you expect me to do about it? [*Coughs.*]

SABRİ: I'm not scolding anyone! But what I'd like to do to the man who had the bright idea of placing the bed right under the hole in the roof . . .

GRANDFATHER: Tahsin Bey.

SABRİ: And his wife! Heaven help me! When I heard the thunder at midnight, I had an idea of what was going to happen. I wanted to leave everything and go home—but can you do that? Oh no, there is not a thing in hell you can do.

SABİHA: It was not like a summer rain at all; it was a . . . calamity! What did my poor little Saadet do, alone with those strangers? Lightning has always frightened her.

GRANDFATHER: Saadet is in a warm house; she sleeps on a soft bed. Let's look after ourselves.

SABİHA: How should I know? I felt strange all of a sudden, thinking of her.

GRANDFATHER: The girl is safe, safe. Her bread and water are provided for her.

SABRİ: And we are left to ourselves, like a tomato stake after the tomatoes are gathered. A fine thing!

GRANDFATHER: She's been gone only three or four days. If you begin to long for her so soon . . .

SABRİ: Who's longing? I'm cursing. [*Throws the rag angrily into the pail.*]

SABİHA: Sabri, if you don't rinse out that rag, the mud will spread everywhere.

SABRİ: I get it. It is written on my forehead that I'm to return to work tonight without having had a moment's rest. [*Goes to the faucet.*]

GRANDFATHER: [*As he's folding a sheet.*] Was it so necessary for these to be ironed right away?

SABİHA: I don't want them underfoot. Sabri, since you've put your hand to it . . .

SABRİ: [*Angrily.*] I haven't put my hand to anything, understand? I wish I hadn't!

SABİHA: [*Pointing at a corner of the room.*] I think it's leaked in that corner as well, or something. I was going to say, you might wipe it dry before the paint peels off entirely.

SABRİ: Hell, instead of building this house, we should have pitched a tent in the open! What's the difference? It would rain there; it rains here. [*As he wipes the wall dry, a large piece of plaster falls off.*] Hey! Hey!

GRANDFATHER: What's happened now?

SABRİ: To hell with you!

GRANDFATHER: Mind your language!

SABRİ: I'll show you language!

SABİHA: Don't worry, Sabri, for heaven's sake. It's just a bit of plaster. The painters can replace it when they come.

SABRİ: There's going to be no paint, you hear? I'm not spending another penny on this ruin. I don't care if all the plaster falls off and the walls follow. I'll sell it all by the pound and be a free man.

SABİHA: It's anger that makes you say these things.

SABRİ: [*Gets even angrier.*] Anger! You've said it! Anger!

GRANDFATHER: I've finished the ironing. [*To* SABİHA.] See that you get up before the rest are dry. I'm through. [*Bumps into* SABRİ *on his way to the door.*]

SABRİ: [*Snarls.*] Go to hell!

GRANDFATHER: What is the matter with you?

SABRİ: Don't keep getting under foot!

GRANDFATHER: For God's sake, is it now forbidden to move?

SABRİ: It's forbidden, yes! [*Tries to open the door, which is stuck.*] Damn door! [*Kicks it.*] Open up! Open, I say!

SABİHA: Sabri, I beg of you . . .

GRANDFATHER: This boy is out of his mind today.

SABRİ: [*Opens the door.*] That's it, come to heel, you hunk of wood. [*Empties the pail.*] If the doors swell at the first rain and refuse to open, we're going to be nice and busy this winter.

SABİHA: We'll shave off a bit at the bottom.

SABRİ: Now that's a good idea. We'll shave and shave until there is nothing left of this scrap.

SABİHA: If you're going to curse while you work, you might as well stop.

SABRİ: So that's it. We're supposed to smile through it all. [*Shows his teeth and pretends to smile.*] Is this what I should do?

SABİHA: I'll get up in a little while, and . . .

SABRİ: You can't get up. You've got TB. You're finished!

GRANDFATHER: Think before you speak. You're overdoing it!

SABRİ: If you haven't got TB, then wait until the September rains, and we'll all get it.

SABİHA: May the wind take those words right out of your mouth!

SABRİ: This is not a house; it's a tomb, a mausoleum! It's not enough that we are wet right through; let's not be surprised if next we have an invasion of worms!

GRANDFATHER: All right, pull it down, then! Pull it down and leave us standing stark naked in the middle of nowhere.

SABRİ: Damn it, I'll demolish it, that's what I'm going to do. I'll pull it down! What do you think? If I don't destroy it, it will destroy me.

SABİHA: [*Shouts.*] Stop it, for heaven's sake! [*Coughs.*] My life is such endless suffering! If we devour each other like this . . . [*A spasm of coughing interrupts her.*]

SABRİ: [*Softly.*] That's really a bad cold you've got.

SABİHA: It's right down in my chest. I'm rattling inside.

SABRİ: Father, heat a little water on the burner.

GRANDFATHER: Oops!

SABRİ: [*To* SABİHA.] Have we got some linden tea in the house?

SABİHA: In the bottom of the mesh cupboard.

GRANDFATHER: Not a moment of peace!

SABRİ: Forget it, forget it. I'll do it. [*Goes to the burner.*]

SABİHA: I was longing for some in the back of my mind, but didn't dare say anything.

SABRİ: [*Opens the mesh cupboard.*] Pay no attention to the way I behave. For five days now, it's as though there were a fist right here. [*Puts his fist to his chest.*] Must be that I'm tired, what else?

SABİHA: You lie down and sleep a while. Before evening I'll have tidied up everything. You have a rest!

SABRİ: [*Suddenly shouts.*] What's this? My God, what's this?

SABİHA: Sabri!

SABRİ: The wall behind the burner . . . it's all black!

SABİHA: The plaster's rough there. I've scrubbed and scrubbed, and it's still . . .

SABRİ: No, you mustn't scrub it. [*Imitates* TAHSİN's *voice.*] You must appreciate its charm the way it is, Sabiha Hanım. [*In his own voice.*] Heaven help me! [*Lights the burner.*]

GRANDFATHER: I'm taking one of these glasses, Sabiha.

SABİHA: Good God, in the middle of all this mess . . .

[GRANDFATHER *takes a glass and busies himself with his stamps.*]

SABRİ: Damn!

SABİHA: What's happened now?

SABRİ: Is this all the linden tea there is? [*Holds up a jar.*]

SABİHA: I guess so.

SABRİ: Why don't you say, "The boy must have drunk it"?

SABİHA: Oh, Sabri, you're making me a drop of linden tea, and you're turning it into poison! Forget it, I don't want any.

SABRİ: Well, isn't that what you always say? "The boy must have gorged himself on it." "The boy must have scraped the bottom!"

GRANDFATHER: Sure thing!

SABRİ: You keep out of this!

GRANDFATHER: Heavens, what is going on?

SABRİ: [*To* SABİHA.] Why did he light that cigarette in front of his elders, eh, why?

SABİHA: How should I know!

SABRİ: He makes us feel like he doesn't think anything of us.

GRANDFATHER: You're making a mountain out of a molehill.

SABRİ: That is so, that is so. He doesn't like his father, that dog. He doesn't like me, that's all there is to it.

SABİHA: What have you ever done to him, other than buy his clothes and fill his stomach?

SABRİ: Nothing else, to be sure, but nevertheless the bastard doesn't like me. [*The teapot boils over; his hand on the handle gets scalded.*] Ow!

SABİHA: Do be careful, Sabri dear.

GRANDFATHER: Never mind, there isn't a dry spot in the house. So what if the burner gets wet?

SABRİ: My hand's scalded, and look what he's talking about!

SABİHA: Turn it off, since there's no tea left.

SABRİ: There's enough for you. [*Fills the pot again.*]

GRANDFATHER: Sabiha, where are the scissors?

SABİHA: What are you going to do with the scissors?

GRANDFATHER: What's it to you?

SABRİ: And this is my father—admire him if you can!

GRANDFATHER: What do you mean by that?

SABRİ: I mean, one is the son of one's father. That is what I mean.

GRANDFATHER: And whose son would you be, if you please?

SABRİ: Hell, I don't like you either. You get it?

GRANDFATHER: You are completely out of your mind today.

SABRİ: You are my father, aren't you? And I don't give a damn about you.

GRANDFATHER: Are you going to leave me in peace?

SABRİ: You're going to answer to me now; you can't escape.

GRANDFATHER: Get on with your work!

SABRİ: You could say I'm a chip off the old block! Thanks to you I have become a proper servant, bragging of serving this or that person!

GRANDFATHER: Heaven forbid!

SABRİ: You . . . shithead!

SABİHA: Sabri, I beg of you, I kiss your feet.

SABRİ: Wait, Sabiha, don't you interfere! I'm going to say to him all the things that the boy was not able to say to me, and then perhaps I'll feel better!

GRANDFATHER: Is that it . . . whatever you can get away with?

SABRİ: Whatever you can get away with . . . isn't that what you taught me?

SABİHA: Sabri, he's your father, no matter what.

SABRİ: [*Totally angry.*] Respect him for what, I ask you? Ever since I've known him, his head has been bowed, he's been bent in two . . .

GRANDFATHER: You're insolent!

SABRİ: It was not enough that you kissed the hand you licked, but you made me kiss it, too!

GRANDFATHER: We've seen you at it, too. Easy enough to curse and shout now.

SABRİ: Of course you've seen me at it. We're so cowed, the lot of us, that when we see anyone with a bit of fat about him, we turn to jelly! Two or three sweet words, and I melt altogether! Am I any better than you?

GRANDFATHER: Why do you keep nagging, then?

SABRİ: This is shameful, that is not. Who taught me that, eh? Who? I didn't look for the meaning myself. It's as though those posh customers of yours made you gobble it all up, and then you me. I tried to fool the boy in turn, but I didn't succeed! He's clever, that one, not a fool!

SABİHA: I'm going to faint right now. Sabri, for heaven's sake.

SABRİ: Of course he has no respect! If I had any sense, I wouldn't have asked him. What's he going to respect about a fellow who guards other people's property all night, then comes home in the morning to mop floors?

SABİHA: And yet you are working hard; you are striving as best you can. But he doesn't even lift a finger.

SABRİ: Why should he lift a finger? If it's a matter of not starving to death, he manages not to starve, anyway. [*With bitter irony.*] His father is loaded, rolling in money and real estate. [*Points to the shanty with a sweeping gesture.*] His father has worked his tail off, toppled many mountains, erected enormous building so that his son can gobble it all up.

SABİHA: Because he has confidence in you . . .

SABRİ: [*Interrupting.*] That's why he's behaving like a tough guy, is that it? And here we are, clinging onto these four walls. Just to make sure no one will grab our property, we keep kowtowing even if they shit all over us.

SABİHA: If he got up and left, it's because of his own worthlessness. Don't find fault with yourself.

SABRİ: As easy as that, eh? Fine! And what about Saadet . . . did she up and go because of her worthlessness?

SABİHA: [*Unhappily.*] The linden tea must be done. Don't let it boil away.

SABRİ: This world is so much shit! [*Takes the pot from the burner.*] Shall I pour the tea into a glass?

SABİHA: If it's no trouble.

GRANDFATHER: [*As* SABRİ *pours the linden tea into a glass.*] If it's the girl that's bothering you, why couldn't you say so? Because of a pup no bigger than one's thumb, you have called your father every name under the sun! You ought to be ashamed.

SABRİ: I am ashamed, but not for the reason you think.

SABİHA: Please, don't begin again!

GRANDFATHER: [*To* SABRİ.] Say what you like, I've had enough! I'm sick to death of living with you. It's nag, nag all day long.

SABRİ: [*Points to the door.*] No one is holding you. God be with you!

SABİHA: Sabri!

SABRİ: What's come over you both? You are at each other's throats all the time, but if I once in a blue moon lose my temper, then you rally to each other's support!

SABİHA: It's not that, but . . .

SABRİ: You're now in a tizzy because you're afraid your life is going to be a mess.

GRANDFATHER: And what a life!

SABRİ: Whatever it is. [*Brings the glass.*] Here's your tea.

SABİHA: Bless you.

GRANDFATHER: [*Mutters to himself.*] In the end, the pumpkin falls on my head!

SABRİ: The pumpkin was on your head already.

GRANDFATHER: What's that supposed to mean?

SABRİ: Too subtle for you. That's enough now, all right? Today I've forgotten everything I had learned up to now, I want you to know that.

GRANDFATHER: What's it to me? Every sheep hangs by its own leg.

SABRİ: That's not the way the cookie crumbles.

SABİHA: [*To change the subject.*] The linden tea is delicious, Sabri.

SABRİ: A swashbuckler all of a sudden, that boy of mine! And how right he was!

GRANDFATHER: You should have thought of that before you threw him out. But you wouldn't listen to reason.

SABRİ: It has just now dawned on me. It's not the advice of a bit waiter I'm going to ask for!

GRANDFATHER: Don't rub it in, don't rub it in!

SABİHA: Stop, both of you! Sabri, you must be hungry . . . that's why you're so edgy. You must be hungry.

SABRİ: So, at last you've thought of me. Of course I'm hungry.

SABİHA: I'm going to get up and heat some food, right now.

SABRİ: No, you're not going to get up. You're going to have your own food brought to you in bed.

SABİHA: What next, Sabri? It's not your job to fix a meal.

SABRİ: I'm not going to fix a meal. Have we or have we not someone here whose job it is to produce meals?

GRANDFATHER: [*Hastily.*] I'm going out for a little.

SABRİ: No, no running away, please!

GRANDFATHER: I run away or I don't run away—what's it to you?

SABRİ: What's it to me? Your son returns from work tired and weary, your daughter-in-law is ill in bed, and you cannot place a dish of food in front of them?

GRANDFATHER: Am I to have this job forced upon me?

SABRİ: So what did you think? That you were always going to wait on the gentry, on cabinet ministers and the like? If they're the people's representatives, I am the people! I am going to sit here, crossing my legs, and I expect my food to be placed right in front of me!

GRANDFATHER: Get a grip on yourself! Know your place, understand?

SABRİ: It's because I've always known my place that all this has happened. From now on, no one can hold me back!

GRANDFATHER: That's fine, go bash your head against some other rock. Leave me in peace!

SABRİ: It's you I've got to bash against. I'm my father's son, haven't I said so?

SABİHA: My God!

SABRİ: [*To* SABİHA.] As for you, stay well out of it! Relax, wait for your food. [*To* GRANDFATHER.] Come on, now, get going.

GRANDFATHER: You're completely crazy, my son. Hunger must have gone to your head.

SABRİ: If I want to be treated as a man, does it mean I'm crazy? Come on, come on, I know where you hide those stamps you've cut off envelopes. If I were to whisper a word to Sabiha . . .

GRANDFATHER: [*Walks to the gas burner.*] Goddamn you!

SABRİ: Stop cursing! Just tend to your task!

GRANDFATHER: [*Muttering to himself.*] What the son does to his own father . . .

SABRİ: [*Interrupting.*] When Saadet left, did you not say it was one mouth less for me to feed? You keep complaining, and I'll place you in a home and have even less to worry about. Don't you forget it.

GRANDFATHER: [*As he lights the gas burner.*] I shall think of some way to fend for myself, no doubt.

SABRİ: You will, I know. Two somersaults, three kowtows, and some Tahsin Bey will be found to adopt you, just you wait. Saadet can mop floors and wash dishes. What can you do? If you want to become an unpaid servant, this is a good time to practice!

GRANDFATHER: [*Nervously.*] For heaven's sake!

SABİHA: [*Quietly.*] Sabri!

SABRİ: Hmm?

SABİHA: You think they make her mop the floors? She's no bigger than a doll.

SABRİ: Who cares how big she is? They may even make her clean the toilet.

SABİHA: Oh!

SABRİ: Yes, oh! Too late for *oohs* and *ahs,* now!

SABİHA: Was it my fault? Don't blame me for it now!

SABRİ: Who's blaming you for it! It's my own stupidity. Hell! Did we entertain guests, or was it our unlucky day? Tell me if you can!

GRANDFATHER: What am I supposed to warm up?

SABİHA: There are a few potatoes from yesterday in the small pot.

SABRİ: Potatoes again . . . I won't eat them!

SABİHA: Why do you say that, Sabri, when I struggle to make them last?

SABRİ: I won't eat them! Don't let them last! I don't give a damn!

SABİHA: As if you didn't know that the grocer won't let me have anything more on credit.

SABRİ: To hell with him! I'm not going to pay my bills. I'm not going to pay my back debts either. Let the son of a bitch deduct it from the times he's overcharged us. I've had enough!

SABİHA: Are we to become the disgrace of the neighborhood, then?

SABRİ: If it is a disgrace to have no money, then by all means, and the devil take . . .

SABİHA: We had a bit of self-respect.

SABRİ: Our head was in the sky with all that self-respect! Wait, those words sound familiar. Where have I heard them before?

SABİHA: Never mind now.

SABRİ: That's right! They're your words! Right!

SABİHA: A figure of speech . . .

SABRİ: You are free and easy with figures of speech when you want to be. So what happens when I feel like using a few?

SABİHA: But these potatoes are so delicious . . .

SABRİ: Forget the potatoes! I'm not going to eat potatoes, all right? Today I'll go hungry, tomorrow I'll rob a man or break into a safe. I'll decide which later.

SABİHA: As though you could!

SABRİ: I can—what do you think? Am I the only man for whom things are forbidden, things are sinful? What about swindling and black marketeering? You've got to sell nonstop, I tell you. Don't let go of anything without selling it. Say you are a pimp; you start by selling your wife!

SABİHA: God forbid!

SABRİ: Plant yourself on the corner of the street, whisper a thing or two, drive a bargain, let the fellow in here. Then I'm on the doorstep, and he's inside with you.

SABİHA: Father, you give him a piece of your mind.

GRANDFATHER: Who's going to listen to me?

SABRİ: Since we've got shit, then let us be without self-respect as well! Once I get going, I'll buy you all the best kind of self-respect. The kind that money buys.

SABİHA: God grant that this fellow's wits return to him!

SABRİ: That's it, pray to God in the end. But did you not try to scalp me because I didn't help myself to the safe the night the thief got into the factory?

SABİHA: Did I know what I was saying?

SABRİ: Well, I know what I'm saying. I know . . . so sit down now and wail about your troubles. Honesty is too expensive for me, get it? I can't pay the next installment, so I'm sending it back to the shop.

SABİHA: [*Makes a final effort to appease him.*] I'll send to the butcher's for a quarter pound of ground meat, add it to the potatoes, and . . .

SABRİ: I want a gentleman's meal. Write it down somewhere! If ever I dip my bread into potatoes boiled in plain water . . .

GRANDFATHER: Well, I'm going now.

SABRİ: Wait! [*To* SABİHA.] Isn't there anything else?

SABİHA: There's some fresh bread I bought this morning. You could have a bit of goat cheese with it.

SABRİ: [*To* GRANDFATHER.] Light the burner! With this head on my shoulders, I should be grateful even for this! [*To* SABİHA.] There I go quoting you again.

GRANDFATHER: [*To* SABRİ.] You could set the table at least.

SABRİ: Whether we have anything to feast on or not, I don't give a damn. Come on now, go ahead and say again, "Forks go on the right, the knives on the left."

GRANDFATHER: Forks on the left . . .

SABRİ: Damn it, he's still talking! [*A knock on the door.*]

SABİHA: I wonder what that could be? I hope it's not bad news.

SABRİ: Come in! [*Someone pushes the door, but can't open it. Knocks again.*] I said come in, you jerk!

SABİHA: Sabri! There's a knock on the door.

SABRİ: Come in, damn it!

SABİHA: It's stuck again. It won't open, see!

SABRİ: [*Walks to the door. Angrily.*] I'm going to wreck this shack! [*Pulls the door open.* TAHSİN *is seen on the doorstep.* SABRİ's *anger melts like foam.*] Sir . . .

GRANDFATHER: [*Alarmed.*] Good God!

TAHSİN: Good morning.

SABİHA: [*Pulls herself together.*] Sir, I am going at once to . . .

TAHSİN: Please don't bother!

SABİHA: God forbid! It's no bother. [*Picks up the quilt and goes to the bedroom.*]

SABRİ: Come in, sir.

[TAHSİN *enters with an alarmed expression. He is still careful when he speaks, but his forced smile in Act I has disappeared. He is more himself. He takes a step into the room and stumbles against some of the furniture piled up in front of the door.*]

TAHSİN: Damn it!

GRANDFATHER: You haven't hurt yourself, I hope?

TAHSİN: There's no place to take a step in this house!

SABRİ: We weren't expecting you, sir.

TAHSİN: Did I do something wrong by coming?

GRANDFATHER: You bring us honor, sir.

TAHSİN: [*Looks at the mess the house is in.*] What's going on? Are you moving out?

SABRİ: [*Embarrassed.*] Not moving out, exactly, but . . .

TAHSİN: I see, summer cleaning. [*Trying to joke.*] And you've certainly made a thorough job of it. There's not a spot the size of one's hand left dry.

SABİHA: [*Returns, having hurriedly dressed.*] Sit down here, sir, on the divan. The rain didn't get that far. [*While she speaks, she pulls the clothes off the rope and tosses them into a corner.*]

TAHSİN: No, not the divan. Three minutes on that divan and all my bones begin to ache.

SABRİ: Is that so?

TAHSİN: Yes! You're young, Sabri. What do you know about aching bones? [*To* GRAND-FATHER.] Isn't that so, sir?

GRANDFATHER: I myself can never sit on the divan.

TAHSİN: Hard or not, this chair is better for me. [*Walks to the chair.*]

GRANDFATHER: Sabiha, bring a cushion.

SABİHA: [*Places one of the cushions from the divan on* TAHSİN's *chair.*] Please forgive us, sir, everything's in a mess, but I couldn't tidy up because I've got a cold.

TAHSİN: [*Indifferently.*] Too bad. I hope you get well soon.

SABİHA: Thank you.

TAHSİN: [*Sits down. After a short pause, just to make conversation.*] Ahhh, it's downright cool in here. Outside, it's hell! If it hadn't rained last night, the heat would be simply unbearable!

GRANDFATHER: [*Kowtows.*] Yes, it's very warm, sir.

TAHSİN: Fortunately, it didn't rain; it poured. It made things a bit cooler, thank heaven!

SABRİ: [*Bitterly.*] Yes, it made things cooler.

TAHSİN: The rain is fine, but not the mud! Your road's a real quagmire—only a bright fellow can find his way up here. The car got stuck at the bottom of the slope.

SABİHA: Oh my God, it must have sunk.

TAHSİN: It did and how. Oh Sabri, can you get two kids from around here to wash it for a few pennies? The sun's come out now. It would dry in no time.

SABRİ: [*Reluctantly.*] Shall I do it, sir?

TAHSİN: No, no, you sit down. I want to talk to you.

SABRİ: Father!

GRANDFATHER: Hmm?

SABRİ: [*Deliberately.*] You could toss a couple of pails of water on the gentleman's car.

TAHSİN: [*Half-heartedly.*] I don't want the gentleman to get tired.

GRANDFATHER: Think nothing of it, sir.

TAHSİN: [*To* GRANDFATHER.] You're putting me to shame.

SABRİ: The pail is under the faucet, Father, and there's a rag inside.

GRANDFATHER: [*Crossly.*] I know. [*Walks to the pail.*]

TAHSİN: Just the surface mud. That will be enough.

SABRİ: Don't worry, sir, my father is very thorough. Right, Father?

GRANDFATHER: [*As he fills the pail, softly so that only* SABRİ *can hear.*] Asshole!

SABİHA: The house is absolutely bare. I don't know what to offer you, sir.

TAHSİN: No need to trouble yourself. But how about giving me a brush?

SABİHA: I'll get it right away. [*Goes to get a brush.*]

TAHSİN: I've got mud all over my cuffs. [SABİHA *comes with a brush.*] Thank you. [TAHSİN *waits indifferently for* SABİHA *to brush his cuffs.* SABİHA *bends down.*]

SABRİ: [*Rushing, just as* SABİHA *is about to start brushing.*] Don't do it, Sabiha! [*Takes the brush out of her hand.*]

TAHSİN: [*Realizing his gaffe.*] Please don't bother, Sabri. Thanks. [*Takes the brush out of* SABRİ's *hand and stands brushing his cuffs.*] What was I saying? Oh yeah, I came to discuss something with you. [SABRİ *and* SABİHA *look at each other with a strange intuition.* TAHSİN, *uneasy about this pause, tries to change the subject.*] Where is the young man? Yılmaz?

SABRİ: He's not here.

TAHSİN: Has he found a job for himself?

SABRİ: We don't know. He's gone.

TAHSİN: Gone? How gone? You mean for good?

SABİHA: For good. We haven't seen him since the day you and your wife came to dinner.

TAHSİN: Why, for heaven's sake?

SABRİ: [*Fidgety.*] He's gone . . . that's all. I was a bit sharp with him that day.

SABİHA: Why blame yourself, Sabri? Weren't you in the right?

SABRİ: I don't know, maybe I was, maybe I wasn't, and as for him . . .

TAHSİN: Don't worry, Sabri! I'm sure you were right. I've seen the boy, he is . . . how shall I say . . . a strange fellow. A bit headstrong. No fool, mind you . . .

SABRİ: [*Interrupts.*] Not at all!

TAHSİN: That's right, clever but headstrong. One of those people who can't be happy with what they have. I didn't say anything that day so as not to worry you. In fact, when we got home, Nezahat said, "You should have taught that boy a lesson."

SABİHA: So the lady was annoyed, too?

TAHSİN: [*Softening.*] No, I don't think she was annoyed or anything like that. [*To* SABRİ *in a good-humored voice.*] A child is bound to leave home eventually. Perhaps it is better this way. Let him be without a home for a while, and he'll soon be toeing the line.

SABRİ: He won't.

TAHSİN: I've seen his kind, I've seen all kinds. Throughout the years, so many headstrong youngsters working for me. If they go hungry for three days, they turn into obedient monkeys.

SABRİ: Turn into a monkey?

TAHSİN: What did you think? Of course he will. What I do for these kids who work for me is act like their older brother or their father. One of these days he'll come slinking back, you'll see.

SABİHA: Sure thing, he'll come back.

TAHSİN: Between you and me, he was up to no good. [*Sees that* SABRİ *is unhappy.*] All right, all right. Let's close the subject! [*A silence.*] Look, Sabri . . . er, you don't doubt my good intentions, I am sure.

SABRİ: [*Half-heartedly.*] I wouldn't dream of it, sir.

TAHSİN: Fine. As for me, I'm as fond of you as though you were my son.

SABRİ: Thank you, sir.

TAHSİN: No, no, don't thank me. It's only right that it should be so. Think of why I came to your house . . . because I trust you. Someone else would have gotten spoiled. But you . . . [*Hems and haws.*] I mean . . . that is why we adopted your child.

SABİHA: [*Suddenly alarmed.*] Saadet hasn't done anything she wasn't supposed to do . . .

TAHSİN: No! [*Embarrassed, stammers.*] It's not that. Now, this morning, Saadet went to the grocer's because she ran out of soap to clean the floor. The grocery shop is at the corner of our street, barely a hundred feet away. She really learned about the street and the neighborhood. That's why the cleaning woman sent Saadet there . . . then the hall porter saw her . . .

SABRİ: [*Worried.*] She can't have . . . no, she doesn't know what money means!

TAHSİN: [*Stammers.*] I haven't made myself clear. What I mean is, on the way to the grocer's, someone went up to her . . .

SABİHA: What!

TAHSİN: Yes, some guy.

SABİHA: [*With great alarm.*] What could the fellow be after? She's such a little girl!

TAHSİN: The porter saw them in the distance. He tried to run after them, but they were gone!

SABİHA: [*On the point of panicking.*] Oh, my child, my little girl!

SABRİ: [*Nervously.*] Wait a moment, Sabiha, let's listen carefully.

TAHSİN: To cut a long story short, Saadet has not returned!

SABİHA: Oh, God, what misfortunes are piling on us! [*Sobs.*]

SABRİ: Didn't she shout for help? Didn't she resist?

TAHSİN: The porter says he couldn't understand it. The fellow simply grabbed her by the arm and flung her into a car, then he drove away.

SABİHA: My baby, my poor child! [*Having panicked, she cries and paces the room.*]

SABRİ: How can it be . . . in broad daylight? [*Stammers.*] In broad daylight?

TAHSİN: In the early hours, there's practically nobody in the street, of course.

SABİHA: My poor child! [*Paces the room.*]

TAHSİN: That's what the porter had to say.

SABRİ: What time did this happen?

TAHSİN: I told you, it was early. We weren't up yet. [*Catches his gaffe.*] That is, of course, she goes to bed before we do and so . . . when I saw the porter on my way out and he told me, it must have been half past nine. The stupid jerk didn't wake us up. Though for a reason like this we wouldn't have minded, of course. I bawled him out later.

SABİHA: [*In a panic.*] They've kidnapped my daughter! They've kidnapped my daughter! [*Paces back and forth.*]

TAHSİN: If I hadn't had a board of directors meeting, I'd have come earlier. And you don't have a telephone. I did come the moment the meeting was over.

SABRİ: [*Bitterly.*] Thank you.

TAHSİN: To tell you the truth, I'm not quite sure whether she was kidnapped, or just . . . ran away!

SABRİ: Ran away? How could she?

TAHSİN: True enough, where would she be as comfortable as she was in our house? Nevertheless, I've a suspicion that she might have run away. It is known that adopted children—children about to be adopted . . . turn their minds to . . . [*Stammers.*] An acquaintance of ours had an adopted child . . . a child . . . who when she was alone in the house took in the fruit vendor's apprentice. You know the familiar story!

SABRİ: [*Defiantly.*] What are you saying? She's a tiny little girl!

TAHSİN: Of course she is! And certainly I didn't say anything like this happened. But who knows, maybe for a little money . . . they seduced her.

SABİHA: Can't be! It's just out of the question! Oh my daughter! [*Paces around the room.*]

TAHSİN: [*Changing his statement.*] Of course, of course . . . and if she did run away, she would have come straight to you because she missed you, isn't that right?

SABİHA: Sabri, I beg of you, run to the police station right away!

SABRİ: Sabiha dear, my boss must have already notified the police.

TAHSİN: No. That is . . . I thought it best to let you know first. Now if we put our heads together, we'll think of something.

SABİHA: [*To herself.*] Who'd kidnap her . . . of what use would she be to anyone?

TAHSİN: We did our best. Do not hold us responsible, Sabiha Hanım.

SABİHA: [*Not knowing what she is saying.*] We wouldn't dream of it.

TAHSİN: She goes to the grocer once in a blue moon, and see what happens! Believe me, we have never allowed her out of the house. When we went out ourselves, we told the cook she was to stay in. Or if the cook was out, then Nezahat put the child in the hall and locked all the doors! After all she might have fallen out the window. We were responsible for her!

SABRİ: You were, yes!

TAHSİN: Surely we did not want her to run away! Just as she was getting used to odd jobs around the house . . . [*Stammers.*] . . . that is, Nezahat said she was beginning to be a help to her.

SABİHA: I'm sure she was!

TAHSİN: She's a clever child, an able child! You have to tell her something only once. I mean, Sabri, the other day she polished the parquet floors so well you could see your eyelashes in them! You'd be proud of her if you saw . . .

SABRİ: [*Gets up abruptly. Determinedly.*] Don't you worry, Sabiha, I'll be back in a minute.

SABİHA: Wait, let me get a wrap. I'm coming with you!

TAHSİN: [*Hurriedly.*] Now, now, don't be in too much of a hurry. You know the saying about the devil and those in a hurry. Let's first sit down and think.

SABRİ: [*Loudly.*] What's there left to think about, sir? It's twelve thirty. Some five and a half hours have gone by since the incident. The damage is done!

TAHSİN: [*Impatiently and loudly.*] You don't seem to understand. [*Seeing that* SABRİ *is startled, he continues more gently.*] Look, Sabri, listen to me, my boy. You are fond of me, are you not? You owe me more than a little. You wouldn't like my name to be mixed up in so unseemly an affair, would you? Come now, would you?

SABRİ: I wouldn't, of course . . . but I don't understand very well.

TAHSİN: [*Tries to be calm.*] What do you not understand? Think a little. An item in the newspapers—a foster child in the house of a well-known businessman has been kidnapped. This "foster child" business is a bit awkward. You understand now?

SABRİ: [*Comes to his senses.*] Yes, I understand now!

TAHSİN: That's how it is. You wouldn't like to be in my place, would you?

SABRİ: I don't know.

TAHSİN: Of course you don't know. Your name is not likely to get into the papers, so you don't know! [*Containing his anger.*] See here, my boy, one has enemies, just as one has friends. One cannot put a padlock on people's mouths. They'll say things like, "They were beating her, that's why she ran away," "They put her to work, that's why she ran away." That sort of thing. There's no way to force people to keep quiet about such things. In this evil world, who could possibly convince people that we loved Saadet as though she were our own daughter?

SABİHA: [*Has come to her senses.*] But what shall we do, then? How are we to find our child?

SABRİ: Do you mean we must not go to the police?

TAHSİN: [*Softly.*] Of course you'll go to the police. But without making a lot of fuss. Quietly, right? And without involving us in any way.

SABRİ: What are we to say, if they ask us? Did they not kidnap Saadet outside your house?

TAHSİN: What difference does it make, for heaven's sake? She could have been kidnapped from right here.

SABİHA: But isn't that going to make it more difficult for the police?

TAHSİN: [*Suppressing his anger.*] Come, now, Sabiha Hanım, why do you complicate things? I don't understand you. Do I have the time to waste at the precinct, my dear? Remember the saying: "If you have a lot of money, guarantee somebody else's loan; if you have nothing to do, serve as a witness." If she is to be found, she can be found this way as well as that.

SABİHA: [*Fearfully.*] You mean it's possible that they won't find her?

TAHSİN: That was just an expression. Of course she will be found. Where do you think we live?

SABRİ: So we are not to tell the police that Saadet lived in your house?

TAHSİN: That's it, that's all. She was playing in front of your house, you called her in to breakfast, she didn't come. You looked everywhere in the neighborhood. When you couldn't find her, you notified the police.

SABİHA: Of course you know best, but . . .

TAHSİN: Don't imagine for a moment that we don't want her back. Saadet is still our daughter. The moment you find her, you bring her to us. She will be most welcome.

[SABRİ *and* SABİHA *are silent.*]

SABRİ: [*In a soft voice.*] Let's find her first.

TAHSİN: That's right. If need be, we'll officially adopt her. But if we were to search for her now, it would look strange. Won't they ask us why we're looking for a child who is a stranger to us?

SABRİ: [*In pain.*] Yes, they would ask.

TAHSİN: In the precincts of poor neighborhoods, such matters are taken care of more easily. I mean . . . if it becomes necessary to spend a few pennies . . . don't you worry about it. [*Noticing that* SABRİ *and* SABİHA *are keeping quiet.*] Of course, you're her real father and mother, no matter what. I thought it would be right for you to report her loss. Am I wrong? It's not that I'm evading my responsibilities. I swear to you that Nezahat has been crying all morning.

[SABİHA *and* SABRİ *silently look at* TAHSİN *as though they are seeing him for the first time. He is embarrassed.*]

Do we understand each other?

[SABİHA *looks at* SABRİ, *then goes straight into the bedroom.*]

SABRİ: [*Expressionless.*] We do.

GRANDFATHER: [*Comes in through the street door huffing and puffing. Puts down the pail.*] Ugh!

TAHSİN: Are you tired, sir?

GRANDFATHER: [*Sulking.*] Well . . .

TAHSİN: [*Trying to look cute.*] I appreciate what you did.

GRANDFATHER: I can't say it's as bright as new, but it's better than it was. [*Pointedly.*] I'm not used to washing cars, you know.

TAHSİN: [*Pretends he doesn't understand.*] I'm sure it looks fine. It's no equivalent for what you've done, but . . . [*Pulls out his wallet.*] Would you accept a little gift?

GRANDFATHER: [*Offended.*] Please, sir!

TAHSİN: But why not?

GRANDFATHER: [*Curtly.*] Because!

SABİHA: [*Comes out of the bedroom in her coat.*] Come on, Sabri.

SABRİ: With your permission, sir.

TAHSİN: As I said!

GRANDFATHER: [*To* SABRİ.] What's up?

SABRİ: I'll tell you later, I'll tell you later. [SABRİ *and* SABİHA *walk toward the door.*]

GRANDFATHER: What's come over you? Where are you going in such a hurry?

SABİHA: They've kidnapped Saadet!

GRANDFATHER: What?

TAHSİN: Our porter saw it happen. In a car . . . so I ran here.

GRANDFATHER: May God punish them! A child no bigger than that!

SABRİ: So we are going to the police station, Father. Keep your eyes open until we return.

GRANDFATHER: You should have gone earlier! Get going now! [*Truly overcome by emotion.* SABİHA *has red eyes from crying. He pats her on the shoulder with a closeness that we witness for the first time.*] I'll tidy up the house before you return.

SABİHA: [*Warmly.*] Bless you, Father.

GRANDFATHER: [*With awkward kindness.*] She'll be found. Of course they'll find her! The moment you tell them. [*Angrily.*] What a dastardly affair!

TAHSİN: [*To* SABRİ *and* SABİHA.] Let me give you a lift. [*They all walk to the door.*]

GRANDFATHER: I want to hear at once. Don't keep me worrying. [*Sincerely.*] The poor child!

[*As* SABRİ *is about to pull on the door, it opens from the outside.* YILMAZ *stands on the doorstep, holding* SAADET *by the hand.*]

SABİHA: My baby! My little girl! [*Runs to* SAADET *and puts her arms around her.*] My baby! [*Hugs her tightly. The others seem turned to stone. They all are facing the door and*

YILMAZ, *who is still standing tall on the doorstep without a trace of guilt on his face. A long silence.*]

TAHSİN: Well, really, this is too much! [*To* SABRİ.] Aren't you going to say anything, Sabri?

SABRİ: [*Tries to hide his joy.*] What shall I say, sir?

TAHSİN: [*Sternly, to* YILMAZ.] Where did you find Saadet, my son? [YILMAZ *does not reply.*] I must confess I thought of the possibility. [*A pause.*] But why did you do it? [YILMAZ *looks at him.*] Your aunt Nezahat and I have been worried all morning. We didn't know what to do. I came here to tell your father and mother. They nearly died of fright. Was it worth it? [YILMAZ *is silent.*] I hear you have stayed away from home for several days. Don't you think you have caused your family enough worry?

SABİHA: [*Hugs* SAADET.] We've found my daughter. I care nothing about the rest!

TAHSİN: No, you must not say that, Sabiha Hanım. This young man has deserved a lesson for some time now. [*To* YILMAZ.] Yes? Aren't you even going to defend yourself? [YILMAZ *keeps quiet and looks him straight in the eye.*] Have you found yourself a job, my son? [YILMAZ *remains silent.*]

SABRİ: [*Tries to protect his son.*] Never mind, sir, that is how he is. Thank heaven I earn enough to . . .

TAHSİN: [*Sternly.*] Do not interfere, Sabri. [*To* YILMAZ.] You do not reply. That's something at least! It means you realize your guilt.

GRANDFATHER: It's not that he hasn't looked for a job, sir. He's complained many times to me that he simply couldn't find decent work. Many times.

TAHSİN: [*Interrupting.*] That I cannot believe, sir. I've said it before, and I say it again, there is plenty of work to do, and no bread for him who refuses to work. [*To* YILMAZ.] I offered you a job as my chauffeur. Why did you not accept? [*A pause.*] If you love your sister so much, it would have given you opportunities to be with her. What's wrong with that?

SABRİ: [*Butts in.*] I'll speak to him later, sir. I don't know . . . he just doesn't want it . . . he doesn't want to be a chauffeur. It's best not to insist.

TAHSİN: [*Sternly.*] What is it, Sabri? There's something strange about you today. Instead of bawling out your son, you're trying to give me advice.

SABRİ: Sir, I wouldn't dream of it. Please forgive me.

TAHSİN: [*Noticing that* YILMAZ *is looking him straight in the eye and that* SABRİ *is averting his gaze.*] Well . . . since you all appear to be pleased with each other, there is nothing further for me to say. [*After a pause, to* SAADET.] Come on now, Saadet, my child, let's go and stop your aunt Nezahat from worrying. [SAADET *does not move.*] Kiss your mother good-bye. [SAADET *looks at* YILMAZ *as though for help. The others also look at* YILMAZ, *who still says nothing.* TAHSİN *loses his composure, but tries not to show it.*] Come on, my child. [SAADET *frees herself from her mother's arms and runs to grab* YILMAZ's *legs. She looks pleadingly at her brother.* TAHSİN *cracks a forced smile.*] What's that supposed to mean?

SAADET: That's the way it is!

[SABRİ *and* SABİHA *look at each other with doubt, but also with pleasure, which they are trying to conceal.*]

TAHSİN: Come on, come on, you haven't forgotten your blond dolly, have you? She must be missing you. What will we do if she cries?

SAADET: [*Her eyes glitter suddenly. To* SABİHA.] Where's my dolly? You haven't given her to the bogeyman, have you?

SABİHA: [*Touched.*] Never! She's there . . . under the bed.

SAADET: [*Runs to the bed and pulls out her rag doll. To her doll.*] Did you cry a lot? You mustn't cry anymore! [*Plays with her doll and hums "rock-a-bye, baby." A nervous pause.*]

TAHSİN: [*Nervously.*] Well, Sabri?

SABRİ: [*Hesitating.*] Sir . . . it's this way. We cannot force her to . . .

TAHSİN: [*Thoroughly put out.*] Whatever you say, then. I thought I was doing you a favor. I didn't just think so; it *was* so. It wasn't for our convenience that . . . [*Unable to continue.*] All right then, if you want to doom your child to lifelong poverty, that's your business. [*No one replies.* YILMAZ *looks* TAHSİN *straight in the eye; the others look away as if they are afraid* TAHSİN *will notice their joy.*] Very well, then, very well. [*Walks to the door.*]

SABRİ: [*As though waking up.*] Good-bye, sir!

SABİHA: Come again!

GRANDFATHER: Be well!

TAHSİN: [*Stops as he is about to go out.*] Hey, Sabri, let me tell you right now. Be extra careful when you're making your rounds, OK? You caught the thief after he broke in. Now that's fine. But it could be that next time he'll get away, and there's nothing we can do about it. [*Just as he is stepping out, he bumps into furniture as he did when he came in.*]. Damn it. Why they ever give permits for such ramshackle shanties, I don't know!

SABRİ: [*Flatly.*] There's no permit, sir.

TAHSİN: Hell, whatever! [*Goes out, banging the door behind him.*]

[*The family stands absolutely still while* TAHSİN *gets his motor started, and the car is heard going down the hill. Then they all turn to face* YILMAZ, *who is still standing by the door. A tense silence.*]

SABRİ: [*Jittery; cannot find the right words.*] Well, hmm! It rained hard last night, so we were flooded. [*A pause.*] Where were you?

YILMAZ: [*Timidly.*] I was staying with a friend.

SABRİ: [*Without coming close to* YILMAZ.] Good. [*After a pause, blurts out.*] The roof leaked. The plaster's peeled off here and there.

YILMAZ: We'll repair it all.

SABRİ: Should we repair? [YILMAZ *keeps quiet.*] If I demolish it altogether, would I be more of a hero, eh? [YILMAZ *doesn't answer.*]

SABİHA: [*Softly.*] Are you hungry, Yılmaz?

YILMAZ: [*Hesitatingly.*] Well, a little.

GRANDFATHER: Of course he's hungry. How could he be anything else? You lie down again, Sabiha; I'm going to warm up the food. [*Lifts the lid of the pot.*] Oh boy, we can't celebrate with only boiled potatoes.

YILMAZ: I have a few pennies if you like.

GRANDFATHER: Cut that out, will you? I'm used to living on my son's money, but I haven't sunk low enough to live on my grandson's.

SABRİ: Why not? It's not for nothing that I brought up this young man who is as tall as I am.

SABİHA: For shame, Sabri! The poor boy's earnings . . .

SABRİ: I told you I was going to change the head on my shoulders.

GRANDFATHER: [*Grabs the string bag from beside the gas burner.*] I'll fill the string bag with food worthy of you all.

[*The shanty comes alive again. Only SABRİ and YILMAZ stand far away from each other and aloof. YILMAZ is in no mood to apologize. SABRİ is anxious to have his son approve of him. They both are restless for the other to make the first move.*]

SABRİ: Fill the string bag to your heart's content, old man, but from now on you're not going to have to stick your nose into anything, get that? Whatever you want to do . . . getting busy with your stamps or whatever your heart desires. Well, whatever . . .

SABİHA: You'll get the biggest glass, I promise you!

SABRİ: You're going to sit in your corner, and we'll come and pay you our respects every holiday.

GRANDFATHER: Now what does all that mean?

SABRİ: That means you are old, you are finished. You are not—What do they say?—in fashion anymore. Isn't that so, Yılmaz?

YILMAZ: [*Smiles broadly.*] Looks like it.

GRANDFATHER: Shame on you, boy!

SABRİ: As for Sabiha and me, we're not finished yet . . . not finished. The paint is peeling off here and there, bits of rust are showing through.

SABİHA: Honestly, Sabri, you're talking like a dictionary.

SABRİ: [*Kiddingly jabs SABİHA.*] Don't you like it, girl?

SABİHA: [*Giggles coquettishly.*] I don't know.

SABRİ: [*Swaggers center stage.*] Damn it, I really feel good. This could mean trouble.

GRANDFATHER: Tahsin Bey was in a huff when he stormed out.

YILMAZ: I thought you weren't going to meddle in such talk, Grandpa?

GRANDFATHER: Get out of here! What's going on here, huh? [*Sulks like a child.*]

SABRİ: I've got nothing to lose! I can just dump this guard's uniform. To hell with it! [*To* YILMAZ.] To hell with the world! I can fuck off this world, can't I?

YILMAZ: You sure can.

SABRİ: There you go!

YILMAZ: Still and all, let's not get too excited and let this thing slip out of our hands just when we've grabbed hold of it.

SABRİ: Now listen to that! This guy begrudges his dad a bit of fun! [*Joking.*] We tidied up the house inside and out. Man, we can sure find a way out for the rest. [*Suddenly remembers.*] Heey, remember that burglar, the guy I caught red-handed? You know what that guy said to me?

SABİHA: [*Giggles.*] Sure, sure.

SABRİ: Come off it. Wait before you call me stupid. The guy said: "Look, you're never going to see such a bundle of money even if you stay away from food and drink and save all that for a thousand years. Come, let's split it half and half." He said he could give me a bang on the head . . . a swelling—and scram! That way it would appear as if I had a fight with a burglar who managed to get away. That's it . . .

SABİHA: And what did you say to that?

SABRİ: I grabbed the bastard by the collar. [*Timidly turns toward* YILMAZ.] Now, does that make me stupid?

[YILMAZ, *with an embarrassed smile, just shakes his head.* SABRİ *regains his self-confidence, but still cannot go near his son.*]

Tell me, where did you find the car? They said you drove her away in a car.

YILMAZ: I got a job driving a taxi.

GRANDFATHER: [*Once again he cannot help butting in.*] Good for you! So you're on the straight and narrow path at last.

YILMAZ: [*Softly.*] I'm not on the path you mean, Granddad. I've simply got a job, that's all.

GRANDFATHER: [*Contented, without listening to the rest.*] Well, whatever, whatever . . .

[FATHER *and* SON *stand and stare face to face without uttering a word.*]

SABRİ: [*Trying to keep a stiff upper lip.*] What were you waiting for all this time? Since you had the girl, why didn't you bring her back right away?

YILMAZ: I hadn't made up my mind.

SABRİ: Made up your mind about what?

YILMAZ: About bringing Saadet back here . . . and coming myself.

SABRİ: [*Bursting with enthusiasm.*] Since you're back, why not cuddle up, you son of a dog? [*Hugs* YILMAZ.]

[As SABRİ *and* YILMAZ *give each other a tight embrace, it's as if the invisible wall between them tumbles. Their enthusiasm spreads to the others.*]

GRANDFATHER: You son of a dog! You dirty rat!

SABRİ: [*Shoves his son center stage.*] Take a close look at this boy. This guy has a lot going for him! I tell all of you, he's the sort that will stick a handle on the world and spin it.

YILMAZ: [*All smiles.*] Dad, you sure are different today . . .

SABRİ: Stop making fun of me, bastard, or else I'll beat the hell out of you. [*Embarrassed.*] Son of a gun, whatever I do, I do to please you, to make you appreciate me. [*They all chuckle.* SABRİ's *enthusiasm is boundless.*] Hey, what're we waiting for? Dad, you go to the grocer's. [*Hands the string bag, which* GRANDFATHER *had laid aside, to the old man and pushes him toward the door.*]

GRANDFATHER: I'll be back in a jiffy. [*As* GRANDFATHER *rushes out as fast as he can,* SABRİ *grabs* SABİHA *and forces her on to the divan.*]

SABRİ: Jump into bed, Sabiha, my girl!

SABİHA: [*Giggling.*] Stop that, will you! With the kids around . . .

SABRİ: Yılmaz and I better get to work right away! [*To* YILMAZ.] Aren't we supposed to repair the shanty?

YILMAZ: [*Gets going.*] There was supposed to be a bit of plaster under the sink.

SABRİ: Right . . . the trowel's there, too.

YILMAZ: [*From underneath the cupboard, he takes out the trowel and a sack with a little plaster left at the bottom.*] Is there a cup to mix some plaster in?

SABİHA: Take one of the trays. I'll wash it later.

SABRİ: No, dear, let's not dirty the tray. [*Looks around.*] Hey, Saadet! On top of the radio there's a dish, silver or tin, whatever. Grab that and bring it over.

SABİHA: Sabri, that won't do!

SABRİ: Why not? Once the plaster dries, whatever you have used is useless. What should we do, dump the plate in the junkyard? [*As* SABRİ *laughs heartily,* SAADET *brings over the silver plate that was the gift from* TAHSİN *and* NEZAHAT. SABRİ *makes believe he is reading the inscription on the plate.*] "To our heroic watchdog Karabaş . . ."[5]

SABİHA: [*Cannot help laughing.*] What a tease you are!

SABRİ: [*Fondling his wife.*] What an artful dodger you are! [*As* SABİHA *puts on airs,* SABRİ *flings the silver plate to* YILMAZ.] Mix the plaster real well, lad. We don't want to work on this again every time it rains.

YILMAZ: [*Turns the silver plate up and down.*] Plate, don't go astray!

SABRİ: That's good. [*Examining the walls of the shanty.*] Unless we scrape off these swollen surfaces, we'll have done all this work for nothing. [*Knocks loose large chunks of plaster with his hammer.*] There you go . . . I'd better scrape off the whole wall and be done with this damn wreck! [*As* YILMAZ *keeps mixing the plaster,* SABRİ *relentlessly pounds on the swollen plaster. He gets elated as pieces fall off. He gasps and pants, then suddenly stops.*] So we're not done yet, huh?

---

5. Karabaş: Anatolian sheepdog; used here as a name.

YILMAZ: Not done.

SABRİ: We're just starting, huh?

YILMAZ: Just starting.

[*As* SAADET, *who is clutching her rag doll, and* SABİHA, *who is watching her* HUSBAND *and* SON *with pleasure from her bed, look on admiringly,* SABRİ *hammers once again. A big slab of plaster falls off the wall.* YILMAZ *approaches holding the trowel and the plaster-filled silver plate to begin work, and* SABRİ *stands beside him in utter dignity.*]

SABRİ: From now on . . . if anyone tries to honor me, I'll make mincemeat of him!

CURTAIN

The Mikado Game

MELİH CEVDET ANDAY

Translated by Nermin Menemencioğlu

An Editor's Note

Melih Cevdet Anday (1915–2002) stands as a towering figure in modern Turkish literature. He achieved impressive success in many genres. As a poet, he was in the forefront of a decisive innovative movement in the 1940s and later forged a powerful synthesis by adding many abstract features and philosophical dimensions. His seven novels rank among the best of contemporary fiction. His masterly essays on literature, culture, and politics—hundreds of them published in the socialist daily *Cumhuriyet*—shaped the ideas and tastes of his large following. Anday excelled in travel writing as well. His impeccable translations of classics and major modern works, ranging from Molière, Plato, Gogol, and Turgenev to Caldwell, Lagerkvist, and Pasternak, are among the best available to Turkish readers. Some of his early versions of American poems (by Edgar Allan Poe and Langston Hughes, for instance) have enchanted generations of Turks.

Anday's plays brought vigor and sophistication to the Turkish theater from the mid-1960s to the early 1980s. His *İçerdekiler* ('Those Inside) and *Mikado'nun Çöpleri* (presented in this anthology as *The Mikado Game*) had a strong impact on Turkish dramatic writing. The latter, which was premiered and published in 1967, introduced an "absurdist" strain, firing the imagination of avant-garde theatergoers.

Anday had limited exposure to higher education—after only two years in Belgium on a State Railways scholarship, he was forced to return home when World War II erupted. In Turkey, he worked for brief stints at the Publications Office of the Ministry of Education and the Ankara City Library. He later held jobs as arts and literature editor for numerous major Istanbul dailies. For many years, he taught diction at the Istanbul City Conservatory. He also served as a member of the executive board of the Turkish Radio and Television Administration.

Anday's poetry, plays, translations, and contributions to literature won many awards. *Mikado'nun Çöpleri* earned two prestigious awards. His works have been translated into a variety of languages—Russian, French, German, Serbian, English, Hungarian, Bulgarian, and others. In 1971, Turkish newspapers reported that UNESCO cited him as one of the prominent figures of world literature.

See p. 216 in the introduction to *A Shanty in Istanbul* for the biography of translator Nermin Menemencioğlu (Streater).—TSH

Characters

MAN

WOMAN

ACT I

[*The foyer, also used as a living room, of a second-floor apartment in a residential build-ing. The main door at the back; doors to left and right of the foyer lead to other rooms. Another door on the right opens onto a corridor. A coatrack by the main door. To one side a sideboard and a gas stove. Bookshelves. On the walls, abstract paintings, a clock, a mirror. A cot. Several chairs.*]

2:00 A.M. on a winter night.

As the curtain goes up, the stage is dark. A dog can be heard barking on the first floor. A key turns in the lock of the apartment door. The MAN *enters and turns on the light. His hair and overcoat are covered with snow. He is about twenty-eight or thirty. He has been drinking.*]

MAN: [*Stamps his feet lightly on the doormat, shakes the snow off his hair and clothes, looks behind him.*] This is it. Come in. [*The* WOMAN *comes in, holding in her arms a child muffled in woolen wraps, a baby. The* WOMAN *is thirty to thirty-five years old. She, too, is covered with snow. She surveys the room timidly from the threshold.*] I told you, my parents are home. You have nothing to fear.

WOMAN: It's not that. I don't want to be a nuisance. [*Enters.*] Thank you.

MAN: [*Points to the cot.*] You can put the child down there.

WOMAN: [*Places the child on the cot, brushes the snow off it,[1] uncovers its face.*] It's sleeping. [*Goes to the doormat and stamps her feet; tidies her appearance, breathing deeply and occasionally sighing.*]

MAN: What weather! We'll all be buried alive if this snow continues. Not a bad idea at that. [*Hangs his coat on the rack.*] Take off your coat; you can hang it up here! [*Crumples up a piece of newspaper, lights it with a match, and tosses it into the stove, which starts burning.*] How long had you been waiting there?

WOMAN: [*Reluctantly takes off her coat and hangs it up.*] I don't know. One hour, perhaps, or two.

MAN: You waited for nothing. Taxi drivers do not work on nights like this. An unheard-of winter. The snow's right up to the doors. Perhaps it's the beginning of a new Ice Age, man's last night on earth. Tell me, are you educated?

---

1. In Turkish, there is no gender indicated in the third-person singular verb; therefore, the translator has opted for the use of *it*.

WOMAN: I suppose so.

MAN: Well, I'm not. If I say the wrong things, you mustn't mind. Were you going to catch a boat?

WOMAN: [*Back beside the child.*] Yes.

MAN: Which boat? The car ferry?

WOMAN: Yes, the car ferry.

MAN: [*Bends down to make sure the stove is working, then straightens up.*] It may seem to be working, and then it suddenly goes out. [*Lights a cigarette.*] Perhaps the car ferry isn't working either. There's not much visibility, is there? They say the ferries are fitted out with radar, but nothing works; the ferries that use radar all run aground. [*Looks at the* WOMAN.] Why don't you sit down? [*She does so.*] Say the ferries are working. You still won't be likely to find a taxi on the other shore. [*Puts out his cigarette.*] Where did you want to go?

WOMAN: I was just going to stay on the ferry, waiting for morning. [*The* MAN *looks at her.*] I had nowhere to go. [*He appears determined not to ask too many questions.*] And no money. [*Hides her face in her hands.*]

MAN: [*In a normal tone of voice.*] So, you were going to go back and forth on the ferry all night, is that it?

WOMAN: Yes, back and forth until morning. It's warm on the ferry.

MAN: It is warm on the ferry. [*Silence.*]

WOMAN: You've been very kind. It's not me, it's the child I'm thinking about. [*Weeps quietly.*] I'm disturbing you. I could have spent the night down in the entrance hall.

MAN: It's better here, isn't it?

WOMAN: [*Stands up.*] Please let me go downstairs, down to the entrance. [*Wants to pick up the child.*]

MAN: This is no time for madness. You'd freeze.

WOMAN: In a house that I don't know . . .

MAN: No time to be touchy, either. If I were in your place, I'd have broken down a door, any door. Sit down where you are.

WOMAN: Very well. [*Leaves the child.*] You said your mother and father were at home.

MAN: If you don't mind my saying so, that's irrelevant, too. My mother may well get up after a while to see whether I'm back or not. [*Looks at himself in the mirror.*] I take it my face does not inspire confidence. Not a very good face, I know, but I didn't make it. You can't very well expect me to accept responsibility for it.

WOMAN: I'm sorry; it was uncalled for, I know. For someone in my position to ask questions must seem odd, to say the least. [*Sits down.*] I wonder what you're thinking about me—a woman out on the streets on a winter night, with a child. [*Sighs and becomes lost in her dreams.*]

MAN: I'm not thinking anything at all about you. I may later, but at the moment I've got other things to think about. The discussion I was involved in tonight. I can think of arguments that would have clinched it, much good it does now. Makes me feel on edge.

WOMAN: I thought I'd spend the night with a friend, but she wasn't there. I tried perhaps ten times.

MAN: These things happen. [*Begins to take off his shoes.*] My socks are wet through. [*Rubs his toes.*] It's obvious you didn't go out for fun in this kind of weather. [*Takes off his socks.*] Take yours off too—that is, if you want to. [*Places his shoes by the outside door, holds his socks in his hand.*] Are you hungry?

WOMAN: No, no. I'm a married woman.

MAN: [*Doesn't understand that these are two unrelated statements.*] Well, as I'm a dark-haired man, I am hungry.

WOMAN: You didn't understand. I was going to say something else.

MAN: How could I not have gotten hungry? I haven't eaten a thing since morning. I've been drinking, that's all. Do you know, there are people who look down on the hungry? It's a crime to be hungry, in fact. But crimes mean nothing to me, so I can be hungry without the least embarrassment. Except that I never eat during the day, just at night. And by nighttime I begin to feel old, that's the worst of it. [*Goes toward the door leading to the corridor.*] I'm going to see what I can find in the kitchen. [*When he goes out, the* WOMAN *quickly opens her handbag, looks into it, then shuts it, and places it beside her. She bends over the child, murmuring to it softly. Then she walks on tiptoe toward the apartment door, but on hearing the man's footsteps hurriedly returns to her place. He comes in with cheese, sausage, and bread on a tray, which he puts down on the sideboard while he takes out a bottle of brandy and two glasses.*] The poor do not like to watch one eat. It's a good thing to eat secretly, if you have any food. The way beasts do. Have some brandy?

WOMAN: Thank you, no.

MAN: You won't mind if I forget and ask you again. [*Pours himself a drink.*] What does the child eat?

WOMAN: I'll find some milk for it tomorrow.

MAN: There may be some in the kitchen. [*Sits down and helps himself to some of the food.*] It wasn't the fault of the host, mind you. Thoughts, arguments, clashes, even fights are to him like the tidbits that go with drink; they just keep the conversation going. He is so tolerant, no idea provokes him. Hasn't got a belief to his name, in other words. [*Starts to pick up his glass, but puts it down instead.*] Don't misunderstand me; I don't mean to praise people with beliefs. If someone were to stick a knife into my belly, I don't know which of the ideas in my head would stay and which would disappear. One mustn't brag. [*Points at one of the doors.*] My room's in there. You can sleep out here or in there.

WOMAN: I don't want to sleep. I'll just sit here, near the child.

MAN: I think it would be better for you to go into the other room, though, so that my folks don't see you. [*Smiles.*] I can stretch out on the cot here.

WOMAN: [*Timidly.*] Will they mind very much?

MAN: They'll be surprised. They're not used to outsiders, you see. A stranger means a thief or a murderer to them. I once brought home the girl I was going to marry for them to meet. They met, they talked. What do you think they said after she had left? "This is a respectable house, what do you mean bringing a woman here like that, without a wedding ceremony?" Believe it or not. [*The* WOMAN *makes a start toward the apartment door.*] No, no . . . don't be afraid! Those days are past. [*Hits the table with his fist.*] I could burn this place down if I felt like it.

WOMAN: I don't want to cause any trouble.

MAN: No need to get excited. I've never yet done anything I wanted to. And that means plenty of things other than burning down this place. You do what I tell you: go and lie down in my room.

WOMAN: [*Frightened.*] Very well.

MAN: And don't just lie down, go to sleep. One should be either drinking or sleeping.

WOMAN: Very well.

MAN: You understand?

WOMAN: Yes.

MAN: But of course you must have something to eat if you are going to sleep. Food after midnight is as good as a sleeping pill. [*Points to the tray.*] Help yourself!

WOMAN: Thank you, I simply can't.

MAN: [*Lost in his thoughts.*] "If the socialists win, they'll kill all the intellectuals." The guy who said this is a blasted ignoramus. "So what's it to you?" I should have said. "You've nothing to worry about." [*Mockingly.*] He thinks himself an intellectual! [*Stands up, as though grasping someone by the throat.*] Or I should have done this to that fellow. Do you know what he said? He said, "Nations that engage in rebellion should get the atom bomb right on top of their heads." "Might makes right," he said. I should've got hold of him by the neck and squeezed and squeezed. "Now say it again. Does might make right, huh? Does it?" [*Sits down again.*]

WOMAN: I'd like to tell you something about myself. I think I should. You are seeing me for the first time and under peculiar circumstances. I don't want to bore you with all the details, of course.

MAN: The way he ate was enough to make you sick. When his mouth was already stuffed with food, he kept sticking bread into it. You know the way a mouse tail sticks out of a cat's mouth. Well, a fishtail stuck out of his.

WOMAN: You're right, there are people like that. It's not that I'm anxious to talk about myself.

MAN: It isn't just some people, but everybody eats that way. That's why I can't stand going to a restaurant. Donkeys and horses eat more neatly than we do. Would you like a drink?

WOMAN: No, thank you. Although it must have been very cold outside, I'm just beginning to realize it. It was time for the call to prayer when I left, so it must have been . . .

MAN: They must have increased the number of calls to prayer, don't you think? They sound more frequent to me these days.

WOMAN: Perhaps, I don't know. [*Sits clasping her hands, then making up her mind.*] I mustn't disturb you any longer. [*Stands.*]

MAN: Off to sleep, then? I'll turn on the light for you. [*Goes toward the bedroom.*] Let me give you a pair of slippers. [*Goes into the room. The* WOMAN *kisses the child, murmurs to it, weeping. He returns, barefoot, holding a pair of slippers.*] Here, put these on. I like going around barefoot. [*Places the slippers in front of the* WOMAN.] One's hands and feet should be bare. It's faces that should be covered. What faces there are! God's own ghastly collection, that's what we are.

WOMAN: [*Takes the slippers, looks at her feet.*] The melting snow has ruined the carpet! I'm so ashamed, so ashamed!

MAN: You'd do better to be hungry, I can tell you.

WOMAN: [*Takes off her shoes and places them beside the* MAN's, *then puts on the slippers.*] I'll leave very early in the morning; they needn't see us. [*Takes the child in her arms and moves toward the bedroom.*] And neither need you. I insist on it. You must put it out of your mind or I'll be a constant nuisance to you. I was going to explain, briefly, and then hold my tongue. But then, when I saw you didn't want to listen, it made me cringe. Don't worry, please don't worry!

MAN: I didn't realize how sensitive you were. But, after all, how could I? We don't know each other.

WOMAN: You mustn't think that I want our acquaintanceship to grow!

MAN: I understand, I understand. But I wasn't even aware that I wasn't listening to you earlier. Don't look for motives where there aren't any. Nothing I've done tonight has had a motive. My going to that house, my staying there an hour, or whatever it was, my wandering about in the streets afterward—none of it was planned. And I do not like that house. The way they keep comparing me to a movie star when I'm with them.

WOMAN: You keep talking about that house. It's very much on your mind, obviously. So much that you have forgotten meeting me at the corner and asking me to come to your house.

MAN: No, I do remember, but other things keep getting on my mind as well.

WOMAN: [*Curiously.*] Such as?

MAN: Sit down. [*The* WOMAN *sits down, with the child in her lap.*] You see, I can't remember what you and I talked about because I was thinking of other things.

WOMAN: Well, it's important to me. How can you forget? Did you not offer to help me?

MAN: Don't misunderstand me. I haven't forgotten that. Yes, I know I offered to help you.

WOMAN: Weren't we talking right here, in this room, only a minute ago?

MAN: So we were.

WOMAN: About how I was going to take the car ferry and go back and forth until morning.

MAN: That's right. But I was carrying on two conversations at the same time, one with you and the other with the people in that house.

WOMAN: But you're sure of the one with me, aren't you?

MAN: Do you think I'm out of my mind?

WOMAN: Not you, not you. But you made me feel maybe I was. I was confused. Good night. [*Goes into the bedroom.*]

MAN: [*Finishes his brandy in one gulp, fills the glass again, and takes a sip.*] She doesn't want to listen.

WOMAN: [*Returns with a pair of pajamas in her hand.*] I thought you might want these.

MAN: Put them down there. [*Points at the cot.*] But I'm not sleepy. I'm just going to sit here until morning.

WOMAN: [*Leaves the pajamas on the cot, hastily picking up the handbag she had left there. He watches her. She hesitates, then goes up to him.*] I'm not sleepy, either. My mind's working so fast I can hear it rumbling. Somehow I can't stop it.

MAN: You see? We're both thinking of something else. It's pointless to try to talk. But that's not altogether unusual; all conversation is rather like that. I conducted an experiment once. I didn't listen to a word of what the other fellow was saying; I thought of other things all the time, and at the first opportunity I said the first thing that came to my mind. "I want to spit," I think it was. The fellow came back with, "That's exactly what I was suggesting." So I had come up with exactly the right reaction!

WOMAN: May I sit down?

MAN: Do, it's warmer here than in the other room; you'll feel better. Sit here by the stove. Did you cover up the child? There was a loose blanket.

WOMAN: I did. [*Goes near the stove.*] I'm shivering. Not from the cold, though. It's nerves.

MAN: I walked for miles, up one street, down the other. I kept falling, and each time I cursed out loud.

WOMAN: [*Wants to talk, fumbles for a beginning.*] I'd reached the end of my tether. It's not that I like wandering about at that sort of hour.

MAN: As for me, I prolonged the walk in order to curse to my heart's content. There was a light at some windows. Whenever I saw a light, I stopped and shouted, "Bastards!" The light would be turned off at once. I was like one of those men who used to walk in the street with a snuffer to put out the streetlamps. "Bastards!" And that did it. Only one time a window opened, and a man looked out. The fool was curious. I made him regret his curiosity. "Greetings, bastard!" I shouted, louder than ever. Wasn't I right? I shouted for bastards, and he opened his window. [*Laughs.*] He must have told his wife it was some bum disturbing the quiet of the night. Insults are of no avail at such times; they don't touch one's honor. When the temperature is minus ten, honor retires, shutting the doors and windows tightly, and the streets are left to bums.

WOMAN: There's something I want to say.

MAN: [*Paying no heed.*] It's not really the cold that makes them cringe; it's their bitchiness. They've got hold of a bone and are looking for a place to hide in. [*Drinks.*] You said your nerves made you shiver; one doesn't shiver because of nerves. One must get used to the cold. Had you never been out in it before?

WOMAN: I come from a good family.

MAN: [*Indifferently.*] I'd like to know who doesn't.

WOMAN: [*Hurt, bows her head.*] A woman left in the streets deserves such irony.

MAN: [*Fills a second glass with brandy and offers it to her.*] Drink this, it will warm you up! [*The* WOMAN *shakes her head thoughtfully and refuses.*] I won't think of you as low class because I first saw you in the street. If those living in houses can all be said to be of good family and those in the street of low breeding, the good families would win by a long shot. [*Drinks.*] Whether you belong to a good family or not has absolutely no importance tonight. I saw you at the corner, your face covered with snow, a small child in your arms. I asked you whether you needed any help. You said you were looking for a taxi. I ran about looking for one, couldn't find one, and came back to you. You see? I haven't forgotten what happened.

WOMAN: Yes, I see.

MAN: I asked you what you intended to do. You said you were going to wait there. You obviously had no place to go. But you couldn't stand there waiting until morning. So I asked you to come to my house. You came, that's all. What's odd about it? A simple occurrence.

WOMAN: I wish now I hadn't come.

MAN: You were right to come. I couldn't have left you out in the street. You're here, you'll spend the night here, and you'll go in the morning.

WOMAN: I'll go in the morning.

MAN: When you meet a woman with a child at midnight in the snow, you don't say to her, "I can see that you're from a good family, so I'll invite you to come into my house." [*Begins to remove his tie as though he is all alone in the room.*]

WOMAN: It's all true, what you say. A good deed is a good deed, even toward a bad woman. [*Looks at the* MAN.] I could be a bad woman, couldn't I? [*He shrugs his shoulders.*] For instance, I could be a thief. [*He repeats the gesture.*] Or I could be insane.

MAN: You could.

WOMAN: Of course, those are the sorts of things one thinks about, aren't they?

MAN: One does or one doesn't. Man's mind is completely indecent; it can conjure up the most unreasonable, the most revolting thoughts.

WOMAN: You mean, I mustn't worry about it?

MAN: Something like that. Did you meet anyone else tonight?

WOMAN: People went by.

MAN: Anyone who offered help, I mean.

WOMAN: No.

MAN: You see! I didn't choose you, any more than you chose me. A situation simply brought us together. [*Drinks.*] A coincidence. All sorts of other things must have been happening at the same time—a cat meowing, a man embracing a woman, a man knifing another man, a child crying. One of all those things happened to us, that's all. Not worth making a fuss about.

WOMAN: You're right, it's pointless to worry.

MAN: Pointless, indeed. Suppose you'd been taken to prison instead. Would you have worried about what the other prisoners thought of you?

WOMAN: It may be very simple for you, but if you only knew how uncomfortable it makes me feel.

MAN: You may feel uncomfortable now, but outside you'd have frozen.

WOMAN: That's right, and my child, too. [*Becomes pensive.*]

MAN: You see?

WOMAN: I still think there's some injustice in all this.

MAN: All what?

WOMAN: Forgive me, but I don't want you to think bad things about me.

MAN: You're really scared. So what I think of you is more important than my not leaving you in the lurch? Forget it. Let me think what I think, let everybody think what he thinks.

WOMAN: I didn't worry out there. It began when I came into your house. It may seem funny to you, but it's so. I'm not alone now, so, of course, I worry about what you think.

MAN: Well, I'm relaxed in that respect. I always assume people think the worst, and I accept that.

WOMAN: Please, it's not the same. I didn't bring you into my house. I was the one found in the street.

MAN: All right, I'm not thinking badly of you.

WOMAN: [*Unsatisfied.*] Thank you.

MAN: Furthermore, I'm not in a position to think very hard. I've been drinking, and I've got a headache. [*Drinks.*]

WOMAN: I don't want to bore you with what I'm going to say. What I mean to say . . .

MAN: Go ahead, I didn't mean to change the subject.

WOMAN: To be alone with a man I don't know, in a house I don't know, you must admit, makes my situation a bit peculiar. You are a good person; you have been kind to me. You could have passed by without asking me what I was waiting for, could have pretended not to see me. You could have thought, "This is no time for adventures; I'd better go home and sleep." If you'd acted that way, could I have thought it wrong of you?

No one else would have thought it wrong. There was no one to see you. When there's no one to see, people can run away from things more easily.

MAN: According to this description, I'm a brave do-gooder. Obviously, I haven't flinched from duty. You're the only witness.

WOMAN: I'm saying these things, I'm thanking you, I admire you, I shall never forget your kindness. But later on, when you think about this, do not unjustly belittle a woman you don't know.

MAN: I don't know you, so I can't think anything about you.

WOMAN: And I don't know you, so I can't imagine what you think of me.

MAN: I'm afraid we're not getting anywhere in that case. You don't know me, I don't know you, there's no one to see us. This is a simple event between two people who don't know each other. Even less than that. Imagine that I gave you my seat in the bus, that's all.

WOMAN: You're making it even more humiliating. I've no intention of altering the situation in any way. I'm not going to pursue you because you gave me your seat in the bus. That's all I was afraid of, in any case. There must not, there will not, be a change in our relationship.

MAN: But if I try to make you talk now, the relationship would change. I'd be giving myself the right to question you simply because I had invited you into my house. Furthermore, I'd be putting myself in the position of one who has helped not just a human being, but a definite person—say, someone's spouse. Perhaps tomorrow I'd find myself unable to keep quiet about it. I'd start bragging. People always do that. Why? Because if there were no one to help, then we'd be unable to display our humanity. So really you shouldn't want this.

WOMAN: Want what?

MAN: Want me to know you. Want me to know whether you have, say, quarreled with your husband tonight, been beaten by your husband, run away, or, for all I know, kidnapped your child or lost your mind.

WOMAN: You may not be interested, but aren't you afraid a little bit?

MAN: Afraid of your being out of your mind?

WOMAN: Yes.

MAN: [*Laughs.*] Why are you not afraid of me? What if I'm crazy?

WOMAN: Of us two, I'm the unknown. Who am I, where do I live? You don't know, do you?

MAN: What about you, then, are you not curious about me?

WOMAN: You are someone who has a home of his own, isn't that enough?

MAN: And you are someone who hasn't. What's the difference? If you absolutely insist, I'll try and be frightened, but you haven't convinced me that you're insane.

WOMAN: Doesn't the thought occur to you that I might have killed someone?

MAN: If it's your husband, I can only approve. I think all husbands should be killed.

WOMAN: You're my partner in crime. You're hiding me in your house.

MAN: I won't lose sleep over it; I'm not sleepy anyway.

WOMAN: And you're not afraid I'll kill you?

MAN: You're prolonging the suspense, aren't you? The papers will tell the story tomorrow. Anyway, whether you're mad or a murderess, I couldn't very well leave you stranded in the street. [*Drinks.*] Shall I tell you something? You don't look like a killer or a mad woman, but you are a peculiar woman. The more I try to reassure you, the more you try to frighten me. No use!

WOMAN: I'm simply trying to show you that you're not telling the truth when you say you don't think anything at all about me. Hasn't it occurred to you that I might very well kill myself tonight?

MAN: You'd have done it before if you wanted to. [*Drinks.*] Waiting for hours in the snow, thinking to oneself, "Oh, if I could only find a house in which to commit suicide"— that's not very likely. [*Suddenly remembers the child and looks toward the bedroom, then gets up to fill his glass from the bottle on the sideboard.*] Of course, there's the child. You might say, "for the child's sake." I hadn't thought of that. [*Looks at the* WOMAN *intently.*]

WOMAN: [*Regretting that she brought up the subject of suicide. Hurriedly.*] Neither had I . . . not at all. Don't misunderstand me! What I meant was, you must have thought of a number of possibilities, but you won't admit any of them, and as long as you don't, then I bear the burden of them all. Don't you see why I want to talk? I refuse to have you think of me merely as a woman left alone in the street; it just isn't good enough. I'm a human being, not a cat.

MAN: If you insist. [*Finishes his brandy, pours another one, and sits in a chair. Looking uninterested, he prepares to listen.*] I'm listening.

WOMAN: You must admit this is not a normal situation. I couldn't go into the other room and sleep as though it were. I want to have some esteem in your eyes. My being here forces me to speak.

MAN: And me to listen. We've plenty of time.

WOMAN: [*Sighs.*] When I left the house this evening—I'm going to tell you only about this evening. Let me tell you, it wasn't my house . . . I . . . [*Begins to weep quietly.*] It's no good, I can't do it, I can't tell you . . . oh, I wish I hadn't come. I wish I were in the street, in some doorway; no one would ask me anything then.

MAN: No one's asking anything now, as you know perfectly well. Have I asked you anything?

WOMAN: [*Louder.*] Well, you should. Because you are asking yourself.

MAN: I should ask what?

WOMAN: Anything, any question. Invent one, to make my difficult situation a little more bearable. You could have asked whether I'd had my money stolen, for instance. That would have given me a chance to say something. Maybe not the truth, maybe I'd have invented something. Your not asking any questions deprived my situation of . . . how shall I say? . . . meaning. It made me feel like a . . . a kitten. You took the kitten by the scruff of the neck, you brought it into your warm room. What can be the history of a kitten abandoned in the street? It was as though you had come home alone. You spoke to yourself, you took off your shoes, you took off your socks, you took off your tie.

MAN: I thought I was being natural. [*Hides his feet under the chair.*]

WOMAN: What would your mother think if she suddenly came in, I'd like to know? [*Seriously.*] You weren't being natural; you were simply ignoring me. Because you were obliged to assume I wasn't there. A man who is so courteous as to ask no questions of a woman he brings into his house from the street is more afraid of being natural than he is of anything else. You were really protecting yourself. You behaved that way so that I wouldn't think myself worthy of your noble generosity. I wasn't important; you were. [*Imitates the* MAN.] "I've done my duty," you were saying to yourself. But I wasn't the object of your duty, merely a pretext for it. [*Puts her head in her hands.*] My husband was just the same. A heartless do-gooder!

MAN: I can't speak for your husband, but I have no sense of duty. I'm heartless, I admit that.

WOMAN: Even if you're only pretending, it's nothing to brag about!

MAN: If I were to say that I was anguished by the sight of you in the snow, that it made my heart bleed, then I'd be sensitive, I suppose. How easy!

WOMAN: You said you were thinking of something else at the time, so your reactions to me were entirely mechanical. How easy!

MAN: You won't mind if I laugh, but we seem to be having a fight like a husband and wife. You said I reminded you of your husband, anyway.

WOMAN: You behave toward me the way he behaves toward "the people." That was a phrase he never tired of using. [*Mimics.*] "The people must be fed," he used to say, as though talking of cats and dogs. I'll tell you what, I've had enough of honest, serious men. So severe, too! When he puts on his serious act, I say to myself, "Who knows what evil intent he has, what harm he's done to some unfortunate creature."

MAN: [*Startled and slightly annoyed.*] I trust you cannot say that I have done you any harm.

WOMAN: You've done me no harm, but you've been thoughtless, that's all. It's the first time something like this has happened to you, I suppose?

MAN: Don't tell me it's happened to you often? I had merely been at the house of a friend.

WOMAN: You'd been drinking. You thought it a good thing to end your evening on a heroic note. And so you did. Whereas I began to squirm the moment we first spoke—I was a human being while I was by myself, but now I'm just a subject, a nothing. That's what you turned me into. Even my body seemed to grow smaller and smaller. Small enough to hide under the carpet, small as a flea. [*Cries a little louder.*]

MAN: Stop crying, you can't talk and cry at the same time. I had no intention of making you feel small. What did I say, what did I do?

WOMAN: You said there was no one who did not belong to a good family. Fallen women and servants always say that they belong to good families, don't they? It's a lie, in other words, to make one's low status seem more exceptional, more respectable. I was lying, too, in the same way, to make my situation seem more important. Look how you forced me into such a situation!

MAN: You appear to attach some importance to lineage. I don't give a damn about it myself. Snow falls upon the lowly, and it's all right; it falls upon those of noble birth, and it's a tragedy—is that it? It's still the same old snow, quite incapable of making a distinction.

WOMAN: Even this boorishness is better than your previous callous attitude.

MAN: I like that, you know. You are getting to know me, even if I don't know you. I'm a boor, not a show-off.

WOMAN: No offense meant, but people who do favors to show off are still kinder than you.

MAN: [*Harshly.*] I wasn't doing a favor.

WOMAN: You saved us.

MAN: Saving is one of the things I hate the most. There are so many vulgar creatures with a hankering for saving others. Haven't you seen them walk? Their legs well apart, as though recovering from a prostate operation. Like this. [*Mimics.*] A rigid face, eyebrows raised, ears well back, a muffled voice pausing between words, like this. [*Imitates.*] "As I was saying." [*To the* WOMAN.] I have no idea how to go about doing good, let alone save anyone, I assure you.

WOMAN: If there has been no good deed, then there is also no one to think that there was. That's exactly why you don't wish to listen to me . . . to assume that I don't exist.

MAN: [*Rapidly draining his glass.*] Since you're so full of subtleties, you might as well know that if I had listened to you as though, to all intents and purposes, I believed in what you said, that would have been a pretense.

WOMAN: You see . . . you see, you think I'm not good enough to be subtle. Of what use are subtle thoughts to a homeless woman? I am merely someone who has been done a kindness, someone who has created an excuse for an act of kindness. I've no right to anything more. Whether I am this or that kind of person is the least of your concerns.

MAN: [*Pacing up and down in his bare feet.*] Very well, then, you are well born. Proceed from there. You . . .

WOMAN: [*Interrupts him.*] Oh shut up! Please shut up!

MAN: [*Continues.*] . . . are full of subtle thoughts; you have suddenly been faced with an injustice, a disaster such as no one before you has known. Anything more to say? [*Stands in front of the* WOMAN.] I am delighted to have made your acquaintance.

WOMAN: You have every right, including that of exercising your sense of humor.

MAN: You see? You refuse to believe anyone in my place, no matter what he says, what he does.

WOMAN: You didn't listen.

MAN: You didn't talk.

WOMAN: Listen now, then. [*Trembling.*] Give me some brandy! [*The* MAN *fills her glass. She takes a sip.*] My husband fell in love with someone else.

MAN: Wonderful! Have some more brandy. [*Pours more into her glass.*] To our health!

WOMAN: I want to drink and drink. [*Drinks.*] He sent us there, to his aunt's house, to get us away from him. [*The* MAN *takes the tray to her; she absentmindedly helps herself to some food.*] He left us there. And that was it. No money, no letters. [*Sits by the table and continues to help herself from the tray.*]

MAN: Every man has a right to leave his wife, but courtesy demands that he should write her a letter. He could have said, "Our souls are incompatible" or "I know that I can't make you happy" or "None of us is responsible for his acts," or, best of all, he could have said, "Society is to blame for everything."

WOMAN: Will you give me a cigarette?

MAN: [*Hands the* WOMAN *a cigarette, lights it for her.*] I saw an Arab film once. The fellow finds his wife in bed with another man. What a dramatic scene. You wait with bated breath for what is to follow. He leans against the door and produces the punch line. "This is one of the evils from which our society is bleeding," he says.

WOMAN: My cigarette's out!

MAN: [*Relights it.*] Wait, that's not all. On hearing these brave words, the woman wraps herself in the bedsheets and, going up to her husband, says to him. "I'm not to blame, society is!" It was a film with a social message.

WOMAN: I'm not trembling so much now. Give me another brandy, please.

MAN: [*Pours the brandy.*] By all means. Drink is the cure for the ills of society. Drink, drink!

WOMAN: As I talk, I can see that it all must seem very ridiculous. [*Inhales deeply, then takes another sip from her drink.*]

MAN: I'm a stranger; you've no reason to be reticent.

WOMAN: I've changed my mind. My story isn't a very interesting one.

MAN: So much the better. Get it off your chest, and you'll be free of it. [*The* WOMAN *is silent.*] And don't forget, I may have a few stories to tell you myself, without asking for your reactions afterward.

WOMAN: Thank you.

MAN: Don't thank me, I wasn't being polite. If you weren't here, I'd be talking to myself. This is an opportunity, so let's make the most of it. [*Goes up to the* WOMAN *and looks intently into her face.*] When I came up to you in the street, you were muttering something to yourself.

WOMAN: [*Looks up at the* MAN.] And so were you.

MAN: Yes, but you didn't find me alarming.

WOMAN: No, there was no time.

MAN: You see! That's a kind of equality between us. Lift up your head. Look at me! [*The* WOMAN *does so.*] Smile a little! [*She smiles.*] Your husband had left you in his aunt's house.

WOMAN: [*As if left alone.*] It's a big house, crowded. They're rich. They showed me to a room. [*Drinks.*] I knew that my husband was not coming back. They knew it, too, but we didn't talk about it. They didn't want the subject to come up. Just the way you didn't want to listen to me at first, they were afraid of creating some human bond between us. They thought the end would come by itself. They waited impatiently for the day when I would say good-bye and quietly go away. [*Drinks.*] I, too, was waiting for that day. If I said good-bye too soon, it might embarrass them. They'd cringe in front of me and lean against that door they wanted to shut behind me at once. The whole time they would look in discomfort at each other and at me.

MAN: Their embarrassment would have lasted only until they shut that door.

WOMAN: That would be much worse than simply being thrown out, don't you agree? [*Stops, listens.*] Was that the child crying? [*Goes into the bedroom.*]

MAN: I didn't hear anything.

WOMAN: Wait a moment. [*The* MAN *goes into the kitchen and returns with another plate of food. She returns.*] Sleeping. [*Drains her glass.*] The first few days they called me to the table when meals were served. Then they began to forget. [*Mimics.*] "Oh, haven't you had your lunch? Help yourself to some food in the kitchen. You can take it up to your room." So I was made unwelcome at the family table.

MAN: A good thing, too. A hell of a family table, if you ask me.

WOMAN: So I shut myself up in my room. I had no money, no place to go. I didn't know what to do. I used to lie awake all night, thinking. One night . . .

MAN: You tried to kill yourself?

WOMAN: No!

MAN: You didn't, then what?

WOMAN: Did you read that somewhere?

MAN: When what is read is forgotten, it's as if it was lived. But go on, go on!

WOMAN: If you'll be patient for a little longer, as soon as I've told you, I'll go into the bedroom. I'll leave you alone. If I don't tell you, then I can't stay in this house, do you understand? One night . . .

MAN: Don't lose the thread of your story. I'll be right back. [*Goes out into the corridor.*]

WOMAN: One night the aunt came into my room. "Aren't you sleeping yet? she asked. "I'm not," I said. "The light was on, that's why I came in," she said. "Turn it off," she said, "it's a waste." [*Goes to the light, like a sleepwalker, and turns it off. Continues to speak in the dark.*] So I kept it off. After that night I sat in the dark.

MAN: [*Returns to find the room dark, turns on the light. He is wearing shoes.*] Are you sitting in the dark?

WOMAN: Night after night I sat in the dark.

MAN: [*Looks at the* WOMAN *intently.*] Did you think I had gone to bed?

WOMAN: One night the child was in pain. It began to cry. I rocked and rocked it in my arms. It wouldn't stop. Suddenly the door opened, and the aunt came in. She turned on the light. "Shut that bastard up!" she shouted at me.

MAN: [*Jumps up.*] What was that? What did she shout?

WOMAN: [*Rises to her feet.*] "Shut that bastard up," she shouted at me.

MAN: [*Shouts.*] You're lying!

WOMAN: Wasn't it that way in the book?

MAN: What book?

WOMAN: That book you've forgotten.

MAN: To hell with books. Suppose the child heard what you just said.

WOMAN: It's only a baby; it wouldn't understand.

MAN: Go on, what happened then?

WOMAN: [*Harshly.*] What could have happened? I said, "It won't shut up, it's in pain."

MAN: Monster!

WOMAN: Who?

MAN: That woman, of course.

WOMAN: That's not the end.

MAN: You're inventing these things on purpose. [*Drains his glass.*]

WOMAN: [*Drinks.*] On purpose?

MAN: Yes, on purpose, to arouse my interest. Because I asked no questions, didn't give a damn, you want to get me worked up. What happened then? Go on!

WOMAN: "We're fed up," she shouted. "You look out for yourself. We've had enough!"

MAN: [*Excitedly, his eyes bulging.*] Shut up, that's enough now!

WOMAN: You promised to listen. That's not the end.

MAN: Not the end?

WOMAN: Give me a little brandy. [*The* MAN *does so. She takes a sip.*] Bitter, isn't it?

MAN: The brandy?

WOMAN: No, what I had to go through.

MAN: [*Harshly.*] I thought you meant the brandy.

WOMAN: Why are you getting excited?

MAN: I'm not excited.

WOMAN: You said, "Shut up, that's enough now."

MAN: You surprised me.

WOMAN: I don't understand.

MAN: Do you think I do? Anyway, what's it to you?

WOMAN: I'm going to continue.

MAN: Yes, go on.

WOMAN: "Shut that bastard up," she said.

MAN: [*Loudly.*] You got that far already! Go on from there!

WOMAN: "You look out for yourself," she said.

MAN: You keep repeating.

WOMAN: I can stop if you're bored.

MAN: [*Nervously.*] Go on!

WOMAN: What's come over you?

MAN: [*Stands in front of the* WOMAN *nervously.*] I'm suspicious all of a sudden.

WOMAN: Of what?

MAN: Look here!

WOMAN: I'm listening.

MAN: Were you waiting for me at that corner?

WOMAN: [*Stands up, frightened.*] It was the first time I'd ever seen you!

MAN: You're lying!

WOMAN: What on earth do you mean?

MAN: I feel I know you somehow.

WOMAN: [*Goes toward the bedroom.*] I'd better leave.

MAN: [*Catches hold of the* WOMAN's *arm and turns her around.*] Don't be silly. Stop! [*Rubs his forehead.*] I must be confused. What nonsense! Don't go! Continue!

WOMAN: [*Turns back.*] You're frightening me.

MAN: And you're frightening me.

WOMAN: All right then, I won't talk.

MAN: No, do talk, please do!

WOMAN: [*Looks at him.*] Where was I?

MAN: "We're fed up," said your husband's aunt.

WOMAN: [*Again, as though to herself.*] Then one day I heard them talking; they'd had a letter from my husband. It appears he'd said, "Haven't you got rid of them yet?" Meaning us.

MAN: You never left your room, remember? So how did you know? They weren't reading the letter out loud, were they?

WOMAN: You don't want to listen, so I'm skipping some of the details.

MAN: Skipping a few details—strange courtesy! Let's have the details. How did you learn what was in your husband's letter?

WOMAN: I went into their living room one day. They were reading a letter. They stopped when they saw me. I pretended not to notice, but could see out of the corner of my eye that the aunt had tossed the letter into her workbasket. Just then the doorbell rang. A guest had arrived. They all jumped up from where they were sitting. So when nobody was looking, I took the letter from the basket.

MAN: [*Tries to appear calm.*] The other was a better story.

WOMAN: What other?

MAN: How you heard the letter from inside your room. For future renderings, might I suggest the following version: "They came right up to the door of my room and read the letter at the top of their voices."

WOMAN: [*After a long silence.*] Very well, I'll use your version. [*Pauses.*]

MAN: [*Paces the floor.*] It's not what happens to people that's important; it's how they react. [*Mimics.*] "They did this, this, and this to me. They were unjust, they were cruel." So what? People are unjust, they are cruel, they have nothing better to do. [*Shouts.*] But what did you do, for heaven's sake? If you just did nothing, then say, "I'm helpless, I'm hopeless." Go ahead, say it! Don't be afraid to! Let's have some more helpless, hopeless people. [*Pours drinks for both of them.*] Why did you shut yourself up in that house? Wasn't there anything you could do?

WOMAN: You're not listening.

MAN: Never mind me, just go on talking!

WOMAN: One day I took the child and went looking for a job. [*They drink.*] Who'd give me one? It's not easy, is it?

MAN: An excuse.

WOMAN: Whose excuse, mine?

MAN: Yes, yours. You said you'd had schooling. Why shouldn't you be able to get a job? Women are used to men supporting them, so they avoid work. I can think of any number of educated women who gave up their jobs after marrying. I once knew a woman doctor who said to me, "I'm not going to spend the rest of my life working; I'll get married sooner or later." She did and gave up her practice. Marriage is the most secure of jobs for you, that's what it is.

WOMAN: Just how secure must be evident in my case.

MAN: You say this only because you have lost your security.

WOMAN: Not so loud, you'll wake your parents. My husbands forced me to stay at home.

MAN: Husbands? How many have you had?

WOMAN: Two, or maybe three.

MAN: When you say you were looking for a job, you mean you were looking for a husband.

WOMAN: You wouldn't talk that way if you had any idea how dull, how sickening, house-work is. Cook, wash, iron. One can go mad doing these things over and over again. And in the evening flit reassuringly around your husband, who comes home sulking because he's been working all day.

MAN: Did you really look for a job?

WOMAN: I did!

MAN: Where did you go, then?

WOMAN: Oh, to several people I knew. I couldn't very well just ring any doorbell.

MAN: And you had no luck.

WOMAN: Some told me to go to the municipality; some gave me the address of well-off people they knew. One petted the child and said, "What a darling. What's its name?"

MAN: What is its name?

WOMAN: Sibel.

MAN: So it's a girl.

WOMAN: It's a girl.

MAN: Well, then?

WOMAN: When I got back to the house that evening, they would not let me in. I rang and rang and rang the doorbell. Then I banged on the door with my fists.

MAN: Where was the child when you were using your fists on the door? Lying on the doorsill?

WOMAN: I mean my fist. I used one fist, as though that's important! I hit and hit and hit with one fist. The neighbors saw me; they opened their windows. It was like a scene from a play! A few came down to where I was; they shouted up the stairs. Much later, the aunt opened the door. She had been taking a nap, she said, so she didn't hear, and there was nobody else in the house.

MAN: Not true!

WOMAN: Of course not. All the neighbors felt sorry for me.

MAN: Neighbors are dishonest, you should know that. They merely pretend to be sorry for you so as to find out what it's all about. Gives them something to discuss in the evening.

WOMAN: After that, I left the child behind when I went out—to make sure they wouldn't lock the door against me.

MAN: [*Tense.*] Couldn't you have killed her?

WOMAN: The aunt, you mean?

MAN: No, no, I mean the child, of course.

WOMAN: [*Jumps up.*] The child? You wanted me to kill my child?

MAN: It would have been more dramatic if you had thought of it. [*Mimics.*] "I killed my child so that it might not have to suffer." [*Short pause.*] It's quite the thing nowadays to think of death, of killing, as a solution. People advocate euthanasia for hopeless cancer patients, for instance. The logic is that the person is doomed in any case. Cancer cases today, bedridden patients tomorrow, then idiots, morons. And why not the lame, the hunchbacked, the blind, the one-armed while we are about it? Think of states passing laws to that effect. [*Mimics.*] "Bring me the dossier of the cross-eyed," shouts the dictator.

WOMAN: You were angry earlier, and now you're making fun of me. I simply don't understand you.

MAN: I understand myself so well that it makes me sick and tired. I know what's going to happen inside of me, just as I know in the morning, when I have my first cigarette, how weak at the knees with drunkenness I am going to get. An unpleasant sensation. I feel like a stupid scientist who keeps repeating the same experiment again and again. But for you, I am someone new, not easy to understand. A pleasant thought. Come, let's finish the story. What happened tonight?

WOMAN: [*Looks at the* MAN *fearfully.*] Tonight? Had we come to that point?

MAN: If you don't skip, we'll never get there.

WOMAN: [*Drinks.*] Tonight . . . what happened tonight? That bitch said, "You're immoral." She insulted me. We fought. The others joined in; they all began to beat me. Look.

[*Lifts her skirt and points at her leg.*] They kicked me. [*Stops.*] So I ran away. How could I remain in that house any longer? Wasn't I right to run away?

MAN: You were right.

WOMAN: Do you believe me now?

MAN: I do.

WOMAN: You're only saying that.

MAN: Very well, then, I don't believe you.

WOMAN: No one believes me.

MAN: You've told someone else?

WOMAN: Told what?

MAN: The events of this night.

WOMAN: I haven't seen anyone else tonight.

MAN: Well, then, who is it that doesn't believe you?

WOMAN: People never believe me; they never think I'm right.

MAN: I don't follow you. Weren't you telling me about something that happened tonight? Or has it happened before? Does it happen often?

WOMAN: You see! You, too, suspect me. I told you only a little so as not to bore you.

MAN: [*Inquisitively.*] You mean all this had happened to you before?

WOMAN: Nothing ever happens twice the same way, of course. There are variations.

MAN: [*Surprised.*] Well, as I haven't heard about the other times, I can't express an opinion about them.

WOMAN: You can't, I know. And if you did, what of it? It wouldn't help me. No one helps me, in fact. People feel sorry for me and then forget all about it. And you'll do the same. You're sorry for me . . . you were, you know, when you saw me in the street. You brought me to your home. You did me a favor.

MAN: Let's not have that all over again. I don't know that I did you a favor.

WOMAN: You don't like that word . . . but it's not because of the nobility of your spirit.

MAN: You're quite right. It's to protect myself against you.

WOMAN: You're waiting for the morning, so you can see me go away and be able to forget me.

MAN: [*Nervous.*] Of course, I'll forget you. What else can I do?

WOMAN: [*After a short silence.*] What about love?

MAN: Love?

WOMAN: Yes, because I am a human being. [*Pause.*] Is it so difficult?

MAN: [*Surprised.*] I'm not used to that sort of thing.

WOMAN: But if one doesn't love the person one is kind to, then one turns cruel. Tonight you have saved me from freezing to death, but because you have no feeling for the person you saved, you are cruel. So were the people who came to help me when the door wouldn't open. They were cruel! As for that fellow I came upon when looking for a job, the man who offered me money, that tyrant! [*Shouts.*] I don't mind the people who looked the other way, I'm telling you. I'm angry at those who helped, those who were kind. I'm angry at you!

MAN: You're right to be angry. There's no one who does not deserve anger. Even the dead make me angry. Once in a blue moon, I wake up feeling actually joyful, but it turns to hatred in no time. We are alike in this. I'm not sure I know why you should want to be loved, though.

WOMAN: I sure want to be loved. Is that too much to expect?

MAN: Maybe it's too little. But it's impossible.

WOMAN: Don't you ever want to be loved?

MAN: No, and there's no one I love.

WOMAN: Then why did you bring me here?

MAN: You mean I shouldn't have?

WOMAN: You shouldn't have. One should think of consequences when one acts. Give me some brandy.

MAN: [*Pours her a drink.*] The greatest kindness I can do to people is to pay no heed to them. But you're different.

WOMAN: How am I different?

MAN: You're a woman. The most I can do is to kiss you, go to bed with you . . . that would be love.

WOMAN: You can't talk to yourself like this.

MAN: I'm not saying these things to myself.

WOMAN: But isn't that what we said? That each of us would talk, but not to each other?

MAN: I have plenty of opportunities to talk to myself.

WOMAN: Does it not disgust you to think of sexual relations with a woman whom you saved from freezing in the streets?

MAN: When it comes to that, I can't think of anything I've ever done that did not disgust me.

WOMAN: That did not lower your self-esteem?

MAN: And why only me? What if a woman wants this?

WOMAN: Is that what you thought I meant?

MAN: It isn't, but that doesn't change anything.

WOMAN: What do you mean?

MAN: I met a woman whose husband had just died in a bus accident, and she was crying. The way I met you, except that it wasn't snowing. That's because it wasn't winter. I accompanied her to her house. She was the only one of the survivors who had no one to turn to. She was dreadfully upset. So to console her, we went to bed, amidst her tears. Best way there is to console a woman.

WOMAN: That's the easy way out.

MAN: What other way is there?

WOMAN: If you'd done that to me, it would be better than it is now. There's an equality in making love.

MAN: [*Looks at the* WOMAN *intently as he pours her a drink.*] You think so?

WOMAN: I do! We'd have settled accounts. Your pride would have taken a fall.

MAN: You think me proud?

WOMAN: You're lonely; it's the same thing.

MAN: Come, then, let's make love.

WOMAN: Only if you'll say that that's what you had in mind when you brought me here.

MAN: I didn't have it in mind.

WOMAN: What did you have in mind, then?

MAN: I simply happened to stop beside you. And having spoken to you, I couldn't just say good-bye and walk away. Nobody likes being good; either one is forced into it, like I was, or one does it to impress others. If I had shown any interest in you once you were here, then I'd be savoring my good deed, enjoying it. Best not to give a damn. So I took off my shoes and socks, my tie, and made myself comfortable. [*Sips his brandy.*] You do the same; you owe me no debt!

WOMAN: I wish I hadn't told you.

MAN: I knew it was going to be like this . . . you have told your story, but have found no release. The more people talk about themselves, the farther away they get from each other. It was nicer when you were a complete stranger. [*Walks about with his arms outstretched.*] We might as well now that there's nothing left to do. [*Turns to the* WOMAN.] Let's make love!

WOMAN: [*Sadly.*] I didn't choose to get into this mess. You have no need for being loved. [*Drinks.*]

MAN: It's not anything that anyone can force on me. When we talk of wanting people to love us, we mean we want them to love our defects, our vices.

WOMAN: What about making love, then? You were saying, "Let's make love."

MAN: That has nothing to do with love.

WOMAN: It must be really horrible for you!

MAN: [*Shouts.*] I'm not the one to compare them, it's you! You wanted me to love you simply because I had done you a kindness. Was it going to bed together that you wanted?

WOMAN: No!

MAN: Well, you see?

WOMAN: I merely asked whether you could not feel some affection for me. I didn't expect you to fall in love with me.

MAN: If you had, I still wouldn't have fallen in love with you. You take the fun out of everything. That's because you live in an artificial world.

WOMAN: [*Picks up her glass.*] The story I told you was made up. Did you know?

MAN: True or made up, it was a lot of nonsense. We're talking so as not to be silent.

WOMAN: I feel myself going down, down. [*Drinks.*] I can't see a way out. [*As though to herself.*] I was right. It's not madness. I was right. [*Turning to the* MAN.] If I had not met you, I'd have perhaps weakened toward morning.

MAN: First time anyone's gained strength from me. Now that's something new. I'm going to see myself in a different light in a moment.

WOMAN: Aren't you alone?

MAN: No, I've found someone to talk with. And what a conversation! [*Laughs.*] Love, and again love. Shall I tell you something? You do not give a damn, really, about the things that have happened to you.

WOMAN: Nothing's happened to me. [*Drinks.*] I'm a woman of the streets.

MAN: It's because you are not a woman of the streets that you are enjoying your situation so much. Isn't that right? Be frank, now. You'd even enjoy freezing if it made someone feel sorry for you.

WOMAN: What a boor you are! [*Looks at the* MAN *inquisitively.*]

MAN: You've no idea. If I were to give you details, you'd flee.

WOMAN: I've no place to flee to. The world's a narrow little place all of a sudden. And I haven't a leg to stand on. I was afraid when I met you. And surprised when I came to your place. I thought everything would begin again, that I'd be taken in again, that I'd be willing to put up with things. But I must be grateful to you because you gave me no chance to soften. Now go on and tell me, tell me the worst so that there is nothing left to hope for.

MAN: Good. We'll get to the morning that way. Tonight's an opportunity. We're not going to see each other again, in any case. So I'll tell my story, then you tell yours—there needn't be any order to it. Just the way it comes. Are you game? [*The* WOMAN *nods.*] Fine. Make no judgments—but then I don't give a hoot about what you are or what you say. Go ahead and judge me if that is what you want to do. [*Shuts his eyes and sways, then opens them.*] Wait a moment, who am I talking with? I think I must be drunk. [*Strokes the* WOMAN's *hair.*] It's a good thing you've come. I'd have drowned myself in drink if you hadn't.

WOMAN: I didn't come.

MAN: [*Sways.*] What's that? Weren't you waiting for me at that corner?

WOMAN: I wasn't waiting for you.

MAN: Who were you waiting for, then?

WOMAN: Nobody.

MAN: So we just met at that corner by chance, is that it?

WOMAN: Yes.

MAN: A coincidence. There's no such thing in this world, no coincidences.

WOMAN: About what?

MAN: We were looking for each other.

WOMAN: I wasn't looking for anyone. There wasn't anyone I could be looking for.

MAN: Do you know the story from Rumi? Seems he was looking at the countryside out of his window. Way in the distance he saw a stork and a woodcock hopping together on the ground. He wondered what could have brought together two creatures so dissimilar.

This friendship intrigued him, you see. So he went out and walked right up to them. And he saw that they both were lame.

WOMAN: I feel a little better now.

MAN: Come on, then, who shall begin?

WOMAN: It's your turn.

MAN: But weren't we going to make love?

WOMAN: No, we were going to talk.

MAN: Should we make love first and talk afterward, or the other way around? [*Pauses.*] Why don't we toss a coin—heads or tails? [*Takes a coin from his pocket.*] If it's heads, we make love; if it's tails . . . [*To the* WOMAN.] Now don't forget which is which. [*Flips the coin and catches it in his palm.*] It's tails. What was it we were going to do if it was tails?

WOMAN: We were going to talk. It's your turn.

MAN: Very well, we'll make love afterward. But don't let me forget!

WOMAN: I won't.

MAN: Here I go. Brace yourself. [*Drinks.*] I lied to you, did you know?

WOMAN: [*Drinks.*] Yes, I did.

MAN: What was it, then?

WOMAN: Your parents are not in the house.

MAN: Bravo! So you knew!

WOMAN: I did.

MAN: I'm not a liar, mind you.

WOMAN: You're not?

MAN: And you weren't afraid.

WOMAN: I've nothing to look forward to, so I'm not afraid.

MAN: You came here knowing?

WOMAN: I came here knowing.

MAN: [*Drunk now.*] You may have come knowing, but you seemed to believe me when you came in.

WOMAN: I wanted to find out.

MAN: [*Shouts.*] Why did the child have to be dragged into this? That's what I don't understand. Why couldn't you leave her behind?

WOMAN: You mean since I was looking for a customer? [*Drinks.*] Oh, you are really vulgar. But I like it when you talk that way. It puts me at ease. So you think I was out looking for a man? Wonderful, wonderful. I've nothing to worry about now. When things get as vulgar as this, then there's really no sense in worrying.

MAN: Yes, one is more at ease in a vulgar world. I lied to you in the street, all right, but you certainly spun some tall tales once we got here. Because you fancy yourself as the heroine of a tale, you spin yourself lovely stories of unhappiness, and then, in order to believe they are real, you dash off into the streets, like tonight. I bet you have a comfortable home of your own. Isn't that right? Were you not inventing that sad story a while ago?

WOMAN: What's it to you whether I was inventing it or not?

MAN: Right, we said we would not pass judgment. I must play according to the rules.

WOMAN: [*Sways drunkenly as she walks about.*] Must be the drink. I feel as though I've traveled to a foreign country.

MAN: Are you going to travel to my lap?

WOMAN: No! I'm looking for the bathroom.

MAN: Through that door. [*The* WOMAN *opens the outside door. He has his back turned and is not aware that she goes out. She realizes she has made a mistake, and stands for a while looking at him. He then realizes from the cold air coming in that the apartment door has been opened. He turns to the door and sees her standing there. He does not get up. After the* WOMAN *sways outside for a while, she reenters. The dog on the first floor can be heard barking. The* WOMAN *shuts the door.*] I didn't say through there.

WOMAN: [*Returns to her place.*] I felt dizzy; the cold air was nice.

MAN: [*Hands her a plate of food.*] You shouldn't drink on an empty stomach. Better have something to eat.

WOMAN: [*Takes a bite.*] I'm not used to it.

MAN: Do you know, if you had shut the door quietly and gone, I wouldn't have known. [*The* WOMAN *looks at him.*] I'd still be wondering whether it was your turn or mine.

WOMAN: It was yours.

MAN: We'll toss the coin again for the lovemaking, don't let me forget.

WOMAN: I won't.

MAN: Listen! [*Walks back and forth, looking at the* WOMAN.] When I was in primary school, I shared a desk with a boy, a puny, silent fellow. He studied hard, didn't play much. Used to wander about the school grounds all by himself. I can't forget his face. Listen to what I did to him one day. "Do you like your mom better, or your dad?" I asked him. "My dad," he said. But his father wasn't his real father, see, only he didn't know this. "He's not your dad," I snickered. At first he thought I was joking. He smiled. I swore it was true; he was puzzled but still didn't believe me. So I insisted. "What do you want to bet?" I said. "You nut," I said, "I wouldn't say so if it weren't so, if I didn't really know. Go look in the mirror. Do you look like your dad at all? Everybody knows it but you," I said.

WOMAN: [*Stands up.*] Why did you do this?

MAN: For fun, I suppose, I'm not sure why, really. Perhaps to show off my superior knowledge.

WOMAN: What happened then?

MAN: The boy went off in a daze; he stayed away from school for three days.

WOMAN: It's not true, what you're saying. You're making it up like you did about your parents being here when they weren't.

MAN: [*Seriously.*] I'm not making it up.

WOMAN: Swear.

MAN: I swear.

WOMAN: [*Walks up to him.*] Why are you telling me this story?

MAN: I'm telling myself, really.

WOMAN: Did the boy return on the fourth day? Go on, tell me!

MAN: [*Louder.*] What's your hurry? I'm talking. The third day, it seems, his mother came to our house to complain. My mother was very angry. During supper she said to my father, "We must not talk of such things when he is around." [*Pauses.*] Would you like some brandy?

WOMAN: Yes, I would.

MAN: [*Opens a new bottle.*] I like drinking brandy at night. On top of raki, it really wipes out a man.

WOMAN: [*Slowly comes up to the* MAN, *speaks harshly.*] What happened after that?

MAN: After that . . . after that the boy came back to school. [*Fills her glass and his own.*] He looked downcast. His eyes were red; he must have cried a good bit. He slunk into his seat beside mine. [*Feeling greatly ashamed.*] He wouldn't look at me. "How about it," I asked him, "was I right or not?" "Yes," he said, hesitatingly, "it's true. They hadn't told me, but they were going to when I was older." If I had touched him, he'd have burst into tears. Or perhaps he would have thrown his arms around me and hugged me and kissed me.

WOMAN: How do you know he was going to kiss you? You're just trying to soothe your conscience. You're trying to say he wasn't hurt by what you'd done, that he still loved you. [*Shouts.*] You wanted to crush him into loving you.

MAN: Don't shout; you'll wake the child.

WOMAN: Let her wake up and listen to this story!

MAN: [*Smashes his glass against the floor.*] This brandy is foul. [*To the* WOMAN.] Does it taste foul to you?

WOMAN: No, it doesn't!

MAN: You haven't tasted it yet. Try it and then speak.

WOMAN: [*Drinks.*] Mine tastes fine. [*Her eyes are on him.*]

MAN: [*Takes another glass from the sideboard, fills it from the same bottle.*] This time I said to him . . . [*Takes a sip.*]

WOMAN: [*Drinks.*] What did you say to him?

MAN: I was about to tell you! "There's something else you don't know," I said to him.

WOMAN: [*Surprised.*] Something else?

MAN: Yes, there was something else he didn't know.

WOMAN: So you told him that as well?

MAN: I did.

WOMAN: Still for fun, eh?

MAN: I suppose so.

WOMAN: What did you tell him?

MAN: I said, "Your mom isn't yours, either."

WOMAN: Brute! You were lying, of course.

MAN: Certainly not, I wasn't lying. He was an adopted child; everybody knew it except him.

WOMAN: Why did you do this? Why did you want to hurt that boy?

MAN: Yours not to judge, remember? [*Drinks.*] This time he didn't cry. He just looked at me. What I'd said about his father had turned out to be true, so now he believed me. His eyes were glazed; he fled from school. [*The* WOMAN *begins to cry.*] Crying won't help, just listen! He stayed away from home for a whole week. That small, frail boy slept on the rocks by the seashore, under the trees, in the rubbish heaps. The police found him at last. When they got him back home, he was running a fever; he was in bed for days. [*Pauses.*] They changed his school, and I never saw him again. [*Drinks.*] Now it's your turn.

WOMAN: [*Wipes her eyes.*] I've no story to tell.

MAN: No story to tell, that's a good one! Let me ask you a question in that case. Why don't you sue your husband for child support?

WOMAN: [*Shouts.*] Because the child is not his! Does that satisfy your curiosity? [*Drinks.*] Let me have some more brandy.

MAN: [*Pours her drink.*] Now we're getting somewhere! So you betrayed your husband!

WOMAN: No!

MAN: Deny it as much as you please. One thing I don't get is, how did your husband catch on? Or did you tell him?

WOMAN: No!

MAN: The earlier stories are nothing next to this. This is what I'd call a story. Did your husband get an anonymous letter?

WOMAN: No!

MAN: No, no, no! We're not playing at riddles. Are you going to tell me, or are you going to make a mess of this beautiful night?

WOMAN: The child's father was my first husband, I think.

MAN: [*Bursts into laughter.*] Your first husband? You think? So the child was already in its cradle when you married again. Obviously one can't talk of betrayal in that case.

WOMAN: Of course one can't.

MAN: You could, then, sue your first husband for child support.

WOMAN: But he refuses to recognize the child.

MAN: How is that?

WOMAN: I couldn't figure it out either. I was still married to my first husband when I had an affair with the man who was to become my second husband. I became pregnant. My first husband was sterile, so of course we separated. Then I married the other man. For some reason, my second husband had himself examined by a doctor, who told him he couldn't father a child. When he got this opinion, he didn't begin to argue with me right away; he saw other doctors first. But when they all said the same thing, he came home and screamed at me. "That's another man's child you're trying to pass off as mine!" He would not have minded it if the child had been my first husband's, but the thought of a third man drove him crazy! Funny, isn't it? He drove me out of the house in the middle of the night in a snowstorm.

MAN: A beautiful story! So it was not your husband's aunt from whose house you fled tonight; it was your husband who drove you out of his house!

WOMAN: [*Quietly.*] That's right.

MAN: [*Drinks.*] So the child's father is nowhere to be seen.

WOMAN: That's right.

MAN: [*Paces up and down, stops in front of her.*] You don't suppose I could be the father of that child?

WOMAN: You still don't believe me, do you?

MAN: I believe you, but I'm trying to help you find the father. Every child must have a father.

WOMAN: [*As if talking to herself.*] Neither of them loved me, really, or they wouldn't have left me because of a child. [*Drinks.*] One of them could very well have accepted the child. [*Turns to him.*] If my second husband had not been to the doctor, if he hadn't had himself examined, would he have known, do you think? He wouldn't have known a thing. And since I don't know either, we could have carried on somehow. It makes me see red. Am I obliged to find my child's father?

MAN: You're not, of course.

WOMAN: Very true, I'm not obliged. I keep thinking about it, and I simply can't tell. Everything is so confusing. What am I to do?

MAN: You might go to a doctor.

WOMAN: Why should I go to a doctor?

MAN: He might tell you that you're not fertile either.

WOMAN: [*Drains her glass.*] What was that, what was that you said?

MAN: I said perhaps you cannot bear a child.

WOMAN: [*Laughs softly, then louder and louder.*] Cannot bear a child! [*Her laughter turns to tears.*] What a wonderful night! If I had not met you, what an opportunity I would have missed! It's been a long time since I've had such fun. Give me another brandy! [*The MAN pours her a drink.*] Go on, now it's your turn.

MAN: Who're you trying to fool?

WOMAN: Fool?

MAN: Your story isn't over.

WOMAN: It's over.

MAN: I say it isn't over!

WOMAN: [*Shouts.*] And I say it is, do you hear?

MAN: [*Shouts.*] It isn't, it isn't, it isn't! Tell me the end!

WOMAN: [*Frightened.*] I won't go on.

MAN: [*Threatens her.*] I tell you to go on.

WOMAN: I won't, I won't!

MAN: You will! All the dirt will come to the surface! You're not going to get away with your Virgin Mary role. What did your husband say to you? "Get rid of the child, and you can come back," isn't that what he said?

WOMAN: [*Crying.*] Yes, it is.

MAN: And isn't that what you were going to do? Weren't you going to drop your child somewhere and sneak back into that dirty bastard's bed?

WOMAN: No, no, I was going to kill myself. [*Cries.*]

MAN: [*Paces back and forth.*] She was going to kill herself! I just don't get it. Life is a dirty thing, to be lived in a dirty way. To want to kill oneself is to believe that it can be clean after all. Where would one get such a belief? Why should one have it? [*Stops.*] In order to build up enough nerve to kill oneself, maybe. [*Drinks and paces.*] Well, more power to them! [*Stops in front of the* WOMAN.] Why didn't you kill yourself?

WOMAN: [*Sits down at the table and begins to eat.*] I couldn't find a suitable place. The less I feel like sleeping, the hungrier I get. My father used to say that one should die by one's own hand.

MAN: Crying makes you hungry, too. . . . Say, I just thought of something. Do men who are condemned to death feel hungry?

WOMAN: [*Surprised, puts a piece of food back onto the plate.*] I don't know.

MAN: [*Looks at her.*] Neither do I.

WOMAN: Why are you asking me?

MAN: Well, whom should I ask? Do you think I ought to wake up the neighbors in the middle of the night to ask them? [*Laughs.*] There's a fellow upstairs, a fat smuggler. He's the one to wake up. "Say, friend, do you get hungry when condemned to death?" I wonder what the bastard would do? Half asleep, he might imagine that he was being taken to be shot. "Help, help!" he would shout.

WOMAN: Don't shout, you will wake up the neighbors.

MAN: Let them wake up, the sons of bitches. Are we sleeping? We're not sleeping, but what are we doing? Are we making love? No! But why aren't we making love? Go on, tell me!

WOMAN: [*Absentmindedly, her eyes on the morsel she had put back onto the plate.*] We tossed a coin, and it came up tails, that's why.

MAN: That's right, it was tails. If it had been heads, we would now be making love, isn't that so?

WOMAN: [*Absentmindedly.*] Yes.

MAN: If you ask me, that's exactly what married couples should do. Heads or tails every night—love if it's heads, talk if it's tails. The counterfeiter upstairs, being no longer a man, could no doubt mint himself a coin that was tails on both sides. Tails every night—an orgy of talk! What do you suppose that fellow would talk about? What do such people talk about? Have you noticed?

WOMAN: No, I haven't noticed.

MAN: Why not? When you women get together, you talk about nothing but marriage. Who wants to marry whom? How much does he make? Does he own his house? Is he going to buy an apartment? If he should die, what will his wife inherit? What's he like sexually? How many times a week?

WOMAN: My second husband used to brag, too. Not every man could equal his prowess, he used to say. It seems he went to bed with some woman and that woman was most impressed by his prowess. "Oh yeah," he used to say, all puffed up, "I've been loved."

MAN: No doubt you supported him, told him there was no one else like him.

WOMAN: Of course I did; he expected me to.

MAN: You know the stories of newly married girls? How she first met him, how the man looked at her, how she was annoyed at first and was going to give him a piece of her mind, then they're alone and he kissed her. A fellow told me once about running after a girl for a whole year.

WOMAN: A whole year?

MAN: Yes. If you follow a girl about for a whole year, of course you start to think of her as the culprit. Then the first time you're with her, you kill her.

WOMAN: Did he kill her?

MAN: No. They sat side by side in a public park, and he asked her if she'd ever had an affair with another man. "No," she said, "you're the first."

WOMAN: [*Laughs.*] You'd think she was going into business. My first husband talked about politics all the time. He just repeated the things he'd read in the papers, but he made them sound as though they were his own thoughts.

MAN: A man was talking politics with me once and picking his nose at the same time. When I caught him at it, he pressed the snot against his cheek with a finger. So I kept my eye on that finger. He worked it up gradually toward his forehead; he was pretending to be thinking of a name. [*Rubs his forehead.*] "What was that name, now what was it?"

WOMAN: They talk endlessly.

MAN: A silly thing to do.

WOMAN: That's exactly what it is.

MAN: Let's not talk, then.

WOMAN: [*Looks up.*] It's your turn.

MAN: It's my turn. Listen! We were four friends in a boat, devil take us all. Three of us were real pals; the fourth had sought us out to join our group. We were a little distant with him; he realized this, and it upset him. He worked awfully hard to make us like him—eagerly agreed to everything we suggested. The more he tried to ingratiate himself with us, the less successful he was, of course. That day I lost my wallet. We looked everywhere, turned the boat upside down, nothing doing.

WOMAN: What happened to the wallet?

MAN: We suspected him.

WOMAN: Your friend?

MAN: Yes.

WOMAN: Why him and not the others?

MAN: Because the three of us were good pals, and, besides, he'd remained alone in the boat the longest, while the rest of us went swimming.

WOMAN: Was that enough?

MAN: Perhaps not, but the three of us talked it over, and we decided he must be the one.

WOMAN: Perhaps he really had taken the wallet.

MAN: No, when I got back home, I found my wallet there. I had forgotten to take it with me.

WOMAN: You should have told the truth.

MAN: But I didn't.

WOMAN: Why not?

MAN: I didn't want to spoil the relationship between the three of us. People have to live in little clans, you know. We didn't like the other fellow, and this was a bond between us; it made us feel stronger, if you will. If you can make someone feel small, you feel like you've got something to be proud of. If there's no one smaller than you, how can you feel superior?

WOMAN: For shame! You disgust me. That's really going too far. Anyone doing what you did should die of shame.

MAN: [*Laughs.*] Yours not to judge, don't forget!

WOMAN: [*Angrily.*] Are you pulling my leg? Are you making all this up?

MAN: Wait, it's not over yet.

WOMAN: [*Drains her glass.*] Well, my glass is empty. You might fill it.

MAN: [*Does so.*] He knew we suspected him. He was wiggling in his seat as though to say, "I didn't do it!" But he couldn't bring himself to say anything. And whenever he seemed about to broach the subject, we would look coldly at each other and say, "What makes you think such a thing?" He resigned himself to remaining under suspicion. Only later, once or twice, he asked me, shyly, "Did you ever find your wallet?" "What wallet?" I said, as though I had forgotten all about it. He was trying to keep calm. "That day . . . in the boat," he stammered. "Oh that," I said. "It wasn't important." So we humiliated him, destroyed him, and he parted ways with us. [*Drinks.*] Now it's your turn.

WOMAN: No one could compete with you in vileness.

MAN: This is not a competition. We're talking as though to ourselves.

WOMAN: As though I'm talking to myself . . . to myself. You're right. Hasn't it always been that way? Only I didn't realize it was so, didn't realize it at all. It's getting clearer all the time that you're right. I owe this to you. I've been talking to myself all along. [*Silence.*] I had a teacher once who was accused of being a lesbian and lost her job.

MAN: What of it?

WOMAN: She wasn't. She was a strict grader; she kept flunking the children. So to get rid of her, my classmates made up these rumors.

MAN: And you joined them?

WOMAN: Yes!

MAN: [*Drinks.*] Bravo! Now who is vile?

WOMAN: An inspector came to the school, questioned us one by one. My classmates had told me what to say. I did as they told me. I didn't even know what the word meant! [*Cries.*]

MAN: I'm afraid there's nothing left to eat in the kitchen. A pity!

WOMAN: [*Weeping.*] That teacher had a daughter. When her mother was fired, she threw herself into a well.

MAN: Wait, I'll tell you a nice story. I went into a low-class nightclub one evening. I invited a shriveled, cross-eyed hag to my table. I think her throat must have been hurting— she had it wrapped in a scarf, and she was coughing. She was really a low-class tart, that one! I suddenly thought it might be amusing to lead her on a bit. [*Mimics.*] "Do sit down, dear lady." I stood up meanwhile. "What may I order for you?" The woman was sizing me up out of the corner of her eye. Was I pulling her leg? That's what she wanted to know. Heaven help me if she thought I was!

WOMAN: Why?

MAN: She was a tough one; she could have beaten me up. But I played my part well, and she wasn't all that used to respect, poor thing. She may have thought that I had acquired this polish abroad. An innocent who didn't know that manners are unnecessary with a woman of her sort. I helped her along that train of thought. "I've been away for a great many years," I said to her. She began to put on airs. [*Mimics.*] She was from a good family, had been brought up by nannies, had had her own horse to ride at the family farm.

WOMAN: You were much more vulgar than she.

MAN: Listen to the rest! She had known German at one time, but had forgotten it. "I'd like to ask you something," I said, "but you must reply in German." She snickered. "Go on, ask me!" she said. "May I kiss your hand?" I said. "Ya," she said and held out her hand.

WOMAN: [*Begins to laugh, but is nervous.*] Is that all?

MAN: There's more. [*Mimics.*] I bent to her ear, and with an innocent face I said, "Dear lady, I'd like to ask you something, but I don't dare!" "What is there to be timid about?" she said. "We're friends, aren't we?" "Dear lady, are you a virgin?" [*Laughs. The* WOMAN *joins him.*] Do you know what she said? [*He can hardly speak in his amusement. Mimics with a sad expression.*] "Unfortunately, I'm not." [*They both laugh nervously.*] Would you like some brandy?

WOMAN: Yes.

MAN: [*Fills her glass.*] Come now, it's your turn.

WOMAN: The child in the other room is not my child, did you know that?

MAN: You created it. [*Laughs loudly.*] Whose is it, then?

WOMAN: Children belong to all of us, one might say.

MAN: [*Laughs.*] True, true.

WOMAN: Ask whose child this is, and the answer follows: this one is mine, that one is yours. Think what it means to divide children up like so much property. It's ridiculous!

MAN: Absolutely ridiculous. [*Silence.*] You haven't kidnapped her, have you?

WOMAN: No, listen! I told you my first husband could not have children. He was sterile, as I explained. Not that he minded. He was a show-off, too! "I understand women," he used to say. "I understand a woman's soul. Any woman I've ever had a chat with can never forget me. Why? Because I'm a man from head to toe." He was vulgar, too, a low breed. [*Mimics.*] "There goes the old clothes peddler. Shall I give you to him," he'd say, "and get a new one?" From time to time he'd slap me on the buttocks. [*Mimics.*] "I've skimmed your cream; you're reduced to nothing!" Another slap. [*Mimics.*] "Go find me a girl with your own hand." [*Lost in her thoughts.*] The way you don't give a damn about people, you can act just like him.

MAN: There is a certain resemblance between our vulgarities, but you can't say that I'm impotent since you haven't tried me yet. Time to flip a coin. [*Brings out his coin again.*] Heads or tails?

WOMAN: You're determined to prove that you're a man, aren't you?

MAN: Heads or tails?

WOMAN: Put that coin back in your pocket.

MAN: Heads or tails? Go on, make a choice! Why are you silent? You're not shy, are you? Tell me if you are! I adore a woman who's shy at the beginning. First she's shy; then she begins to scratch, to bite . . .

WOMAN: You may be a man, but you are not human.

MAN: I'm not insulting you.

WOMAN: But you are. Why did you tell me that story about the tart in the nightclub? Will you tell me why?

MAN: You tell me!

WOMAN: [*Mimics.*] She was from a good family, she had been brought up by nannies, she had had her own horse to ride at the family farm. You were comparing her to me, weren't you?

MAN: I wasn't comparing.

WOMAN: Well, I am like her. What have you got to say to that? I used to speak German when I was a child.

MAN: Pity it wasn't French. We could be speaking French now.

WOMAN: [*Mimics.*] Why don't you ask me, "Dear lady, are you a virgin?"

MAN: Dear lady, are you a virgin?

WOMAN: Unfortunately, yes!

MAN: That might be. There ought to be centers for the elimination of virginity in every neighborhood, you know. That would do away with a great deal of nastiness and stupidity. A girl came up to me one time, all out of breath. Do you know what she said?

WOMAN: She wanted you to take care of it?

MAN: Precisely. She was in luck; she was going to marry a wealthy man. "If I let that conceited fellow have my virginity, I'll be disgraced!" she shouted. Then she began to plead with me. "Please," she said, "solve my problem."

WOMAN: What did you do?

MAN: I did what she wanted, but it didn't do any good.

WOMAN: What do you mean?

MAN: Her engagement to the other fellow fell through, and she married me. So I accomplished two tasks in one. Think of it—what a foundation for a marriage. Work yourself to the bone for someone else, then . . .

WOMAN: I hope you didn't hold it against her.

MAN: Of course I did! She'd throw her arms around my neck. "Do you remember that day, darling?" she'd say. She meant the day the center for the elimination of virginity had done its job. What sort of a memory was that for me?

WOMAN: Did you divorce?

MAN: Most certainly.

WOMAN: Because of this?

MAN: Certainly because of this. It meant that she wasn't as afraid of me as she was of that other man. She had no respect for me.

WOMAN: You shouldn't have married her, then.

MAN: If I hadn't married her, I couldn't have divorced her.

WOMAN: One needs a reason for divorce.

MAN: The tip of her nose was always cold. Isn't that reason enough?

WOMAN: Brandy, please!

MAN: [*The bottle is in his hand.*] Not before you've finished your story, though.

WOMAN: Which story? I'm getting them all mixed up.

MAN: The one about your first husband, who was sterile.

WOMAN: I'll hurry, then. Do you know what cured him of being a show-off? Our neighbors were gossiping about there being no child. This upset him. He came home as meek as a lamb one evening. "I beg of you, tell me the truth, have you been talking?" There were tears in his eyes. He said he'd kill himself. This frightened me, so I told him I'd think of a way out. I did, too.

MAN: Was there a way out?

WOMAN: We moved to the suburbs. I stayed shut up in the house for months. We didn't know any of the neighbors. The nearest house was a distance away. One night, he came home with a baby, not more than three or four days old. He'd bought it for five hundred from a poor family in the shantytown. [*Begins to laugh.*] "Get into bed," he said to me.

I undressed and got into bed. He placed the baby near us. "Now scream," he said. So I began to scream as loud as I could, as though I were having labor pains. My husband kept saying, "Louder, louder!" as he opened all the windows wide. Some of the neighbors heard me and came to see if there was anything the matter. "It's all right. She's only giving birth," my husband said. "Haven't you had children? It's a perfectly normal thing to happen." [*They both laugh.*] Not so loud, you're going to wake the child. Give me my brandy. [*Takes a sip.*] Do you want to know what happened after that?

MAN: There's more to it?

WOMAN: Of course there is. He was now as full of his own importance as ever and back to his old tricks. A slap on my buttocks. [*Mimics.*] "Now would you like another child?"

MAN: Wait a minute, are you putting me on?

WOMAN: Putting you on?

MAN: You weren't pregnant when you married your second husband; you already had a child.

WOMAN: I don't get it.

MAN: She doesn't get it. Your second husband knew perfectly well that the child wasn't his, so why did he tell you that you were trying to palm it off on him?

WOMAN: What makes you think he knew it was an adopted child?

MAN: Don't talk nonsense. You did say, a minute ago, that you were pregnant when you married again.

WOMAN: [*Shuts her eyes, puts her hands to her head.*] Wait, wait, I'm getting so confused. What was it I said?

MAN: [*Shouts.*] Is this your child, or is it the child that you bought in the shantytown?

WOMAN: Which child?

MAN: The child in that room.

WOMAN: But that isn't a child.

MAN: Not a child?

WOMAN: It's not a child—it's just a doll. Go and look if you don't believe me! [*The* MAN *rushes into the bedroom. She throws herself down on the cot and shuts her eyes.*]

CURTAIN

ACT II

[*The* MAN *returns slowly from the bedroom, looks at the* WOMAN.]

MAN: She's sleeping.

WOMAN: [*Her eyes closed.*] She's been sleeping all the time. She hasn't uncovered herself, has she?

MAN: [*Thoughtfully.*] No.

WOMAN: Let her sleep.

MAN: We've been damn silly, you know.

WOMAN: [*In a begging tone.*] Do you think if we were to start again, from the beginning, we might do better this time?

MAN: I don't think so at all.

WOMAN: Neither do I. Never mind. We've just not been very successful. We'll never know why. It doesn't really matter.

MAN: Weren't you the one who was so eager to talk, to explain?

WOMAN: The more I talk, the more confused things become. I swear to you, it isn't my fault!

MAN: It's because you're trying to hide the truth.

WOMAN: And you're trying to make everything sound simple. I can see things are not. I'm not trying to make them sound so.

MAN: Well, in that case, let's get things thoroughly confused. Let's make our minds whirl.

WOMAN: I don't know anything.

MAN: Then I won't ask you any questions.

WOMAN: Don't.

MAN: But earlier you were angry because I didn't ask you questions.

WOMAN: I'm completely muddled.

MAN: Strange! You'd think I was the one who wanted conversation.

WOMAN: It was you. You brought me here to carry on a conversation with yourself. Frightened me to pieces.

MAN: I knew you were; that's why I didn't want to ask any questions.

WOMAN: But what's happening to me?

MAN: Don't worry, you're exactly the same.

WOMAN: So, you see, it didn't do any good.

MAN: I've never much cared to listen to other people's experiences.

WOMAN: It's the end you should bear in mind. Was I or was I not forced into the streets? That should be enough. Whether my stories are contradictory, what does it matter?

MAN: After all that, you come around to my view.

WOMAN: Did you really not care at all? Why did you want the child to sleep in the other room?

MAN: [*Surprised.*] Why? Well, why was it?

WOMAN: Because if we, the child and I, had slept here, then you would have had to sleep in your room.

MAN: [*Listening.*] So?

WOMAN: But here, the apartment door is nearer.

MAN: So it is.

WOMAN: There's no one between this cot and the apartment door. So you get up in the morning . . . and suddenly you see . . . [*The dog is heard barking from the first floor. Both stop and listen.*]

MAN: [*Jokingly.*] The hound of the Baskervilles. What a horrible night!

WOMAN: Horrible . . . let's not pretend—that's what you were afraid of, isn't it?

MAN: I don't understand. We can't be thinking of the same thing. All we can do is talk, that's all. [*The dog barks again.*]

WOMAN: Suppose morning never comes.

MAN: That's something I cannot accept responsibility for. [*Makes up a song and sings it off-key.*] Suppose morning never comes. [*Whirls around as he sings, staggers, fails to catch hold of a chair, and falls, sprawling on the floor. He appears to be unconscious. The* WOMAN *stands looking, then goes over to him, and, bending down, shakes him by the shoulders. He does not respond. She struggles to her feet, smoothes her hair, then seems to reach a decision. She swiftly goes to the apartment door, puts on her coat and shoes, lifts up her collar, opens the door noiselessly, goes out, and pulls the door so that only her hand can be seen for a while through the crack in the door. Then the hand disappears, too. The man sits up, looks at the door calmly, then stretches out again. The door opens, she comes in again, looking crestfallen, removes her coat and shoes, puts on his slippers. She shuts the door and walks to the sideboard, where she pours herself a drink. She looks at the* MAN. *Just then the* MAN *moves.*]

WOMAN: Are you all right?

MAN: [*Sits up.*] I don't seem to be dead, so I must be all right. I was going to say something, but I can't say it now.

WOMAN: Why not?

MAN: It's one of those things that come to mind when one is about to die. I've forgotten it now.

WOMAN: A pity!

MAN: Yes. Have you ever been near someone who was about to die?

WOMAN: No!

MAN: I have. People apparently discover happiness at just that moment. In the case I know of, it was an old woman. She said, "I'm going to tell you the way to be happy. Would you like to know?" "Yes," I said, and I was all ears.

WOMAN: What did she say?

MAN: She said, "You wouldn't understand if I told you," and then she died. [*Stands up.*] Do you know the Mikado game?

WOMAN: What's that?

MAN: Don't you know?

WOMAN: No, I don't.

MAN: It's a very easy game to play. Come, let's play it. [*Takes a small transparent plastic bag out of the sideboard drawer. It is full of little sticks, striped in bright colors. He takes out a fistful of them, holds them straight up with their tips on the table, and suddenly lets go. They fall in a small tangled heap.*] Come here!

WOMAN: What does one do with these?

MAN: We're going to take turns picking them up one at a time.

WOMAN: You mean taking turns again?

MAN: That's right. But none of the other sticks must move when you're picking up yours.

WOMAN: I see, it's easy! Let's begin!

MAN: Wait ... [*Picks up one of the sticks.*] This one's the Mikado; it counts for twenty points. [*Picks up another.*] This one's called the Mandarin, fifteen points. [*Picks up another.*] This one's the Samurai, ten points. The others are worth three, four, or five points according to the number of stripes on them. You get it? You've got to pick up the most points in order to win. If you pick up the Mikado or the Mandarin, you can use them to pick up other sticks. Now watch, I'll start. [*Picks up the sticks again and lets them drop onto the table. Carefully picks up the top stick without moving any of the others.*] There you are, you see?

WOMAN: I see. My turn now?

MAN: No, as long as one goes on without moving any of the other sticks, the turn doesn't change. [*Picks up another stick.*] There's another. [*Bends down to pick up one more.*] Blast, the Mikado has moved. Your turn now. [*Drinks.*]

WOMAN: [*Goes up to the table.*] It's a good game. [*Bends over the sticks.*]

MAN: Pick up the stick on top of the Mikado, then you can take the Mikado, too.

WOMAN: [*Stretches two fingers.*] My hand's trembling. Suppose the Mikado moves?

MAN: Don't hurry. Here, take my place. It's easier from here.

WOMAN: [*Changes places with him.*] The Mikado's twenty points, isn't it?

MAN: That's right. It's the best stick to pick up.

WOMAN: First, the one on top. Go ahead, go ahead. [*Picks it up.*] Hooray! I've got the one on top!

MAN: Bravo! Now try for the Mikado. Let's see you do it! [*While the WOMAN is concentrating on the game, he edges his hand toward her handbag, which is lying on the cot, finally picks it up, and hides it behind his back. But she has seen him.*]

WOMAN: [*Sharply.*] Give me my bag!

MAN: [*Still holding the bag behind him.*] I won't.

WOMAN: Give it to me, I say! [*They chase each other around the table.*] You've no right to do this! It's my bag! Give it to me! [*Throws herself at him. They struggle and fall together on the cot. She bites his hand; he cries out and lets go of the handbag. She is out of breath, her hair disheveled. She stands up.*] Come on, let's play! [*Smoothes her hair with one hand.*] It was my turn. [*Walks backward to the table. She holds one hand behind her back and with the other picks up a stick.*] There, I've got the Mikado!

MAN: [*Also out of breath.*] That's twenty points for you. Now with the other hand, you can use the Mikado, too. You've got yourself an assistant!

WOMAN: I can use both the fingers of my hand and the Mikado?

MAN: Both your hand and the Mikado.

WOMAN: [*Her bag in one hand, the Mikado in the other.*] You stand back! [*He takes a step.*] Back, back! [*Puts the bag down on the table and with the help of the Mikado picks up another stick.*] Hooray! How many points is this?

MAN: Three.

WOMAN: Why three?

MAN: Because there are three colored stripes on it, see?

WOMAN: Move back. [*Bends over the sticks.*] That boy wasn't your friend.

MAN: What boy?

WOMAN: [*Intent on the sticks.*] My hand is trembling so much I'm afraid I am going to move them. [*To the* MAN.] What did you say?

MAN: I said, "What boy?"

WOMAN: That orphan at grade school.

MAN: The one in my story?

WOMAN: Yes. [*Still intent on the game.*]

MAN: [*Nervous.*] Who was he? I wonder. I'd like to know.

WOMAN: You do know. It was you.

MAN: [*Shouts.*] Go on, make things up! You mean the boy I bullied? [*Laughs nervously.*] The one who shared my desk? That's very funny! [*Gets closer to her.*] What in the world makes you think . . . ?

WOMAN: Wait, wait, wait. [*Shows him a stick she has just picked up.*] How many points is this?

MAN: Five.

WOMAN: Good! [*To one of the sticks.*] Now it's . . . now it's your turn. [*Bends over the table.*] That frail boy . . .

MAN: [*Drains his glass.*] Go on, make up stories to your heart's content. Look at my face. Do I resemble him? Do I look sallow?

WOMAN: The boy whose eyes glittered like glass.

MAN: It wasn't me, it wasn't me!

WOMAN: Wait, wait, wait, wait. [*Picks up another stick.*] How many points is that?

MAN: Two!

WOMAN: Fine! I'm not going to give you a chance. It's still my turn! [*Bends over the table.*]

MAN: That boy killed himself.

WOMAN: [*Straightening up.*] You killed him! You're more cruel to yourself than to the people you hate! You've done things to yourself that they wouldn't do! You've scraped love out of yourself. You're like those women who have had their wombs scraped so many times that they can never have children! You've worked hard to achieve your loneliness; you've built walls all around yourself, only to find there was nobody inside!

MAN: And you're telling me all this?

WOMAN: Yes, I am.

MAN: You? Who are so desperate you don't know what to do? [*Shouts.*] A fine teacher to give me lessons. But I don't want to go on.

WOMAN: What can you say? That's all you're worrying about. You were afraid of my talking because you've really destroyed yourself. And that's why you shout—you want to be able to hear yourself.

MAN: Would you prefer me to act as you did?

WOMAN: [*Surprised.*] What did I do?

MAN: [*About to speak, changes his mind, shrugs a shoulder.*] I mean . . . you didn't do anything at all.

WOMAN: You haven't as good an excuse as I have!

MAN: That's what you think.

WOMAN: One can't live with hate alone.

MAN: Are you going to shut up?

WOMAN: I'm not going to "shut up," as you say! Stop hiding behind yourself!

MAN: What on earth are you trying to say?

WOMAN: And another thing.

MAN: What's that?

WOMAN: It was you the others thought had stolen it. Tell me that's a lie.

MAN: Stolen what?

WOMAN: Don't pretend you don't understand! The wallet in the boat.

MAN: [*Shouts.*] They thought . . . am I responsible for what they thought? Should I take that bunch of bastards on my shoulders? Or maybe you'd like me to feel love for them? You're talking nonsense! Let's say my mother left me in someone's house and went off to kill herself. Is that my fault, perhaps? Should I feel shame because of it? Go on, tell me! You see, you're silent! I tell you our world is not a world of right and wrong; it's only . . . a world of balance!

WOMAN: So . . . you've created a balanced world with your hatred. Is that what you would like me to believe?

MAN: Completely. I hate everyone. There is no one I love, no one I respect. To hell with love and respect! And the same with mothers and fathers, schools and teachers. Nothing is sacred as far as I'm concerned. Any further objections? [*Raises his voice even more.*] I am shouting; I can hear my own voice. Hey, listen, this is my voice! You can hear it, too. That means there is someone in this house. I'm saying the world disgusts me.

WOMAN: You're forcing yourself to shout; you want to make yourself believe in the strength of your hate.

MAN: Whether you believe in what I'm saying or not doesn't change anything.

WOMAN: The point is, you don't believe in what you're saying, that's why you're scared.

MAN: One can't be scared of nothing.

WOMAN: Because you keep talking to yourself, you think the world is nothing.

MAN: I'm not the only person guilty of that.

WOMAN: In the war between you and the world, you must help the world.

MAN: You talk like a book.

WOMAN: We're talking. The more we talk, the more you'll seek shelter in me.

MAN: [*Bursts into laughter.*] Turn to you for shelter!

WOMAN: [*With an expression of disgust.*] Yes, just as I've come to you for shelter! Your boorishness is another result of fear.

MAN: [*Goes on laughing.*] If I were to look for shelter . . . it would not be with you. I can assure you . . . [*Stops.*]

WOMAN: Go on, finish your sentence. I'm not angry. I'm not going to get angry at anything you say.

MAN: Just where would you shelter me?

WOMAN: [*Wonders where all the things the* MAN *is saying might end.*] What do you mean?

MAN: Would you shelter me inside your handbag, for instance?

WOMAN: [*Looks at her bag, raises her head.*] I'm talking about a one-time shelter. The shelter that changes a person.

MAN: You want to change yourself before you leave here?

WOMAN: [*Sadly.*] No.

MAN: Then give me your bag. [*Reaches for it.*]

WOMAN: [*Steps back.*] It's my bag.

MAN: [*Pointing at himself.*] And this is mine, mine! We're both free to hold onto our property.

WOMAN: If it were so, then you wouldn't want to know what's in my bag; you wouldn't try to take it away from me.

MAN: I wouldn't like to make anyone change his route.

WOMAN: [*Tense.*] My route . . . [*Lost in her thoughts.*]

MAN: [*Quickly jumps up and fills the two glasses.*] Let's go on with the game. One can't play it alone. Come on, sooner or later it will be my turn. You can be as careful as you please, but you're bound to move one of the sticks when you're not supposed to. [*Drinks.*] To your good health!

WOMAN: To yours! [*Drinks.*]

MAN: Bitter, isn't it?

WOMAN: The brandy?

MAN: No, losing one's turn. It wasn't your turn to preach at me.

WOMAN: Ah, well, there's plenty of time until morning.

MAN: Let's play.

WOMAN: I like the Mikado game. It's exciting. I hope it will be your turn soon.

MAN: I'm waiting. Go ahead!

WOMAN: [*Bends over the table and picks up one more stick.*] Isn't this one the Samurai?

MAN: Well done, well done! That's ten points for you. [*As the* WOMAN *bends over the table again, he picks up a book from the bookshelf and leafs through the pages. Reads.*] "He killed himself, like a Samurai whose honor has been violated."

WOMAN: What's a Samurai?

MAN: It's the name given to Japanese warriors in ancient times.

WOMAN: Let me see that book. [*The* MAN *hands it to her. She finds the line and reads it, mumbling.*] "A Samurai whose honor has been violated." [*Lifts her head.*] You know what this means?

MAN: Yes.

WOMAN: You wouldn't like to make anyone change his route, is that right?

MAN: I would not.

WOMAN: What time is it?

MAN: [*Looks at the clock on the wall.*] That clock hasn't been working for some time.

WOMAN: The clock isn't working. The dog downstairs keeps barking. So what are we going to do?

MAN: Perhaps you are crazy, after all.

WOMAN: Are you sure?

MAN: Or else you're a coward.

WOMAN: How do you know? What makes you think so?

MAN: If you're not crazy and you're not a coward . . .

WOMAN: Then why have I not killed myself, like you, is that it?

MAN: I haven't killed myself. Nor did I intend to.

WOMAN: Well, I haven't killed myself, but I did kill my aunt. [*Laughs.*]

MAN: Don't make things up. Anyway, she wasn't your aunt. The woman in your story . . . she was your second husband's aunt.

WOMAN: Why should one kill only one's second husband's aunt? Couldn't one kill one's own aunt?

MAN: Then you think that the things that go through your mind have actually happened. Go on with the game.

WOMAN: How many points was the Samurai?

MAN: Ten.

WOMAN: [*Counts the sticks in her hand.*] I've got quite a few points: twenty plus ten is thirty . . . plus three . . .

MAN: [*Mockingly.*] What did you kill her with, then?

WOMAN: Thirty-three . . . a gun.

MAN: The gun in your bag?

WOMAN: Plus three . . . yes.

MAN: You're sure it's not a toy gun?

WOMAN: If you thought it was a toy gun, you wouldn't have tried to take it away, would you? [*Takes the gun out of her bag.*] Here, smell it! You can still smell the gunpowder. Here!

MAN: Let's have a look.

WOMAN: You're not to grab.

MAN: All right, I won't touch.

WOMAN: [*Holds onto the gun with both hands.*] Put your hands behind your back! [*The* MAN *does so.*] Fine, now come closer, closer. [*His nose is to the muzzle.*] Boo! [*He jumps.*] Now who's a coward? [*Both laugh.*] Can you smell the gunpowder?

MAN: Let me smell it again.

WOMAN: [*Thrusts the gun back into her bag.*] You have no sense of smell. [*Finishes her drink.*] Brandy, please!

MAN: [*Swaying as he approaches her with the brandy bottle in his hand.*] I don't believe a word you say. You can say anything you like.

WOMAN: It's not my turn.

MAN: [*Pours both of them a drink.*] It's my turn?

WOMAN: It's your turn.

MAN: [*After a short silence.*] What nonsense, all this!

WOMAN: Yes, it's nonsense. [*Bows her head, maybe weeping. Silence.*]

MAN: So it's nonsense. [*Looks at her.*] The difference between us is that I may have turned myself into stone, but I'm still alive.

WOMAN: I've always been happy, and you unhappy.

MAN: [*Indifferent.*] Try unhappiness for a change!

WOMAN: [*Goes up to him.*] Look into my eyes and repeat that!

MAN: [*Mockingly.*] In your eyes, I see an ocean.

WOMAN: It's not for me, but for you . . . I beg of you, stop this mocking. You've helped me, haven't you? Perhaps for the first time in your life you've helped someone. Go a little farther, don't be afraid, take another step!

MAN: [*Pointing at the Mikado sticks.*] How many points have you got so far?

WOMAN: I'll count them up. [*Counts up her sticks.*]

MAN: You take everything seriously, and I don't. That's the difference between us.

WOMAN: Forty-two. I don't see any difference. Forty-five . . .

MAN: [*Laughs.*] Having birth pangs and pretending to have birth pangs is the same, you mean?

WOMAN: [*Softly.*] Was your shouting because you were in pain? If we look for reasons for your rebellion, what are we going to find? Nothing.

MAN: You can't unnerve me, so stop trying.

WOMAN: Do you know what that old woman was going to say to you before she died?

MAN: She was going to tell me how to be happy. But she learned it herself only when she was about to die—if then. So it was of no use to me. I might discover it myself—just as I am dying.

WOMAN: I can show you how to be happy.

MAN: [*Pretends to recoil in fear. Jokingly.*] Are you about to die, perhaps?

WOMAN: No . . . not yet . . .

MAN: How about telling yourself the secret?

WOMAN: It was just helplessness in my case. I didn't know what hit me. But it was beautiful just the same.

MAN: You'd like me to believe it was.

WOMAN: I'm scared for the first time. That's why. [*The dog can be heard barking again. The* MAN *suddenly looks at her. She looks at the door. The doorbell rings.*]

MAN: [*Startled.*] At this hour? [*Goes to the door and presses the button that releases the door of the apartment building. He opens the door slightly and takes a couple of steps outside. Footsteps and voices can be heard. The dog stops barking. The* MAN *comes in; shuts the door.*] It's the people upstairs. They dropped their key, couldn't get in . . . so they tried my bell. The son of a bitch seems to think I'm the caretaker. How did he know I wasn't sleeping? He was holding his wife's arm; she was helping him up the stairs.

WOMAN: Your fate is to help those who are left in the street tonight.

MAN: They'd been to a wedding. I bet they're tearing the occasion to pieces right this moment. The man is lurching left and right as he utters gross remarks. "They must be having a great time," he says of the bride and groom. He has a dirty grin. A shitty wedding! [*Mimics.*] "The happy bridegroom . . . a sweet smile upon his face." . . . As though one's happiness must be displayed upon one's features. The fool is probably feeling stupefied. With the same smile, he greets everybody who shakes his hand to congratulate him. And, as for the bride . . . I swear to God, tonight she has already started laying down the law. [*Mimics.*] "Not so much to drink, darling, put down your glass. And throw away that pack of cigarettes. Good boy! Do you love me?" She can't show her love without interfering with his habits. The guests, watching this tear-jerking display of happiness, are beside themselves with excitement. Heads are tilted to one side, gazes deepen, jaws drop! I can see that smuggler upstairs playing the sycophant. Not that it will prevent him from acting as witness at the divorce proceedings, tomorrow or the day after. [*Goes up to the table and fills his glass. The* WOMAN *is very drunk by now and not following his remarks very closely. She gives a jump whenever he sounds excited, then slumps down again.*] And they talk about the sacredness of the family. [*Mimics.*] "It's sheer wanton destruction, sir!" What are you but a ruin yourself, you so-and-so! Traditions, ceremonies, sacred institutions . . . for those fellows, they are the sticks of the Mikado game. [*Pretends to be playing the game.*] "Wait, morality's been joggled, it's my turn. Look, without joggling tradition at all I'm going to pick up twenty points with my two fingers." [*Changes his voice.*] "Wait, you've joggled tradition, so it's my turn. If I can get hold of one of those sacred institutions, then I have it made! I can go on picking up all the sticks. I've got it, well done!" [*Changes his voice again.*] "I'm after the Samurai, my dear. Once I've got him, the day is mine!" They're playing a game—they're gambling, I tell you! [*Goes up to the table and hits the Mikado sticks with his fists, scattering them.*] To hell with you all! [*Looks up toward the ceiling.*] Hey, usurer, sycophant! Can you hear me? Or are you snoring in the arms of your wife? You bear, why don't you just stay asleep, hibernate in your cave, to give us a break? [*To the* WOMAN.] Why do you keep looking at my face? Drink your brandy instead! [*Both drink.*]

WOMAN: It's nice to drink. [*Sways, laughing.*] I'm not used to it.

MAN: It's as though I got the habit in my mother's womb!

WOMAN: Do you drink like this every night?

MAN: Every day and every night I drink like this. Anything more to say? [*Sings an old tango.*] "Suuuunaaaa . . . your eyes have enslaved me, Suna!" [*To the* WOMAN.] So they went to a wedding. Can't we go to a wedding? Come, let's dance. Let's pretend we're at a wedding. I'm coming over to invite you to dance. Now you pretend . . . you have seen me out of the corner of your eye, but you act as though you haven't. [*The* WOMAN *does as he says. He crosses the stage toward her, still singing.*] May I have the next dance, please?

WOMAN: That's very old-fashioned. Nobody goes through that rigmarole nowadays. Go back to your place. [*The* MAN *does so. She goes up to him, throws her arms around his neck. They dance, humming the tune.*]

MAN: [*Lifts his head, singing at the top of his voice.*] "Suuuunaaa!"

WOMAN: [*Bursts into laughter, drops her arms.*] No need to shout.

MAN: Let's drink.

WOMAN: We've had an awful lot.

MAN: So what? You know what dear old Omar Khayyam says, don't you? I don't drink like this every day, he says, only on Tuesday, Wednesday, Thursday, Friday, Saturday, and also Sunday and Monday.

WOMAN: [*Laughs hilariously.*] Tuesday, Wednesday, Thursday, Friday, Saturday, and also Sunday and Monday. I do not drink like this every day.

MAN: [*His speech is slurred.*] No, not every day like this. Tuesday, Tuesday evening, Wednesday, Wednesday evening, Thursday . . .

WOMAN: Thursday evening, Friday evening . . . not every day, not every evening.

MAN: [*Goes up close to her. Seriously.*] Not drink . . . listen to a lot of balderdash instead? [*Mimics.*] "The world of freedom, a regime based on rights and discipline, the structure of the nation . . . " Who's going to swallow that lot? It all happens behind my back: the government of the nation, the government of the world . . . all hidden from me. I'm just a number, among the millions whose destruction is planned . . . not even a name. I'm going to die in any case, aren't I? Well, that's none of your business! I want to go to the cinema tomorrow, to walk ankle deep in the snow, you get it? I want to live in order to hate. I want to look into the eyes of those I hate. And that's why I'm drinking. I cannot tolerate anyone if I do not drink, not even those I love.

WOMAN: In that case, give me a drink!

MAN: You give me one.

WOMAN: [*Picks up the bottle and pours the* MAN *a drink.*] I didn't quite understand the last bit.

MAN: I was talking to myself.

WOMAN: You said something about those you love. What has happened to those you love?

MAN: Don't imagine that you're going to build a link between me and love because of that offhand remark. My head is whirling. "You see," you're going to say, "there are people you love!" I'm rocky. I'm going to see two of you in a moment.

WOMAN: I'm already seeing two of you! You're like you were earlier, and you're different. You have two heads, one with a long face, and one with almost a smiling face. Sometimes the two heads come together and are one, and then I look and they have come apart. Please stop it! You're making me dizzy.

MAN: I'm not rocky, you are! But no matter which one of us rocks, we'll both see double.

WOMAN: If both of us rock, what happens?

MAN: Then we see one of everything.

WOMAN: Come, let's both rock! Begin from the left! [*They move their heads beginning at the same side.*] How lovely! Now you begin from the right! And I'll begin from the left. [*Then they turn their heads in opposite directions.*] Now let's do it this way, then that way. [*They do as she says. One, two, one, two.*]

MAN: Enough of this game; it makes one drunker than drink does.

WOMAN: I haven't been drunk at all.

MAN: You mean you haven't ever or you haven't tonight?

WOMAN: I don't know. I cannot answer such complicated questions.

MAN: [*Comes and stands by the* WOMAN.] You promised you'd remind me, why didn't you?

WOMAN: Remind you of what?

MAN: Heads or tails, remember? To make love.

WOMAN: There's plenty of time until morning. Don't hurry.

MAN: There's nothing else left to do.

WOMAN: Nothing else left? What a pity! Were we not going to talk? Is this all there is to the story of our lives? Not enough to fill one night! I thought so much had happened. I loved so much . . . was so happy! [*Her eyes fill with tears.*] Not enough to fill one night. Go to bed, go to sleep! I'll go into the bedroom. Perhaps I'll leave, we'll leave, while you're sleeping. Let's say good-bye now. [*Gets up.*] Good-bye, it's all over.

MAN: It's not over yet. [*Murmurs.*] I'm going to tell you a secret. If you promise you won't tell anyone.

WOMAN: I promise. Your secret shall be buried with me, you can count on it.

MAN: I don't want it to be buried, merely to stay with you, warm and alive.

WOMAN: You want me to keep your secret alive?

MAN: Yes, because it can only live on with you.

WOMAN: Tell me your secret, then.

MAN: I'm afraid you might not understand.

WOMAN: What makes you think I wouldn't understand?

MAN: You see, it's not my secret. It's yours.

WOMAN: I'm going to destroy my secret.

MAN: You don't know what it is, so how can you destroy it?

WOMAN: [*Mockingly.*] Tell me so that I'll learn.

MAN: You've got absolutely nothing that you can destroy, but you think you have. It's just a poor figment of your imagination.

WOMAN: You can't surprise me.

MAN: Have you ever looked at your face in the mirror for a long time?

WOMAN: I must have . . . I am a woman.

MAN: Not that way. [*Lifts the mirror off the wall, brings it up to the* WOMAN, *and holds it to her face.*] Look, look well, look closer! Your eyes, your eyelashes. Look closely! Your eyebrows, your lips . . . that mouth, that chin . . . look at your forehead, too. Now try to look at all of them at once. They fade, they swim away, don't they? They drift away from each other—each one pulls in a different direction, and they go in separate directions! Look carefully! Are those your eyes, your eyebrows? Those pretty lips, are they yours? They aren't. You don't know that mouth; it's someone else's mouth. This face is someone else's face. The hair you caress as you run a comb through it . . . place your hand on it now. [*The* WOMAN *does so.*] It's like thorns, like thorns pricking your hand, isn't it? It scratches. [*She pushes the mirror away, looks at the* MAN.] You're afraid of yourself. Yet you used to love your hair, to love your eyes. You used to open and shut your lips in the mirror, to love them better. Never look at them again when sober. They're not yours, so you can't destroy them.

WOMAN: You're not drunk. [*Walks up to the* MAN *slowly.*] You're merely pretending to sway as you walk. You're shouting on purpose. [*Shouts.*] You're pretending to be angry. Pretense, pretense, pretense! You've got some sort of plan; you're carrying it out step by step. Everything you do and say is calculated. You're trying to pin me down; you want me to repent, to change my mind. You want to crush me! It's not worth it, you say, it's not worth it for things that don't belong to you! Well, if you don't love me, why do you want to save me? If you can make me despise myself and the world, then you shall have made me rise above the world and myself, is that it? That's your plan, your calculation. But don't forget that I live in that world you find disgusting. Hate me, as you hate everyone else. Get out of my way! You want to achieve in me what you haven't achieved in yourself. You've given up hope for yourself, so you want to change me. Look, I'm stroking my hair—it's my hair, it's soft, not at all like thorns. My eyes, my eyebrows are mine. This body is mine. I'm mistress of all these things. I do what I want to do. Do you understand that? None of them belongs to someone else. Even if you are the Devil, you can't deceive me; you can't estrange me from myself. [*Opens the door of the room where the child is sleeping.*] Come here! [*The* MAN *goes, swaying, up to her.*] Look inside! Look at the child sleeping there. That's you! You're an abandoned child! That is the source of your strength, your boldness, your selfishness.

You're stronger than anybody else. I want her to be like you, not like me. Not weak, not pathetic, not soft. Don't try to stop me! [*Chokes and bursts into sobs.*]

MAN: Look at what you've done to yourself while trying to change me. [*Paces back and forth, waiting for her sobs to subside.*] Do you know what you are? The accidental meeting place of a number of events . . . a precarious balance established between a number of acts. Don't magnify your own importance.

WOMAN: [*Swaying drunkenly.*] Say it again, say it again!

MAN: [*Slaps her hard.*] Just listen! You don't have to understand!

WOMAN: [*Rubs her cheek.*] That hurt.

MAN: It hurt because I hit you. You're simply a consequence, a result; a consequence cannot take revenge.

WOMAN: I'm not seeking revenge.

MAN: That proves you have a low opinion of yourself. Come here! Let me show you what's on the other side of this door! [*Takes the* WOMAN *by the arm and pulls her toward the door, opens it.*] Look at this ocean! Where the waves are hurling themselves against each other there is a smooth spot, there in the middle. Do you see it? It is calm, it is sleeping. It cannot destroy itself; that is not in its power. [*Drops her arm.*] Shut the door! We destroy ourselves only because we cannot create ourselves.

WOMAN: [*Shuts the door, looking at him intently.*] I don't recognize you.

MAN: You speak as though you knew me when you came.

WOMAN: [*Walks to the cot.*] I'm tired all of a sudden. What's happening to me? [*Stretches out slowly, face down.*] I'm going to lie down for a little. There's nothing like sleep! [*Gently raises her head, her eyes shut.*] Please go on talking. Your voice sounds beautiful, as though it comes from afar, from the depths. Why have you stopped?

MAN: Do you know how mummies are made?

WOMAN: [*Sleepily.*] I don't understand.

MAN: [*Louder.*] I asked you whether you know how mummies are made.

WOMAN: What mummies?

MAN: Egyptian mummies.

WOMAN: I don't know.

MAN: Or how to pickle fish?

WOMAN: I said I didn't know.

MAN: It's the same process. First, you disembowel it, then wash off the blood with plenty of water, then rub it with salt. [*Yawns.*]

WOMAN: I just want to go to sleep.

MAN: [*Yawns.*] We had a cat once that would eat nothing but liver. While my wife was in the hospital, it was my job to look after the cat. This is my chance, I thought. I'll train that cat to eat other kinds of food. I tried bread, eggs, spaghetti, but nothing doing. So I thought I'd starve her for a while, figuring that ought to do the trick. Far from it—that tame cat simply grew wild. She began to attack me. I had difficulty throwing her out the door. She yowled and hurled herself against it. I really got scared; I'll never forget it. I was cowed, beaten by a small cat. I finally gave her what she wanted. [*Sits down.*] Then we had a dog. It saved my life once. It was lame. I had fallen into the pond. [*Picks up the bottle of brandy and holds it to the light. There's nothing left in it. Puts it down on the table.*] It's empty. [*To the audience.*] If you ask me what happiness is, I say it's being able to scratch yourself. I was nearly happy once. I had a sudden pain in the belly. Writhing in pain, I fell into bed. It turned out to be a kidney stone. I thought I was going to die of pain. Shortly before dawn a doctor came and gave me a morphine injection. That dreadful pain was all gone; it was a beautiful world all of a sudden. I could hardly believe it. I was happy, in the fullest sense. I wanted to savor my happiness. Just then I began to itch behind the ear as though an insect had stung me. I wanted to lie absolutely still so as not to spoil my state of euphoria, but that itch spoiled everything. In the end, I was forced to lift an arm to scratch myself behind the ear. Then I let my arm fall back. A minute later that itch started again. I scratched myself once again; that itch, once again I scratched. It wouldn't stop. That damned itch wouldn't stop; it made a mess of my happiness. So now, whenever I seem to feel something approaching happiness, I wait for the itch to begin. And it always does.

WOMAN: [*Jumps up hastily from the cot.*] Is it morning already?

MAN: No.

WOMAN: I don't think it will ever be morning. I'm going now.

MAN: Stay a little longer, wait. Children should not be awakened in the dark. There's no window in this room, but I'll turn off the light when it's morning, and you can watch the room fill with blue, like the bottom of the sea. The blue of daytime, seeping through the walls. Perhaps it will spread right into us, too. The blue is worth waiting for. Don't rush!

WOMAN: [*Picks up her handbag, then drops it again.*] Let me have that mirror again. [*The MAN brings it to her. She examines herself.*] I don't look the way I did earlier.

MAN: They woke me up in the dark. My earliest memory is of that darkness. Do you know what it did to me? For years afterward I was unable to discern the blue of morning.

WOMAN: I had a dream. I was lying in bed. My school friends were all around, each telling a story . . . beautiful stories. I hoped they would never come to an end. A man all dressed in black kept tugging at my hand. "It's over, come along," he said. My friends felt sorry for me. "But it's not over," they kept saying. I pleaded with that man, "Can't you see? They're still talking. Please let them all tell their stories, and I'll come later." "No use putting it off," he said, "you're coming now." I was so scared!

MAN: I, too, saw a dream, once. There was a beautiful garden ahead, a dark green garden, steeped in flowers. It was as though I were in the garden yet unable to see the path that led to it. So I felt the frustration of being outside the garden although I was really inside. A numbing frustration . . . [*The clock on the wall suddenly begins to tick. Both hear the sound.*]

WOMAN: Hadn't that clock stopped?

MAN: So it had.

WOMAN: It's started again. [*Silence. The clock can be heard ticking.*] What time was it when I came here?

MAN: [*Thinks.*] I don't know.

WOMAN: Where was it you found me?

MAN: Where? [*Scratches his head.*] I was drunk. I don't remember. [*Silence.*]

WOMAN: Is the child in that room?

MAN: Yes, it is.

WOMAN: Did it wake at all?

MAN: No, it didn't. [*Silence.*]

WOMAN: I must have gone to sleep.

MAN: Yes.

WOMAN: All night?

MAN: I don't know.

WOMAN: [*Stands up.*] I must go now.

MAN: Wait, wait! Let's wait for the blue. It should begin any moment now. Let me turn off the light. [*Gets up and turns off the light. The stage does not dim—it is multicolored, and toward the end of the act it slowly becomes blue.*]

WOMAN: The Mikado sticks are scattered on the floor. I'll pick them up and put them back into their bag. [*Stoops and picks up the sticks, one by one.*] I've never been able to choose anything, up to now, to do anything of my own accord, to be myself. [*As in a dream.*] I've always found myself either in the street or in a strange house. But I was always happy, without quite knowing what it meant; happiness was my job. Either they forced me to go away, or they forced me to join them. I didn't change; whether I was caressed or pushed away, I was always the same. Any blind devil could make me laugh, make me cry. I existed only because others wanted me to. Only once did I really want to be myself. Last night I wanted this. Do you know what my father used to say?

MAN: Yes, I do.

WOMAN: I must have told you, then.

MAN: You did tell me.

WOMAN: [*Puts the sticks into the bag.*] There, that's done. I won the game, didn't I?

MAN: It was never my turn.

WOMAN: If it was my turn, then surely yours was to follow. This is a game one can't play by oneself. [*Goes up to him.*] We both won.

MAN: Look, look! The room is filling with blue! Can you see? [*They look.*]

WOMAN: How beautiful! Don't you like it, too?

MAN: I'm usually passed out at this time. I don't like to feel myself growing old in the morning.

WOMAN: Have you never seen this blue before, then?

MAN: Never, I've merely thought about it.

WOMAN: I thank you!

MAN: The worst of it is, the brandy's all gone. I must keep a stock of it on hand in the future. On a snowy morning, there is nothing so pleasant as a drink of brandy before you go out into the street. I remember having done that once, long ago, with a poet friend when we were very young. We had spent the night talking at the home of another friend. Toward morning that friend placed a bottle of brandy on the table. "Can you drink this?" he asked. He had no idea that we would be able to, and, frankly, neither did we. To keep up the joke we filled our glasses. But now we couldn't stop; the glasses were waiting. So, for a joke, we drained them. I'll never forget it; the world was like paradise. Then we went off into the snowy streets. [*The* WOMAN *tiptoes gently into the other room. He watches her go, then stretches out on the cot, using her handbag for a pillow. He falls asleep.*]

CURTAIN

İbrahim the Mad

A. TURAN OFLAZOĞLU

Translated by Murat Nemet-Nejat

An Editor's Note

When the Kent Players Theater, Turkey's premier independent theater, presented its engrossing production of *Deli İbrahim (İbrahim the Mad)* in 1967, with its world-class actor Müşfik Kenter in the title role, the fledgling playwright A. Turan Oflazoğlu was catapulted into fame. Born in 1932, Oflazoğlu did not start writing plays until he was past the age of thirty. In his twenties, he had published his translation of Franz Kafka's *Penal Colony*, earned degrees in philosophy and English literature at the University of Istanbul, and published numerous essays and translations in literary magazines. In 1963 and 1964, he studied playwriting and drama at the University of Washington (Seattle) on a Fulbright scholarship.

Oflazoğlu's fame rests first and foremost on *İbrahim the Mad*, which won for him the coveted Drama Prize of the Turkish Language Society; was translated into English, Russian, and Hungarian; and enjoyed success on Radio Budapest. It was certainly a major hit when it premiered in Istanbul in 1967 and had a lavish production in Ankara later that year. Most Turkish critics rank *İbrahim the Mad* and Oflazoğlu's 1970 tragedy *IV. Murat* (Murat the Fourth) as two of the best Turkish plays ever written about Ottoman history. Some consider *İbrahim the Mad* the best such work of Turkish drama ever.

İbrahim, who came to be dubbed "the Lunatic," reluctantly acceded to the Ottoman throne in 1640 and reigned desperately but, according to what the playwright once said, "with a conscious and studied madness" until he was deposed and executed in 1648. He had come to the throne straight out of a "cage" where he had been incarcerated for many years because of his presumed madness. Once in power, he divided his time between the harem and interminable festivities, the likes of which had never been seen in Istanbul. Cinci Hoca,[1] a diabolical sorcerer, supposedly restored the impotent Sultan İbrahim to manhood and thus acquired great power over the empire.

Oflazoğlu observed in the play's program guide that "*Deli İbrahim* is a tragedy of power—sexual, political, and spiritual power." İbrahim, who grew from impotence to egregious sexuality, becomes an easy prey to the manipulations of his ambitious and clever mother, Kösem Sultan, who maintains tight control over the harem—and over her

---

1. *Hoca*: Generically means "teacher," more specifically "teacher of Islam." In Ottoman times, it was also used to designate a scholar, scientist, or learned person.

son. The grand vizier harbors hopes of toppling the sultan and assuming power himself. The play tells a story of corrupt people corrupting power.

İbrahim, as depicted by Oflazoğlu, rules with a "divine madness," but his lunacy is self-consuming and inexorably brings about his downfall. He typifies a new type of existence because he tries to defend himself against madness by committing insane acts. Ironically, both his entourage as well as the people join in this game of power and play into his hands. But madness is all. And madness destroys İbrahim, although at times he appears more sane than the vultures around him. He debunks too many beliefs, chops off too many heads, and commits the unforgivable error of seating his favorite concubine on the imperial throne for the sake of love and in defiance of the establishment.

Out of these sorry episodes of Ottoman history, Oflazoğlu has created a modern tragedy in the grand manner. *Deli İbrahim* has a conventional structure, but its techniques, concepts, and psychological orientation are thoroughly modern. The play has no heroes in the classical sense. All its protagonists are devoid of moral values. Only İbrahim acquires—as the play progresses—intimations of greatness in spiritual terms, but he, too, fails to attain the stature of a tragic hero. Classical heroes almost always rise, decline, and perish. İbrahim starts out in defeat, achieves little, and comes full circle back to defeat and destruction.

Oflazoğlu's earliest plays, *Keziban* and *Allahın Dediği Olur* (God's Will Shall Prevail), written when he was studying in Seattle, deal with backwardness in villages. The latter, a one-act verse tragedy, was produced in Seattle. *Deli İbrahim,* too, is essentially in free verse.

In later decades, Oflazoğlu wrote many fine plays about themes and vicissitudes in rural Turkey, a dramatization of Socrates' trial, a play about Mustafa Kemal Atatürk, and nearly a dozen major plays dealing with tragic events in the Ottoman Empire. He also published two collections of poetry and a volume of his critical essays; produced books about Shakespeare and Molière; and translated many volumes featuring selected poems by Rilke and Hölderlin, Nietzsche's *Thus Spake Zarathustra,* as well as plays by Lorca (*The House of Bernarda Alba* and *Blood Wedding)* and by Shakespeare (*Othello, Winter's Tale,* and *Romeo and Juliet),* many of which had successful productions. Some of Oflazoğlu's plays received Turkey's most prestigious awards and prizes.

İbrahim the Mad is notable for combining the drama of one of the Ottoman Empire's most striking episodes with the skills of a powerful playwright and the virtuosity of an accomplished translator. It is a play that promises to achieve success if ever it is produced on the American or British stage.

The English-language version of *Deli İbrahim* is by the poet Murat Nemet-Nejat, who ranks as one of the leading translators of Turkish poetry into English. In addition to numerous collections of his own poems, he has published his translations from the work of the Turkish poets Orhan Veli Kanık and Ece Ayhan. He is also the editor of a critical anthology entitled *Eda: An Anthology of Contemporary Turkish Poetry* (Jersey City, N.J.: Talisman House, 2004), which includes many of his translations. His play entitled *Parakeet* was produced in New York City in 1980.—TSH

Characters

ŞEYHÜLİSLÂM, chief religious dignitary

KARA MUSTAFA PASHA, a grand vizier

MINISTERS

SULTAN İBRAHİM

KÖSEM SULTAN, İbrahim's mother

HEAD OF THE HAREM

STEWARDS

PALACE OFFICIALS

ATTENDANTS

JANISSARIES[2]

MILITARY BAND

SOLDIERS

SİLÂHTAR YUSUF AĞA,[3] personal bodyguard of the sultan; later YUSUF PASHA, army commander

MUSTAFA AĞA, Janissary commander in chief

MUSLİHİDDİN AĞA, a Janissary commander

KARA MURAD AĞA, a Janissary commander

BEKTAŞ AĞA, a Janissary commander

KEEPER OF THE GATE OF FELICITY

STREET CRIER

FOUR INHABITANTS OF ISTANBUL

CONCUBINES

TURHAN, a harem girl; later TURHAN SULTAN, the sultan's first wife

HOBYAR

CİNCİ HOCA, an exorcist

COURTIERS

HÜMAŞAH, a concubine; later HÜMAŞAH SULTAN

DİLÂŞUB, a concubine

CHIEF GARDENER (CHIEF EXECUTIONER)

---

2. Janissaries: Elite corps of Ottoman infantry units organized in the fourteenth century and abolished in 1826. Some of the janissary units served as the sultan's household troops and bodyguards.

3. *Ağa*: A palace title similar to "lord in waiting"; also used as a title for a person in a position of authority or for a commander.

JESTER IN CHIEF

MEHMED PASHA, a grand vizier

KARA ALİ, executioner

HAMAL ALİ, Kara Ali's aide

ACT I

Scene 1

[*Morning. Topkapı Palace. The Ottoman throne in front of the Gate of Felicity. The* ŞEYHÜLİSLÂM, GRAND VIZIER KARA MUSTAFA PASHA, *and the other* MINISTERS *are waiting. Noises are suddenly heard from the left. The people on stage, amazed, concerned, and worried, look in that direction.* SULTAN İBRAHİM *is dragged in by his mother,* KÖSEM SULTAN; *the* HEAD OF THE HAREM; *a* STEWARD *of the palace; and a few other* PALACE OFFICIALS.]

SULTAN İBRAHİM:

I do not want it, I say! I do not want it, I don't, I don't!

You are playing tricks on me, trapping me.

What shall I do with the throne? Let my brother have a long life.

KÖSEM SULTAN:

Which of your brothers, my dear son?

You just saw your brother's corpse inside.

Didn't you just lift the cover from his face and look?

Go and look again if you will.

SULTAN İBRAHİM:

[*Goes out running and soon returns.*]

Yes, but what if he isn't really dead?

KÖSEM SULTAN:

My son, my dearest İbrahim,

You are the only son I have left in this world,

You are the one who can claim this throne.

SULTAN İBRAHİM:

They had taken my other brothers, too, in this way.

They had taken them out by tricks from their princely rooms;

None of them has ever returned.

KÖSEM SULTAN:

My İbrahim, my royal son, pull yourself together.

I gave you life; tell me, if their intentions were bad,

Would they have sent me to you like that?

Would they have chosen me as your death trap?

You know how ruthless your brother was;

He would not have used sly methods like that.

He would have consigned you to the hangman's hand.

That would have been your end.

SULTAN İBRAHİM:

Impossible. I do not want it. My black dungeon is enough for me.

KÖSEM SULTAN:

[*Very upset, anxious that the* MINISTERS *may see her son in this condition. To the* GRAND VIZIER.]

Grand Vizier, how about your having a talk with the sultan?

[*As the* GRAND VIZIER *moves a bit forward and bows with respect,* İBRAHİM *jumps back, frightened by the* VIZIER's *majesty.*]

SULTAN İBRAHİM:

But you had told me he was dead! You are lying:

It was not the corpse of my brother you showed me!

KÖSEM SULTAN:

This is your mentor, my child, your grand vizier.

He will carry your seal from now on.

He will rule, in your name, the Ottoman Empire.

KARA MUSTAFA PASHA:

Your stately brother, Sultan Murad, has passed into eternity;

May you live long; the throne and sultanate are yours.

May your sovereignty be blissful.

SULTAN İBRAHİM:

[*Seemingly dizzy; his eyes disturbed by the light, he covers them with his hands.*]

May both the throne and sultanate be yours!

Take me to my cell.

KÖSEM SULTAN:

[*Angrily.*]

All right, then, return to your dungeon! Return

And let this glorious throne be vacant!

Let the age-old Ottoman dynasty end! Because of bandits

Vying for the throne, let turmoil reign among the people,

Let the empire fall apart. And you rot in your dark dungeon!

Of course, if the new owners of the throne let you live.

[SULTAN İBRAHİM *looks once in the direction of the throne and once in the direction of the door from which he has entered. He suddenly nods his head in consent.*]

[*Relieved,* KÖSEM SULTAN *to the* GRAND VIZIER.]
I will take the sultan to be dressed quickly.
Pasha, let the ceremonies be prepared.

[*The* GRAND VIZIER *salutes, bowing. As* İBRAHİM, KÖSEM, *and her* ATTENDANTS *leave, the* GRAND VIZIER *looks for a moment with worry and suspicion at the other* MINIS- TERS. *The* GRAND VIZIER, *the* ŞEYHÜLİSLÂM, *and the other* MINISTERS *are confused and preoccupied.*]

KARA MUSTAFA PASHA:

[*To himself.*]
You, poor, dead Sultan Murad. Your presence filled
Not only this small armchair, but the whole empire.
May you rest in Heaven.

ŞEYHÜLİSLÂM:

How can one afraid of the throne sit on the throne?
Also, in our religion, a child of sound mind
May reign, but a mature man
Of unbalanced mind is not entitled to claim that right.

KARA MUSTAFA PASHA:

What you say is true, my dear sir;
The manners of the new sovereign have us worried, too.
Luckily, the commanders were not here.
A soldier demands a sovereign who is master of his throne.
But in fact we are in no position to make a choice;
Good or bad, we must have a head;
Otherwise, this huge body will disintegrate.
Sultan İbrahim is the sole heir; that is,
He became sultan against his will; and
Against our will, we have to accept him as sultan.

ŞEYHÜLİSLÂM:

Let me hope it will be good for the country. God willing,
You won't make us miss Sultan Murad;
You should assist the new sultan in all his steps;
You should, with authority, pull the strings of state.
After all, you have served as the grand vizier
Of the great ruler, Sultan Murad.

[*The other* MINISTERS *nod their approval.*]

KARA MUSTAFA PASHA:

You are kind, my lord.

We must get ready for the ceremony.

The sultan will be here soon.

[*Exits to supervise the ceremony.*]

MINISTERS:

[*Draw together and speak in low voices.*]

—How he shied away from the grand vizier!

—The sultan will never forget this.

—To have such majesty is not always very good.

—Mighty trees draw lightning.

—Seeing that the sultan is weak, the grand vizier will get ideas.

—He won't be able to restrain his ego.

—The sultan will more and more be crushed under the grand vizier's majesty.

—The grand vizier will almost see himself as the sultan.

—But there is the mother of the sultan.

—She will remind her son of his imperial position.

[*As the* GRAND VIZIER *reenters, they hush. They withdraw to a corner and wait. In front of the throne the* JANISSARIES *and on either side of the throne the queen's* ATTENDANTS *and the* OTHER ATTENDANTS *of the court take their places. The Gate of Felicity slowly opens. With a plumed turban on his head and with timid gestures,* SULTAN İBRAHİM *enters.*]

SULTAN İBRAHİM:

[*Stands in front of the throne, raising his arms in the air.*]

O God Almighty! You saw your humble servant fit to be sultan. I desire that no one be hurt during my rule; may my people be happy with me, and I with my people. If I am unjust, if I spread misfortune through my land, let me be punished. Let me be cursed quickly, my Lord!

[*All in attendance, in particular the* MINISTERS, *are amazed and pleased, as though they are ashamed of their previous concerns. As* İBRAHİM *sits on the throne, the* MILITARY BAND *begins to play. The* SOLDIERS *cheer and applaud, "Peace, and let God's will be done." The* HEAD OF THE HAREM *stands on the right side, and the sultan's personal bodyguard,* SİLÂHTAR YUSUF AĞA, *stands on the left side of the throne. They have vowed their allegiance to the sultan beforehand, inside. Two* STEWARDS *of the palace come toward the* MINISTERS, *and, tapping their scepters on the floor, they beckon them to the ceremony. The* GRAND VIZIER *advances first and salutes, prostrating himself to the ground.* İBRAHİM *gets up, and the* SOLDIERS *and the* ATTENDANTS *of the court applaud again with the words, "Long live the sultan!" This time and during each subsequent applause,* İBRAHİM *cringes. Kneeling, the* GRAND VIZIER *kisses both feet of the* SULTAN *and then, passing to the right of the throne, stands in front of the* HEAD OF THE HAREM. *After him, the other* MINISTERS *come up, pledge their allegiance, and step back*] to their former places. İBRAHİM *gets up each time and is applauded with the words,* "Long live the sultan!" *Then the* ŞEYHÜLİSLÂM *comes up, pays his respects with slight bows, and kisses the* SULTAN *on the collar and the shoulder.* İBRAHİM *is again startled. The* ŞEYHÜLİSLÂM *walks a few steps back, recites a prayer, and exits. The* JANISSARY COMMANDERS *pledge their allegiance next.*]

ALL TOGETHER:

[*To the* SULTAN.] Let your luck be abundant! Let your life be long! Let your road be open! Do not be too proud in your rule, our sultan! God is greater than you.[4]

[İBRAHİM *descends from the throne accompanied by the cheer,* "Long live the sultan!" *The* GRAND VIZIER *takes his right arm and the* KEEPER OF THE GATE OF FELICITY *his left. They take a few steps, but, near the gate, leaving the right arm of the* SULTAN *to the* HEAD OF THE HAREM, *the* GRAND VIZIER *whispers something into* İBRAHİM's *ear and steps back.*]

SULTAN İBRAHİM:

[*In a low voice.*] I grant double pay and promotions to my soldiers. Let it be done!

KARA MUSTAFA PASHA:

[*In a high and powerful voice because the* SOLDIERS *have not heard these words.*] I grant double pay and promotions to my soldiers. Let it be done!

[*Aware of the difference between the voices of the* SULTAN *and the* GRAND VIZIER, *the* MINISTERS *look at each other. Then* İBRAHİM *leaves by the Gate of Felicity with his* ATTENDANTS. *The others exit slowly, and in an orderly fashion.*]

Scene 2

[*Toward noon. A* STREET CRIER's *voice is heard:* "The realm and sovereignty are Sultan İbrahim's! The realm and sovereignty are Sultan İbrahim's!" *From the right and left,* INHABITANTS OF ISTANBUL *slowly enter the stage; they gather together timidly. Distant echoes of the* CRIER's *voice are heard.*]

FIRST INHABITANT:

The realm and sovereignty are Sultan İbrahim's!
Thank God! That nightmare called Sultan Murad
Has lifted from our heads. Congratulations, fellow citizens.

SECOND INHABITANT:

Even two or three of us could not come together;
He left neither coffeehouse nor tavern in the land;

4. It was customary in the Ottoman state for the crowd, including common people, at some ceremonies or on certain occasions to remind the sultan that he did not have holy status and that God was always greater than the sultan.

Tobacco and liquor were banned.

THIRD INHABITANT:

Don't talk like that. Sultan Murad was a great ruler.

If he had not used stern measures, had not flown

Like a keen-eyed eagle over our heads,

How could he have saved the land from chaos?

How could he have finished off the bandits?

FOURTH INHABITANT:

It's true. If the head cannot assert its will,

No one can tell where the legs will go.

The new sultan seems to be good and even tempered.

I hope chaos will not find its chance to rise again.

FIRST INHABITANT:

Yes. The people can't be let loose,

Or everyone will run wild!

But too much pressure also stifles the people.

From time to time, the devil also must receive his due.

FOURTH INHABITANT:

[*To the* THIRD INHABITANT.]

You restaurant owners are in good shape now!

Now that the fear of Sultan Murad has lifted from your heads

You can sell meat and rice at the price you wish.

THIRD INHABITANT:

You think of the wool you'll pull over our eyes at your coffeehouse!

How many times were you cheated at my place, tell me?

You used to eat forty pieces of fried liver for one asper;

You will still do so.

You used to eat a hundred pieces of broken rice for the same;

You will still do so.

FOURTH INHABITANT:

If you give thirty-five pieces instead of forty, who will count?

If you count ninety pieces instead of a hundred, who will be any wiser?

THIRD INHABITANT:

Shame, shame! There is God above us, what will He say?

FIRST INHABITANT:

[*Laughing.*]

Yes, but you live on earth.

There is the devil in you, what about that?

[*They all laugh.*]

SECOND INHABITANT:

> I hear that the new sultan has said:
> "I wish that my subjects will be happy with me,
> That no one gets hurt in my land." Strange thing . . .
> No sultan has ever talked like this before,
> None has ever considered his subjects.
> Do you have any tobacco?

THIRD INHABITANT:

> You see. The happiness of the subjects has already started.

SECOND INHABITANT:

> [*Rolls with pleasure the tobacco he has received from the* FIRST INHABITANT.]
> But they say the new sultan is a bit . . . strange.
>
> [*The others turn to him, doubtful of his meaning.*]
> This is the way the world turns. Some lose their heads
> Trying to be sultan, and some must be dragged
> Onto the throne.

FOURTH INHABITANT:

> The day is rising for his mother, Kösem Sultan.
> Her other son, Sultan Murad, did not want his throne shared.
> Consequently, for a while, she could not call the tune.

THIRD INHABITANT:

> After a bird of prey like Sultan Murad,
> A turtledove like Sultan İbrahim.

FIRST INHABITANT:

> After all, who cares? The wheels of fortune keep turning.
> Murad or İbrahim, Ali or Veli!
> As long as someone rules us,
> Let him be a wise man or a lunatic!

ALL INHABITANTS:

> Let him be a wise man or a lunatic!

Scene 3

[*Topkapı Palace.* KÖSEM SULTAN'*s chamber. Night.*]

KÖSEM SULTAN:

> You made me suffer a lot, Murad, you made me suffer a lot!
> Still, may you rest in Heaven! I bore you, after all.
> You also were part of my flesh. Suddenly, you grew up,
> Pushed me aside; no one heeded my words.

I, Kösem, who had shared power in so many sultanates,
Became a sort of retired concubine.
To be pushed aside like that, to be kept away from power,
For me it was like being buried alive. May you
Rest in Heaven; your death
Has been a new birth to me—and to İbrahim.
You were almost going to kill him, too, the only heir to the throne;
How much I had to struggle to keep him from your hands.
Poor boy, how he is used to his dungeon.
His eyes were shying away from the light. It was not good
That the ministers saw him in that state, particularly the grand vizier!
How they whispered among themselves!
The pasha is a man who can mold what he grips,
A strong man. What if he covets the throne
Or obtains an edict from the *şeyhülislâm*
That the sultan is mad and unfit
To sit on the throne? What if he ends the dynasty?
One must do something before it's too late.
We must comb the entire harem, the entire empire, if necessary,
From the Atlantic Sea to the Indian Ocean,
From the Russian steppes to the Abyssinian plateau,
The entire Ottoman Empire, to graft
At once the seed of the new sultan.
Why is this girl not back yet? All the others came back empty-handed.
I hope this one is more able. If she can but stir İbrahim's blood . . .
Oh God, how long this has been!

[*Listens to footsteps.*]
Is she coming? If she can but make us smile.

[*A* CONCUBINE *enters;* KÖSEM *runs toward her, yet when the* CONCUBINE *bows her head guiltily . . .*]
Have you not been able to untie the knot either?
And you call yourself a woman! You eat the bread of this throne,
Your happiness depends on this throne,
But you cannot please the first man of the dynasty.
[*Motions to her to leave; the* CONCUBINE *leaves.*]
Perhaps the child is under the spell of an angry witch.
Have they tied his manhood with charms?

[*A noise is heard at the door.*]

Who is it? I say, who is it? Heavens!

[*Walks toward the door.* IBRAHİM *enters slowly, panting.*]

Is it you, my dear child? My lion!

What is wrong with you, İbrahim? Come and sit with me.

SULTAN İBRAHİM:

I am getting smothered, Mother, I am being suffocated,

As though an iron claw is tightening in my breast,

Making the whole world small for me. I am dying.

[*Cries. Puts his head on the shoulder of his* MOTHER, *sitting next to him.*]

KÖSEM SULTAN:

[*Caresses his head.*]

Do not worry, İbrahim. You are

The mightiest ruler in this world.

No one in your empire can ignore your will.

SULTAN İBRAHİM:

Mother, what good is sovereignty to me?

What is the use of countries, continents to me,

If I cannot breathe easily, if I gasp for breath?

All my roads opening outward are blocked.

This air enjoyed by wolf and bird alike

I cannot inhale.

I cry so much at night my eyes bulge.

KÖSEM SULTAN:

Tomorrow let all the palace doctors come together

And try to understand the root of your trouble.

SULTAN İBRAHİM:

I called for a few doctors this afternoon;

No one could tell me anything definite.

As each of them played a different tune, my distress got worse.

KÖSEM SULTAN:

[*Sounds him out, but tries not to scare him.*]

There are many beautiful women in your harem, my son,

Why don't you play with them a bit?

If you do not like them, one can find others,

Tawny Arab girls, fair-haired, sky-eyed Russian

And German concubines, thin-waisted Circassian maidens . . .

Which kind do you lack in your harem?

I expect healthy princes, sultans from you, my lion;

Soon our walls will ring with sounds of cradles.

SULTAN İBRAHİM:

[*Ashamed and hopeless.*]

But, Mother . . . but . . .

KÖSEM SULTAN:

[*Concerned and anxious.*]

My child, didn't any of the girls cheer you up tonight?

SULTAN İBRAHİM:

[*Straightening up angrily.*]

Mother! Mother!

[*Walks out hastily, panting.*]

KÖSEM SULTAN:

My poor İbrahim.

My last words hurt his pride. He is ashamed.

Since the work of physicians is of no use,

We shall try other means.

[*Claps her hands. A harem girl,* TURHAN, *enters.*]

Come over close to me, my child.

[*Examines the girl closely, as if she is seeing her for the first time.*]

Hmm. All right, Turhan. Go and ask the sultan's bodyguard to come to me.

Then go to sleep. It is late.

TURHAN:

[*Tries to appear as attractive and coquettish as possible.*]

Yes, my queen. Let me relay your wish.

But let me wait on you till you sleep, if I may.

KÖSEM SULTAN:

[*Smiles.*]

No, no need. It is late. Go to sleep.

[TURHAN *exits.*]

Devilish girl, how she understood my purpose.

She began to move in a new way as she saw

That I watched her for the sultan. Ah, I wish it were true.

I wish you could untie the knot in the boy,

And become the first wife of the sultan.

There are hundreds of women in his palace,

Each more beautiful than the other, all dying

To enter his arms, yet the poor boy can leave his seed

In no one. He is the sultan,

But still not rid of his jail; that black dungeon

Has embraced his soul like armor.

I wonder which woman will melt down

His thick crust with the flames of her thighs.

[SİLÂHTAR YUSUF AĞA, *the sultan's personal bodyguard, enters.*]

Come here, Yusuf, come. Where have you been?

SİLÂHTAR YUSUF:

Please, tell me your desire, my lady. I pray for your health.

KÖSEM SULTAN:

I troubled you in the middle of the night.

SİLÂHTAR YUSUF:

Not at all, my lady. For your subject Yusuf,

Living is serving you.

KÖSEM SULTAN:

The problem is great, Yusuf Ağa, great.

SİLÂHTAR YUSUF:

What is it, my lady? Is there untimely news?

Has anything happened against your wish?

KÖSEM SULTAN:

Yes, indeed, it has. The sultan is in distress!

Haven't you sensed anything?

SİLÂHTAR YUSUF:

Yes, he seems depressed. He is almost stifled

When he breathes. And sometimes

He loses himself, staring at unseen things.

If I call him gently, "My sultan," he jumps

Like a bird that has just noticed a hawk.

KÖSEM SULTAN:

He was here, just now.

SİLÂHTAR YUSUF:

Who, the sultan?

KÖSEM SULTAN:

Yes.

SİLÂHTAR YUSUF:

Why did he visit your chamber so late?

KÖSEM SULTAN:

Poor child, his head on my shoulder, how he cried, my İbrahim.

I want to say, "Oh, Murad, may you not rest in your grave!" but I can't.

Finally, it hurts me.

Yusuf Ağa, let us find a remedy, a remedy!

Let us not wait with our hands tied like this;

A sultan should not go to waste

At the head of such a limitless empire.

SİLÂHTAR YUSUF:

I am ready to serve you, my lady.

Both you and my sultan.

KÖSEM SULTAN:

The work of the doctors has been in vain, Yusuf Ağa.

But this does not mean that there are no other remedies

Outside the limited knowledge of doctors.

I want exorcists with sharp breath, men of mystery, to be found.

One of them will I hope find a cure.

SİLÂHTAR YUSUF:

Starting tomorrow, I shall mobilize the whole palace

For this purpose. I shall comb the capital;

From east to west, from north to south, I shall comb all the cities

Of the empire—Kayseri, Erzurum,[5] Baghdad,

Buda, Belgrade, Cairo, Algiers.

If any shelters a soul who knows the cure,

My lady, one way or another, I shall have him tracked down.

KÖSEM SULTAN:

Thank you, Yusuf Ağa. With your words

The bud of hope has sprouted in my heart

And its flowering depends on you!

My request from you now . . .

SİLÂHTAR YUSUF:

Your command, my lady?

KÖSEM SULTAN:

Listen to me, Ağa! You are the closest person to İbrahim.

He calls you "my Yusuf."

He calls you "the guardian of his sleepless nights."

He says, "Talking to Yusuf is an inexhaustible pleasure."

SİLÂHTAR YUSUF:

What bliss your words are to me, my queen.

I wish I could find a remedy for his ills.

KÖSEM SULTAN:

Just now he left this place as if obsessed by demons.

He must have been angry at my questions.

---

5. Kayseri and Erzurum: Cities in eastern Anatolia.

SİLÂHTAR YUSUF:

What did you ask him, my lady?

KÖSEM SULTAN:

[*As though confiding a secret.*]

You are no stranger, Yusuf Ağa. To keep this from you

May block the way to the solution. He has not touched

Any of the concubines I sent him.

You are close to him, his peer. Why don't you sound him out?

I may be his mother, but I am, after all, a woman. He may be embarrassed.

Why don't you talk to him?

He may talk to you. Do this for us, Yusuf Ağa,

Let my İbrahim not stay alone tonight.

The sultan will not let your efforts go unrewarded.

SİLÂHTAR YUSUF:

My life is dedicated to serving my lord.

Both my lord and you.

KÖSEM SULTAN:

Thank you, Yusuf Ağa. I wish you well. Good-bye.

Thanks to you, I shall get some sleep tonight.

Scene 4

[*Morning. The* INHABITANTS OF ISTANBUL.]

THIRD INHABITANT:

I saw a wench from the palace this morning;

She asked me for the house of Molla[6] Hüseyin.

She looked worried, as though the world would come to an end

If she did not find the house of our exorcist.

SECOND INHABITANT:

In every street somebody from the palace is asking for some

Hoca's name. I wonder if Sultan İbrahim has pledged himself to God

And wants to open new symposia on faith with wise gentlemen?

FIRST INHABITANT:

It always works like this: the one who can't

Grasp what he sees, clings to unseen things.

What a place our world is. What is the use of ruling the whole world,

If you can't rule a woman . . . ?

6. *Molla*: High-level religious teacher; frequently anglicized as *mullah*.

FOURTH INHABITANT:

> Watch your language. Do you want to cast a shadow
>
> On the limitless authority of our great ruler?
>
> All you do is steer to the fearsome
>
> Waters of evil, while the clear waters of goodness
>
> Stand before you.

FIRST INHABITANT:

> In those waters you are talking of only
>
> Simple ducklings swim. If you use your mind a little bit,
>
> What kinds of mysteries you may unravel.
>
> Your heart may expand with so many pleasures.

> [*The* THIRD *and* FOURTH INHABITANTS *stare at him without comprehending.*]

SECOND INHABITANT:

> [*Laughs.*]
>
> They say that Sultan İbrahim is very low.
>
> Neither hunting nor orgies on the Bosphorus nor concubines
>
> Nor maidens—nothing seems to lighten his depressed heart.
>
> He seems to travel from one chamber to another,
>
> All that huge palace just too small for him.

FIRST INHABITANT:

> [*Slyly.*]
>
> Of course it is too small. For such a man,
>
> The whole world, not only the palace, is too small.
>
> Black clouds hang constantly in his sky.
>
> They say Kösem is very alarmed.

THIRD and FOURTH INHABITANTS:

> Why?

FIRST INHABITANT:

> Kösem is constantly scolding the concubines, giving them
>
> A hard time, but if the cock does not crow with majesty among the hens,
>
> How can the hens sparkle with light?

Scene 5

[*Toward noon. Topkapı Palace.* SULTAN İBRAHİM's *private chamber. The* SULTAN *is preoccupied and walking back and forth. He tries to take deep breaths; from time to time, his hand goes to his back, which is in pain.*]

SİLÂHTAR YUSUF:

> [*Enters and bows.*]

May your day be light and happy, my lordship.

SULTAN İBRAHİM:

[*Turns back, startled.*]

Is it you, Yusuf? I am glad you have come.

Once again, my heart was very heavy

After you left last night.

SİLÂHTAR YUSUF:

I wish I had stayed longer with you, my lord.

SULTAN İBRAHİM:

How can I let you do it, Yusuf? Should your life be spent

Waiting on my insomnia? Is that fair to you?

I am all gloomy inside.

SİLÂHTAR YUSUF:

I wish I had a thousand lives to burn

To light your soul.

SULTAN İBRAHİM:

Thank you, Yusuf. Your love is the

Richest jewel in my treasury.

SİLÂHTAR YUSUF:

My lord is drowning me with honor

And happiness.

SULTAN İBRAHİM:

Any news from the ministers?

What is the grand vizier doing?

SİLÂHTAR YUSUF:

There is a message from him.

SULTAN İBRAHİM:

What does he request?

SİLÂHTAR YUSUF:

The pasha says: [*Reads the communiqué.*] "For a long time, we have been unable to look at the blessed face of the sultan. The ministers worry deeply over his health. Would it please the honor of his majesty to show himself today before us, his subjects? There are deep problems needing solutions, awaiting his lordship's decisions. If his majesty does not wish to appear even today, let me prostrate myself right away before his blessed presence."

SULTAN İBRAHİM:

Yusuf, please go to the pasha and

Let him know I don't feel well.

Even today I do not wish to appear before the chamber.

Let him please come here, so we can discuss the problems.

SİLÂHTAR YUSUF:

Would you care to write it on one side of the communiqué, my lord?

SULTAN İBRAHİM:

Write it? Oh, yes! To the grand vizier's communiqué

The sultan responds in the imperial script.

This is the palace protocol,

Isn't it, Yusuf?

[*They laugh. Reading aloud,* İBRAHİM *writes.*]

"My dear tutor, I have received your communiqué. Your concern over my health has brought me joy. Not feeling well today, I will not be able to come to the ministers' chamber. I implore you, come to my private chamber so that we can discuss those deep problems waiting for solutions; and, perhaps together we can find out the way of destroying that madness oppressing my heart more and more, that monster feeding on my blood. Master, do not fail me."

[*Gives the message to* YUSUF AĞA. *At that moment,* KÖSEM *enters majestically.*]

KÖSEM SULTAN:

Give me that communiqué, Yusuf Ağa.

[SİLÂHTAR YUSUF *gives the communiqué to* KÖSEM.]

My child, you are the sultan. You cannot plead,

You can just order. The grand vizier is your servant;

You must return his wishes with your orders.

You call for him, and he will come. Take this letter,

Change all the "you's" into "thou's"

And replace "implore" with just "come."

SULTAN İBRAHİM:

[*Annoyed, but being afraid of his* MOTHER, *can say nothing. Revises the text and gives it formally to* SİLÂHTAR YUSUF AĞA.]

Silâhtar Yusuf Ağa,

I am waiting for the grand vizier here.

[SİLÂHTAR YUSUF *exits.*]

KÖSEM SULTAN:

[*Mildly.*]

Have I made you unhappy, my sovereign child?

Yusuf is your bodyguard; he is, night and day, with you.

With him you do not have to be formal;

With him you can talk freely. But . . .

SULTAN İBRAHİM:

Yes, but?

KÖSEM SULTAN:

But the grand vizier is different. He carries your seal;

He governs the whole empire.

The whole might of the state is in his hands.

Never let him forget that you are the sovereign.

I have lived through many sultanates;

Your ancestors never let a grand vizier shine more than necessary.

They jealously kept their authority from others.

SULTAN İBRAHİM:

Did they keep it from their mothers, too?

KÖSEM SULTAN:

[*Upset.*]

From their mothers, too, but . . .

SULTAN İBRAHİM:

But?

KÖSEM SULTAN:

When it becomes necessary . . .

SULTAN İBRAHİM:

Then they do not keep their authority from their mothers.

Is that it, Queen Mother?

KÖSEM SULTAN:

[*Alarmed because* İBRAHİM *calls her "Queen Mother" instead of "Mother."*]

Should my pain go in vain?

How I suffered to save you from your brother's rage!

Can I ever leave you, my child, to fly with your own wings?

SULTAN İBRAHİM:

[*To himself.*]

Until I learn how to fly with my own wings.

[*Regretting having taken a wrong step,* KÖSEM *looks at* İBRAHİM *with anxiety. Just then* KARA MUSTAFA PASHA *enters and prostrates himself before the* SULTAN. *Bending down right away,* İBRAHİM *lifts the* GRAND VIZIER, *then guiltily looks at* KÖSEM.]

Welcome, dear mentor. How are you?

KARA MUSTAFA PASHA:

Having seen your face, my lord,

I am happier.

SULTAN İBRAHİM:

[*Ill at ease, he looks toward his* MOTHER.]

Master, for many nights, I have not been able
To close my eyes.

[Because İBRAHİM *looks at* KÖSEM *on and off,* KÖSEM *leaves.*]

I am being tortured in the grip of an unspeakable pain,
As though a thick cloud is rising from my head,
Cold sleet is falling within me.
There are days I am torn, separated
From my body. As though these arms, these legs
Are not mine. I am like an island floating
In the void.

KARA MUSTAFA PASHA:

My lord,
If you could put your body to work a little,
To get it tired.
Exclusively used, the brain exploits
The body, weakens its core. Then,
The body takes bitter revenge on the soul.

SULTAN İBRAHİM:

As far as work is concerned,
Dear mentor, my body is tired enough.
Why should I tire it more?

KARA MUSTAFA PASHA:

That tiredness derives from not working, my lord;
It cannot rest; that is why it is dangerous.
If the muscles can work to their hearts' content,
They can also rest to their hearts' content
And renew the body.

SULTAN İBRAHİM:

What you say makes good sense, my dear teacher.
I feel better listening to you.
What kind of work do you advise?

KARA MUSTAFA PASHA:

What shall I say? For example, dueling,
Javelin throwing, mace wielding, riding,
Bow bending, especially bow bending . . .
Then, one day,
Like your brother, you will take command of the army,
Start new campaigns, expand the empire.

The souls of your warrior ancestors may then rest in Heaven.

When the sultan leads them, the soldiers fight differently.

SULTAN İBRAHİM:

My life has passed in a dark dungeon;

My hand has felt no hilt up to now;

I cannot make myself the laughingstock of the soldiers.

Such a move would be ruinous for me.

KARA MUSTAFA PASHA:

Through trying, even the toughest crust can be cracked, my lord.

SULTAN İBRAHİM:

[*Examines the* GRAND VIZIER *with admiration.*]

I have heard that you are very masterful at archery—

The famous archer of Sultan Murad,

Kara Mustafa Pasha.

KARA MUSTAFA PASHA:

May he rest in Heaven!

Your brother did love me.

SULTAN İBRAHİM:

We also love you, Tutor.

KARA MUSTAFA PASHA:

Your love gives me life, my lord.

SULTAN İBRAHİM:

I wish it so, Teacher.

KARA MUSTAFA PASHA:

With which one shall we start, my lord?

SULTAN İBRAHİM:

[*Preoccupied.*]

Start what, Master?

KARA MUSTAFA PASHA:

The review of state affairs.

SULTAN İBRAHİM:

With whichever one you wish.

KARA MUSTAFA PASHA:

First, the borders . . .

SULTAN İBRAHİM:

Master!

KARA MUSTAFA PASHA:

My lord?

SULTAN İBRAHİM:

I saw my mother in my dream last night.

KARA MUSTAFA PASHA:

>   [*A bit irritated, but respectful.*]

>   I hope it's a good omen, my lord.

SULTAN İBRAHİM:

>   [*Reliving the dream.*]

>   My mother put a thick, heavy coat on me,

>   Which I just can't carry; I am smothered in it.

>   I want to breathe again by slipping out of the coat,

>   But my mother will not let me. Each time I attempt

>   To take it off, she makes me wear it again.

>   She puts her arms around me, keeps kissing me.

>   I feel I am drowning. I push her far away from me,

>   But she comes back.

>   I woke up last night in a cold sweat.

KARA MUSTAFA PASHA:

>   Your mother loves you very much, my lord.

>   The borders . . .

SULTAN İBRAHİM:

>   Yes! The borders . . .

KARA MUSTAFA PASHA:

>   The Venetians have been seen carrying on

>   Suspicious activities at Klis. Precautions are necessary.

SULTAN İBRAHİM:

>   Is Kilis not in Anatolia, Tutor?

>   What are the Venetian infidels doing there?

KARA MUSTAFA PASHA:

>   That is Kilis, my lord; this is Klis.

SULTAN İBRAHİM:

>   My bodyguard Yusuf does not like the Venetians at all.

>   Always he tells me, "Let's teach them a lesson

>   At the first opportunity." Let me tell him when he comes in a little while,

>   "It is time for me to take care of your Venetian infidels,

>   Yusuf. Congratulations."

>   What do you say to that, Mentor? Shall we send an army against them?

>   [*The* GRAND VIZIER *frowns.*]

>   Why are you frowning, Mentor? Have I done something wrong?

KARA MUSTAFA PASHA:

>   My lord, one cannot gratuitously send an army

>   To please a bodyguard.

>   Besides, these matters must be discussed between you and me.

SULTAN İBRAHİM:

> I hold my bodyguard very dear to me, Master;
>
> I would like you to love Yusuf, too.

KARA MUSTAFA PASHA:

> Love your bodyguard, my lord; love him as much as you wish,
>
> But that is one thing and this another. Your brother,
>
> Let him rest in Paradise, had asked me one day, "Mentor, you have offended
>
> My bodyguard. You have not included him in any state matters.
>
> Why is that?" And I . . .

SULTAN İBRAHİM:

> [*Curiously.*]
>
> Yes? What did you say to him, Mentor?

KARA MUSTAFA PASHA:

> I said to him: "My sovereign lord,
>
> First, tell your humble servant, is your bodyguard
>
> Partner to your throne, or is he not? If he is,
>
> Then you are right. My neck is thinner
>
> Than a thread before your will. If he is not, then these matters
>
> Must be discussed between you and me."

SULTAN İBRAHİM:

> [*Amazed and filled with admiration.*]
>
> Did you tell my brother all this, Master?

KARA MUSTAFA PASHA:

> Yes, my lord.

SULTAN İBRAHİM:

> But my mother, this morning,
>
> Told me, "No Ottoman sultan
>
> Has let his grand vizier shine more than necessary."
>
> [*The GRAND VIZIER is annoyed.*]
>
> You are sullen, Mentor. Are you angry with me, possibly?

KARA MUSTAFA PASHA:

> You are the sovereign, my lord.
>
> How dare a servant get angry with his master?

SULTAN İBRAHİM:

> Mentor!

KARA MUSTAFA PASHA:

> My lord?

SULTAN İBRAHİM:

> Why was my mother clinging with such fury to my neck,
>
> Choking me with her kisses?

KARA MUSTAFA PASHA:

> Apparently, your mother loves you a great deal, my lord,
>
> A bit more than necessary. Now for the Persian border . . .

SULTAN İBRAHİM:

> Do they also have evil designs against us, Mentor?

KARA MUSTAFA PASHA:

> My lord, among nations good intentions can only be a trap.
>
> We must always be alert against Persia.
>
> We must keep great armies in the East
>
> To preserve the Kasr-ı Şirin Agreement.[7]

SULTAN İBRAHİM:

> [*Impatient now that his interest is spent.*]
>
> Mentor, you do as you see fit.

KARA MUSTAFA PASHA:

> And also there is a Persian called Yusuf Khan.
>
> He was the confidant of Sultan Murad.
>
> He found young boys, wine bearers for the late sovereign.
>
> Addicting him to pleasure, he led him to destruction.
>
> He is an immeasurably corrupt man.
>
> We heard that he has been arrested escaping to Persia. Who knows
>
> What sorts of plots he would have hatched against us there.

SULTAN İBRAHİM:

> What do you think we should do, Master?

KARA MUSTAFA PASHA:

> [*Makes the sign for execution.*]
>
> Let him be disposed of, my lord, if you so decree.

SULTAN İBRAHİM:

> [*Repeats the sign for execution.*]
>
> Let him be disposed of.

KARA MUSTAFA PASHA:

> We must change the amount of silver in our coins.

SULTAN İBRAHİM:

> Let it be changed, Mentor. Each sultan has
>
> New coins minted for himself.
>
> When will mine be minted?

KARA MUSTAFA PASHA:

> At the first suitable opportunity, my lord.

---

7. Kasr-ı Şirin Agreement: Treaty signed in 1639 by Murad IV with the Persians confirming that Iraq would be under Ottoman control and that Erivan and parts of the Caucasus would be left to Iran.

SULTAN İBRAHİM:

> I would like it done as soon as possible, Pasha.

KARA MUSTAFA PASHA:

> [*This slight change in* IBRAHIM *has attracted his attention.*]
>
> As you will, my lord.

SULTAN İBRAHİM:

> Let's govern this state in the best way possible,
> Pasha, so my people will say,
> "What a sovereign this is, what a grand vizier."
> If someone intends to split my land,
> Sow rebellion among my subjects, let him
> Be hanged.
> [*Gets more and more excited.*]
> Let living in my land be like breathing easily.
> Bandits and muggers be wiped out.
> Cruel people meet a most terrible cruelty.
> If anyone unjustly makes others live in terror,
> Let him taste the same terror a hundredfold.

KARA MUSTAFA PASHA:

> [*In amazement.*]
>
> My sovereign's blessed wish shall be carried out.

SULTAN İBRAHİM:

> [*Tired and preoccupied.*]
>
> The dark birds of sadness . . .

KARA MUSTAFA PASHA:

> [*Worried.*]
>
> Are you not feeling well, my lord?

SULTAN İBRAHİM:

> [*Absentmindedly.*]
>
> The dark birds of sadness flit before my eyes
> Clouding the sky.
> —Why don't you toil a bit for me, too, Teacher?
> You who are my grand vizier and carry my seal.

KARA MUSTAFA PASHA:

> My life is pledged to my sultan, my lord.
> Have you consulted the chief physician, my emperor?

SULTAN İBRAHİM:

> So many times, Mentor! No use. They are looking now
> For exorcists with sharp breath.

They file into my chamber one after another.

But it's no use. No use, I say. No use.

KARA MUSTAFA PASHA:

What can come of an exorcist, my lord?

Those charlatans!

SULTAN İBRAHİM:

Mentor, when you are in dire straits,

You grab at anything.

[*As* KÖSEM *and* YUSUF AĞA *enter.*]

Are we through with state affairs, Pasha?

KARA MUSTAFA PASHA:

Yes, we are, my lord.

SULTAN İBRAHİM:

You may leave now.

[*The* GRAND VIZIER *prostrates himself before the* SULTAN *and exits.*]

KÖSEM SULTAN:

My sovereign son, Yusuf Ağa has good news for you.

SULTAN İBRAHİM:

What is it, Yusuf?

SİLÂHTAR YUSUF:

We have found a new exorcist for your lordship.

They say he has eyes that see the unknown.

[İBRAHİM *is interested.*]

Among the palace porters you have a subject.

He is called Hacı[8] Mehmed the Arab. Walking in the street,

He lost his purse to a bearded pickpocket,

Who got away with all the gold coins the man had saved all his life.

People advised him to see somebody called Cinci Hoca,

And Hacı Mehmed found this holy man.

The *hoca* right away cast his sheep's knuckles.

SULTAN İBRAHİM:

What are sheep's knuckles, Yusuf?

SİLÂHTAR YUSUF:

My lord, they are one of the ways to see the unknown.

He cast his sheep's knuckles; then to Hacı Mehmed

He said, "I see a ruin at the end of our street,

I see something under the marble column there,

8. *Hacı:* A person who has made a pilgrimage to Mecca, often used as a title; frequently anglicized as *hajji.*

I see something like a purse with something like shining gold coins.

Our *hacı* flies to the place that the *hoca* tells him about.

SULTAN İBRAHİM:

Yes . . . ?

SİLÂHTAR YUSUF:

Not one coin was missing from the purse, my lordship.

SULTAN İBRAHİM:

[*Somewhat hopefully.*]

Do you think this holy person can find my gold as well?

KÖSEM SULTAN:

Hobyar told us, my sovereign son—

She is a palace woman who takes care of things in the city;

I had sent her yesterday to look for the *hoca*—

Hobyar told us that she searched every corner of the city the whole day.

Finally, whom should she find but . . .

[İBRAHİM *looks at her questioningly, interested to find out the name.*]

She found no other than the *hoca*, Cinci, whom Yusuf talks about.

[İBRAHİM *is surprised and pleased.* KÖSEM *signals to* HOBYAR.]

HOBYAR:

[*Moves forward.*]

Wrapping a scarf around my head

I went to the abode of the *hoca*. And I saw

That this holy man, this man who would not accept this worldly realm for a penny,

Who rules in the limitless empire of the soul,

Lives in a poor, lonely hovel. What do you think he said to me

When he saw me? He said, "You did not come here for yourself.

You came here for your master. You did well to come.

For a long time, I have been waiting to be called."

It seems I fainted the moment I heard those words.

Then, I don't know how, I woke up in a dream . . .

I am near the pool brimming with heavenly wine,

The wind of Heaven caresses my skin all over;

Lionlike young men whirl around me.

Each one of them brightens a new side of my joy.

I say to myself, a whole life can be sacrificed

For such a moment.

[*Retires.*]

SULTAN İBRAHİM:

I think I feel a little better.

Even hearing this man's name has brought me comfort.

KÖSEM SULTAN:

I have asked the gatekeeper
To bring that holy man to you unharmed.
Any moment now . . .

[*Voices are heard from outside.* CİNCİ HOCA, *with the* HEAD OF THE HAREM *and other* COURTIERS *accompanying him, enters majestically. He has a full beard, fiery eyes, simple clothing, and decisive, authoritative gestures. He seems to live in a spiritual world. Without even trying to bow, he moves toward the* SULTAN. *Everybody is surprised.* YUSUF AĞA, *afraid that* CİNCİ HOCA *will do something to the* SULTAN, *tries to intervene, but* CİNCİ HOCA *dismisses him with a sign of his hand.* İBRAHİM *is quite bewitched.* CİNCİ HOCA *looks piercingly into* İBRAHİM*'s eyes.*]

CİNCİ HOCA:

[*Frowning. To the people around him.*]
What have you done to this man?
[*Everybody is petrified.*]
They live it up in every corner of the palace.
Do you all have designs on this poor man?
How can you tolerate all these goings-on?
The Prophet himself would be bewitched here.
I'd say this man withstood it well.
Right away, bring me some incense. Put out some of the lights.

[*Some of the lights are put out. To the people around him.*]
You wait outside the door. Do not put a foot
Over the threshold. Otherwise,
You will meet the spirits I will chase away.

[*As everybody, including* İBRAHİM, *runs toward the door.*]

You wait here, İbrahim!
[İBRAHİM *stops. The* HOCA *beckons him. As* İBRAHİM *approaches, spellbound.*]
Stay right in the middle. Do not move.
Now, İbrahim, sit down.
[İBRAHİM *sits down.* CİNCİ *takes the incense vial to him and, going from one place to another, begins to chase away the spirits, as if shooing away chickens.*]
O God in Heaven . . . heavenly fly his angels . . .
Beelzebub in Hell . . . hellfire roasts his wings . . .

[*Circles around* İBRAHİM.]
I am drawing a circle around you, İbrahim;
Don't ever leave it until I tell you to do so.

[*Sits down in front of* IBRAHİM, *bending his legs under himself and raising his voice gradually.*]

Bitter, litter, clutter, curses, nurses, faster, rooster,

Sea, road, hurdle, brother, jumper, humble, evil, loony,

Burning, castle, rustle, lemon, stop, terror, mountain, jump, skip,

Warm, embrace . . . oh, love, love!

[IBRAHİM *jumps. For a while,* CINCI, *his eyes closed, is lost in thought. He begins to speak, deeply, as if from a faraway place.*]

İbrahim! İbrahim! Your soul is

In the castle of the Sultan of Fairies, Ezreke Bânû, the Blue Witch.

For a long time, you have been living

Far away from yourself; this sickness

Is the hardest yearning to cure, to quench.

But if now you trust me from the depths of your heart,

If you join all your will to my will,

Your thirst can stop; you can rejoin

Yourself, İbrahim.

[*Opens his eyes slowly, as if returning from a long trip, and bends toward* IBRAHİM.]

İbrahim, leave yourself entirely in my hands!

Believe that my breath is a divine breath!

Keep your heart pure; do not think of anything,

I will think for you. Do not look either to the left or to the right,

I will look for you. İbrahim, now

We are going on a long trip.

[*Changes his tone and speaks in a more matter-of-fact way.*]

During the trip, whenever I tap your arm, repeat my last words with me. Now, close
    your eyes. Have a good trip.

[*They get up. During the ensuing scene,* IBRAHİM, *his eyes closed, will remain within the circle and mark time. The* HOCA *will do the same at his place.*]

We will scale the mountains on our path one by one.

We will distill into ourselves the secret strength of each mountain.

Do not be distracted by the things you will see on the way.

Your soul is waiting impatiently for you at that place,

In the arms of Ezreke Bânû.

Now we are climbing the black mountains, İbrahim.

These violet flowers, with wide leaves, opening and closing,

Haven't you encountered them often on the steep hills of grief?

Poison that drops from the moon feeds them at night.

Let us absorb their essence and proceed.

[*Taps* IBRAHIM's *arm.*]

CİNCİ HOCA and SULTAN İBRAHİM:

Let us absorb their essence and proceed.

CİNCİ HOCA:

Now we are climbing the blue mountains, İbrahim.

These heavy birds perching on the rustling leaves,

Haven't you seen them making arcs in the skies of sadness?

Listen, they are answering the moon's last melody!

Let us absorb their voices and proceed.

[*Taps* IBRAHIM's *arm.*]

CİNCİ HOCA and SULTAN İBRAHİM:

Let us absorb their voices and proceed.

CİNCİ HOCA:

Now we are climbing the yellow mountains, İbrahim.

While a harsh winter was reigning in your soul,

Did not a warm breeze sometimes roll over your icy waters?

Let us absorb its warmth and proceed.

[*Taps* IBRAHIM.]

CİNCİ HOCA and SULTAN İBRAHİM:

Let us absorb its warmth and proceed.

CİNCİ HOCA:

[*Joyfully.*]

Now we are climbing a red mountain, İbrahim.

The castle of the Sultan of Fairies is at its peak.

But first let us cleanse ourselves in the golden waters of this lake.

[*Taps* IBRAHIM. *They cleanse themselves.*]

Now we can come to the gate of the castle.

Defend yourself against the black girls guarding

These copper-wrought gates. Their gestures,

Their dreamy eyes, the maddening titillation of their breasts,

Are all the many snares of lust.

[IBRAHIM, *wanting to hold one of the girls, extends his hand.* CINCI *hits* IBRAHIM's *arm.*]

Don't ever!

My trip ends in the arms of Ezreke Bânû!

[*Taps* IBRAHIM.]

CİNCİ HOCA and SULTAN İBRAHİM:

> My trip ends in the arms of Ezreke Bânû!

CİNCİ HOCA:

> [*Excited.*]
>
> We are at the threshold to the Sultan of Fairies.
>
> Now, stop here, İbrahim!
>
> [*They stop.*]
>
> Your soul is on the other side of the door,
>
> Lost in the pleasures of Paradise.
>
> [*Speaks matter-of-factly.*]
>
> You will repeat my words all by yourself.
>
> You, the sultan of the kingdom of spirits,
>
> Ezreke Bânû!

SULTAN İBRAHİM:

> You, the sultan of the kingdom of spirits,
>
> Ezreke Bânû!

CİNCİ HOCA:

> I am İbrahim,
>
> The greatest sultan in the kingdom of man.
>
> [*Taps* İBRAHİM.]

SULTAN İBRAHİM:

> I am İbrahim,
>
> The greatest sultan in the kingdom of man.

CİNCİ HOCA:

> For very long, my soul has been dwelling with you.
>
> I have come to claim it.
>
> [*Taps* İBRAHİM.]

SULTAN İBRAHİM:

> For very long, my soul has been dwelling with you.
>
> I have come to claim it.

CİNCİ HOCA:

> I have not been fooled by the black maidens at your gate.
>
> My eyes were constantly attracted to your golden hair.
>
> [*Taps* İBRAHİM.]

SULTAN İBRAHİM:

> My eyes were constantly attracted to your golden hair.

CİNCİ HOCA:

> [*In a low voice.*]
>
> Open the door, İbrahim. Go in. Embrace her tightly.

Let all ecstasies flow

Warmly from her soft flesh

To your cold body.

[İBRAHİM *embraces her passionately.* CİNCİ *whispers.*]

Enough, İbrahim. It is enough. You possess your soul now.

Blessed Ezreke Bânû!

Like a long milky lake,

Your skin shines in the night.

Anyone who plunges into your depths once,

Can never have enough pleasure;

Your craving settles so deeply inside you.

[*Taps* İBRAHİM.]

SULTAN İBRAHİM:

[*In rapture.*]

Can never have enough pleasure;

Your beauty settles so deeply inside you.

CİNCİ HOCA:

Now we are mounting a Phoenix, İbrahim.

You are on one of its wings, and I on the other.

The trip will be very short this time;

We'll be back the moment you open your eyes.

Now open your eyes, İbrahim!

[İBRAHİM *opens his eyes as if reborn.* CİNCİ, *with a powerful, joyful voice.*]

Now I have returned to my arms; I have returned to my legs;

Now I have returned to my body.

[*Signals to* İBRAHİM.]

SULTAN İBRAHİM:

[*With a powerful, joyful voice.*]

Now I have returned to my arms; I have returned to my legs;

Now I have returned to my body.

CİNCİ HOCA:

Now I have returned to my loins; I have returned to my spittle;

Now I have returned to my body.

[*Signals to* İBRAHİM.]

SULTAN İBRAHİM:

Now I have returned to my loins; I have returned to my spittle;

Now I have returned to my body.

CİNCİ HOCA:

The worlds before and behind me are returned to me

In their beauty!

[*Signals to* IBRAHIM, *blowing on him.*]

SULTAN İBRAHİM:

The worlds before and behind me are returned to me

In their beauty!

CİNCİ HOCA:

The worlds below and above me are returned to me

In their beauty!

[*Blowing, he signals to* IBRAHIM.]

SULTAN İBRAHİM:

The worlds below and above me are returned to me

In their beauty!

CİNCİ HOCA:

[*Holds* IBRAHIM *by the hand.*]

Come, İbrahim. O God . . . close enough . . . O God, close to health . . .

O God, close to plenty . . . rid of sickness . . . washed of sickness . . .

The spirits fly away . . . the father of grief fly away . . .

Sixty, seventy,

Health come quickly

And all grief wash away . . .

Now leave the circle I drew for you, İbrahim.

[*Takes* IBRAHIM *out of the circle.*]

Let your new health bring you joy, my lord.

SULTAN İBRAHİM:

A sweet fire is now awakening in my loins;

The black clouds in me have begun to disperse.

A red song is marching into my veins.

[*As if waking up from a dream, the people waiting outside the door enter.* IBRAHIM *to* CİNCİ.]

I should always like to see you near me. Stay in my palace.

[*To the* HEAD OF THE HAREM.]

Make preparations for tonight, Ağa.

[*Exits with majesty.*]

KÖSEM SULTAN:

[*Clasps* CİNCİ's *hand.*]

My *hoca* with holy breath,

We owe this day of happiness to you.

CİNCİ HOCA:

[*Panting.*]

For me, only a glass of water.

KÖSEM SULTAN:

Bring some icy sherbet to my *hoca*.

CİNCİ HOCA:

[*Draws* KÖSEM *to one side.*]

My lady, a concubine never seen by the sultan is necessary,

Golden haired, blue eyed, with skin white as milk.

KÖSEM SULTAN:

Hoca, do not worry, the girl is ready. She is of Russian stock,

Not more than fifteen, only a bud, impatient

To be opened. Her name is Turhan.

CİNCİ HOCA:

[*As he drinks the sherbet brought to him.*]

Excellent! Preparations must begin immediately.

She must be perfumed with attar and ambergris

From her hair to her ankles. Let her turn

Her body into an early morning garden

Out of which no exit is possible.

And let the sultan chew on wild pears

Constantly, let him smell and swallow

Ambergris until the nuptial.

KÖSEM SULTAN:

Your words will be carried out to the letter, Hoca.

[*To the people around her.*]

Make my *hoca* comfortable.

[*Exits with the others.*]

SİLÂHTAR YUSUF:

[*Goes near* CİNCİ.]

May you have a long life, Hoca.

Now that you have untied the knot,

There is a wide plain before you.

Ride your horse at full tilt.

CİNCİ HOCA:

But, my dear lord, I have no eyes

For worldly matters; my science is enough for me.

SİLÂHTAR YUSUF:

You had a hard trip, Hoca,

Will you not move to your chamber? Do rest a little.

Scene 6

[*Night. The* INHABITANTS OF ISTANBUL.]

THIRD INHABITANT:

It is very late. You must forgive me, gentlemen.

[*Yawns, attempts to leave.*]

FOURTH INHABITANT:

I must be going, too, friends,

With your permission.

SECOND INHABITANT:

Where are you going? Why don't you stay

A bit longer?

FIRST INHABITANT:

Many of the seeds sown during the day

Sprout only in the late hours of night.

What do you say to this business, friends?

FOURTH INHABITANT:

What business?

FIRST INHABITANT:

The very fact that our Cinci has not yet

Returned from the palace.

THIRD INHABITANT:

Who cares? Whether he is back or not,

Is it any of our business?

FIRST INHABITANT:

I have been spying on his house

Since he has left.

FOURTH INHABITANT:

Whether he returns or he doesn't return,

What difference does it make?

FIRST INHABITANT:

[*Insinuatingly.*]

Do you think Cinci's magic was powerful enough?

SECOND INHABITANT:

[*Laughs.*]

Enough . . . to melt his blocks of ice?

THIRD INHABITANT:

Come off it! Our sovereign sultan

Must be in a deep sleep now.

FOURTH INHABITANT:

Or he must be sitting with his wise men

Talking about God and religion.

SECOND INHABITANT:

You were not carrying a lantern with you, gentlemen, were you?

FOURTH INHABITANT:

A ban on walking in the streets without a lantern

Was imposed on us by Sultan Murad.

FIRST INHABITANT:

[*Laughs.*]

True, true! The ban has disappeared

With the imposer of the ban. In the age of Sultan İbrahim

We can walk without a lantern in the pitch darkness of the streets.

Our evil thoughts can run wild.

Long live the darkness!

SECOND, THIRD, and FOURTH INHABITANTS:

Long live darkness, long live darkness!

THIRD INHABITANT:

Good night, friends.

FOURTH INHABITANT:

Good night, gentlemen.

[*The* THIRD *and* FOURTH INHABITANTS *exit arm in arm.*]

FIRST and SECOND INHABITANTS:

Have a good night, dear friends.

SECOND INHABITANT:

Either Cinci's key hasn't fit the door either, and they axed his head—

Else why wouldn't he come out of the place for so long?

Or he has been more clever than all the others,

And opened İbrahim's doors all the way.

FIRST INHABITANT:

[*Listens to the ground.*]

Rivulets of water are wandering

In dark spaces underground,

All yearning to gather into a spring.

It is hard to resist the sea's pull, hard!

Water cannot hide in spigots

And become stagnant. It desires to be startled

Into rivers.

SECOND INHABITANT:

Sooner or later . . . the Ottoman rooster

Will crow.

FIRST INHABITANT:

I hope it will bring a lucky morning to us.

Scene 7

[İBRAHİM's *bedchamber. Predawn. His back turned,* İBRAHİM *is panting heavily. He throws a cover over the half-naked body of* TURHAN. *He kisses her on the forehead.*]

SULTAN İBRAHİM:

Run to my mother at once. Kiss her hand.

TURHAN SULTAN:

Do you mean right now, my lord?

SULTAN İBRAHİM:

Of course! Immediately!

TURHAN SULTAN:

Should we not wait for the morning?

SULTAN İBRAHİM:

No, this news cannot wait!

Let them know that my reign has started.

[TURHAN *stares without comprehending.* İBRAHİM *caresses her face with his hands.*]

They put me on the throne, Turhan,

But it was you who made me a sultan. Go now.

[*Kisses* TURHAN *once more.*]

TURHAN SULTAN:

What will she say to me, my lord,

If I go and kiss her hand at this hour of the night?

SULTAN İBRAHİM:

She will drown you in gifts. Besides,

I don't think she has slept tonight.

And is she the only one? Countless people living in the palace

Are at this moment listening to this chamber, Turhan.

[TURHAN *exits.* İBRAHİM *turns around slowly.*]

How many torches have lit

All the caverns of my being!

[*Dawn approaches, as if rising with* İBRAHİM's *body. While* İBRAHİM *moves to the front of the stage, the light increases gradually.*]

The silver lances of the armies of the morning, rising

Over the tops of dark, faraway mountains,

Erect their pennants at the towers of my empire.

[*Pauses.*]

I, İbrahim, grew up in the dark,

Fear was my nurse. Sensing the greased

Rope of the hangman at my neck all the time,

My being was shaped in darkness. And then,

When they took me into the light and called me "sultan,"

I felt myself a stranger to the world and to myself.

My soul was gripped by a feeling of powerlessness and inadequacy.

It tyrannized and ruined me; my thighs could not feel

The throne I sat on. I didn't exist under my turban

Or in my fur tunic.

I just didn't exist.

My mother, my mentor, my chief guard, and Cinci

Were all truer sultans than I, particularly Cinci.

For a moment, he was the sultan of sultans.

[*Pauses.*]

Now . . .

Herds of stars, startled by the sun,

Are filling my expanding veins.

I am the world before me, I am the world behind me;

I am the world below me, I am the world above me.

I am İbrahim, the sultan,

Sultan İbrahim.

[*Pauses.*]

My manhood boiling from the depths

Will burst out foaming till the very end.

And the world will know İbrahim now.

CURTAIN

ACT II

Scene 1

[*Morning.* İBRAHİM's *private chamber.* HÜMAŞAH *and* DİLÂŞUB *are arranging flowers in vases.*]

DİLÂŞUB:

> I am sick and tired of playing with the same flowers!
>
> I wish the sultan would come so we'd be freed.

HÜMAŞAH:

> What is your hurry? He will be here sooner or later.

DİLÂŞUB:

> The mother of the sultan is quite something.

HÜMAŞAH:

> In what way, Dilâşub? Not that I disagree,
>
> But in what way? She has so many tricks.

DİLÂŞUB:

> Yes, she does, and she uses them all
>
> To call her own tunes.
>
> Why do you think she sent us here this morning?

HÜMAŞAH:

> [*Feigning incomprehension.*]
>
> Why, dear girl? To arrange in the vases
>
> The sultan's favorite flowers!

DİLÂŞUB:

> Well, we have arranged the flowers,
>
> Why are we not leaving?

HÜMAŞAH:

> Because . . .

DİLÂŞUB:

> Because the sultan's mother wanted it this way.
>
> She told us, "Don't move
>
> Until the sultan has seen you arranging the flowers," didn't she, Hümaşah?
>
> Why do you think she is using us as bait?
>
> Because the sultan can't resist such bait, that's why.
>
> By stealing her son's wind away from him in sweet ways,
>
> She is filling her own sails.

HÜMAŞAH:

> But all the girls of the harem
>
> Are dying to be bait for her tackle.

DİLÂŞUB:

> Who wouldn't? If you catch the eye of the sultan,
>
> And if he is stirred by you and takes you to his bed for one night,
>
> And if you offer him in nine months
>
> And ten days a prince or a sultan,
>
> You will be saved from dying a servant in the harem.

You were his concubine, you will become his wife,

And you will be called Mother Sultan.

HÜMAŞAH:

This place will be teeming with mother sultans soon.

What is the use of that?

But if you were the only wife, then . . .

DİLÂŞUB:

You are flying too high, Hümaşah!

Yet, why not? Your beauty is a fruit

To be picked from the remotest branches.

[TURHAN *enters.* HÜMAŞAH *and* DİLÂŞUB *stop talking.*]

TURHAN SULTAN:

What are you doing here?

DİLÂŞUB:

We were arranging the sultan's flowers.

TURHAN SULTAN:

[*To the* HEAD OF THE HAREM, *who enters.*]

What are they doing in the sultan's chamber?

Can't only one person arrange a few flowers?

HEAD OF THE HAREM:

[*To* HÜMAŞAH *and* DİLÂŞUB.]

Who has sent you here?

[*To* TURHAN.]

I know nothing about it, my lady.

DİLÂŞUB:

The sultan's mother sent us here.

[TURHAN, *eyeing them with hatred, particularly* HÜMAŞAH, *suddenly holds her stomach and staggers.*]

HEAD OF THE HAREM:

[*Runs to* TURHAN's *aid.*]

Let me take you to your chamber, my lady, please.

[*Helps* TURHAN *out.*]

DİLÂŞUB:

[*Imitates him.*]

"Let me take you to your chamber, my lady, please."

She is showing off as though she has given birth to a prince.

She is about ready to burst with envy.

Did you notice how she looked at you with hatred?

HÜMAŞAH:

> Why at me? She was also angry with you.

DİLÂŞUB:

> She is not paying too much attention, either to me
>
> Or to the other girls in the harem.
>
> She doesn't believe we are her equals. But you,
>
> You drive her crazy. She knows that the sultan
>
> Will not easily get tired of you in one night.
>
> All the brilliance of her beauty fades near you.
>
> Hümaşah, the sultan is coming! Arrange the flowers!

> [İBRAHİM *enters with* SİLÂHTAR YUSUF.]

SULTAN İBRAHİM:

> [*Lethargic, sniffing ambergris.*]
>
> I was tired of that potion, Yusuf.
>
> It was clever of our *hoca* to think
>
> Of boiling the figs in milk. And once you have added
>
> The white ambergris to them, it is impossible to resist their taste.
>
> I was so tired after last night.
>
> I was black inside; I was swimming in cold waters again.
>
> But this morning, the moment I ate the figs with white ambergris,
>
> A nimble fire began to move in my veins.

SİLÂHTAR YUSUF:

> My lord, your *hoca* has all sorts of keys
>
> To open the gates of pleasure.

SULTAN İBRAHİM:

> Because of him, I cracked my first crust, Yusuf.
>
> I wonder what will happen now? When he is near me,
>
> I feel mysterious forces flowing
>
> From his body to mine. Do you like Cinci, Yusuf?

SİLÂHTAR YUSUF:

> Anything that brings goodness to you
>
> Is good, is beautiful for me, my lord.

SULTAN İBRAHİM:

> [*Notices the* CONCUBINES; *his eyes glitter.*]
>
> I wondered. Because the grand vizier does not like him that much.
>
> When I promoted the *hoca* to chief scholar,
>
> The pasha was wild with anger. What can I say?
>
> We had decided to pay our debt to the *hoca* as a sultan should.
>
> [*Moves toward the* CONCUBINES.] What are your names?

DİLÂŞUB:

> [*Jumps forward.*]
>
> Your servant Dilâşub, my lord.

SULTAN İBRAHİM:

> [*Caresses her cheek, then smells a flower he picks up from* HÜMAŞAH's *vase.*]
>
> I asked you,
>
> "What is your name?"

HÜMAŞAH:

> [*A bit aloof.*]
>
> I could not tell which one of us you were asking, my lord.

SULTAN İBRAHİM:

> [*Affected.*]
>
> Hmm . . . all right, what is your name?

HÜMAŞAH:

> Hümaşah, my lord.

SULTAN İBRAHİM:

> [*Excited, begins to pant heavily. He comes near* YUSUF *and looks in the direction of the* CONCUBINES.]
>
> What do you say? Is there time, Yusuf?

> [*Without waiting for an answer, he goes back to the* CONCUBINES. *He caresses* HÜMAŞAH, *but she remains aloof. He then caresses* DİLÂŞUB; *she responds coquettishly.* İBRAHİM *is seething with desire. He moves back quickly to* SİLÂHTAR YUSUF's *side.*]
>
> When is the grand vizier expecting us, Yusuf?

SİLÂHTAR YUSUF:

> [*Uneasy.*]
>
> Soon, my lord . . .

SULTAN İBRAHİM:

> [*Exploding.*]
>
> Goddamn that council chamber! I am sick
>
> Of all those ambassadors kissing the ground in front of me
>
> And talking in strange tongues.

SİLÂHTAR YUSUF:

> But you were not going to the council chamber today, my lord;
>
> The grand vizier himself is going to come here soon.

SULTAN İBRAHİM:

> Oh, I see! Did I say I wasn't going to the council chamber today?

SİLÂHTAR YUSUF:

> You had willed it that way, my lord.
>
> The grand vizier will be coming here soon.

[*On tenterhooks,* İBRAHİM *turns his back on the* CONCUBINES. SİLÂHTAR YUSUF *motions them to leave. The* CONCUBINES *leave.*]

SULTAN İBRAHİM:

Do you like the grand vizier, Yusuf?

SİLÂHTAR YUSUF:

He is very adept at turning the wheel of state, my lord.

He is not very learned, but his experience is wide.

KÖSEM SULTAN:

[*Enters.*]

May this be a wonderful day for you, my royal son.

[*To* SİLÂHTAR YUSUF *she nods her head in greeting.*]

Did my lion like his flowers this morning?

SULTAN İBRAHİM:

Thank you, dear mother.

KÖSEM SULTAN:

Well, have they arranged the flowers in their vases nicely?

SULTAN İBRAHİM:

[*Does not understand at first; then suddenly his eyes glitter.*]

Who is that girl Hümaşah, Mother?

KÖSEM SULTAN:

[*Pretends not to understand. Pretends to rearrange something out of place on* İBRAHİM's *shoulder.*]

What careless person dressed you this morning?

[*Looks* İBRAHİM *over.*]

I have a small request from my lion.

SULTAN İBRAHİM:

[*Worried.*]

What kind of request, Mother?

KÖSEM SULTAN:

There is a certain Mustafa Ağa, one of my retinue.

He has done much for us, particularly for you.

SULTAN İBRAHİM:

What did he do for me, Mother?

KÖSEM SULTAN:

When I was saving you from the rage of your brother,

He helped us a great deal.

SULTAN İBRAHİM:

[*Gradually getting annoyed.*]

What do you want me to do for him?

KÖSEM SULTAN:

> If the head of the army is one of us, my son,
>
> Our place will be secure. Do you not think so, Yusuf Ağa?

SİLÂHTAR YUSUF:

> The head of the army needs an iron-fisted man, my lady;
>
> I wonder if Mustafa Ağa can assert his authority on the soldiers?

KÖSEM SULTAN:

> [*Looks at* İBRAHİM.]
>
> If the sultan wishes, he can assert it very well.
>
> Authority is not a matter of fists,
>
> But of heart. Mustafa Ağa has a lion's heart;
>
> He is somebody who can carry out his duties.

SULTAN İBRAHİM:

> [*Worried.*]
>
> What about the grand vizier? Hell will freeze over
>
> Before he says yes to this matter.

KÖSEM SULTAN:

> [*Angrily.*]
>
> Is he a partner to your throne, this man?
>
> Whatever I want from you, you bring up his name!
>
> What is this? Are you not the sultan?
>
> Pretty soon, you will sit and get up by his edict.
>
> By his permission you will take the concubines to your bed.
>
> Don't you hear the rumors going around?
>
> They say the grand vizier is sending sackfuls of pure flour
>
> And sugar to the soldiers. He is telling them,
>
> "Go and make halvah for yourselves." One day
>
> You will find him sitting on your throne, and you,
>
> Hands folded, bending yourself before him.

SULTAN İBRAHİM:

> [*Startled; speaks haltingly because of tension.*]
>
> What do you mean, Mother? When Nasuhpaşazade
>
> Marched on Istanbul with his army, was it not the grand vizier
>
> Who saved my throne
>
> And both me and you?

KÖSEM SULTAN:

> To this pure-hearted son of mine
>
> You tell the truth, Yusuf Ağa!

SULTAN İBRAHİM:

> What is she talking about, Yusuf?

SİLÂHTAR YUSUF:

> The rumor has it that Nasuhpaşazade had said,
> "My quarrel is with the grand vizier;
> My neck is thinner than a thread before my sultan."
> Supposedly, Kara Mustafa Pasha had him killed first,
> And then received your decree for his death.

SULTAN İBRAHİM:

> But the grand vizier is carrying my seal.
> To oppose him is to oppose me.
> But I know nothing about the matter of the decree. Hmmm . . .

KÖSEM SULTAN:

> My son, before he uses your own authority against you,
> Why don't you give your seal to someone else,
> To a more able, more powerful hand?

SULTAN İBRAHİM:

> [*Nervously.*]
> Do you know anybody, Yusuf?

SİLÂHTAR YUSUF:

> Just any hand is not mighty enough to carry that seal,
> My lord. Kara Mustafa Pasha has been seasoned in state affairs
> For years.

KÖSEM SULTAN:

> Look here, Yusuf Ağa. Aren't your hands, too,
> Mighty enough to carry that seal?

SULTAN İBRAHİM:

> [*Pleased.*]
> Yes, truly, Yusuf. It would be so good.
> I am used to you, and you to me.

SİLÂHTAR YUSUF:

> Forgive me, my lord; during the life of Kara Mustafa Pasha
> I cannot see myself deserving that position.

KÖSEM SULTAN:

> All right, on his death?

[*Both* YUSUF *and* İBRAHİM *are amazed and startled.* GRAND VIZIER KARA MUSTAFA PASHA *enters and prostrates himself before the* SULTAN.]

SULTAN İBRAHİM:

> [*In a confusion of feelings.*]
> Good day, Pasha. Where have you been?

KARA MUSTAFA PASHA:

I did not want to come early and disturb you, my lord.

SULTAN İBRAHİM:

What were the matters today? Were there again

Any ambassadors around?

KARA MUSTAFA PASHA:

There was one from the new Russian czar, Alexi, my lord;

He brought many worthy gifts to our sultan.

SULTAN İBRAHİM:

[*Pleased.*]

Really? Let them all be sent to my treasury.

I will look them over sometime today.

Is an answer written to the czar?

[*Looks at* KÖSEM. *As she frowns, he assumes a majestic air.*]

Here is my edict to the new Russian czar: "The former Muscovite

Czars used to send their taxes to the Crimean governor on time.

You should also send your taxes on time."

[*Looks at* KÖSEM. *She smiles.*]

KARA MUSTAFA PASHA:

This czar is new to the throne. If you could wish him well.

Also, if we could thank him for the gifts!

SULTAN İBRAHİM:

[*Annoyed.*]

Let the scribes add that, too!

KARA MUSTAFA PASHA:

As you will, my lord! Also,

The English ambassador has a request from my sovereign

About the English ships entering and leaving our ports more easily,

Their trading in our empire more expeditiously.

SULTAN İBRAHİM:

No. Neither the British nor the Venetians,

No privileges to anybody.

Why, after all, should they enter or leave our ports more easily?

Are our ports wayside inns? But wait a minute!

According to my Cinci Hoca, the English sailors

Bring the best ambergris from the Indian ports.

And there are hundreds of women in my harem—German,

French, Italian, Spanish, Hungarian, Arab—

But not one English girl. How can there be a harem like that, Pasha?

Tell that ambassador . . .

KARA MUSTAFA PASHA:

[*Frowns.*]

Not possible, my lord; it is not our practice, not wise.

Such behavior stains the very essence of a state. Besides,

Is your Cinci not enough for those affairs of yours, my lord?

Am I your grand vizier, or your . . . ?

SULTAN İBRAHİM:

[*Bites his lips and looks periodically at* KÖSEM.]

All right! All right!

KARA MUSTAFA PASHA:

Also, my lord, there is the execution of a few bandits.

SULTAN İBRAHİM:

[*Happily.*]

Let them be executed in the palace. I want to watch, too.

KARA MUSTAFA PASHA:

It is not proper, my lord, to execute

Any small-time bandit in the palace;

That requires an important person. In Rumeli . . .[9]

SULTAN İBRAHİM:

[*Interrupts him.*]

Do you mean someone like Nasuhpaşazade, Pasha?

KARA MUSTAFA PASHA:

In Rumeli there is a very famous bandit recently caught.

They call him the Bloody Knife. He will soon be brought here.

As soon as he is here, we will hang him with ceremony in the palace

In your presence.

SULTAN İBRAHİM:

[*Shouts.*]

I asked you,

Do you mean someone like Nasuhpaşazade?

KARA MUSTAFA PASHA:

[*A little curtly.*]

What about Nasuhpaşazade, my lord?

SULTAN İBRAHİM:

[*His anger rising.*]

What about the sackfuls of flour and sugar, the purses full of gold?

9. Rumeli: Ottoman territories in Europe.

KARA MUSTAFA PASHA:

> [*Looks at* KÖSEM *and then at* SİLÂHTAR AĞA.]
>
> I don't understand at all, my lord!

SULTAN İBRAHİM:

> What are these things you call procedure and reason?
>
> Whatever I want goes against them.
>
> Every sultan's name is mentioned at Friday prayers,
>
> Coins are minted in his name.
>
> I have asked you so many times:
>
> Why aren't coins minted in my name?
>
> Can it be that I am not the sovereign?

KARA MUSTAFA PASHA:

> God forbid, my lord!

SULTAN İBRAHİM:

> Or do you plan to have coins minted for yourself?
>
> [KÖSEM *signals to* SİLÂHTAR YUSUF; *they exit.*]

KARA MUSTAFA PASHA:

> [*Angrily, but respectfully.*]
>
> I, your servant, did not receive such an insult
>
> Even from Sultan Murad, my lord.

SULTAN İBRAHİM:

> [*To himself.*]
>
> Even from Sultan Murad?

KARA MUSTAFA PASHA:

> [*Takes the royal seal from his breast pocket, kisses it respectfully, and presents it to* İBRAHİM.]
>
> Here it is, my lord—your seal!
>
> Give it to a servant of yours more deserving than I,
>
> More capable, more worthy of your trust.

SULTAN İBRAHİM:

> [*Startled, his voice trembling.*]
>
> No, Mentor, no, I do not want it; keep it.
>
> I do not have a servant more deserving than you.

KARA MUSTAFA PASHA:

> [*Is moved and softens.*]
>
> My lordly sovereign, I am your grand vizier;
>
> My authority is your authority.
>
> As you trust me, I become stronger,

More useful to you. Every labor of mine

Is to increase the vast majesty of your sovereignty;

Let not only one Kara Mustafa Pasha, but a thousand viziers fall

In order to make the powerful star of your state brighter.

My lord, we spent too much money on the fleet,

All because the Venetians were restive in the Mediterranean;

We must teach them a lesson at the first opportunity.

The funds in the treasury have considerably decreased;

Only I know what I have to do to meet the pay of the soldiers.

Let the taxes come from the governor-general.

I will have your coins struck in no time.

SULTAN İBRAHİM:

All right, Mentor, as you see fit.

Can we have peace?

KARA MUSTAFA PASHA:

My lord, how can you say that?

Can the servant be angry with his lord?

We have peace.

SULTAN İBRAHİM:

All right, your time is yours, Master.

KARA MUSTAFA PASHA:

Let me not be late to the council chamber, my lord.

[*Kisses the* SULTAN's *hem and exits.*]

Scene 2

[*Night. A room in* KARA MUSTAFA PASHA's *mansion. The* GRAND VIZIER *enters and locks the door. He ceremoniously moves to a throne standing covered in the middle of the room. He removes the cover and strokes the throne. Then he sits with majesty on it. A voice,* THE VOICE *of his alter ego, speaks. The* GRAND VIZIER *follows what it says with changes in the expression on his face.*]

THE VOICE:

Kara Mustafa Pasha! Kara Mustafa Pasha!

Sultan Murad's grand vizier, who crushed the Persian army!

Who made this foolish, blind law?

Yes, one may inherit land, one may inherit money,

But how can one inherit a throne?

Sovereignty, that slut,

Must be won with the strength of arms, of heart, of head.

Only the one who can fill the throne should sit on the throne.

[*Strokes the arms and seat of the throne.*]

True, Sultan Murad had also received the throne from his father

When he was still a boy! But that lion of lions

Managed to push his mother into a corner the moment he grew up;

With his own strength, he recaptured the throne; then he became the sovereign.

His presence was a blessed weight on your shoulders.

To serve him was to live by the laws of your own nature.

You know well that in serving a great man, one also becomes great.

But this new master of yours, this so-called sultan,

This caricature of a man who was dragged to the throne,

How can he rule the greatest empire in the world when he cannot handle himself?

Kara Mustafa Pasha! Kara Mustafa Pasha!

The great commander who makes his presence felt in the heart of every soldier,

The wise man who was born to turn the wheel of state,

Be worthy of the darkest, the noblest desire in your heart,

Be worthy, be worthy, be worthy!

[*The* GRAND VIZIER *is frightened by these words. He shuts his ears. There is a sudden knock at the door.* KARA MUSTAFA PASHA *recovers himself immediately; covering the throne, he hides it in a corner.*]

KARA MUSTAFA PASHA:

Who is it?

[*The door is opened.* SİLÂHTAR YUSUF *enters anxiously.*]

Is it you, Yusuf Ağa? What is it? At this hour . . .

SİLÂHTAR YUSUF:

[*Panting.*]

The governor-general of Rumeli is in danger, Pasha.

KARA MUSTAFA PASHA:

What kind of danger?

SİLÂHTAR YUSUF:

The sultan had Faik Pasha put in chains

And brought secretly from Sofia—and personally interrogated him.

All at the instigation of Cinci Hoca!

KARA MUSTAFA PASHA:

That is not possible! How can he put

A full governor-general in chains without asking me?

And, without consulting me, how can he question him?

The council of ministers must first investigate, then make a determination, then
  advise the sultan.

What was the poor fellow's crime?

SİLÂHTAR YUSUF:

> Faik Pasha was supposedly behaving ruthlessly in Rumeli,
>
> Was first hanging the thieves and bandits he had caught
>
> And then getting the edict
>
> For their execution from the judge of Sofia.

KARA MUSTAFA PASHA:

> Was he supposed to give the thieves and bandits gifts instead?
>
> Of course he would hang them right away.
>
> Well! Who brought the complaint against the pasha?

SİLÂHTAR YUSUF:

> The judge of Sofia, Sancarlı Mehmed,
>
> Cinci Hoca's man.

KARA MUSTAFA PASHA:

> I see! He was Cinci Hoca's man.

SİLÂHTAR YUSUF:

> Something must be done, Pasha!
>
> Faik Pasha is one of the few honest men left
>
> In the land. No effort must be spared to save him.
>
> In the hands of charlatans, the pillars of state
>
> Are falling one by one. The whole edifice is tumbling.
>
> Something must be done. Shoulder to shoulder, together
>
> Let us prevent this crumbling, Pasha! Let us prevent it!

KARA MUSTAFA PASHA:

> [*Angry, but controls himself.*]
>
> Thank you, Yusuf Ağa. I do believe
>
> You are the only unrotten one left in the Ottoman palace.
>
> I will talk to the sultan tomorrow morning. Yes,
>
> Something must be done, even at the cost of our own lives.
>
> [SİLÂHTAR YUSUF *salutes him and exits.*]

Scene 3

[*Morning.* İBRAHİM's *private chamber. As* İBRAHİM *paces back and forth restlessly,* CİNCİ HOCA *enters.*]

SULTAN İBRAHİM:

> [*Sniffs the air.*]
>
> What is the perfume you have put on yourself?
>
> It is not ambergris. Is it anthurium or what?

CİNCİ HOCA:

> Our sultan's senses do not err anymore.

SULTAN İBRAHİM:

> What is there about beautiful smells, my *hoca,*
>
> That brings light to the darkest recesses in my brain?

CİNCİ HOCA:

> Is a woman not like that also, my lord? Only,
>
> If you always smell the same odor,
>
> Your nose gets used to it; finally, you cannot sense it.
>
> A woman is like that also.

SULTAN İBRAHİM:

> Very true. After my return from the castle of Ezreke Bânû,
>
> I embellished my nights with white women,
>
> But, in the end, they became like winter suns, all light but no heat.
>
> Then I turned to dark ones. First, I found in them
>
> The very savor of summer nights that melts the heart,
>
> But, in the end, they were a puff of smoke
>
> Without fire or burning coal.

CİNCİ HOCA:

> One must change them according to a measure, my lord;
>
> New ecstasies can spring only from new bodies; and
>
> Only with new ecstasies can life renew itself.

SULTAN İBRAHİM:

> [*Preoccupied.*]
>
> Only with new ecstasies can life renew itself . . . Hoca,
>
> My mentor is majestic like a mountain summit.
>
> How can one reach its top?

CİNCİ HOCA:

> How is this possible, my lord? That summit
>
> Can be made flat with one word of yours.
>
> My sultan, if you can use this opportunity . . .

SULTAN İBRAHİM:

> Which opportunity, Hoca?

CİNCİ HOCA:

> You witnessed the guilt of Faik Pasha,
>
> The judge of Sofia isn't lying after all.
>
> You saw him say, "This pasha did me no harm.
>
> I came here to complain because I could not bear
>
> The cruelty done to the people."
>
> That the pasha is guilty is clear as daylight.

SULTAN İBRAHİM:

> [*Ill at ease.*]

But the grand vizier . . .

CİNCİ HOCA:

The blow you will deal to Faik Pasha

Will diminish the majesty of the grand vizier, my lord.

SULTAN İBRAHİM:

[*Nervously thinks for a while, then suddenly.*]

Chief Gardener!

[*The* CHIEF GARDENER (CHIEF EXECUTIONER) *enters.*]

Let Faik Pasha be disposed of!

[*The* CHIEF GARDENER *exits prostrating himself. As* İBRAHİM *walks up and down very ill at ease,* KARA MUSTAFA PASHA *enters with majesty and prostrates himself.* İBRAHİM *becomes excited.*]

What is it, Mentor? What wind blew you

Here so early in the morning? Is there a state matter

That needs immediate solution?

KARA MUSTAFA PASHA:

[*Controls his fury with difficulty.*]

What kinds of happenings are these, my lord?

SULTAN İBRAHİM:

[*Pretending ignorance, but excited.*]

What happenings, Mentor?

KARA MUSTAFA PASHA:

[*Unable to control his fury any longer.*]

Can a full governor-general be strangled like a sheep,

Without questioning, without determining his guilt?

Am I carrying your seal for nothing?

Are all the governors-general not responsible to me,

And am I not responsible for them to you?

How can a pasha be executed without asking the grand vizier?

SULTAN İBRAHİM:

[*With a slightly sharp edge in his voice.*]

Am I not the sovereign? Can I not impose my will?

KARA MUSTAFA PASHA:

To be a sultan, above all, is to be just,

To protect the rights of everyone, even of every object!

Sovereignty can't go hand in hand with cruelty for long.

Before long, one falls into the lap of ruin.

On what evidence did you kill Faik Pasha?

SULTAN İBRAHİM:

>I don't give a damn about evidence.
>
>I just killed him.

KARA MUSTAFA PASHA:

>If so, put an end to all institutions, my lord!
>
>Let there be no council of ministers, no grand vizier,
>
>No council of state! What need is there for tribunals
>
>If you dispense justice according to your whim?
>
>I am sure your *hoca* will not fail to be of help to you.

CİNCİ HOCA:

>[*To the* GRAND VIZIER.]
>
>It is the judge of Sofia who has complained about Faik Pasha, my lord.
>
>The man has traveled all that distance to come here.

KARA MUSTAFA PASHA:

>Well! That Mr. Justice,
>
>In whose hands did he leave the judicial affairs
>
>Of a whole province to come here?
>
>From whom did he get the permission?
>
>[CİNCİ *is uncomfortable, does not know what to say. The* GRAND VIZIER *takes the seal out of his breast pocket.*]
>
>I cannot serve injustice, my lord. Forgive me.

SULTAN İBRAHİM:

>[*Is worried. Points to the seal.*]
>
>No, no, Mentor, put it back in your pocket!

KARA MUSTAFA PASHA:

>[*Quietly but sadly.*]
>
>It was a great pity to have Faik Pasha killed, a great pity.
>
>My lord, without justice, not only two men,
>
>But two objects even, cannot exist together.
>
>One slight injustice upsets the balance of the whole empire;
>
>One slight injustice may even shake the throne of God, my lord.

SULTAN İBRAHİM:

>[*Guilty and timid.*]
>
>You are still going to keep my seal,
>
>Aren't you, Mentor?

KARA MUSTAFA PASHA:

>As long as you see fit,
>
>I will, my lord.

SULTAN İBRAHİM:

>Then we have made peace. Now go, Mentor.
>
>A dark sadness has coiled in my heart again.
>
>[*The* GRAND VIZIER *prostrates himself and leaves. As* İBRAHİM *walks back and forth absentmindedly, the noise of a drum is heard outside.* İBRAHİM *and* CİNCİ *look at each other surprised.*]

KÖSEM SULTAN:

>[*Enters happily.*]
>
>A new Ottoman man has just honored our world.

CİNCİ HOCA:

>[*Pleased. To* İBRAHİM *who does not understand what's going on.*]
>
>Congratulations, my sultan!
>
>You have taken a step into eternity. Glory be!

KÖSEM SULTAN:

>My royal son, you have a son!

SULTAN İBRAHİM:

>[*Reins in his joy, stops a moment.*]
>
>Good, Turhan! My son, my eternity!
>
>[*Kissing* CİNCİ *on the cheek, he runs out.*]

CİNCİ HOCA:

>[*To* KÖSEM.]
>
>Congratulations, my queen. Blessed news.

KÖSEM SULTAN:

>May you be happy forever, my *hoca*.
>
>Thanks to you, we have this happiness. Let me go
>
>And prepare the cradle and crib for my prince.
>
>[*Controls her joy with difficulty. To herself.*]
>
>Finally! The prince I was waiting for is born.
>
>The tortuous and dark roads of my fate are lit up now.
>
>This princely sun will feed your daylight, Kösem.
>
>My prince is born, my prince is born!
>
>[*Exits.*]

CİNCİ HOCA:

>[*To himself.*]
>
>Everything went well up to this point, Hoca.
>
>Now you have understood that you are not a common little man.
>
>You must take steps according to your size from now on.
>
>This grand vizier's neck should be rung,

He should be removed from my path.

SULTAN İBRAHİM:

[*Returns with an overflowing joy.*]

He is lively like a lion's cub, Hoca!

As if I had gone to faraway countries on a campaign,

And when I was on the verge of being defeated and destroyed in a battle,

New armies had come to my help from the motherland.

Well done, Turhan! But no, one flower does not a spring make.

In every chamber of my palace, one of my babes must smile,

The walls echo with sounds of cradles.

With their unformed faces, my children are teeming in my loins;

I must expand like armies, expand

Against death, against void. Hoca . . .

CİNCİ HOCA:

My lord?

SULTAN İBRAHİM:

[*The brilliance of resolution in his eyes.*]

If I had my mentor, my grand vizier, killed right away,

Would my subjects be angry with me?

CİNCİ HOCA:

On the contrary, my lord; they would pray for your health

Because you have saved the land from the awesome power of Sultan Murad.

SULTAN İBRAHİM:

[*To* SİLÂHTAR YUSUF, *who enters at this moment.*]

Quickly, Yusuf, call the grand vizier to my presence!

SİLÂHTAR YUSUF:

[*In amazement, looks at* CİNCİ *and then at* İBRAHİM.]

Do you mean right away, my lord? He is in the council now.

Is it wise to break up the meeting? Or is there something wrong?

SULTAN İBRAHİM:

[*Panting with joy.*]

I have a son, Yusuf, haven't you heard?

SİLÂHTAR YUSUF:

May it be an auspicious occasion. I had just heard.

I was coming to wish my lord well.

SULTAN İBRAHİM:

Call the grand vizier to my presence right away!

SİLÂHTAR YUSUF:

[*Frightened.*]

Yes, my lord.

SULTAN İBRAHİM:

[*To himself.*]

Even Sultan Murad didn't treat you like that,

Isn't that so, Pasha? Even Sultan Murad, eh?

CİNCİ HOCA:

It seems that the grand vizier was goading the soldiers constantly

To rebel against the palace.

SULTAN İBRAHİM:

[*In great rage.*]

From whom did you hear this? Tell me quickly!

CİNCİ HOCA:

From someone belonging to the Janissary Corps. "You are close to the sultan,"

He told me. "The intention of the grand vizier is evil. He is

Goading the soldiers toward discord. He is telling them that the state

Is in the hands of a madman."

KARA MUSTAFA PASHA:

[*Enters anxiously.*]

You have called for me, my lord?

[*Attempts to prostrate himself before the* SULTAN *and kiss his hem.*]

SULTAN İBRAHİM:

[*Withdraws and turns his back.*]

Yes, I have called for you.

KARA MUSTAFA PASHA:

What is the will of my sultan?

SULTAN İBRAHİM:

Last night, the water of the baths was not heated, Pasha.

Why is the wood that I have requested not given

To the woman caretaker in the harem?

KARA MUSTAFA PASHA:

[*His anger flaring up suddenly.*]

Have you had me called for this, my lord?

For this, have you had the council meeting interrupted?

Such a thing has not been seen in the Ottoman realm before.

By what law are you behaving, my sovereign?

SULTAN İBRAHİM:

[*Turns around.*]

By the law of Sultan İbrahim, Pasha . . . my seal.

[KARA MUSTAFA PASHA *takes the seal out of his breast pocket, kisses it, and extends it slowly and timidly.*]

[*The* SULTAN *once again turns his back and shouts.*]

Chief Gardener!

[*The* CHIEF GARDENER, *at least as majestic as the* GRAND VIZIER, *appears at the door; he salutes.*]

Take this!

[*The* CHIEF GARDENER *takes the seal.*]

Not only the seal.

[*There is a stony silence.*]

CHIEF GARDENER:

[*To* KARA MUSTAFA PASHA.] Please come, my lord.

[*The* CHIEF GARDENER *and* KARA MUSTAFA PASHA *exit. Extremely nervous, trying to assimilate this difficult decision,* İBRAHİM *walks back and forth.* CİNCİ HOCA *exits quietly.*]

SİLÂHTAR YUSUF:

[*With a deep grief showing on his face, kneels at* İBRAHİM's *feet.*]

Please spare the life of your servant Kara Mustafa Pasha, my lord.

He is the mainstay of your state.

His life is your life. Don't kill him.

The chief gardener is ready to deliver him to the executioner.

Don't put out that majestic life.

SULTAN İBRAHİM:

[*In inner turmoil, hardly able to control himself.*]

No, Yusuf. This decision has cost me so much effort

I cannot retract it. I must believe in myself.

Don't insist, ever!

[*Scared,* SİLÂHTAR YUSUF *becomes silent.*]

The first day I ascended the throne I was afraid of him.

His manners, Yusuf, his manners. Words used to come out of him

Like victorious soldiers. Like my brother Sultan Murad—

May he rest in Paradise—he seemed majestic.

Near him, I went back to my dark cell.

[*Absorbed. To himself.*]

Oh, these dark birds of sadness that cover the sky . . .

[*Raises his voice suddenly.*]

No, I do not want these birds to cover my sky any longer.

These birds belong to my dark room.

I fed each one of them with the blood, the core, of my heart.

I feel a stranger before everything, Yusuf. I'm cold, I'm shivering.

I have to steep this heart in fire to get some heat.

The stars have set such a life for me,

Between intense noises and intense silences,

To achieve balance, burning and being burned, burning and being burned.

[*Turns his back to* YUSUF, *who turns away from him.* YUSUF *exits, stunned and mournful.*]

Here the wind of madness awakened is wafting from the open seas.

Yes, I must act more quickly, blow harder than it does.

If it is a tempest, I must become a whirlwind,

And act, like this, more insane than my madness,

Play my life to the end, so

That the white rose of consciousness

Does not fade away.

Scene 4

[*Night. The* INHABITANTS OF ISTANBUL.]

FIRST INHABITANT:

When things go too well, one must worry.

How can old Kösem not know this fact?

SECOND INHABITANT:

The princes she waited for came one after another,

The women in the harem are not one,

Not five, but hundreds. She also made

The man of her choice the grand vizier. Somebody

Whom she can easily put the reins on.

Was Sultanzade Mehmed Pasha ever anybody to become the grand vizier?

FIRST INHABITANT:

Especially after the archer Kara Mustafa Pasha?

THIRD INHABITANT:

The cunning of Cinci toppled the grand vizier, eh?

FIRST INHABITANT:

He has settled into the Ottoman palace so well

That he has no intention of budging.

Judgeships, governorships are sold to any old fool.

Graft has almost become the official thing.

FOURTH INHABITANT:

Under what star was that bastard Cinci born?

SECOND INHABITANT:

Under the same star as Sultan İbrahim, I guess.

SULTAN İBRAHİM:

> [*Enters from the left disguised as a* JESTER. *To the audience.*]
>
> Not only I watch, so do those,
>
> Those unblinking, eternal eyes of God—
>
> Those witnesses of
>
> My virginal, magnificent madnesses.
>
> —Let me just enter among the people,
>
> And look at myself from the outside.
>
> [*Approaches the* INHABITANTS.]
>
> Good evening, friends.

ALL INHABITANTS:

> And good evening to you, Jester in Chief!

FIRST INHABITANT:

> It is a pity about Kara Mustafa Pasha.
>
> How his iron grip is needed at this moment
>
> To take hold of this chaos and give it shape.
>
> How can such a man be killed? And besides, for nothing.
>
> As far as I can see, Sultan İbrahim cut off the branch on which he sat.

SULTAN İBRAHİM:

> It seems that he interrupted the council to call him.
>
> [*Plays the* SULTAN.]
>
> Last night, the water of the baths was not heated, Pasha.
>
> Why is the wood that I have requested not given
>
> To the woman caretaker in the harem?
>
> [*Plays the* GRAND VIZIER.]
>
> Have you had me called for this, my lord?
>
> For this, have you had the council meeting interrupted?
>
> Such a thing has not been seen in the Ottoman realm before.
>
> By what law are you behaving, my sovereign?

FIRST and SECOND INHABITANTS:

> Good for Kara Mustafa Pasha!

SULTAN İBRAHİM:

> [*Laughing.*]
>
> Yes, good for him! Yes!

FOURTH INHABITANT:

> Please keep quiet! The spies of the sultan might overhear you.

SULTAN İBRAHİM:

> So what, friends? Let them, then!

[*Plays the* SULTAN.]

By the law of Sultan İbrahim, Pasha . . . my seal.

SECOND INHABITANT:

God, no! What are you doing, Sultan İbrahim?

SULTAN İBRAHİM:

[*Plays the* SULTAN.]

Chief Executioner!

FIRST and SECOND INHABITANTS:

[*Frightened.*]

God forbid!

THIRD INHABITANT:

Now, if we must tell the truth,

Kara Mustafa Pasha went a bit too far.

After all, he is addressing a sultan.

Is it proper for him to ask, "By what law, Sultan?"

FOURTH INHABITANT:

That's true, gentlemen. To be a sultan

Means to eat from everybody's garden.

SULTAN İBRAHİM:

[*Reprimands him in order to draw him out.*]

He should eat dirt instead! So what if he is a sultan?

Is he God, this İbrahim? Does he reside in eternity?

As far as I know, he also should have limits.

FIRST INHABITANT:

A sultan must know his sultanhood

For a subject to know his place.

But you will protest,

How can a mad ruler have wise subjects?

SECOND INHABITANT:

He has turned his new grand vizier into a fool.

What did he say to Mehmed Pasha, his new mentor?

SULTAN İBRAHİM:

[*Plays the* SULTAN.]

Look here, Mentor! My ancestors, for years, have sent

Jewels, gold to Mecca, to the Holy Land.

Bring all of them back for my treasury so that

The great star of Sultan İbrahim may shine brighter than ever.

THIRD and FOURTH INHABITANTS:

[*Surprised.*]

Good heavens! Well?

SULTAN İBRAHİM:

> [*Plays* GRAND VIZIER MEHMED PASHA.]
>
> Yes, my sovereign lord.
>
> [*Plays the* SULTAN.]
>
> My former mentor Kara Mustafa Pasha used to contradict me sometimes.
>
> He used to tell me that this act goes against the rules,
>
> That it is against reason.
>
> I have not ever heard anything similar from you. Why is this so, Pasha?
>
> [*Plays the* GRAND VIZIER.]
>
> You are the caliph. You are God's shadow on this earth.
>
> Can you do any wrong? All of your actions, even if they seem contrary,
>
> Convey deep meanings.
>
> The duty of your subjects is to understand them.

FIRST and SECOND INHABITANTS:

> You sycophantic dog!

SULTAN İBRAHİM:

> [*Plays the* SULTAN.]
>
> Disappear from my sight, you watermelon-headed pimp!
>
> Find in this, too, profound significance!

ALL INHABITANTS:

> Good for you, Sultan İbrahim! Good for you, Mad İbrahim!

FIRST INHABITANT:

> He should have gone to conquer Crete himself . . .
>
> He should have made the Mediterranean too small for the Venetians . . .
>
> Ah, then, with a conquest not destined for Sultan Murad,
>
> Our sultan would have cracked another nut.

SECOND INHABITANT:

> It seems that, at first, he was interested and wanted to go to Crete himself,
>
> But then he changed his mind. What can he do?
>
> The battlefield is not the harem!
>
> Suddenly he is sending Silâhtar Yusuf Pasha in his place,
>
> And leaving himself in desire's caressing hands.

SULTAN İBRAHİM:

> He is seeing Yusuf Pasha off and calling for the head of the harem.
>
> [*Plays the* SULTAN.]
>
> In our heart there has been a certain amount of sadness again lately.
>
> Let the imperial host get ready for a campaign tonight.
>
> Our army should not lag behind Yusuf Pasha's.

We must attack the old walls of the unknown with new pleasures

And fill up our inner voids with new measures.

[*Plays the* HEAD OF THE HAREM.]

To every wish of our sultan our neck is as thin as a thread.

The whole army of the harem will be ready for campaign tonight.

[*The* INHABITANTS *laugh.*]

Is the world getting out of joint, or what, friends?

What are these madnesses of the sultan?

FIRST INHABITANT:

It is better for you, Jester in Chief!

Let the world be distorted by mad hands,

That, mirroring it, you make us laugh.

SULTAN İBRAHİM:

[*Smiling devilishly.*]

I am warning you, the end of the world is coming,

But you all think this is a new kind of clowning and laugh!

SECOND INHABITANT:

An old sage said that if things go to the devil,

Put on the armor of humor and take the field.

Pretty soon you'll be friendly with all the hardships.

Even though they do not get better, you'll feel better.

SULTAN İBRAHİM:

[*Toward the outside of the stage.*]

Let the devil play his tune then!

Let the pot boil! Let the pot boil!

[*It gets semidark. A stamping tune begins.*]

ALL INHABITANTS:

[*Upon a signal by* İBRAHİM.]

Let the pot boil! Let the pot boil!

SULTAN İBRAHİM:

[*Holds the* FIRST INHABITANT *by the hand.*]

Give me your hand, dear friend, give me your hand!

[*Signals to the others to join them. They form a circle and begin to dance a* hora.[10]]

Let us gnaw at the foundations of the world with laughter!

ALL INHABITANTS:

Let us gnaw at the foundations of the world with laughter!

10. *Hora:* Folk dance of the Black Sea region.

SULTAN İBRAHİM:

Laughing and dancing, friends, laughing and dancing!

ALL INHABITANTS:

Yes, yes! Yes, yes!

Laughing and dancing, laughing and dancing!

SULTAN İBRAHİM:

This is living in the arms of madness!

Tell me, is it worth it to be diverted by dreams?

ALL INHABITANTS:

Yes, yes! Yes, yes!

To be diverted by dreams! To be diverted by dreams!

SULTAN İBRAHİM:

How can the heart take such stretching?

Now good-bye, friends, to desires and cares.

ALL INHABITANTS:

To desires and cares! To desires and cares!

SULTAN İBRAHİM:

Now that the world has shown us all its tricks,

Let us end the world on a final applause!

ALL INHABITANTS:

Let us end the world on a final applause!

SULTAN İBRAHİM:

Laughing and dancing, friends, laughing and dancing!

ALL INHABITANTS:

Yes, yes! Yes, yes!

Laughing and dancing, laughing and dancing!

Scene 5

[İBRAHİM's *private chamber.* CİNCİ *is waiting for the* SULTAN.]

SULTAN İBRAHİM:

[*Enters.*]

Did you use this breath of yours a bit too much, Hoca?

Your spirit has entered my soul like a raging storm;

I cannot keep pace with my suddenly galloping desires.

It is as if I am tied to the tail of a mule running full tilt.

Why don't you use your breath again and rein this in?

CİNCİ HOCA:

Lust gives speed to what death slows down, my lord.

As for living, it is a constant speeding against death.

To pull at the reins now will be to give up the race.

SULTAN İBRAHİM:

No, no, I won't give up the race. I meant to say,

Let's stop and rest for a while,

To figure out what's happening.

CİNCİ HOCA:

What if resting becomes stopping altogether?

SULTAN İBRAHİM:

That is true, too . . .

CİNCİ HOCA:

What did we say in one of our recent lessons, my lord?

SULTAN İBRAHİM:

What did we, Hoca?

CİNCİ HOCA:

One must refresh the sources of ecstasy in some measure.

SULTAN İBRAHİM:

And we added: new ecstasies can spring only from new bodies.

CİNCİ HOCA:

You remember everything, my lord, I am amazed!

You never let go of what you have once grasped.

Every race has its special taste; the Spanish,

The Italians, the Greeks, the Arabs—particularly the Arabs—

Their women inflame a man with a special fire.

SULTAN İBRAHİM:

[*Excited, panting.*]

Particularly the Arab women, you say? They inflame a man?

CİNCİ HOCA:

Melt him like a candle!

SULTAN İBRAHİM:

[*Clasps* CİNCİ *by the neck.*]

O God! My *hoca* . . .

CİNCİ HOCA:

My lord!

SULTAN İBRAHİM:

You are right. I know the taste of all the races

You have just listed. But I have been wondering from the very beginning,

How is the English woman? How is lovemaking with her?

CİNCİ HOCA:

As far as I know, my lord, her skin is the color of white silk.

SULTAN İBRAHİM:

You mean, of the same race as the Sultan of Fairies, Ezreke Bânû?

CİNCİ HOCA:

Yes, my lord. But I do not know

How well they compare with others in the field of love.

[GRAND VIZIER MEHMED PASHA *enters with a sable coat on each of his arms and two* CONCUBINES. *Their faces are covered.* İBRAHİM *excitedly moves toward the* CONCUBINES.]

SULTAN İBRAHİM:

[*To the* GRAND VIZIER *and pointing to the* CONCUBINES.]

From which clime, Pasha?

MEHMED PASHA:

You guess, my lord. As soon as you touch their skin,

You'll be able to tell which clime, which race.

SULTAN İBRAHİM:

[*Pleased, parting the* CONCUBINES' *veils, caresses them.*]

I am not familiar with this skin. I wonder . . .

[MEHMED PASHA *nods, smiling.*]

Good for you, Mehmed Pasha. You have served us well.

My former grand vizier could not do what you have done.

He had left me deprived of the taste of the English woman.

[*Going near* CİNCİ.]

Their skin is really like white silk, Hoca.

Let us see how hot their flames are.

[*Goes back near the* CONCUBINES; *as he is caressing them one after the other,* MEHMED PASHA *approaches.*]

MEHMED PASHA:

My lord, your servant Mustafa is a peerless soldier.

What if we make him commander of the Janissaries?

SULTAN İBRAHİM:

[*Drunk with caressing the* CONCUBINES, *not comprehending the* GRAND VIZIER'S *words.*]

Whatever you say, Mentor . . . do as you wish.

MEHMED PASHA:

[*Presents the furs.*]

They are sables from Russia, priceless, my lord.

SULTAN İBRAHİM:

> [*Takes the furs, caresses them with delight.*]
>
> This sable also is arousing like a woman's skin, isn't it?
>
> Good, Pasha, very good! This is the way to serve the sultan.
>
> [*Wraps the* CONCUBINES *in the furs.*]
>
> Give them right away to the caretaker of the concubines
>
> That he add them with a special ceremony to the armies of the harem.
>
> Let him put them tonight with others who are waiting for their turns;
>
> We are out on a very big campaign tonight.
>
> Are there any state matters as well, Pasha?

MEHMED PASHA:

> Everything is in order.
>
> Let your royal heart enjoy itself.
>
> I will carry that load all by myself.

SULTAN İBRAHİM:

> Good, very good! But let the harem be ready tonight.

> [MEHMED PASHA *prostrates himself and exits with the* CONCUBINES.]

> Why wait for the night, Hoca,
>
> Since we can renew our speed right away?
>
> I am very curious about this new flavor.

CİNCİ HOCA:

> In this business, my lord, to wait
>
> Is to reinforce the strength, to accelerate the speed of desire.
>
> Besides, pleasure can be felt
>
> More powerfully at night.
>
> Also, if you can get help from ambergris until nuptial time . . .

SULTAN İBRAHİM:

> That is to say, I should not get caught flatfooted
>
> In the English land. Is that it, Hoca?

CİNCİ HOCA:

> No, with God's help, you won't when your *hoca* is around.
>
> You will be galloping tonight, too, my lord!

SULTAN İBRAHİM:

> [*Smacks* CİNCİ *on the shoulder.*]
>
> May you live long, Hoca! I have made you the chief military judge.
>
> You are fit to be the *şeyhülislâm*.

CİNCİ HOCA:

> My lord, my young İbrahim will be very glad about this.

SULTAN İBRAHİM:

>Your young İbrahim? Who is he?

CİNCİ HOCA:

>My son, my lord. To bring me luck
>
>I named him İbrahim
>
>Because he was born the day you were enthroned.

SULTAN İBRAHİM:

>[*Flattered.*]
>
>Really! How old is your son, Hoca?

CİNCİ HOCA:

>He has just turned six, my lord.

SULTAN İBRAHİM:

>Very good. What about finding him a governorship
>
>Or something?

CİNCİ HOCA:

>[*Bows.*]
>
>My sovereign!

SULTAN İBRAHİM:

>What do you say to the governorship of Erzurum?

CİNCİ HOCA:

>That post is not vacant, my lord.

SULTAN İBRAHİM:

>What about Sivas?[11]

CİNCİ HOCA:

>That post is taken, too.

SULTAN İBRAHİM:

>God, what is this?
>
>Are all these damned posts filled? What about Damascus?

CİNCİ HOCA:

>That too.

SULTAN İBRAHİM:

>Well, if it is filled, so it is!
>
>I have made our son, İbrahim, the governor of Damascus!
>
>Let them send the former governor to another place.

>[CİNCİ *bows.*]

11. Sivas: City in central Anatolia.

Scene 6

[IBRAHİM's *bedchamber. Night.* IBRAHİM *enters, girded with a sword, a helmet on his head like an emperor returning from battle, and accompanied by music.* CINCI *is with him.*]

SULTAN İBRAHİM:

With such rich spoils we have returned from the Caucasus!

The delight of Georgian and Circassian girls is terrifying, Hoca.

CİNCİ HOCA:

They are created for lovemaking, my lord!

SULTAN İBRAHİM:

[*Draws his sword.*]

We must review the sources of pleasure constantly.

My navy! Get my navy ready immediately!

Sultan İbrahim is going on a campaign to the British Isles!

[*Music plays as he moves toward the bed.*]

CİNCİ HOCA:

[*Quietly to the* HEAD OF THE HAREM, *who enters.*]

Prepare those English girls now.

Do not forget to use the perfumes I have mentioned.

[*The* HEAD OF THE HAREM *bows and leaves.*]

Scene 7

[KÖSEM's *chamber.* KÖSEM *and* GRAND VIZIER MEHMED PASHA.]

KÖSEM SULTAN:

You have done well, Pasha; you have served us well

By having Mustafa made the Janissary commander.

MEHMED PASHA:

To serve you, my queen,

Is the highest sovereignty for your servant Mehmed.

KÖSEM SULTAN:

Thank you. What the sultan has denied me

He granted you somehow. Ever since he had his former grand vizier killed,

He is overruling every wish of mine.

All this business depended on two concubines, it turned out.

You say that he has developed a new passion for sables now?

MEHMED PASHA:

Yes, my lady. As the sultan touched those soft things,

He began to soften up. And when I said to him,

"Should we make your servant Mustafa the Janissary commander?"

He did not even ask who Mustafa was. He said, "Yes." To secure

Your wish pleased me immeasurably, made me happy.

KÖSEM SULTAN:

The day the sultan had the former grand vizier killed,

He faltered, asking, "To whom is this seal to be given now?"

We thought of you then. We recommended your name.

MEHMED PASHA:

From that day on, I also

Have not forgotten who my real master is.

KÖSEM SULTAN:

[*Proudly.*]

We are very happy with you, Pasha. You should know that.

As long as your endeavors look in our direction,

Your value will increase daily in our eyes.

We would like to repay your recent service with a gift.

The sultan's former bodyguard and dearest friend, Yusuf Pasha,

Is about to return from Crete as the conqueror of Chania.

MEHMED PASHA:

I have heard that the sultan loves him very much.

KÖSEM SULTAN:

He is the only person whom he trusts and believes, that Yusuf.

He loves him with unfailing affection.

The trust the sultan has in him, Pasha, is dangerous for you.

MEHMED PASHA:

You have perched this lucky bird of state on my head.

My lady, I should learn from you, too, how not to scare it.

KÖSEM SULTAN:

It seems that Yusuf Pasha has conquered the fortress through consent,

That is, without looting;

It means he will return to Istanbul empty-handed,

Whereas the sultan likes

Both giving and receiving many gifts.

[*Extends her hand to the* GRAND VIZIER *to be kissed.*]

MEHMED PASHA:

[*Kneels and kisses the extended hand.*]

Let your servant Mehmed stay tied always at your door;

Do not deny me this favor, my sovereign lady.

[KÖSEM *smiles, nodding her head. The* GRAND VIZIER *exits.*]

KÖSEM SULTAN:

> [*To herself.*]
>
> After all, my man has been installed as the Janissary commander
>
> Either through my wish or the grand vizier's!
>
> Well, I also have a prince who will ascend the throne.
>
> That infidel Cinci, how he has settled himself at the helm!
>
> Before the people and army rear their heads and end the dynasty,
>
> We should smoothly remove İbrahim from the throne; otherwise,
>
> His tumble will take us all.
>
> After all, the prince is very young; even his mother is a child.
>
> They cannot move out from under my wing yet.
>
> [TURHAN SULTAN *enters.*]
>
> Come here, my girl, come. How is my prince, is he well?

TURHAN SULTAN:

> Very well, my lady. In perfect health, thank God!
>
> If he, too, happened to be sick, my life would be unbearable.

KÖSEM SULTAN:

> What is wrong, Turhan? What is troubling you?

TURHAN SULTAN:

> My son's father, my lady,
>
> Who else could it be?
>
> He does not speak to me, even for a day.

KÖSEM SULTAN:

> You are merely a woman of the sultan now, Turhan.
>
> That first night is now an old story. Besides,
>
> The sultan does not summon his other women, either,
>
> Neither Muazzez or Dilâşub. They, too,
>
> Have borne princes, sultans for him.

TURHAN SULTAN:

> That's true. All he thinks of now is Hümaşah,
>
> His dearest Hümaşah.

KÖSEM SULTAN:

> That girl has turned out to be quite something. But it seems that
>
> She has not managed to enter the sultan's arms even for one night.

TURHAN SULTAN:

> The girl herself does not want it, my lady,
>
> And the sultan does not want to force her.
>
> Somehow Hümaşah has managed to control herself, and consequently

Her stock has risen in the sultan's eyes.

Your son is tied to her slightest wishes now.

KÖSEM SULTAN:

Do not worry yourself too much, my girl. You are, after all,

The mother of the eldest son; your place is secure.

TURHAN SULTAN:

I am also worried by the strange mannerisms of the sultan, my queen.

He is, after all, my husband, my son's father.

When he begins joking with that jester . . .

KÖSEM SULTAN:

That jester?

TURHAN SULTAN:

The man enters the sultan's chamber

As if it were his own room. "You are my master, my jester in chief."

It seems as if he is saying to him, "In my eyes you are higher than the grand vizier!"

He is walking the streets at night, disguised.

I am worried that something will happen to him.

[*About to leave.*]

KÖSEM SULTAN:

Don't let things bother you.

Look into our prince's room once more before you go to sleep, my dear girl.

TURHAN SULTAN:

Yes, my lady. May God never separate me from my Mehmed.

[*Exits.*]

KÖSEM SULTAN:

[*To herself.*]

Then it seems that Hümaşah is no ordinary concubine.

She knows how self-restraint brings power.

One must be alert against her from now on.

But why is İbrahim not taking her to his bed?

Why does he not shout, "Bring me Hümaşah,"

In one of his rabid nights? Or is this

Another aspect of his madness?

Hümaşah is not to be trusted; she must be plotting something.

Is she trying to have the sultan fall into her net, or what?

Scene 8

[IBRAHIM's *private chamber.* IBRAHIM *is sitting with* HÜMAŞAH *on a divan. Whereas the* SULTAN *constantly looks at her, she looks in the other direction.* IBRAHIM *wants to touch her and reaches out, but she ignores him. Sighing, İBRAHİM withdraws his hand. HÜMAŞAH smells the rose in her hand first; then she holds it to İBRAHİM's nose. He smells the rose devouringly. İBRAHİM suddenly stretches toward HÜMAŞAH; the girl withdraws immediately. She begins to kiss the flower. Crawling, İBRAHİM advances; the moment he is about to kiss her, she tosses back her head. With sly coquetry, she holds the rose to İBRAHİM's lips. İBRAHİM kisses and smells the flower passionately.*]

SULTAN İBRAHİM:

[*To himself.*]

This is an utterly new thing in my life.

HÜMAŞAH SULTAN:

What is a new thing, my lord?

SULTAN İBRAHİM:

[*Without turning his head to her, kisses the flower.*]

As you keep yourself away from me like that,

A new spring is welling within me,

Its waters flowing toward you.

HÜMAŞAH SULTAN:

Those waters that I awaken,

Let them all flow to me.

SULTAN İBRAHİM:

Why do you not then submit to the authority of my love,

And admit me to your beauty as a guest even once?

HÜMAŞAH SULTAN:

[*Showing her body.*]

This land is from tip to toe yours, my lord;

You can rule here, according to your will.

[İBRAHİM *advances toward her.*]

But I wish that all your love

Grow only in my virginal garden.

[İBRAHİM *embraces her.* HÜMAŞAH *pulls her head to one side.*]

Also . . .

SULTAN İBRAHİM:

Yes?

HÜMAŞAH SULTAN:

Should I not know that I am the favorite of my lord?

SULTAN İBRAHİM:

Hümaşah, is anybody preventing you?

HÜMAŞAH SULTAN:

I would not like my lord to worry.

[*Kisses* İBRAHİM *quickly.*]

My love is stronger than all evil intentions.

SULTAN İBRAHİM:

My dear Hümaşah, anyone who does not recognize you as my sultan

Is going against my will.

HÜMAŞAH SULTAN:

I am not yet your sultan, your first wife, my lord.

I have not borne you a child, nor have I even become your woman.

SULTAN İBRAHİM:

You have not wanted it, Hümaşah. Tell me, what is making you unhappy?

HÜMAŞAH SULTAN:

Your sisters don't accept me as a human being.

Whenever they see me in the harem, they giggle behind my back,

Mock me in front of the concubines,

Send me for menial chores.

SULTAN İBRAHİM:

[*Inflamed suddenly.*]

Somebody come here!

HEAD OF THE HAREM:

[*Enters.*]

What is your command, my lord?

SULTAN İBRAHİM:

[*Nervous.*]

Right away, call my sisters here!

[*Points to* HÜMAŞAH.]

They will serve my one and only sultan!

[KÖSEM *appears at the door.*]

HÜMAŞAH SULTAN:

[*Worried.*]

Forgive your sisters this time, my lord,

Spare them. Your mother . . .

SULTAN İBRAHİM:

[*Angry.*]

What about my mother, Hümaşah?

HÜMAŞAH SULTAN:

[*On tenterhooks.*]

Your mother, my lord . . .

SULTAN İBRAHİM:

Am I not the sultan?

KÖSEM SULTAN:

>*[Enters furiously.]*
>
>You are the sultan, my son, yes, you are,
>
>But you do not behave like one!
>
>*[In anger, she looks at* HÜMAŞAH *belittlingly.]*
>
>What stories did you tell my son, the sultan, girl?
>
>*[*HÜMAŞAH *remains silent, defiant; she looks at* İBRAHİM, *who is at the peak of his anger. His hands are shaking, and he is hardly able to control himself.]*
>
>I am talking to you, you sly snake, answer me!

SULTAN İBRAHİM:

>I want them to serve my sultan.
>
>I want them to see what it means to mock her.

KÖSEM SULTAN:

>So what if they have mocked her? They are the daughters of sultans.
>
>This one, she is a mere concubine from the slave market.
>
>How many princes, sultans has she born you that she has become your favorite
>>wife?
>
>It seems that you are forgetting the Ottoman rules, my son.

SULTAN İBRAHİM:

>Rules, rules, rules! Were rules not set by my ancestors?
>
>Shall I live by the laws of dead people?
>
>Will I not do what I want?

KÖSEM SULTAN:

>You shall do what you want,
>
>But according to the laws.

SULTAN İBRAHİM:

>Yes, according to the laws I set.
>
>Let my sisters come. They shall serve my sultan.

HÜMAŞAH SULTAN:

>*[Anxious, timid.]*
>
>My lord . . .

SULTAN İBRAHİM:

>Let them come right away. Or else . . .

KÖSEM SULTAN:

>As long as I am alive, your sisters shall not serve
>
>A two-bit concubine of unknown parentage.
>
>Get hold of yourself, Son!

SULTAN İBRAHİM:

>You are talking to the sultan of the land, Mother!
>
>Do not forget that for a moment!

KÖSEM SULTAN:

> The sultan of the land is my son!
>
> Do not forget that either, my sultan.

SULTAN İBRAHİM:

> [*Turns his back.*]
>
> Leave immediately and gather your belongings.
>
> Move to the pavilion of İskender Çelebi. Your presence in the palace
>
> Has become too burdensome for us.

KÖSEM SULTAN:

> [*Upset but not without composure.*]
>
> I carried you for months in my womb. That was not too burdensome for me.
>
> When your brother wanted to turn you over to the hangman,
>
> I withstood his anger. That was not too burdensome for me.
>
> When you refused to ascend the throne,
>
> I dragged you to the throne. That was not too burdensome for me.
>
> Well, İbrahim, this is how, finally, you are going to repay me?

SULTAN İBRAHİM:

> A mother does not lend her child,
>
> A mother gives. Whereas you
>
> Consider everything you give me to be a loan.
>
> And you demand high interest on it.
>
> Our decision is definite, Mother.
>
> Make preparations to leave immediately.

KÖSEM SULTAN:

> Very well, İbrahim! Now that you have learned how to bite,
>
> You show your teeth to your mother, too.
>
> Truly, your sun has climbed to the very zenith;
>
> Eyes are dazzled by its brilliance.
>
> But the zenith is the beginning of descent.
>
> [*Looks at* HÜMAŞAH *with hatred. Exits.*]

HÜMAŞAH SULTAN:

> My lord, is your mother's being away from here
>
> Not more dangerous than her being under our eyes?

> [GRAND VIZIER MEHMED PASHA *and* YUSUF PASHA *enter.* HÜMAŞAH *exits.*]

SULTAN İBRAHİM:

> [YUSUF PASHA *prostrates himself in front of* İBRAHİM, *who helps him rise to his feet.*]
>
> Welcome, Yusuf. We have missed you. Are you well?

YUSUF PASHA:

> My lord, I am so happy that I am at a loss for words!

SULTAN İBRAHİM:

> I welcome the conqueror of Chania.
>
> Let your battle and your victory be blessed!

MEHMED PASHA:

> Yusuf Pasha has done a glorious deed, my lord.
>
> He has finally put the Venetians in their place.

YUSUF PASHA:

> My lord, if things had not gone wrong,
>
> I would have opened all of Crete to your rule.

[YUSUF PASHA *looks at the* GRAND VIZIER *furtively;* MEHMED PASHA *becomes worried.*]

SULTAN İBRAHİM:

> That too may happen one day, Yusuf. Thanks to you!

YUSUF PASHA:

> Thanks to my sultan!

SULTAN İBRAHİM:

> You must rest a little now. We'll have our noon meal together
>
> So that we can assuage our longings.

[YUSUF PASHA *prostrates himself and exits.*]

> You also love Yusuf Pasha, don't you, Mentor?

MEHMED PASHA:

> Of course, my lord. He did a great deed.

SULTAN İBRAHİM:

> He achieved a glorious deed, Mentor. He used to tell me,
>
> "My lord, the control of Crete by the Venetians
>
> Is a great danger to the Ottoman Empire.
>
> This island is a lance pointed at our heart."

MEHMED PASHA:

> Yusuf Pasha did a great deed, my lord.
>
> One end of the lance is in our hands now. Only . . .
>
> [İBRAHİM *looks at him questioningly.*]
>
> He let the infidels in the castle go scot-free,
>
> Whereas thousands of our soldiers were martyred there.
>
> Besides, what about the thousands of sacks of gold spent on this battle?
>
> They say that the Cretans are very rich,
>
> And that there are no women excelling theirs.
>
> Yet Yusuf Pasha returned to Istanbul very much empty-handed.
>
> He brought merely two stone columns for my sultan.
>
> But perhaps these columns are some unknown jewel.

I wonder if he let those infidel merchants go free

Without getting anything in return?

SULTAN İBRAHİM:

Call Yusuf Pasha to me immediately!

[*To himself.*]

Is it possible? Can Yusuf do this to me?

[*To* YUSUF PASHA, *who has rushed back.*]

Yusuf, go and take all of Crete.

YUSUF PASHA:

[*Surprised, looks at* MEHMED PASHA *and* İBRAHİM *alternately.*]

Gladly, as my sultan wishes, but the season

Is not fit for a naval campaign now.

A rocky island like Crete cannot be taken in the winter.

SULTAN İBRAHİM:

You think you have served your sultan, don't you,

When you have spent so much of my treasury? Besides,

You let a great many infidels go.

YUSUF PASHA:

I have spent gold, but I have conquered a huge fortress.

True, I did not touch the inhabitants' lives or honor, but

It was your honor I gave them in my promise of pardon.

It is true I could have put them all to the sword;

Could have chained their wives, their daughters, and brought them here;

But that would have been murder, plunder, not conquest.

How has the mighty Ottoman Empire stood on its legs for so many years?

Have you ever thought of that, my lord?

I have done everything I could,

And that despite many acts of treachery . . .

Let your other servants serve you the way I have.

SULTAN İBRAHİM:

You are saying strange things to me. I'm telling you to go capture the island.

YUSUF PASHA:

It is not the time. One cannot go.

SULTAN İBRAHİM:

I told you to go and take the whole of Crete and come back!

YUSUF PASHA:

Crete is not a ship, my lord,

That I can tie to the back of my galley and bring back.

Since you were interested, so interested, in this island,

You could have been a bit more interested in those who would take the island.

For weeks, my soldiers went hungry. They ate grass.

I sent message after message to Istanbul,

I sent for help. There was no answer.

My eager soldiers who had gone to conquer an island

Became an army encircled by misery there.

Was the grand vizier occupied with harem matters,

Or did he employ all his strength to serve the Venetians?

[İBRAHİM *looks at the* GRAND VIZIER.]

MEHMED PASHA:

[*Stuttering.*]

Slander! Great lies!

YUSUF PASHA:

First to prevent the Cretan campaign, then to abort it,

How many thousands of gold coins the grand vizier took from the Venetian ambassador—

Would he like me to tell about that?

MEHMED PASHA:

They are all lies, my lord! All lies!

He is envious of your love for me. His eyes are on my post.

SULTAN İBRAHİM:

Give me my seal, you pimp! Yusuf does not lie.

In fact, he speaks the truth a bit too much.

[*The* GRAND VIZIER *takes the seal from his breast pocket, kisses it, and hands it to the* SULTAN.]

SULTAN İBRAHİM:

[*Takes the seal.*]

You slander my heart, pimp.

I have never dirtied it with any love of you.

My mother let you loose on me. Away!

I wish never again to smell your stench in my palace.

[*The* GRAND VIZIER *exits.* İBRAHİM *gives the seal to* YUSUF PASHA.]

Take it, Yusuf. You are the only person who can carry it.

Once, you were my bodyguard, the closest person to my heart.

Then you became my commander, conquered a new castle for me.

Now become my grand vizier, govern my state.

YUSUF PASHA:

> This is too great an award to bestow on your servant, my lord.
>
> I cannot carry such a heavy burden.

SULTAN İBRAHİM:

> You can, Yusuf. Take it.

YUSUF PASHA:

> No, my lord. I cannot take it.

SULTAN İBRAHİM:

> [*His hand remains raised. Confused about what to do, he becomes nervous.*]
>
> Do you mean you don't want it?

YUSUF PASHA:

> No, I do not, my lord.

SULTAN İBRAHİM:

> It is opening like a pit before me,
>
> This "no" from your mouth, Yusuf.
>
> You talk to me
>
> As though the soul of my former mentor, Kara Mustafa Pasha, has entered you.

YUSUF PASHA:

> Since my youth, my lord,
>
> I have longed to become a man of state like him.
>
> I have not forgotten how Kara Mustafa Pasha was killed
>
> For the sake of nothing.

SULTAN İBRAHİM:

> Am I not the sultan?
>
> I can kill anybody for the sake of something or for the sake of nothing.

YUSUF PASHA:

> To be a sultan is not to kill people at random.

SULTAN İBRAHİM:

> Then what is it to be a sultan, Yusuf?

YUSUF PASHA:

> To be a sultan is, above all, to know how to leave the harem behind.

SULTAN İBRAHİM:

> [*Stifling his anger, turns his back to* YUSUF PASHA.]
>
> Executioner!

[*The* CHIEF GARDENER *appears at the door. He waits for* İBRAHİM'*s order.*]

YUSUF PASHA:

> [*Shouts with fury.*]
>
> What are you waiting for? Have me strangled, too!

Perhaps then you will be double the sultan you are now!

SULTAN İBRAHİM:

[*His back turned, speaks to the* CHIEF GARDENER.]

Be quick! Either his life or yours!

[*The* CHIEF GARDENER *exits with* YUSUF PASHA. İBRAHİM *paces back and forth, breathless.*]

If anyone comes before me and says, "No, I will not . . . "

I find myself inside that dark dungeon.

[HÜMAŞAH *enters slowly.* İBRAHİM *moves toward her, showing the seal.*]

What will become of this? Who will be made the grand vizier now?

HÜMAŞAH SULTAN:

[*Takes the seal.*]

My lion should not worry about it.

There is an Ahmed Pasha among your servants.

Nobody can handle this job better than he.

You should rest a little and enjoy yourself;

I'll have this seal sent to Ahmed Pasha.

[İBRAHİM *agrees with a nod of his head.* HÜMAŞAH *exits.*]

SULTAN İBRAHİM:

[*To himself.*]

Yusuf, my darling Yusuf, your death

Like a black halo is encircling my heart.

I myself cannot become a sword, and I am destroying those

Who act as my sword.

Destruction, by what confusing laws you wreak your havoc!

[*Shouts with anguish.*]

Right away, call the head of the harem to me!

[*The* HEAD OF THE HAREM *enters; anxious and timid, he prostrates himself.*]

Let the whole harem be mobilized and adorned with lights.

No soul in my palace shall fall asleep tonight.

Call all the boy dancers, all the girl dancers

From the city. Red wine must gush forth tonight,

Singing must stop the dark noises awakening within me.

Let Cinci not stay idle either. Go and seek him.

He should arm me and the forces of the harem

With love's weapons. We must conquer the night with pleasures.

This is a great death; it can be healed only with great revelries.

CURTAIN

ACT III

Scene 1

[*A room in İskender Çelebi's pavilion.* KÖSEM *and* JANISSARY COMMANDER MUSTAFA AĞA. KÖSEM's *face is covered with a black veil.*]

KÖSEM SULTAN:

A madness, with a thousand arms and a thousand legs,

Is dancing to the tune of destruction in the Ottoman palace.

The ship of state will soon hit the straits of nothingness.

We must act in time, Ağa. Anarchy is about to break out.

MUSTAFA AĞA:

We know in what hands the wheel of state is left now, my lady.

All the Janissary commanders, Bektaş, Muslihiddin, Kara Murad, and myself,

Often come together and discuss the matter,

Trying to find solutions to the problem.

This new grand vizier, Ahmed Pasha, is a worse bootlicker

Than Mehmed Pasha. All he does is serve the sultan's lust.

Somebody from the dynasty must sympathize with our cause.

We are waiting for a sign, my lady, a sign.

Except we want no blood spilled during this business;

The memory of Young Osman[12] is too fresh on us yet.

KÖSEM SULTAN:

Replacing the grand vizier is not enough, Ağa.

You would have changed the poker, but what is the use

If the hand holding it remains the same?

Sultan İbrahim is my son, yes, true enough.

I do not want anything ever to happen to him,

Even though he has exiled me from the palace, after

I put him on the throne, made him sultan.

MUSTAFA AĞA:

You are right, he should not have gone that far.

His action wounded each one of us very deeply.

KÖSEM SULTAN:

Your loyalty is my greatest support, Ağa.

The state and sovereignty depend on you.

You can either raise it or sink it with your hands.

Particularly your stature—the stature of our brave Mustafa Ağa

---

12. Osman III: Ottoman sultan who ruled from 1754 to 1757.

Is very lofty in our eyes and in our heart.

MUSTAFA AĞA:

You are drowning your humble servant in honor, my lady.

Consider my worthless life pledged to you.

KÖSEM SULTAN:

We think of higher places for our *ağa.*

MUSTAFA AĞA:

[*Bows.*]

My lady!

KÖSEM SULTAN:

I do not want the life of the sultan touched.

He is part of my flesh, after all!

But he is used to living in a dark cell.

Besides, the one to take his place is the prince, his own son,

Yet the prince is still too young, and so is his mother.

MUSTAFA AĞA:

[*Jumps in immediately.*]

But what about my lady?

Both your experience and superior personality

Will make up for the defects of the prince and his mother.

We, the Janissary commanders, think along these lines.

KÖSEM SULTAN:

You are very kind, Ağa! Now listen to me:

The sultan has sent me gifts, asking me to forgive him.

It seems that he has missed his mother and wants to see her again in the palace.

I am returning to Topkapı Palace, Mustafa Ağa.

MUSTAFA AĞA:

Will it not be difficult to keep in contact then?

My sultan, how are we going to communicate with you?

KÖSEM SULTAN:

I will find some way, Mustafa Ağa.

I will relay the events one by one to you.

My moving to the palace will be very good for our cause.

On that great day of action, one of us must be there.

In military parlance, that means conquering the castle from the inside,

Isn't that so, Ağa?

MUSTAFA AĞA:

In the face of your falconlike insight,

My mind is stranded, my sultan!

KÖSEM SULTAN:

> To the fire that Sultan İbrahim has started
>
> I am moving with a pair of bellows, Ağa.
>
> Then we will put it out all together,
>
> If you know how to arrive on time.
>
> They will come to take me soon.
>
> Let them not see you here, Mustafa Ağa.

MUSTAFA AĞA:

> [*Kisses the hand extended by* KÖSEM.]
>
> The soldiers will wait for the signal from you;
>
> You should give the signal right on time, my lady.

KÖSEM SULTAN:

> The sultan's insanity will provide the signal.
>
> Good-bye.
>
> [MUSTAFA AĞA *exits.* KÖSEM *is joyful.*]
>
> The Janissaries are in my hands now.
>
> It would have been good if I had secured the cavalry, too,
>
> But it is not right to open too many fronts.
>
> [*Raises her voice passionately.*]
>
> I will attack my enemy from his weakest point.
>
> Your calling me back shows that you are scared of me, İbrahim.
>
> You are a fruit now, ripe on the tree of insanity.
>
> If I give the tree a jolt, you'll fall off,
>
> But I'll shake that tree, I'll shake it to its roots.
>
> You and your lover will tumble to the ground.
>
> Did you say that my presence in the palace was too unbearable for you?
>
> But I have grown even more unbearable with my hatred, İbrahim!
>
> And I'll wipe out every obstacle to the throne before me.
>
> Whatever it is, whoever it is, I'll wipe it out.
>
> [*Settles on the sofa, as though sitting on the throne.*]
>
> In this land, from east to west,
>
> From north to south,
>
> Only my rule will pass,
>
> Only mine, mine, mine!
>
> [*Speaks as if the* GRAND VIZIER *were in front of her.*]
>
> Grand Vizier! Give triple pay to my soldiers,
>
> More than ever given by a sultan previously!
>
> [*Pleased.*]

Yes, I know, Pasha, I know. These rolls of silk, this Indian shawl,
These pearl necklaces, topaz rings, emerald bracelets—
All are gifts from all the corners of the world.
Let them be added to my treasury.

[*Nervous.*]
Look here, Pasha. Gifts are coming from every part of the world,
But why does the shah of Persia not remember us?
Perhaps he finds his own sun brighter than ours!
Start a new campaign toward the eastern borders.
We are not very happy with the governor of Egypt, Pasha.
He seems unable to send his taxes on time. Get someone
More able, more competent in his place. The governor-general,
It seems, is lax in his business
Around Bosnia; the enemy is stirring up trouble.
Discuss some solutions immediately. From now on, then,
Either in internal matters or in foreign matters,
Without asking me, without discussing with me,
No important decision will be taken!
Is this clear?

[*Rapt in her dream, she extends her hand to the imaginary grand vizier in front of her to be kissed. Steps are suddenly heard from outside. Recovers herself.*]
Now, great Kösem, let your path be open.
Let your rule be long, very long.
[*Exits with decisive steps.*]

Scene 2

[İBRAHİM's *bedchamber. When light appears,* İBRAHİM's *roar is heard.*]

SULTAN İBRAHİM:
[*Jumps out of his bed. His eyes bulging out of their sockets,* İBRAHİM *is hardly able to stand up.*]
You, head of the harem! Where are you, you castrated dog!
Has a plague hit the harem? Why are they not coming?
Did I not tell you that they must line up and wait for my orders?
Whenever I yell, "Attack!" one of them must enter.
Why am I not obeyed? Am I not the sultan?

[*Darts to the door. Pulls in a* CONCUBINE *passing down the corridor outside.*]

Is it your turn, girl, is it? Where do you come from?

Tell me, is it from the deserts of Arabia or from the Caucasus?

Goddamn those frozen English girls,

Nothing is like my Circassians!

CONCUBINE:

[*Very scared, struggling desperately.*]

I am not Circassian, my lord! It is not my turn!

SULTAN İBRAHİM:

[*Pulls her to the bed.*]

Doesn't matter, doesn't matter!

[*The* CONCUBINE *frees herself and runs away.* İBRAHİM *darts after her like a bird of prey. Outside, the* CONCUBINE's *scream is heard; then groans come, and then there is silence. The* HEAD OF THE HAREM *and* CİNCİ *carry* İBRAHİM *in with difficulty. He is half unconscious; they take him to his bed.*]

CİNCİ HOCA:

[*Leaving worried.*]

My God, how am I going to restrain now

This force that I have let loose?

[*Exits.*]

SULTAN İBRAHİM:

[*Groans.*]

Hümaşah! Hümaşah! Hümaşah!

HEAD OF THE HAREM:

[*Going out, encounters* HÜMAŞAH *at the door.*]

The sultan is repeating your name, my lady!

HÜMAŞAH SULTAN:

[*Angry.*]

Keep your overheated mares in check from now on!

And tell that infidel bastard called Cinci Hoca

That he should pack right away and leave the palace with all his tricks!

[*The* HEAD OF THE HAREM *exits, bowing.*]

SULTAN İBRAHİM:

[*Groans, twisting in bed.*]

Hümaşah! Hümaşah! Hümaşah!

HÜMAŞAH SULTAN:

[*Gets undressed slowly.*]

It falls on me to calm down that stallion stirred up inside him.

Scene 3

[*The* INHABITANTS OF ISTANBUL.]

FOURTH INHABITANT:

But they had made the poor man sultan by force,

And now he is taking his revenge upon the world.

SECOND INHABITANT:

Should one smile or cry at this condition of the world?

THIRD INHABITANT:

[*Marking time with his foot. To himself.*]

Let us gnaw at the foundations of the world with laughter!

FIRST INHABITANT:

[*Keeping time with his foot. To himself.*]

Laughing and dancing, friends, laughing and dancing!

SECOND INHABITANT:

No, really, our jester in chief was telling the truth.

What are these ravings of the sultan?

FIRST INHABITANT:

[*Teases the* FOURTH INHABITANT.]

To be a sultan means

To eat from everybody's garden!

FOURTH INHABITANT:

He should eat dirt instead! So what if he is a sultan?

THIRD INHABITANT:

Is he God, this İbrahim? Does he live in eternity?

FOURTH INHABITANT:

As far as I know, he also should have limits.

Scene 4

[İBRAHİM's *private chamber. Both* İBRAHİM *and* HÜMAŞAH *are cloaked in sable.*]

HÜMAŞAH SULTAN:

But were you not going to smell any rose after me?

SULTAN İBRAHİM:

After long and despairing nights

A wave of fire stirs within my loins,

I want to burn and to be burned, burn and be burned.

Besides, do you know, Hümaşah,

That after the storm of such lust-ridden nights

I look for you even more, seek your shelter,

Just as a ship seeks harbor

After being tossed on open seas

For a long time?

HÜMAŞAH SULTAN:

The storm raged too hard last night, it seems.

The hull of the ship was taking water as it entered the harbor,

Its sails were riddled with holes.

SULTAN İBRAHİM:

It is good that you kicked Cinci out.

He has almost turned my desire

Into a monster that would swallow me, too.

HÜMAŞAH SULTAN:

Of course! The man knew that was

The only way for him to remain in this stud farm of a palace.

I am tired of this place, my lord.

SULTAN İBRAHİM:

Why are you sulking so, my dear Hümaşah?

Am I not building a new palace for you near the Hippodrome?

It will be furnished like that palace in the story,

The story we heard together in the course of our sweetest night.

HÜMAŞAH SULTAN:

[*Mockingly.*]

Let us see if your treasury will be enough

To finish that fairy-tale palace.

SULTAN İBRAHİM:

My empire is the greatest empire in the world.

People of three continents work for me,

Vie with each other to satisfy my wishes. Or are you,

My dear Hümaşah, not of the palace?

Are you tired of me? Is your beauty tired of my love?

HÜMAŞAH SULTAN:

If the love of my lord is withdrawn,

My beauty turns into an untended garden.

SULTAN İBRAHİM:

The treasury of my mother is no less than mine;

I am sure she'll help, too, in the building of the palace.

HÜMAŞAH SULTAN:

I am very happy that your mother is returning;

Her being away gave me concern.

SULTAN İBRAHİM:

Why? She is my mother after all.

It was she who made me the sultan.

Besides, she knows how deeply I love you.

HÜMAŞAH SULTAN:

That she is strong enough to make you the sultan,

Does this not bother you at all?

KÖSEM SULTAN:

[*Enters with feigned joy.*]

Thank God that I have seen this day, my sovereign ones!

SULTAN İBRAHİM:

[*Clasps his* MOTHER's *arm.*]

Welcome among us, Mother.

I was talking about you with Hümaşah a while ago.

We were saying how much we missed you.

HÜMAŞAH SULTAN:

[*Kisses* KÖSEM's *hand.*]

You are welcome, my sultan; your presence has brought us happiness.

KÖSEM SULTAN:

Thank you, Hümaşah Sultan!

What happiness to see you again.

HÜMAŞAH SULTAN:

If you had called me daughter, instead of sultan,

You would have made me happier.

KÖSEM SULTAN:

[*Kisses* HÜMAŞAH.]

But, my child, I feel like calling you "my sultan"

When I see such beauty that is beyond words

And that soars so high!

[HÜMAŞAH *is worried.*]

SULTAN İBRAHİM:

[*Glad.*]

Isn't she, Mother? Forget the harem.

In the whole world, is there one more beautiful

Than your daughter-in-law?

KÖSEM SULTAN:

A beauty fit for the majesty of my sultan son.

HÜMAŞAH SULTAN:

It unfolded under your care, my sultan.

KÖSEM SULTAN:

[*After smiling at* HÜMAŞAH, *addresses* İBRAHİM.]

The enemy has entered Bosnia and conquered the fortress of Klis.

And they say other fortresses in the area are also being besieged.

SULTAN İBRAHİM:

It is not the fortress of Klis they took, Mother, but *kilise,* a church.

That is what the new grand vizier has told me.

KÖSEM SULTAN:

I see . . . only a church. Then it doesn't matter.

SULTAN İBRAHİM:

Mother, I am building Hümaşah such a palace

That fairy-tale palaces will pale beside it.

KÖSEM SULTAN:

Whatever you do is not enough for her, my royal son.

The Venetians have closed the Dardanelles,

Our fleet is unable to leave the Marmara,

Our army in Crete is helpless because of that.

SULTAN İBRAHİM:

Mother, the grand vizier says that the Dardanelles are a month's distance from
here.

KÖSEM SULTAN:

That is true, too. Until the enemy comes from a month's distance . . .

SULTAN İBRAHİM:

This palace will have gates made of pure gold,

Decked with emeralds, rubies, and other precious stones.

KÖSEM SULTAN:

Not enough! The rooms should be furnished with sable.

I am ready to give all the sable I possess.

SULTAN İBRAHİM:

[*Caresses his sable coat.*]

Did I not say so, Hümaşah? My mother loves me

And holds dear everything I hold dear.

KÖSEM SULTAN:

[*Removes the necklace she is wearing from her neck and puts it on* HÜMAŞAH's.]

This was the most precious gift from your father to me.

No treasury in the world has its equal.

[*Caresses* HÜMAŞAH's *neck.* HÜMAŞAH *is startled.*]

Your neck is like a swan's, my royal daughter,

So soft, so white, so imperial!

HÜMAŞAH SULTAN:

[*Worried.*]

Because of your love, my lady.

SULTAN İBRAHİM:

Do you think my treasury will not be enough, Mother,

To finish Hümaşah's palace?

KÖSEM SULTAN:

How can the richest treasury in the world

Not be enough to build a palace?

Besides, my royal son, you have millions of subjects,

All dying for you to continue your reign.

If the gold and the silver in your treasury is not enough,

You will just collect taxes from your subjects;

You will just ask for sable from all the merchants

And the people and the pashas and the generals.

SULTAN İBRAHİM:

That's it. Let the head of the harem come immediately . . .

[*The* HEAD OF THE HAREM *enters.*]

This is my edict to the grand vizier Ahmed Pasha:

"All the sable that exists in the houses and shops of Istanbul will be confiscated, and all the owners of great estates, rich men, money changers, pashas, merchants, generals, all sorts of shop owners will remember that their riches are in reality the possessions of the sultan and will give half their property to him."

Now, send this immediately to Ahmed Pasha,

And let him act even faster than you do.

[*The* HEAD OF THE HAREM *exits.*]

HÜMAŞAH SULTAN:

[*Extremely nervous.*]

My lord! That is a little too much.

KÖSEM SULTAN:

[*Jumping in.*]

What do you mean, my royal daughter?

The sultan must live like a sultan, and you must live like his wife!

JESTER IN CHIEF:

[*Enters, reading from a piece of paper in his hand.*]

Our royal, gracious, munificent lord . . .

SULTAN İBRAHİM:

> [*Excited.*]

> Oh, my jester in chief, come here, Master.

> [HÜMAŞAH *looks at* KÖSEM, *embarrassed.*]

KÖSEM SULTAN:

> Laughter is a good thing, my royal daughter;

> It sprinkles a person's heart with light.

SULTAN İBRAHİM:

> We have missed your jokes for so many days.

> What is in your hand, our expert of laughter?

JESTER IN CHIEF:

> It is a petition from your dejected flatterers, my lord.

> [*Reads.*] "Every year, when the sacred Ramadan arrives, we go to the feasts, invited or un-invited, to break fast. We eat at the tables of theologians, statesmen, and other prominent people. There we help ourselves to delicious dishes, liqueurs, jams, puddings, pastries, halvah, baklava with thick cream, and all sorts of other desserts and compotes . . . "

SULTAN İBRAHİM:

> Let them enjoy all that!

> What else do they petition for, I wonder?

JESTER IN CHIEF:

> [*Reads.*] " . . . followed by tobacco and sweet coffee."

SULTAN İBRAHİM:

> God, how many sultans are there in this land?

JESTER IN CHIEF:

> [*Reads.*] "But . . . " [*Stops and looks at* İBRAHİM.]

SULTAN İBRAHİM:

> Hmmm! I see the tune is changing now.

HÜMAŞAH SULTAN:

> [*Goes near* KÖSEM.]

> If you would be my guest for dinner tonight,

> If I could have the honor of serving you again, my sultan!

KÖSEM SULTAN:

> Would it not be too hard on you, my royal child?

HÜMAŞAH SULTAN:

> It would be a source of pleasure.

JESTER IN CHIEF:

> [*Reads.*] "But certain ill-bred ones among us, behaving against the proper etiquette, are degrading the ancient and noble profession of flattery. If the profession of flattery is not controlled by firm rules, we shall obviously all die of hunger."

[*They laugh.*]

SULTAN İBRAHİM:

When did this profession start, honorable master?

JESTER IN CHIEF:

From the day that haves and have-nots appeared among men,

The profession of flattery also grew, my lord.

With time, it assumed different shapes and finally,

Reaching its zenith in our days, produced its masterpieces in our land.

SULTAN İBRAHİM:

All right, but what is the function of these parasites?

What is their place in my land?

JESTER IN CHIEF:

The sycophant, my lord, is an accomplished magnifier

Who keeps vigil, for a fee, near the sovereign.

Clothing the puny essence of man in furs,

He shows him majestic to himself.

SULTAN İBRAHİM:

I see. Then he is performing an important function.

Without being supported by such lying witnesses,

Can anyone in the world tolerate himself?

Continue, my friend.

JESTER IN CHIEF:

[*Reads.*] "We request that this time-honored profession be restructured; that the ones misbehaving among us be expelled; that Şakir Ağa, whose manners and actions are highly esteemed by us, be appointed our warden; and that the document announcing his appointment be passed to his hands in due manner. The decision and the decree belong to our royal, majestic sultan."

SULTAN İBRAHİM:

[*Chuckling.*]

Look here, Master! The petition of your colleagues . . .

JESTER IN CHIEF:

[*Interrupts him. Proudly.*]

My lord! By confusing the sycophant with the clown,

You are insulting the highest of professions.

Haven't you called me "master" many times?

I had thought that you had a profound understanding of this art.

[*Pauses.*]

When insanity masses its troops on the borders of consciousness,

And startled thoughts and dreams begin to desert you . . .

SULTAN İBRAHİM:

> [*Preoccupied.*]
>
> Then?

JESTER IN CHIEF:

> Then the laughter I make will blossom on the secret branches of your being,
>
> Will enable you to withstand the awesome face of existence.

SULTAN İBRAHİM:

> I did not intend to hurt you, Master. Only,
>
> Make us laugh a little—you certainly know how!
>
> Then we shall grant the request of our flatterers.

JESTER IN CHIEF:

> [*Assumes a majestic air, raises his voice.*]
>
> If anybody is afraid, let him return to the arms of his woman!
>
> I can face single-handedly Shah İsmail's army!

SULTAN İBRAHİM:

> [*Laughs aloud.*]
>
> Good for you, Sultan Selim,
>
> Good for you a thousand times!

> [*Embarrassed,* HÜMAŞAH *looks at* KÖSEM.]

KÖSEM SULTAN:

> [*Smiles.*]
>
> The clown is mirroring Sultan Selim's majesty so well.

SULTAN İBRAHİM:

> [*Cackles with laughter.*]
>
> Isn't he, Mother, isn't he?
>
> More, Master, more!

JESTER IN CHIEF:

> [*Assumes a different air.*]
>
> If even one strand of my hair knows my secret,
>
> I would pluck it and burn it!

SULTAN İBRAHİM:

> [*Surprised.*]
>
> Who is this?

JESTER IN CHIEF:

> [*In the same manner, but vehemently.*]
>
> Attack, my lions, attack!
>
> Our banner is waving on her ramparts,
>
> Istanbul is now ours!

SULTAN İBRAHİM:

Long live Sultan Mehmed! Long live the conqueror!

My jester in chief, how many people are you?

You were Sultan Selim; you are now Sultan Mehmed!

How is this possible?

JESTER IN CHIEF:

This one is from my mother, my lord, and that one was from another.

[*Laughter.*]

SULTAN İBRAHİM:

Oh Master, you have made me laugh too much today!

JESTER IN CHIEF:

They have another wish, my lord, your flatterers!

SULTAN İBRAHİM:

[*Laughs.*]

Tell me, tell me.

JESTER IN CHIEF:

They want a change in the price schedule, a certain raise in their fees. For example, to twitch the nose of a sycophant is today twenty pennies per twitch. My lord, you'd appreciate this, it's too little! [IBRAHİM *nods, laughing.*] A twitch must be at least twenty-five pennies. Now, to throw a flatterer down the stairs is one hundred and eighty pennies (also the joker must pay for the expense of the doctor and the surgeon if any part of the flatterer's body gets hurt or broken). Have pity, my lord; you are throwing the man down the stairs and paying him a mere hundred and eighty pennies. You just try it yourself. You will see the unfairness of the current price schedule. This thing must be at least two hundred and twenty pennies, and, besides the expenses of treatment, one must pay a certain amount of compensation. [IBRAHİM *nods, laughing.*] It also says here: the shaking of the beard with five or ten hairs remaining in the hand and the teeth clattering like a crane's beak—sixty pennies. Come on, now! How can this convulsion be so cheap, my sultan? It must be at least seventy pennies.

SULTAN İBRAHİM:

I espouse from my heart the cause of my flatterers;

All their wishes will be granted.

As for you, my dear master,

I was noticing during your recent performance

That you can be an excellent commander in chief.

I have made you the head of the Janissaries. Assume your functions immediately.

JESTER IN CHIEF:

[*Laughs.*]

My lord, you are going to take my profession away from me soon!

How well you have mastered this art!

SULTAN İBRAHİM:

[*Adamant.*]

I am serious!

You should assume your functions immediately! I do not want any laxness.

JESTER IN CHIEF:

[*In terror, throws himself at* IBRAHİM's *feet.*]

Please, my lord, spare me this favor!

How can a jester possibly serve as the commander in chief of the Janissaries?

SULTAN İBRAHİM:

Why not . . . if I want it?

JESTER IN CHIEF:

[*Pleads.*]

Your soldiers will tear me to pieces, my lord.

SULTAN İBRAHİM:

[*Angrily.*]

How dare they? Am I not the sultan?

Can I not put at the head of the Janissaries anyone I choose?

You tell me, my dear mother, can I not do it?

KÖSEM SULTAN:

The power of the sultan knows no limit; his will is absolute.

How dare anybody cross him?

HÜMAŞAH SULTAN:

[*Worried.*]

My lord, your Janissaries may be offended by this action!

SULTAN İBRAHİM:

[*Flaring up.*]

What do you mean? Am I not the sultan?

I can make anyone I want not only commander in chief, but even sultan.

Is that not so, Mother?

KÖSEM SULTAN:

The sultan stands for God on this earth.

SULTAN İBRAHİM:

[*Kicks the* JESTER IN CHIEF.]

Get up, you dog! Take hold of your duties!

The responsibility of the army lies with you from now on.

[*The* JESTER IN CHIEF *darts out.*]

HÜMAŞAH SULTAN:

> [*Anxious.*]
>
> My lord, my lord!

SULTAN İBRAHİM:

> I can make anyone I want sultan,
>
> Anyone I choose!
>
> [*Looks at* HÜMAŞAH's *face, grins.*]
>
> Yes, anyone I want! You, Hümaşah, you!
>
> Bring my throne from the audience chamber immediately.

HÜMAŞAH SULTAN:

> Please, my lord, what are you doing?
>
> [*Helpless, she looks at* KÖSEM, *asking for assistance.* KÖSEM *smiles.*]

SULTAN İBRAHİM:

> [*Takes* HÜMAŞAH's *face in his hands.*]
>
> Every beauty looks for a throne to sit on.
>
> My love and my boundless power will provide yours, Hümaşah.

HÜMAŞAH SULTAN:

> It is enough for me to rule in your heart, my lord.
>
> How can a harem room receive the throne from the audience chamber?
>
> [*The* HEAD OF THE HAREM *and a few other* COURTIERS *bring the throne.*]

SULTAN İBRAHİM:

> It's here already! Because I have demanded it!
>
> [*Holds* HÜMAŞAH *by the hand. To the* HEAD OF THE HAREM.]
>
> Whoever is outside, let him come in. The sultan should observe
>
> Her subjects, and the subjects their sultan.
>
> [*The* HEAD OF THE HAREM *exits and reenters with other* COURTIERS. *As* İBRAHİM *leads* HÜMAŞAH *toward the throne, she looks at* KÖSEM *and waits for assistance.*]

KÖSEM SULTAN:

> [*Nods, smiling.*]
>
> Beauty needs to rule, my sultan!

HÜMAŞAH SULTAN:

> [*Implores.*]
>
> My lord, my lord! This is your throne.
>
> As long as you sit on it, both of us remain sultans!
>
> But if someone aside from Sultan İbrahim sits there,
>
> Either myself or someone else, then . . . my lord, oh my lord.

SULTAN İBRAHİM:

> [*Sits* HÜMAŞAH *on the throne, showing it to the people around.*]

This act is witnessed by my authority. Bow!

[*In amazement and fear, staring at each other, they bow.* HÜMAŞAH *looks at* KÖSEM *in despair; she tries to rise.* KÖSEM, *smiling, bows all the way down.*]

HÜMAŞAH SULTAN:

Give me permission to descend from this shaky place, my lord.

You have raised me to a fearsome height.

SULTAN İBRAHİM:

[*Bows down as if worshipping.*]

There, I have pushed you away from my inner monster!

There you are . . . up there now! Alone by yourself.

As for myself, all alone, with my love, in the depths.

Scene 5

[*Stage left, the lights go on. The* INHABITANTS OF ISTANBUL.]

FIRST INHABITANT:

If you don't sit on your throne, others will make it their own.

THIRD INHABITANT:

He wants us to donate half of what we own.

FOURTH INHABITANT:

To finish the palace of his favorite.

FIRST INHABITANT:

[*With his foot puts out the cigarette butt thrown down by the* SECOND INHABITANT.]

Please be careful. Put out the butt after you have smoked;

Otherwise the firemen of the neighborhood will have a blazing celebration.

SECOND INHABITANT:

How riotous they have grown lately!

As though they are not fire extinguishers,

But a committee of fire feeders. When the flames grow,

They only watch over rich men's mansions,

Holding their hoses from the roofs of poor men's shacks.

THIRD INHABITANT:

The meals I sell during the whole day do not fill more than ten pots,

And with what I earn I must feed a family of six.

My lord wants half of it as a donation!

I can't even live on all my income, Sultan İbrahim!

FOURTH INHABITANT:

All in all, I have two rooms.

Take one of them to Topkapı, Sultan İbrahim.

Your palace will grow a bit bigger.

SECOND INHABITANT:

Do I have any sable, friends?

FIRST, THIRD, and FOURTH INHABITANTS:

Where would we get any?

FIRST INHABITANT:

If you don't sit on your throne, others will make it their own.

You wait, Sultan İbrahim, you wait!

We heard sable softly cuddles the flesh!

SECOND INHABITANT:

He forced his concubine to sit on the throne.

FOURTH INHABITANT:

He himself was made sultan by force.

The Ottoman palace is at the peak of revelry.

That means destruction is rampant.

FIRST INHABITANT:

The jester in chief should have been here now

And enacted for us the events, blow by blow.

SECOND INHABITANT:

[*Marking time.*]

Laughing and dancing, friends, laughing and dancing!

FIRST, THIRD, and FOURTH INHABITANTS:

[*Marking time.*]

Yes, yes! Yes, yes! Laughing and dancing!

[*It grows dark. Stage right, the lights go on.* JANISSARY COMMANDERS MUSTAFA AĞA, MUSLİHİDDİN AĞA, KARA MURAD AĞA, *and* BEKTAŞ AĞA.]

KARA MURAD AĞA:

What are we waiting for, Ağas? Destruction is coming full speed.

He is saying, "People should give me as gifts half their possessions.

They should remember that all of them belong to me."

The Venetians are at the Dardanelles;

They are not letting our fleet venture out. While all he is saying is,

"The Dardanelles are a month's distance from here."

BEKTAŞ AĞA:

The enemy has taken the Klis fortress of Bosnia, and all the sultan can say is,

"It is only *kilise,* a church, they took."

KARA MURAD AĞA:

And what about the ones fighting in Crete, Ağas,

What about them? Hungry and in rags, they are conquering castles.

Can you tell us, Mustafa Ağa,

When is the signal coming from the sultan's mother?

MUSTAFA AĞA:

She said that the sultan's madness will give us the signal.

Those were our lady's words!

[*It grows dark. Stage left, the lights go on. The* INHABITANTS OF ISTANBUL.]

FIRST INHABITANT:

Hümaşah's palace is going up at the Hippodrome.

Gold is needed for this building, emeralds are needed, rubies and sables are needed.

Where do we get rubies, emeralds, and sables?

SECOND, THIRD, and FOURTH INHABITANTS:

Where do we get rubies, emeralds, gold?

FIRST INHABITANT:

You wait, Sultan İbrahim, you wait!

SECOND, THIRD, and FOURTH INHABITANTS:

You wait . . . you wait . . . !

[*It grows dark. Stage right, the lights go on. The* JANISSARY COMMANDERS.]

KARA MURAD AĞA:

[*Shouts after someone who has just left.*]

So he wants two sables and two hundred sacks of ambergris, eh?

Who does he think his Janissary commanders are? This is not a fur shop.

The army is a place for men! We only hear from others the names of sable and
    ambergris.

As for money, we have to borrow it ourselves.

Except for fine-grained powder and greased bullets, we have nothing.

Ağas, isn't this the signal?

MUSTAFA AĞA:

When the signal comes, it will speak in a clear tongue.

Then no one will have to ask whether it is the signal or not!

[*It grows dark. Stage left, the lights go on. The* INHABITANTS OF ISTANBUL.]

FIRST INHABITANT:

If you don't sit on your throne, others will make it their own.

SECOND, THIRD, and FOURTH INHABITANTS:

Others will make it their own . . . others will make it their own!

FIRST INHABITANT:

You wait, Sultan İbrahim, you wait!

SECOND, THIRD, and FOURTH INHABITANTS:

> You wait . . . you wait . . . !

FIRST INHABITANT:

> Sable softly cuddles the flesh . . .

SECOND, THIRD, and FOURTH INHABITANTS:

> Softly . . . very softly!

FIRST INHABITANT:

> Sable softly cuddles the flesh!

SECOND, THIRD, and FOURTH INHABITANTS:

> Softly . . . cuddles very softly!

[*It grows dark. Stage right, the lights go on. The* JANISSARY COMMANDERS.]

BEKTAŞ AĞA:

> This is the last straw! A commander in chief out of a jester?

MUSLİHİDDİN AĞA:

> The poor man has cried and implored,
>
> "Your Janissaries will tear me to pieces, my lord!"

KARA MURAD AĞA:

> They certainly will;
>
> The Janissaries will tear the person to pieces!
>
> [*To* MUSTAFA AĞA.]
>
> What do you say, Ağa, is this the sign?
>
> [MUSTAFA AĞA *remains silent.*]

[*It grows dark. Stage left, the lights go on. The* INHABITANTS OF ISTANBUL.]

FIRST INHABITANT:

> [*Remembering.*]
>
> But, really, the jester in chief was telling the truth.
>
> Is Sultan İbrahim God? Does he reside in eternity?
>
> As far as I know, he also should have limits.

SECOND, THIRD, and FOURTH INHABITANTS:

> As far as I know, he also should have limits.

[*It grows dark. Stage right, the lights go on. The* JANISSARY COMMANDERS.]

MUSLİHİDDİN AĞA:

> Now the whole world has turned upside down. Look at this artistry of madness!
>
> Bringing the Ottoman throne from the audience chamber, Sultan İbrahim
>
> Has put Hümaşah, his concubine, on the throne!

[*It grows dark. Stage left, the lights go on. The* INHABITANTS OF ISTANBUL.]

FIRST INHABITANT:

If you don't sit on your throne, others will make it their own.

SECOND, THIRD, and FOURTH INHABITANTS:

Others will make it their own!

[*It does not grow dark. Stage right, the lights also go on.*]

MUSTAFA AĞA:

If you don't sit on your throne, others will make it their own.

MUSLİHİDDİN AĞA, BEKTAŞ AĞA, and KARA MUSTAFA AĞA:

Others will make it their own!

FIRST INHABITANT:

Is Sultan İbrahim God? Does he reside in eternity?

As far as I know, he also should have limits!

ALL INHABITANTS:

[*Slowly move toward the* JANISSARY COMMANDERS.]

As far as I know, he also should have limits!

MUSTAFA AĞA:

Is Sultan İbrahim God? Does he reside in eternity?

As far as I know, he also should have limits!

MUSLİHİDDİN AĞA, BEKTAŞ AĞA, and KARA MUSTAFA AĞA:

He also should have limits!

INHABITANTS OF ISTANBUL and JANISSARY COMMANDERS:

He also should have limits!

[*Growing louder, the words echo outside.*]

Scene 6

[İBRAHİM's *private chamber.*]

SULTAN İBRAHİM:

[*Tries to make out the words echoing outside.*]

What are they shouting about? What are they saying?

This room is stronger than the strongest fortress.

I have already ordered that the palace retinue and guards should arm themselves!

If they try to break in, I will kill all of them.

But the roars are coming closer and closer.

[*Grabs the* HEAD OF THE HAREM, *who has entered anxiously.*]

These roars should have stopped

Against the walls of the outer court, Ağa!

Or are my orders not obeyed in my palace anymore?

HEAD OF THE HAREM:

> [*Panting.*]
>
> The chief gardener has opened the outer door, the Imperial Gate!
>
> Thousands of soldiers, all armed and shouting the name of God, are filling the court!

> [*The cries of "Allah! Allah!" are becoming more audible.*]

SULTAN İBRAHİM:

> [*Haltingly.*]
>
> Why did the chief gardener open the gate? By whose order?

HEAD OF THE HAREM:

> By your mother's, my lord, Kösem Sultan's!
>
> With majesty, she came to the chief gardener and said,
>
> "Open the doors. The subjects have come to see the new sultan.
>
> One must not stand between the sultan and his subjects."

SULTAN İBRAHİM:

> Ah! I let her out of the palace; she became dangerous.
>
> I brought her back to the palace; the palace became dangerous.
>
> My mother, my real mother! Did you say "the new sultan"?

HEAD OF THE HAREM:

> It appears they are going to put Prince Mehmed on the throne, my lord.

SULTAN İBRAHİM:

> Go, see how far they have come!
>
> I will confront these dogs with my palace retinue!

> [*The HEAD OF THE HAREM exits.*]

HÜMAŞAH SULTAN:

> [*Enters anxiously.*]
>
> They have filled the second court, my lord.
>
> They are advancing toward the Gate of Felicity.

SULTAN İBRAHİM:

> The palace will fight to the last man.
>
> I'll kill all of them, this rabble!

HÜMAŞAH SULTAN:

> Everybody in the palace is hiding in a corner,
>
> Each worried about his own life.

HEAD OF THE HAREM:

> [*Enters.*]
>
> From the harem entrance, they have poured
>
> Into the third court.

> [*The chanting is heard quite near.*]

SULTAN İBRAHİM:

Are the palace people going to defend their sultan, Ağa?

They have been eating my bread for so many years.

HEAD OF THE HAREM:

Countless people live in this palace, my lord,

But it's as if they have vanished into thin air.

SULTAN İBRAHİM:

What shall we do, Ağa? Is there any exit?

HEAD OF THE HAREM:

Remember how you ascended the throne, my lord?

You were the only Ottoman heir.

They dragged you to the throne!

SULTAN İBRAHİM:

Meaning? How is this related to my survival?

HEAD OF THE HAREM:

[*Timidly.*]

Still you may remain the sole owner of sovereignty.

SULTAN İBRAHİM:

[*Surprised.*]

How?

HEAD OF THE HAREM:

The princes!

SULTAN İBRAHİM:

[*Startled, stepping backward.*]

What? My own sons?

HÜMAŞAH SULTAN:

[*Approaches and caresses* İBRAHİM *timidly.*]

You have three sons, my lord, and can have three more,

But Sultan İbrahim is the one and only.

If he goes, no one can take his place.

SULTAN İBRAHİM:

No, no, not possible. They are my eternity,

My infinity!

HEAD OF THE HAREM:

[*Listens to the noises outside.*]

They have also entered the fourth court, my lord.

They will soon be here.

HÜMAŞAH SULTAN:

[*Anxiously.*]

You are late, my lord, you are late!

They are about to break in.

Your princes are in the next room.

[*Shakes* İBRAHİM, *who is in a daze.*]

Wake up, my lord, get hold of yourself!

[*The* HEAD OF THE HAREM *sneaks out.*]

See how many mouths death has?

All are opening together toward us!

[*From outside, in a chorus, the crowd is clearly heard chanting, "Is Sultan İbrahim God? Does he reside in eternity? As far as I know, he also should have limits."*]

SULTAN İBRAHİM:

[*Startled, in terror.*]

My own words are coming back to haunt me,

My own words . . . !

Everything is against Sultan İbrahim,

Everything . . . everything . . .

[*Pauses suddenly.*]

Through the work of others, I broke the first crust.

If I could pull apart the second, then my presence

Would transcend the palace, the borders of my land.

I would be a sovereign like my great ancestors.

Well, let me tear apart with my death, at least,

What I could not crack with my living.

Let me be the sultan of my own death.

And while my sun plunges into darkness, let my sons,

Like new constellations, burn in my sky.

[*The* JANISSARY COMMANDERS *and the* ŞEYHÜLİSLÂM *enter slowly from the right.*]

MUSTAFA AĞA:

The head is bare, our cause rare, and our sword bloody.

The heads we cut off in this place no one can question.

KARA MURAD AĞA, BEKTAŞ AĞA, MUSLİHİDDİN AĞA, and the ŞEYHÜLİSLÂM:

No one can question! No one can question!

MUSTAFA AĞA:

Let our swords and our anger fall on the enemy.

Our loyalty goes to our sultan!

KARA MURAD AĞA, BEKTAŞ AĞA, MUSLİHİDDİN AĞA, and the ŞEYHÜLİSLÂM:

Our loyalty goes to the sultan!

SULTAN İBRAHİM:

> [*Shouts.*]

> What kind of a sultan can a knee-high child be?

ŞEYHÜLİSLÂM:

> [*Reads his official pronouncement.*]

> For a mature man of unbalanced mind to be sultan in our land

> Is illegal. But for a child of sane mind to be so is legal.

SULTAN İBRAHİM:

> [*Gets angry.*]

> I spit in your face and at your decree, too!

> You have entered my palace, usurped my sovereignty,

> But nobody can dare question the balance of my mind.

> My madnesses were my defense against insanity.

> Tell me, you traitors, did you not bow before me,

> And did you all not applaud me when I ascended the throne?

> Tell me, dogs, am I not the sultan?

> I am the sovereign sultan, am I not?

> [*Slowly, the rebels encircle* HÜMAŞAH *and* İBRAHİM, *and lead them toward the door.*]

> This throne was left to me by my ancestors.

> How can you take from my hands the sovereign right

> Granted me by centuries? Am I not the sultan?

> Have I not ascended the throne with full ceremony?

MUSTAFA AĞA:

> Whoever is worthy of it is entitled to the state.

KARA MURAD AĞA, BEKTAŞ AĞA, and MUSTAFA AĞA:

> Whoever is worthy!

> [İBRAHİM *shouts repeatedly,* "Am I not the sultan?" *At the door, other* JANISSARIES *apprehend* İBRAHİM *and* HÜMAŞAH. *The* AĞAS *return.* KÖSEM SULTAN *enters with majesty, a black veil covering her face. The* AĞAS *fully prostrate themselves before her.*]

KÖSEM SULTAN:

> [*On her face a feigned grief.*]

> Is it right to stir up disorder like this?

> Are you not eating the bread of this dynasty?

> [*In utter amazement, the other* AĞAS *and the* ŞEYHÜLİSLÂM *stare at* MUSTAFA AĞA.]

MUSTAFA AĞA:

> [*Continues the game in secret agreement.*]

You are right, my sovereign queen, you are right.

It is wrong to mix in internal affairs

The forces prepared for use against the enemy. It is like

Pitting the foot against the head, inviting chaos to our dear land.

But, my sovereign queen, you yourself know full well

The sultan's madness has long since changed places with the laws of the land.

KARA MURAD AĞA:

On one side, the army on Crete is struggling with the Venetians;

On the other side, it fights against hunger. Yet Istanbul does not listen.

BEKTAŞ AĞA:

On all our borders, the enemy puts on a show of force,

Not feeling our formidable power of the old days.

MUSLİHİDDİN AĞA:

There is nothing left in the land that cannot be bought;

All values are upside down.

They must be reestablished, my sultan.

KÖSEM SULTAN:

Listen, Ağas. My son has been sovereign for exactly eight years.

His mad habits changed shape constantly, but none of you

Ever raised his voice. If, joining hands, you had advised him,

He would have had to set limits to his power. Then none of you

Would have been conspirators in the crimes.

[*Except for* MUSTAFA AĞA, *everybody becomes anxious.*]

Besides, what kind of a sultan can a seven-year-old child be?

MUSTAFA AĞA:

Our prince is fit for the throne, my lady.

The decree of the *şeyhülislâm* testifies to that.

ŞEYHÜLİSLÂM:

[*Shows the edict.*] It testifies to that!

KÖSEM SULTAN:

You are insisting, then?

ALL TOGETHER:

Yes, my lady!

KÖSEM SULTAN:

You are declaring that, otherwise,

You will not return to your barracks?

There will be bloodshed?

ALL TOGETHER:

Yes, my lady!

KÖSEM SULTAN:

>You all have come together; you have secured a decree from the *şeyhülislâm;*
>
>You insist on putting the prince on the throne?

ALL TOGETHER:

>Yes, my lady!

KÖSEM SULTAN:

>[*Sighs.*]
>
>Well, what can we do? We have to accept our fortune. Let me go,
>
>At least, and have the turban of the innocent child wound and bring it here.
>
>Let the throne be placed in front of the Gate of Felicity,
>
>And let you get ready for the ceremonies. But at the same time,
>
>As a precaution, let the doors of the room where Sultan İbrahim will stay
>
>Be closed tightly, its windows sealed with bricks.
>
>Let only a small hole remain under one window to let in a plate of food.

MUSTAFA AĞA:

>Your will be done, my lady.
>
>[KÖSEM *begins to move.*]
>
>My lady?
>
>[KÖSEM *stops, waits without turning.*]
>
>What will happen to the sultan's favorite?

KÖSEM SULTAN:

>It is not for us to rend asunder what love has joined.
>
>They have walked this path together; let them rest together.

MUSTAFA AĞA:

>Your will be done, my lady.

[*The* JANISSARY COMMANDERS *and the* ŞEYHÜLİSLÂM *prostrate themselves.* KÖSEM *exits.*]

Scene 7

[*Morning. The* INHABITANTS OF ISTANBUL.]

FIRST INHABITANT:

>Sultan İbrahim could not sacrifice his sons for his throne.
>
>Let us see what Kösem Sultan will do.

THIRD INHABITANT:

>But he is, after all, her own son.

FIRST INHABITANT:

>The new sultan is the size of this hand, his mother very inexperienced.
>
>Kösem is the sole owner of the state now. She may do anything to keep it.

SECOND INHABITANT:

> I have heard that the cavalry is restive.

FOURTH INHABITANT:

> They say: "When the prince was put on the throne, we were not consulted.
>
> We recognize only Sultan İbrahim as our ruler."

THIRD INHABITANT:

> Even the people of the palace cannot endure anymore
>
> The screams of the sultan and his wife.
>
> They are whispering, "We have eaten Sultan İbrahim's bread for so many years;
>
> Let us not tolerate anymore his being buried alive.
>
> Let us join together and save him from his prison."

SECOND INHABITANT:

> If the palace officials and the cavalry join hands,
>
> All hell will break loose!

FIRST INHABITANT:

> Kösem Sultan is encircled by fire again.
>
> Let us see how she will put it out.

Scene 8

[Stage right, the lights go on. The JANISSARY COMMANDERS.*]*

BEKTAŞ AĞA:

> How shall we handle this thing, Ağas? Do you think it can work?
>
> There is no precedent for issuing an edict
>
> Or a *ferman* to strangle the sultan.

MUSLİHİDDİN AĞA:

> When we began this business, our purpose was
>
> To bring the sultan down and put the prince on the throne.
>
> The purpose is accomplished; therefore, the job is done.

KARA MURAD AĞA:

> It is no small thing to shed the blood of a sultan;
>
> But, because it requires more work from us,
>
> It means our job is not yet done.
>
> We have arrived at the middle of the river.
>
> We must cross to the other side;
>
> Returning is at least as dangerous as forging ahead.

MUSTAFA AĞA:

> When the sultan's mother handed me the edict of the new sultan,
>
> She whispered these words in my ear, Ağas, "If İbrahim

Breaks out of his jail now, he would leave neither you nor me alive.

Be careful."

BEKTAŞ AĞA:

Why don't you read this new edict again, Mustafa Ağa?

MUSLİHİDDİN AĞA:

Yes, read it again!

MUSTAFA AĞA:

[*Reads the edict.*] "My father, Sultan İbrahim, with some people who have fallen in with him, is sowing discord and rebellion. His presence has become a great danger to the security of the empire and the populace. Let this danger be eliminated."

MUSLİHİDDİN AĞA:

What beautiful edicts our young sultan has learned how to write now!

MUSTAFA AĞA:

Ability, Ağa, is not in the years but in the mind.

BEKTAŞ AĞA:

Only the seal is the sultan's.

KARA MURAD AĞA:

We go by the words not the speaker. The decree is in our hands.

We must act immediately, Ağas,

Before the unfinished business backfires.

[*It grows dark. Stage left, the lights go on outside the room where* İBRAHİM *and* HÜMAŞAH *are imprisoned. The* JANISSARY COMMANDERS *enter with the executioner,* KARA ALİ, *and his aide,* HAMAL ALİ.]

MUSTAFA AĞA:

[*Shows the door of the room to the* EXECUTIONERS.] Now, brave men, show your craft!

KARA ALİ:

[*Gulps to control his feelings.*]

My lord . . .

MUSTAFA AĞA:

What's wrong, Kara Ali?

KARA ALİ:

I don't know how to put it . . .

I cannot bring myself to do this, my lord.

How can you possibly have a sultan strangled?

HAMAL ALİ:

And a caliph, too. The caliph of all Islam!

KARA ALİ:

Shut up, you!

KARA MURAD AĞA:

> You talk as though you are new to this work, coward.
>
> Go, obey the decree right away.

KARA ALİ:

> True, I am not new in this trade.
>
> How many viziers and grand viziers have passed through my hands!
>
> But I have not killed a sultan yet.
>
> No executioner has ever strangled a sultan.

HAMAL ALİ:

> Nor has he strangled a caliph!

KARA ALİ:

> [*Raises his hand.*]
>
> I told you to keep quiet!

KARA MURAD AĞA:

> We have a decree in our hand, you dog!
>
> How dare you contradict the sultan?

KARA ALİ:

> God forbid, my lord! My neck is thinner than a thread before the decrees of my
>> sultan,
>
> But I can bring neither my heart nor my hand to do this.
>
> Please, let somebody else do it. Spare me, my lord.
>
> [*Tries to run away. The* JANISSARY COMMANDERS *prevent him. Shoving and slapping,*
> *they force* KARA ALİ *and his* AIDE *toward the door.*]

BEKTAŞ AĞA:

> Hurry up, man! Finish this business quickly!
>
> Let both you and us finish it off.

MUSLİHİDDİN AĞA:

> After all, we all must obey orders.
>
> We follow edicts where they take us.

MUSTAFA AĞA:

> Go in!

VOICE OF SULTAN İBRAHİM:

> [*From within.*]
>
> What is going on there? What are you hatching?
>
> Let me just get out of this place, and you'll see.
>
> You'll rue the day you were born, you dogs!

KARA MURAD AĞA:

> [*Draws his dagger.*]
>
> Go in, damn it, dirty Gypsy. Forget this innocence of yours,
>
> And put on your bloody face. Or else I'll put it on you!

[*Under the pressure of the dagger, the executioner* KARA ALİ *and his* AIDE *open the door and enter the room. The* AĞAS *lock it from the outside and press against it. Noises and a woman's screams are heard from inside.*]

VOICE OF SULTAN İBRAHİM:

Tell me, you bastards, by what book,

By what law are you killing me? Am I not the sultan?

Am I not the . . . ? I . . . I . . . !

[*A deep silence descends. Relaxed, the* AĞAS *let go of the door. With greased ropes in their hands, crushed under the weight of the act they have committed,* KARA ALİ *and* HAMAL ALİ *appear at the door. The* AĞAS *are at a loss as to what they should do. The* EXECUTIONERS *exit slowly.* KÖSEM *enters quietly. Startled, the* AĞAS *prostrate themselves on the floor.*]

KÖSEM SULTAN:

[*Stands right in the middle of the stage, majestic and decisive.*]

A tongue that spoke deliriously,

Is now silent. Bury Sultan İbrahim and his lover

In the courtyard of Saint Sophia.

MUSTAFA AĞA:

Your will be done!

KÖSEM SULTAN:

And before the people hear about this event and talk,

Dispense with the two executioners right away.

MUSTAFA AĞA:

Your will be done!

[*The* JANISSARY COMMANDERS *bow and then exit, while* KÖSEM *lifts the black veil from her face.*]

CURTAIN

◆　◆　◆

Çiçu

AZİZ NESİN

Translated by Allan R. Gall

An Editor's Note

Aziz Nesin (1916–95) has been a household name in Turkey for decades thanks to his hilarious humor, biting satire, and courageous political stands. "Straight out of Aziz Nesin" is a common expression among Turks. When a situation is incredibly funny, many people describe it as "almost going beyond Nesin." His more than one hundred books—fiction, poetry, essays, plays, memoirs, diaries, children's books, correspondence, travelogues, and so on—have enchanted his devout readers since the 1940s. He was so popular in Iran that some smart-aleck publishers started putting his name on books that he had not written.

Yet the man whose name became synonymous with humor and satire led a life battered with literally hundreds of arrests, trials, convictions, and prison terms—all because of his leftist ideology and relentless attacks against inequity and injustice. When Nesin first published *Çiçu* in 1969, he added a note that he had written the play in 1950 in an Istanbul prison and rewrote it with revisions in 1963.

The made-up word *Çiçu* has no meaning. Nesin seems to have intended it as a neutral international name without any specific linguistic identification. The same is true in the case of virtually all other names he uses in this play, except for Adam (Man) and a few other references.

In his vast literary corpus, Nesin concentrates on social and political issues from a leftist ideological standpoint. In some of his plays, however, he dwells on the psychological crises of individuals. *Çiçu* is a paragon of this latter genre. A rueful portrayal of a solitary man's misery, it is notably devoid of the broad humor that characterizes most of the playwright's other works. It strives to delineate estrangement and loneliness in universal terms.

Nesin, whose fiction also achieved wide popularity in France and Italy, in many countries of the Muslim world, and in the countries of the former Communist bloc, failed to attract the attention of the English-speaking world. In Turkey, he was showered with awards. *Çiçu* won the prestigious 1970 Best Play Award of the Turkish Language Society. His non-Turkish honors include first prize in Italy's Bordighera International Humorous Stories Competition, 1956 and 1957; the Soviet Union's Krokodil Prize, 1969; the "Lotus" prize of the Union of Asian-African Writers, 1974; the International Press Freedom Award of the U.S. Committee to Protect Journalists, 1994; the Soviet Union's

Tolstoy Gold Medal, 1989; and the Contribution to World Peace Award, Editha Morris Foundation, Sweden, 1995.

The translator of *Çiçu,* Allan R. Gall, holds a Ph.D. in Near Eastern studies from the University of Michigan. He wrote his dissertation on the political and satirical themes in the works of Aziz Nesin. From 1962 to 1964, he served in Turkey as a Peace Corps volunteer, teaching English in the provincial capital of Çankırı. He is currently deputy director general of the Peace Corps.—TSH

Characters

CEST, a ceramic figurine

VAVU, another ceramic figurine

FISH, in an aquarium

YUMUŞ, a caged bird

NİREY, a musical clock

MAN, a middle-aged bachelor

ÇİÇU, an inflated female rubber dummy

PİKİ, a dog

LAMİ, a cat

NEIGHBOR, a voice offstage

NEIGHBOR'S WIFE, a voice offstage

BEYTİ, a turtle (or a porcupine)

RİSAMİ, a potted flowering plant

RADIO ANNOUNCER

GUEST, played by the MAN

WOMAN'S VOICE, a voice offstage; member of love triangle, played by the MAN

MAN'S VOICE, a voice offstage; member of love triangle

LOVER, member of love triangle, played by the MAN

WOMAN ON THE PHONE, a voice offstage

NEWSPAPER BOY, a voice offstage

MAILMAN, a voice offstage

WOMAN'S VOICE (LETTER WRITER); later WIFE

JANITOR, a voice offstage

ACT I

[*Combination sitting and dining room of a penthouse apartment. The general clutter and confusion of things give an impression of a bachelor's apartment. Toward the right-hand corner of the backstage wall is the outside door, which opens onto the stairway of the apartment building. Another door in the stage-left wall opens into another room. In the stage-right wall, toward stage front, is an open doorway coming from a hall (back-stage, in this case). Toward the rear of the stage-left wall is a window, the upper half of which is covered with yellowed newspaper. Along the stage-rear wall is a couch; an oil painting of a woman hangs on the wall above it. In addition, the room contains a table placed toward stage-right center; three chairs; an armchair; a telephone; a tape recorder; a radio; a record player; a cupboard; books,* CEST, *and* VAVU *on bookshelves;* FISH *in an aquarium;* YUMUŞ, *a bird in a cage; and* NİREY, *a musical clock.*

It is a stormy night. When the curtain opens, the stage is dark. Nothing can be seen. The MAN *is sitting in the armchair by one of the bookshelves.* ÇİÇU *is lying on the couch. During the first few minutes of the play, lightning will strike five times, lighting up* ÇİÇU'S *naked body. Thus, the impression should be given to the audience that a real, naked woman is lying on the couch.*

As the curtain opens, the musical clock begins to play. As the clock's tune dies out, the MAN *speaks.*]

MAN: [*Flatteringly, as though trying to make up with a capricious wife whom he has offended.*] Çiçuuuu! [*Softer.*] Çiçuuuu. [*Tries various tones of voice that express different emotions.*] Çiçu! Çiçuuuuu . . . Çiiiiiiçu . . . Çiiiiiiçuuuuuu. [*Lightning strikes.*] Çiçu dear. Çiçu dear! Why don't you say something? [*Faint sound of thunder in the distance.*] Çiçu! Çiçuuu . . . [*Pause.*] Say something, dear, please say something. [*Pause.*] Come sit beside me, love. So . . . now I understand. Çiçu doesn't love me anymore. [*Lightning strikes for the second time, harder than the first.*] Are you mad at me or something? What are you mad about? [*The second clap of thunder, louder than the first.*] Look, dear, you can't just lie there naked; you'll catch cold. Cover yourself. [*Pause.*] Shall I get a blanket? So, you've swallowed your tongue? [*Pause.*] A home is no place for anger, sweetheart. Anyway, I didn't do anything for you to get sore about. [*Lightning strikes for the third time, harder than the second.*] Come on, sit here beside me. Let's make up. Shall I come over there? Will you get mad if I come over there? [*A louder clap of thunder.*] Çiçu . . . my Çiçu . . . shall I turn on the light? [*Lightning strikes for the fourth time.*] Honey, you'll freeze like that. [*Pleadingly.*] Darling, sweetheart, my dearest Çiçu . . . my one and only Çiçu . . . what have I done to make you mad at me? Look, if I've done anything to hurt you, forgive me. [*Thunder.*] I didn't mean to hurt you. Shall I turn on the light? [*Lightning strikes for the fifth time, very hard, long, and bright.*] For goodness' sake, say something!

[*From where he's sitting, the* MAN *flicks the switch on a cord, and the bulb hanging above him goes on. The right-hand portion of the stage lights up. The side where* ÇİÇU *lies is dim.*]

Çiçu! [*A thunder clap louder yet than all the previous ones.*] Did you fall asleep or something? [*Gets up and haltingly tiptoes over to her. Kisses her bare feet. Then slowly caresses her from her legs to her hips and upward toward her breasts.*] See, you're cold, frozen. You're like ice. You'll get sick. Come on, get up and get dressed. [*Sits down on the floor at the foot of the couch and caresses* ÇIÇU.] My dear Çiçu, have I done something to hurt you? If only I knew why you're angry. Please tell me. You're gonna catch cold, dear. Let me dress you.

[*Flicks on the switch on the wall, and the stage lights up. Exits through the door on the left.* PİKİ's *sharp barking is heard from offstage. Returns with woman's underwear and begins to dress* ÇIÇU, *putting on her underpants first, then the rest of her underwear. Simultaneously talks to her and kisses her on the shoulders, back, and breasts while dressing her.*] Ahh, you're freezing, freezing. Your legs are like ice. Dear, dear, dear, what are you doing lying here in this cold. OK, OK. don't get angry, sweetie! What did I say, anyway? First thing tomorrow I'll go out and buy you anything you want, honey, you hear? First thing I'm gonna do is buy you a present. No, it's still a long time till your birthday; you can have another present for your birthday, a different one. [*Puts her robe on her.*] I see, now I get it. You're just playing another little game with me, pretending to be angry! [*Sits down beside* ÇIÇU.] Little lady, these games of yours are hard on me. [PİKİ *begins barking.*] Quiet, Piki, quiet, I say! What are you griping about? [*To* ÇIÇU.] I have only one Çiçu in this world. [*To* PİKİ.] OK, quiet, so I have you too, Piki. Your stomach empty? Settle down, I'm coming. Just wait a minute. You're not about to die of hunger. [*Puts* ÇIÇU *in one of the chairs beside the table.*] You just sit here pretty and proper while I go to feed Piki.

[*Exits through the right-hand door. From behind the curtain comes* LAMİ's *meowing. The* MAN *enters carrying* PİKİ's *food in one hand, opens the door on the left, and leans over to give the food to* PİKİ *from the doorway. Remains bending over while speaking to him.*] You were really hungry, weren't you? Glutton! Eat slowly! You'll choke. I've never seen such a greedy dog.

[*Closes the door and sits down in the chair next to* ÇIÇU's. LAMİ *begins to meow.*] All right, now tell me, my dearest Çiçu, what have I done to make you angry with me? Did I say something rude? I don't remember doing anything to hurt or offend you. [*To* LAMİ, *who is meowing.*] Lami, did you have to start fussing, too? Quiet! These guys don't give a man a moment's peace, always interrupting, never letting me get a word in edgewise. One stops, the other starts. [*To* ÇIÇU.] Tell me, do you think they're jealous? You're my one and only love, my first and last. Believe me, Çiçu, I have no other woman, no lover, no friend, no companion except you. You're everything to me.

[*To* LAMİ.] Quiet! I put up with such crap from you guys. I'm sick and tired of it. [*To* ÇIÇU.] How about the women before you? [*Pauses. Depressed.*] What about them?

They all left me alone, completely alone. They shoved me into your lifeless arms, Çiçu. Now all I want is to distract myself with your soulless body and hide in your heartless breast. I inflate you with my own breath and give you life strictly for my own sake. And when I please, I let out your air and kill you. I can't live without love, Çiçu. All those people without love. All those days unlived. We've been together all these years now, and we'll stay like this right here together side by side. [*More painfully.*] You're not at all like the rest—not in the least. You don't make me a stranger to myself like they did. You don't make me pretend to be anything I'm not. You don't know how to be insensitive, you don't know jealousy, you don't fight, you can't commit adultery. [*Eyes begin to fill with tears.*] You have no life, no soul, no tongue. You can't speak, you can't laugh, you can't cry, you can't be happy. I laugh for you. [*Smiles with tear-filled eyes.*] I speak for you. If necessary, I cry for you. I'm so very happy with you. [*Takes* ÇIÇU *in his arms.*] My beautiful blond baby. [*Coquettishly.*] Lovey-dovey. [*To* LAMI, *whose meowing has increased.*] Quiet, Lami, is this anytime to make such a fuss? Can't I have any time to myself? You'd think you were dying of hunger. Ugh, no rest for the wicked. All right! Be quiet, will you? I'm coming, can't you see? [*Exits through the right-hand door to feed* LAMI. *Meowing ceases. The* MAN *returns shortly.*]

Gobbled that enormous can of cat food right up. Yes, that's the way it is, Lady Çiçu; we aren't jealous of each other. To me, you're the most lovable woman in the world. You're my one and only, my forever. [*Hugs and kisses her.*] What's the matter? What're you looking so down in the dumps about anyway? [*Looks at the wall.*] Oh, I see. [*Pointing to the woman's picture on the wall.*] Is this what you're jealous of? Are you jealous of her? Jealous child. Silly girl. That's a picture of my aunt. Surely you're not going to be jealous of my long-dead aunt? OK, all right. [*Climbs up on the couch and turns the picture around so it faces the wall. Returns to* ÇIÇU's *side and takes hold of her chin.*]

I have a surprise for you, dear. [*Quickly goes to his briefcase, gets out a velvet box, removes a necklace, and places it around her neck. Then steps back to look at it.*] It looks marvelous on you. Do you like it? It's nothing. There's no need to thank me. It's not worth it. You deserve a much more valuable one. [*Looks at the birdcage.*] Just a minute, let me give Yumuş his food and water. Then we can talk in peace. [*Exits by the right-hand door. Enters with* YUMUŞ's *food and water, gets up on a chair, and begins talking with* YUMUŞ *while giving them to him.*]

Were you hungry, my little Yumuş? My little yellow Yumuş. [*Simulates canary sounds.*] Are you lonely, too? My poor little Yumuş. [*Simulates canary sounds.*] So you are lonely, too? [*At this moment, a family quarrel is heard from next door. The* MAN *eagerly steps down, gets his tape recorder, places it in front of the door, opens the door slightly, and turns on the recorder. The* MAN *listens exuberantly while the tape records the neighbors' noisy fight.*]

NEIGHBOR: [*Voice from offstage.*] Where were you so late last night?

NEIGHBOR'S WIFE: [*Voice from offstage.*] I was where I was. What's it to you? You leave me here alone for days on end, then show up and wonder where I am.

NEIGHBOR: I asked you a question. Answer me! Where were you? Where were you hanging around?

NEIGHBOR'S WIFE: [*Shouts.*] You're a great one to be talking. Where do you hang out every night? Have you ever once come home on time since we got married? You're the one who's always hanging around in the bars. I need some companionship, too.

[*The* MAN *is visibly pleased the more the fighting goes on; he even begins jumping for joy.*]

NEIGHBOR: Shut up! For God's sake, shut up. Everyone will hear.

NEIGHBOR'S WIFE: Let them hear; let them hear all about you. Why should I shut up? If you expect to be treated like a husband, you'll have to act like one. Night after night expecting my husband to come home, I get all dressed up, set the table, and wait for you. I'm human, too, you know. Do you ever think about me?

NEIGHBOR: I'm sick of your long faces and nagging. That's why I don't come home. You understand? When a man comes home tired from working all day, he expects his wife to greet him with a smile. Here I am dying of loneliness, and you make me even more lonely.

NEIGHBOR'S WIFE: Whose fault is that? Yours. You think I'm not dying of loneliness?

NEIGHBOR: Do you really care about my problems? Should I come home early just so I can fight with you? The less I see your face, the less we fight. What do we have to say to each other?

NEIGHBOR'S WIFE: It's true—we don't even have anything to talk about anymore, do we? [*Crying.*] I can't take this any longer. I can't take it.

NEIGHBOR: I can't either.

NEIGHBOR'S WIFE: [*Shouts louder.*] I'm getting out of here. I'm leaving.

NEIGHBOR: Leave, for God's sake. [*The more the woman cries, the more her husband gives in, increasingly warming up as he talks.*] Stop, don't cry! What did I say, anyhow? You're the one who was yelling at me. First you yell and make a fuss, then you cry. Don't cry. Did I say something to make you cry? I didn't say anything to hurt your feelings, did I?

NEIGHBOR'S WIFE: [*Crying, but weakening.*] What didn't you say? Is there anything you didn't say?

NEIGHBOR: [*More gently.*] Honey, can't we even discuss anything? Can't I even open my mouth? All I said was, "Where were you today, dear?" in order to start a conversation. If you'd just given a nice answer, instead of shouting right away . . .

NEIGHBOR'S WIFE: If you'd asked nicely, I would have given you a nice answer.

NEIGHBOR: OK, OK, let's drop the subject. Come on, smile a little.

[*Pause. The* NEIGHBORS' *fight is over. The* MAN *puts his ear to the slightly open door and tries to listen to what is said. Finally closes the door. Places the tape recorder back on one of the shelves and rewinds the tape. The last part of the* NEIGHBORS' *row is heard again, only this time from the tape recorder and somewhat louder and clearer.*]

MAN: [*After the tape is finished.*] They already made up. [*Pleased.*] By now they're in each other's arms making love. [*Happy.*] The heat of their bodies will warm them and drive out the cold. They make up after every fight and make love all over again. [*Depressed.*] A man ought at least to have someone to fight with. Even fighting is happiness. You can't fight with me, Çiçu. You never get mad at me. I get mad at me for you, and then I make up with myself for you, too. I can't make you lose your temper and get angry at me. I can't please you and make up to you. [*Sits down in the chair next to* ÇIÇU'*s. Places his elbows on the table and rests his head between his hands. To himself.*] Hey you, who do you live for? No one! You always wanted to do some great work to be remembered by. You looked for somebody to inspire those great deeds, someone to give you strength. You looked, waited, and did nothing. You wanted to pledge your life to her. Someone who understands you. Someone to save you from your loneliness. Someone who would share herself with you. [*As if suffocating, he runs his hands around his neck.*] Well, where is she? Where is that somebody for whom you were going to do your greatest, most wonderful work, the world's most creative and immortal work? Where is the hand that was to instill in you a love for living? [*Gets up and stands. Brief pause.*]

It's this silence. This silence will drive me crazy someday. [*Silence. Pantomimes the actions of his speech.*] The more tightly you close your ears, the more you will hear the waterfall of silence inside you. [*Begins to pace back and forth. His shoes squeak noticeably, all the more so because of the complete silence.*] Wear the squeakiest shoes you can find.

MAN'S OWN VOICE: [*From offstage, mockingly.*] You can't drown out the silence inside with little external noises like squeaky shoes. It's useless to hope that the barking of the dog, the meowing of the cat, the chirping of the bird, the neighbors' fights, and the melody of the musical clock will save you.

MAN: Yes, it's hopeless. I know it. [*Goes through all the motions of the actions he is describing.*] I'll become deaf from the noise of this silence inside me. Every night when I come home, the cold metallic sound of the key in the keyhole and the tumbling of the lock rushes to my brain as though to choke me. I take a step inside . . . not a sound, nary a sound! My cold loneliness spreads to my innermost being; I can feel it throbbing against my spine. The silence of the darkness chills me, and I dash in fear to flip on the light switch. I look at the telephone, hoping someone, anyone, will call. I wait for the clock to strike up its tune, for the dog to bark, for the cat to meow.

[*After a long pause, suddenly shouts.*] Çiçu, Çiçuuuuu! Say something, Çiçu. Lami, Lami, will you please meow! Piki, open your mouth. Say something, Piki. External noises—tell me I'm alive!

[*Casts a glance at his surroundings, possessions,* ÇIÇU *with a pained mocking smile.*] What are all of these things for, all these foolish playthings of mine? To pass the time, to escape. This silence sinks its teeth sharply, deeply into my brain. [*Walks over and stands behind* ÇIÇU *with his hands dangling at his sides and his shoulders drooping. A long silence.*] Oh, for a sound! Any sound! [*Lightning strikes, followed by thunder. Pause.*]

It's as though my door were about to open suddenly and . . . [*The window is heard being whipped open by the storm and slamming shut, making a great noise. The newspaper covering the top half of the window is torn away. The* MAN *is at first frightened by the noise, then places a chair under the window, climbs up on it in order to close the window, and looks outside. When he steps down off the chair, it is apparent from the look on his face that something he has seen outside has pleased him. He takes* ÇIÇU *in his arms and carries her out through the left-hand door. Returns, gets a pair of binoculars out of the cupboard, tiptoes across the room—periodically glancing back over his shoulder to see if someone might be watching—and climbs up on the chair. He watches out the window with the binoculars. It is apparent by the motions of his back, legs, and arms that he is spying on one of his neighbors and that he enjoys it immensely. Watches for a while until suddenly startled by* PIKI's *barking. Then resumes peeping and finally closes the window and steps down off the chair.*] Nuts, they closed the curtain. Why'd they have to go and do that? [*Returns the binoculars and the chair to their places and calls* ÇIÇU.]

Çiçuuuu, Çiçuuuu! Are you hungry, sweetie? [*Exits through the left-hand door, returns with* ÇIÇU, *and sets her down at the table. Angrily.*] So you're looking for an excuse to fight, eh, Çiçu? Now what'd I do? What're you being so grouchy about? [*As though* ÇIÇU *has said something and he is answering.*] Who? Me? When have I spied on the neighbors? You should be ashamed of yourself. How can you suspect such a thing of a respectable man like me? Come on now, don't start a fight over nothing. Let's eat our meal in peace. [*As though angered by something* ÇIÇU *has said.*] That's enough of that, I said, I'm not gonna stand for any more of your accusations! [*Suddenly changes his tone so that it is apparent his heart had not been in the previous shouting.*] I'll just feed the fish, and then we can sit down to eat. [*Exits through the right-hand door. Returns, talking to the* FISH *as he feeds them.*] My little fish. Especially you with the enormous fringe, just look at you! What greedy little things you are! If your food is the least bit late, you eat your own offspring.

[*To* ÇIÇU, *delightedly.*] You know what's going to happen someday? Some evening I'm going to walk in through this door, and you know what I'm going to see? You, with Piki's food in your hand, feeding him. I'll freeze in my tracks right there.

"Çiçu is walking," I'll say, flabbergasted. I'll stand in the door and watch you from behind without moving or saying a word. Then you'll feed Lami and give Yumuş his food and water, completely unaware that I've come home and am watching you. Next you'll change the fish's water, and I'll slowly tiptoe up behind you. [*Tiptoes. Comes up behind* çiçu *and pauses, suddenly shouting.*] "Booooo!" I'll shout, and you'll jump. "Oh, it's you!" you'll say. "You scared me out of my wits!" You're gonna talk someday, Çiçu. [*Picks up* beyti, *the turtle, from the floor and speaks to him.*] And how are you, Mr. Beyti? Ohh! Are you hungry too? It's your turn, Beyti. No, you may not go into the yard in this weather. Anyway, you know well enough I barely managed to save you from the neighbors' kids yesterday. Come on, let's fill your tummy, too. [*Exits from the right-hand door with* beyti *in his arms. Returns with lettuce leaves and* beyti. *Opens the left-hand door and puts down the lettuce leaves and* beyti. *Turns toward* risami, *the potted plant.*] Poor Risami, you're practically drying up from lack of water. [*Pours a cup of water into the plant pot.*] You don't say anything, like the rest. You can't sing or meow or bark or eat your offspring like these fish when you get hungry. [*Loudly, angrily.*] Say something, Çiçu! You say something, too! Please open your mouth! [*Pause.*]

[*From behind the right-hand door comes the noise of a glass container falling, rolling, breaking. The* man *is overjoyed.*] Lami's knocked something over in the kitchen again. Knock 'em over, Lami! Make noise! I want noise! Noise! Tell me I'm alive, Lami!

[*Takes the figurines from the shelf and talks to them.*] My greetings to Mr. Vavu and Mrs. Cest. You don't need food or water. You don't get old or suffer loneliness or die. [*Kisses both of them.*] But your existence gives me pleasure, my dear undemanding friends!

[*Turns to* çiçu.] I understand why you're jealous of Lami, Piki, my fish, Beyti, and even Risami, but don't be jealous of my two poor, lifeless friends! [*Places the figurines back in their places and sits down on the chair next to* çiçu'*s, tired, collapsing in a heap.*] Boy, am I tired, Çiçu.

[*Pause. Gets up. Walks around. He is edgy and doesn't know what to do with himself. If nothing else, he would like to get into a fight with someone just to prove his existence. Picks a fight with* çiçu, *imitating his* neighbor'*s voice.*]

Where were you till all hours of the night? [*Pause.*] I asked you a question. Answer! Where were you? Where were you hanging around? [*Shouting.*] Quiet! Shut up! Enough! I'm sick and tired of your nagging. I'm sick and tired of living. [*Pause.*] Have you ever given a damn about my problems? Look at your own life! What do I have to talk to you about? As soon as I step into the house, you start a fight.

[*Pause. Speaks increasingly softer and more sympathetically, as if* çiçu *were crying and he were trying to comfort her.*] Can't I say anything? All I said was, "Where were you today, dear?" If you'd just answer nicely . . . [*Pause.*] Don't cry, dear. What's there to cry about? Please stop, Çiçu. I didn't mean to hurt you. [*Goes to* ÇIÇU's *side, takes her by the shoulders, and kisses her on the neck.*] Don't cry anymore. [*Takes* ÇIÇU *in his arms, carries her to the couch, sits her down, and settles beside her.*] Smile, smile a little, Çiçu. Come on now, shall we throw shadows? What do you say?

[*Adjusts the lights for throwing shadows. Throws shadows on the wall by making different shapes with the fingers of both hands. He throws the silhouettes of various animals, such as a wolf, a dog, a fish. These silhouettes should be large. He tries to entertain and comfort* ÇIÇU *by imitating the sounds of the same animals. He himself gets caught up in the pleasure of the game and keeps up continuous laughter in* ÇIÇU's *place.*] Look at this dog, Çiçu, an enormous sheepdog. Woof, woof, woof . . . he's gonna bite you. Run, Çiçu! [*Laughs, barks, snarls.*] See what a nice donkey! You like donkeys, don't you? So do I. [*Brays, laughs, brays. Bursts out laughing. Brays.*] Ohh! I've laughed so hard, I've got tears in my eyes. Stop it, Çiçu, I'm gonna collapse in a heap! And this is a sheep! [*Baas.*] Look at the rooster! A rooster. [*Crows. Drops the shadow and waves his arms like wings while imitating a rooster and dances around* ÇIÇU. *He leaps on* ÇIÇU *and bites her on the back of the neck like a rooster mounts a chicken.* ÇIÇU *falls on the floor. The* MAN *leaps onto the table and proudly flaps his wings and crows. Then starts to tickle* ÇIÇU. *Moves away, comes back, and tickles her again, then moves away again. Begins laughing as though he were the one being tickled. Laughing, he tumbles on the couch with* ÇIÇU; *then they fall rolling on the floor.*] Don't tickle, please don't tickle me, Çiçu, I'm gonna faint. Ooohhh. [*Gets up and slowly begins to come to himself.*] Oh, it's ten o'clock. Nirey says it's time to eat. Boy, am I hungry, dear! Let's prepare a good meal for ourselves.

[*Flips on the light switch, illuminating the room as before. Takes off his jacket, tie, and sweater and puts them on a hanger. Exits through the right-hand door. Puts on an apron and returns with a tablecloth, which he spreads out on the table.*] Would you like to have a guest for dinner? OK, I'll prepare a meal for three.

[*Turns on the radio, which the audience hears while the* MAN *is going back and forth to the kitchen off to the right, bringing plates and food. He is very happy—whistles, waltzes around with the plates, jumps around, dances. At first, he pays no attention to the talk on the radio, then finally he stops to listen with plates in hand.*]

RADIO ANNOUNCER: Man's greatest selfishness is his subconscious desire to use his friends only as vehicles to bear the burden of his own problems. Although selfish people continuously complain of their loneliness and of being misunderstood by those close to them, they do not want to share the loneliness of others or attempt to understand them. This selfishness does not save them from their loneliness; on the contrary, it leaves them totally depressed and alone. Yet when they force themselves to seek groups in an attempt to escape from the loneliness they have created, the crowd merely increases their loneliness. Permanently sentencing themselves to the loneliness in which they bury themselves, these selfish people hold their friends responsible and blame those around them for their loneliness. However, a man's escape from loneliness lies not in burdening others with his loneliness, but in bearing the loneliness of others, in sharing the problems of those around him.

MAN: Good grief, Çiçu, aren't you tired of listening to this chatterbox?

RADIO ANNOUNCER: Man's escape, man's winning of friendship . . . [*The* MAN *turns off the radio.*]

MAN: [*Places three chairs around the table.*] Çiçu, this is your place, this is our guest's, and this is mine. [*Places* ÇIÇU *on a chair. On the back of the chair for the* GUEST *he places the jacket he had taken off and hung up. To the* GUEST.] Won't you sit down, please? [*From here on, throughout the meal he will act like a child playing house and will speak for* ÇIÇU *and the* GUEST. *Pours drinks for the three of them.*] Won't you have a drink? Please do. [*Raises his glass to the* GUEST.] Here's to your health!

[*Moves to the* GUEST*'s chair and sits down, putting himself in the* GUEST*'s place. Raises his glass to* ÇIÇU *and speaks in the* GUEST*'s voice.*] To our happiness, madam. [*Raising his glass, this time to his own empty chair. With the* GUEST*'s voice.*] To your health and honor!

[*Quickly goes to his own chair, sits down, and raises his own glass.*] Thank you. [*Drinks.*] If you like, I could put some light music on the record player.

[*He places a record on the record player, and it begins. The volume is low. He steps behind* ÇIÇU *and says with a woman's voice.*] What a lovely evening.

[*Sits in his own chair.*] Tonight I want to get drunk. Let's drink. [*Drinks. To the* GUEST.] Won't you have some meatballs?

[*Takes the* GUEST*'s seat. In the* GUEST*'s voice.*] I have some, thank you. [*With the* GUEST*'s voice to* ÇIÇU.] You're a marvelous cook. The meatballs are very good . . . delicious!

[*Steps behind* ÇIÇU *and with a woman's voice.*] Thank you, sir. Won't you have some more? You haven't eaten anything, really. How about a little salad?

[*Returns to his own chair.*] My wife fixes excellent meals. She's not only an intellectual, but an excellent housewife. I don't mean to brag to her face, but . . . I don't say it just because she's my wife, either. Really, I mean that. No one can criticize her as a housewife. Why don't you have some pickles? [*Places some pickles on the* GUEST*'s plate.*] I'm so glad you came. [*Turning to* ÇIÇU.] Really, we are very pleased, aren't we, dear?

[*Steps behind* ÇIÇU. *In a woman's voice.*] Oh, of course, delighted. Who wouldn't be? We're delighted, delighted. [*Laughing with a woman's voice.*] Have some fries.

[*Sticking his hands under* ÇIÇU*'s arms, he puts some fries on the* GUEST*'s plate. Returns to his own chair, pours some whisky in his glass, and drinks.*] In our family life, there's not the least little, least little . . . [*Can't think of the word.*] What do they say? Oh yes, thing, thing, not the least little thing interfering with our happiness. [*Growing increasingly drunk.*] Nothing. Because we . . . who are we? We, I would like to submit that . . . please permit me, I was speaking . . . I haven't finished what I was going to say yet.

[*Steps to the* GUEST*'s chair. With the* GUEST*'s voice.*] You know, I'm jealous of your family life. I'm forever pointing you out as the ideal family to all my married friends. [*Laughs indifferently, then suddenly becomes very serious.*] Your financial position is very good . . . your sex life is exceptional . . . a family that's really moving forward. Soon you'll be prospering.

[*Steps behind* ÇIÇU , *addresses the* GUEST *in a woman's voice.*] To this day we have never hurt each other's feelings. My husband has never hurt me.

[*Moves to the* GUEST*'s chair and slides the chair toward* ÇIÇU. *Familiarly in the* GUEST*'s voice.*] You, Lady Çiçu . . . I don't quite know how to say it . . . in comparison with your husband . . . that is, what I mean is, you are more . . . well, yes, you deserve a better life. I can't tell you how much I admire you . . . your beauty . . . your special something. . . . Please, I hope you won't think I've had too much to drink. I . . . I . . . I . . . I'm not a man to withhold my feelings.

[*Steps behind* ÇIÇU, *speaking flirtatiously in a woman's voice.*] You're flattering me . . . hee, hee, hee . . . you're too kind. Really, I'm embarrassed. I don't know what to say. [*Coquettishly.*] Thank you very, very much. I'll never forget you.

[*Goes to his own chair, addresses the* GUEST *firmly in a harsh voice that betrays his jealousy regarding* ÇIÇU.] Have some beef, you ox! You're not eating anything. Ahaa . . . I think you're drunk. Are you nauseated? [*Looks knowingly several times at* ÇIÇU *and the* GUEST.] I mean, my stomach's a bit upset, too.

[*Steps behind* ÇIÇU. *Addresses the* GUEST *with a woman's voice.*] Try some of my beans, or I'll be offended. [*Coquettishly.*] Really, I'll get angry. Come on, have some . . . for my sake. I'll die if you don't eat some. At least take one spoonful. Just taste 'em, darling.

[*Sits in his own place. In his own voice.*] It's hot in here, I'm uncomfortable. If you'll permit me, I'll take this off. [*Takes off his shirt and steps behind* ÇIÇU *in his undershirt. In a woman's voice.*] What next? Don't do that, you're embarrassing me. Aren't you ashamed to sit across from our guest like that?

[*Sits in his own chair.*] I will if I feel like it. Is he some kind of a stranger, for cryin' out loud? He's an old family friend. I'll sit next to him in my shorts if I feel like it. [*To the*

GUEST.] What's the matter? Your stomach? The bathroom? It's here. [*Gets up, takes the* GUEST *by the arm, and leads him, drunkenly staggering out through the right-hand door. Comes back and turns to* ÇIÇU *angrily.*] You look at me . . . look me square in the eye. If you think I don't know what you're up to, you've got another think coming. You can't fool me, you hear, you can't fool me! Nobody, but nobody, puts anything over on me. [*Drunkenly.*] You're not dealing with a fool, you know. You're not gonna put any horns on me, not on me. I . . . I . . . I . . . the woman ain't been born who's gonna put horns on me.

[*Steps behind* ÇIÇU *and answers himself in a woman's voice.*] Oh, for God's sake, don't start that again! I've had it up to here with your jealous rages. What am I supposed to do if he's got his eyes on me? It's no sin to be pretty. It's not my fault if you pick up every tramp in the street and bring him home to dinner.

[*The* MAN *to* ÇIÇU.] What the hell do you mean, jealous rage? You've been taking advantage of my tolerance and plotting under my nose.

[*Steps behind* ÇIÇU *and begins crying with a woman's voice.*] How can you say such a thing?

[*Cries loudly with* ÇIÇU's *voice, then gets up and speaks in his own voice.*] If you didn't encourage him, he wouldn't start drooling at the mouth! I saw him pinching your leg under the table.

[*Steps behind* ÇIÇU. *With a woman's voice.*] Aaahhhh, I thought that was your hand. How could I know it was his hand? To hell with him anyway; he made my whole leg one black-and-blue mark.

[*The* MAN *stands, shouting.*] I'm not the fool you think I am. [*The right-hand door suddenly opens by itself.*] I . . . I . . . I'm an honorable man and a faithful husband. [*Suddenly laughs coldly as if seeing the* GUEST *enter from the opening door.*] Is that you? [*Can't remember what he was going to say.*] Did you manage all right? Good, good, you must feel better now. That's great, Çiçu and I were just discussing the world situation. What a bunch of crap our foreign policy has turned out to be. Eskimos want our Kınalı Island[1] again. Have a seat. [*Pulls out the* GUEST's *chair for him.*] You're not drinking anything. [*The* MAN *drinks.*] What do you think of the state the world's in? [*Pretends to listen carefully to what the* GUEST *says and expresses surprise.*] Really? You don't say! Incredible! What's this world coming to, anyway? And then? [*Listens to the* GUEST *and slowly begins to laugh harder and harder, until in tears with laughter.*] Stop, stop, you'll kill me with laughter. [*Doubles up.*] You're killin' me! [*Suddenly straight-*

---

1. Kınalı Island: One of the islands in an archipelago of nine (the so-called Princes' Islands) in the Sea of Marmara, near Istanbul.

ens up.] Hey, what's your hurry? It's still early. You can go later. We're having such a good time. Do you have to get up early tomorrow? Well, it's up to you. [*Stands as though exchanging good-byes with the* GUEST. *Finally goes toward the door and opens it. Shakes the imaginary man's hand, smiling.*] We'll expect you again sometime.

GUEST: [*Voice from offstage.*] Good night!

MAN: Good-bye!

GUEST: Good-bye!

MAN: We won't count this brief visit; you must come again. We'll expect you.

GUEST'S VOICE: Thanks for your hospitality.

MAN: [*Mockingly waves his hand.*] Goood-byyyye, gggooodd-bbyyye, good-byyyye. Respects to your wife. Good-byyyye. [*Closes the door. Suddenly becomes very serious. Sits down in his own chair. Downs drinks in rapid succession. Very drunk. After considerable silence and after finishing the drinks, he stands up. Staggers to the record player and turns it off. To* ÇIÇU.] Did you say I should get married? [*Staggers aimlessly.*] Let's say I got married. [*As if playing a game.*] OK, let's say I'm married. I tell my wife I have to go on a business trip and won't be coming home for a week. [*As though* ÇIÇU *were is wife.*] Well, good-bye, sweetheart. It'll be a long week without you. Of course I'll write every day. I'll miss you terribly.

[*Exits by the outside door and immediately reenters.*] And now I secretly return home that evening. I tiptoe slowly into her room. What's this? Whispering in my bedroom. And a very meaningful whispering. I open the bedroom door, and well, well, well, what's all this? My darling wife is dancing in bed in the arms of some stallion! Shameless bitch! [*Takes his gun from the cupboard.*] As I grab my gun, my wife and her lover race out in their underpants, and I go after them. [*Exits quickly through the right-hand door. His shouting is heard from backstage.*] You bastard, rapist! Despicable ass! Come out, wherever you are. Come out like a man. I'll have your blood for this. Bastards, and in my own house, in my own bed! I'll kill you like a mad dog!

[*Loud noises, sounds of running. A* WOMAN *screams and then enters in a nightie from the right-front corridor. It is the* MAN *in a woman's disguise. The* WOMAN (MAN), *with her hair completely disheveled, is in a state of panic and runs from side to side. Runs to the outside door, hoping to escape, but is unable to open it.*]

WOMAN'S VOICE: [*The* MAN *speaking in a woman's voice.*] Ooohh God, he locked the door. I'm ruined, my whole home and family are wrecked.

[*The* WOMAN *exits through the right-hand door. A great tumult is kept up offstage. From off-stage the* WOMAN'S *screams are heard.*] Please don't kill me! Please don't kill me! I beg of you, spare my life. I swear I wasn't committing adultery—really, I wasn't. Believe me, I did nothing wrong. Believe me, please believe me. I'm innocent. That man, that man is a . . . that is . . . he forced his way into my bed while I was asleep. I had no way of knowing.

MAN'S VOICE: And what was he looking for in my bed?

WOMAN'S VOICE: I guess maybe he'd lost his watch or something.

MAN'S VOICE: You mean I've been raising a snake in my own house all these years?

WOMAN'S VOICE: I'm no snake. I'm a dove, your little dove.

MAN'S VOICE: Traitor! I'll kill both of you!

[*Tumult, sound of running. The* LOVER *enters from the corridor on the right. It is the* MAN *disguised as the lover. He is barefoot and wearing only his shorts. In a panic, he runs from one side to the other. Tries hiding under the couch and under the table, but fails.*]

LOVER: [*Mumbles.*] God, I've had it. This guy means business. [*Exits through the right-hand door. From backstage we hear the* LOVER *pleading.*] Don't kill me, please don't shoot me, sir; I have a wife and family! Have pity on my children! I swear to God I didn't mean anything bad. I didn't mean any harm. Your wife called me in to fix the faucets. Don't shoot, don't shoot. I beg of you. Spare my life.

MAN'S VOICE: I'll kill the both of you. Where are you? You won't catch me wearing any horns. You can't escape me.

MAN: [*Enters from the corridor on the right and moves to the front of the stage. He has on his undershirt again and is in the role of the* MAN. *With a gun in his hand, he walks to the table and fills his glass with alcohol and drinks it.*] Where are they hiding? [*Looks under the couch and the table. Suddenly smiles.*] I was gonna kill the two of them, but that's a waste of bullets.

[*The phone rings. The* MAN *adopts a serious manner that shows the previous antics were all an act.*] And who could that be? I wonder who wants me at this time of night, Çiçu? Or are they looking for you? [*Takes another drink and carries the bottle and his glass to the telephone. The telephone is beside the couch. Stretches out on the floor and rests his head up against the couch. Picks up the receiver. Listens. While he listens, he continues to drink.*] Hello, hello!

WOMAN'S VOICE ON THE PHONE: [*Voice audible to audience.*] This man is driving me nuts.

MAN: What man?

WOMAN ON THE PHONE: My husband, who else? What haven't I put up with from that man? I can't begin to tell you. I'd have committed suicide long ago if it weren't for my children. [*The* MAN *takes a drink.*] This torture is unbearable. Can anyone stand such treatment? If a person were made of stone, he couldn't stand this kind of punishment. See, it's already midnight, and he hasn't come home yet!

MAN: Who hasn't come home yet?

WOMAN ON THE PHONE: Aren't you listening to me? What did I just say? My husband, my husband, I said! Don't you understand?

MAN: What happened to your husband?

WOMAN ON THE PHONE: All day I wait for him to come home. I prepare his dinner. I straighten up the house. I get all dressed up, and then he doesn't show up until after midnight. Some nights he doesn't come home at all. [*Weeping.*] Sometimes he doesn't come home for days at a time. [*The* MAN *drinks.*] He often comes home drunk toward morning. He never has anything nice to say. If he does come home early once in a blue moon, he starts a fight, yells and screams, then leaves again. He plays cards at the club. I'm sick of his insults and insensitivity. My life is poison. That man . . .

MAN: What man?

WOMAN ON THE PHONE: I've just been telling you! My husband! Who knows where he is now. Believe me, it's been this way ever since we were married. Not even once has he shown enough interest to ask how I was or what I was doing.

MAN: But, lady, if you'll permit me . . .

WOMAN ON THE PHONE: He spends his time shooting the breeze at the coffeehouse, playing cards at the club, and drinking at the bar. I'm human, too, you know. [*Weeping.*] Don't you see? I'm alive too! I'm fed up with being alone. I was much happier before I got married. At least I lived with the hope of escaping loneliness. Now I've even lost that hope.

MAN: [*Thickly.*] But . . . lady . . . if . . . just a minute . . . please, just hold on a second. [*Drinks.*]

WOMAN ON THE PHONE: You can't possibly understand the loneliness of a woman. There's nothing worse than not having someone to share yourself with.

MAN: Well, I'm very sorry lady, but I don't even know you.

WOMAN ON THE PHONE: Of course you don't know me. If you knew me, would I have called you? I'm telling you all this precisely because you're a stranger. I just rang a number at random, and you answered. [*The* MAN *falls asleep stretched out on the floor with his head propped up against the couch and lets the receiver fall from his hand onto the floor. The* WOMAN's *voice continues, becoming louder, echoing.*] I'm overcome with loneliness. Of course you don't know me. I don't know you, either. I'm so alone I haven't anyone to tell my troubles to. I'll burst if I don't tell someone. I've written your number down in my notebook. I couldn't possibly tell my troubles to people I know. They'd immediately start gossiping. Worst of all, they'd outwardly give me sympathy but inwardly be pleased. So what could I do? I told my problems to you, someone I've never seen before. [*Sobs.*]

CURTAIN

ACT II

Scene 1

[*Same place, toward morning. The situation is the same as in Act I. The curtain opens with music—Mussorgsky's* Pictures at an Exhibition *would be appropriate. As the cur-*

tain opens, the stage is dark. The MAN is sleeping, stretched out on the floor with his head propped up against the couch. The telephone receiver is on the floor. The basic elements of the room are unchanged, and the furniture is in the same place. A dark blue, fairylike, lavishly star-studded sky is lowered into the room, taking the place of the walls, while the rest of the room and its furniture remain as they were. This star-studded night demonstrates that in this scene the MAN is dreaming.

The stars twinkle slowly. Dim blue rays of light fall on the place where the MAN is sleeping. Stretching, the MAN slowly awakens and gets up. During this entire scene, all of the MAN's movements are in time with the music and in the form of a dance.

He goes over to ÇIÇU. Dancing, he makes ÇIÇU do a striptease act. After each dance movement, he removes one of her undergarments. The MAN's dance is a comic, amateurish effort, but this is deliberate. During the striptease dance, real ballet dancers appear on stage. By dancing around ÇIÇU, they aid in giving an aura of reality to her. The MAN finally removes even her underpants. The blue light spreads out somewhat and turns to a deep purple. The MAN performs several dance movements with ÇIÇU. The music stops. The sound of great applause is heard. With their backs to the audience, the MAN takes ÇIÇU's hand, and they bow, turning from side to side, as though acknowledging the applause of the imaginary audience. The applause increases. The MAN presents ÇIÇU. As the applause slowly dies away, the lights turn red.]

MAN: Boy, am I tired, dear. [*Kisses* ÇIÇU.] Go on, take your bath. [*Takes* ÇIÇU *out the left-hand door and returns. As he walks toward the door on the right, which has remained dark, a red light spreads toward the right, disclosing* ÇIÇU *in the right-hand doorway. The* MAN *is surprised and afraid. Music begins.*] Çiçu? Is that you? [*To himself.*] I just took her to the bathroom and left her there! [*Timidly, hesitantly, frightened, he approaches* ÇIÇU *and touches her. He takes her in his arms and carries her out the right-hand door and returns. Walks toward the couch. A red light spreads toward the back of the couch, and we see* ÇIÇU *standing there. Very frightened, the* MAN *steps back and shouts.*] It's not true! It can't be! [ÇIÇU's *laughter is heard from a loudspeaker.*] It can't be.

ÇIÇU's VOICE: [*Laughing loudly.*] Why can't it?

MAN: [*Hesitatingly approaches* ÇIÇU, *stands watching her, then picks her up and carries her out the left-hand door and returns, locking the door. As he approaches the door on the other side, the red light spreads toward that door, and* ÇIÇU *is seen in front of the door.* ÇIÇU's *laugh mockingly echoes. He shouts.*] Çiçu! You can't walk. You stay where you're put. You can't laugh.

ÇIÇU's VOICE: Why? Why can't I walk? Why can't I laugh?

MAN: [*Steps back, afraid.*] She's talking, she's talking.

ÇIÇU: Why are you so surprised?

MAN: Quiet! Stop talking!

ÇİÇU: You were the one who always wanted me to talk. And now that I'm talking, you're afraid of me.

MAN: [*Pleads.*] Be quiet, Çiçu. Please don't talk! You're lifeless. Don't you realize that? Wherever I put you, you stay there; you can't move!

ÇİÇU: You see, it's not like you thought at all. I'm walking, I'm talking, and I'm laughing, too. [*Laughs.*]

MAN: [*Shouts in fear.*] You can't talk! This isn't you talking. You don't have a voice!

ÇİÇU: Weren't you the one who wanted me to save you from your loneliness? Now here I am, being as you always wanted me to be. [*Lovingly, in a sweet voice.*] Come here, dear! Hold out your arms to me. Let's hold hands and fly up to the clouds.

MAN: [*Steps back, stuttering.*] But I . . . but I didn't really . . .

ÇİÇU: Even fighting is happiness for you. Wasn't it you who said, "If only I had someone, even if only to fight with." You may fight with me as you please. After every spat, we'll make up and love each other more, even more than before. And when you come home late, and when you don't show enough interest in me, I'll sulk. We'll get married, and I'll be your wife.

MAN: [*Bewildered.*] No, you won't. I can't marry you.

ÇİÇU: Why not? Don't you love me? Why can't you marry me? So, you've been taking me for a ride all along. You've been lying to me.

MAN: You aren't alive, Çiçu. You can't have children.

ÇİÇU: But I won't grow old. I'll always stay young and beautiful just as I am now, just the age you wanted. Just like this, see. Just like dead people, just memories, without growing old. [ÇİÇU's *laughter grows louder, echoing. Sound of music also grows louder.*]

MAN: [*Shouts.*] Quiet, stop it, Çiçu! [*Covers his ears with his hands and tries to escape. Runs toward the left-hand door, but the sound of* PİKİ's *barking added to the music and the laughter scares him away, and he turns toward the right-hand door. From the right-hand door,* LAMİ's *meowing is added to the other noises and music. The* MAN *turns from the right-hand door and runs to the outside door, from which comes the sound of the husband-wife fight he taped. This noise is added to the previous noises and the music. He shouts.*] Quiet! Stop that! [*Rushing in this direction and that, he steps toward the radio, from which the previous program emerges. He retreats madly. From the record player is now heard the music he put on while drinking with his pretend* GUEST. *He turns toward the telephone, only to hear the sobbing voice of the* WOMAN *with whom he'd spoken earlier, repeating her tale. All these noises and the music mix together. Racing madly back and forth, he begins to scream like a wild beast. As though having experienced a terrible nightmare, he suddenly retreats in fear, crouching in a corner. Then he rushes over and stretches out on the floor with his head propped up against the couch as he was at the beginning of this scene. First the barking, then the meowing, then the record player, then the taped quarrel stop, one by one. The ambient music grows soft.*]

RADIO ANNOUNCER: . . . whereas man's escape from loneliness lies not in burdening others with his loneliness but in bearing the loneliness of others and sharing it. [*Radio program stops; music grows still fainter.*]

WOMAN ON THE PHONE: I'm choking with loneliness. Of course you don't know me. You can't understand. There's no greater pain than not having someone to share your loneliness with. [WOMAN's *sobbing is heard; then silence.*]

[*The* MAN *is sleeping. The music softly disappears. The musical clock gets louder, and the red light decreases. From the window, a pinkish yellow morning light falls upon the* MAN.]

Scene 2

[*The continuation of the previous scene, minus the star-studded sky effect. Morning. The* MAN *is asleep on the floor with his head propped up against the couch.* ÇIÇU *is seated at the table, fully dressed. The musical clock is playing. As the melody of the clock dies out, the* MAN *awakens and looks around in surprise at having slept there.*]

MAN: [*Sleepily.*] Çiçu! Çiçuuuuu! [*Suddenly noticing* ÇIÇU.] Oh, there you are. I guess I fell asleep here. Did we drink that much last night? I must've really tied one on. I must've collapsed right here and not moved an inch. I don't even remember stretching out. God, my head is splitting. How do you feel, Çiçu? [*Stretches. Sits in the chair next to* ÇIÇU's.] God, what a terrible dream I had, Çiçu. [*Suddenly stands up.*] Let me go wash my face; then I'll come and tell you about it. [*Exits through the right-hand door.* LAMI *meows several times. The* MAN *enters, drying his face with a towel.*]

A terrible dream! You know what happened? You were alive. That's right. You talked just like a real person. And laughed. What a sweet warm voice you had. If you were like my dream, I'd marry you and never be lonely again. Strange how a man can think his dream is real and be scared to death. But you can't know that; you can't dream. In my dream you said, "Let's get married." What do you think of that? Isn't that a frightening idea? That was a crazy idea, wasn't it? Supposing this rubber bag I've blown up with my own mouth came alive and talked to me. It'd scare the hell out of me, wouldn't it? Everything here began to close in on me. [*Picks up the two ceramic figurines from the shelf.*] Even Vavu and Cest came alive and descended on me, howling as though they'd become rabid. The fish leaped out of the aquarium by the thousands, tens of thousands, and began hovering above my head. [*Points to the flower in the flowerpot.*] Risami grew and grew until he was an enormous tree with live branches and reached out for me wherever I tried to escape. I can't tell you what a horrible night I had. Strange how a man can think his dream is real and . . . [*Paces back and forth.*]

I'm fed up with all of you. With all of this absurdity. I'm repulsed by everything in this house. I'm afraid I'll go mad someday in this desolate prison I've sentenced myself to. [*Collapses on a chair, holds his head between his hands. Pause. When he raises his head, his eyes are filled with tears.*]

Are you hungry? Should I get breakfast ready, Çiçu?

[*The doorbell rings. Runs to open the door but finds no one there.*] Who's there? [*No answer. He closes the door. As he turns away, the bell rings again. Opens the door and looks out for a while, but sees no one and closes the door again. Exits through the right-hand door. The bell rings again several times. The* MAN *returns with a breakfast tray, places the tray on the table, opens the door, and looks outside. Seeing no one, he closes the door. He returns to the table, sits down, and breaks off a piece of bread just as the doorbell rings again. In an effort to catch the culprit, he moves very slowly toward the door on his tiptoes and swings the door open suddenly. He sees no one and shouts.*] Who's ringing the doorbell?

[*Leaves the door completely open and returns to the table. Crossly to* ÇIÇU.] Come on, come on now, eat your breakfast! [*Yells.*] What are you waiting for, eat your breakfast!

[PIKI *begins barking;* LAMI *begins meowing.*] To hell with the lot of you!

[*The doorbell rings several times in a short, sharp staccato fashion. The* MAN *approaches the door fearfully and looks out. The doorbell continues to ring. He angrily rips the doorbell from the wall and flings it on the floor. The doorbell rings even more loudly. Then the right-hand door, followed by the left-hand door, also start ringing. Then a bell begins ringing at the window and finally from various places in the walls. The* MAN *closes the outside door in fear, and all the bells simultaneously stop ringing. A deep silence. The* MAN *listens.*]

NEWSPAPER BOY: [*Voice from outside.*] Newspaper! [*Shouts.*] Newspaperrrr! [*Footsteps are heard on the steps. The sound of the footsteps gets louder and nearer. The doorbell rings.*]

MAN: [*Opens the door and talks to the* NEWSPAPER BOY, *who is unseen on the other side of the door.*] Did you ring this bell a little while ago?

NEWSPAPER BOY: [*From outside.*] No, I just now came to the door and rang the bell once. Here are your newspapers.

MAN: Thanks. [*With his newspapers and magazines in hand, he closes the door and returns to sit in the armchair. Reads one of the newspapers. Looks at a magazine. Picks up a pair of scissors and carefully cuts out a picture of a nude woman and puts it up on the wall. To* ÇIÇU.] What are you staring at? I don't care anymore what you think. Come on over and look at it closely. [*Grabs* ÇIÇU *by the back of the neck, drags her over to face the nude on the wall, and knocks her head against the picture a couple of times.*] Now, did you get a good look? You know what it is? It's a picture of a nude woman. You got anything to say about it? [*Doorbell rings. He drops* ÇIÇU *in the armchair.*]

MAILMAN: [*Voice from outside.*] Mail. [*Doorbell rings.*] Maaiil.

MAN: [*Opens the door and addresses the unseen* MAILMAN.] Did you ring the doorbell earlier this morning?

MAILMAN: [*Voice from outside.*] No, this is the first time I've been here this morning. You have a letter.

MAN: [*Takes his letter.*] Thanks. [*Closes the door. Reads the address on the envelope. Very pleased, he tears open the envelope and begins reading the letter.*] My dear friend. [*The* MAN *stands holding the letter in his hand. What is written in the letter is heard through the voice of the* WOMAN (LETTER WRITER) *from whom the letter has come. The* MAN *is obviously thrilled.*]

WOMAN'S VOICE (LETTER WRITER): [*Reads the contents of the letter.*] My dear friend. At this moment your letters are piled in front of me. I have read them over and over again, enjoying them more with each reading. They take my mind off my loneliness. [*The* MAN *is obviously pleased.*] There is something, a secret force, that continuously draws me toward you, and I can no longer resist it. I don't have the strength to resist it. I'm afraid I won't be able to express my feelings very well in this letter, but if you were to extend your hand toward me and place it over my heart, you would understand my feelings better.

MAN: [*Spitefully to* ÇIÇU.] You hear what she said? You hear?

WOMAN'S VOICE (LETTER WRITER): [*From the letter.*] Sir, I try to enjoy life, but until now I have not been able to taste happiness for a single day. My life is nothing more than a burden I have to bear.

MAN: [*Answers the* WOMAN (LETTER WRITER) *who is reading the letter.*] Believe me, mine is the same. I've been alone for years. At night when I come home, I shiver at the cold sound of the key turning the lock. Loneliness is a cold, damp thing. I enter my house and listen to this deep darkness, the darkness of my loneliness. Finally, a confusion of sounds, a waterfall of sounds, drums, pipes, a deafening noise. [*Talks as though the* WOMAN *who is reading the letter were right in front of him.*] I immediately race to the light switch. As soon as the light comes on, the noises stop. Sometimes I become terrified that I might go crazy. I don't need the false noises buzzing in my ears; I need real noises. I come to think that the neighbors' quarrels, even the most unimportant overheard bits of conversation, will save me. Listen, listen. [*Looks at his own shoes and walks a little, making them squeak.*] You hear them, don't you? You hear how they squeak? When I buy shoes, I always check whether or not they squeak. I always wear squeaky shoes like these. I need sounds, noise. I want to hear real sounds, so that I can escape from the noise of the tens of thousands of orchestras overpowering my brain. So I try to distract myself even with the squeaking of my shoes; I try to rid myself of loneliness. Some people think I wear these squeaky shoes to attract attention. [*Smiles.*] That's also why I bought this bird. The same goes for the dog and the cat and this musical clock. [*Tears in his eyes.*] Look here, look at all the loneliness here beside me. This inflatable rubber dummy . . . all of these things are my escape from loneliness. Every night I take a bunch of sleeping pills and fall asleep curled up on the floor for a couple of hours without even getting into bed. I have terrible dreams. When I put out my arm in bed at night, there's nothing there but loneliness. It makes me afraid, and I put out my other arm. I hold myself—cold, damp, shivering. [*Collapses on the floor in front of the chair. Wraps his arms around its legs as though encircling a woman's legs and rests his head against it.*]

WOMAN'S VOICE (LETTER WRITER): [*Reading the letter.*] The actions of those around me seem phony, artificial. I don't like it; I don't feel at ease. The women seem like wild beasts with their arms, necks, and fingers decorated in pearl beads and their faces all painted up. I want to make you understand how and why I am suffocating from spiritual loneliness. I wonder if I've been able to? I don't feel a part of this society. And consequently I suffer without end. I would like to escape far away, very, very far away. I wonder if I will ever be able to find the happiness I seek even in that unknown and possibly nonexistent faraway place.

I have a tremendous need to be loved compassionately, to take an interest in someone else. I feel like I'm in an oarless boat in the middle of a stormy sea. Maybe someday the boat will strike a sharp rock, and I'll be torn to pieces. Or maybe it'll find a sandy beach, and I'll find the peace and quiet I need. If you accuse me of living in a dream world, you're probably right.

MAN: [*Gets up with the letter in his hand.*] No, I don't think you're mistaken at all. You shall save me from here. Close your palms, squeeze your hands, dig your fingers in until your nails enter your flesh. Hold tight and don't run away. Don't let happiness escape. Bite off a hunk of happiness with your teeth.

I'll do anything you want. For you I'll throw birds by the handful to the bottom of the sea. I'll fill the skies with fish by the handful. Then with my head in the sky and my feet in the sea . . . [pɪkɪ *barks,* LAMɪ *meows.*] My wounds are bleeding. See, they are calling to me. [*Doorbell rings. The* MAN *calls from where he is.*] Who's there? What do you want?

JANITOR: [*From outside the door.*] It's me, sir, the janitor.

MAN: [*Angrily.*] What is it? What do you want?

JANITOR: Remember you said you were going to have the apartment painted. I've brought the painter.

MAN: It's not necessary. I'm not going to have it painted. I'm leaving here. I'm moving. [*Happily. To himself.*] I'm going to escape.

[*Lights dim while the musical clock plays.*]

[*When the stage lights up again, the* MAN *is not there.* ÇIÇU *has been placed stretched out on one of the emptied bookshelves. Sound of the key turning in the outside door is heard. Door opens. The* MAN *enters, leaving the door slightly ajar. He is very happy, whistles.*]

MAN: No more squeaky shoes for me; I'm saved. Shoes ought to be soft. [*Goes to the shelf where* ÇIÇU *is.*] I'm getting married, you hear? I am getting mar-ri-ed. [*Pause.*] What're you sulking about? Why aren't you crying? [*Pause.*] You just stay there on that shelf getting dusty, old, and dry. Let the moths chew you full of holes, eat you up. You never lived, and you're not going to. You won't die either. But you'll get old lying there. [PIKI *barks.*] Piki, I'm taking you with me. [LAMI *meows.*] You too, Lami. Fish, Yumuş, Beyti, Risami, Nirey, Cest, Vavu—all of you are coming along. We're going to our new home. You'll like your mistress, really you will. Only Çiçu will be left behind. I'm gonna leave her here. She'll be passed from hand to hand. Kids will play with her. They'll poke her with needles, fill her with air, let the air out again, and make fun of her. [*Pulls a chair over to feed* YUMUŞ.] Yumuş, you're glad I'm getting married today, aren't you, my Yumuş? [*Makes canary sounds. Then feeds the* FISH.] I'm going to the marriage ceremony. Today we're having the marriage ceremony. [*To* PIKI, *who is barking.*] From now on you, too, will escape from this depressing loneliness, Piki. My wife'll take you out for a walk every day. [*Sits down in the armchair. Takes off his shoes and puts on his slippers. He then decides to take off his socks. Smells his socks and throws them to one side. Gets up and starts undressing. Whistles. Once down to his shorts, his eyes light on the window. Takes the binoculars from the shelf, places the chair under the window, gets up on it, and looks out with the binoculars. Turns his head to* ÇIÇU.] Look all you want. That was in the old days. See, I'm peeping right in front of your eyes. Be furious, see if I give a damn! [*Looks outside with the binoculars, then gets down off the chair.*] Don't get the idea I'm doing this for you. From now on, there'll be no more spying on women with binoculars from behind a window. That's forbidden. I can't betray my wife. These binoculars should be put away somewhere, hidden. [*Puts the binoculars away. Gets up on the couch and straightens the picture he'd hung backward.*] I don't care how jealous you are; from now on, you mean nothing to me.

[*Exits from the right-hand door. A moment later, the telephone rings. The* MAN *enters in a bathrobe and picks up the receiver.*]

WOMAN ON THE PHONE: [*The volume of her voice is raised.*] Sir, I'm so sorry to bother you again. The first time I dialed a number at random, and you answered. I wrote your number down.

MAN: What do you want?

WOMAN ON THE PHONE: Thank you in advance for listening to me.

MAN: [*Yells.*] What do you mean? Damn, what a nuisance.

WOMAN ON THE PHONE: Last night he didn't come home again. Who knows where he spent the night?

MAN: Who didn't come home?

WOMAN ON THE PHONE: My husband.

MAN: I don't give a damn about your husband. Everybody has his own problems. [*Slams the receiver down. But even though the receiver is down, the* WOMAN'*s voice is still audible. In fact, it is even louder than when the receiver was up. The* WOMAN'*s voice periodically echoes. The* MAN *exits by the right-hand door.*]

WOMAN ON THE PHONE: I can't tell you what I've suffered. Nobody can take this kind of suffering. And to think of the hopes I had when I got married! Now I even miss my former loneliness. I was much happier then, but I didn't realize how well off I was. But I know now that I have no escape. The more I try to escape, the deeper I get trapped in the swamp of my loneliness. [*Sobs.*] I want to thank you for listening to me. It's easier to talk to a stranger, to someone whose face you have never seen. Thanks. [*Sobs. Then a pause.*]

[*The* MAN *has finished his bath and enters in clean underwear with an electric razor in his hand. He is very happy and active. Puts on aftershave lotion. Combs his hair. Puts on new clothes from the closet and his new shoes that don't squeak. The* WOMAN'*s talking should be audible during these activities, but the* MAN *is impervious to it, seemingly doesn't hear it, and whistles a tune. Finished dressing, he looks around him. He takes* ÇIÇU *down from the shelf and holds her up opposite him. Mockingly laughs at her.*]

MAN: I'm saved, you cold, bleeding wound of loneliness! [*Removes the necklace he had put on her in Act I and tosses it on the floor.*] I love someone I believe I was created for and who believes she was created for me. Now I can succeed at everything I always wanted to do. The successes she will inspire! I will dedicate to her whatever I do. I am erasing all the loveless, lonely days of my life and beginning all over. [*Angrily flings* ÇIÇU *to the floor.*] You . . . you . . . you can't even commit adultery. [*Kicks* ÇIÇU *and sends her rolling along the floor.*] I'm never coming back. [ÇIÇU'*s crying begins echoing in the background as the* MAN *shouts.*] Good-bye, lifeless days! [*The musical clock begins playing. The* MAN *ecstatically twirls around several times and then turns off the clock.*]

CURTAIN

ACT III

Scene 1

[*The stage is the same as at the end of Act II. The time is three years later. It is evening. The* MAN *is not on stage.* PİKİ *barks weakly a couple of times.* LAMİ *meows. Then silence. The sound of a key turning the outside lock is heard. The* MAN *enters. He is wet from the rain. Going directly to the table to put down the package of food for* PİKİ, LAMİ, *and the others, he stumbles over* ÇIÇU *on the floor, but pays no attention. Puts the package on the table. He has the look of a man who is not happy with himself, a hopeless look, but who is trying not to let it show. Runs his hand along the seat of the chair he's about to sit on. It's dusty; he blows on it as though to remove the dust, then places his handkerchief on the seat and sits down very lightly.*]

MAN: There's a definite, moldy odor of loneliness in here. [PIKI *barks weakly.*] Just a minute, Piki. I'm exhausted. Let me rest a minute, then I'll come. [*Lights a cigarette.* LAMI *meows.*] Lami, I can't bring you food and water every day. I have my own work, my own troubles. I give you a week's worth of food at a time. What more do you want from me? Don't gobble it up and stuff yourself all at once. [*Pause.*] What could I do? My wife didn't want any of you. If only she'd taken all of you in, too. What difference would it make to her? [*Gets up, goes to* RISAMI.] Poor little Risami, your leaves are getting yellow. I gave you water when I was here just ten days ago. My wife doesn't want me to keep anything from before I knew her. [*Strokes* RISAMI'S *yellowing leaves.*] She's jealous of my past, of my memories. That's why she didn't want any of you. She filled the house with flowers, and all of them are lovely, but none of them is you. [*Takes lettuce leaves from the package and picks up* BEYTI *from the floor.*] Beyti, my wife is jealous. You know what? It makes me kind of happy to have her jealous. [*Exits with the lettuce and* BEYTI *through the right-hand door. Returns immediately with a glass of water and pours it in the flowerpot.*] There, now you have plenty of water; that should last you for a week. I can't come by so often as I used to. Well, the baby has grown up, Risami. My daughter has just turned two, and my wife is pregnant again. [*As though* RISAMI *has said something and he doesn't understand it.*] What? How's that? Have I forgotten all of you? [*Smiles painfully.*] What nonsense, Risami! [*Puts his ear down toward the plant.*] What? Of course not. Just because I don't come as often anymore doesn't mean I've forgotten you. [*Turning toward the figurine named* CEST, *as though it has said something.*] What? What did you say? [*Going closer to* CEST.] Listen to that; she says I'll forget them completely after a while. [*As though that suggestion were very funny, he begins to laugh loudly until tears come to his eyes.*] What a riot you are, Cest, always cracking a joke from the very beginning.

MAN'S OWN VOICE: [*From offstage.*] It's all right to cry. You may cry in comfort. Why do you fool yourself by pretending to laugh? It's no use trying to hide tears behind laughter! Here at least is a place where you can cry in peace. [*Pause.*] You are suffering from loneliness. You thought you could escape loneliness by burdening your wife with it. You actually never wanted to escape from loneliness at all; you wanted to escape from yourself. Now you miss even your old loneliness. You will keep on coming back. You will keep on returning, but at the same time you will be ashamed of doing so.

MAN: [*Shouts.*] Who will make me ashamed?

MAN'S OWN VOICE: Çiçu. You are embarrassed about Çiçu. [*Pause.*] Are you happy? Are you rid of your loneliness? Are you happy?

MAN: [*Pretends not to hear the question.*] Nirey, I could have taken you with me at least. What difference would that have made? If only she'd have let me. Nirey, what's happened to you? You've stopped. [*Takes* NIREY *the clock in his hands as though trying to comfort it.*] Don't make me feel bad, Nirey. Your heart was meant to beat continuously. [*Winds* NIREY, *sets it by his wristwatch, and places it back in its place. Takes the fish food from the package and goes over to the aquarium.*] Oh, there are fewer of you. Next time I come, I'll clean your water, too. My poor little fish. [*As though angered by something the* FISH *have said.*] That's right! She doesn't know I come here. So what if I hide the fact that I come here and feed you? What's it to you? My wife thinks I emptied this place long ago and sold everything. [PIKI *barks.*] I . . . I'mmm coomming. [*Removes* PIKI*'s food from the package, opens the right-hand door, and bends down to talk.*] Piki, Piki, you've gotten thin. That's too bad. Next time I come, I'll take you for a walk and give you a bath. [*Returns. Removes* LAMI*'s food from the package, goes to the left-hand door, and leans down to talk to* LAMI.] You look good, Lami. You've gained a little weight even. I'll bet you've managed to snitch a bit from the neighbors.

MAN'S OWN VOICE: [*From the upper-right-hand side of the stage.*] Are you happy? [*From the upper-left-hand side of the stage.*] Are you happy? [*From the rear of the stage.*] Are you happy? [*From several places at once.*] Are you happy? Are you happy? Are you happy?

MAN: [*Shouts.*] I'm happy, I'm happy! [*Suddenly softens and speaks in a subdued voice.*] We're people from two different worlds. Of course, it's not easy to adjust. In the morning, I cough something terrible. Smoker's cough. Every morning I cough as though I were going to choke, and it makes my wife very angry with me. But I can't stand her . . . her quivering leg gets on my nerves. As soon as she sits down and crosses her legs, her left leg starts quivering. For one or two days a person can ignore it. But it drives a man crazy to have a woman sitting across from him year after year with one leg quivering. I never say anything. She doesn't either. [*Pauses. Then suddenly.*] You see, I'm happy! [*Looks absentmindedly at the telephone for a few minutes. Approaches* CEST.] Remember that woman who used to call me every once in a while to tell me her troubles? [*Neighbors' quarrel is heard from the door.*]

NEIGHBOR'S WIFE: Last night I waited up until morning, thinking you'd come and I'd open the door for you. I didn't sleep a wink all night. Where were you?

NEIGHBOR: Did you really want me? I'm sick of being together but living at a distance, sick of your indifference. I've had it.

NEIGHBOR'S WIFE: And I suppose you're the understanding one?

MAN: [*Walks quickly to the door and closes it. The* NEIGHBORS' *fight can no longer be heard.*] I wonder why they fight? [*To* VAVU.] Anybody call while I was gone, Vavu?

MAN'S OWN VOICE: The phone kept ringing. Perhaps it was that unknown woman you hung up on. The one you're now wondering about. But Çiçu can't answer the phone, you know. Çiçu can't talk. Çiçu can't walk . . . lifeless, soulless, dumb Çiçu. Çiçu, whom you kicked and sent rolling across the floor when you left. Çiçu, whom you never ask about, never pay any attention to whenever you return here. Çiçu is not alive; she never lived. [*The* MAN *is sad.*] Your own breath is still in this woman-shaped inner tube. Are you happy? [*Pause.*] Don't you hear me? I am your loneliness that you abandoned and sent rolling across the floor with a kick as you left. [*Pause.*] What's the matter? Can't you hear your own voice anymore?

MAN: Stop it! Shut up! Stop it!

MAN'S OWN VOICE: If you stop thinking, I'll be quiet. So, you mean you can't stand to hear your own voice. Would you like to speak with your wife?

MAN: No, no, I don't want to do that.

MAN'S OWN VOICE: But deep down you would like to.

MAN: No, I don't want to. Don't bring her here! I want to run away from her and escape.

MAN'S OWN VOICE: Just like you once ran away from here. Your wife's going to come here. She wants to settle everything with you, get everything out in the open. You want that, too. You have to understand who the guilty person really is. Your wife is coming! [*The outside door slowly opens by itself and closes again.*]

MAN: [*Begins to retreat in fear. Then speaks as though his* WIFE *has actually entered the room.*] Come on in. Have a seat. [*Speaks as though his* WIFE *has taken a seat on the chair he pointed to.*] This is the one place I didn't want to meet you. You see, I come here once in a while to take refuge in my loneliness. At least when I'm all by myself, I'm only as alone as myself; with you, I'm doubly alone.

WOMAN'S VOICE (LETTER WRITER): [*This is the same voice as that of the* WOMAN *who read the letter in Act II, Scene 2. The voice comes from under the chair on which she is presumably sitting.*] And me? I had hoped that you would draw me out of my loneliness and save me from it. But you didn't share anything of mine. Now I even miss my former loneliness.

[*The* MAN *and his* WIFE *tell each other their troubles, but neither listens to the other. What each says is not necessarily in relation or response to what the other says.*]

MAN: All my life I have longed for a woman to whom I could devote myself. You fooled me by saying, "I am that woman."

WIFE: You weigh me down with your burdens. You burden me with yourself.

MAN: You make me carry you.

WIFE: You don't let me share myself with you.

MAN: You make me a stranger to myself. Leave me alone. Let me be myself.

WIFE: I'm shivering with loneliness.

MAN: The damp coldness in me grows even worse when I'm with you. Every day you make me more alone than the day before. The hopelessness of being lonely keeps making me try to love you again and again, even though I know it's useless. Because I have to live, and to live I have to love . . .

WIFE: You lost me and didn't even know I was gone. I pick up and leave before your eyes, and you aren't even aware that I'm gone. Even when our bodies touch, you don't sense how you've exhausted me.

MAN: It's your fault; it's all your fault.

WIFE: You're the one at fault.

MAN: In that case, would you read what you have written in your diary?

WIFE: Of course. [*As if reading.*]

May 21: It was a beautiful spring day. We met in the country. We talked and talked and talked. But somehow I couldn't bring myself to say what I really wanted to say.

July 11: I saw him in my dream. In my dream, I told him everything I've been unable to tell him.

September 4: It's been three months since we met. Yesterday we spent the whole day in one room. I kept silent all day; we had nothing left to say to each other.

November 1: I can't imagine how we used to talk on end, how we always found something to talk about.

December 13: I'm terribly bored. I'm going crazy with boredom. Continuous tension; a continuous state of not knowing what I'm going to do. I'm continuously tired, sleepless, and nervous.

[*Pause.*] How about you? Would you read the diary you've secretly kept?

MAN: Of course I will. [*Takes a notebook out of his inside pocket, opens it, and begins reading.*]

March 18: When a woman yells at a man, "What do you want from me?" it is no longer possible to want anything from her. This morning I called to my wife, and she yelled, "What do you want from me?"

April 22: Last night in bed I asked, "What do I mean to you?" and she yelled, "You mean nothing to me!" The woman for whom I gave everything, who was everything to me, and who I thought was my everything told me I meant nothing to her.

[*Sound of a woman sobbing. The* MAN *turns to the wall, places his arm up against it, and rests his head against his arm. After a while, he turns his head toward the chair.*] Are you leaving? [*The outside door slowly opens, seemingly unassisted, and closes again. The* MAN *again turns and rests his head against the wall. The telephone rings almost immediately. The* MAN *goes quickly to the telephone and picks up the receiver.*] Hello, hellooo!

WOMAN ON THE PHONE: [*The* MAN *listens very attentively at first.*] I've called you often. You haven't been home for a long time. Your telephone never answers. Me? I talked anyway, even though the telephone didn't answer, even though no one was listening. If I hadn't, I would have exploded.

MAN: I was hoping you'd call. If I'd known your number, I would have called you.

WOMAN ON THE PHONE: I was desperate to talk to someone.

MAN: Me, too.

WOMAN ON THE PHONE: The other day I absentmindedly found myself talking to the cat. I was telling her my troubles. When I suddenly realized what I was doing, I was scared I was going crazy. [LAMİ *meows.*] In the kitchen, I find myself talking to the pots and pans and the stove. Yesterday, to the potted plants . . . [*Pause.*]

MAN: Yes? Go on, go on!

WOMAN ON THE PHONE: I want to love my husband. And he wants to love me.

MAN: I try to love my wife. I think she tries, too.

WOMAN ON THE PHONE: I can't even bear my own loneliness, yet he . . .

MAN: She doesn't share herself with me.

WOMAN ON THE PHONE: When I think that I've come into the world only once . . . [*Both begin talking simultaneously without paying any attention to the other. They keep repeating the same sentences. The musical clock begins to play. As the sound of the clock fades out, so do the voices of the* MAN *and the* WOMAN ON THE PHONE. *Stage slowly darkens.*]

MAN: I can't bear my loneliness.

WOMAN ON THE PHONE: I can't stand my loneliness any longer.

MAN: I can't bear my loneliness.

WOMAN ON THE PHONE: I can't endure my loneliness any longer. [*Both repeat the same sentences.*]

Scene 2

[*Ten years have passed since the events of the previous scene. The same place. The room, furniture, and* ÇİÇU *are as left in the previous scene. When the curtain opens, the stage is dark. A faint light moves toward the outside door. The sound of a key turning a lock is heard. The door squeaks and opens slowly. The* MAN *enters. He flicks on his cigarette lighter and looks around. He enters from a rainy night. His hat and raincoat are soaking wet. With the flame from his cigarette lighter, he finds the light switch and flips it on, but nothing happens.*]

MAN: They've cut off the electricity. [*Lights several candles he finds on one of the shelves. Puts the candles at the base of the walls, in the corners, on the floor. The stage lights up slightly. The* MAN *has aged a great deal and looks depressed. Removes his wet coat and hat and places them across one of the chairs. Runs his hand along the walls, along the shelves, across the books, the table, the chairs, touching his possessions.*] Everything's filthy with dust. [*Pause.*] Something smells here. [*Opens the left-hand door and looks inside. Slams it shut.*] Little Piki. [*Cries.*] My poor little Piki. [*Takes one of the candles in his hand and goes over to the clock.*] Nirey, did Piki die a long time ago? And you stopped ages ago, too. [*Tries to wind* NİREY, *but the key comes off in his hand.*] You went silent years ago, Nirey. You've grown rusty and fallen apart. You can't sing to my loneliness anymore. [*Takes down the birdcage and looks in it; the bird is dead.*] Yumuş, Yumuş. [*With a candle in hand, he goes over to the aquarium and looks in. Puts his hand in the empty aquarium and takes it out. There is not even any water left. Goes over to* RİSAMİ. *The plant has completely dried up. There is nothing left but a pot full of dirt.*] I planted you myself, Risami. I watered you. I raised you. I smelled your flowers. [*Weeps. Then suddenly shouts.*] Which one of you is still alive? Say something! [*Lifts the telephone receiver.*] Not a sound. It was cut off long ago. [*Loudly and sadly.*] Are all of you mad at me? Even the walls? The table, too? Are even the chairs mad at me? [*Yells.*] Ceeeessst, Vavuuuu, answer me; you say something. [*Goes over to the figurines with the candle in hand. Picks up the figurines. Looks at them. Puts them back again. Pauses. Opens the right-hand door. The wind whips through, banging the window open and blowing out all the candles.*] It's as though I've come to my own funeral; I keep wanting to weep. [*Flicks on his cigarette lighter and relights the candles. Gets up on a chair and closes the window.*] There's no light in the windows of the houses across the street. [*Gets down off the chair.*] I want to hide in the cold, bleeding wounds of my earlier loneliness and warm up.

WOMAN ON THE PHONE: It's not others who make you feel cold, who make you lonely. It's you.

MAN: [*Afraid.*] Who's that?

WOMAN ON THE PHONE: You, it's you.

MAN: Are they still there? Haven't those voices inside me dried up and disappeared yet?

WOMAN ON THE PHONE: If that's what you want, stop thinking. As long as you live, you will hear yourself. In fact, especially now that you're really lonely. You have fallen into the pit of your self-centeredness. Save yourself, if you can. Tell me, what is it that you shared with your friends?

MAN: [*Runs to the telephone.*] I, too, have problems to tell someone I don't know. [*Lifts the receiver, listens, throws it down on the floor. Picks up a candle and trips over* ÇİÇU *on the floor. Drops down beside her. Painfully.*] Çiçu, Çiçu. I've come back to you with all my bitter regrets. I've come back to you, see? Is it too late, Çiçu? [*Picks up the necklace he had removed from* ÇİÇU *and thrown on the floor when he left to get married and puts it on her again.*] Çiçu, I've come to make up; I've come to ask your forgiveness. [*Lifts up* ÇİÇU *and props her up on the couch.*] Çiçu, let's play like in the old days. Smile again like you used to. Let's start all over again, Çiçu, as though all these years had not gone by. Come on, what do you say? Let's start anew. [*Exits through the outside door in haste. Closes the door. Sound of the key turning the lock open again. The* MAN *enters smiling. Tiptoes up behind* ÇİÇU *and puts his hands over her eyes.*] Guess who? Yeah, how did you know? I'm the first and last man in your life, ehh? [*With a false air of lightheartedness.*] Come on, let's throw shadows. I'll make you a cat, a dog, and a wolf. [*Making the shapes with his fingers, he moves quickly from one side to another, trying to cast the animal shadows on the walls. Frightened, he yells.*] My shadow! My shadow! My shadow is gone! I'm left without a shadow. [*Puts his head on* ÇIÇU's *knees and starts to weep.*] Çiçu, I don't have a shadow anymore. I don't even have a shadow. You've taken it. You've taken it. Give me back my shadow, Çiçu. Give me my shadow! I can't live without my shadow. I came back to you, Çiçu. Give me my shadow!

MAN'S OWN VOICE: [*After laughing a great, echoing laugh.*] You know very well Çiçu can give you nothing.

MAN: [*Lifts* ÇIÇU *up in his arms and walks to stage center. Standing there, he pleads with her.*] Forgive me, Çiçu. Give me loneliness. I don't even have my loneliness anymore. [ÇIÇU *gradually begins to lose air.*] All the while I was trying to escape my loneliness and find happiness, I succeeded only in losing even my loneliness. Çiçu, Çiçu, give me back my old loneliness. Give me back my shadow. [ÇIÇU *is losing air. The* MAN *shouts.*] Çiçu! Don't leave, Çiçu! Don't leave! At least you should stay. Çiçu, don't go, don't abandon me. [ÇIÇU *has completely deflated in his arms and is nothing but a limp piece of rubber. The* MAN *weeps. Pause.*]

MAN'S OWN VOICE: Why did you create Çiçu? Why are you looking for Çiçu? What do you want with her? Selfish man! Go find people with loneliness to share and save yourself from yours!

MAN: It's too late, much too late.

MAN'S OWN VOICE: You are alive. You are living. As long as you are alive, it's not too late for anything. As long as you are alive, you can start anew from a thousand defeats.

MAN: It's too late. My wife has left. I have no one, no one at all.

MAN'S OWN VOICE: The streets are full of lonely people. The lonely people of the cold rainy night are waiting for you. Go find them.

[*The stage lights up very slightly. It is lit by lights from both above and below. The telephone rings, even though the receiver is off the hook. The* MAN *picks up the receiver; the phone rings again. The* MAN *is surprised. The* WOMAN *begins to talk.*]

WOMAN ON THE PHONE: Last night he didn't come home again. And when he left the house . . . ohh, I'm desperate to tell my troubles to someone.

MAN: [*Drops the receiver and talks.*] Lady, your husband has troubles, too. He, too, needs someone to tell his troubles to.

WOMAN ON THE PHONE: You? Is that you talking? Why didn't you tell me that before?

MAN: I didn't know it then. It's a difficult thing to learn, a very difficult thing to learn. [*Smiles.*] I'm going out to find some other people.

[*As he heads for the outside door, the musical clock begins to play. The* MAN *returns, greatly pleased, and picks up the clock, kissing it.*] Nirey, Nirey, I'm not alone anymore.

CURTAIN

Biographical Notes

◆　　◆　　◆

Acknowledgments

Biographical Notes

TALAT S. HALMAN is a critic, a scholar, and a leading translator of Turkish literature into English. His books in English include *Contemporary Turkish Literature, Modern Turkish Drama, Süleyman the Magnificent Poet,* three books on Yunus Emre, *Mevlana Celaleddin Rumi and the Whirling Dervishes* (with Metin And), *A Brave New Quest: 100 Modern Turkish Poems, Shadows of Love* (his original poems in English), *A Last Lullaby* (his English/Turkish poems), *Living Poets of Turkey, Turkish Legends and Folk Poems,* and many books featuring modern Turkish poets (Dağlarca, Kanık, Anday). He is the editor of *A Dot on the Map: Selected Stories and Poems* and *Sleeping in the Forest: Stories and Poems* by Sait Faik. His book *Nightingales and Pleasure Gardens: Turkish Love Poems* was named one of the ten best university press books of 2005 by *ForeWord Reviews.*

Among Halman's books in Turkish are eleven collections of his own poetry, including *Ümit Harmanı* (his complete poems); a massive volume of the poetry of ancient civilizations; the complete sonnets of Shakespeare; the poetry of ancient Anatolia and the Near East; Eskimo poems; ancient Egyptian poetry; the *rubais* of Rumi; the quatrains of Baba Tahir Uryan; two anthologies of modern American poetry; and books of the selected poems of Wallace Stevens and Langston Hughes. Halman was William Faulkner's first Turkish translator; he has also translated works by Mark Twain and Eugene O'Neill.

Halman has published nearly three thousand articles, essays, and reviews in English and in Turkish. He has served as a columnist for the Turkish dailies *Milliyet, Akşam,* and *Cumhuriyet.* Many of his English articles on Turkish literature have been collected in *Rapture and Revolution: Essays on Turkish Literature.* Selections from Halman's Turkish articles and essays have been collected in two volumes, *Doğrusu* and *Çiçek Dürbünü.* His English reviews of works of Turkish literature have been collected in *The Turkish Muse: Views and Reviews, 1960s–1990s.* Some of his books have been translated into French, Hebrew, Persian, Urdu, Hindi, and Japanese. He won Columbia University's Thornton Wilder Prize for his work as a translator.

His translations of Robinson Jeffers's *Medea;* Jerome Kilty's *Dear Liar,* a play adaptation of the correspondence of George Bernard Shaw and Mrs. Patrick Campbell; Eugene O'Neill's *The Iceman Cometh;* and Neil Simon's *Lost in Yonkers* were produced in Turkey. *Dear Liar* and *The Iceman Cometh* won best-translation awards. His English version of Güngör Dilmen's one-woman play *I, Anatolia* was presented by Turkey's premier actress

Yıldız Kenter in North America, England, Europe, and Asia. Halman also wrote a one-actor Shakespeare-based play entitled *Kahramanlar ve Soytarılar* (Heroes and Clowns), which was presented in the 1986–87 season by the prominent actor Müşfik Kenter in Istanbul. It was published in book form in 1991. Later, Halman himself presented it as a dramatic reading. In recent years, he has been doing a revised version with Yıldız Kenter in both English and Turkish. The script was published as a book under the title *"Türk" Shakespeare* in 2003. Halman was chosen to write the 2006 World Theater Day proclamation for Turkey.

Talat Halman served as Turkey's first minister of culture and later as its ambassador for cultural affairs. He was a member of the UNESCO Executive Board. Between 1953 and 1997, he was on the faculties of Columbia University, Princeton University, the University of Pennsylvania, and New York University (where he was also chairman of the Department of Near Eastern Languages and Literatures). In 1998, he founded the Department of Turkish Literature at Bilkent University, Ankara, and has since then been its chairman. He also serves as Bilkent's dean of the Faculty of Humanities and Letters. He is currently the president of the Turkish National Committee for UNICEF and editor in chief of the *Journal of Turkish Literature*. He was also the general editor for a four-volume history of Turkish literature published in Turkish.

Halman's honors and awards include many literary prizes, two honorary doctorates, a Rockefeller Fellowship in the Humanities, the Distinguished Service Award of the Turkish Academy of Sciences, the UNESCO Medal, and Knight Grand Cross (GBE), the Most Excellent Order of the British Empire, conferred on him by Queen Elizabeth II.

JAYNE L. WARNER is director of research at the Institute for Aegean Prehistory in Greenwich, Connecticut. She holds a B.A. in classics, an M.A. in ancient history, and from Bryn Mawr College a Ph.D. in Near Eastern and Anatolian archaeology. Her publications include *Elmalı-Karataş II: The Early Bronze Age Village of Karataş*. Warner has served as assistant editor for the American School of Classical Studies at Athens and executive director of the Poetry Society of America (New York). She has also served as director of the American Turkish Society (New York) and director of the New York Office of the Board of Trustees of Robert College of Istanbul. She is the editor of *Cultural Horizons: A Festschrift in Honor of Talat S. Halman*, *The Turkish Muse: Views and Reviews, 1960s–1990s*, and *Rapture and Revolution: Essays on Turkish Literature*. She is the associate editor of *Sleeping in the Forest: Stories and Poems* by Sait Faik, *Nightingales and Pleasure Gardens: Turkish Love Poems*, and *A Brave New Quest: 100 Modern Turkish Poems*.

Acknowledgments

The editors offer their thanks to the following individuals for their assistance with various aspects of the production of this book: Tuncel Acar, Ceyda Akpolat, Gönül Büyüklimanlı, Günil Özlem Ayaydın Cebe, Demet Güzelsoy Chafra, Yıldız Kenter, Ela Şengündüz, and Yalçın Tura.

Also the editors are grateful to the following for permission to print these translations: Suna Anday, Cahit Atay, Şakir Eczacıbaşı, Clifford Endres and Selhan Savcıgil-Endres, Allan R. Gall, Murat Nemet-Nejat, Ali Nesin, A. Turan Oflazoğlu, Başar Sabuncu, Osman Streater, Demet Taner, Leyla Tecer, the Turkish Ministry of Culture and Tourism, and Şen Yalman.

DATE DUE

GAYLORD   PRINTED IN U.S.A.